DiMaio's Forensic Pathology

Third Edition

CRC SERIES IN
PRACTICAL ASPECTS OF CRIMINAL AND FORENSIC INVESTIGATIONS

VERNON J. GEBERTH, BBA, MPS, FBINA *Series Editor*

Serial Violence: Analysis of Modus Operandi and Signature Characteristics of Killers
Robert D. Keppel and William J. Birnes

Practical Aspects of Rape Investigation: A Multidisciplinary Approach, Fourth Edition
Robert R. Hazelwood and Ann Wolbert Burgess

Bloodstain Pattern Analysis: With an Introduction to Crime Scene Reconstruction, Third Edition
Tom Bevel and Ross M. Gardner

Tire Tread and Tire Track Evidence: Recovery and Forensic Examination
William J. Bodziak

Officer-Involved Shootings and Use of Force: Practical Investigative Techniques, Second Edition
David E. Hatch and Randy Dickson

Practical Drug Enforcement, Third Edition
Michael D. Lyman

Cold Case Homicides: Practical Investigative Techniques
Richard H. Walton

Principles of Bloodstain Pattern Analysis: Theory and Practice
Stuart James, Paul Kish, and T. Paulette Sutton

Global Drug Enforcement: Practical Investigative Techniques
Gregory D. Lee

Practical Investigation of Sex Crimes: A Strategic and Operational Approach
Thomas P. Carney

Principles of Kinesic Interview and Interrogation, Second Edition
Stan Walters

Practical Criminal Investigations in Correctional Facilities
William R. Bell

Practical Aspects of Interview and Interrogation, Second Edition
David E. Zulawski and Douglas E. Wicklander

The Practical Methodology of Forensic Photography, Second Edition
David R. Redsicker

Quantitative-Qualitative Friction Ridge Analysis: An Introduction to Basic and Advanced Ridgeology
David R. Ashbaugh

Footwear Impression Evidence: Detection, Recovery, and Examination, Second Edition
William J. Bodziak

The Sexual Exploitation of Children: A Practical Guide to Assessment, Investigation, and Intervention, Second Edition
Seth L. Goldstein

Practical Aspects of Munchausen by Proxy and Munchausen Syndrome Investigation
Kathryn Artingstall

Practical Fire and Arson Investigation, Second Edition
David R. Redsicker and John J. O'Connor

Interpretation of Bloodstain Evidence at Crime Scenes, Second Edition
William G. Eckert and Stuart H. James

Investigating Computer Crime
Franklin Clark and Ken Diliberto

Practical Investigation Techniques
Kevin B. Kinnee

Friction Ridge Skin: Comparison and Identification of Fingerprints
James F. Cowger

Tire Imprint Evidence
Peter McDonald

Practical Gambling Investigation Techniques
Kevin B. Kinnee

DiMaio's Forensic Pathology, Third Edition
Vincent J.M. DiMaio and D. Kimberley Molina

DiMaio's Forensic Pathology

Third Edition

Vincent J.M. DiMaio, MD
D. Kimberley Molina, MD

CRC Press
Taylor & Francis Group
Boca Raton London New York

CRC Press is an imprint of the
Taylor & Francis Group, an **informa** business

CRC Press
Third edition published 2022
by CRC Press
6000 Broken Sound Parkway NW, Suite 300, Boca Raton, FL 33487-2742

and by CRC Press
2 Park Square, Milton Park, Abingdon, Oxon, OX14 4RN

First edition published by CRC Press 1992
Second edition published by CRC Press 2001
CRC Press is an imprint of Taylor & Francis Group, LLC

Library of Congress Cataloging-in-Publication Data

Library of Congress Cataloging-in-Publication Data
Names: Di Maio, Vincent J. M., 1941- author. | Molina, Kimberley, author.
Title: DiMaio's forensic pathology / Vincent J.M. DiMaio, M.D. and
Kimberley Molina, M.D.
Description: Third edition. | Boca Raton, FL : CRC Press, 2021. | Series:
Practical aspects of criminal and forensic investigations | Revised
edition of: Forensic pathology / Vincent J. Di Maio, Dominick Di Maio.
2nd ed. c2001. | Includes bibliographical references and index. |
Identifiers: LCCN 2020053726 (print) | LCCN 2020053727 (ebook) | ISBN
9780367251482 (hardback) | ISBN 9780429318764 (ebook)
Subjects: LCSH: Forensic pathology.
Classification: LCC RA1063.4 .D5 2021 (print) | LCC RA1063.4 (ebook) |
DDC 614/.1--dc23
LC record available at https://lccn.loc.gov/2020053726
LC ebook record available at https://lccn.loc.gov/2020053727

ISBN: 978-0-367-25148-2 (hbk)
ISBN: 978-1-032-00450-1 (pbk)
ISBN: 978-0-429-31876-4 (ebk)

Typeset in Minion Pro
by KnowledgeWorks Global Ltd.

To my wife Theresa G. DiMaio, BSN for her support and to my children, Samantha DiMaio, JD, and Dominick DiMaio, MD, and my grandchildren Vincent, Geovanni and Gemma.

Dr. DiMaio

To my wonderful husband, Jose, and our amazing son, Emeshaw.

Dr. Molina

Contents

Acknowledgments

The authors would like to thank Nancy Hebert whose hard work made this edition possible as well as the numerous autopsy technicians and physicians we have worked with over the years and with whom we have shared these cases.

> *I looked, and there before me was a pale horse!*
>
> *Its rider was named Death, and Hades was following close behind him. They were given power over a fourth of the earth to kill by sword, famine and plague, and by the wild beasts of the earth.*

Revelation 6:8 (New International Version)

About the Authors

Vincent J.M. DiMaio, MD, was the Chief Medical Examiner for Bexar County in San Antonio, Texas for over 25 years. He was also an Adjunct Professor in the Pathology Department of the University of Texas Health Sciences at San Antonio, School of Medicine and the Editor-in-Chief of the *American Journal of Forensic Medicine and Pathology* from 1992 to 2017. He has published a large volume of peer-reviewed scientific articles in his field in addition to several textbooks on the topics of forensic pathology, gunshot wounds and excited delirium, including the present book that was originally written with his father, Dr. Dominick DiMaio, also a forensic pathologist and a former Chief Medical Examiner of New York City. Dr. Vincent DiMaio is an internationally renowned leader in forensic pathology and is highly respected for his expertise in gunshot wounds and firearms, often being consulted by attorneys and law enforcement officials from across the country.

D. Kimberley Molina, MD, is currently the Chief Medical Examiner for the Bexar County Medical Examiner's Office located in San Antonio, Texas. She is also the Editor-in-Chief of the *American Journal of Forensic Medicine and Pathology* and serves as an Adjunct Professor in the Department of Pathology at the UT-Health Medical School. She has written numerous articles and book chapters regarding the field of forensic pathology, including *The Handbook of Forensic Toxicology for Medical Examiners* with Dr. Veronica Hargrove.

Death is not an end. It is a new beginning.

—Allan Hamilton

Medicolegal Death Investigation

1

Nothing matters but the facts. Without them, the science of criminal investigation is nothing more than a guessing game.

—**Blake Edwards**

Forensic pathology is a branch of medicine that applies the principles and knowledge of the medical sciences to problems in the field of law. The major duties of a medicolegal system in handling deaths falling under its jurisdiction are:

- To determine the cause and manner of death
- To identify the deceased, if unknown
- To determine the time of death and injury
- To collect evidence from the body that can be used to refute or corroborate an account of how the death occurred
- To document injuries or lack of thereof
- To deduce how the injuries occurred
- To document any natural disease present
- To determine or exclude other contributory or causative factors to the death
- To provide expert testimony if the case goes to trial

Deaths that come to the attention of the office of the medical examiner or the coroner generally fall into the following categories: violent deaths (accidents, suicides and homicides), suspicious deaths, sudden and unexpected deaths, deaths without a physician in attendance and deaths in an institution. There are, of course, variations to these categories, depending on the local jurisdiction.

Definition of Death

Because of advances in medical science, what was formerly not a problem has now become one – the definition of death. In simpler times, death was defined as the permanent cessation of cardiac and/or respiratory function. Today, instrumentation can keep a heart beating and an individual breathing in spite of the fact that if this machinery were turned off, heart and respiratory activity would cease. This has brought about the concept of *brain death*. There is extensive literature on this subject, and the definition of brain death in adults and children is not necessarily the same.[1]

The declaration of an individual as brain dead, with all the requirements to be met, is mostly of academic interest to the medicolegal system in that a case is not reported until a clinician has pronounced the individual dead. However, cases do sometimes occur where the pronouncement of brain death can be obscured by the concomitant presence of sedative medications that may also impact the cause and manner of death.[2]

Other issues that may arise are the procurement of organs or the moving of brain-dead individuals. In most jurisdictions, if harvesting of organs is intended and family permission has been obtained, and if the case is to be a medical examiner's or coroner's case, prior to the removal of the organs, approval must also be obtained from the medical examiner or coroner. This is because, once the individual is "dead," he or she comes under the medicolegal jurisdiction. Procurement of organs without such consent of the medicolegal authority could be interpreted as interfering with the duties of the medicolegal system and could, therefore, constitute a crime. The procedure for obtaining permission to procure the organs after pronouncement of death is a matter of routine in most medicolegal systems. A strong relationship between medical examiner/coroner offices and the local organ procurement organization is paramount in maintaining best practices for both entities. The importance of organ procurement and transplantation is well understood by medical examiner/coroner offices and, with proper coordination and communication, organ procurement can often be performed without interfering with the subsequent medicolegal examination of the body.

Another issue the authors have seen is when an individual who has been declared brain dead has been transferred outside the jurisdiction of the medicolegal authority for the purpose of organ procurement. Once the organs are procured and the machines turned off, the question arises of who will perform the examination of the body. Because the body has been moved out of the legal jurisdiction where it was pronounced dead, does it have to be moved back to that jurisdiction or does the medicolegal authority in the area where the body is now located take jurisdiction? Does this medicolegal authority have the legal right, since the individual "died" in another jurisdiction? While there may be subtle differences depending upon jurisdiction, for the most part, the medicolegal authority where the death was pronounced retains the jurisdiction for investigation. Such issues are best settled beforehand with conferences involving the organ procurement organizations and other medicolegal entities.

One other minor point should also be mentioned. An individual may be pronounced dead, yet be maintained on a life support system for 2–3 days after pronouncement. This has sometimes resulted in confusion in the documentation of the date of death, though this is more a problem of bureaucracy than science.

Death Certification — Cause, Manner and Mechanism of Death

Two of the most important functions of the medical examiner's or coroner's office are the determination of the cause and manner of death. Clinicians, lawyers and the lay public often have difficulty understanding the difference between cause of death, mechanism of death and manner of death. Simply put, the *cause of death* is any injury or disease that produces a physiological derangement in the body that results in the death of the individual. Thus, although differing widely, the following are causes of death: a gunshot wound to the head, a stab wound to the chest, adenocarcinoma of the lung and coronary atherosclerosis.

The *mechanism of death* is the physiological derangement produced by the cause of death that results in death. Examples of mechanism of death would be hemorrhage, septicemia and cardiac arrhythmia. One must realize that a particular mechanism of death can be produced by multiple causes of death and vice versa. Thus, if an individual dies of massive hemorrhage, it can be produced by a gunshot wound, a stab wound or a malignant tumor of the lung eroding into a blood vessel. The reverse of this is that a cause of death, for example, a gunshot wound of the abdomen, can result in many possible mechanisms of death, for example, hemorrhage or peritonitis.

Medical examiners often have to review death certificates produced by clinicians. Not infrequently, the cause of death is listed as "cardiac arrest" or "cardiopulmonary arrest." Simply stated, this means that the heart stopped or the heart and lungs stopped. Experience tells us, however, that when any individual dies, the heart and lungs stop. These are not causes of death and, to a degree, are not even mechanisms of death. Yet, clinicians continue to list these diagnoses on the death certificate, and some government organizations accept them as causes of death.

The *manner of death* explains how the cause of death came about. Manners of death can generally be categorized as natural, homicide, suicide, accident or undetermined. The authors also use the category "unclassified." Just as a mechanism of death can have many causes and a cause can have many mechanisms, a cause of death can have multiple manners. An individual can die of massive hemorrhage (the mechanism of death) due to a gunshot wound to the heart (the cause of death), with the manner of death being homicide (somebody shot the individual), suicide (they shot themselves), accident (the weapon fell and discharged) or undetermined (one is not sure what occurred).

The manner of death as determined by the forensic pathologist is an opinion based on the known facts concerning the circumstances leading up to and surrounding the death, in conjunction with the findings at autopsy and the laboratory tests. The autopsy findings may contradict or agree with the account of how the death occurred. Thus, if the story is that an individual shot himself and the autopsy reveals a gunshot wound to the back inflicted from a distance, there is obviously inconsistencies between the account and the autopsy and further investigation is warranted. If, however, it is a contact gunshot wound of the temple, then the autopsy findings are consistent with the account. It must be realized that the manner of death can be changed if subsequent information that alters the circumstances surrounding the death is discovered. Thus, if we have an individual found with a contact gunshot wound to the temple, with no weapon present and no history of any suicidal threats, one might then conclude that this case is a homicide. If, subsequently, it turns out that the individual had a clinical history of suicidal ideations after embezzling a half a million dollars from his company being indicted by the grand jury, and his body was found by his wife, who removed a gun and suicide note from the scene, the manner of death would be changed to suicide.

Just because a forensic pathologist makes a determination as to the manner of death does not mean that it will be accepted by either families or other agencies. The authors have certified homicides in a number of cases that police agencies have determined to be accidents. Sometimes, families will challenge a manner of death opinion and go to court to have it overturned. In most instances, the court will support the medical examiner. The medical examiner should not be upset, however, if the court rules the manner of death differently, because juries, especially in cases of suicide, do not necessarily utilize the same medical knowledge, training or experience as the medical examiner and may base their opinion more on emotion and supposition. For example, if a widow, challenging a medical examiner's opinion of suicide so that she can collect insurance, brings two young children to the trial, it would not be surprising if the jury should decide to rule the death an accident, no matter how much objective evidence had been presented to the contrary.

Occasionally, there are cases in which the cause of death would ordinarily be considered natural, but the manner is homicide, for example, a homeowner who surprises a burglar, engages him in a violent struggle and then collapses and dies of a heart attack. The mechanism of death is a cardiac arrhythmia and the cause of death is severe coronary atherosclerosis, but the manner of death is homicide, as the arrhythmia was brought on or precipitated by the struggle. Some individuals will even determine a case to be a homicide even if there is no physical struggle, just sufficient psychological stress to have precipitated the arrhythmia and death, though this can be controversial.

While manner of death is mainly determined by circumstances, the autopsy findings can still be important in making the determination of the cause of death. For example, in one case, a young woman stood at the end of a pier, placed a gun to her chest and pulled the trigger. The bullet struck her in the chest and she fell backward into the harbor. Her body was subsequently pulled out of the water by a police boat. At autopsy, she had a through-and-through gunshot wound of the left breast, with the bullet producing only soft-tissue injury and not entering the chest cavity. The actual cause of death was drowning with the manner of death of suicide.

The undetermined manner of death is used when there is insufficient information about the circumstances surrounding the death to make a determination, or, in some instances, when the cause of death is unknown. Thus, if one finds the skeletonized remains without evidence of trauma, one cannot say whether the manner of death was accident, homicide or suicide, because the cause of death is not known. In other instances, there may be insufficient information concerning the circumstances surrounding the death to explain the manner of death. This situation often occurs in deaths due to drug overdoses such as the case when individual may have a long history of overmedicating but, at the same time, has also previously attempted suicide. Is this a case of suicide or did the individual just take too much medication inadvertently, because that was his or her normal habit?

In some instances, based on the circumstances surrounding a death, a manner of death can be determined without a cause of death. For example, the decomposing body of a 32-year-old female was found in a ditch 2 mi from her burglarized house. She was clad in pajamas, barefoot (with the soles of her feet clean), and her hands were bound behind her back. An autopsy failed to reveal a cause of death. The cause of death was ruled undetermined; the manner homicide. The manner of death was based on the circumstances surrounding the death and not the autopsy findings. In some jurisdictions, the term "homicidal violence" is used as the cause of death, though the connotation is the same – the exact cause of death is unknown though the circumstances are indicative of homicide.

In addition to the usual classifications of manners of death, some forensic pathologists, ourselves included, use the term "unclassified." This refers to a death in which the cause and circumstances are known, but the death does not readily fall into any of the aforementioned categories. An example is the case of a woman who came into the hospital for an abortion. A hypertonic saline solution was injected; the woman went into labor and delivered a live 450-g infant. The infant displayed chemical bums of the skin due to the hypertonic saline solution and survived an hour and a half without mechanical assistance, prior to dying. The death does not fit neatly into any of the categories of natural, accident, suicide or homicide and it is not truly undetermined as the cause and circumstances surrounding the death are accurately known. Thus, a manner of death of unclassified may be used. The authors also place in the unclassified category cases that some individuals call *medical misadventure* such as a case of a perforated heart due to an intravascular catheter or an air embolism complicating spinal fusion.

One must also understand that sometimes the classification of manner of death is based on local precedent or office policy. If two people are "kidding around" with a gun and one individual points the gun at another and pulls the trigger, in some localities, this is classified as an accident; in others, as a homicide. An individual walking down the street is hit by an automobile and the driver stops, this is an accident; if the driver continues on their way, in a number of jurisdictions, this is classified as a homicide. If one drinks too much alcohol and dies of acute alcohol intoxication, this is an accident. If one drinks too much alcohol every day for 15 years and develops cirrhosis of the liver and chronic liver failure due to the alcohol, then the manner of death is classified as natural.

Delayed deaths often cause issues with death certification as well as investigation. What people often fail to realize is that the cause of death may still be traumatic even if there is a long delay between injury and death, as long as the death was a result of injuries. Thus, if an individual suffers a head injury resulting in irreversible coma and dies 2 or 3 years later of pneumonia, the cause of death is still head injury and a medicolegal death investigation is still required. In another case, an individual died of chronic renal failure within a few hours of admission to a hospital. However, renal failure was due to chronic pyelonephritis, complicating paraplegia, which had in turn been caused by a gunshot wound to the spine 25 years prior. Not only was the cause of death in this case the gunshot wound, but the manner of death was also homicide.

Death Certification — Importance

Accurate death certification is an important duty of the medicolegal authority. Death certificates are not only used by families for legal and financial purposes, but also they often provide emotional closures for families being the decedent's last medical record (Figure 1.1).

They may be used to determine familial genetic propensities or in genealogy studies. They are also used to identify emerging diseases, gauge the health of a population and direct public health initiatives. Unfortunately, inaccuracy in death certification is an international issue. Information that certifiers may view as important, such as whether or not tobacco contributed to death or if the decedent was pregnant at the time of death, can have widely impacting implications.[3] Medical examiners and coroners, as routine certifiers of deaths, should be particularly mindful of these issues and the importance of accuracy in death certification. They should have a strong working relationship with their local death registrar and a thorough understanding of their local death registration system.

Statistics

While one of the main duties of medicolegal death investigation systems is to investigate non-natural deaths, natural deaths still comprise a large portion of any medical examiner/coroner office. Most of these are the sudden and unexpected deaths of individuals out functioning in the community, but who may not have significant medical history or who did not routinely see a physician. The other large category of deaths is usually accidental

1. LEGAL NAME OF DECEASED (Include AKA's if any) (First, Middle, Last) | (Maiden) | 2. DATE OF DEATH – ACTUAL OR PRESUMED

3. SEX | 4. DATE OF BIRTH | 5. AGE-Last Birthday (Years) | IF UNDER 1 YR: MO, DAYS | IF UNDER 1 DAY: HOURS, MIN | 6. BIRTHPLACE (City & State or Foreign Country)

7. SOCIAL SECURITY NUMBER | 8. MARITAL STATUS AT TIME OF DEATH ☐ Married ☐ Widowed ☐ Divorced ☐ Never Married ☐ Unknown | 9. SURVIVING SPOUSE (If wife, give name prior to first marriage)

10a. RESIDENCE STREET ADDRESS | 10b. APT NO | 10c. CITY OR TOWN

10d. COUNTY | 10e. STATE | 10f. ZIP CODE | 10g. INSIDE CITY LIMITS? ☐ Yes ☐ No

11. FATHER'S NAME | 12. MOTHER'S NAME PRIOR TO FIRST MARRIAGE

13. PLACE OF DEATH (CHECK ONLY ONE)

IF DEATH OCCURRED IN A HOSPITAL: ☐ Inpatient ☐ ER/Outpatient ☐ DOA | IF DEATH OCCURRED SOMEWHERE OTHER THAN A HOSPITAL: ☐ Hospice Facility ☐ Nursing Home ☐ Decedent's Home ☐ Other (Specify)

14. COUNTY OF DEATH | 15. CITY/TOWN, ZIP (if outside city limits, give precinct no) | 16. FACILITY NAME (If not institution, give street address)

17. INFORMANT'S NAME & RELATIONSHIP TO DECEASED | 18. MAILING ADDRESS OF INFORMANT (Street and Number, City, State, Zip Code)

19. METHOD OF DISPOSITION ☐ Burial ☐ Cremation ☐ Donation ☐ Entombment ☐ Removal From State ☐ Other (Specify) | 20. SIGNATURE AND LICENSE NUMBER OF FUNERAL DIRECTOR OR PERSON ACTING AS SUCH | 21. ☐ Unknown Section ____ Block ____ Lot ____ Space ____

22. PLACE OF DISPOSITION (Name of cemetery, crematory, other place) | 23. LOCATION (City/Town, and State)

24. NAME OF FUNERAL FACILITY | 25. COMPLETE ADDRESS OF FUNERAL FACILITY (Street and Number, City, State, Zip Code)

26. CERTIFIER (Check only one):
☐ Certifying Physician - To the best of my knowledge, death occurred due to the cause(s) and manner stated.
☐ Medical Examiner/Justice of the Peace – On the basis of examination, and/or investigation, in my opinion, death occurred at the time, date, and place, and due to the cause(s) and manner stated.

27. SIGNATURE OF CERTIFIER | 28. DATE CERTIFIED (Mo/Day/Yr) | 29. LICENSE NUMBER | 30. TIME OF DEATH (Actual or presumed)

31. PRINTED NAME, ADDRESS OF CERTIFIER (Street and Number, City, State, Zip Code) | 32. TITLE OF CERTIFIER

CAUSE OF DEATH

33. PART 1. ENTER THE CHAIN OF EVENTS – DISEASES, INJURIES, OR COMPLICATIONS – THAT DIRECTLY CAUSED THE DEATH. DO NOT ENTER TERMINAL EVENTS SUCH AS CARDIAC ARREST, RESPIRATORY ARREST, OR VENTRICULAR FIBRILLATION WITHOUT SHOWING THE ETIOLOGY. DO NOT ABBREVIATE. ENTER ONLY ONE CAUSE ON EACH LINE. | Approximate interval: Onset to death

IMMEDIATE CAUSE (Final disease or condition ——→ resulting in death) a. ____
Due to (or as a consequence of):
Sequentially list conditions, if any, leading to the cause listed on line a. Enter the UNDERLYING CAUSE (disease or injury that initiated the events resulting in death) LAST. b. ____
Due to (or as a consequence of):
c. ____
Due to (or as a consequence of):
d. ____

PART 2. ENTER OTHER SIGNIFICANT CONDITIONS CONTRIBUTING TO DEATH BUT NOT RESULTING IN THE UNDERLYING CAUSE GIVEN IN PART I. | 34. WAS AN AUTOPSY PERFORMED? ☐ Yes ☐ No | 35. WERE AUTOPSY FINDINGS AVAILABLE TO COMPLETE THE CAUSE OF DEATH? ☐ Yes ☐ No

36. MANNER OF DEATH ☐ Natural ☐ Accident ☐ Suicide ☐ Homicide ☐ Pending Investigation ☐ Could not be determined | 37. DID TOBACCO CONTRIBUTE TO DEATH? ☐ Yes ☐ No ☐ Probably ☐ Unknown | 38. IF FEMALE: ☐ Not pregnant within past year ☐ Pregnant at time of death ☐ Not pregnant, but pregnant within 42 days of death ☐ Not pregnant, but pregnant 43 days to 1 year before death ☐ Unknown if pregnant within the past year | 39. IF TRANSPORTATION INJURY, SPECIFY: ☐ Driver/Operator ☐ Passenger ☐ Pedestrian ☐ Other (Specify)

40a. DATE OF INJURY (Mo/Day/Yr) | 40b. TIME OF INJURY | 40c. INJURY AT WORK? ☐ Yes ☐ No | 40d. PLACE OF INJURY (e.g., Decedent's home; construction site, restaurant, wooded area)

40e. LOCATION (Street and Number, City, State, Zip Code) | 40f. COUNTY OF INJURY

41. DESCRIBE HOW INJURY OCCURRED

42a. REGISTRAR FILE NO. | 42b. DATE RECEIVED BY LOCAL REGISTRAR | 42c. REGISTRAR

Figure 1.1 Sample death certificate.

deaths, which encompass automobile collisions and drug overdoses as well as falls in elderly persons. Only a minority of medicolegal cases are actually homicides, which is often contrary to popular belief. Table 1.1 highlights the cases seen by several large medical examiner offices in the United States.

Table 1.1 Breakdown of Case Types Investigated by Manner of Death for ME Offices (Calendar Year 2016)

Office Location	Natural (%)	Accident (%)	Suicide (%)	Homicide (%)	Undetermined (%)
Office of the Chief Medical Examiner, Baltimore, MD[4]	30	23	8	11	28
Los Angeles County Medical Examiner, Los Angeles, CA[5]	43	37	10	8	2
Cook County Medical Examiner, Chicago, IL[6]	40	35	7	15	3
Bexar County Medical Examiner, San Antonio, TX[7]	40	39	9	8	4

Death Investigation Systems

The Coroner System

There are two general types of medicolegal investigative systems in the United States: **coroner** systems and **medical examiner** systems. As of 2000, 12 states had coroner systems, 19 states had state medical examiner systems, 3 states had county or regional medical examiner's offices but no coroner's offices and 16 had a mixture of medical examiner and coroner systems.[8] Over the years, there has been a gradual decrease in the number of coroner systems, with replacement by medical examiner systems, though this seems to have slowed down recently. Coroner systems, however, still make up a significant proportion of the medicolegal coverage of the American population.

The coroner system, dating back to feudal England, is the older of the two medicolegal systems. The earliest reference appears in the Articles of Eyre (1194).[9] In the pure form of this system, an individual who is not a physician is elected the coroner. He then makes rulings as to the cause and manner of death in cases that fall under the coroner law. As a general rule, these cases constitute violent deaths, sudden and/or unexpected deaths, suspicious deaths and cases in which a physician is not in attendance at the time of death. In making a determination, the coroner is not required to consult a physician for advice, may or may not order an autopsy and may or may not rule in agreement with autopsy findings if one is performed. The training the coroner receives for the position can range from absolutely none to a few hours or 1–2 weeks. Based on this training – or lack of it – the coroner makes decisions as to cause and manner of death that may have significant criminal and civil consequences.

In some areas of the country, this system has been modified such that the coroner must be a physician, though not necessarily a pathologist. This gives a scientific veneer to the system. We now have physicians making decisions in a medical field usually having absolutely nothing to do with their areas of expertise. Thus, we have the obstetrician-coroner, the general practitioner-coroner and so on. Occasionally, by chance, a forensic pathologist actually gets elected coroner, as is the case in several jurisdictions in Colorado, for example.

In some jurisdictions, the roles of the Coroner and Law Enforcement intersect, such as the case in California where, in a number of counties, the coroner is also the sheriff. Thus, a deputy sheriff might kill a civilian and his boss, the sheriff, rules as to the cause and manner of death. Sheriffs also operate jails. The sheriff acting as the coroner thus makes determinations as to the cause of death of inmates dying in his jail. Obviously, this may create at least the appearance of an ethical conflict. This conflict was recently on display when a sheriff-coroner in California was stripped of his death investigation duties after his impartiality was called into question.[10]

The issue of impartiality is not limited to law enforcement, however. In some cases, the coroner is also a funeral director and here again, there may be at least the appearance of a conflict of interest as some unscrupulous coroners are more interested in obtaining a family's permission to conduct the funeral than to make an accurate determination as to cause and manner of death. This may also occur if the coroner is simply a politician and the death being investigated involves a wealthy donor or prominent community member.

The coroner system was developed at a time when the lay public knew as much about the science of medicine as the physicians practicing it. Times have changed. Medicine has become an extremely complicated, specialized, scientific field. Specialized knowledge is necessary not only to practice medicine in general, but also to practice any of its numerous subspecialties. Thus, a dermatologist would not consider doing neurosurgery, nor would a neurosurgeon practice obstetrics/gynecology. The practice of forensic medicine has also become such a specialty. Neither average hospital pathologists nor physicians who are not pathologists can adequately practice in this field no matter how well intentioned they are – and they are often very well intentioned.

Some non-forensic pathologists claim that any anatomical pathologist with a basic knowledge of pathology can handle 85% of medical examiner cases, with the remaining 15% needing a forensic pathologist in a fully equipped medicolegal facility. Therefore, only a small corps of experienced forensic pathologists is needed, to which the difficult 15% of cases can be referred.

Even accepting this somewhat dubious premise, the problem is how does one know ahead of time which of the cases are the 15% needing the forensic pathologist and the fully equipped medical examiner's office? Not even a forensic pathologist knows for sure in every case. One never knows when the simplest autopsy will turn out to be a complicated case with the most extreme repercussions. For example, the authors know of cases where a witnessed "automobile accident" turned out, at autopsy, to be a capital homicide involving an armed robbery; where a simple carbon monoxide suicide in a garage eventually ended up with a million-dollar lawsuit involving the flying characteristics of lightplanes; and where a simple case of sudden death in infancy ended up as the final death in a decades-long chain of infanticide.

The Medical Examiner System

The medical examiner system was first introduced in the United States in 1877 in Massachusetts. The state was divided into a number of sectors, within each of which was designated a physician who functioned as a "medical examiner" to determine the cause and manner of death. Originally, medical examiners did not have the right to order autopsies. This was not corrected until the 1940s. It was only in the 1980s that a true state medical examiner system was established in Massachusetts.

The first true medical examiner system came into existence in 1918 in New York City.[11] A medicolegal system was established in which the individual designated as chief medical examiner was to be a physician experienced in the field of pathology (forensic pathology did not become a subspecialty until 1959). The system described the type of cases that fell under the Medical Examiner Law; it stated that the medical examiner could perform autopsies in cases where it was necessary, and it established a postmortem laboratory. The cases that fell under the medical examiner system were violent deaths (accidents, suicides, homicides), suspicious deaths, sudden, unexpected deaths and deaths occurring without the attendance of a physician. Most medical examiner systems in this country are variations of the original New York concept. Some of the newer systems specify that the chief medical examiner must be a forensic pathologist.

However, the creation of a medical examiner system does not necessarily mean that a community actually has a functioning or effective medical examiner system, nor does the fact that it once had one guarantee that it will continue to operate in an effective manner. For example, in the mid-1980s, New York City changed the law allowing families to prevent the performance of autopsies in cases in which the manner of death did not appear to be homicide; that is, the forensic pathologist had authority to perform an autopsy only in cases that were obviously homicide. Unfortunately, it is not always possible to recognize a homicide until an autopsy is performed. For instance, in 10% of children beaten to death, there is no external evidence of trauma. In addition, without an autopsy, an accurate cause of death, the presence and extent of disease or injury, the incapacitation produced by them and knowledge of whether there was any pain or suffering involved in an injury (an important question in civil cases) become sheer speculation.

In some instances, medical examiner's offices have not been funded adequately. In other instances, the offices are placed under state government agencies that should not be supervising the medical examiner's office. As discussed previously with coroners, no medical examiner's office should function under a police agency as this is a direct conflict in values, goals and philosophies. Police agencies are tasked with determining if a crime occurred while medical examiners determine the cause and manner of death, independent of who did what. While these functions often coincide, in some cases, they do not. One of the most controversial types of death is that of a civilian killed by police. By virtue of being a subdivision of a police agency, the impartiality of the medical examiner's office in such cases is open to serious question.

In some areas, the medical examiner's office functions under the public health department. This may or may not work out. Public health departments often have only a vague concept of the duties and functions of a medical examiner's office, which is a medicolegal agency rather than a pure medical agency. Ideally, the medical examiner's office should be reportable to only the highest authority, for example, the mayor, county commissioners or governor. However, as a general rule, while some medical examiner's offices are handicapped by defective laws, underfunding and political interference, they do a much better and more scientific job than a coroner. It is easier to convince ("coerce") a politician subject to election to change a death determination than a physician who can usually make more money in private practice doing the same work.

One argument for retention of the coroner system is that it is more economical than a medical examiner system. The coroner system, while cheaper in some jurisdictions in the short run because no experts or scientific investigations are used, becomes more expensive in the long run. Savings are lost when cases are invariably mishandled with resultant expensive and protracted litigation, both criminal and civil, retrials, the hiring of outside experts and so on. More important than money, however, is that the coroner system often produces inferior and inaccurate results. Nonphysicians cannot make medical decisions, no matter how many weeks of training they have. Mismanagement of cases can result in the imprisonment of innocent individuals and the release of the guilty. Just as we are guaranteed certain basic rights by our legal system, we should also have the right to a competent scientific medical investigation following a death, especially if there is the potential for civil or criminal litigation.

Some coroners argue that they can and do produce excellent work because they retain competent physicians and rely on them to make decisions. This is true. But, if coroners rely that much on their physicians, then what purposes do the coroners serve? They are just elected administrators subject to political influence who, if they desire, can ignore their experts. In addition, a conscientious, competent coroner may be defeated at the next election to be replaced by a venial incompetent.

A modern, well-organized medical examiner system is relatively inexpensive to operate, considering its benefits once the population serviced exceeds approximately 1,000,000. Cost to the community for a good system is approximately one-half the cost of a movie ticket per person per year. This money will fund a fully staffed medical examiner's office, including an investigative staff and a toxicology laboratory. Some states or counties claim to be too big, with a population too scattered, for a state system. This can be handled by establishing either regional offices or a central state office to which bodies can be transported.

Operation of a Medical Examiner System

To perform its duties, a medical examiner system requires a number of basic essentials. First is an adequate law under which to operate. Under such a law, violent deaths (accidents, suicides and homicides), suspicious deaths, sudden and unexpected deaths, deaths without a physician in attendance and deaths in jails and penal institutions should fall under the medical examiner's jurisdiction. In many areas, there is also a broad "24-h death" report law. That is, the death of any individual dying within 24 h of admission to a hospital must be reported to the medical examiner as a possible medical examiner case. This law is useful in picking up cases that might otherwise be missed.

After indicating the type of cases that fall under the medical examiner's jurisdiction, the law should then state that medical examiners have the right to perform an autopsy on any cases that they feel need one to accurately determine the cause and manner of death or to document injuries or disease processes. The law should also give medical examiners the right to subpoena records and individuals, if necessary, to help in making such determinations. The law should state that deaths are to be reported to medical examiners immediately after they occur or are discovered and that, at any death scene, medical examiners have jurisdiction over the body. Overall jurisdiction of the scene, of course, lies with the police agency involved. The law should also provide medical examiners with a certified toxicology laboratory.

The right of the medical examiner to perform autopsies in any cases falling under the Medical Examiner's Law is especially important. This is because accurate determination of the cause and manner of death can be accomplished only by a complete autopsy. The absence of any external evidence of injury does not rule out massive internal injuries and the possibility that the case is a homicide. Thus, in the authors' experience, 10% of all children dying of blunt traumatic injuries show no evidence of injury externally. If one could not perform an autopsy in such cases, these homicides would be missed and death ascribed to natural causes. Obvious homicide cases are less of a problem than the more subtle ones that initially appear to be natural deaths or accidents.

It is also highly desirable that the medical examiners have some civil service protection. This is because medical examiners make unpopular decisions, decisions that politicians, police agencies and sometimes the public may not want to hear. There is always the natural tendency of humanity to want to "kill" the bearer of bad news.

The second requirement for an adequate medical examiner system is qualified personnel. The chief medical examiner should be a **board-certified forensic pathologist** with a number of years of experience. Under the chief medical examiner, there should be assistant medical examiners who are also board-certified forensic pathologists. If the assistant medical examiners are initially not certified, the individuals should be given a certain time limit (2–3 years) to obtain certification. To acquire and retain such qualified personnel, they must command competitive salaries.

What is a board-certified forensic pathologist? A **board-certified forensic pathologist is a physician** who has successfully completed a graduate medical education program either anatomical or anatomical and clinical pathology accredited by the Accreditation Council for Graduate Medical Education (ACGME) or the Royal College of Physicians and Surgeons of Canada and has successfully passed a board examination administered by the American Board of Pathology in this (these) field(s) of medicine. They have then completed at least one additional year of supervised training in forensic pathology in an ACGME-accredited program and passed an examination designed and administered by the American Board of Pathology in the field of forensic pathology.

Third, the medical examiner's office needs adequate staffing. Medical examiners alone do not constitute an office. There must be competent investigative, administrative, secretarial and technical support staff.

Fourth, there must be an adequate facility. One cannot practice forensic medicine in the subbasement of a county hospital or in the back of a funeral home. The facility must have sufficient space; an appropriate floor plan; electrical, plumbing and cooling capabilities; and furnishings.

Fifth, there must be adequate instrumentation available for the scientific investigation of death, including X-ray equipment or even CT scan capability. There should also be equipment in the toxicological laboratory capable of an accurate, precise analysis for the presence of drugs. The equipment should be of high quality and be in sufficient quantity to handle the caseload. Computerization of an office has now become mandatory.

There must also be consistent and adequate funding of the institution. Without this, a qualified staff is not possible, nor are adequate facilities or equipment. And lastly, the office should be accredited by an appropriate accrediting body. The National Association of Medical Examiners (NAME) offers a voluntary inspection and accreditation program for medicolegal offices. The program offers **a minimum set of qualifications** of an office to ensure an adequate death investigation system. In addition to accrediting offices, NAME has also issued Autopsy Performance Standards that offer guidelines for practicing forensic pathologists. These requirements are available to all interested parties on the NAME website, as is a list of NAME-accredited offices (www.thename.org).

Death Investigation

How should a medicolegal death investigation be approached? Medically – just like any other physician approaches a patient. In medical school, one is taught that, to make a correct diagnosis, one must take a history, perform a physical examination and order relevant laboratory tests. Based on this, a diagnosis is made. The forensic pathologist performs all of these functions but with some variance. Firstly, the history is not obtained from the patient, but from witnesses, relatives of the deceased, police agencies, treating physicians and/or records (medical, nonmedical, police, governmental, etc.). It is an account of the events leading up to and surrounding the death.

After a review of this background information, the medical examiner determines what type of exam is necessary. The medical examiner then performs a physical examination and laboratory tests. The procedures may range from an external examination of the body to a complete internal autopsy. This will be determined by the information that has been provided to the medical examiner by the investigator, the type of case, the medical examiner's expertise and local or regional differences. Not all deaths require full autopsies, as doing so places additional strains on often tight resources.

Photographic documentation of autopsies is often also necessary. At a minimum, it is recommended that photographs of the body be taken prior to examination with at least one photograph of the face and head for use as an identification photograph. Additionally, there should be photographic documentation of any significant injuries, including close-up photographs of all gunshot wounds, stab wounds and patterned injuries.

Samples should be retained on every case for future testing, if needed. Often blood, urine and vitreous samples are obtained. Routine drug screens should be performed on almost all investigated deaths, with the exception being deaths that occurred after a prolonged period of time since the incident, and where samples from that time are no longer available. However, even in these deaths, toxicology may be helpful, for instance, in the case of a death due to a remote head injury where the patient was administered terminal morphine. Additionally, a genetic sample, such as a blood spot card, is obtained and retained for every case, should future DNA testing be required.

At the time of autopsy, tissue should be retained for possible microscopic examination, although this is not necessary in every case. Such tissue, as well as any toxicology samples, should be retained for as long as possible, though the National Association of Medical Examiners requires them to be retained for at least one year.[12] If microscopic slides are created, NAME requires retention of at least 10 years for the paraffin blocks and indefinite retainment of the slides.[12]

Additional specialized tests or examinations may also be completed at the autopsy, such as sexual assault examinations, and evidence may also be collected. This evidence should either be released to the investigating agency or the appropriate forensic laboratory or be retained as required by the local applicable laws.

Investigators

In most major medical examiner systems in this country, reports of deaths do not come directly to medical examiners, but to lay investigators employed by the medical examiner's office, who are trained to screen the cases and make a determination as to whether a death is a medical examiner's case. If it is not, it is then released back to the reporting physician. If the case falls under the medical examiner's jurisdiction or if there is no physician to sign the death certificate, the case is accepted. Whether a case is accepted or not, documentation of the death and subsequent report is necessary. In cases that are not accepted, the report should be reviewed by a medical examiner as soon as possible so that if there is any disagreement with the conclusion of the investigator, the medical examiner may still order an examination.

If investigators accept the case as a medical examiner's case, they often also attend the scene and take possession of the body. If the body has been moved from the scene to a hospital, a scene examination is usually not necessary and the body can be brought directly to the ME office. If the body is still at the scene, the investigator should go to the scene and document all the findings at the scene regarding the body and to obtain a detailed history of the circumstances leading up to and surrounding the death. In addition to preparing a detailed scene report, investigators should document the scene with diagrams and/or photographs. Even if the body has been removed from the scene, a scene investigation may still be necessary, this is particularly true for sudden infant deaths.

In some jurisdictions, physicians routinely make all scene investigations or at least all violent death scenes. While this is satisfactory in small, low-volume offices, it is generally not practical for larger jurisdictions. In some areas of the country, a physician who visits a scene has the right to sign out the case without bringing it into the medical examiner's office – the authors do not condone this practice as there is no way to adequately examine a body at a scene. If a body is a medical examiner's case, it should come into the office, where, at the minimum, a complete external examination can be performed in an environment with adequate lighting, equipment and support personnel, and the necessary toxicology samples can be obtained.

Depending upon jurisdiction, investigators come from a variety of backgrounds, including criminal justice, nursing and anthropology; some have degrees in biological, psychological or physical or other sciences. Regardless of previous training, investigators should be well versed in the local laws governing medicolegal death investigation and should become certified as medicolegal death investigators by the American Board of Medicolegal Death Investigators.[13]

Forensic Consultants

As part of a thorough death investigation, consultation with additional forensic experts may be of assistance. In addition to interacting with forensic scientists (see Chapter 23), the forensic pathologist may require assistance from a forensic odontologist, especially for issues of dental identification or bite mark analysis. Or in skeletal case, a forensic anthropologist may be of assistance. In cases where forensic consultants are utilized, the authors recommend only working with consultants who are certified by the appropriate specialty boards, such as the American Board of Forensic Odontology and the American Board of Forensic Anthropology.

References

1. United States. President's Commission for the Study of Ethical Problems in Medicine and Biomedical and Behavioral Research (1981). Defining death: a report on the medical, legal and ethical issues in the determination of death. Retrieved November 7, 2006 from The President's Council on Bioethics web site: http://www.bioethics.gov/reports/past_commissions/defining_death.pdf
2. Molina DK, McCutcheon JR, and Rulon JJ, Head injuries, pentobarbital and the determination of death. *Am J For Med Pathol* 2009; 30(1):75–77.
3. Baeva S, Archer NP, Ruggiero K, Hall M, Stagg J, Interis EC, et al., Maternal mortality in Texas. *Am J Perinatol* 2017; 34(6):614–620.
4. 2016 Annual Report, Office of the Chief Medical Examiner, Baltimore, MD.

5. 2016 Annual Report, Los Angeles County Medical Examiner, Los Angeles, CA.
6. 2016 Annual Report, Cook County Medical Examiner, Chicago, IL.
7. 2016 Annual Report, Bexar County Medical Examiner, San Antonio, TX.
8. Hanzlick R and Combs D, Medical examiner and coroner systems: history and trends (special communication). *JAMA* 1998; 279(11):870–874.
9. Mant AK, The evaluation of the coroner's system and the present status in Great Britain. *Forensic Sci Gazette* 1971; 2(4):1–6.
10. Small J, San Joaquin county sheriff stripped of role in death investigations. https://www.kqed.org/news/11664465/san-joaquin-county-sheriff-stripped-of-role-in-death-investigations accessed 8 August 2019.
11. The office of the Medical Examiner of the city of New York. Report by the Committee on Public Health, New York Academy of Medicine. *Bull NY Acad Med* 1967; 43:241–249.
12. NAME Inspection and Accreditation Checklist Adopted November 2018.
13. American Board of Medicolegal Death Investigators: St. Louis, MO.

Postmortem Changes, Time of Death and Identification

2

I'd like to introduce you to the mortifying Mortis Brothers. They are … Pal, Al, Rig, and Liv Mortis.

—Artem Cheprasov

Determination of the time of death is important in both criminal and civil cases. In criminal cases, it can set the time of the murder, eliminate or suggest suspects, and confirm or disprove an alibi. In civil cases, the time of death might determine who inherits property or whether an insurance policy was in force. Unfortunately, all methods now in use to determine the time of death are, to a degree, unreliable and inaccurate. They usually give vague or dubious answers. The longer the postmortem interval, that is the time between death and the attempt to determine time of death, the less precise the estimate of the interval. One obvious facet of time of death determination often not considered is that the time the fatal injury is incurred is not necessarily the time of death. One can incur massive fatal injuries, yet linger in an unconscious state for hours prior to death (Figure 2.1).

Many postmortem changes have been used to try to determine the time of death, including livor mortis, rigor mortis, body temperature, decomposition, vitreous electrolyte composition, digestion of stomach contents, insect activity, flow cytometry, DNA degradation and circumstantial information; however, none proved adequate enough to establish a definitive time range.

Livor Mortis

Livor mortis (lividity, postmortem hypostasis) is a reddish-purple coloration in dependent areas of the body due to accumulation of blood in the small vessels in these areas secondary to gravity (Figure 2.2A).

Postmortem lividity is occasionally misinterpreted as bruising by people unfamiliar with this phenomenon.

Dependent areas resting against a firm surface will appear pale in contrast to the surrounding livor mortis due to compression of the vessels in this area, which prevents the accumulation of blood. Thus, areas supporting the weight of the body, for example, the shoulder blades, buttocks and calves in individuals lying on their backs, show no livor mortis, but appear as pale or blanched areas (Figure 2.2B and C).

Tight clothing, such as brassieres or belts, can also compress soft tissues, collapsing the vessels and producing pale areas.

Livor mortis usually, but not invariably, has a cherry-red to pinkish color in deaths with elevated concentrations of carboxyhemoglobin such as those due to carbon monoxide. Identical coloration may be caused by exposure of a body to cold temperatures, and in

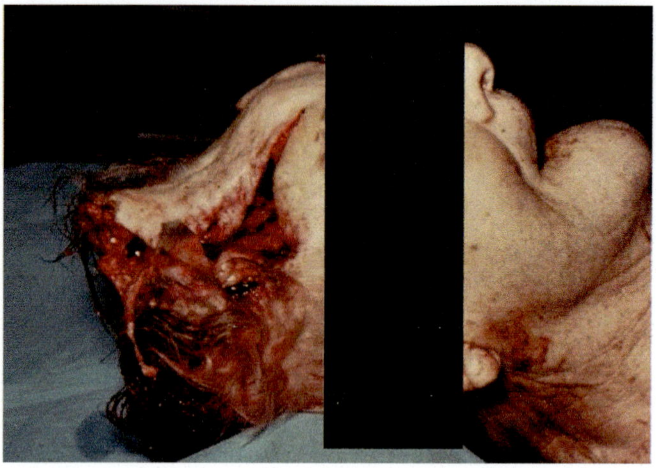

Figure 2.1 Contact wound of right temple with .357 Magnum. The deceased lived 1 h and 34 min with no life support systems.

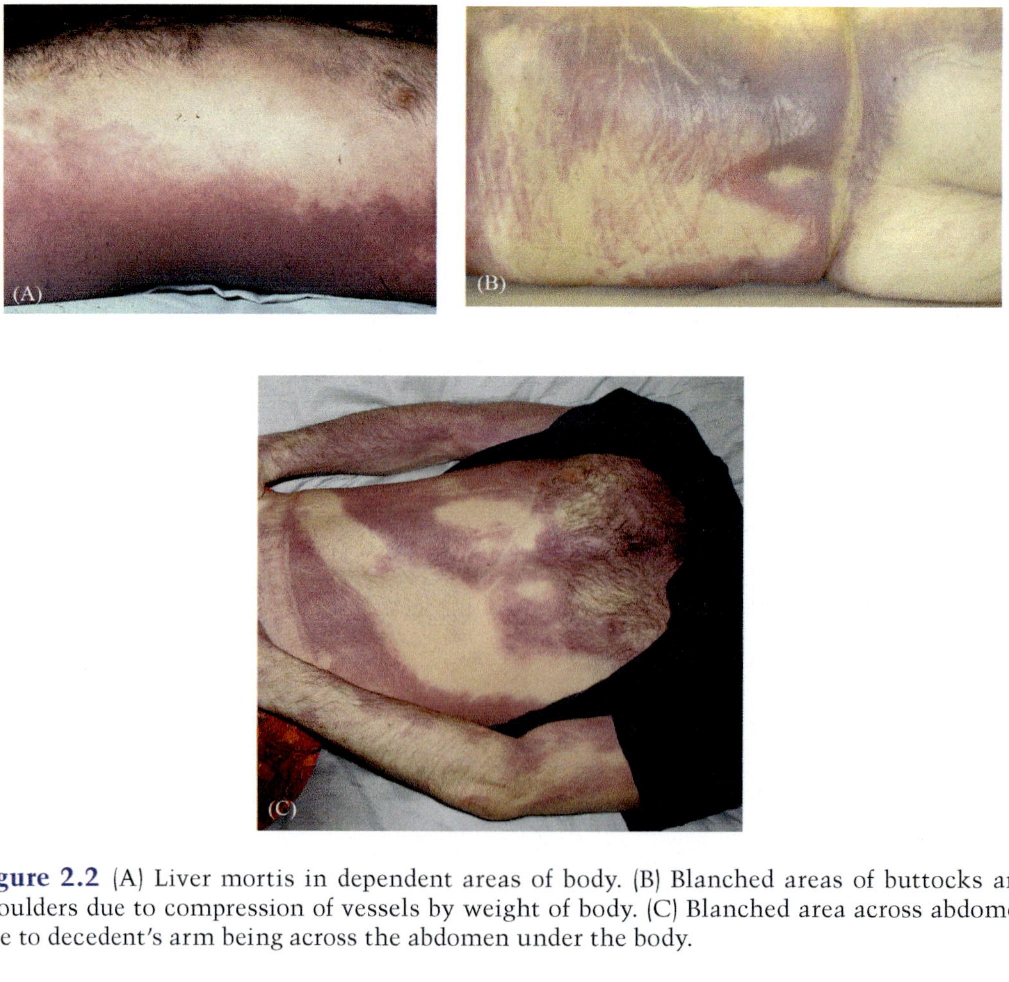

Figure 2.2 (A) Liver mortis in dependent areas of body. (B) Blanched areas of buttocks and shoulders due to compression of vessels by weight of body. (C) Blanched area across abdomen due to decedent's arm being across the abdomen under the body.

deaths due to cyanide. Localized areas of bright red livor mortis are also seen adjacent to chest tubes and contact gunshot wounds. In the first three of the aforementioned entities, the coloration is caused by predominance of oxygenated hemoglobin, while the coloration surrounding gunshot wounds is due to carboxyhemoglobin.

Livor mortis is usually evident within 30 min to 2 h after death. In individuals dying a slow lingering death with terminal cardiac failure, livor mortis may actually appear antemortem. Livor mortis develops gradually, usually reaching its maximum coloration at 8–12 h. At about this time, it is said to become "fixed." Prior to becoming fixed, livor mortis will shift as the body is moved. Thus, if an individual dies lying on his back, livor mortis develops posteriorly, that is, on the back. If one turns the body on its face, blood will drain to the anterior surface of the body, now the dependent aspect. Livor mortis becomes "fixed" when shifting or drainage of blood no longer occurs, or when blood leaks out of the vessels into the surrounding soft tissue due to hemolysis and breakdown of the vessels. The absence of fixation can be demonstrated by applying pressure to a dependent discolored area and noting the subsequent blanching at the point of pressure. Fixation can occur before 8–12 h if decomposition is accelerated, or be delayed up to 24–36 h if the body is kept cool. Thus, the statement that livor mortis becomes fixed at 8–12 h is really just a vague generalization.

Although livor mortis may be confused with bruising, bruising is rarely confused with livor mortis. Application of pressure to an area of bruising will not cause blanching and incision into an area of contusion or bruising shows diffuse hemorrhage within the soft tissues. In contrast, an incision into an area of livor mortis may reveal faint erythema due to the congested vessels, and fails to show hemorrhage within the soft tissue.

It is important to note that livor mortis also occurs internally, with settling of the blood in the dependent aspects of an organ. This is most obvious in the lungs.

As the blood accumulates in the dependent areas, the pressure of the settling blood can rupture small vessels, with the development of petechiae or minute hemorrhages also called Tardieu spots after Auguste Tardieu. These spots can aggregate to create purpura (patches of purplish discoloration) (Figure 2.3). This usually takes 18–24 h and often indicates that decomposition is fast approaching. This phenomenon is more common slow deaths such as in asphyxia. Unfortunately, as time passes, it cannot always be determined with certainty whether the purpura produced are ante- or postmortem. The presence of petechiae and purpura only in dependent areas suggests a postmortem origin. In limbs hanging over the side of a bed or the legs and forearms of an individual who is hanging, Tardieu spots may develop even more rapidly, appearing as early as 2–4 h after death

Livor mortis can cause difficulty in interpreting head injuries in decomposed bodies. In a body lying on its back, blood accumulates in the posterior or dependent half of the scalp due to gravity. In advanced decomposition, with lysis of red blood cells and breakdown of the vessels, there is seepage of blood into the soft tissue of the scalp. This gives the appearance of confluent bruising and cannot always be differentiated from true antemortem bruising. There will, of course, be no abrasion or laceration of the scalp, but all forensic pathologists have seen extensive scalp contusions without abrasions or lacerations. In decomposed bodies, blood collecting in the occipital areas of the brain due to gravity may escape through small vessels, producing very thin localized films of blood in the subarachnoid or subdural spaces coating the occipital lobes. The rest of the brain does not show subarachnoid or subdural hemorrhage. In drownings where the body floats head

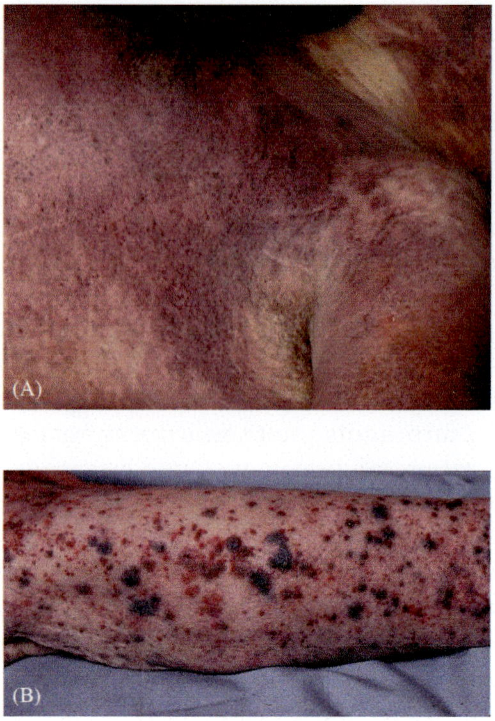

Figure 2.3 Tardieu spots: (A) petechiae in area of livor mortis and (B) petechiae and purpura in arm hanging over a bed terminally.

down, decomposition produces the picture of diffuse scalp hemorrhage. Rarely, postmortem leakage of blood into the soft tissue and muscle of the anterior aspect of the neck may also occur in drownings; however, when present, this hemorrhage is minimal.

Due to the variables involved, livor mortis is not very useful in determining the time of death. However, it can be immensely valuable in determining terminal position and whether the body has been moved.

Rigor Mortis

Rigor mortis, or the stiffening of the body after death, is due to the disappearance of adenosine triphosphate (ATP) from muscle. ATP is the basic source of energy for muscle contraction. Muscle needs a continuous supply of ATP to contract because the amount present is sufficient to sustain muscle contraction for only a few seconds. The three metabolic systems responsible for maintaining a continuous supply of ATP in the muscle are the phosphagen system, the glycogen-lactic acid system and the aerobic system. Under optimal conditions, the phosphagen system can provide maximal muscle power for 10–15 s, the glycogen-lactic acid system for 30–40 s and the aerobic system for an unlimited period of time.[1] After exercise, these three systems need time to be replenished. After death, generation of ATP stops, though consumption continues. In the absence of ATP, actin and myosin filaments become permanently complexed and rigor mortis sets in. This complex remains until decomposition occurs.

Any violent muscular exertion prior to death will produce a decrease in ATP and speed up the onset of rigor mortis, since no ATP is produced after death. Some factors that cause a marked decrease in ATP prior to death are violent or heavy exercise, severe convulsions and high body temperatures. All of these factors may cause rapid onset of rigor mortis, with onset appearing within minutes in some cases, and, in rare instances, instantaneously. The instantaneous appearance of rigor mortis is known as **cadaveric spasm**. In one instance, a man was chasing his wife with a straight razor when she turned and fired one shot, striking and killing him instantly. The deceased collapsed to his knees, holding the razor in his right hand in an upward position. At the scene, he was found dead, kneeling, with his right arm extended upward with the razor clasped in the hand. In cadaveric spasm, the object will be firmly clenched in the hand (Figure 2.4).

Rigor mortis disappears with decomposition. Cold or freezing will delay the onset of rigor mortis as well as prolong its presence. Rigor mortis can be "broken" by passive stretching of muscles. After rigor mortis is broken, it will not return. If only partial rigor mortis has set in prior to stretching, then the residual unbroken rigor mortis can still set in.

Rigor mortis usually appears 2–4 h after death and fully develops in 6–12 h. This can vary greatly. In a case seen by one of the authors, a young woman died following an overdose of aspirin. The emergency medical system was activated while she was in an agonal state. On arrival, she was still breathing and had a heart rate. Almost immediately, she suffered a cardiopulmonary arrest. Attempts at resuscitation were made and continued for approximately 15–20 min. Following this, she was pronounced dead. The body was then made ready to be transported to the medical examiner's office. At this time, it was realized that she was in full rigor mortis, only minutes after being pronounced dead. Two hours later, at the morgue, she had a rectal temperature of 106°F.

Rigor mortis, when it develops, involves all the muscles at the same time and at the same rate. However, it becomes most evident in the smaller muscles. Thus, rigor mortis is said to appear first in the smaller muscles, such as the jaw, and then to gradually spread to large muscle groups, such as the thighs. The classical presentation of rigor mortis in its

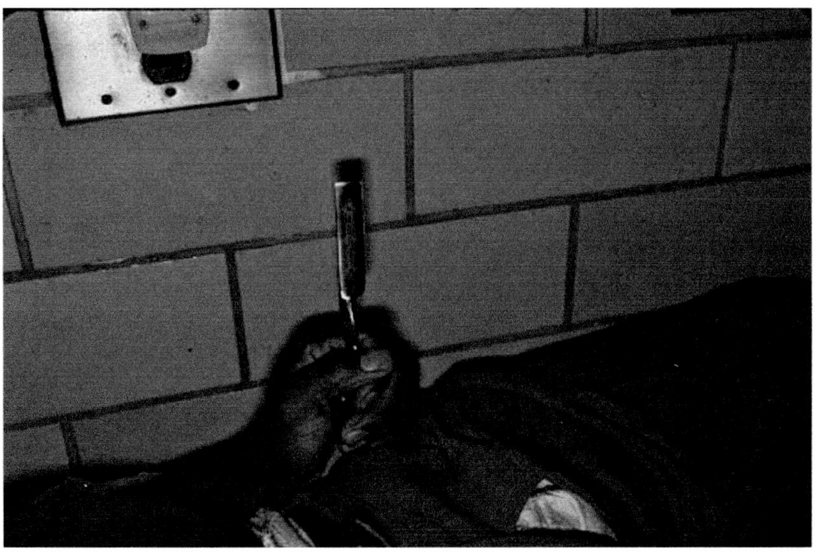

Figure 2.4 Cadaveric spasm in a 43-year-old male with razor in the right hand.

order of appearance is jaw, upper extremities and lower extremities. It passes off in the order in which it appeared. Rigor mortis is lost due to decomposition. In temperate climates, rigor mortis disappears in 36 h, but may be present up to 6 days. In hot climates, a body can be in a moderately advanced to advanced state of decomposition in 24 h, in which case, there will be no rigor mortis present.

In a case seen by one of the authors, the decomposing body of a 14-year-old boy was pulled from a cold lake. He had drowned 17 days prior. The body was in an early-to-moderate state of decomposition externally with a swollen face and discolored skin with slippage and marbling. The internal organs were in an early state of decomposition – not as decomposed as one might expect with the external changes. The most unusual aspect of the case was that the body was still in full rigor mortis. One can only speculate that the immersion in the cold water was the reason the rigor mortis persisted.

Rigor mortis may be delayed or be very weak in emaciated individuals. Its onset may also be very rapid in infants. Poisons, such as strychnine, that produce convulsions can accelerate the development of rigor mortis. Any disease or environmental factor that raises body temperature accelerates the development of rigor mortis. Thus, hyperthermia, loss of body regulatory temperature due to cerebral hemorrhage, sympathomimetic drugs, excited delirium and infection may accelerate the development of rigor mortis.

In drowning deaths, rigor mortis may develop fully within only 2–3 h. This is apparently due to exhaustion of ATP through violent struggling while drowning. Individuals who are being chased prior to their deaths may show more rapid development of rigor mortis in their legs than in the rest of their musculature. This, again, is due to exhaustion of ATP by the muscles of the legs caused by running.

Like livor mortis, rigor mortis displays far too much variability to be used to determine time of death, however, it can indicate whether a body has been moved (Figure 2.5).

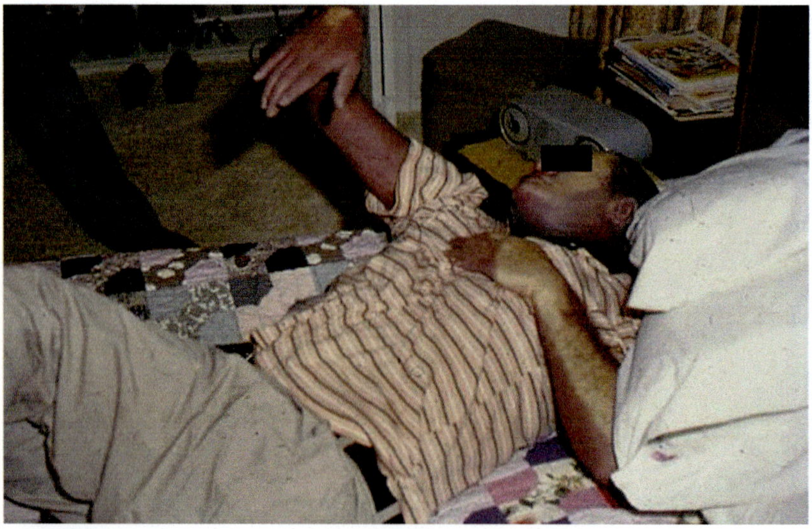

Figure 2.5 Body originally found face down, but now turned onto back. Left arm in air, blanching of the right side of face, back of right hand and forearm and back of the left wrist.

Body Temperature

After a person dies, and metabolic processes cease, it has long been believed that the body temperature will slowly begin to decrease, until decomposition sets in, when the temperature may rise again. Some have attempted to quantify this change to determine how long an individual has been dead. However, these determinations have been shown to be fraught with errors. First, one must assume that the body temperature at death was normal, and second, that body cooling follows a predictable pattern such that one can project what the prior body temperature was and what it will be.

Determination of the time of death by body temperature usually involves using a formula. A number of formulas have been devised, some of which are quite complicated. However, the easiest of the formulas is simply a rough estimate that:

$$\text{Time since death} = 37e°\text{C} - \text{Rectal temperature } (°\text{C}) + 3$$

Others rely on the Glaister equation or temperature nomograms (Figure 2.6):

$$\text{Time since death} = \frac{98.6\ °\text{F-Rectal Temperature } (°\text{F})}{1.5} (\text{Glaister equation})$$

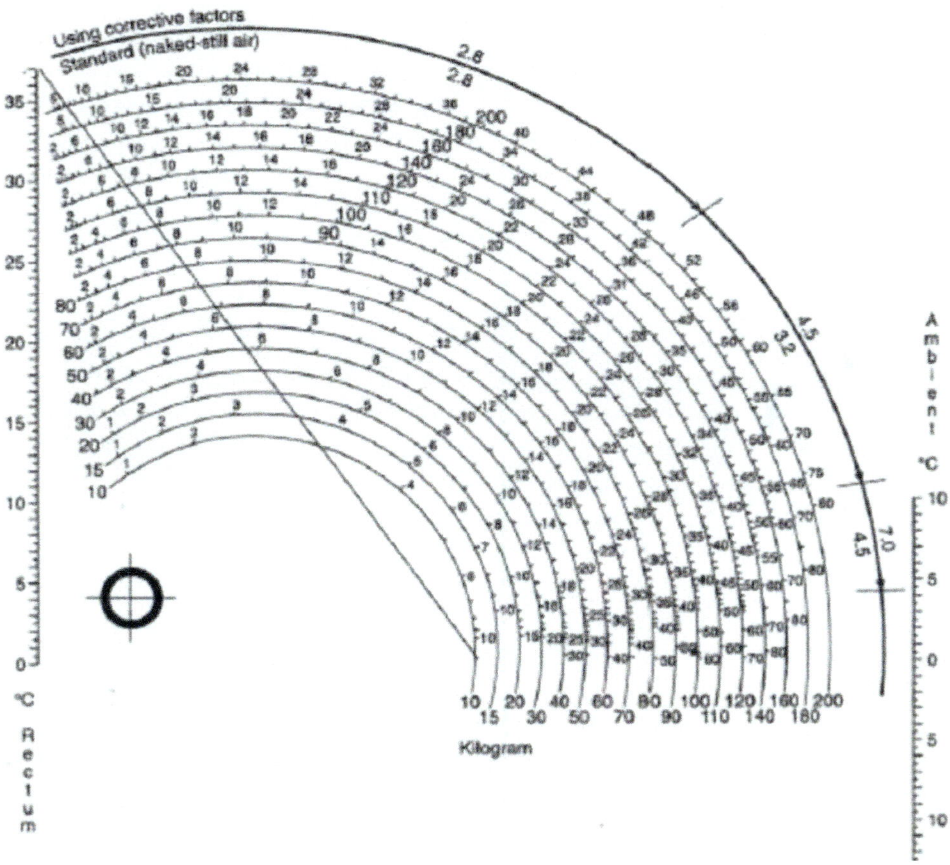

Figure 2.6 Temperature nomogram for determining time since death.

The problem with all formulas using body temperature to determine time of death is that they are based on the assumption that the body temperature at time of death is "normal." What is normal? "Normal" body temperature is an average. Some people have higher and some have lower body temperatures. Traditionally, the normal mean oral temperature has been said to be 98.6°F (37.0°C). These figures are based on testing done during the 19th century. More recent work indicates that mean oral temperature, for healthy adults age 40 or younger, is really 98.2°F (36.8°C) with 99.9°F (37.7°C) the upper limit of the normal temperature range.[2] Body temperature also varies with time of day, with the nadir at 6 a.m. and the zenith at 4–6 p.m. Women showed slightly higher normal temperatures.

A second problem is that even if we knew what the deceased's normal temperature was, was the temperature normal at the time of death? Strenuous exercise can raise rectal temperatures up to 104°F. Infection obviously causes a rise in body temperature. Intracerebral hemorrhages or injury to the brain can cause dysfunction of the thermoregulatory system of the brainstem, which causes increased body temperatures. Exposure to cold can cause hypothermia (low body temperatures).

In other words, body temperature varies from the site where it was taken (oral or rectal, brain or liver), from individual to individual, by time of day, by the activity of the individual and by the health of the individual. To make matters even worse, it appears that body temperature may not consistently decrease after death. Hutchins compared recent premortem rectal temperatures with postmortem rectal temperatures and found postmortem temperatures increased in the early postmortem period.[3] Utilizing linear regression analysis of the pre- and postmortem rectal temperature difference as a function of time, he concluded that, on the average, postmortem rectal temperature took about 4 h to return to premortem levels after death. He hypothesized that continuing metabolic activity of body tissues and bacteria in the bowel was the cause of this effect.

Another factor to be considered is that death may not occur immediately following an assault. Patients could be injured and lie in a coma for several hours. They might develop pneumonia, increasing the body temperature, or die slowly in coma, becoming hypothermic. Thus, even if one knew exactly when an individual died, the time might not correspond to the time of the assault.

An additional issue is the logistics of actually obtaining the postmortem temperature as care must be taken not to introduce injury to the body when doing so. If the forensic pathologist decides to take rectal temperatures, the rectum must always be examined prior to insertion of the thermometer. In cases of possible sexual assault, swabs should be taken prior to insertion of the thermometer. The authors recommend against taking internal temperatures, such as rectal or liver, at the scene, as the body cannot be adequately assessed prior to doing so.

In addition to the aforementioned problems with "normal" body temperatures, there is the confounding issue that body cooling does not necessarily follow a uniform, predictable pattern such that one can project what the body temperature was. In a dead body, heat is lost by conduction (absorption of heat by objects in contact with the body), radiation (loss in the form of infrared heat rays) and convection (movement of air). Thus, we can see that loss of body heat is passive. If the temperature of the environment surrounding the body is greater than 98.6°F, the body will get warmer; if the same, the body will remain at 98.6°F; and, if colder, the body will cool. There is, unfortunately, no control over environmental temperature.

At a scene, there may be air conditioning or heating. A body lying in sunlight will retain heat longer than in shade. But the sun moves, changing the conditions of exposure to sunlight, and thus, heat. A wet body conducts heat more rapidly. Is the body lying on stone, which is excellent for conduction, or on a bed, which acts as an insulator? Is the individual fat or thin? Clothed or nude? Clothing and fat act as insulators that tend to retain heat. Children and infants cool rapidly because they have a large surface area relative to mass. The opposite occurs with obese individuals, that is, they have a small surface area relative to their mass. Cachectic (emaciated) individuals, of course, cool faster than obese individuals.

Thus, like both rigor and livor mortis, body temperature displays far too great variation to allow for prediction of time of death based upon its measurement. That being said, it may be useful in the investigation of certain types of deaths, such as hyperthermia, hypothermic and excited delirium, but its routine use for determination of time of death should be discouraged.

Decomposition

Decomposition involves two processes: autolysis and putrefaction. Autolysis is the breakdown of cells and organs through an aseptic chemical process caused by intracellular enzymes. Since it is a chemical process, it is accelerated by heat, slowed by cold, and stopped by freezing or the inactivation of enzymes by heat. Organs rich in enzymes will undergo autolysis faster than organs with lesser amounts of enzyme. Thus, the pancreas autolyzes before the heart.

The second form of decomposition, which to most individuals is synonymous with decomposition, is putrefaction. *This is due to bacteria and fermentation.* After death, the bacterial flora of the gastrointestinal tract spread throughout the body, producing putrefaction. This is accelerated in septic individuals because bacteria have already spread throughout the body prior to death.

When we talk about decomposition, we usually mean putrefaction. The onset of putrefaction depends on two main factors: the environment and the body. In hot climates, the more important of these two factors is environment.

Most authorities would give the following sequence of events in decomposition of bodies. First, there is greenish discoloration of the lower quadrants of the abdomen, the right more than the left, usually in the first 24–36 h. This is followed by greenish discoloration of the head, neck and shoulders, swelling of the face due to bacterial gas formation and "marbling." Marbling is produced by hemolysis of blood in vessels with reaction of hemoglobin and hydrogen sulfide and development of greenish-black coloration along the vessels (Figure 2.7).

The body soon undergoes generalized bloating (60–72 h) followed by vesicle formation, skin slippage and hair slippage. By this time, the body is a pale green to green-black color.

Bloating of the body is often noted first in the face, where the features are swollen, the eyes bulge and the tongue protrudes between the teeth and lips. The face has a pale greenish color, changing to greenish black, then to black (Figure 2.8).

Decomposition fluid (purge fluid) will drain from the mouth and nose (Figure 2.9).

This is often misinterpreted by the inexperienced as blood, and trauma is suspected. Decomposition fluid will also accumulate in body cavities and should not be confused with hemothorax in the case of the pleural cavities. Usually, the fluid accumulating in each pleural cavity is less than 200 mL.

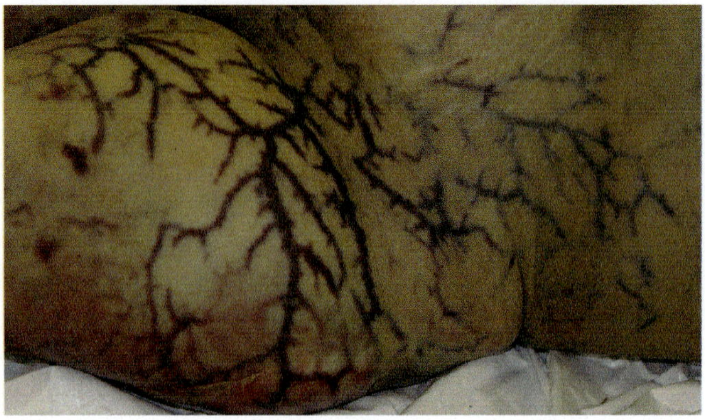

Figure 2.7 Marbling.

As decomposition continues, hemolyzed blood leaks out into the tissue. Especially in the scalp, this cannot readily be differentiated from antemortem bruising. Thus, in the dependent areas of the head in decomposed bodies, one must be very cautious in interpreting blood in the tissue as a contusion.

This description of the gradual decomposition of a body assumes a temperate environmental climate. With high temperature, this process can be accelerated. Thus, in South Texas, a body left in a car during the summer may take less than 24 h to go from a fresh

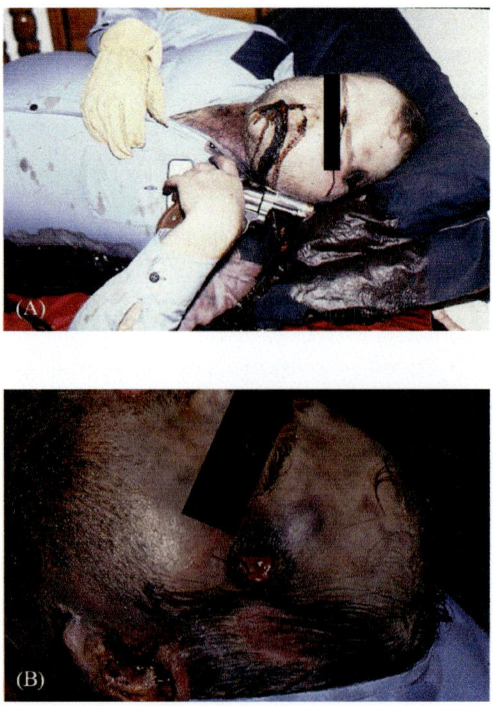

Figure 2.8 (A) Decomposition with discoloration and early marbling. (B) Same individual 12 h prior. Body was immediately refrigerated after discovery, yet decomposition continued.

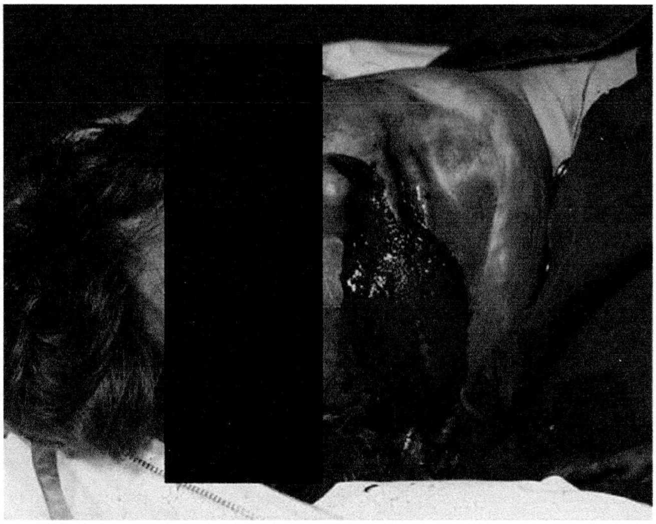

Figure 2.9 Early decomposition with bloody purge fluid flowing from nostrils.

state to a swollen, greenish-black body with marbling, vesicle formation, skin slippage and purge fluid. Cold weather slows down and may even stop decomposition. A frozen body will not undergo decomposition until it defrosts. Extreme examples of this are mammoths frozen in Siberia for thousands of years.

Decomposition is hastened by obesity, heavy clothing and sepsis, all of which keep the body warm. Decomposition is delayed by tight clothing or by the body's lying on a metallic or stone surface that will rapidly cool it by conduction. In the case of generalized sepsis, the authors have seen bodies undergo accelerated decomposition in spite of the fact that they were immediately refrigerated. A septic body dead 6–12 h may have the appearance of one dead 5–6 days even if refrigerated.

Even in the non-septic body, if decomposition has set in, immediate refrigeration of the body may not necessarily stop decomposition completely (Figure 2.7). Thus, the authors have seen a number of bodies in which there was early decomposition with opaque eyes, a reddish tinge to the skin of the face, and bloody purge fluid in the mouth and nostrils when the body was initially viewed at the scene. When the body came to autopsy 6–12 h later, after having been refrigerated the whole time, the face was bloated and greenish black.

As decomposition progresses, hair slips off the head and skin from the hands. Thus, one finds "gloves" of skin. Hair may be taken by birds in the area and used to build nests. As the body decomposes and swells, one often gets the impression of a very heavy individual. When the body is actually weighed, however, the weight will be found to be significantly less than estimated on gross examination of the body. As decomposition proceeds, the weight of the organs decreases; the internal organs will autolyze, becoming soft, clay-like or liquify. **Agonal** or **postmortem esophagomalachia** and **gastromalacia** (autodigestion of the lower esophagus and stomach) can also occur, even in the absence of decomposition. The gastric mucosa turns grayish-white to black in appearance and is extremely friable; ruptured sites may also be seen. Microscopically, there is an absence of any inflammation. This phenomenon occurs either immediately prior to death or, more probably, immediately after death and is of no clinical significance.

In hot, dry climates, the body can dehydrate rapidly and may go into mummification rather than decomposition. While the skin will have a brown to black leathery appearance, the internal organs will continue to deteriorate, often reduced to a blackish-brown putty-like consistency. The uterus and prostate are two of the last organs to decompose.

Bodies are embalmed to delay decomposition. The success of embalming is variable and depends on the quality of the embalming, the climate and the nature of the ground where the body is buried. Rarely will a body be perfectly preserved for years. One of the authors disinterred the body of an elderly white female buried for 6 years that was in perfect condition and could have been "viewed" at a funeral. There was no odor, no observable changes to the outside of the body and no fungus present. Microscopic sections from the embalmed organs were perfectly preserved. The body of another female buried the same length of time, but in ground where water leaked into the coffin, was completely skeletonized. The authors have seen bodies buried for a year perfectly preserved, except for some drying of the fingertips and patches of fungus, while other bodies buried 2–3 weeks are in an advanced state of decomposition.

The time necessary for skeletonization of a body is also variable. In areas where the body is exposed to the elements and scavengers, it can proceed quite rapidly, occurring in 9–10 days. In rare instances, it may be even faster than this.

Occasionally, a decomposing body will undergo transformation to adipocere (Figure 2.10). Adipocere is a firm, grayish-white to brown wax-like material composed of oleic, palmitic and stearic acids. It is produced by conversion of neutral fats during putrefaction to the aforementioned acids. It is most prominent in subcutaneous tissue, but can occur wherever fat is present. Adipocere is really a variation of putrefaction. It is seen most commonly in bodies immersed in water or in damp, warm environments. In adipocere, fat undergoes hydrolysis to free fatty acids by virtue of endogenous lipases and bacterial enzymes. Bacterial enzymes, principally from *Clostridium perfringens,* convert these free fatty acids to hydroxy fatty acids.[4] Adipocere is said to take several months to develop, though development can be as short as several weeks. It is relatively resistant to both bacteriologic and chemical degradation.

Figure 2.10 Adipocere.

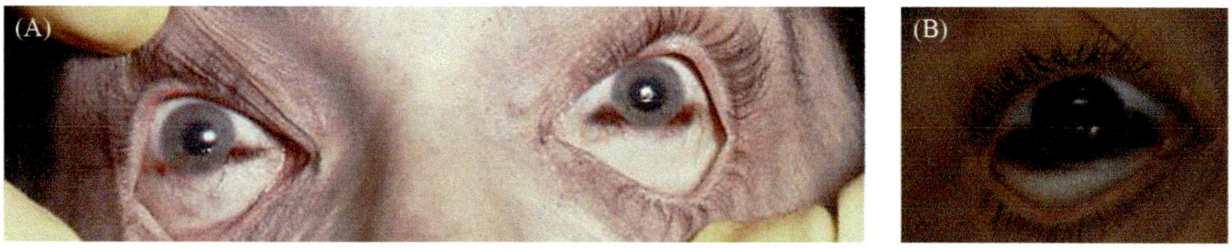

Figure 2.11 *Tache noire.* Postmortem drying of sclera of eyes. (Photo B courtesy of Dr. Rajesh Kannan.)

A brief mention should be made of maceration of infants in intrauterine deaths. This is not truly putrefaction, but rather an aseptic autolytic process. It is described in a separate section.

Eye changes postmortem are difficult to interpret. Changes depend on whether the eyes are open or closed and on the environment. *Tache noire* is an artifactual drying consisting of a brown to black band of discolored sclera where the eyes are partly open and exposed to the air (Figure 2.11).

In closed eyes, by 24 h, there is usually a white scummy deposit on the cornea, which, in turn, is cloudy.

Insect Activity

Often present along with decomposition, are changes of the body as related to scavenger or insect activity. Just as in life, after death the tissues of humans are still attractive to a variety of predators and insects. Even domesticated animals often prey upon the recently dead, commonly on the face and extremities (Figure 2.12).

Additionally, dead bodies provide an attractive food source for a variety of insects. Different insects are involved at different stages of decomposition of the body. These insects follow a set pattern of development in or on the body. Identification of the type of insects present and their stage of development, in conjunction with knowledge of the rate of their development, is sometimes used to determine approximately how long a body has been dead. In addition, this identification might indicate that the body has been moved from one area to another.

In their development from egg to adult stage, insects undergo either complete or incomplete metamorphosis. In incomplete metamorphosis, small versions of the adult hatch from the egg. These subsequently mature into the full adult form. In complete metamorphosis, the insect hatches from the egg as a larva that is markedly different in appearance from the adult. For example, the maggot that develops into a fly begins as a larva, then after a series of molts, the larva enters a resting stage, the pupa, and from the pupa emerges the fully formed adult insect.

The insects that are attracted to a dead body fall into three categories: the necrophagous species, which feed on the body itself; the predators and parasites, which feed on the necrophagous insects; and the omnivorous species, which feed on both the body and on the other insects. The necrophagous species are the most important in determining the time of death. Depending upon the time of day and the species of insect, insects may settle on the body and begin to feed immediately after death. As the body decomposes,

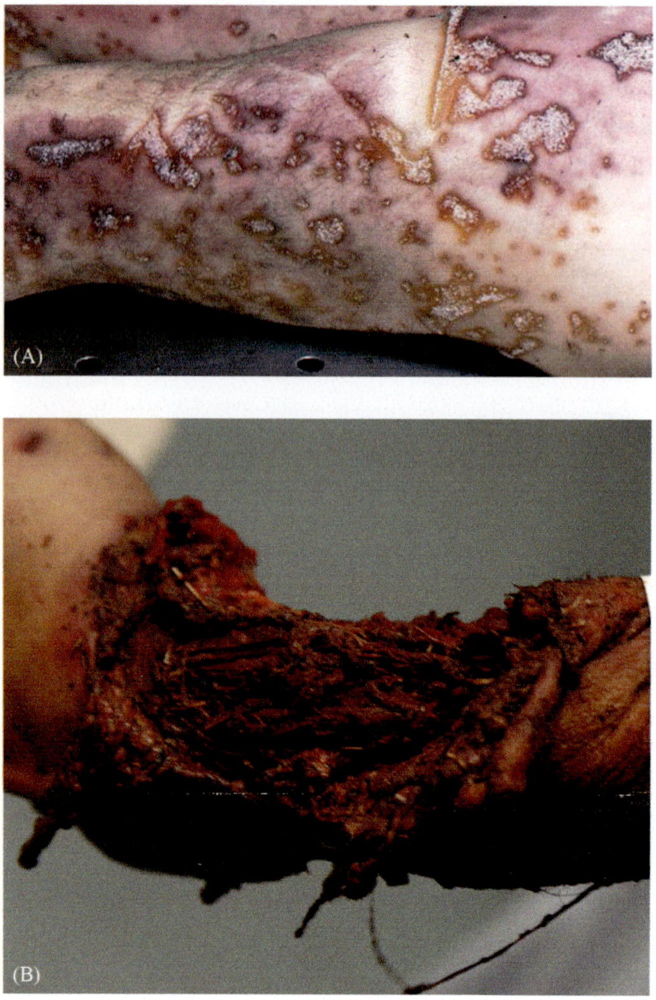

Figure 2.12 Postmortem depredation by (A) insects and (B) a pet dog.

successive waves of insects settle on the body. Varying factors, such as the rate of decomposition, burial, immersion in water, mummification and geography, determine how soon and how many types and waves of insects will attack the body. The temperature and humidity of the environment are the major factors controlling the laying of eggs and the rate of development of the necrophagous insects. Extremes of temperature may impair, prevent or cause cessation of insect development. Obviously, temperature and humidity are tied into the season of the year, which also controls what insects are available. Temporary storing of the body in an area where there is no access for insects will prevent the laying of eggs on the body and thus impair determination of the time of death. In addition, moving the body from one area to another may interfere with the cycle of insect development and introduce new species.

Flies are the most common form of insect associated with decomposing bodies. They tend to lay their eggs in orifices of the body and in open wounds. This latter attribute may result in either destruction or alteration of the appearance of a wound. Eggs are generally deposited immediately after death in the daytime. Blowflies do not normally lay eggs at night. If the body has not been moved and only eggs are present on the body, one can assume that the duration of death has been about 1–2 days. This is quite variable, however, depending on the temperature and humidity, as well as the species of fly. After hatching, the maggots grow progressively larger until they reach the pupa stage. This can take anywhere from 6 to 10 days under ordinary conditions. The adults emerge in 12–18 days. All of these figures, however, are quite variable and greatly dependent on the species involved and the temperature of the environment.

It is the authors' opinion that any attempt to determine time of death using entomological evidence from bodies should be done only with the aid of an entomologist. For more detailed information concerning methods and techniques used and the different species of insects, the authors recommend consulting a forensic entomology text, such as *A Manual of Forensic Entomology* by Kenneth G.V. Smith and *Forensic Entomology The Utility of Arthropods in Legal Investigations* edited by Jason H. Byrd and James L. Castner.[5,6]

Other Methods for Determining Time of Death

Vitreous Potassium

Quantitation of vitreous potassium has been put forward as a reliable method of determining the time of death. It is known that, as time since death increases, so does the concentration of potassium. Sturner and Gantner developed a formula for estimating the time of death based on a uniform increase in vitreous potassium.[7] However, this formula has since been proven inaccurate with the variability becoming greater with an increasing postmortem interval. Graphs published in the same article are also of little help due to their wide margin of error. Though this study has been widely repeated, an accurate method for determination of time of death from vitreous potassium has not been developed. The wide variation is because increases in potassium concentration in the vitreous are controlled by the rate of decomposition. Anything that accelerates decomposition, for example, high temperature, will increase potassium rise.

DNA, RNA and Protein Degradation

After death, biological markers, including DNA, RNA, and proteins, are degraded by proteases, nucleases and bacteria. Recently, several studies have investigated the temporal relationship of this degradation in various tissues with postmortem interval in order to predict time of death. Techniques such as flow cytometry, electrophoresis and RT-PCR (reverse transcriptase polymerase chain reaction) have all been investigated and while all show positive correlations between time of death and amount of degradation, the predictive function is too variable to allow for practical use, not to mention that most forensic pathologists to do have routine access to this equipment and these techniques.

Gastric Emptying and Digestion

One way of attempting to determine the time of death is by establishing the time interval between eating and death and then finding the time the deceased last ate. A perusal of standard forensic textbooks gives a number of estimations of how long it takes to digest a meal. Spitz and Fisher state that a small meal (a sandwich) is digested in 1 h and a large meal takes 3–5 h.[8] Adelson says gastric emptying depends on the size and content of the meal, with a light meal taking 1/2–2 h to digest, a medium size meal 3–4 h and a heavy meal 4–6 h.[9]

For stomach contents to be of value in making an estimate of the time of death, a knowledge of gastric emptying is necessary. The introduction in 1966 of radioisotopic methods measuring gastric emptying has led to more accurate measurement of gastric emptying than the old barium contrast meal and tube recovery technique. Thus, it is now possible to simultaneously measure gastric emptying of both liquid and solid components of normal meals without an invasive technique. Such studies have shown that there are no significant differences in solid food emptying rates between young and aged men, though a delay in liquid emptying has been observed in aged men.[10]

Dual-radionuclide methods employing noninvasive simultaneous monitoring of liquid and solid meal gastric emptying have been used to determine the influence of weight and caloric content of a meal on gastric emptying. These methods have revealed that, if water is ingested with a solid meal, the water is emptied rapidly and separately and is not influenced by either the weight or total calories of the accompanying solid meal. The rate of emptying is exponential and identical to that of non-nutrient liquid meals ingested without solid portions. In contrast, the emptying pattern of calorie-containing liquids is slower and more linear, which indicates a more constant rate of emptying. Thus, in a study by Brophy et al., the mean liquid half-emptying time for 150 g of orange juice was 24 ± 8 min (range 12–37 min).[11]

If the caloric content of a meal is kept stable but the weight is increased, the result is an increase in the rate of emptying; that is, the emptying rate (expressed as grams of solid food emptying from the stomach per minute) increases directly with meal weight. This is felt to be due to activation of gastric wall stretch or volume receptors stimulating peristalsis of the antrum by the increased meal weight and volume. In contrast, if the meal weight is held constant and the caloric content is increased, there is a progressively slower rate of emptying.[12,13]

Most studies done on gastric emptying utilize an artificially structured meal, unlike what the ordinary person would eat. This meal is designed to give a certain weight and/or a number of calories. The favorite of many of the experimenters seems to be beef stew, though one used lettuce. In contrast, a study by Moore et al.[12] allowed the subjects to self-select a meal that included meats, seafoods, vegetables, soups, salads, pastries, desserts and a variety of beverages. The subjects were allowed to eat as much as they wanted and to stop when they felt full. The meals were consumed in 30 min. The total amount of food ingested ranged from 1024 to 2408 g with a mean of 1692 g. The weight of the solid food consumed ranged from 693 to 1279 g with an average of 865.5 g. The gastric half-emptying time ($t^1/_2$) for these meals ranged from a low of 60 to a maximum of 338 min with an average half-emptying time of 277 ± 44 min. There was also great variability in meals of approximately the same weight. Thus, a 1474-g meal in one individual had a half-emptying time of 195 min, a 1549-g meal 126 min in another, a 1562-g meal 60 min in a third, a 1260-g meal 143 min and a 1923-g meal 124 min. This study also revealed that, in several subjects, there was a long lag time following ingestion of the meal during which no emptying occurred. As expected, the liquids emptied significantly more rapidly than the solid food. For the liquids, the mean half-emptying time was 178 ± 22 min, compared with 277 ± 44 min for solids. Also as part of the study, the same individuals were given 900- and 300-g meals and it was observed that the larger meals were associated with a longer emptying time.

The half-emptying time of 277 ± 44 min for an ordinary meal is much longer than most of the studies in the literature.[12] Most studies, however, usually involved smaller meals that were artificial in composition. Studies show that the longer emptying times are associated with larger meals and that gastric emptying appears to be more closely correlated with the total number of calories in the meal than with meal weight.[12,13]

Brophy et al. investigated differences in emptying rates in healthy subjects fed the same meal on separate days.[11] Both solid and liquid times were studied. The meal administered consisted of 150 g of beef stew and 150 g of orange juice, with both elements isotopically labeled. As a result of these experiments, it was concluded that meal-emptying time is a variable phenomenon in healthy subjects with significant differences from day to day in the same and in different individuals. Thus, for liquids, the half-emptying time was an average of 24.88 ± 8.66 min. In one individual, however, over 4 days, the half-emptying time for 150 g of orange juice was 30, 12, 28 and 12 min. The range of half-emptying times for the whole group was from 12 to 38 min. For solid food, the half-emptying time was 58.58 ± 17.68 min. The overall range was from 29 to 92 min. Thus, this study demonstrates that the gastric emptying of either liquids or solids is subject to relatively wide differences in the same and different individuals even if the same meal is ingested. If, in addition to this, we added differences in the weight, caloric content and composition of the meal, we would see even greater differences in half-emptying time.

It can, therefore, be concluded that even when the exact timing and amount of the last meal is known, there is a great deal of variability in predicting digestion. Thus, trying to use the amount and type of food present in the stomach at death to predict the time of death should not be attempted.

Scene Markers

One of the most reliable ways of predicting time since death is simply to investigate when the decedent was last seen alive and when they were found dead – indicating that the death occurred sometime in between. Though unscientific and often imprecise, this method does give the most reproducible and accurate account of the postmortem interval.

In order to narrow this window, investigators may also utilize markers present at the scene in an attempt to determine the last known alive time. Helpful scene markers may include:

- Cell phone calls or text messages
- Uncollected mail or newspapers
- Whether the lights are on or off
- How the individual is dressed
- Any food that is out or dirty dishes in the sink
- Sales receipts or dated slips of paper in the deceased's pockets
- Witness statements – for example, if a decedent typically went for a walk every evening and suddenly is no longer seen, then one might conclude that death occurred on or about the day they failed to take his walk

Identification

Visual

The most commonly used method for identifying a decedent is visual. This is used every time there is a witnessed collapse and a family member or friend says "that's Uncle Joe" or when police officers match a decedent based upon their driver's license or some other form of photo identification. Though common, visual identifications can be fraught with error. Family members or friends may not desire to look at the deceased and may simply glance that looks like Uncle Bob, or the police, being unfamiliar with the deceased may feel the resemblance is "good enough" to the ID found, or witnesses may intentionally give an incorrect identity for possible financial gain or other fraudulent purposes. In other cases, such as with decomposition or severe trauma, a visual identification may just not be possible (Figure 2.13).

Fingerprints

The second most common method for identification is fingerprint comparison. Fingerprints are easy to obtain and relatively quick and easy to compare, and unlike visual identifications, fingerprints are considered a scientific identification technique. Like the other scientific methods, fingerprints require a reference standard to make the identification – meaning antemortem prints need to be available for comparison. While antemortem prints are not always available, such as with minors, several databases do exist, which allow readily accessible and easily searchable references samples, the most notable of which being the Integrated Automated Fingerprint Identification System (AFIS). Several states also maintain their own databases, particularly if fingerprints are required when obtaining a driver's or other licenses, and if the decedent has a criminal history. Aside from utilizing local law enforcement databases, the FBI and Department of Homeland Security also maintain searchable databases accessible to law enforcement for the purpose of identification.

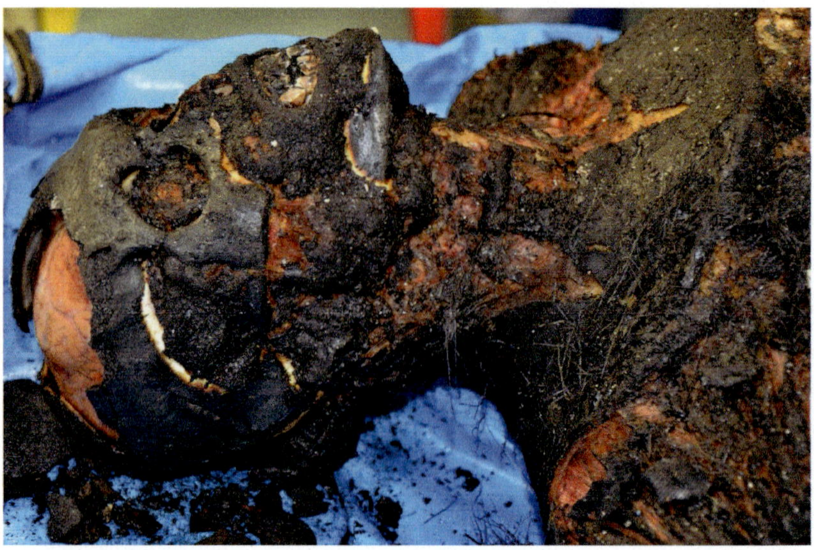

Figure 2.13 Decedent burned in a fire where visual identification was not possible.

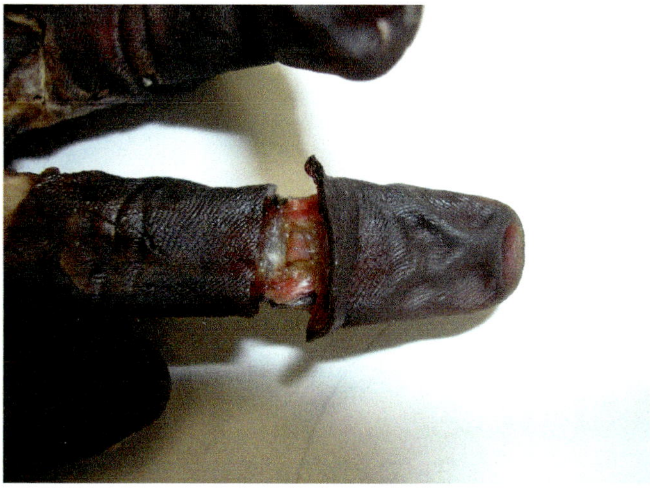

Figure 2.14 Removal of the finger pad of a mummified hand in order to obtain fingerprints for identification.

Depending on the state of decomposition, fingerprints may still be obtainable as mummified hands can be rehydrated and adequate prints obtained and degloved skin can be placed over a gloved finger to yield excellent prints. Several such techniques exist though they can be time-consuming and require precision and patience (Figure 2.14).

Unfortunately, however, on some bodies, fingerprints simply cannot be obtained especially in cases of skeletal or burned bodies.

Circumstantial

While circumstantial information itself is insufficient to determine a positive identification, it can often be used to make a presumptive or tentative identification that can then be used to obtain information necessary for a scientific positive identification to be made. Circumstantial information includes information that can be obtained from the scene such as the name on the car registration where the decedent was found, or the owner of the home, or the name on the mail. It may also include characteristic clothing or jewelry on the decedent. A search through the decedent's wallet or cell phone may lead to a helpful business card such as a lawyer or parole officer or a phone number to a relative such as "mom" or "dad."

Circumstantial information may also include findings on the body itself such as distinctive tattoos or scars. Even identifying features such as height, weight, eye color and hairstyle can be useful. Internal findings can be of assistance as well. For instance, previous surgeries such as an appendectomy or hysterectomy, unique congenital abnormalities like a horseshoe kidney and certain disease states such as cancer can be helpful identifiers.

Establishing a presumptive identification is often the critical first step to a positive identification as it can be used to obtain the records necessary for comparison for a scientific positive identification.

Anthropology

Like circumstantial findings, anthropologic findings are often helpful in establishing a presumptive identification that may lead to a positive identification by additional means.

Identifying characteristics such as sex, height, age and ancestry can often be estimated. In addition, more unique features such as bony abnormalities can be used to establish identification. While most forensic pathologists are well trained in forensic anthropology, it is often useful to consult a forensic anthropologist for such examinations. When consulting a forensic anthropologist, the authors recommend using someone with the appropriate credentials, such as board certification from the American Board of Forensic Anthropology.

Dental

When a body is unable to be identified either visually or through fingerprints, usually due to trauma, decomposition and/or fire, dental is usually the next preferred method. Dental identifications are relatively easy and quick and can be completed on burned and decomposed bodies. Even in the absence of teeth, dental identification can often be established utilizing root morphology or comparing sinus anatomy. Unfortunately, dental identifications require antemortem radiographs to establish a positive identification and no "dental databases" exist, such as those for fingerprints or DNA. Thus, a presumptive identification is usually necessary so that the antemortem records can be obtained for comparison.

To make a dental identification, dental charts should be prepared and X-rays of the jaws obtained. These can be used to compare with the dental X-rays and charts of the individual who is believed to be the deceased (Figure 2.15).

While dental charts and X-rays can be made with the teeth in situ, it is often simpler to remove the jaws, especially for adequate X-raying. The jaws then can be split down the

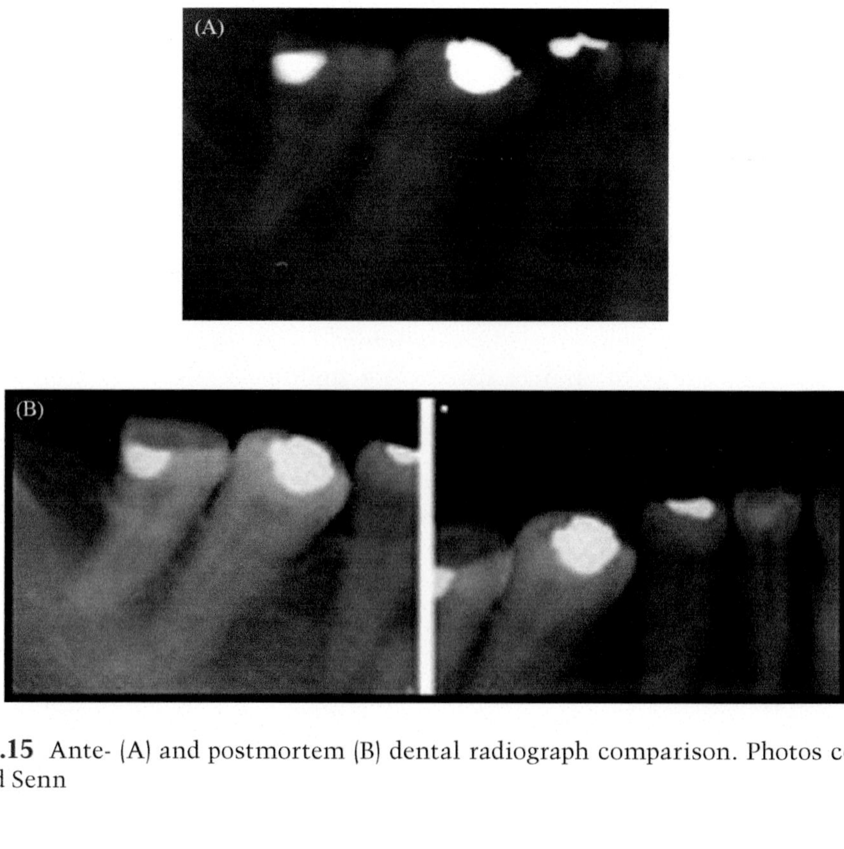

Figure 2.15 Ante- (A) and postmortem (B) dental radiograph comparison. Photos courtesy of Dr. David Senn

middle and more accurate lateral X-ray films taken.[14] While it may seem destructive, often when dental identification is needed, the body cannot be viewed because it has already been disfigured by fire, trauma or decomposition. It should be realized that dental identification utilizing X-rays does not require the presence of fillings but can be made on the bony structure of the jaws and the orientation, and the structure and appearance of the teeth alone.

While some dental identifications may be straight forward, others may be complex and require expert interpretation. For cases such as these, the authors recommend consulting a forensic odontologist who is board certified by the American Board of Forensic Odontology or equivalent. When properly used and interpreted, dental identification is just as reliable as fingerprinting.

Radiographic and Medical Identifications

Another method of identification that can be just as reliable as dental identification, but is less commonly utilized, is the comparison of postmortem X-rays to the antemortem X-rays of the individual the deceased is suspected of being. If one has a tentative identification on a body, one should inquire whether the individual ever had any trauma or even a routine chest X-ray. These X-rays can then be obtained to use for comparison with those of the unidentified body. X-rays of virtually any area of the body can potentially be suitable for comparison. Identification can be based not only on peculiarities of the bones but also on soft-tissue calcification, enteric accretions (e.g., gallstones, kidney stones, etc.) and opaque stints, filters, clips, surgical screws, retained projectiles, etc. Positive identification might be made on either a cluster of relatively common changes or a single unique finding.

Additionally, implanted surgical hardware can be used to establish positive identification (Figure 2.16).

Implanted pacemakers, defibrillators and orthopedic hardware such as knee and joint replacements are often embossed with unique lot and serial numbers that can be matched to antemortem medical records. Unfortunately, obtaining the antemortem records requires knowledge of where and when the surgery was done, though often the manufacturer of the hardware can be contacted and may be able to direct the forensic pathologist to a particular hospital and time period where that lot was shipped. It is often asked if breast implants can be used for identification purposes and while they are usually embossed with a lot number, they often lack unique serial numbers.

DNA

With the advancement in DNA technology and improvements in the rapidity of testing, DNA has become the main method of scientific identification after fingerprinting and dental comparison. Additionally, DNA is often used as a confirmatory method of identification even after other scientific methods have been employed. It is also used if identification cannot be made by any of the above mechanisms.

A thorough review of DNA technology is beyond the scope of this book though it is explored more in-depth in Chapter 22. In brief, DNA analysis can be very specific depending upon the reference sample used for comparison and can be utilized on decomposed, skeletal and burned remains. It is, however, time-intensive, often taking several days to complete, and relatively expensive. Additionally, DNA

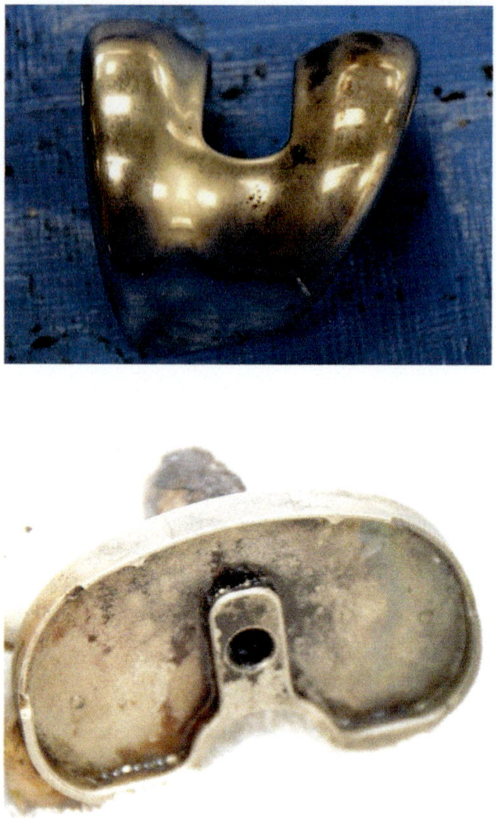

Figure 2.16 Implanted hip joint embossed with serial numbers that was used to positively identify an individual.

comparison requires a reference standard for comparison. This reference standard may be obtained from the decedent's biological mother, father or children and used for parentage analysis, a sibling may be tested for kinship analysis, or a reference sample may be obtained from a toothbrush or other biologic material known to have come from the decedent. In all of these cases, however, the material compared must be biologically related otherwise the analysis will be at best inconclusive and at worst erroneous.

Several searchable DNA databases do exist, including the Combined DNA Index System (CODIS). CODIS is a national crime justice database that houses information regarding convicted felony offenders and unknown criminal samples. It was not designed for nor meant to be used to identify missing persons, though it can support that functionality. NamUs, on the other hand, is a national clearinghouse designed specifically for missing person information. NamUs is a web-based, searchable database funded by the National Institutes of Justice that consists of two databases – unidentified decedents and known missing persons. It houses data from both unidentified remains and familial samples from those searching for their loved ones. However, in order for either NamUs or CODIS to be useful, identifiable information must have been created and uploaded into the system – whether that be a DNA profile for CODIS or medical, dental and/ or DNA information for NamUs.

References

1. Guyton AC and Hall JE, *Textbook of Medical Physiology* 10th ed. WB Saunders Co. Phil., 2000.
2. Mackowiak PA, Wasserman SS, and Levine MM, A critical appraisal of 98.6 degrees F, the upper limit of the normal body temperature and other legacies of Carl Reinhold. *JAMA* 1992; 268(12):1578–1580.
3. Hutchins GM, Body temperature is elevated in the early postmortem period. *Hum Pathol* 1985; 16:560–561.
4. Cotton GE, Aufderheide AC, and Goldschmidt VG, Preservation of human tissue immersed for five years in fresh water of known temperature. *J Forensic Sci* 1987; 32:1125–1130.
5. Smith KGV, *A Manual of Forensic Entomology*. London, British Museum (Natural History); Cornell University Press, Ithaca, NY, 1986.
6. Byrd JH and Castner JL (Eds), *Forensic Entomology The Utility of Arthropods in Legal Investigations* 2nd ed. CRC Press, New York, NY, 2009.
7. Sturner WO and Gantner GE, The postmortem interval: a study of potassium in the vitreous humor. *Am J Clin Pathol* 1964; 42:134–144.
8. Spitz WV and Fisher RS (Eds), *Medicolegal Investigation of Death* 2nd ed. Charles C Thomas, Springfield, IL, 1980.
9. Adelson L, *The Pathology of Homicide*. Charles C Thomas, Springfield, IL, 1974, p 111.
10. Moore JG, Tweedy C, Christian PE, et al., Effect of age on gastric emptying of liquid-solid meals in man. *Digestive Dis Sci* 1983; 28:340.
11. Brophy CM, Moore JG, Christian PE, et al., Variability of gastric emptying measurements in man employing standardized radiolabeled meals. *Digestive Dis Sci* 1986; 31:799–806.
12. Moore JG, Christian PE, Brown JA, et al., Influence of meal weight and caloric content on gastric emptying of meals in man. *Digestive Dis Sci* 1984; 29:513–519.
13. Moore JG, Christian PE, and Coleman RE, Gastric emptying of varying meal weight and composition in man. *Digestive Dis Sci* 1981; 26:16–22.
14. Norton LE, The Norton technique for dental identification. *Forensic Sci Gaz* 1978; 9(4):1–2.

3 Sudden Deaths Due to Natural Disease

Ring around the rosie
A pocket full of posies
Ashes, ashes
We all fall down

—English nursery rhyme

Most natural deaths do not fall under the jurisdiction of a medical examiner; those that do fall under the category of sudden and unexpected. At the time of the medical examiner's involvement, the death is an unknown death, only to be diagnosed as natural after an autopsy examination. Again, the majority of these types of deaths are sudden; however, the definition as to what constitutes sudden death is variable. It is based on the amount of time between the onset of symptoms and death. Depending on one's definition, the maximum time interval varies anywhere from 1 to 24 h. Most witnessed deaths handled by the medical examiner are what are called instantaneous deaths. Literally, the individual falls down dead. In such cases, everyone agrees that these are sudden deaths. In other cases, the individuals usually die within 1 h of the onset of symptoms.

This chapter focuses on the most common causes of sudden, natural death seen in a forensic pathology setting.

Deaths Due to Cardiovascular Disease

The most common cause of death in men and women in the United States is cardiovascular disease, representing approximately one in four deaths.[1] Cardiovascular includes a large group of diseases, including atherosclerosis, cardiomyopathies and valvular disease, all of which can result in sudden death; this chapter will attempt to briefly discuss the most common of these disease processes.

Sudden death in association with coronary artery disease can occur at any time of the day, during any activity; however, they seem to show a circadian variation, with a peak incidence in the early morning. Willich et al. reported the peak incidence of sudden cardiac death as between 7 and 9 a.m. (after discounting individuals found dead during this time), which was 70% higher than the average rate during the rest of the day.[2] They suggest that one possible explanation for this is increased activity of the sympathetic nervous system, known to occur in the morning, which may predispose to cardiac arrhythmias. Sudden cardiac deaths are also associated with environmental changes and strenuous activity. Severe climatic conditions such as heat and cold may stress the heart, predisposing to anginal attacks and sudden deaths.[3] Strenuous activity also predisposes a person to sudden cardiac death.[4–6] In individuals over the age of 35, coronary atherosclerosis is the most common cause of death in exercise-related deaths.[4]

The mechanism of sudden death in most individuals dying from cardiovascular disease is the sudden onset of ventricular tachycardia, which either is sustained or, in most cases, progresses to ventricular fibrillation (approximately 80%). This has been demonstrated in individuals wearing portable cardiac monitors who collapsed and died with the terminal event's being recorded. Asystole or a bradyarrhythmia accounts for the remaining 20% of cases of sudden cardiac death.[7,8]

Coronary Artery Disease

Coronary Atherosclerosis

Zipes and Wellens estimate that up to 80% of individuals dying suddenly of cardiac disease die of coronary artery disease,[9] most commonly coronary atherosclerosis. Approximately half the individuals with coronary artery disease die suddenly. Sudden death is, in fact, the initial symptom in approximately 25% of individuals dying of coronary atherosclerosis. In the authors' experience, coronary artery disease accounts for approximately 75% of adults' dying suddenly and unexpectedly of cardiovascular disease who come to autopsy. The frequency will change to some degree depending on the population handled by a particular office and the criteria used for selection of cases for autopsy.

In contrast to the number of individuals who die in the hospital of coronary artery disease, in a medical examiner's office, acute coronary thrombosis and acute myocardial infarcts are the exception rather than the rule. In a study of 500 consecutive autopsies of individuals aged 20–99 years who died suddenly and unexpectedly of coronary artery disease, only 67 (13.4%) showed acute thromboses, grossly.[10] The left coronary artery and its branches showed a slightly higher incidence of thrombosis compared with the right. The low incidence of thrombosis in individuals' dying suddenly is in agreement with other authorities though it is in contrast which studies of hospitalized patients that show a higher rate of thrombosis, approximately 87%.[11] Gross myocardial scarring representing previous areas of old infarction has been reported as being present in 34.8% of individuals dying suddenly, with 8.4% demonstrating evidence of acute myocardial infarction, grossly.

What is present in all deaths due to coronary atherosclerosis is severe atherosclerosis of the coronary vessels. Significant obstruction of the coronary artery lumen usually requires 75% narrowing of the lumen (Figure 3.1).

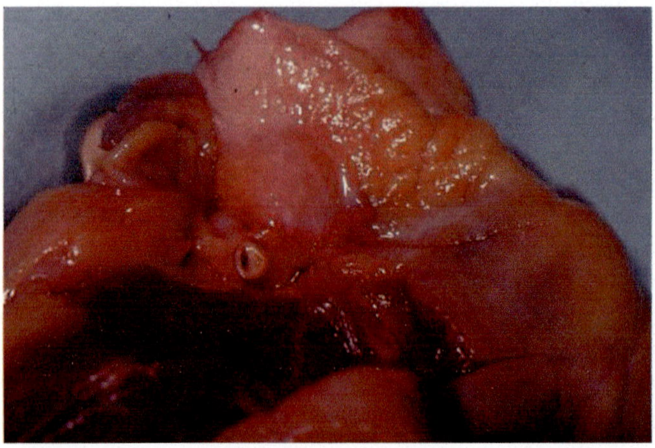

Figure 3.1 Left anterior descending coronary artery of a 21-year-old male with 75% narrowing of lumen due to atherosclerosis.

In individuals with hypertensive cardiovascular disease, one often does not see the classical eccentric narrowing due to plaque formation of pure coronary atherosclerosis, but rather concentric thickening of the walls by atherosclerotic deposits. In these cases, while the lumen may be technically patent, the severe concentric narrowing of the vessels accomplishes the same hemodynamic effect as the eccentric plaques, that is, a reduction in blood flow to the myocardium. In individuals older than 60 years of age, the coronary arteries may present yet another picture. While the lumina are patent, the vessels are rigid calcified tubes because of calcium deposits in the walls of the vessels.

In some individuals, while the epicardial coronary arteries appear non-occluded, microscopic examination of the myocardium reveals severe, occlusive dysplasia of the intramural coronary arteries.[12] The dysplasia is characterized by severe medial thickening, with smooth muscle disorganization and marked luminal narrowing. Burke and Virmani describe four sudden deaths due to this entity in young (12–31 years) individuals.[12]

In most individuals who die suddenly and unexpectedly of atherosclerosis of the coronary arteries, at least two vessels are involved. Occasionally, an individual will die with single vessel disease with a single strategically located atherosclerotic plaque. This plaque, which produces at least 75% narrowing of the lumen, is usually found in the proximal portion of the left anterior descending coronary artery (the "widow-maker") almost immediately after its origin. This is an extremely critical point in this vessel, in that the left coronary artery begins supplying significant myocardial tissue shortly after its origin. In contrast, the right coronary artery does not supply any significant amount of myocardial tissue until it gives off the posterior descending vessel. In a study of 451 deaths due to CAD, in 54 of the cases (11.9%), significant disease was confined to one vessel. The vessel was the left anterior descending coronary in 40 cases; the circumflex in four and the right coronary in ten.

Bridging

Sudden death has been described in a condition called bridging.[13,14] In this entity, the left anterior descending coronary artery (very rarely the right coronary), instead of lying in the epicardial fat of the heart, dips down into the myocardium (Figure 3.2).

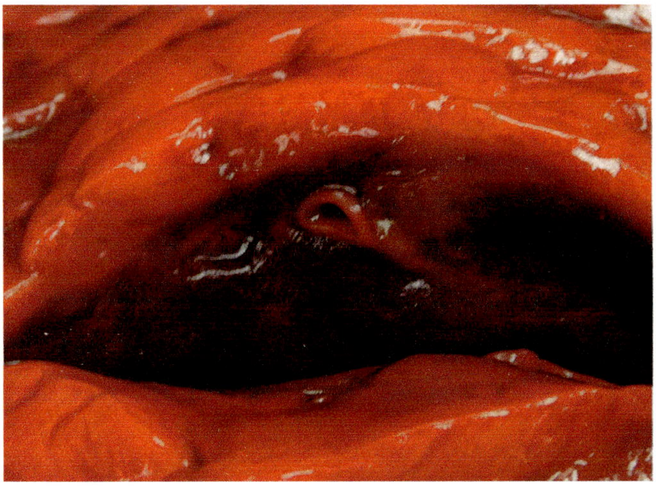

Figure 3.2 "Bridging" of left anterior descending coronary artery.

Coronary angiography has demonstrated bridging in from 0.5 to 1.6% of individuals.[14] In adults with hypertrophic cardiomyopathy, bridging occurs in 30–50% of individuals.[14] In bridging, there is compression of the vessel during systole with either partial or complete occlusion of the lumen. Generally, this is a benign phenomenon, because nearly all coronary blood flow to the left ventricle occurs during diastole. However, with tachycardia, there is a shortening of diastolic perfusion that may allow the systolic compression to become significant resulting in angina, myocardial ischemia, acute coronary syndrome, left ventricular dysfunction, arrhythmias and even sudden cardiac death.[15] Septal fibrosis from repeated systolic compression may also occur. This would explain the observation that sudden death in bridging is seen more often in association with exercise.

Dissecting Coronary Aneurysm

A dissecting aneurysm of the coronary artery may be either secondary to extension of an aortic root dissection or primary and limited to the coronary artery. Primary dissecting aneurysms may be either spontaneous or due to trauma (e.g., chest trauma, coronary angiography). Spontaneous coronary artery dissection is a rare condition, usually presenting as sudden death.[16–18] It consists of an intramural hematoma of the media of the vessel wall, which flattens and occludes the lumen, reducing blood flow (Figure 3.3).

Communication with the lumen may occur. There may be a diffuse adventitial inflammatory reaction consisting mainly of eosinophils present. This is felt to be reactive and

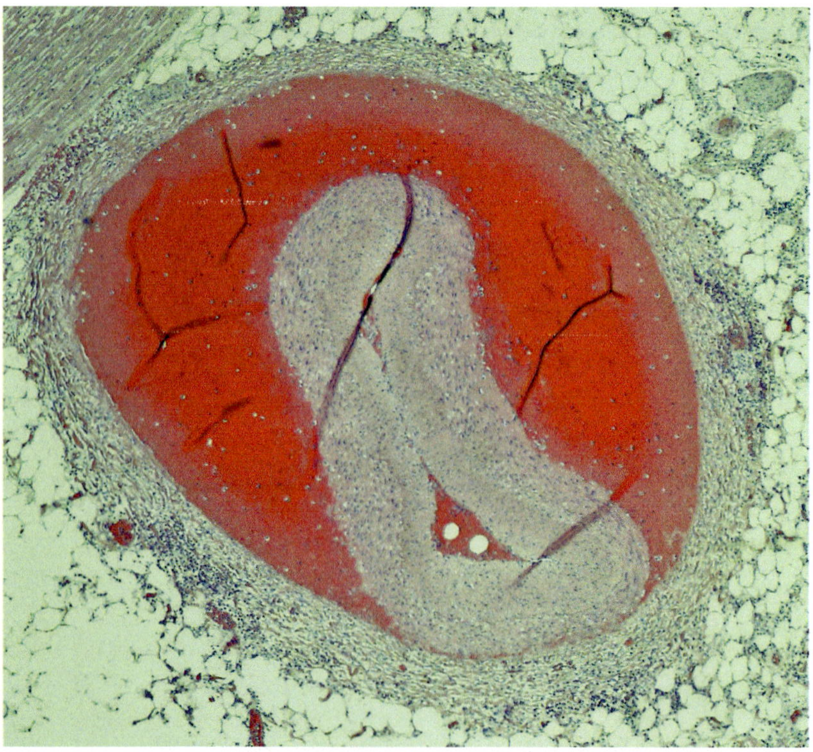

Figure 3.3 Microscopic section of a coronary artery dissection showing the flattening of the artery and occlusion of the lumen.

not related to causation. Most (80%) spontaneous dissecting aneurysms occur in females, particularly in the peripartum period. Three quarters of the cases involve the left anterior descending coronary artery. In men, dissection of the right coronary artery appears to be more frequent.[18] Changes of cystic medial necrosis may be present.

Coronary Artery Spasm

In some individuals, angina coupled with symptoms consistent with development of an acute myocardial infarction occurs immediately prior to sudden collapse and death. At autopsy, however, there is no infarct and the coronary arteries are found to be patent, without significant atherosclerosis or congenital anomalies. Death is believed to be due to transitory coronary artery spasm. The phenomenon of coronary artery spasm without anatomical narrowing of the coronary arteries in association with angina has been demonstrated angiographically and has actually been witnessed during operative procedures.[19–21] Myocardial infarction secondary to coronary artery spasm induced by use of stimulants such as cocaine is also a well-recognized phenomena.

Anatomic Coronary Artery Anomalies

Sudden death in adults and children may be associated with congenital anomalies of the coronary arteries. There are many variations.[22,23] There may be a single right coronary ostium, with the left coronary artery arising from the proximal portion of the right coronary artery (Figure 3.4); the left main coronary artery arising from the right sinus of Valsalva with passage of the artery between the aorta and pulmonary artery; the right coronary artery arising from the left sinus of Valsalva, coronary artery hypoplasia, etc. These anomalies result in reduced blood flow, either continual or intermittent, leading to cardiac ischemia.

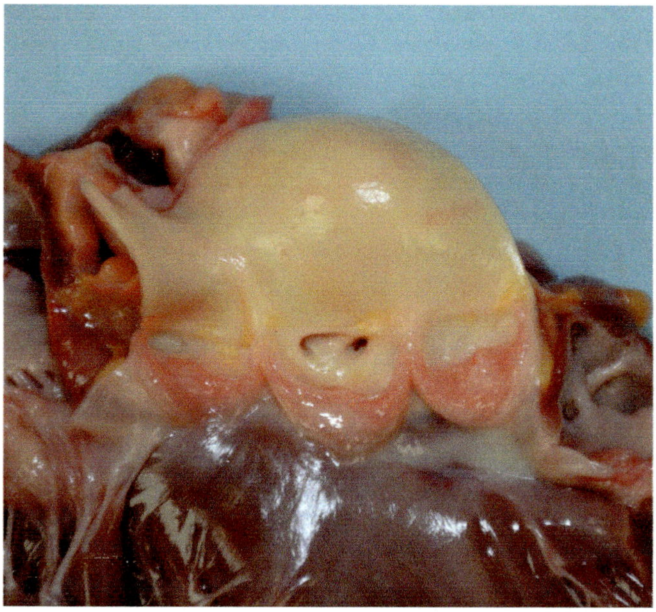

Figure 3.4 Aberrant coronary artery with a single coronary ostium.

Deaths Due to Hypertension

Hypertensive Cardiac Disease

In some individuals with a history of hypertension who die suddenly and unexpectedly, the autopsy will reveal only an enlarged heart, usually 500 g or greater, with marked left ventricular hypertrophy and minimal or absent coronary atherosclerosis.[24] The mechanism of death in these cases is a cardiac arrhythmia, most likely ventricular fibrillation. It has been known clinically for some time that patients with left ventricular hypertrophy have significantly more ventricular premature contractions than normal individuals or individuals with hypertension without left ventricular hypertrophy.[25–27] This clinical observation is in agreement with the observations of forensic pathologists that a small but significant number of individuals who die suddenly and – with a clinical history of hypertension have only left ventricular hypertrophy, without severe atherosclerotic involvement of their coronary arteries or the small vessels of the myocardium.

Aortic Dissection

Aortic dissection occurs when blood dissects between the middle and outer two-thirds of the aortic media, creating a blood filled channel within the aortic wall.[28] The process usually arises in the ascending aorta and is manifested by an intimal tear, a necessary component of a dissecting aortic aneurysm. The tears have sharp edges and run transversely or longitudinally rather than obliquely. A combined longitudinal and transverse tear produces T- or cross-shaped tears. The tear tends to arise in relatively normal appearing areas of the aorta. In some case, the tears are seen to be preceded and arise in areas of intramural hematoma. The dissection then proceeds peripherally down the aorta. It usually breaks out again into the lumen of the aorta. It might, however, rupture into the pericardial sac.

While aortic dissections most often occur in association with hypertension, or underlying hypertensive states such as can occur with cocaine or methamphetamine use, they are also associated with certain disease states, most classically Marfan's syndrome. Marfan's syndrome affects fibrillin, a glycoprotein that sees to the adhesion and alignment of the sheets of collagen in the aorta resulting in fragmentation of the elastic fibers and weakening of the wall, leading to dilatation and dissection.[29] Focal areas of cystic medial necrosis may be seen microscopically leading to the diagnosis.

Other diseases associated with aortic dilatation (aneurysm) and dissection include genetic abnormalities of the collagen, such as those found in osteogenesis imperfecta and Ehlers-Danlos syndrome. Familial degeneration of the aortic media in the absence of any of the well-characterized diseases of the connective tissue can also occur. These cases show cystic medial necrosis. Weight lifting has also been associated with aortic dissection.[29]

Valvular Disease

Sudden death due to valvular disease usually involves either mitral valve prolapse (floppy mitral valve; myxomatous degeneration of the mitral valve) or aortic stenosis. Rarely, sudden death will be due to an acute bacterial valvulitis (Figure 3.5) usually involving the tricuspid valve in individual who use drugs intravenously.

Mitral Valve Prolapse

Until recently, it was estimated that 5–15% of the population had mitral valve prolapse. A study by Freed et al. of 1646 men and 1845 women, representing an unselected,

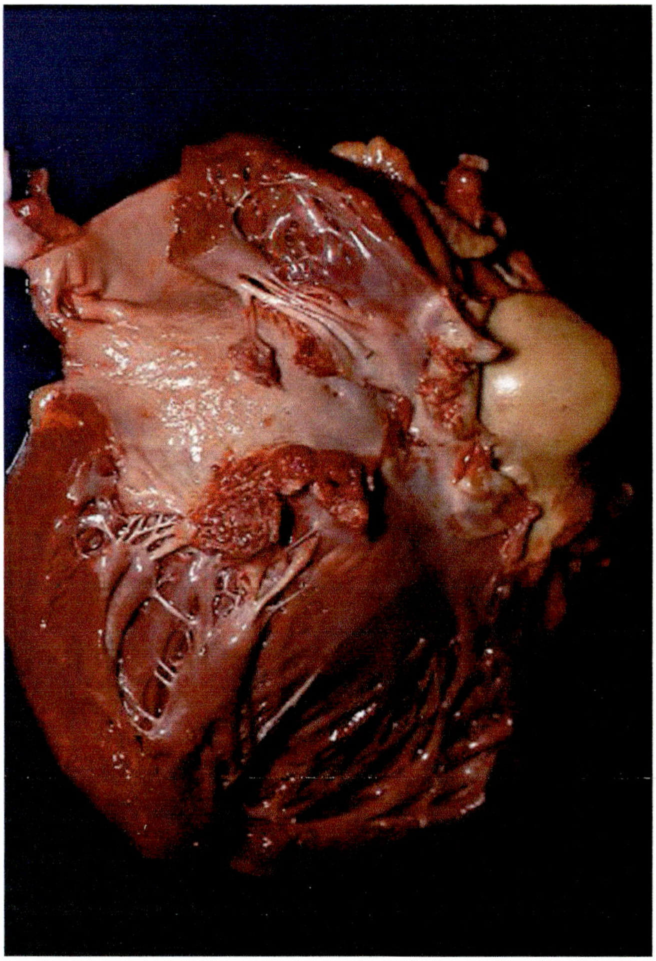

Figure 3.5 Acute bacterial endocarditis involving mitral and aortic valves in a 32-year-old drug addict.

community-based sample of ambulatory patients, and using current two-dimensional echocardiographic criteria, revealed an overall incidence of 2.4%.[30] The mitral valve prolapse syndrome refers to a condition characterized by nonspecific symptoms (dyspnea, fatigue, dizziness, palpitation, anxiety, atypical chest pain), electrocardiographic abnormalities and arrhythmias.[30–32] The characteristic clinical findings are mid-systolic clicks and late systolic murmurs found on auscultation. The arrhythmias are widely varied, with premature ventricular complexes being the most prevalent. The anatomical findings are voluminous, thickened, redundant valve leaflets showing myxomatous transformation of the valve substance, in the absence of any inflammatory change, and dilatation of the mitral annulus (Figure 3.6).

Complications of mitral valve prolapse are sudden death due to ventricular fibrillation, infective endocarditis, transient ischemic attacks and partial strokes secondary to clot or platelet aggregations originating from the prolapsed valve, ruptured chordae tendinae and progression to mitral insufficiency.[30,31]

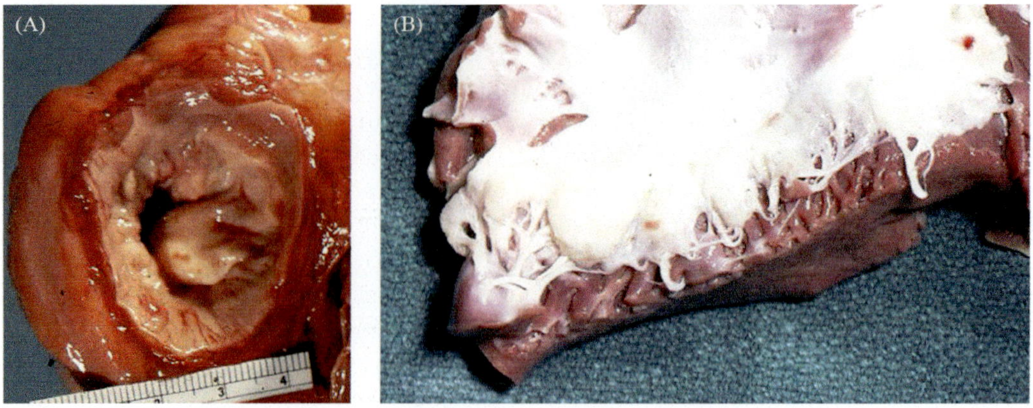

Figure 3.6 Floppy mitral valve. (A) Viewed from atrium. (B) Opened up with lower two-thirds of left ventricle amputated.

Deaths due to mitral valve prolapse are uncommon. Diagnosis of this entity as a cause of death is made by exclusion. One would have to do a complete autopsy, including a thorough toxicological screen, to exclude other possible causes of death before making the diagnosis. In the cases the authors have seen, the myxomatous degeneration of the valves has been extremely marked and has involved both leaflets of the mitral valve. The victims have generally been female, with the youngest 12 years of age and the rest in their late teens, twenties and early thirties.

Aortic Stenosis

After mitral valve prolapse, the next most common cause of sudden death due to valvular disease is aortic stenosis (Figure 3.7).

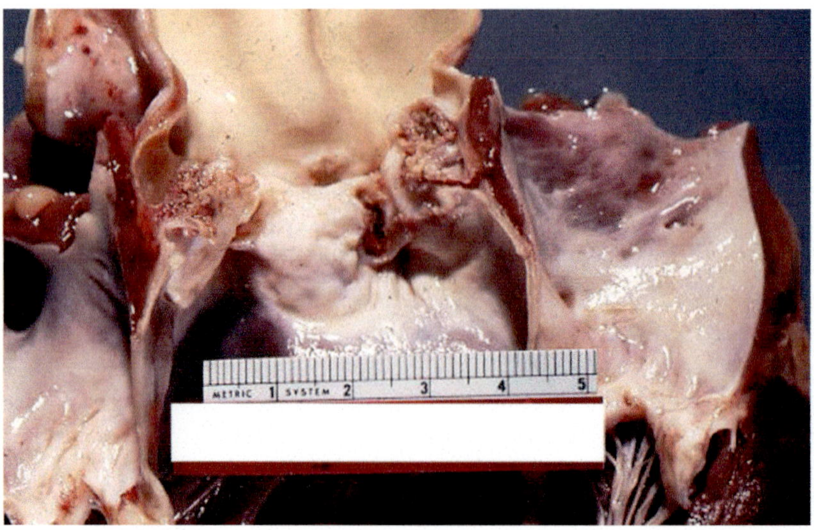

Figure 3.7 Aortic stenosis.

Aortic stenosis (AS) has the propensity for sudden death presumably due to acute myocardial insufficiency secondary to obstruction of the left ventricular outflow. AS has four main etiological causes: congenital malformation of the valve, rheumatic inflammation with fusion of the cusps, secondary calcification of congenital bicuspid valves and primary degenerative calcification of normal aortic valves.[33] Congenital aortic stenosis, which excludes the bicuspid aortic valve, refers to conditions present at the time of birth. Congenital stenotic valves will develop secondary calcification as the individual gets older. This condition is rarely seen in the medical examiner's office because diagnosis has usually been made and treatment administered prior to death.

Rheumatic aortic stenosis, along with mitral stenosis, were once a common finding in the medical examiners' offices, but have almost disappeared today due to the marked decline in rheumatic fever and the available surgical treatments. In rheumatic aortic stenosis, there is fusion of the cusps due to the inflammatory process. Calcification develops in patients as they grow older, generally over the age of 40 years.

In both secondary calcification of the bicuspid valves and primary degenerative calcification of the normal aortic valve, it is the calcium deposit that is the principal cause of the stenosis. With the bicuspid aortic valves, calcification begins in the 6th, 7th and 8th decades of life, developing at the free edges of the cusps and progressing toward the base. In primary degenerative calcification of normal aortic valves, the calcification progresses from the base toward the edges and usually involves individuals in the 8th and 9th decade of life.

At the present time, the most common cause of aortic stenosis is calcification of bicuspid valves. It should be noted that bicuspid aortic valves, the precursor of calcific aortic stenosis, are present in approximately 0.4% of the population.

Cardiomyopathies

The cardiomyopathies constitute a diverse group of diseases of both known and unknown etiology characterized by cardiac dysfunction. Over the years, several classification systems have been proposed including from the World Health Organization and the American Heart Association. These classifications systems are usually based on either the etiology: designated primary or secondary or mixed, genetic or acquired; or on the anatomical and clinical findings usually designated as dilated/congestive, hypertrophic or restrictive-obliterative. Additionally, it has been proposed to add ischemic (i.e., coronary artery diseases), hypertensive and valvular heart disease into the cardiomyopathy categories as well. However, with the understanding of the molecular diagnostics, the use of those categories has become questionable.[34]

The cardiomyopathies related to systemic disease processes, often designated as secondary or restrictive, are rarely encountered by the forensic pathologist, since these are most often diagnosed and treated prior to death and are not as commonly associated with sudden death due to the infiltrative nature of the disease. These include diseases such as amyloidosis, hemochromatosis, sarcoidosis, glycogen storage disease and hypereosinophilic syndrome. The exception is sarcoidosis, which, while uncommon, is occasionally encountered.

In all forms of cardiomyopathy, sudden deaths occur and are recognized by both forensic pathologists and clinicians and are usually the result of arrhythmia (abnormal cardiac rhythm). It is also recommended, when determining the cause of death as being due to a cardiomyopathy that a classification be attempted, if known. For instance, rather than simply using the generic term of "Cardiomyopathy" on a death certificate, "Dilated cardiomyopathy due to chronic ethanol use" or "restrictive cardiomyopathy due to amyloidosis" is preferable.

Congestive or Dilated Cardiomyopathy

The most frequently encountered cardiomyopathy in forensic pathology is the congestive or dilated cardiomyopathy. This condition is characterized by enlargement, sometimes massive, of the heart, with dilatation of all four chambers (Figure 3.8) often resulting in myocardial dysfunction with decreased ejection fraction and congestive heart failure. Mural thrombi are often present. Microscopically, there is degeneration and/or hypertrophy of muscle fibers, focal or diffuse myocardial fibrosis, scattered mononuclear cell infiltrates and, occasionally, fatty infiltrates.

Congestive cardiomyopathies can be idiopathic (without a known cause) or can result from several underlying disease processes including chronic ethanol use, peripartum cardiomyopathy and chronic myocarditis. One of the most common causes of dilated cardiomyopathy in the United States is chronic alcohol abuse. The myocardial damage in this case can be due to the direct toxic effect of the alcohol, the nutritional effects of chronic alcoholism or the toxic effects of an additive to the alcohol (e.g., cobalt). Patients with peripartum cardiomyopathy present with heart failure during the last month of pregnancy or during the first 5 months postpartum.[35] In approximately half the patients, the enlarged heart returns to normal within 6–12 months, though occasionally, sudden death can occur. Congestive cardiomyopathy has also been associated with certain toxic substances such as cobalt and adriamycin.

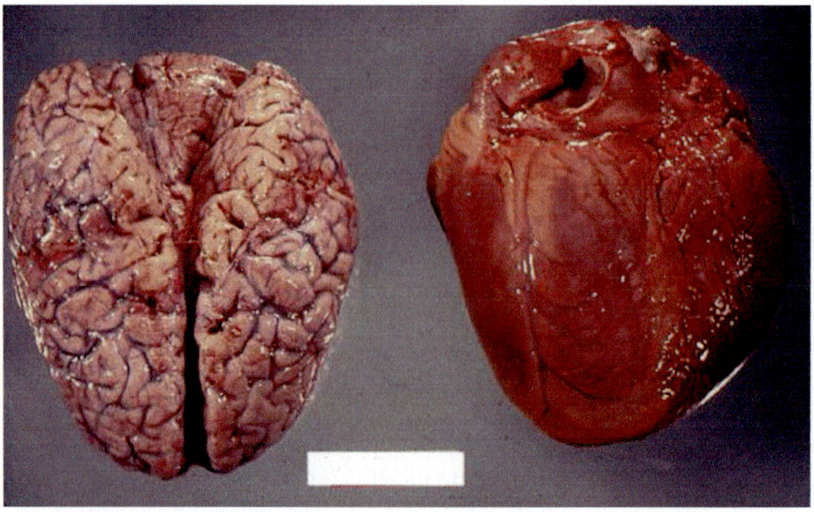

Figure 3.8 Congestive cardiomyopathy. Heart weight 1050 g. Note size of heart in relationship to adult brain of normal size.

Hypertrophic Cardiomyopathy

The most interesting of the cardiomyopathies is hypertrophic cardiomyopathy, also known as idiopathic hypertrophic subaortic stenosis (IHSS) and hypertrophic obstructive cardiomyopathy; however, it should not be confused with hypertensive cardiac disease. Hypertrophic cardiomyopathy is principally a familial cardiac disorder, with an autosomal dominant pattern of inheritance, said to be present in approximately 0.2% of the population.[36] In this condition, there is massive myocardial hypertrophy without ventricular dilatation, in the absence of any cardiac or systemic disease that could produce these changes. The heart usually shows a disproportionate asymmetrical hypertrophy of the interventricular septum compared with the free wall of the left ventricle (Figure 3.9).

In some cases, however, the left ventricular hypertrophy is symmetrical, with thickening of both the septum and free wall. Ninety-five percent of the cases of hypertrophic cardiomyopathy show disarray in the ventricular myocardial fibers, with fibers running in all directions in an apparent haphazard pattern and with the myocardial cells hypertrophied and bizarre. These bizarrely shaped and haphazardly arranged myocardial cells are typically seen in the septum. They are less common in the free wall. The haphazardly arranged bizarre cells are not specific for hypertrophic cardiomyopathy, but have been noted in a number of other conditions usually associated with left ventricular strain. The disarray, however, is not nearly so marked or extensive. Ventricular and supraventricular arrhythmias are common in individuals with this condition.

Echocardiographic evidence of hypertrophic cardiomyopathy is usually present in one or more closely related family members and may present as sudden death in adolescents

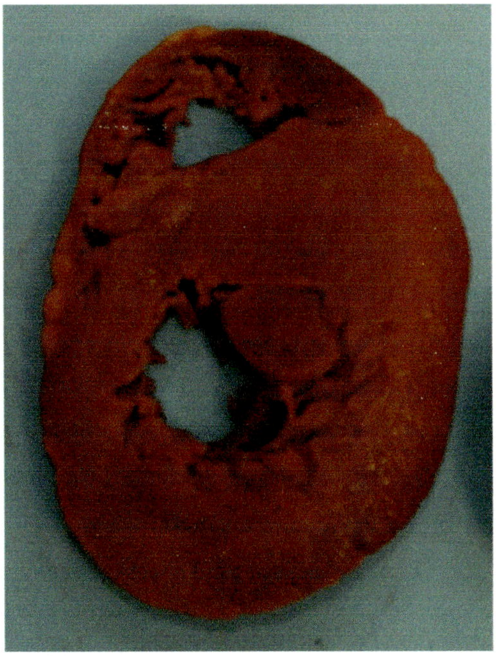

Figure 3.9 Hypertrophic cardiomegaly with asymmetrical hypertrophy of interventricular septum.

and young adults. Genetic testing of both the decedent and surviving relatives is recommended should hypertrophic cardiomyopathy be considered as a cause of sudden death.

Arrhythmogenic Cardiomyopathies

In 1995, the World Health Organization proposed the addition of arrhythmogenic cardiomyopathies to the cardiomyopathy classifications.[37] These include arrhythmogenic right ventricular dysplasia (ARVD) as well as the cardiac rhythm disturbances such as Long QT System.

ARVD is characterized by fibrofatty replacement of the myocardium of the right ventricle and has been shown to cause sudden death particularly in the young and during exercise.[38,39] The majority of ARVD is due to mutations in desmosome genes resulting in myocardial break down and separation. ARVD is associated with the spectrum of arrhythmias including premature ventricular contractions, left bundle branch block, ventricular tachycardiac and ventricular fibrillation.[38]

While ARVD has recognizable anatomic alterations that can assist in identifying the cause of death, sudden cardiac death can also occur due to an arrhythmia without gross cardiac abnormalities.[2,40] Arrythmias due to disorders that prolong the QT interval often have no anatomical abnormalities and unless the disorder was diagnosed prior to death, may leave no findings at autopsy.[41] These disorders are often due to mutations in the cardiac ion channels involving the KCNQ1, KCNH2, SCN5A, KCNE1 and KCNE2 genes.[42] Long QT syndrome (LQTS), Wolff-Parkinson-White syndrome (WPW), primary cardiac conduction system disease (PCCP) and Brugada syndrome have all been associated with prolongation of the QT interval, cardiac ion channel mutations and sudden cardiac death.

Prolonged QT disorders are characterized by a corrected QT interval (QTc) of greater than 450 ms.[43] The QT interval is prolonged because of delayed repolarization as a result of a genetic defect in either potassium or sodium channels. Syncope in patients with LQTS is likely due to torsades de pointes. The onset of symptoms most commonly occurs during the first 2 decades of life. The risk of developing syncope or sudden cardiac death increases with QTc, with lifetime risks of approximately 5% in those with QTc of less than 440 ms but 50% in those with QTc of more than 500 ms. Prolongation of the QT interval can also be seen with electrolyte abnormalities, most commonly hypokalemia but also hypocalcemia and hypomagnesemia, as well as neurologic or endocrine abnormalities. Certain drugs can also cause prolongation, including the methadone and certain antibiotics; this prolongation is most prominent at the initiation of treatment or which any increases in dosages.

The current recommendation for the diagnosis of arrhythmogenic cardiomyopathies is genetic testing or the performance of a "molecular" autopsy.

Genetic Testing in Sudden Cardiac Deaths

Recently, with advances in genetics, "molecular autopsies" have assisted in the diagnosis of sudden cardiac deaths. The mutations in genes leading to diseases such as hypertrophic and arrhythmogenic cardiomyopathies have been identified allowing for these entities to be diagnosed postmortem even in the absence of anatomic abnormalities. Numerous genetic testing panels are now available commercially allowing for detection of such mutations. Specific mutations involving sarcomeric proteins (the myosin heavy chain, cardiac troponins), myosin binding protein C3, desmosomes and cardiac ion channels have all been identified as having a potential role in the development of cardiomyopathies.[44] These genes include MYH7, MYL2, MYL3, MYPBC3, TNNI, TNNT2, KCNE1, KCNE2, KCNH2,

KCNJ2, KCNQ1 and SCN5A. One study of 173 cases of sudden unexplained deaths in individuals aged 1–69 years found potentially pathogenic mutations in 45 with a higher yield in women (38%) than men (18%).[42] Additionally, they found a higher yield in those less than 10 years of age in exercise induced deaths (67%) and in 11–20 year-olds in deaths during sleep (36%).[42]

Genetic testing should be considered in any sudden death, especially in the young, where after a complete autopsy examination including complete toxicological testing and histology, a cause of death is not otherwise apparent. Additionally, genetic testing should be considered for family members of persons who died from cardiac diseases with known genetic propensities, such as hypertrophic cardiomyopathies.

Myocarditis

The clinical manifestations of acute myocarditis may range from none to acute fulminating congestive heart failure to sudden death.[45] The cases that most often involve the forensic pathologist are those of individuals who are asymptomatic or have had only minor complaints and then suddenly collapse and die.

Myocarditis can be caused by infectious agents (bacterial, rickettsial, viral, protozoal, fungal), connective tissue diseases (e.g., rheumatic fever, rheumatoid arthritis), physical agents (chemical poisons or drugs) or can be idiopathic. With infectious myocarditis, injury to the myocardium may be directly due to invasion by the organism or by toxin produced by the organism. Grossly, the appearance of the heart may be normal or pale and flabby with dilated chambers. Microscopically, there are patchy or diffuse areas of myocyte necrosis with interstitial inflammation which may be focal and minor or extensive and severe. The infiltrate may vary from mostly neutrophils to lymphocytes, plasma cells and eosinophils (Figure 3.10).

Figure 3.10 Myocarditis.

Most cases of infectious myocarditis are probably viral in origin. Initially, there is infiltration by neutrophils and lymphocytes accompanied by necrosis of muscle fibers. Subsequently, lymphocytes and macrophages predominate. There may or may not be subsequent interstitial fibrosis on healing. If fibrosis develops, it may be either minor or extensive and may or may not be associated with subsequent arrhythmias. In a case seen by one of the authors, a 17-year-old boy at age 13 had a documented episode of viral myocarditis. Following that, he developed arrhythmias with occasional episodes of ventricular extrasystoles and tachycardia. He was told never to engage in any strenuous activities. At age 17, while participating in a basketball game, he collapsed and died. For the 4 years following his episode of myocarditis, he had been followed by a cardiologist, who had documented his numerous episodes of arrhythmias. It was the expectation of the cardiologist that the heart would show extensive interstitial scarring. At autopsy, the heart appeared grossly normal. Multiple microscopic sections of the heart taken from all areas, including the conduction system, were completely unremarkable highlighting that viral inflammation of the heart can cause injury to the conduction system that may not be detected or evaluated microscopically. This condition may also be the cause of some instances of sudden death in which the autopsy findings are completely negative.

In occasional cases of fatal myocarditis, the myocarditis is not widespread but consists of a single strategically located lesion. Thus, the case of a 32-year-old housewife found dead on the kitchen floor, whose autopsy and toxicological examination were completely negative. Microscopic sections of the heart showed a single focus of acute myocarditis in the conduction system. Death in this case was due to the unfortunate location of a relatively small lesion. This points out the importance of taking multiple sections of the heart, especially through the conduction system, in any complete examination of the heart for heart disease. It should also be realized that a single small collection of mononuclear cells in the myocardium does not necessarily indicate that the individual is suffering from myocarditis. This is often seen in cardiac sections if one takes sufficient microscopic sections; however, in these cases, myocyte necrosis is uniformly absent. In cases where myocardial disease is suspected, the authors recommend taking a minimum of six microscopic sections of myocardium for proper evaluation of the myocardium with at least one of the conduction system.

Cardiopulmonary Resuscitation and Sudden Cardiac Death

The death rate following out-of-hospital cardiac arrests is dependent on the type of arrhythmia that caused the arrest, prompt initiation of cardiopulmonary resuscitation (CPR) and how soon after arrest defibrillation is instituted. The public's perception of the success of CPR is based to a great degree on information communicated to them by the media, especially television, and an unrealistic impression is routinely conveyed. In a television study of CPR, 75% of "patients" survived the immediate arrest, with apparently 67% surviving to discharge.[46] In actuality, short-term success of CPR (the return of the patient's blood pressure and pulse for 1 h) is, at most, 40%, with survival until discharge from the hospital varying from 2 to 30% for cardiac arrests outside the hospital.[8,46] While 83% of the patients on television were non-elderly, in reality, the elderly are the most common group on which CPR is performed. On TV, 28% of the underlying diseases were primarily cardiac, while, in reality, 75–95% are cardiac in origin. For the elderly, long-term survival after cardiac arrest outside the hospital is 5% or less. In arrests due to trauma, the long-term survival rate varies from 0 to 30%.[46]

Who performs CPR can also be a factor. While it has been reported that effective CPR can increase the chances of survival, only about 50% of people worldwide are trained to administer CPR.[47] The presenting rhythm is also a factor in survival. Ventricular tachycardia or fibrillation show the best success rate at 20%, with electromechanical dissociation having a success rate of 7% and asystole 6%.[48] Additionally, a small percentage of patients (2%) have significant neurological sequelae even after successful CPR.

Primary Cardiac Arrest during Exercise

Myocardial ischemia, arrhythmias and sudden death can occur during or immediately after exercise.[49] Cardiovascular function is under the regulatory control of the sympathetic nervous system, with sympathetic stimulation causing an increase in heart rate, force of myocardial contraction and blood pressure. During exercise, there is a progressive rise in systolic pressure, though usually very little, if any, change in diastolic pressure. Diastolic pressure may fall slightly in younger individuals and rise in middle-aged and older individuals.[50] Heart rate increases progressively with exercise before reaching a plateau. The average maximum heart rate is approximately 180–200 beats per minute. Systolic blood pressure increases to between 162 and 216 mm Hg.[50] The increase in systolic blood pressure and heart rate is accompanied by a decrease in peripheral resistance. With isometric exercise such as weight lifting, there is almost no increase in heart rate, an increase in both systolic and diastolic blood pressure and an increase in peripheral resistance.

Sudden death is seen not only during exercise, but often immediately after cessation. The term "post-exercise peril" has been used to refer to the risk of cardiac arrhythmias during the first few minutes after cessation of strenuous exercise.[51] Dimsdale found that the highest levels of catecholamines occurred during the first 3 min after cessation of exercise.[51] During the same period, plasma potassium concentration falls rapidly.[52,53] During exercise, the levels of both norepinephrine and epinephrine increase, with norepinephrine increasing more sharply. Immediately following cessation of exercise, the levels of both these catecholamines, instead of plateauing or decreasing, continue to rise, with norepinephrine levels increasing seven- to ten-fold over baseline values and epinephrine three to eight times. [51,52] Even 10 min after cessation of activity, serum levels of the catecholamines were approximately twice the resting values.[5] During exercise, serum potassium levels increase. Following cessation of exercise, the levels fall rapidly, reaching hypokalemic levels within 1–2 min post exercise.[52,53] The combination of falling potassium and rising catecholamines during the first few minutes post exercise may make the individuals susceptible to post-exercise arrhythmias.

Episodes of sudden death occurring after exercise are probably caused by this phenomenon, with ischemia sensitizing the heart to the arrhythmogenic properties of the catecholamines and hypokalemia.

Sudden cardiac death has also been described in association with psychological stress.[54] It has been documented that psychological stress can induce either fatal or potentially fatal cardiac arrhythmias with and without underlying heart disease. This is apparently caused by stress-induced sympathetic stimulation.

Neurological Deaths

Sudden deaths due to lesions of the brain are considerably less common than those due to cardiac disease. The most common causes encountered by the medical examiner are epilepsy, nontraumatic subarachnoid hemorrhage, intracerebral hemorrhage (ICH), meningitis and tumors. Occasional rare lesions such as cysticercosis or central pontine myelinosis are also encountered.

Epilepsy

Probably the most common cause of a sudden neurological death is epilepsy, often termed sudden unexplained deaths in epilepsy or SUDEP. Epileptic deaths constitute approximately 3–4% of all natural deaths coming to autopsy in a medical examiner's office. The estimated incidence of sudden unexplained death among epileptics is 2–17%.[55] Very few of these individuals die in status epilepticus.

Typically, individuals dying suddenly and unexpectedly of epilepsy are young and show either subtherapeutic levels or absence of epileptic medications on toxicological analysis. Usually, but not always, such deaths are unwitnessed, with the victims often found dead in bed in the morning. If a death is witnessed, there may be no seizures or only one seizure with collapse.[55,56] In individuals found dead in bed, there is usually no evidence of seizures, either in the environment (sheets and blankets undisturbed, no loss of urine) or on the body (bite marks of the tongue are absent in 75% of the cases). That individuals are commonly found dead in bed is probably because sleep predisposes to epileptic attacks and, in fact, is used as a provocative diagnostic technique. Sleep has also been found to affect cardiac vulnerability to arrhythmia in that sudden death secondary to arrhythmias often occurs in the morning, immediately before or at the time of awakening.

Diagnosis of death due to epilepsy is, for the most part, a diagnosis of exclusion. At autopsy, there are no pathonomonic findings. In approximately 25% of the cases, a bite mark of the tongue might indicate a seizure, but seizures as a terminal event can occur in other entities. To make a diagnosis of death due to epilepsy, the examiner must have a clinical diagnosis of epilepsy in the past or a well-documented history of seizures, a scene not inconsistent with such a finding, and a complete autopsy, including removal of the tongue, with no findings, grossly, microscopically or toxicologically, to explain death.

Most epileptic deaths are natural. If, however, the epilepsy was due to trauma, documented and uncontestable, then the manner would more properly be classified as accident. Some epileptics die of accidental means precipitated by an epileptic attack; for example, an individual may have an epileptic attack while in water and drown (Figure 3.11) or fall while seizing and develop a subdural hematoma. No matter what the manner of death, it is very common for epileptics dying suddenly to have subtherapeutic levels or absence of anticonvulsive medication. Careful examination of the brain in most instances does not reveal a lesion that could have caused the epilepsy. The actual incidence of finding such lesions varies considerably, depending on the authority, but, to a degree, is influenced by the type of population being handled. The only thing that one can say is that, in the vast majority of the cases, no lesion to explain the seizure disorder will be found at autopsy. If lesions are found, they may be foci of sclerosis, arteriovenous (AV) malformations or adhesions between cortex and dura. Again, it must be realized that the finding of such lesions is uncommon. One finding, sclerosis of Ammon's horn, is most probably a secondary

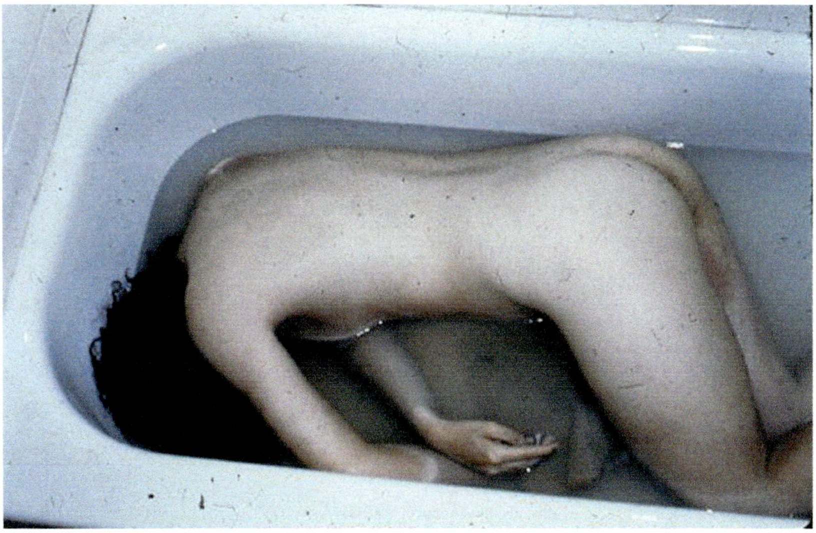

Figure 3.11 A 27-year-old epileptic drowned in the bathtub.

phenomenon related to cerebral edema during epileptic attacks, with compression of the vessels supplying blood to this region (branches of the posterior cerebral artery) against the edge of the tentorium by a herniating hippocampal gyrus.

Because the diagnosis of death due to epilepsy is on an exclusionary basis, the actual incidence of such deaths is probably underestimated. Thus, if an individual dying of a seizure disorder happens to have significant coronary atherosclerosis, the cause of death would probably be ascribed to the coronary artery disease rather than the epilepsy.

The mechanism of death in epilepsy is most probably due to a cardiac arrhythmia precipitated by an autonomic discharge.[55–57] Alterations in cardiac activity and respiration have been documented in individuals dying during an epileptic attack. It is not known, however, why a seizure, apparently no different from those that the patient had previously had in the past, should prove fatal at this particular time. The autonomic nervous system, especially the sympathetic portion, is important in the regulation of cardiac and vascular physiology. Cortical loci exert a more specific autonomic control of cardiovascular changes than do the lower levels of the brain. Cortical stimulation can produce changes in heart rate, blood pressure and cardiac extrasystoles. Stimulation of portions of the hypothalamus can also produce cardiovascular changes, for example, cardiac arrhythmias, because the hypothalamus exerts considerable control over the autonomic function. Production of extrasystoles by stimulation of the hypothalamus is due to the stimulation of the sympathetic pathways to the heart or stimulation of pathways controlling secretion of epinephrine.

The sympathetic nervous system can lower the vulnerable threshold of even electrically stable myocardium, thereby facilitating the onset of ventricular fibrillation, if the activity of the sympathetic nervous system is increased by neural or neurohumoral action. Increased sympathetic nervous activity can predispose to ventricular fibrillation by the direct action of neuroepinephrine on neuroeffector sites in the myocardium. The aforementioned findings indicate that sudden death during epileptic seizures is most likely due to a lethal cardiac arrhythmia induced or propagated by the disorganized neural discharges of a seizure.

Nontraumatic Subarachnoid Hemorrhage

The second most common cause of sudden unexpected death due to natural disease of the brain is nontraumatic subarachnoid hemorrhage. Early in this century, spontaneous subarachnoid hemorrhage was considered a disease entity in itself. With the advancement of medical knowledge, it was realized that it was a syndrome with multiple causes. Berry aneurysms are the most common causes of subarachnoid hemorrhage, followed by ICHs and, to a lesser degree, rupture of AV malformations. Uncommon causes of nontraumatic subarachnoid hemorrhage would be blood dyscrasias; endocarditis with embolic phenomenon; overuse of anticoagulants; tumors, both primary and metastatic; and sickle cell hemoglobinopathy.

Whatever the cause of the nontraumatic subarachnoid hemorrhage, as soon as blood enters the subarachnoid space, it causes a mild inflammatory reaction in the meninges.[58] *Death is due to generalized vasospasm triggered by the subarachnoid hemorrhage, with resultant ischemic injury to the brain.*

If the person survives the subarachnoid bleed, fibrosis subsequently develops in many cases. Following hemorrhages into the subarachnoid space, a meningeal reaction is generally not seen for at least 2 h, when there are small accumulations of polymorphonuclear cells around pial blood vessels. By 4–16 h, a more intensive polymorphonuclear reaction is seen. Lymphocytes begin to accumulate around the pial vessels. After 16–32 h, there are large numbers of polymorphonuclear cells and lymphocytes. Reaction of the mesothelial cells lining the subarachnoid space and arachnoid trabeculae appears 24 h after the subarachnoid hemorrhage. Breakdown of the erythrocytes can be seen as early as 16–32 h after subarachnoid hemorrhage. By the third day, the polymorphonuclear reaction has reached its peak. Because of a rapid increase in lymphocytes and macrophages, however, it accounts for only half of the cells present. Hemosiderin granules can be seen inside macrophages. By 7 days, no more polymorphonuclear reaction is present. At this time, lymphocytic infiltration is most prominent, with macrophages and hemosiderin. Some intact red blood cells are still present. Fibrosis of the pia mater develops in about 10 days. Since slight fibrosis of the pial and arachnoid membranes may be present as a "normal" aspect of these membranes, especially with advancing age, interpretation of minimal fibrosis is difficult.

Berry Aneurysms

In the medical examiner's office, rupture of a **berry aneurysm** is the most common cause of nontraumatic subarachnoid hemorrhage. Berry aneurysms per se are not uncommon – unruptured aneurysms have been reported in 4.9% of all routine autopsies when searched for.[59] While Berry aneurysms are rare in children, they increase in frequency with age. They are located, for the most part, at the point of bifurcation and branching of the cerebral arteries, with approximately 90% found in the anterior cerebral, middle cerebral and internal carotid arteries. Berry aneurysms are thought to be the result of developmental weakness of the vessel walls. This abnormality generally consists of a defect in the formation of the media at the branching point. The intimal elastic lamina and the muscularis terminate at the neck of the aneurysm, with the wall of the sac made up of thickened hyalinized intima and the adventitia. Persistence of incomplete involuted embryonic arteries with residual medial weakness is the explanation proposed for aneurysms away from the point of bifurcation.

Hypertension and cigarette smoking are predisposing factors. Atherosclerosis may also play a secondary role, leading to focal destruction and weakening of the vessels walls. Multiplicity of aneurysms is quite common, multiple aneurysms being reported in anywhere from 12 to 31.4% of cases.[60]

Berry aneurysms almost invariably rupture at the apex and, when rupture occurs, there is generally hemorrhage into the subarachnoid space. Hemorrhage may also occur into the substance of the brain. The patient usually complains of an excruciating headache and loses consciousness almost immediately. Minor leakage from the aneurysm may precede rupture. In such cases, the patient often complains of headache for days or weeks prior to rupture.

Most of the statistical data on ruptured intracranial aneurysms are based on hospital cases, that is, those individuals who survive a rupture long enough to be admitted to a hospital. There are, however, two studies in the literature that include large numbers of individuals who died prior to or on arrival at a hospital.[60,61] These studies more accurately represent the cases seen in the medical examiner system. In both reports, 60% of the patients died immediately after rupture. Of those who survived the initial insult, more than half died less than 24 h after admission to a hospital.

In Freytag's study, the ages of the individuals ranged from 14 to 77, with a mean age of 46 years.[60] Eighty-four percent of the aneurysms were located in the anterior portion of circle of Willis and 16% in the posterior portion; 27% were present in the middle cerebral artery, 25% in the internal carotid artery, 24% in the anterior communicating artery and 10% in the basilar artery. Patients with aneurysms of the posterior circle of Willis or the internal carotid artery showed a greater tendency (69–79%) to die at the time of rupture than those in other areas (49–53%). Of the 24 aneurysms in the basilar artery, 20 were present at the branching point of the posterior cerebral arteries. Evidence of previous bleeding from the aneurysms was present in 13% of the cases.

In ruptured berry aneurysms, massive subarachnoid hemorrhage was present in 96% of the cases, subdural hemorrhage in 22% and ICH in 43%. Subarachnoid hemorrhage was the only lesion in 49% of the cases, with ICH and subdural hemorrhage alone in 1% of each of the cases. ICH was present in 24% of those who died immediately, but in 71% of those who survived some time, thus indicating a better chance of survival if the aneurysm had ruptured into the brain tissue. Hemorrhage into the ventricular system occurred in 17% of the cases with ICH. Such hemorrhage into the ventricular system may be as rapidly fatal as bleeding into the subarachnoid space. Twenty-two percent of the cases showed hemorrhage in the subdural space. Only 5% of the cases, however, were space-occupying (over 50 mL).

In deaths due to subarachnoid hemorrhage from a ruptured berry aneurysm, the largest quantity of blood is on the ventral surface of the brain, with lesser amounts laterally and dorsally (Figure 3.12).

Large pools of blood on the ventral surface of the brain often make it difficult to locate the aneurysm if the brain is not examined when fresh. The arachnoid membrane should be removed with forceps and the ventral surface of the brain flushed with running water. This will allow inspection of the circle of Willis for aneurysms (Figure 3.13).

In approximately 10% of all cases in which subarachnoid hemorrhage is present and in which the presentation is that of a ruptured berry aneurysm, no aneurysm can be found. If we exclude all other causes of the subarachnoid hemorrhage, then, in all probability, the cause is a rupture of a small aneurysm that has been completely obliterated by the blowout of the vessel.

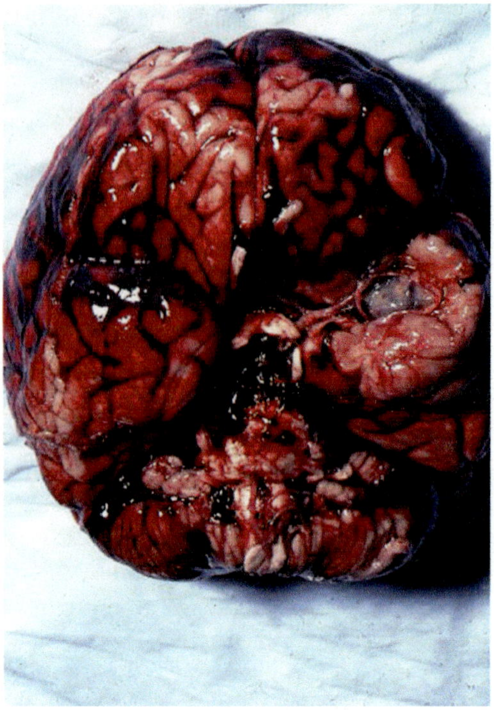

Figure 3.12 Massive subarachnoid hemorrhage from ruptured aneurysm of right middle.

Arteriovenous Malformations

A small percentage of the cases of nontraumatic subarachnoid hemorrhage are due to bleeding from an **AV malformation**. They tend to cluster in the early decades of life, though they can be found at any age and consist of complex tangles of abnormal arteries and veins linked by one or more fistulas.[62] They lack a capillary bed and the small arteries have a deficient muscularis. They range from small to large, cortical to deep. Most of these lesions are visible on the

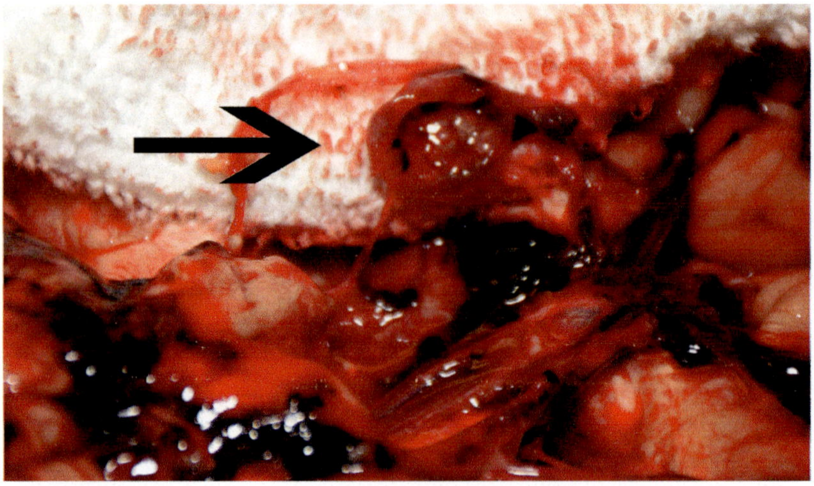

Figure 3.13 A large berry aneurysm along the circle of Willis.

surface of the brain, appearing as a wedge of arteries and veins extending into the subcortical white matter. Deep AV malformations may lie in the white matter, basal ganglia, thalamus or brainstem. The majority of AV malformations of the brain involve the central parietal cortex.

Most AV malformations derive part of their blood supply from at least one branch of the middle cerebral artery. There may be severe bleeding from these lesions into the subarachnoid space or into the substance of the brain, presenting as a massive ICH. It is estimated that 0.1% of the population have AV malformations with 12% of these symptomatic.[62] Sturge-Weber syndrome is characterized by multiple AV malformations of the cerebral hemispheres associated with vascular nevi of the face and/or neck and epilepsy. The most common clinical presentations are intracranial hemorrhage (30–82%); seizures (16–53%); headache and focal neurological deficits.[62] Two percent of all strokes are due to AVs. The death rate from hemorrhage is 10–15%.

At autopsy, there is diffuse subarachnoid hemorrhage distributed evenly over the convexities of the cerebral hemispheres, as well as on the ventral surfaces of the brain. The marked concentration of subarachnoid hemorrhage on the ventral surface of the brain seen in rupture of a berry aneurysm is not present. The brain must be carefully examined to rule out the presence of AV malformations or berry aneurysm.

Intracerebral Hemorrhage

ICHs (strokes) are characterized clinically by an abrupt onset and rapid evolution. ICHs are more common in males and show a higher incidence in blacks than in whites, probably due to the greater incidence of hypertension. Blacks dying of ICHs also tend to be younger than their white counterparts.

Intracerebral hemorrhages (ICHs) are uncommon in the younger age groups, but can occur particularly in association with stimulant drugs such as cocaine and methamphetamine. The hemorrhage usually occurs in individuals who are up and active rather than asleep. In natural ICH events, hypertension is virtually always present. Hypertension leads to small vessel disease in the brain resulting in degeneration of the vessel walls, known as lipohyalinosis. Other vascular diseases can also predispose to hemorrhage, including cerebral amyloid angiopathy. In this entity, there is deposition of amyloid protein within the small vessels, making them prone to rupture. The cause is still unknown, but these deposits can be seen on microscopy.

In ICH, There is usually only one episode of hemorrhage at the time of the attack and recurrence of bleeding is not usually encountered. The patient usually develops symptoms over a period of one to several hours. The primary sites for ICHs are the putamen and adjacent internal capsule, the thalamus, the cerebellar hemispheres, the pons and the white matter (Figure 3.14A–C).

In hemorrhage in the putamen, the speech becomes slurred and the muscles of the face, arms and legs gradually weaken. In thalamic hemorrhage, hemiparesis occurs secondary to pressure on the adjacent internal capsule. The sensory deficit is greater than the motor weakness. Cerebellar hemorrhage usually takes a period of several hours to develop. Loss of consciousness is uncommon. Repeated vomiting, occipital headache, vertigo and inability to walk or stand are symptoms. Occasionally, the individual is thought to be intoxicated. In pontine hemorrhage, consciousness is lost almost immediately.

As in the case of ruptured berry aneurysms, most of the literature about ICH is clinically oriented and concerns hospital cases. The paper by Freytag is probably most relevant

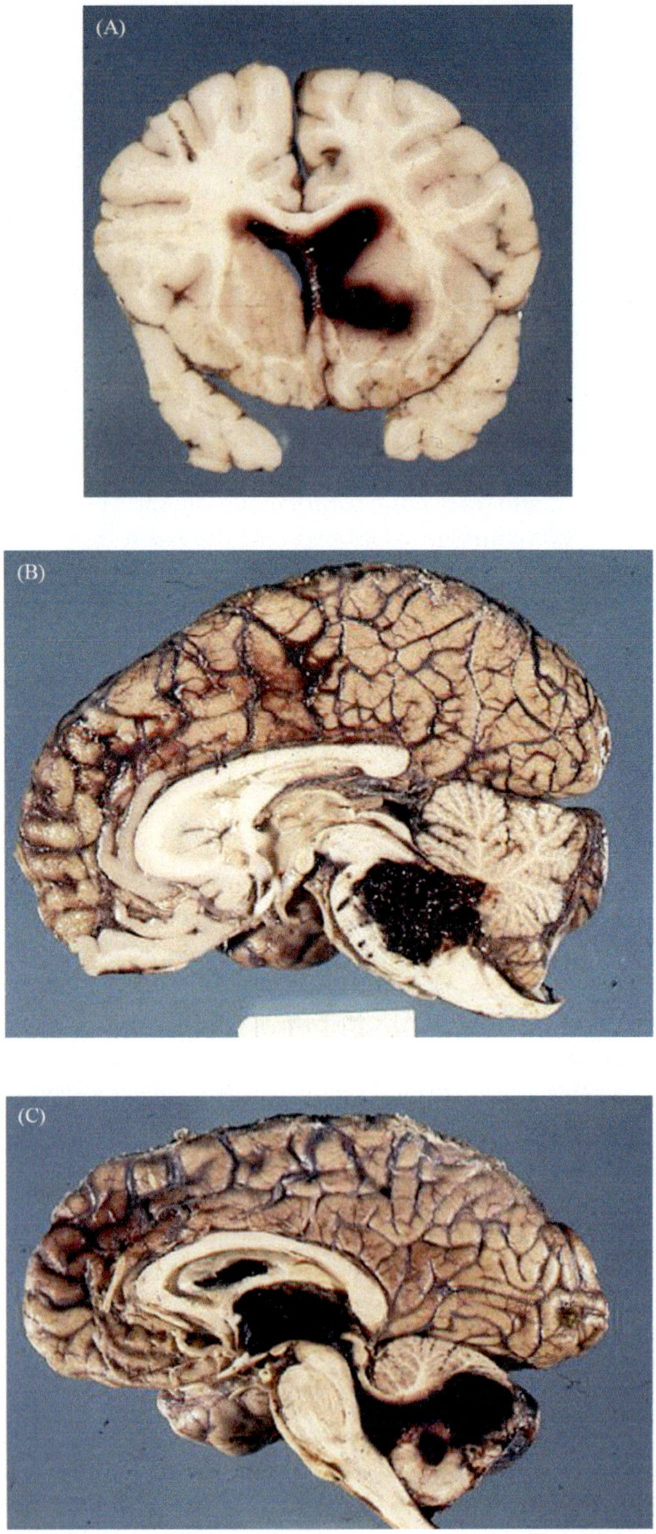

Figure 3.14 Primary intracerebral hemorrhages involving (A) basal ganglia with rupture into ventricular system, (B) pons and (C) cerebellum.

to a medical examiner's office, because 80% of the cases were autopsies carried out in a medical examiner's office.[63] Of the 393 cases studied, 40% of the hypertensive ICHs originated in the striate body area, 16% in the pons, 15% in the thalamus, 12% in the cerebellum and 10% in the cerebral white matter. Neither the cerebral nor cerebellar hemorrhages showed predilection for any side. Three percent of the cases showed multiple areas of origin for the hematomas, with five being the greatest number of multiple sites. There was no direct correlation between the severity of atherosclerosis of the basilar vessels and the development of ICH.

Freytag pointed out that more than 50% of the hematomas occur between 40 and 60 years of age with a range of ages from 30 to 88 years of age and an average of 55.5 years.[63] Eleven percent of the patients, however, were in their thirties. Survival time was relatively short. Thus, 35% of the individuals were found dead or were dead on arrival at a hospital, and 75% were either dead on arrival at a hospital or died within the first 24 h. Only 10% lived longer than 3 days. When hemorrhage occurred in the pons, 95% of the patients died within 24 h. Seventy-five percent of the hematomas ruptured through the ventricular walls into the ventricles. Hemorrhages at sites close to the ventricles penetrated into the ventricles more often than those in remote areas. Thus, 97% of the thalamic hemorrhages ruptured into the ventricles, compared with only 40% of the cerebral white matter hematomas. In 6% of the cases, the intracerebral hematomas penetrated through the cortex and subarachnoid membrane into the subdural space. This was most common with the cerebellar hemorrhages. Only 15% of the ICHs penetrated through the cortex, producing subarachnoid hemorrhage. More than half (54%) of the patients developed secondary brainstem hemorrhages and edema.

In ICH, the brain is asymmetrically swollen, with the swollen hemisphere containing the hemorrhage. Subarachnoid hemorrhage may or may not be present on the base of the brain. On sectioning, the brain tissue adjacent to the hemorrhage is swollen and edematous. No brain tissue is present in the hematoma. Microscopic sections of adjacent brain tissue usually show severely sclerotic hyalinized arteries and arterioles. Occasionally, aneurysmally dilated arterioles and small arteries may be found. Death is generally due to compression and distortion of the midbrain or hemorrhage into the ventricles.

While deaths due to ruptured berry aneurysms or ICH are generally considered natural, in certain circumstances, they might be classified as homicide or accident. Thus, if an individual suffers a stroke, or a ruptured aneurysm, during a fight in which physical violence is involved, the case should be classified as homicidal in manner. Or if either of these occur while intoxicating with cocaine or methamphetamine, accidental would be the better manner. But whether there are any criminal actions involved is something for the courts to decide, not the medical examiner.

Meningitis

Meningitis is an occasional cause of sudden unexpected death.[64] Until the late 1980s, most of the victims were children between the ages of 3 months and 3 years, with the organism involved being *Haemophilus influenzae*. Mass inoculation of children with *Haemophilus* vaccine has resulted in the virtual disappearance of such cases. At present, acute bacterial meningitis is a disease of adults. It is seen in association with infections of the ears and sinuses; alcoholism; splenectomy, pneumonia and septicemia. The most common organisms

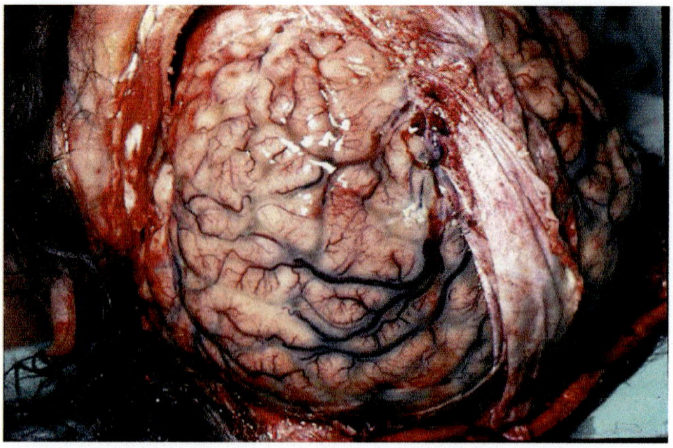

Figure 3.15 A 29-year-old female with pneumococcal meningitis. Purulent exudate in subarachnoid space.

now encountered are *Streptococcus pneumoniae* (80%), *Neisseria meningitidis* (20%); *Listeria monocytogenes* (5%) and *H. influenzae* (8%).[65] In neonates, the coliform bacilli and group B streptococci are predominant. Most cases of meningitis develop secondary to septicemia.

S. pneumoniae may develop secondary to pneumococcal pneumonia. This organism is also the most common organism associated with head trauma in which the dura is disrupted. Haemophilus, pneumococcal and meningococcal meningitis all may develop by direct extension from middle-ear infections. At autopsy, the brain is markedly swollen. The meninges appear cloudy on the ventral surface of the brain and, to a lesser degree, laterally due to purulent exudate (Figure 3.15).

The exudate may be so slight as not to be seen grossly, or severe with copious quantities. In all cases of meningitis, the middle ears should be opened and examined to make sure that this is not the source of the meningitis. Pneumococcal septicemia can also develop, particularly if the patient is asplenic, either through surgery or congenital aberration. Pneumococcal septicemia can usually be diagnosed via blood culture even after refrigeration of the body.

Meningitis caused by *N. meningitidis* is usually spread from the posterior nasopharynx that is the natural reservoir for this organism, with 2–15% of healthy individuals carrying the organism in non-epidemic times[66] and can lead to meningococcemia. **Meningococcemia** may present as a mild febrile illness, a fulminant disease (Waterhouse-Friderichsen syndrome) or a chronic illness. The patient may have chills, high fever, dizziness, nausea, headaches or weakness. Petechiae appear on the body in 75% of cases. They may coalesce, forming purpura and intracutaneous lesions. In 10% of the cases, there is a rapidly progressive course with toxemia, shock and collapse. The individual may die less than 10 h after onset of symptoms. Occasionally, a person who is walking around will suddenly collapse, die and, at autopsy, be found to have meningococcemia. In such a case, one can only speculate that the symptoms were not severe enough to inconvenience the person. At autopsy, there will be cyanosis characterized by a *blotchy erythematous rash, petechiae and purpura of the skin and conjunctivae* and *acute bilateral hemorrhagic adrenal necrosis.* (Figure 3.16A and B).

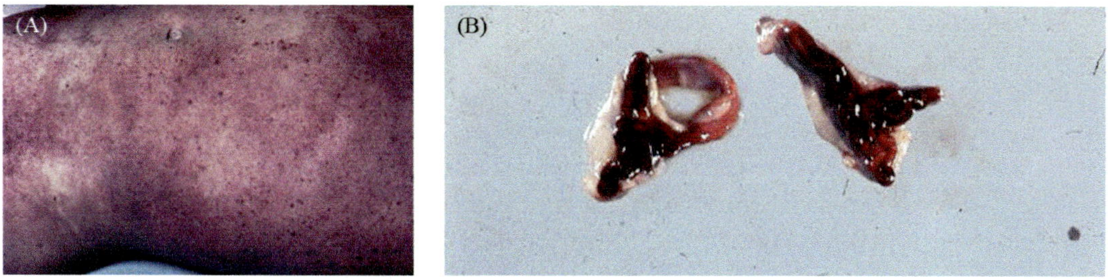

Figure 3.16 Meningococcemia. (A) Blotchy erythematous rash with petechiae and purpura. (B) Bilateral acute hemorrhagic necrosis of adrenals.

Cultures of the blood and spinal fluid for meningococcus are generally negative after refrigeration of the body due to the fragile nature of the organisms and/or antemortem administration of antibiotics. In such cases, diagnosis can be made from blood by detection of specific meningococcal capsular polysaccharides using immunoelectrophoresis, latex agglutination or polymerase chain reaction.[67] These, in the presence of the aforementioned autopsy findings, make the diagnosis of meningococcemia.

Viral, or aseptic, encephalitis is rarely seen in the medical examiner's office due to its protracted course, which leads to a clinical diagnosis. Common etiologic agents include the echo, coxsackie, herpes, cytomegalo and varicella viruses as well as the flavivirus of St Louis encephalitis, West Nile virus.[65] In viral meningitis, the brain will show severe edema with perivascular cellular infiltrates and infiltration of the meninges. The cells are predominantly lymphocytes and polymorphonuclear cells. Acellular plaques of necrosis may be seen throughout the brain. Diagnosis is usually confirmed via PCR for viral markers.

Primary Brain Tumors

The initial discovery of both primary and secondary brain tumors by forensic pathologists is rapidly disappearing due to the wide spread use of pre-mortem radiology especially computerized axial tomography (CT) and magnetic resonance imaging (MRI). However, forensic pathologists are occasionally asked to be involved when there is a perceived association between trauma and tumor development. In most of these cases, the tumor is unrelated to the traumatic event but is found on radiology when done secondary to the trauma. There is no medical proof that a single traumatic event can give rise to a malignant tumor.[68] However, a causal relation between head trauma, such as a fracture of the skull, and the subsequent development of a meningioma has been suggested, with Schiffer et al. reporting three such cases.[69] Trauma has also been linked to the metastatic spread of a preexisting malignant tumor. Multiple episodes of trauma in conjunction with other factors may cause cancer, for example, chronic irritation of the skin and squamous cell carcinoma. If, under the category of trauma, one includes radiation (including ultraviolet light), carcinogenic chemicals and chronic exposure to heavy metals, there is no doubt that, with repeated exposure, an individual can develop a malignant tumor,[68] though tumors developing in these latter cases usually do not come to the attention of a forensic pathologist.

Respiratory Deaths

Sudden death due to diseases of the respiratory system makes up only a small proportion of all sudden deaths, though this has not always been the case. In the textbook by Gonzales et al., published in 1937, diseases of the respiratory tract accounted for 23% of unexpected deaths.[70] Gonzales et al. grouped respiratory deaths into four large categories: asphyxia, hemorrhage from air passages, pneumothorax and infections of the lung.

Nowadays, sudden, unexpected deaths from lung diseases are relatively uncommon. The group that Gonzales et al. referred to as "asphyxia" included asthma and pulmonary embolism. Deaths due to these entities are still seen. Diphtheric or luetic inflammation of the larynx is not seen anymore. Also included in this category were deaths allegedly due to inhalation of vomitus. It is now realized that vomitus in the tracheobronchial tree is almost invariably an agonal event.[71] Vomitus is found in the tracheal bronchial tree in an approximately half the case of individuals dying suddenly. It is only when the airway is completely occluded by foreign material in an individual who has severe neurological impairment that one should attribute death to massive aspiration.

Most natural pulmonary deaths seen currently fall into one of four main categories: infectious disease processes; acute exacerbation of chronic obstructive disease processes; pulmonary thromboemboli; and anaphylaxis; though various other pulmonary processes can also rarely be seen resulting in sudden death.

Infectious Disease Processes

Pneumonia

In most cases, pneumonia is usually a secondary complication of another disease process that has brought the case into the office. Individuals hospitalized for several days or weeks following head trauma from an accident quite commonly will develop bronchopneumonia. Sudden deaths due to primary pneumonia are uncommon, though likely represent the most common cause of sudden respiratory death. In 2018, in Bexar County, Texas, pneumonia accounted for 64% of the sudden natural deaths due to respiratory disease, however this can vary by season and pathogen. For example, during a particularly bad influenza season, pneumonia deaths may increase as was the case during the 2019/2020 COVID-19 pandemic. In cases of sudden death due to pneumonia, either lobar pneumonia or a confluent bronchopneumonia involving at least one lobe is present (Figure 3.17).

In most cases, the decedent may have complained of vague respiratory symptoms prior to death. Often terminal pneumonia is found in alcoholics or chronic drug users where chronic use of intoxicants may result in an impaired immune system or mask symptoms.

Occasionally, one will see a young child with a vague history of some respiratory symptoms over a couple of days, interpreted as being nothing but a cold by the parents. These children are often found to have patchy bronchopneumonia involving all lobes or bronchiolitis, both of which can worsen rapidly, leading to sudden death.

Epiglottitis

While conditions like luetic or diphtheric laryngitis are no longer seen, occasional cases of acute epiglottitis will be seen in the medical examiner's office. Most people think of this as a disease of young children. Increasingly, however, it has become a disease of adults.[72–74]

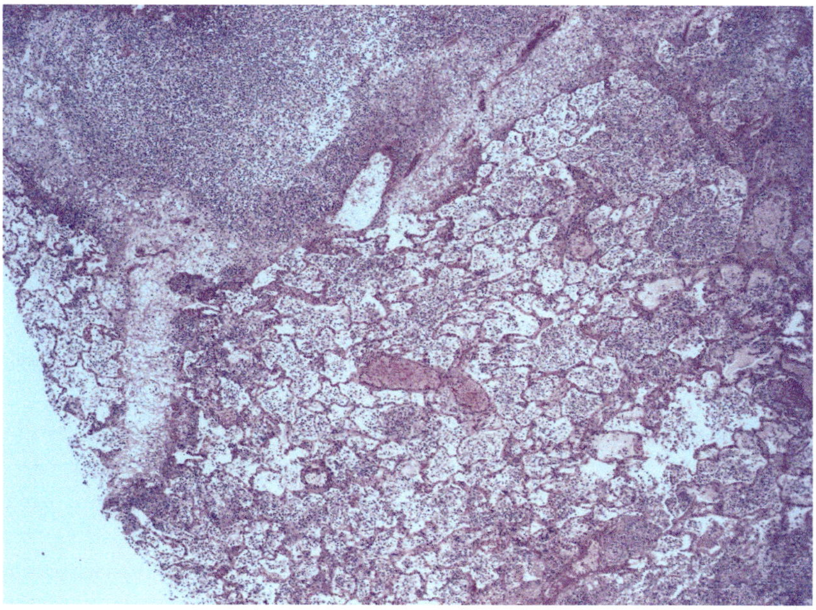

Figure 3.17 Severe, confluent lobar pneumonia with alveolar wall destruction and focal abscess formation.

With acute epiglottitis, there is always the potential for sudden fatal airway obstruction, which can occur extremely rapidly. The individual may have very minor symptoms such as a sore throat, difficulty swallowing and hoarse speech. From there, the patient can rapidly develop airway obstruction, even while talking to a physician. Acute epiglottitis is often a medical emergency, requiring immediate tracheostomy or insertion of an endotracheal tube if the individual begins to develop acute airway obstruction.

H. influenzae has traditionally been the most common cause of this condition in both children and adults. In the last decade, there have been significant changes in the epidemiology of epiglottitis, with its now occurring almost exclusively in adults, and with a lower incidence of *H. influenzae* infection.[72,73] Since the introduction of *H. influenzae* vaccination in Sweden in 1992–1993, there has been a >90% reduction in the incidence of acute epiglottitis in the youngest age group.[73] Other etiologic agents include *S. pneumoniae, Streptococcus pyogenes, Staphylococcus aureus* and *Klebsiella pneumoniae.*

Acute Exacerbation of Asthma or Chronic Obstructive Pulmonary Disease

Chronic pulmonary diseases, such as interstitial lung disease, can all result in sudden death due to lack of oxygen exchange and the resulting hypoxia, but the most common disease entities seen in the medical examiner setting are chronic obstructive pulmonary disease (COPD) and asthma.

COPD is mainly an illness of adults and includes emphysema and chronic bronchitis and is a chronic inflammatory disease of the lungs resulting in destruction of the alveoli and mucus plugging of the bronchi. COPD is most commonly associated with cigarette smoking. Asthma is usually considered a childhood illness, though it is also prevalent in adults, and accounts for approximately 3,500 deaths a year in the United States.[75] Deaths related to asthma are more common in females than males, and African Americans are twice as likely to die from asthma than Caucasians.

Sudden, unexpected death from either asthma or COPD can occur without long-term deterioration or a prolonged attack. The frequency of death is increased at night or in the early morning, possibly due to a pronounced diurnal variation in airflow limitation. Up to one fourth of deaths occur within 30 min of onset of the attack. In an acute exacerbation, there is a reduced airflow rate, air trapping and a ventilation-perfusion imbalance that leads to decreased oxygenation of the blood, elevated carbon dioxide, increased pulmonary vascular resistance, a right ventricular systolic overload and an increase in the effort needed to breathe. These may develop either gradually or in a very short order. If airflow obstruction is not relieved, there will be steady progression to elevated carbon dioxide, metabolic acidosis, exhaustion and death.

At autopsy, the lungs usually appear overexpanded, completely occupying their respective chest cavities. This hyperexpanded state may not be present if extensive CPR has been carried out. In addition to the hyperexpansion of the lungs, a sticky tenacious white mucus deposit will fill the bronchi. In asthma, microscopic sections of the lung show a chronic inflammatory infiltrate with numerous eosinophils around the bronchi associated with hyperplasic of the surrounding smooth muscles. In COPD, there is destruction of the alveolar walls with fibromuscular proliferation of the ends. This alveolar wall destruction can also lead to the formation of air pockets, called blebs, just beneath the pleura (termed blebs); blebs can spontaneously rupture, leading to the sudden development of a pneumothorax.

COPD can also lead to sudden death through secondary pneumonia development and cardiac diseases. COPD has been shown to be associated with an increased risk of sudden cardiac death.[76] In particular, it is associated with changes in the QT interval, both prolongation and shortening, as well as ventricular arrhythmias.

Pulmonary Thromboembolism

Death from massive pulmonary thromboembolus is due to impaction of dislodged thrombi in the pulmonary artery or its main tributaries (Figure 3.18).

Most pulmonary thromboemboli originate in the deep veins of the lower extremities, though they occasionally arise in the pelvic veins, especially in pregnant women. Once a thrombus has formed, it can be subsequently be dislodged and travel through the venous system to the heart and pulmonary arteries, resulting in occlusion of the pulmonary vessels – termed pulmonary thromboembolism. *De novo* formation of blood clots within the pulmonary vessels is rare.

Thrombosis has been classically described as being caused by three factors: stasis, injury to a vein and hypercoagulability. Any trauma to the lower extremities or pelvis may injure a vein and cause the formation of thrombi; however, the classic example of a death due to a pulmonary embolus occurs in an individual confined to bed. Even though there may be no direct injury to the vessel, venous stasis in the immobile individual leads to thrombus formation. If the individual is immobile due to an injury, for instance head trauma, and develops a thrombosis resulting in a massive pulmonary thromboembolus, even though the mechanism of death is natural, that is, a pulmonary thromboembolus, the manner of death would be accident because the individual was confined to the bed due to trauma. If the individual had been assaulted, then the case would be classified as homicide.

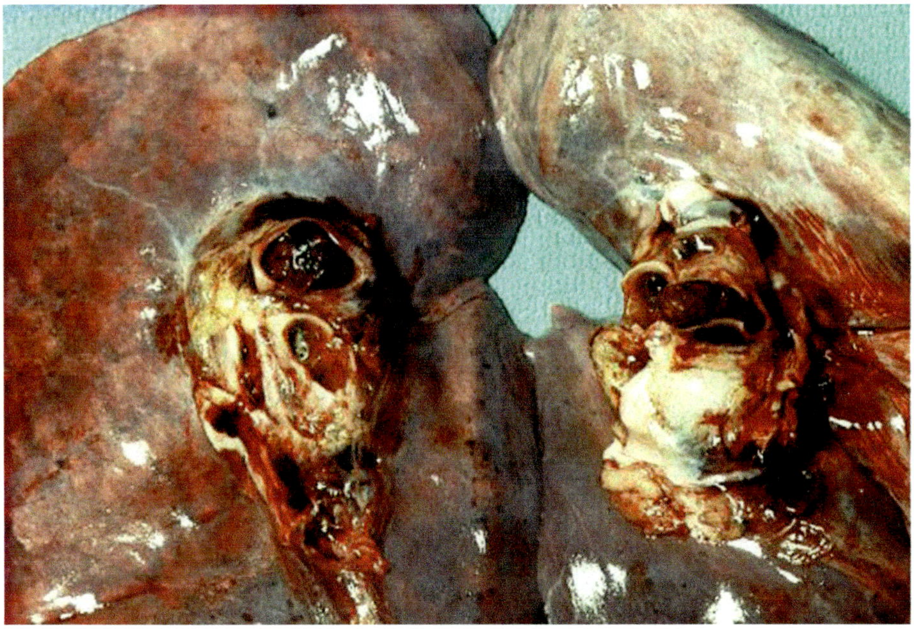

Figure 3.18 Bilateral massive pulmonary thromboemboli.

Hypercoagulability is another risk factor for the development of thrombi and can either be inherited or acquired. Inherited hypercoagulable conditions include prothrombin gene mutation, clotting factor deficiencies such as Protein S or C deficiency and, most commonly, Factor V Leiden. Factor V Leiden is a genetic disorder in which factor V, a normal protein involved in blood clot formation, does not degrade normally and remains active, resulting in excess blood clot formation. This excess clotting normally occurs in the veins, allowing for the formation of thrombi and pulmonary thromboemboli. Factor V Leiden is most prevalent in Caucasians with approximately 5% North American Caucasians having the mutation.[77] It is also estimated that approximately 25% of people with deep venous thrombosis (DVT) or pulmonary embolism have Factor V Leiden.[77] In a study of 43 fatal pulmonary thromboembolism cases, one patient was positive for the Factor V Leiden mutation while four carried the prothrombin gene mutation.[78]

Amniotic Fluid Emboli

Another type of pulmonary embolism that is found exclusively in pregnancy is amniotic fluid embolism. This is an uncommon but highly lethal complication of pregnancy, first described by Steiner and Lushbough.[79] While early studies reported an 86% mortality, more recent work indicates that the mortality is ranges between 11 and 44% and is likely around 20%.[80]

Most cases of amniotic emboli occur during active labor, though cases have occurred as late as 90 min postpartum.[79,81,82] Clark et al. reviewed 46 cases of amniotic fluid emboli.[81] Thirty women had amniotic fluid emboli during labor but before delivery and 13 after delivery. Of these 13 cases, 5 had emboli following vaginal delivery and 8 during cesarean section but after delivery. Three of the patients who had cesarean sections were in labor prior to the section. Of the 13 individuals developing symptoms of amniotic fluid emboli after delivery, 9 (69%) did so within 5 min of delivery. Thus, most of these cases do not come into the medical examiner's office. However, three of the cases reported by Clark et al. involved individuals undergoing second-trimester abortions. Amniotic fluid emboli have also been reported in first- and second-trimester abortions as well as following abdominal trauma and amniocentesis.[83–85]

The clinical presentation of amniotic fluid emboli is sudden dyspnea, hypotension and seizures, followed by cardiovascular arrest.[82,86,87] Of the 40 individuals studied by Clark et al. who had cardiac arrest, all but two arrested within the first hour.[81] If death does not occur immediately, consumptive coagulopathy usually develops evidenced by decreased fibrinogen, elevated levels of fibrin split products, prolonged partial thromboplastin and prothrombin times and thrombocytopenia.

The syndrome of amniotic fluid embolism has been attributed to the acute embolization of amniotic fluid and debris of fetal origin into the maternal venous circulation, with resultant pulmonary microvascular obstruction. On reaching the lung, this material is presumed to produce severe transient vasospasm of the pulmonary vasculature, pulmonary hypertension, right heart failure and hypoxia. Clark et al, however, argue that exposure of the maternal circulation to amniotic fluid triggers a pathophysiologic cascade similar to anaphylactic or septic shock generating the physiological derangements characterizing these syndromes.[81] This would explain the observation that fetal debris is not seen at autopsy in all cases where there is no doubt, clinically, that the patient had "amniotic fluid emboli." Thus, in the 22 cases coming to autopsy in the study by Clark et al., in six of the individuals (27%), no fetal elements (squamous cells, hair, fat droplets, mucin or trophoblasts) were identified in the lungs.[81]

Traditionally, the diagnosis of amniotic fluid embolism was made at autopsy by a combination of clinical signs and symptoms and the finding of mucin derived from meconium, fetal squamous cells, lanugo hair or vernix fat globules in the pulmonary vasculature. These materials can usually be seen on hematoxylin and eosin slides, though special stains might better demonstrate individual elements. Mucin is virtually always present, with cellular elements seen less frequently.[87] As pointed out by Clark et al., in a substantial number of cases where there is no doubt clinically that the patient has had amniotic fluid emboli, no fetal elements are identified.[81] This is especially true in deaths during early pregnancy caused by the less abundant nature of these elements in amniotic fluid at this stage.[84] While, the presence of squamous cells in the pulmonary arterial circulation at autopsy has traditionally been regarded as one of the pathognomonic elements of amniotic fluid emboli, Clark et al. showed that squamous cells are routinely present in the maternal pulmonary circulation of all pregnant women.[87] Thus, the detection of squamous cells alone in the pulmonary arterial blood is not sufficient for the diagnosis of amniotic fluid embolism.

Anaphylaxis

Most anaphylactic deaths seen by a medical examiner are caused by insect bites, drugs or foods such as peanuts. The symptoms of anaphylactic attack are faintness, itching of the skin, urticaria, tightness in the chest, wheezing, respiratory difficulty and collapse. In anaphylactic deaths, the onset of symptoms is mostly immediate or within the first 15–20 min. Beyond that time, one would need a well-documented medical history of gradually developing symptoms to implicate an anaphylactic reaction. Death usually occurs within 1–2 h. In some insects, for example, fire ants, the venom is directly toxic and death can occur without anaphylactic reaction if there were a large enough number of bites.[88] In such cases, death typically occurs after 24 h.

A fatal anaphylactic reaction results in acute respiratory distress or circulatory collapse. Obstruction of the upper airway can be caused by pharyngeal or laryngeal edema while obstruction of the lower airway can result from bronchospasm with contraction of the smooth muscle of the lungs, vasodilation and increased capillary permeability.[89] Cardiac arrest may be caused by respiratory arrest, the direct effects of the chemical mediators of anaphylaxis on the heart or shock caused by a combination of intravascular fluid loss from edema and vasodilatation. Pumphrey and Roberts studied 56 anaphylactic deaths coming to autopsy and found that, in all 16 deaths caused by food allergy, there was difficulty in breathing, with death in 13 of the cases caused by respiratory arrest.[90] In contrast, shock without any difficulty in breathing occurred in 8 of 19 cases caused by insect venom and 12 of 21 caused by iatrogenic reactions.

At autopsy, the findings are often nonspecific. There is often laryngeal edema, but rarely complete obstruction of the airway. Pumphrey and Roberts reported laryngeal or pharyngeal edema in 8 and 49%, respectively, of individuals who died immediately[90] Emphysema caused by the bronchoconstriction might be present. Visceral and pulmonary congestion, edema and pulmonary hemorrhage are present but are nonspecific. In Pumphrey and Roberts' study, 23 of 56 anaphylactic deaths had no macroscopic findings at autopsy.

The circumstances of death are often helpful in making the diagnosis of fatal anaphylaxis. It is most helpful if there is either a history of an allergy known to trigger anaphylaxis or a witnessed collapse and death following an insect bite, ingestion of food or administration of a drug. Most deaths attributed to therapeutic agents involve the administration of either penicillin or an iodine-containing contrast agent used for diagnostic purposes. Death, however, has been associated with a multitude of other therapeutic agents.

The diagnosis of anaphylactic deaths is often augmented by laboratory testing. Both IgE and tryptase have been shown to be of use in diagnosing such deaths. Most anaphylactic reactions are mediated by IgE that interacts with specific antigens, causing activation of mast cells and the release of a number of potent chemical mediators, including beta tryptase and histamine. Both IgE and tryptase can be measured in postmortem blood and have been shown to be useful in diagnosing anaphylaxis deaths.[91–95]

If the etiologic agent is known, it is possible to detect elevated levels of specific IgE antibodies in postmortem blood.[88,90,96] Elevated levels of a specific IgE antibody do not necessarily indicate that an anaphylactic reaction took place, only that the individual is sensitive to the substance. The presence of such an antibody would be confirmatory evidence of an anaphylactic reaction caused by a sting from an insect. However, not all individuals dying of an anaphylactic reaction demonstrate antibodies to the specific insect that stung them. Serum total IgE levels are less specific but, if elevated, can be used along with the autopsy findings, circumstances of death and tryptase concentrations to augment a diagnosis of anaphylaxis.

Upon activation, mast cells release tryptase from their secretory granules. The level of tryptase rises rapidly, becoming detectible within 30 min, with peak concentrations reached in the first 2–3 h. Half-life of tryptase is approximately 2 h. Unfortunately, clinical tryptase concentrations are not applicable postmortem as it has been shown that tryptase concentrations can also be elevated in other causes of death including cardiac deaths, trauma and drug related deaths.[97] The presence of underlying inflammatory processes or systemic mastocytosis, CPR, postmortem interval and sampling technique have all also been shown to affect tryptase concentrations. [97,98] A recent study addressed these issues and suggested a "normal" postmortem tryptase concentration of 23 μg/L be used with concentrations above that level being considered elevated, rather than the clinical level of 11 μg/L.[97]

It should be mentioned that the National Association of Medical Examiners recommends that these types of deaths be classified as accidents.[99] However, the classification may also depend on the conventions of a particular jurisdiction, as some jurisdictions may classify these deaths based on the etiology agents. For example, anaphylactic deaths due to foods and therapeutically administered drugs may be considered natural, those due to toxic envenomations may be considered accidents.

Other Causes of Sudden Respiratory Deaths

Other causes of sudden respiratory deaths are extremely rare. Occasionally, respiratory polyps combined with sudden edema can result in temporary obstruction and cause death. One case the authors saw involved an individual with an undiagnosed squamous cell carcinoma of the larynx that virtually occluded the airway. The individual had had symptoms, but refused to see a physician, when suddenly he developed edema, which completely closed off the airway, and died. Additionally, a tumor can erode into a pulmonary vessel causing massive hemoptysis and exsanguination. Hemoptysis can also develop in cavernous tuberculosis, which is most often seen in individuals with impaired immune systems.

Idiopathic pulmonary hemosiderosis is a rare disease mainly occurring in children that can result in sudden death. The hallmark of the disease is recurrent pulmonary hemorrhage with accompanying hemoptysis and anemia. Another cause of death in children is spontaneous pneumothorax of the newborn.[100,101] This entity is relatively uncommon, occurring in 1–2% of live births and is usually benign, with virtually all term infants having resolution without *sequelae,* often without the condition's being diagnosed. It should be suspected in any apparently healthy newborn who dies suddenly and unexpectedly in a hospital nursery. An X-ray prior to autopsy will usually make the diagnosis (Figure 3.19).

Deaths Related to the Liver, Spleen or Pancreas

Liver

Sudden death in association with liver disease is uncommon. When it does occur, it is usually due to cirrhosis or hepatotoxicity.

Hepatic Cirrhosis

Common mechanisms of sudden death in cirrhosis include liver failure, cardiovascular collapse due to ascites/disruptions in fluid dynamics and gastrointestinal hemorrhage. The most common causes of cirrhosis include chronic ethanol (alcohol) use, chronic hepatitis B and C and nonalcoholic fatty liver disease (Figure 3.20).

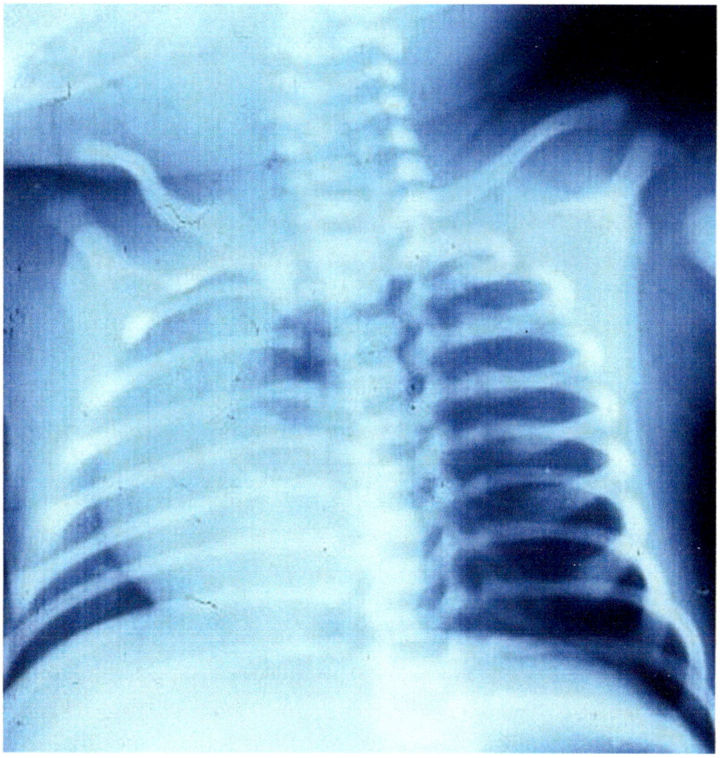

Figure 3.19 Pneumothorax of newborn with left tension pneumothorax and displacement of heart and left lung into right chest cavity.

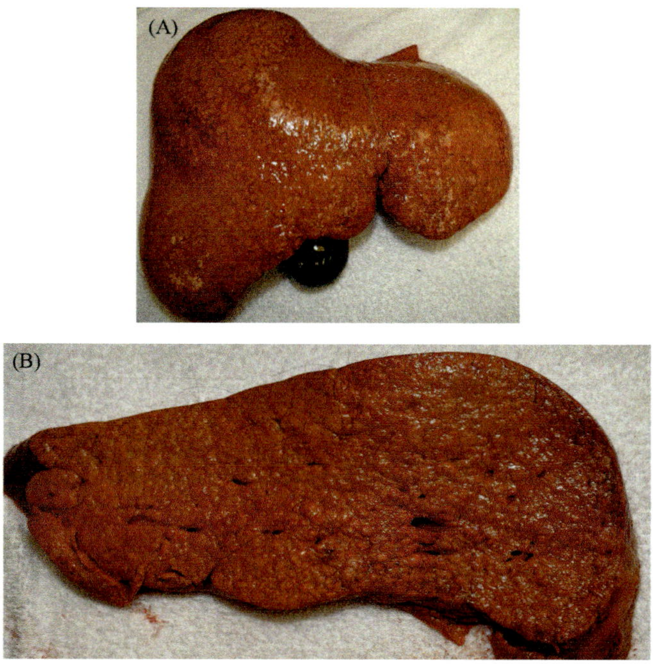

Figure 3.20 (A) Cirrhotic liver (B) on cross section.

Gastrointestinal hemorrhage can occur due to erosion of esophageal varices or due to gastric erosions or ulceration, particularly in alcoholics. Additionally, DiMaio reported three cases of massive nontraumatic intra-abdominal hemorrhage occurring in cirrhotics in which no source for the bleeding was found.[102] Of the three, one who was briefly hospitalized showed evidence of a disseminated intravascular coagulopathy. It is the authors' opinion that cirrhosis was the most likely cause of the intra-abdominal hemorrhage in each case. Similar to the development of esophageal varices, the abdominal vessels can also be affected by cirrhosis including aneurysmal dilation, particularly the splenic artery. These vessels can then rupture, much like a ruptured cerebral artery aneurysm, and the bleeding source not always identified.

Hepatotoxicity

Rarely individuals will die of massive hepatic necrosis caused by fulminating hepatitis. However, one should always worry in such cases that the hepatitis is of a toxic nature such as that caused by an overdose of acetaminophen. Acetaminophen overdoses can be acute or chronic and result in the accumulation of a toxic metabolite (NAPQI). Death due to acetaminophen overdoses usually occurs 3–5 days after ingestion.

In children, Reye's syndrome can cause relatively rapid death, but the condition is usually diagnosed prior to death. Reye's syndrome is an entity of unknown etiology affecting children, in which an upper respiratory tract infection, chicken pox and, rarely, gastroenteritis are followed by vomiting, convulsion, coma, hypoglycemia, elevated blood ammonia and abnormal serum transaminase values. Individuals dying of the entity show fatty metamorphosis of the liver, with multiple small fatty cytoplasmic vesicles in the hepatocytes, myocardial fibers and tubular cells of the kidneys. These are extremely fine vesicles compared with the coarse deposit seen in alcoholic fatty metamorphosis of the liver. Reye's syndrome can be confused with inborn errors of metabolism with which it may share many of the same clinical characteristics. The only way to be absolutely sure of the diagnosis is to demonstrate specific mitochondrial changes in liver tissue. An increased incidence of this syndrome was noted in children who had taken aspirin for flu-like illnesses or chicken pox. Because of this, the use of aspirin in the treatment of children was discontinued in the 1980s. This has led to the virtual disappearance of the entity. Thus, from 1980 to 1997, 1207 cases of Reye's syndrome were reported with a peak incidence of 555 cases in 1980.[103] Since 1994, no more than two cases per year have been reported.

Another cause of massive hepatic necrosis is ingestion of poisonous mushrooms. *Amanita phalloides* is one of the most commonly encountered poisonous mushrooms in the United States. It is the most dangerous, accounting for almost all fatalities. It is found in many regions of the United States, including California, the Pacific Northwest and the Northeast. It contains cyclopeptide toxins,[104] which are potent hepatotoxins with no taste or smell that are not destroyed by cooking. Ingestion of even one mushroom can cause death. Following ingestion, there are no symptoms for several hours. Then, the victims develop nausea, vomiting, severe abdominal cramps and watery diarrhea. They then seem to be getting better, and when they develop hepatic and renal failure, become jaundiced, and develop a coagulopathy and impaired neurologic status. The signs of fulminant hepatic necrosis may not appear for a day or two. The mortality rate for *A. phalloides* poisoning is 20–30%.

Though included here, hepatotoxicity due to an exogenous source, such as acetaminophen or mushroom poisoning, is not considered a natural disease process. They could be accidental suicidal or even homicidal in nature.

Spleen

The most common cause of sudden death due to splenic disease is rupture of an enlarged spleen. Splenic enlargement can be seen with cancers such as leukemia or lymphoma; certain infectious disease processes such as mononucleosis or toxoplasmosis; inflammatory disease processes such as lupus or sarcoid; and with certain genetic diseases such as Gaucher, Niemann-Pick or other glycogen storage diseases. Splenic enlargement can also occur in the setting of cirrhosis. Spontaneous rupture of an enlarged spleen can occur in the absence of trauma resulting in death by exsanguination.

Absence of the spleen, either surgically or congenitally, is associated with pneumococcal septicemia and bilateral adrenal hemorrhages, though in those cases, the death is due to infection, rather than a direct splenic causes.

Pancreas

Sudden death from diseases of the pancreas generally involves two entities, acute fulminating pancreatitis and diabetes mellitus. Deaths from acute pancreatitis in which the patient is mobile and walking around are uncommon. As in instances of unsuspected peritonitis, they are associated with alcoholism and individuals on high doses of antipsychotic medications, which can mask or obscure symptoms.

Sudden, unexpected death due to the acute onset of diabetes mellitus is relatively rare.[105] The classic symptoms of diabetes are polydipsia, polyuria, polyphagia and loss of weight. In some instances however, diabetic coma may be the initial symptom.

Diabetes is a metabolic disorder characterized by hyperglycemia and a failure to a greater or lesser extent to secrete insulin. Approximately one-third of all diabetics are juvenile onset diabetics. In this condition, the lack of insulin may be complete. This type of diabetes is differentiated from the mature onset diabetes by the tendency of the juvenile diabetic to develop ketoacidosis. Most individuals with juvenile onset diabetes present with the classical symptoms of diabetes previously mentioned. Approximately one-third, however, initially present in acidosis or diabetic coma. In a number of instances, the onset of diabetes seems to be triggered by an infective illness. In diabetic ketoacidosis, blood glucose levels are seldom under 300 or over 1000 mg/dL, with an average blood level reported as 736 mg/dL. The biochemical derangement in diabetic ketoacidosis may be extremely severe with increased metabolism of fatty acids, resulting in the formation of ketone bodies and acidosis.

Sudden, unexpected death due to the acute onset of diabetes is a problem to the forensic pathologist in that postmortem blood glucose levels are generally of no value because of the great fluctuation in the level of glucose after death. Elevated blood acetone levels, while suggestive of diabetes, are not diagnostic, because they may be the result of another condition, such as malnutrition. In addition, in the aketotic form of diabetic coma, elevated levels of ketones may not be present. Glucose in the urine is also not diagnostic, because it can occur in many conditions. The presence of glycogen in the cells of the proximal convoluted tubules of the kidney (Armanni-Ebstein lesion) is said to be diagnostic of uncontrolled diabetes. Unfortunately, this lesion is also often absent.

The most reliable indicator of diabetes mellitus in the postmortem state is elevated glucose in the vitreous humor. Vitreous humor provides an easily obtainable fluid for the postmortem diagnosis of diabetic coma. *An elevated vitreous glucose level is an accurate reflection of an elevated antemortem blood glucose level.* (See Chapter 4.)

Miscellaneous Natural Deaths

Deaths Related to the Genitourinary and Gastrointestinal Tracts

Diseases of the urogenital and digestive organs caused 13% of the sudden and unexpected deaths in 1937.[70] Nowadays, such cases are uncommon, with possibly the most common entity a massive hematemesis due to a gastrointestinal bleed either due to cirrhosis or a gastric ulcer. Peritonitis, an infection of the abdominal wall, can also result in sudden death and is most often associated with cirrhosis or a perforated viscus, such as may occur with a perforated gastric or duodenal ulcer or with intestinal ischemia. Other gastrointestinal or genitourinary infections, like appendicitis, diverticulitis or renal infections, can also result in sudden death due to overwhelming sepsis, but again, these causes are rare in the forensic pathology setting due to medical treatment usually being sought prior to death. Gastroenteritis causing profound vomiting or diarrhea can result in death due to electrolyte disturbances (see Chapter 4).

Sudden, unexpected death could be caused by rupture of a tubal pregnancy. The woman may have only vague symptoms of abdominal pain, often ascribed to gastroenteritis. Rupture of the tubal pregnancy can result in massive hemoperitoneum with 2–3 L of blood present (Figure 3.21).

Death Related to the Endocrine Organs

Sudden deaths due to endocrine abnormalities are extremely rare. Pituitary apoplexy due to sudden hemorrhage and infarction of the pituitary gland either due to pregnancy (termed Sheehan's syndrome) or tumor have both been associated with sudden death (Figure 3.22).[106]

Bilateral adrenal cortical hemorrhage can be seen in sepsis, especially with Waterhouse-Friderichsen syndrome classically seen with meningococcemia, though other organisms can produce the same picture. There have been rare sudden deaths in association with a pheochromocytoma of the adrenal gland, a tumor that secretes epinephrine,

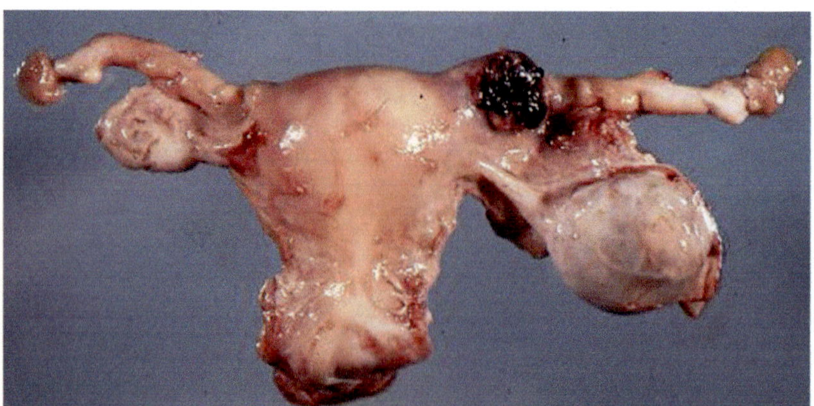

Figure 3.21 Rupture of tubal pregnancy with massive hemoperitoneum in a 28-year-old female. Incidental finding: teratoma of ipsilateral ovary.

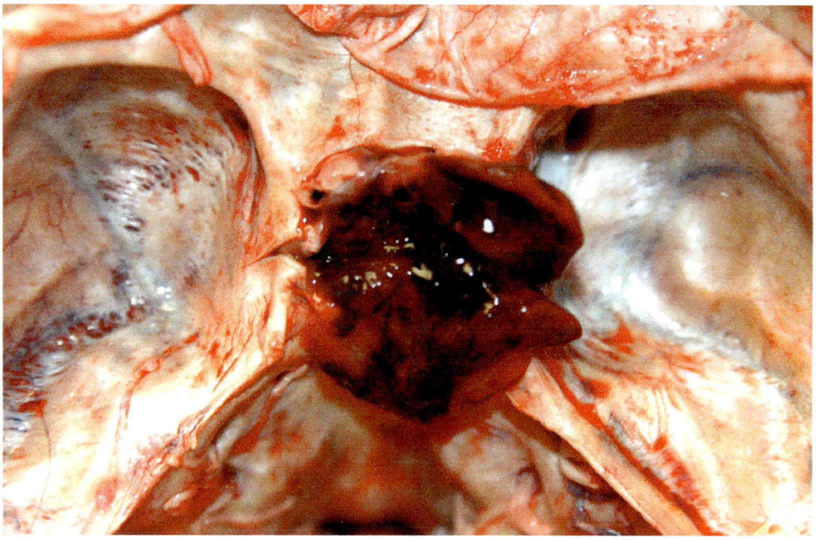

Figure 3.22 Hemorrhagic necrosis of the pituitary gland in a postpartum female.

norepinephrine or both.[107] Sudden death, usually due to the cardiac effects of these chemicals, can occur often after minor trauma or surgery.

Sickle Cell Disease and Sickle Cell Trait

Sickle cell anemia and sickle cell trait are inherited conditions of the oxygen-carrying protein, hemoglobin, in red blood cells, which results in the cells becoming misshapen, taking on a C or sickle shape (Figure 3.23). These sickled red cells can clog blood vessels, impairing delivery of oxygen and removal of harmful metabolites, resulting in severe damage to the involved tissues. Patients with sickle cell disease usually have a chronic, severe anemia in addition to significant complications including chronic pain and infarcts. These patients are usually diagnosed prior to death and are rarely encountered in a medical examiner setting.

Sickle cell trait is generally benign, but during maximal exercise, the oxygen levels in muscles can decrease sufficiently to cause some of the red cells to change from the normal disk shape to a crescent or sickle shape. Individuals with sickle trait inherit one gene for normal hemoglobin and one gene for sickle hemoglobin (hemoglobin S).[108] If oxygen in tissues falls to low levels, the red cells carrying the hemoglobin S can change from the usual disk shape to a crescent or sickle shape. Strenuous exercise can foster sickling: the acidosis and high tissue temperatures "shift to the right" the oxygen dissociation curve, displacing more oxygen from hemoglobin S. This can pose a grave risk for athletes with sickle cell trait during exercise, including death. Fatal sickling collapse in sickle cell trait was first described in 1970, in a report of sudden deaths in 4 of about 4000 Black recruits (about 0.1%) during 1 year of army basic combat training at Fort Bliss.[109]

Deaths in Alcoholics

Occasionally, chronic alcoholics die suddenly and unexpectedly, without any anatomical or toxicological cause of death. At autopsy, the only finding may be an enlarged liver with

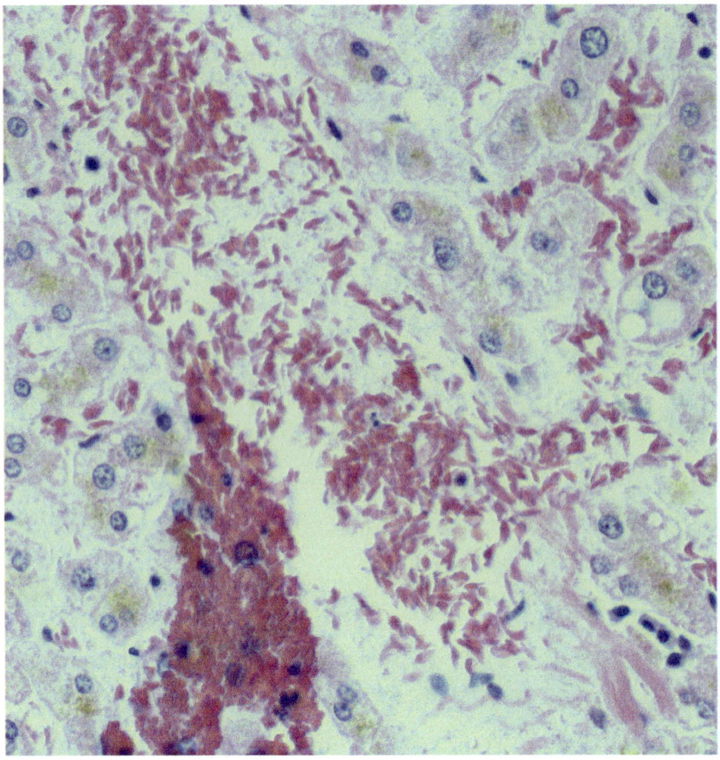

Figure 3.23 Sickling of red blood cells in the liver.

severe fatty metamorphosis or a dilated, non-enlarged heart. The toxicological screen usually shows absence of alcohol.

Alcoholic steatosis was first described by Le Count and Singer in 1926.[110] Alcohol, in both moderate and heavy doses, has a direct toxic effect on hepatic triglyceride metabolism, with resultant accumulation of triglycerides and phospholipids in the liver cells.[76] Large and small vacuoles of fat are present in the hepatocytes and Kupffer cells. While the most common cause of the accumulation of fat in the liver is chronic abuse of alcohol, this condition can also be seen in obesity, diabetes and viral infections as well as due to toxic compounds of phosphorous and chlorinated hydrocarbons.

Alcohol is also directly toxic to the heart and alcoholics have a tendency to develop arrhythmias. Recent study has also demonstrated an increased QT interval and elevated plasma norepinephrine.[111,112] It is thought that the effects of chronic alcoholism on the heart are fatal arrhythmia and death.

Additionally, if an alcoholic abstains from alcohol for a period of time, they may undergo withdrawal symptoms including tachycardia, elevated blood pressure, seizures and even death. It is also possible, depending upon the amount and frequency someone is accustomed to drink, to develop withdrawal symptoms even with measurable ethanol present within the blood.

Psychiatric Patients

Sudden death is occasionally seen in psychiatric patients, usually chronic schizophrenics on antipsychotics, in whom there are therapeutic or high, but not lethal, levels of these

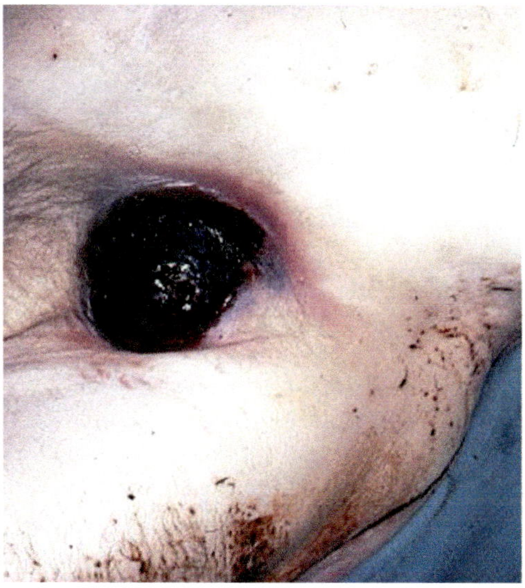

Figure 3.24 Aneurysm of right femoral artery with erosion through skin, perforation and exsanguination in a 75-year-old male. Second uneroded aneurysm is visible in left inguinal region.

drug. Such deaths are believed to be due to cardiac arrhythmias induced by these drugs, all of which have a recognized potential to produce arrhythmias. Deaths may also be due to Bell's mania (see Chapter 19). However, ascribing a death to be due to a mental disorder can be only decided after obtaining a medical history, an account of the circumstances leading up to and surrounding the death, a scene investigation, a complete autopsy and a thorough toxicological analysis.

Miscellaneous

Stasis ulcers of the lower extremities with erosion into an underlying, usually dilated vessel can result in exsanguination, particularly in the presence of the therapeutic use of anticoagulants. Aneurysms of larger arteries can also occur. One of the authors has seen a case of a femoral artery aneurysm with erosion through the vessel wall and skin with massive exsanguination (Figure 3.24).

Undiagnosed malignant tumors are also not uncommonly found in the forensic pathology setting, particularly lymphoma, leukemia and adenocarcinomas of the colon, liver and pancreas.

References

1. Benjamin EJ, Muntner P, Alonso A, Bittencourt MS, Callaway CW, Carson AP, et al., Heart disease and stroke statistics—2019 update: a report from the American Heart Association. *Circulation* 2019;139(10):e56–528.
2. Willich SN, Levy D, Rocco MB, et al., Circadian variation in the incidence of sudden cardiac death in the Framingham heart study population. *Am Cardiol* 1987; 60:801–806.
3. Kavanagh T, A cold weather "jogging mask" for angina patients. *Can Med Assoc J* 1970; 103:1290–1291.

4. Coplan NL, Gleim GW, and Nicholas JA, Exercise and sudden cardiac death. *Am J Heart* 1988; 1(15):207–212.
5. Mittleman MA, Maclure M, Tofler GH, et al., Triggering of acute myocardial infarction by heavy physical exertion. *NEJM* 1993; 329:1677–1683.
6. Willich SN, Lewis M, Lowel H, et al., Physical exertion as a trigger of acute myocardial infarction. *NEJM* 1993; 329:1684–1690.
7. Bigger JT and Coromilas J, Identification of patients at risk for arrhythmic death: role of Holter ECG recording, in Josephson ME (Ed) *Sudden Cardiac Death Cardiovascular Clinics 1513*. FA Davis Co, Philadelphia, PA, 1985, pp 131–143.
8. Weaver W, et al., Use of the automatic external defibrillation in the management of out-of-hospital cardiac arrest. *NEJM* 1988; 319:661–665.
9. Zipes DP and Wellens HJJ, Sudden cardiac death. *Circulation* 1998; 8(21):2334–2351.
10. Maio D and Di Maio VJM, Incidence of coronary thrombosis in sudden death due to coronary artery disease. *Am J Med Path* 1993; 14(4):273–275.
11. De Wood MA, Spores J, Notske R, et al., Prevalence of total coronary occlusion during the early hours of transmural myocardial infarction. *NEJM* 1980 303:897–902.
12. Burke AP and Virmani R, Intramural coronary dysplasia of the ventricular septem and sudden death. *Hum Path* 1998; 29(10):1124–1127.
13. Morales AR, Romanelli R, and Boucek R, The mural left anterior descending coronary artery, strenuous exercise and sudden death. *Circulation* 1980; 62(2):230–237.
14. Cutler D and Wallace JM, Myocardial bridging in a young patient with sudden death. *Clin Cardiol* 1997; 20:581–583.
15. Lee MS and Chen C-H, Myocardial bridging: an up-to-date review. *J Invasive Cardiol* 2015; 27(11):521–528.
16. DiMaio VJM and DiMaio DJ, Postpartum dissecting coronary aneurysm. *NY State J Med* 1971; 71:767–769.
17. Smith JC, Dissecting aneurysms of coronary arteries. *Arch Pathol* 1975; 99:117–121.
18. Basso C, Morgagni GL, and Thiene G, Spontaneous coronary artery dissection: a neglected cause of acute myocardial ischaemia and sudden death. *Heart* 1996; 75:451–454.
19. DeMaria AN, Lee G, Amsterdam EA, et al., The anginal syndrome with normal coronary arteries. *JAMA* 1980; 244:826–828.
20. Manzar KJ, Padder FA, Conrad AR, Freeman I, and Jonas EA, Acute myocardial infarction with normal coronary artery: a case report and review of the literature. *Am J Med Sci* 1997; 314(5):342–345.
21. Yasue H and Kugiyama K, Coronary spasm: clinical features and pathogenesis. *Intern Med* 1997; 36(11):760–765.
22. Perloff JK, Congenital heart disease in the adult, in Braunwald E (Ed) *Heart Disease* 4th ed. WB Saunders, Philadelphia, PA, 1992.
23. Sharbough AH and White RS, Single coronary artery. *JAMA* 1974; 230:243.
24. Kragel AH and Roberts WC, Sudden death and cardiomegaly unassociated with coronary, valvular congenital or specific myocardial disease. *Am J Cardiol* 1988; 61:659–660.
25. Messerli FH, Ventura HO, Elizardi DJ, et al., Hypertension and sudden death. *Am J Med* 1984; 77:18–22.
26. Haider AW, Larson MG, Benjamin EJ, and Levy D, Increased left ventricular mass and hypertrophy associated with increased risk for sudden death. *JACC* 1998; 32(5):1454–1459.
27. Frolich ED, Left ventricular hypertrophy and sudden death (editorial comment). *JACC* 1998; 32(5):1460–1462.
28. Davies MJ, Treasure T, and Richardson PD, The pathogenesis of spontaneous arterial dissection. *Heart* 1996; 75:434–435.
29. Fikar CR and Koch S, Etiologic factors of acute aortic dissection in children and young adults. *Clin Ped* 39(2): 71–80.

30. Freed LA, Levy D, Levine RA, et al., Prevalence and clinical outcome of mitral valve prolapse *NEJM* 1999; 341(1):1–7.
31. Kligfield P, Levy D, Devereux RB, et al., Arrhythmias and sudden death in mitral valve prolapse. *Am Heart J* 1987; 1 13:1298–1307.
32. Scala-Bamett DM and Donoghue ER, Sudden death in mitral valve prolapse. *J Forensic Sci* 1988; 33:84–91.
33. Selzer A, Changing aspects of the natural history of valvular aortic stenosis. *NEJM* 1987; 317:91–98.
34. McCartan C, Mason R, Jayasinghe SR, and Griffiths LR, Cardiomyopathy classification: ongoing debate in the genomics era.*Biochem Res Int* Volume 2012. Article ID 796926. 1-10.
35. Brown CS and Bertolet B, Peripartum cardiomyopathy: a comprehensive review. *Am J Obst Gynec* 1998; 178(2):4091414.
36. Maron BJ, Hypertrophic cardiomyopathy. *Lancet* 1997; 350(9071):127–133.
37. Stone JR, Updates to the WHO classification of cardiomyopathies *Acad Forensic Pathol* 2011; 1(2):202–205.
38. Tavora F, Zhang M, Franco M, et al., Distribution of biventricular disease in arrhythmogenic cardiomyopathy: an autopsy study. *Hum Pathol* 2012; 43(4):592–596.
39. Corrado D, van Tintelen PJ, McKenna WJ, et al., Arrhythmogenic right ventricular cardiomyopathy: evaluation of the current diagnostic criteria and differential diagnosis. *Eur Heart J* 2020; 41(14):1414–1429.
40. Dreifus LS, Haiat R, Watanabe Y, et al., Ventricular fibrillation, a possible mechanism of sudden death in patients with Wolff-Parkinson-White syndrome. *Circulation* 1971; 43:520–527.
41. Basso C, Calabrese F, Corrado D, and Thiene G, Postmortem diagnosis in sudden cardiac death victims: macroscopic, microscopic and molecular findings. *Cardiovasc Res* 2001; 50(2):290–300.
42. Tester DJ, et al., Cardiac channel molecular autopsy: insights from 173 consecutive cases of autopsy-negative sudden unexplained death referred for postmortem genetic testing. *Mayo Clin Proc* 2012; 87(6):524–539.
43. Levine G, *Cardiology Secrets* (Fifth Edition), *Elsevier Philadelphia* 2018.
44. Jacoby D and McKenna WJ, Genetics of inherited cardiomyopathy. *Eur Heart J* 2012; 33(3):296–304.
45. Wynne J and Braunwald E, The cardiomyopathies and myocarditis: toxic chemical and physical damage to the heart, in Braunwald E (Ed) *Heart Disease* 4th ed. WB Saunders, Philadelphia, PA, 1992.
46. Diem SJ, Lantos JD, and Tulsky JA, Cardiopulmonary resuscitation on television - miracles and misinformation. *NEJM* 1996; 334(24):1578–1582.
47. Birkun A and Kosova Y, Social attitude and willingness to attend cardiopulmonary resuscitation training and perform resuscitation in the Crimea world. *J Emerg Med* 2018; 9(4):237–248.
48. Schneider AP II, Nelson DJ, and Brown DD, In-hospital cardiopulmonary resuscitation: a 30-year review. *J Am Board Fam Prac* 1993; 6(2):91–101.
49. Mittleman MA and Siscovic KDS, Physical exertion as a trigger of myocardial infarction and sudden cardiac death. *Cardiol Clin* 1996; 14(2):263–270.
50. Wolthus RA, et al., The response of healthy men to treadmill exercise. *Circulation* 1977; 55:153.
51. Dimsdale JE, et al., Post exercise peril: plasma catecholamine and exercise. *JAMA* 1984; 252:630–632.
52. Young DB, et al., Potassium and catecholamine concentrations in the immediate post exercise period. *Am J Med Sci* 1992; 304(3):150–153.
53. Lindinger M, Potassium regulation during exercise and recovery in humans: implications for skeletal and cardiac muscle. *J Mol Cell Cardiol* 1995; 27:1011–1022.

54. Brodsky MA, et al., Ventricular tachyarrhythmia associated with psychological stress: role of the sympathetic nervous system. *JAMA* 1987; 257:2064–2067.
55. Ficker DM, Sudden unexplained death and injury in epilepsy. *Epilepsia* 2000; 41(Suppl 2):S7–S12.
56. Hirsch CS and Martin DL, Unexpected death in young epileptics. *Neurology* 1971; 21:682–690.
57. Jay GW and Leestma JE, Sudden death in epilepsy. *Acta Neurol Scand* 1981; 63(Suppl 82):1–66.
58. Hammes EM, Reaction of meninges to blood. *Arch Neurol Psychiat* 1944; 52:505–514.
59. Chasson JL and Hindman WM, Berry aneurysms of the circle of Willis. *Neurology* 1958; 8:41–44.
60. Freytag E, Fatal rupture of intracranial aneurysms. *Arch Pathol* 1966; 81:418–424.
61. Dinning TAR and Falconer MA, Sudden or unexpected natural death due to ruptured intracranial aneurysms: survey of 250 forensic cases. *Lancet* 1953; 2:799–801.
62. The Arteriovenous Malformation Study Group, Current concepts: arterio-venopus malformations of the brain in adults. *NEJM* 1999; 340(23):1812–1818.
63. Freytag E, Fatal hypertensive intracerebral haematomas. *J Neurol Neurosurg Psychiat* 1968; 31:616–620.
64. Hirschmann JV, Bacterial infections of the central nervous system 1999, in Dale DC and Federman (Eds) *Scientific American Medicine. Sci Amer.* NY 53A.
65. Putz K, Hayani K, and Zar FA, Meningitis. *Prim Care* 2013; 40(3):707–726.
66. Samore MH and Karchmer AW, Infections due to Neisseria, in Dale DC and Federman (Eds) *Scientific Amer. Medicine. Sci Amer.* NY.
67. Challener RC, Morrissey AM, and Jacobs MR, Postmortem diagnosis of meningococcemia by detection of capsular polysaccharides. *J Forensic Sci* 1988; 33:336–346.
68. Monkman GR, Orwoll G, and Ivins JC, Trauma and oncogenesis. *Mayo Clinic Proc* 1974; 49:157–163.
69. Schiffer L, Avidan D, and Rapp A, Post-traumatic meningioma. *Neurosurgery* 1985; 17:84–87.
70. Gonzales TA, Vance M, and Helpern M, *Legal Medicine and Toxicology.* Appleton-Century, New York, NY, 1937.
71. Knight BH, The significance of the postmortem discovery of gastric contents in the air passages. *Forensic Sci* 1975; 6:229–234.
72. Mayo-Smith MF, Spinale JW, Donskey CJ, Yukawa M, Li RH, and Schiffman FJ, Acute epiglottitis: an 18-year experience in Rhode Island. *Chest* 1995; 108:1640–1647.
73. Garpenholt O, Hugosson S, Fredlund H, et al., Sweden before and after introduction of vaccination against *Haemophilus influenzae* type b. *Ped Infect Dis J* 1999; 18(6):490–493.
74. Bellis M, Herath J, and Pollanen MS, Sudden death due to acute epiglottitis in adults: a retrospective review of 11 postmortem cases. *Am J Forensic Med Pathol* 2016; 37(4):275–278.
75. Asthma FastStats. Centers for Disease Control and Prevention. Available at: https://www.cdc.gov/nchs/fastats/asthma.htm. Accessed 10 February 2021.
76. van den Berg ME, Stricker BH, Brusselle GG, and Lahousse L, Chronic obstructive pulmonary disease and sudden cardiac death: a systematic review. *Trends Cardiovasc Med* 2016; 26(7):606–613.
77. Kujovich J, Factor V Leiden thrombophilia. *Genet Med* 2011; 13:1–16.
78. Fineschi V, Bafunno V, Bello S, et al., Fatal pulmonary thromboembolism. A retrospective autopsy study: searching for genetic thrombophilias (Factor V Leiden (G1691A) and FII (G20210A) gene variants) and dating the thrombus. *Forensic Sci Int* 2012;214(1–3):152–158.
79. Steiner PE and Lushbough CG, Maternal pulmonary embolism by amniotic fluid as a cause of obstetric shock and unexpected deaths in obstetrics. *JAMA* 1941; 117:1245–1254, 1340–1345.
80. Benson MD, Amniotic fluid embolism mortality rate. *J Obstet Gynaecol Res* 2017;43 1714–1718.

81. Clark SL, et al., Amniotic fluid embolism: analysis of the national registry. *Am J Obstet Gynecol*, 1995; 172(4):1158–1169. Liban E and Raz S, A clinicopathologic study of fourteen cases of amniotic fluid embolism. *Am J Clin Pathol* 1969; 51:477–486
82. Cromley MG, Taylor PJ, and Cummings DO, Probable amniotic fluid embolism after first trimester pregnancy termination. *J Reprod Med* 1983; 28:209.
83. Guidotti RJ, Grimes DA and Cates W, Fatal amniotic fluid embolism during legally induced abortion, United States, 1972 to 1978. *Am J Obstet Gynecol* 1981; 141:257–261.
84. Olcott CO, et al., Amniotic fluid embolism and disseminated intravascular coagulopathy after blunt maternal trauma. *J Trauma* 1973; 13:737–740.
85. Clark SL, Amniotic fluid embolism. *Clin Perinatol* 1986; 13:801–811.
86. Sperry K, Amniotic fluid embolism. *JAMA* 1986; 255:2183–2186.
87. Clark SL, et al., Squamous cells in the maternal pulmonary circulation. *Am J Obstet Gynecol* 1986; 154:104–106.
88. Prahlow JA and Barnard JJ, Fatal anaphylaxis caused by fire ant stings. *Am J Forensic Med Path* 1998; 19(2):137–142.
89. Delage C and Irey NS, Anaphylactic deaths: a clinicopathologic study of 43 cases. *J Forensic Sci* 1972; 17:525–540.
90. Pumphrey RSH and Roberts IS, Postmortem findings after fatal anaphylactic reactions. *J Clin Path* 2000; 53(4):273–276.
91. Horn KD, Halsey JF, and Zumwalt RE, Utilization of serum tryptase and immunoglobulin e assay in the postmortem diagnosis of anaphylaxis. *Am J Forensic Med Pathol* 2004; 25(1):37–43.
92. Mayer DE, Krauskopf A, Hemmer W, et al., Usefulness of post mortem determination of serum tryptase, histamine and diamine oxidase in the diagnosis of fatal anaphylaxis. *Forensic Sci Int* 2011;212(1–3):96–101.
93. McLean-Tooke A, Goulding M, Bundell C, et al., Postmortem serum tryptase levels in anaphylactic and non-anaphylactic deaths. *J Clin Pathol* 2014;67(2):134–138
94. Busardo FP, Marinelli E, and Zaami S, Is the diagnosis of anaphylaxis reliable in forensics? The role of beta-tryptase and its correct interpretation. *Leg Med (Tokyo)* 2016; 23:86–88.
95. Cecchi R, Diagnosis of anaphylactic death in forensics: review and future perspectives. *Leg Med (Tokyo)* 2016; 22:75–81.
96. Schwartz HJ, et al., Studies in stinging insect hypersensitivity: postmortem demonstration of antivenom IgE antibody and possible sting-related sudden death. *Am J Clin Pathol* 1986; 85:607–610.
97. Palmiere C, Decline in postmortem serum tryptase levels in anaphylactic deaths. *Am J Forensic Med Pathol* 2017; 38(3):274–275.
98. Garland J, et al., Postmortem tryptase level in 120 consecutive nonanaphylactic deaths: establishing a reference range as <23 μg/L. *Am J Forensic Med Pathol* 2019; 40(4):351–355.
99. Hanzlick R, Hunsaker JC, and Davis GJ, A Guide for Manner of Death Classification. 2002 National Association of Medical Examiners. Available at: https://name.memberclicks.net/assets/docs/4bd6187f-d329-4948-84dd-3d6fe6b48f4d.pdf. Accessed 17 April 2020.
100. Norton LE, DiMaio VJ, and Zumwalt RE, Spontaneous pneumothorax in the newborn: a report of two fatalities. *J Forensic Sci* 1978; 23(3):508–510.
101. Mayo P and Saha SP, Spontaneous pneumothorax in the newborn. *Am Surg* 1983; 49(4):192–195.
102. DiMaio VJM, Sudden unexpected deaths due to massive non-traumatic intraabdominal hemorrhage in association with cirrhosis of the liver. *Am J Forensic Med Pathol* 1987; 8:266–268.
103. Belay ED, Bresee JS, Holman RC, et al., Reyes syndrome in the United States from 1981 through 1997. *NEJM* 1999; 340(18):1377–1382.
104. Pomerance HH, Barness EG, Kohli-Kumar M, et al., A 15-year-old boy with fulminant hepatic failure. *J Pediat* 2000; 137(1):114–118.
105. DiMaio VJM, Stumer WQ, and Coe J, Sudden and unexpected deaths after the acute onset of diabetes mellitus. *J Forensic Sci* 1977; 22:147–151.

106. Shields LB, Balko MG, and Hunsaker JC, Sudden and unexpected death from pituitary tumor apoplexy. *J Forensic Sci* 2012; 57(1):262–266.
107. Primhak RA, Spicer RD, and Variend S, Sudden death after minor abdominal trauma: an unusual presentation of phaeochromocytoma. *Br Med J* 1986; 292:95–96.
108. Randy Eichner E, Sickle cell trait and the athlete. *Gatorade Sports Sci Inst* 2006; 19:4.
109. Jones SR, Binder A, and Donowho EM Jr, Sudden death in sickle-cell trait. *N Engl J Med* 1970; 282:323–325.
110. Le Count ER and Singer HA, Fat replacement of the glycogen in the liver as a cause of death. *Arch Path* 1926; 1:84–89.
111. Bernardi M, Calandra S, Colantoni A, et al., Q-T interval prolongation in cirrhosis: prevalence, relationship with severity, and etiology of the disease and possible pathogenetic factors. *Hepatology* 1998; 27(1):28–34.
112. Day CP, James OFW, Butler TJ, et al., Q-T prolongation and sudden cardiac death in patients with alcoholic liver disease. *Lancet* 1993; 341:1423–1428.

Deaths Due to Electrolyte Abnormalities and Starvation

4

I call supplementing with electrolytes and metals: The Electrical Chemistry of the Human

—Steven Magee, Health Forensics

Electrolyte abnormalities and starvation are often present in many medical examiner cases, but they are usually a secondary factor in the deaths, such as with infections, chronic illnesses or dementia. In infants, vomiting and diarrhea can cause dehydration, electrolyte imbalance and death in a matter of several hours. However, these deaths can also be due to acute intentional acts, such as overdoses of diuretics or potassium chloride pills, water intoxication and repeatedly induced vomiting. Often, in such cases, a thorough examination of the scene, medical history and autopsy is important as well as an understanding of the fiduciary responsibility of the caretaker.

Electrolyte Abnormalities

Electrolyte imbalances most often lead to death due to cardiac arrhythmias or through Central nervous system (CNS) toxicity most often manifested by convulsions. At autopsy, there are no specific findings for any of the electrolyte abnormalities, though in the cases of diabetic ketoacidosis (DKA), the prosector may be able to detect a faint fruity odor due the production of ketone bodies. Unfortunately, the diagnosis of death is made by the vitreous electrolyte findings and/or on the basis of history.

Electrolyte Testing

Analysis of postmortem blood for common electrolyte concentrations gives erroneous results. Sodium and chloride decrease in the blood after death, while potassium increases, due to the breakdown of cells. Thus, one cannot use postmortem blood to accurately determine an individual's electrolyte status immediately prior to death. Fortunately, electrolyte abnormalities in living individuals are often reflected in the vitreous. Because vitreous levels of sodium and chloride are valid, this makes diagnosis of antemortem electrolyte imbalances possible. Unfortunately, this does not hold true for vitreous potassium.

After death, the concentration of vitreous potassium rapidly increases. The concentrations of sodium and chloride are relatively stable in the early postmortem period, but will slowly decrease thereafter. The normal levels of sodium, chloride and potassium in vitreous are 120–155, 105–140 and 3.5–10 meq/L, respectively, if significant cellular and tissue breakdown (decomposition) has not set in.[1] Decomposition of a body is reflected in the vitreous by a potassium level of 15 meq/L or above. When potassium is 15 meq/L or greater, the sodium and chloride values fall, making electrolyte evaluation difficult; however, the elevated potassium concentrations can be used to assess the reliability of the other values.[2]

Vitreous potassium levels are of no help in determining what the potassium status of an individual was immediately prior to death, because potassium is released almost immediately postmortem, even in the vitreous. Elevated levels of potassium, therefore, have no diagnostic value in the vitreous. Low levels of potassium in the vitreous may be indicative of hypokalemia, but the authors have virtually never seen this, even in cases where the individual is known to be hypokalemic.

Normal vitreous glucose concentrations range anywhere from 0 to 120 mg/dL and are of significance only if elevated. Glucose is rapidly consumed after death, so low concentrations are meaningless; however, concentrations significantly above 200 mg/dL are considered diagnostic of diabetes mellitus (DM).[3] Additionally, elevated concentrations of vitreous glucose in the presence of detectable ketones are considered diagnostic of DKA.

Often, if someone dies at the hospital after an acute incident, antemortem testing may show elevated blood glucose concentrations; however, this is often seen due to the terminal release of cortisol and other catecholamines and not due to diabetes or DKA. This is termed "agonal hyperglycemia" and is extremely common, especially if there has been attempted resuscitation. Agonal hyperglycemia is not reflected in the vitreous and, thus, postmortem vitreous testing can be performed to confirm that it simply reflects terminal hyperglycemia and not DM. Coe reported that, in all of 102 nondiabetics in whom postmortem peripheral blood glucose concentration exceeded 500 mg/dL from a terminal rise in blood sugar, the vitreous glucose was below 100 mg/dL.[4] Even if intravenous glucose infusions are administered prior to death, the vitreous glucose levels in normal subjects are generally less than 200 mg/dL.

In individuals with elevated levels of glucose in the vitreous due to hyperglycemia, there is a gradual fall in vitreous postmortem levels. The fall is gradual enough to allow diagnosis of hyperglycemia for a considerable time after death. Unfortunately, because normal individuals start at significantly lower levels of vitreous glucose, the decline is sufficiently rapid that low levels of glucose are the rule. Because of this, one cannot differentiate a low vitreous glucose level caused by hypoglycemia from that of normal postmortem decline in an individual who had a normal glucose level at the time of death. Thus, perfectly normal individuals who die of trauma might be found to have a vitreous glucose level of 0 or 5 mg/dL, which is obviously an artifactual phenomenon.

Vitreous urea nitrogen (VUN) and creatinine are the most stable vitreous components after death and are therefore valuable for diagnostic purposes. The normal ranges are similar to those for blood, with VUN ranging from 7 to 30 mg/dL and creatinine being less than 1.5 mg/dL. Both are also valid for a long period of time and can elevations can be used to diagnose chronic renal insufficiency or acute renal failure. In uremia (renal failure), sodium and chloride are usually within normal limits, with markedly elevated vitreous urea and creatinine, usually greater than 50 and 2 mg/dL, respectively.[5]

Recently, synovial fluid has been used for electrolyte testing with promising results.[6,7] While synovial fluid should not be used as a first-line sample for electrolyte testing, if vitreous is unavailable or needed for toxicologic testing, it may be a valid alternative.

Dehydration

Assuming normal renal function, in individuals with dehydration, sodium is usually greater than 160 meq/L, chloride greater than 145 meq/L and VUN greater than 40 mg/dL. Lethal dehydration most often occurs with natural deaths, such as in the setting of gastroenteritis with severe vomiting and diarrhea, in demented patients who refuse all food and water, in chronic disease patients or in cases of infections. However, it can also occur in exposure (hyperthermic) deaths and in homicides. Most homicides are due to the purposeful withholding of fluids by a caregiver, such as parent. In a review of 37 fatal dehydration deaths of children, Whitehead et al. found that the majority were due to either acute or chronic illnesses (70%), followed by environmental (16%) and abuse/neglect (11%).[8]

Abnormal Salt Ingestion

Rarely, deaths are caused by an overdose of salt tablets or potassium chloride pills. The overdose in these instances might be either suicidal or accidental through abuse of these drugs by an individual who has a history of taking more than the prescribed medication. Obviously, ingestion of large quantities of potassium chloride pills can produce hyperkalemia that can cause cardiac arrhythmias and death. Unfortunately, however, the diagnosis of death caused hyperkalemia can be made only on the basis of history, as postmortem potassium concentrations are not valid for interpretation of hyperkalemia, as discussed previously. Intentional salt intake can result in hypernatremia that can cause gastrointestinal syndromes, muscle weakness, seizures and cardiac arrhythmias leading to death.[9]

Low Salt Syndrome/Water Intoxication

If potassium values are less than 15 meq/L, then sodium values below 120 meq/L and chloride values below 105 meq/L indicate that one is dealing with low salt syndrome or water intoxication. Low salt syndrome is seen most commonly in association with severe fatty metamorphosis of the liver or micronodular cirrhosis, though it can also occur with the over ingestion of diuretics. Coe described six cases of profound salt depletion. In one case, sodium was 106 meq/L, chloride 87 meq/L and potassium 6.2 meq/L due to prolonged use of diuretic therapy.[5]

Low potassium can also occur by taking a diuretic in abnormal amounts and can cause cardiac arrhythmias and death. Unfortunately, like hyperkalemia, the diagnosis of death caused hypokalemia, in most instances, can be made only on the basis of history. While low vitreous potassium concentrations would be valid and indicative of hypokalemia, the authors have almost never seen abnormally low concentrations of potassium in the vitreous, even in the case of individuals who took large amounts of diuretics. This is because, almost immediately after death, cells begin to break down and release potassium. This causes elevated levels of potassium in both the blood and vitreous. Thus, with a low potassium concentration in the vitreous prior to death, unless the vitreous was collected immediately after death, the release of potassium would return the hypokalemic individual to a "normal" or elevated potassium level.

The same picture of a low salt syndrome can be caused by overhydration, or water intoxication. With ingestion or administration of abnormally large quantities of fluid, markedly depressed levels of sodium and chloride could be expected. Deaths resulting from water intoxication are rare. Most of those seen by a forensic pathologist involve psychotic patients who, for some reason, drink large quantities of water.[10] Deaths also have been seen in individuals in jail involved in water-drinking contests. In hospitalized individuals, the administration of large quantities of intravenous fluids devoid of electrolytes can also produce water intoxication. The authors have seen a number of deaths caused by water intoxication and a few caused by repeatedly induced vomiting. In both groups, the individuals were, for the most part, psychotic, though in one case, the water toxicity was in an athlete who consumed too much water for fear of dehydration. In a fatal case of water intoxication seen by one of the authors, vitreous sodium was 115 meq/L, chloride 105 meq/L and potassium 7.6 meq/L.[10]

Starvation

Deaths caused by starvation are relatively rare in America. For the most part, they occur either as a result of child abuse, fasting or mental illness (i.e., anorexia nervosa). A body at rest requires approximately 20–25 cal/kg of body weight per day. Thus, the average 70-kg male, lying in bed, not exerting himself, requires approximately 1400–1750 cal of energy per day. In asleep, he utilizes 65 cal/h and, while awake, uses 77 cal/h.[11] If he walks slowly, he utilizes 200 cal/h, running 570 cal/h, and walking upstairs 1100 cal/h. A manual laborer can require up to 6000–7000 cal/days.

Food can be grouped into three general categories: carbohydrates, fat and protein. Tissues prefer to use carbohydrates for energy. The amount of carbohydrate stored in the body (glycogen in liver and muscle; glucose in blood) has a combined caloric value of approximately 1200 cal, insufficient to supply a 70-kg man with 1 day worth of calories. Therefore, if one stops eating, the body has to utilize fat and protein after the first 24 h of starvation. As fasting continues, there will be a progressive depletion of fat and protein, with fat depletion progressing at a faster rate than protein because fat provides more calories per weight of tissue. As fat is utilized for calories, ketones are produced and appear in the blood. Palmiere et al. reported acetone concentrations between 4 and 158 mg/L in five starvation cases.[12]

As starvation continues, protein is gradually depleted in three different phases. First is a rapid mobilization of protein stores that are converted by the liver to glucose, with the glucose used principally to supply energy to the brain. This is followed by a reduction in the utilization of protein. As total depletion of the fat stores approaches, protein is again rapidly utilized as a source of calories. Death usually occurs shortly after. If one assumes that fat constitutes 20–25% of the body weight in males and 25–30% in females and then assumes 2000 cal are needed per day, for the average individual, there would be sufficient energy supply for 60–70 days. This correlates very well with actual fasting conditions.

Frommel et al. described four individuals who went on a voluntary fast for political reasons.[13] With sedentary activities, no problem was encountered up to 18% of original body loss (28–35 days of fasting). When weight loss exceeded 18%, they developed muscle weakness, syncopal episodes, and decreased mental alertness. Fasting was stopped at 40 days following the development of Wernicke's syndrome by one of the four.

There appears to be no definite level of weight loss that can be considered lethal.[14] When loss of original body weight for adults reaches 35–50%, deaths begin to occur. With semi-starvation over a long period of time, the level is somewhat higher. For children, the level at which death begins is significantly lower.

Leiter and Marlis reported on the fasting to death of 10 young healthy males in Northern Ireland.[15] Information on these cases was obtained from the media, which gave reports of their ages, weights and duration of fasts. Individuals consumed no calories or vitamins, only water. Their average age was 25.6 ± 0.7 years. One died after 45 days of fasting. The other nine survived from 57 to 73 days. The mean survival time for all 10 was 61.6 ± 2.5 days. These authors concluded that the maximum limit of total fasting in healthy, nonobese individuals in their mid-to-late 20s is approximately 60 days. Death in these individuals occurred when approximately 70–94% of the body fat and approximately 19–21% of body protein were lost.

Individuals who have undergone starvation report an initial feeling of hunger and hunger pains, with craving for food wearing off very rapidly. This is followed by both mental and physical lethargy, fatigue and progressive loss of weight.[14,16,17] As the starvation continues, the lethargy becomes extreme, with mental impairment and loss of interest in everything.

At autopsy, there is essentially complete lack of fat in the subcutaneous and deep fat depots (Figure 4.1).

The skin is pale and cadaverous in 82.5% of the cases and dark brown in 17.5% of the cases.[17] Edema is present in one-third of the cases and may mask the amount of weight loss. Peritoneal effusions may occur. There is severe atrophy of skeletal muscles, the heart, liver, spleen and kidneys, but not the brain.[14,17] The small intestinal wall appears swollen, with

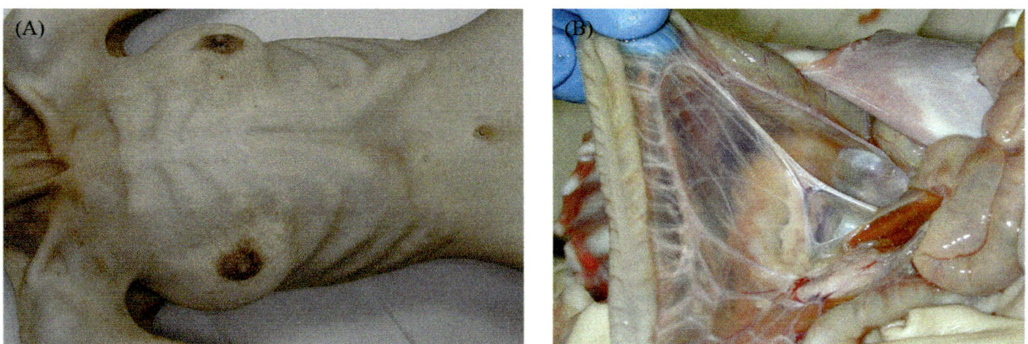

Figure 4.1 (A) Starvation in a 45-year-old with anorexia nervosa; (B) note the complete paucity of mesenteric adipose tissue.

reddish discolored mucosa in 27.2% of the cases. Almost half the cases in one study had ulcerations of the mucosa of the colon, described as "pseudo-dysentery."[17] Pressure sores, dental caries or diaper rash may also be present. Death due to starvation usually occurs due to infections, arrhythmias or hypoglycemia.[18]

In many starvation deaths, dehydration is also present, though a lack of adequate hydration will lead to death faster than lack of caloric intake. Forensic pathologists also need to be able to differentiate true starvation from undernourishment and malnourishment,[18] especially where manner of death may be an issue. Individuals with severe chronic diseases such as cancer or dementia may become chronically malnourished, just as those with mental disease such as anorexia nervosa may refuse to eat. In these situations, the manner of death is considered natural. However, cases where food is intentional withheld, that is, child abuse, are considered homicides. The World Health Organization has developed a checklist items that should be considered when investigating child starvation.[19] For example, information gathered should include feeding history, formula type and preparation, birth records, recent illnesses, ill contacts, deaths of siblings, developmental milestones and immunization status.

The investigation of starvation-related deaths can be difficult. The forensic pathologist must differentiate cachexia and starvation from natural disease processes from the lack of access to appropriate nutrition or the intentional withholding of food. To this end, deaths due to starvation require a thorough death investigation paired with a complete autopsy examination and testing to rule out metabolic or other disease processes. Investigation must also include a review of all pertinent medical records to document the reduction in body mass.

References

1. Coe JI, Postmortem chemistries on human vitreous humor. *Am J Clin Pathol* 1969; 51:741–750.
2. Coe JI, Some further thoughts and observations on postmortem chemistries. *Forensic Sci Gazette* 1973; 4(5):2–5.
3. DiMaio VJM, Sturner WQ, and Coe JJ, Sudden and unexpected deaths after the acute onset of diabetes mellitus. *J Forensic Sci* 1977; 22:147–151.
4. Coe JI, Peripheral blood glucose and cardiopulmonary resuscitation. *Forensic Sci Gazette* 1975; 6(4):1–239.
5. Coe JI, Case # 7, Forensic Pathology Dinner Seminar (# 410), American Society of Clinical Pathology.
6. More DS and Arroyo MC, Biochemical changes of the synovial liquid in corpses with regard to the cause of death. 1: Calcium, inorganic phosphorus, glucose, cholesterol, urea nitrogen, uric acid, proteins, and albumin. *J Forensic Sci* 1985; 30(2):541-546.
7. Madea B, Kreuser C, and Banaschak S, Postmortem biochemical examination of synovial fluid: a preliminary study. *Forensic Sci Int* 2001; 118:29-35.
8. Whitehead FJ, Couper RT, Moore L, et al., Dehydration deaths in infants and young children. *Am J Forensic Med Pathol* 1996; 17(1):73–78.
9. Arambewela MH, Somasundaram NP, and Garusinghe C, Extreme hypernatremia as a probable cause of fatal arrhythmia: a case report. *J Med Case Rep* 2016; 10:272.
10. DiMaio VJM and DiMaio SJ, Fatal water intoxication in a case of psychogenic polydipsia. *J Forensic Sci* 1980; 25:332–335.
11. Guyton AC and Hall JE, *Textbook of Medical Physiology* 10th ed. WB Saunders Co, Philadelphia, PA, 2000.

12. Palmiere C, Tettamanti C, Augsburger M, et al., Postmortem biochemistry in suspected starvation-induced ketoacidosis. *J Forensic Leg Med* 2016; 42:51–55.
13. Frommel D, et al., Voluntary total fasting: a challenge for the medical community. *Lancet* 1984; 1:1451–1452.
14. Keys A, et al., *The Biology of Human Starvation*. University of Minnesota Press, St. Paul 1950.
15. Leiter LA and Marlis EB, Survival during fasting may depend on fat as well as protein stores. *JAMA* 1982; 248:2306–2307.
16. Simpson K, Exposure to cold/starvation and neglect, in Simpson K (Ed) *Modern Trends in Forensic Medicine*. CV Mosby Co, St Louis, MO, 1953.
17. Winick M, *Hunger Disease: Studies by the Jewish Physicians in the Warsaw Ghetto*. John Wiley & Sons, New York, NY, 1979.
18. Madea B, Ortmann J, and Doberentz E, Forensic aspects of starvation. *Forensic Sci Med Pathol* 2016; 12(3):276-298.
19. World Health Organization. *Management of severe malnutrition. A manual for physicians and other senior health workers.* 1999.

5 Blunt Trauma Wounds

What we'll be calling on is good ole fashion blunt force trauma... Heavy duty, cast iron pile driving punches that will ... rattle his ancestors

—Tony "Duke" Evers, Rocky Balboa

The severity, extent and appearance of blunt trauma injuries depend on the following:

- The amount of force delivered to the body
- The time over which the force is delivered
- The region struck
- The extent of body surface over which the force is delivered
- The nature of the weapon

If a weapon deforms or breaks on impact, less energy is delivered to the body to produce injury, because some of the energy is used to deform or break it. Thus, the resultant injury is less severe than one would have if the weapon did not deform or break. Similarly, if the body moves with the blow, this increases the period of time over which the energy is delivered and decreases the severity of the injury.

For any given amount of force, the greater the area over which it is delivered, the less severe the wound. The size of the area affected by a blow depends on the nature of the weapon and the region of the body. For a weapon with a flat surface, such as a board, there is diffusion of the energy and a less severe injury than that caused by a narrow object, for example, a steel rod delivered with the same amount of force. If an object projects from the surface of the weapon, then all of the force will be delivered to the end of the projection and a much more severe wound will be produced. If a blow is delivered to a rounded portion of the body, such as the top of the head, the wound will be much more severe than if the same force is delivered to a flat portion of the body, such as the back, where there will be a greater area of contact and more dispersion of force.

Of course, just with any injury, the effects of blunt force injuries may be worsened in the presence of preexisting natural disease. Injuries and their treatment can lead to cardiac decompensation in patients with heart disease, cerebral damage during shock, uremia in patients with chronic renal disease or even delirium tremens in alcoholics. Thus, the injuries themselves as well as any underlying disease processes must be considered in the death investigation.

Types of Blunt Force Injuries

Blunt force injuries fall into four categories:

1. Abrasions
2. Contusions

3. Lacerations
4. Fractures of the skeletal system

It should be realized that a wound might display more than one type of injury. Thus, one may have a laceration with abraded margins lying in the center of an area of contusion.

Abrasions

An abrasion is an injury to the skin in which there is removal of the superficial epithelial layer of the skin (the epidermis) by friction against a rough surface, or destruction of the superficial layers by compression. Antemortem abrasions have a reddish-brown appearance (Figure 5.1) and heal without scarring. Abrasions produced after death are yellow and translucent with a parchment-like appearance. They are important to the forensic pathologist in that they indicate where a blunt instrument or a blunt force has interacted with the body. They may be the only external evidence of trauma to the body. Abrasions are not always present in areas of blunt force injury.

There are three types of abrasions:

1. Scrape or brush abrasions
2. Impact abrasions
3. Patterned abrasions

In **scrape (brush) abrasions**, the blunt object scrapes off the superficial layers of the skin, leaving a denuded surface. At times, these abrasions may be fairly deep, extending down to the dermis. In such instances, there may be leakage of fluids from vessels with deposit of a serosanguineous fluid on the surface of the abrasion. This dries, forming the familiar reddish-brown scab. One of the most common types of scrape abrasions is the linear abrasion known as the scratch. Extensive scrape-like abrasions (graze or sliding abrasions) are seen in pedestrians who slide across the pavement (Figure 5.1A) after being hit by a motor vehicle. Particles of gravel, dirt or glass may be embedded in such wounds. An incision made into these areas usually fails to reveal underlying soft-tissue hemorrhage (Figure 5.1B).

Similar scrape abrasions may be produced when a victim's body is dragged over a rough surface. Nooses or ligatures can also produce scrape abrasions.

It is quite common to read in textbooks of the heaping up of epidermis at the distal end of a scrape abrasion, enabling one to determine the direction of movement of the blunt object or the body across a rough surface. The phenomenon is more theoretical than real and usually does not occur to a significant degree.

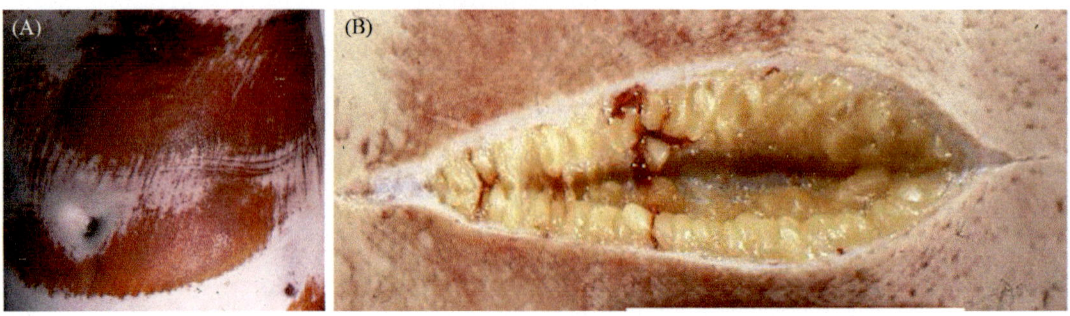

Figure 5.1 (A) Scrape-like abrasion from sliding across pavement. (B) Incision shows injury confined to epidermis.

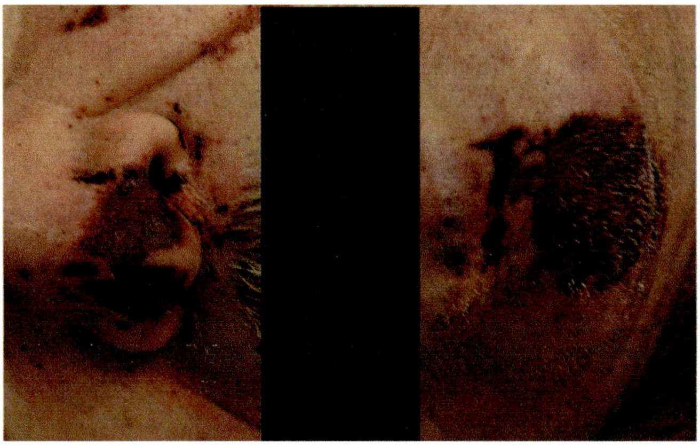

Figure 5.2 Impact abrasions of the tip of the nose and chin.

In **impact abrasions**, the blunt force is directed perpendicular to the skin, crushing it. Such abrasions tend to be focal and are commonly seen overlying bony prominences where a thin layer of skin covers bone. Impact abrasions over the supraorbital ridge (eyebrow), zygomatic arch (cheekbone) and the side of the nose are commonly seen in individuals who are unconscious when they collapse and strike their heads on the ground (Figure 5.2).

A **patterned abrasion** is a variation of an impact abrasion. Here, the imprint of either the offending object, such as a pipe, or intermediary material, such as clothing, is imprinted or stamped on the skin by the crushing effect of the blunt object (Figure 5.3A and B).

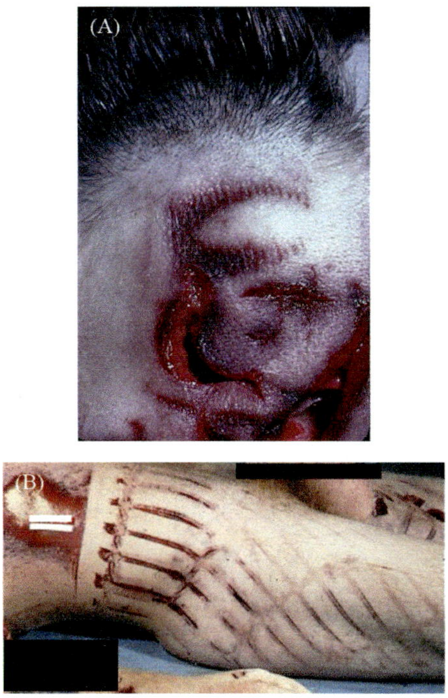

Figure 5.3 Patterned abrasions: (A) thread marks of pipe (lacerations below abrasion) and (B) grill marks in individual who jumped off an eight-story building, landing on a metal grill.

Postmortem insect bites and diaper rash are occasionally misinterpreted as abrasions by the inexperienced physician (Figure 5.4A and B).

Another artifact that can be confused with an abrasion is drying of the skin of the scrotum and, less commonly, of the vulva (Figure 5.4C). The skin in these areas seems to be very susceptible to drying, especially if exposed to the open air. It has a reddish-brown or yellow coloration and may be interpreted as an abrasion.

Dating of Abrasions

Unlike attempts at dating of contusions in which histological examination of the injuries has not been helpful, histological examination of abrasions in an attempt to determine

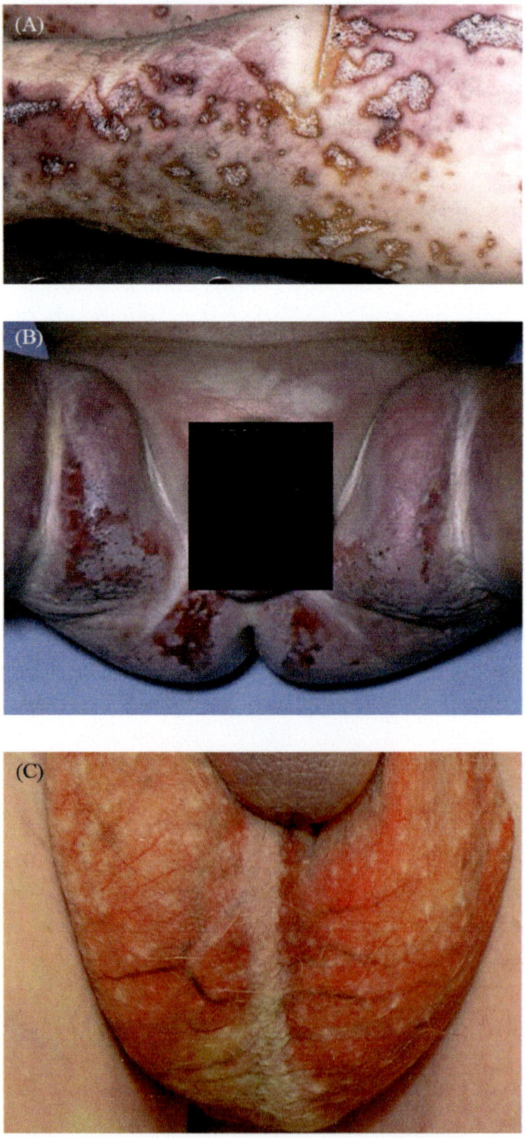

Figure 5.4 (A) Postmortem ant bites simulating abrasions. (B) Diaper rash. (C) Drying of scrotum.

their age is possible to a degree. Robertson and Hodge probably provide the most authoritative and logical method of approach.[1]

They describe four stages in the healing of abrasions:

1. Scab formation
2. Epithelial regeneration
3. Subepithelial granulation and epithelial hyperplasia
4. Regression of epithelium and granulation tissue

The first stage is **scab formation**. Serum, red cells and fibrin are deposited on the abrasion. These are not used for aging but do indicate survival following the injury. The infiltration of polymorphonuclear cells in a perivascular formation signifies that the injury is 4–6 h old. The earliest time for such a cellular reaction is 2 h, but it is usually not clearly visible until 4–6 h. By 8 h, the bed of the scab is marked by a zone of infiltrating polymorphonuclear cells underlying the area of epithelial injury. At 12 h, there are three layers: a surface zone of fibrin and red cells (or crushed epithelium in the case of impact abrasions), a deeper zone of infiltrating polymorphonuclear cells and a layer of damaged abnormally staining collagen. For the next 12–18 h, the last zone is progressively infiltrated by polymorphonuclear cells.

The second stage is **epithelial regeneration**. Regeneration of the epithelial cells arises in surviving hair follicles and at the edges of the abrasion. Epithelial growth may appear as early as 30 h in superficial scrape-like abrasions and is clearly visible by 72 h in most abrasions.

The third stage is **subepithelial granulation**. This becomes prominent during days 5–8. It occurs only after epithelial covering of an abrasion. Perivascular infiltration and chronic inflammatory cells are now prominent. The overlying epithelium becomes progressively hyperplastic, with the formation of keratin. This stage is most prominent during days 9–12 after injury.

The last stage is **regression**. It begins at about 12 days. During this phase, the epithelium is remodeled and becomes thinner and even atrophic. Collagen fibers, which began to appear in the late subepithelial granulation phase, are now prominent. There is a definite basement membrane and the vascularity of the dermis decreases.

Contusions

A **contusion**, or **bruise**, is an area of hemorrhage into soft tissue due to rupture of blood vessels caused by blunt trauma (Figure 5.5).

Contusions may be present not only in skin, but also in internal organs, such as the lung, heart, brain and muscle. A large focal collection of blood in an area of contusion is referred to as a **hematoma**. A contusion can be differentiated from an area of livor mortis in that, in a contusion, blood has escaped into soft tissue and cannot be wiped or squeezed out, as in an area of livor mortis. The extent and severity of a contusion depends not only upon the amount of force applied, but also on the structure and vascularity of the tissue that is contused. Thus, contusions are more readily incurred in areas with thin, lax skin and in fatty areas.

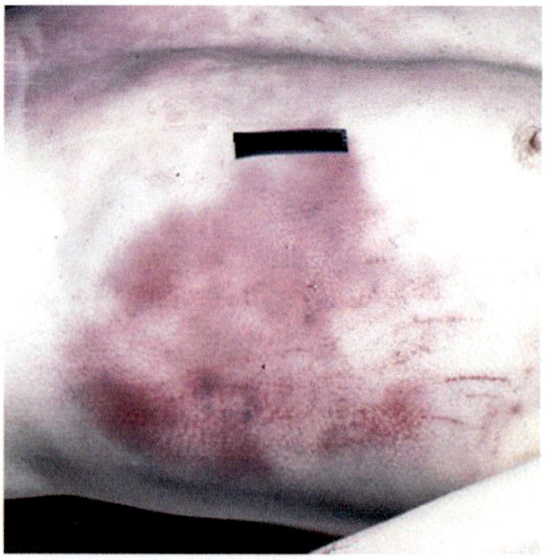

Figure 5.5 Non-patterned contusion. Perpetrator jumped on deceased's chest, rupturing left lung and lacerating liver.

Contusions might reflect the configuration of the object used to produce the contusion; that is, they might be patterned (Figure 5.6).

When an individual is struck with a flat object, such as a board, it is quite common to find parallel linear contusions corresponding to the edges of the board, with normal-appearing tissue in between. A contusion at a site does not necessarily indicate the point of trauma, since soft-tissue bleeding will follow the path of least resistance. Deep bruises may not be visible externally and may be discovered only on incising the soft tissue. In other instances, deep bruises may not become visible externally until hours after death. Scalp bruises are frequently not visible externally unless there is swelling (Figure 5.7A, B).

Bruises can also be difficult to detect in dark-skinned individuals (Figure 5.8A, B).

Contusions, like abrasions, indicate that blunt force has been applied to a particular area. The absence of a bruise, just as the absence of an abrasion, does not indicate that there was no blunt force to that area. This is especially true of the anterior abdominal wall, where there may be massive internal injury in the absence of external evidence of trauma. Another point to remember is that a contusion might be much larger than the object that produced it.

As a rule, bruises are not fatal. However, multiple contusions with extensive soft-tissue hemorrhage may produce shock and death from massive blood loss. This is seen occasionally in battered children.

The size and severity of a contusion is not always indicative of the amount of force applied, though, obviously, the greater the force, the greater the contusion. Certain factors influence the size of a contusion: age, sex, the condition and health of the victim and the site and type of tissues struck. Children and the elderly bruise more easily because of loose delicate skin in the former and loss of subcutaneous supportive tissue in the latter. Senile purpura (ecchymoses) on the forearms of the elderly may be mistaken for bruises. Women, especially if obese, seem to bruise more easily. Well-conditioned, muscular individuals are more resistant to bruising. Soft, lax, vascular tissue, such as in the eyelid, is more susceptible to bruising than areas such as the palm. Alcoholics with cirrhosis, individuals with bleeding diatheses and individuals taking aspirin bleed more easily. A single therapeutic

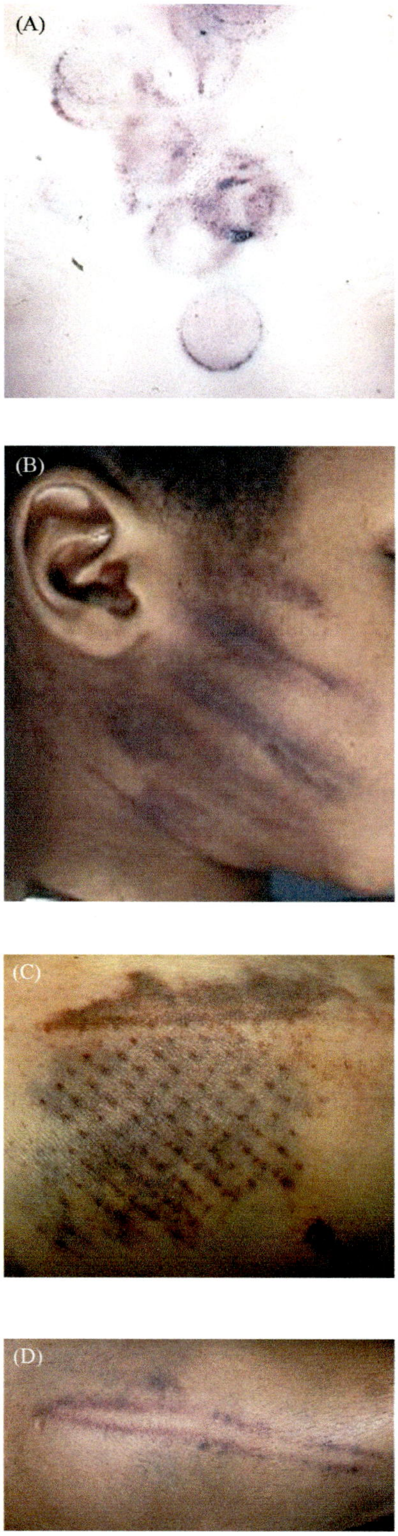

Figure 5.6 Patterned contusions caused by (A) end of flashlight, (B) imprint of the left hand, (C) clothing and (D) pool cue.

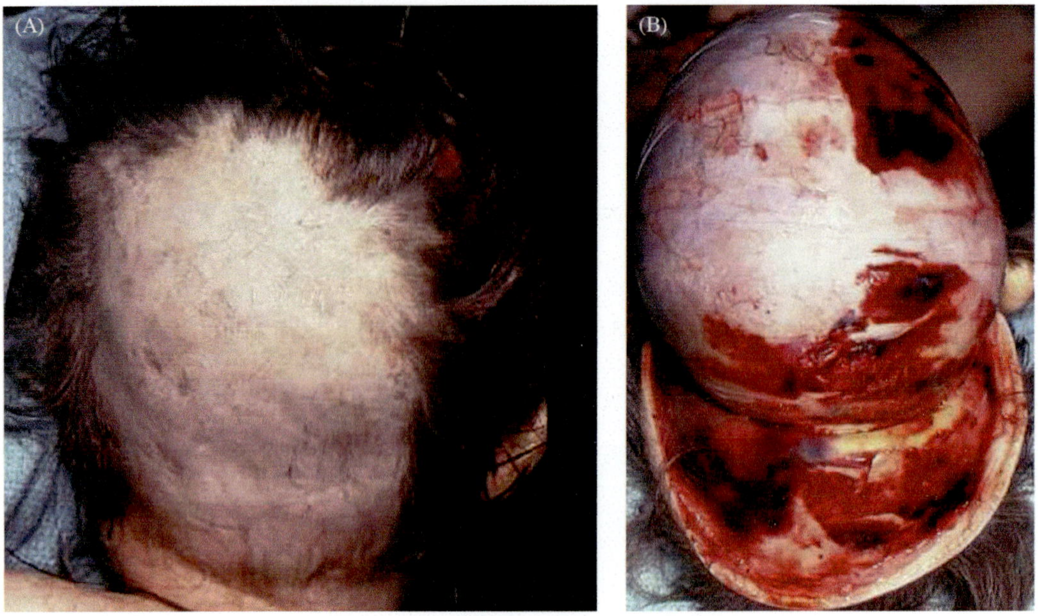

Figure 5.7 External surface of the scalp without obvious contusion (A) The internal surface showing diffuse subcutaneous and subgaleal hemorrhage (B).

dose of aspirin irreversibly inhibits platelet function for the 7-day life of the platelets with resultant inhibition of hemostasis and a prolonged bleeding time.[2]

Dating of Contusions

The forensic pathologist is often asked the age of a bruise, as such information could be of potential importance in a case. Methods used to age a bruise are (1) histology and (2) color changes.

The method most commonly employed in dating contusions is based on the changes in color a contusion undergoes as it heals. The depth of a contusion and skin pigmentation may affect the appearance and detection of the colors. Yellow coloration is visible sooner in superficial bruises than in deep bruises; dark pigmentation may conceal a bruise. The depth and location of the bruise can influence its time of appearance, with superficial bruising and bruises of the eyelids appearing more rapidly; deep bruising may not, appearing for days.

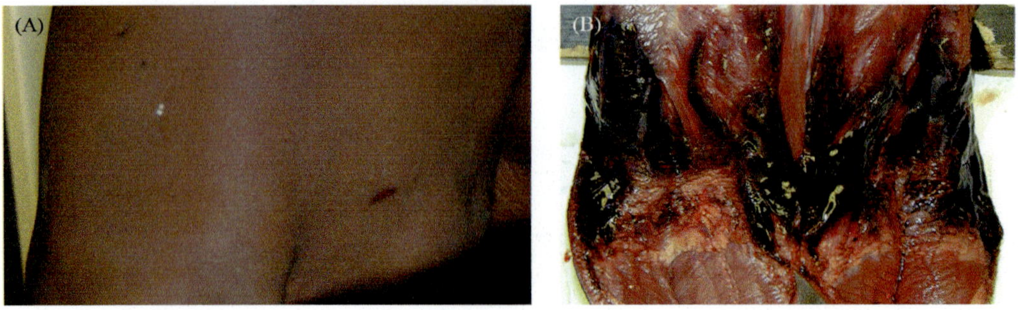

Figure 5.8 External surface of the back of a child with scattered abrasion but without obvious contusions (A) and the internal surface of the same child showing diffuse contusions (B).

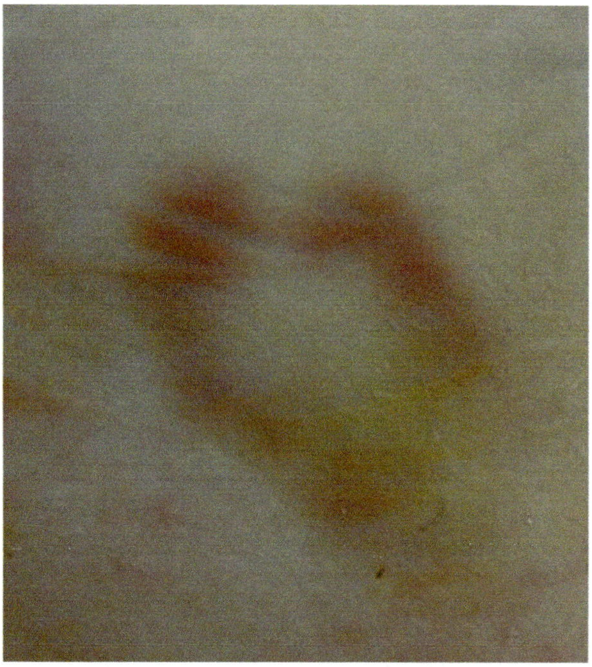

Figure 5.9 Healing bruise on the left buttock showing a brown and yellow pigmentation.

As a bruise ages, it undergoes an evolution in its color due to the degradation of the hemoglobin (Figure 5.9).

The time and order of the changes is how one ages a bruise. Problems arise, however, in individuals' disagreeing on color terminology and the chronology of the development of colors, and that bruises are not consistent in appearance, color or evolution.

There is no standard terminology in use to describe the color of a bruise. The same bruise might be described as violet, reddish purple, bluish purple, purple or blue. Most bruises appear initially as red, dark blue, purple, violet or black. As the hemoglobin in the bruise is broken down, the color gradually changes to violet, green, dark yellow and pale yellow before disappearing. These changes can occur over a matter of days to weeks. Unfortunately, the rate of change is quite variable, not only between persons, but also in the same person and from bruise to bruise. Not uncommonly, the color change goes directly from violet to yellow with no green coloration. In the same individual, one can have two bruises that were incurred at the same time, and one will go from blue to violet to yellow and disappear while the other is still violet. A brown coloration to a contusion is often said to indicate that it is not recent. The authors, however, have seen numerous pale brown contusions of the anterior chest overlying the sternum produced by perimortem cardiopulmonary resuscitation (CPR), and have seen contusions develop a pale yellow color in 2–3 days.

Langlois and Gresham concluded that the only conclusion that can be drawn regarding the coloration of bruise was that a yellow coloration indicted the bruise to be more than 18 h old.[3] They also concluded that the absence of a yellow color does not mean that the bruise is less than 18 h old. Additionally, Maguire et al. reviewed 167 articles regarding aging bruises on children and found conflicting results regarding yellow coloration.[4] They found that in some studies, yellow coloration appears only after 24 h and that red coloration may indicate a more recent bruise (less than 1 week). They also found that clinicians could only correctly estimate a bruise within 24 h of occurrence in less than 4% of cases, though it improved to 55–63% if determining only fresh, intermediate or old. Thus, color changes should be considered only as general guidelines in interpreting how old a bruise is. Additionally, aging of bruises should not be assessed in a photograph as the photograph itself can alter coloration and interpretation.

Histology has also been used to try to date bruises; however, much of the experimental work on this topic is performed on animals and the results are not necessary transferable to humans. Traditional research has focused on the appearance and type of inflammatory cells. Unfortunately, there can be extreme variability in this with neutrophils being shown to appear anyway between 20–30 min and 15 h[5,6] and may not appear for up to 24 h in scalp injuries. Hemosiderin deposition has also been assessed, with equivalent variability, ranging from less than 24 h to up to 3 days. The presence of fibroblasts and collagen is usually indicative of healing, as fibroblasts usually appear around 72 h and collagen begins to form around 3–6 days; however, they may also be present in cases of repetitive injuries to the same location. Other markers have been proposed and studies, including immunostaining, histochemical staining and even DNA degradation; however, none have been successful. It has also been shown that individuals who have suffered from a catastrophic event and are hospitalized prior to death undergo delayed wound healing.[7]

Postmortem Bruising

One of the most commonly heard statements in regard to contusions is that they indicate that the injury was incurred prior to death, because one cannot form a contusion after death. This is not entirely correct. Contusions can be produced postmortem if a severe blow is delivered to a body within a few hours of death.[8] The blow can rupture capillaries, forcing blood into the soft tissue and producing a postmortem contusion identical in appearance to an antemortem contusion. Postmortem contusions rarely occur and are most commonly seen in skin and soft tissue overlying bone or bony prominences such as in the head. Microscopic examination of a contusion to determine whether it is antemortem or postmortem is usually of no help, because, in most cases, the antemortem injuries are incurred immediately prior to death and there is insufficient time for tissue reaction.

Additionally, confluent hemorrhage in eyelids can occur after death in cases of head trauma with fracture of the orbital plates. One can prove this by taking the body of an individual with skull fractures, but without hemorrhage in the eyelids, and placing it face down for a number of hours. Blood will drain from the cranial cavity through the orbital plate fractures into the eyelids. Surgical removal of corneas or the globes of the eyes shortly after death can also result in hemorrhage into the eyelids indistinguishable from antemortem trauma (Figure 5.10A) just as the removal of vitreous fluid shortly after death can result in scleral hemorrhage at the puncture site (Figure 5.10B).

Techniques to identify antemortem injuries involve the same techniques as dating injuries,[9] with the premise being that any presence of reaction indicates the decedent was alive at the time of the injury. Unfortunately, however, the reverse is not also true. The absence of reaction does not necessarily mean the decedent was dead at the time of injury.

Decomposed Bodies

In decomposed bodies, especially in the scalp, hemolysis of erythrocytes produces a diffuse discoloration of the soft tissue, which makes attempts to distinguish between an

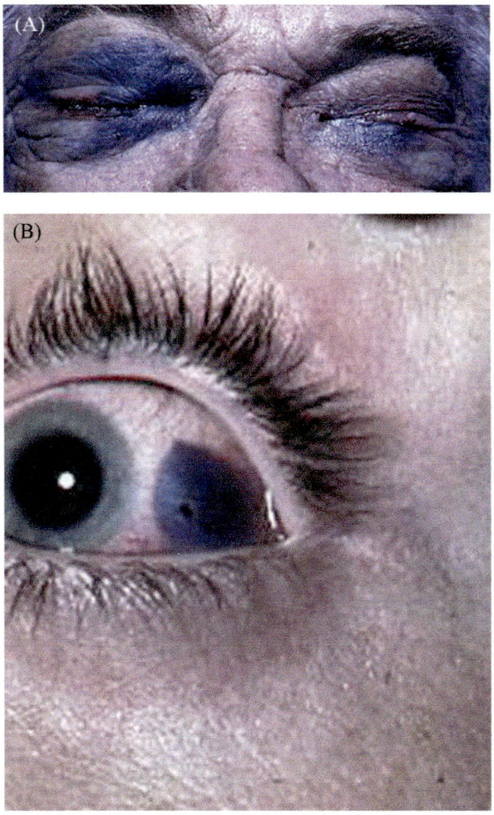

Figure 5.10 (A) Hemorrhage into eyelids following removal of corneas and (B) scleral hemorrhage following removal of vitreous.

antemortem contusion and an area of livor mortis impossible. In areas of livor mortis, blood vessels break down with leakage of erythrocytes into the soft tissue. Erythrocytes still in the vessels and those that diffuse into soft tissue hemolyze. Erythrocytes in soft tissue from bruising will also hemolyze, giving identical appearances to these lesions.

Lacerations

A laceration is a tear in tissue caused by either a shearing or a crushing force (Figure 5.11).

Just as with contusions, one can have lacerations of internal organs as well as the skin. Lacerations of the skin tend to be irregular with abraded and/ or contused margins.

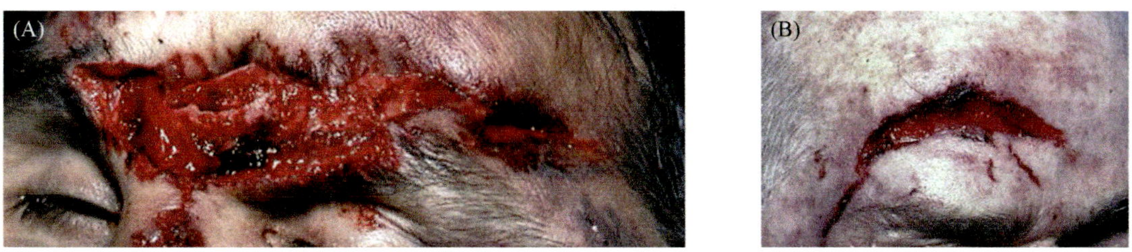

Figure 5.11 (A and B) Lacerations.

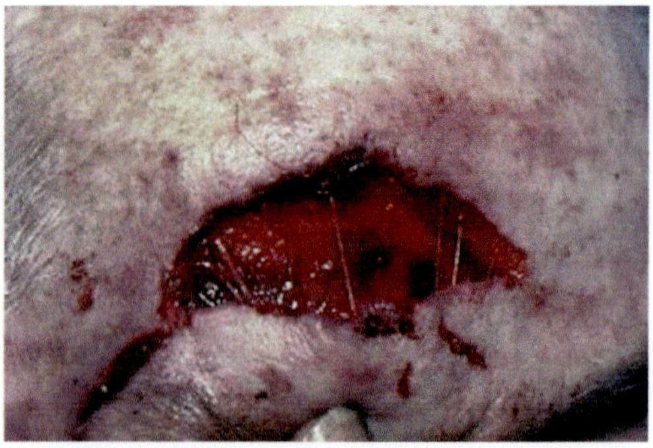

Figure 5.12 Laceration with bridging.

They are caused by blows from blunt objects, falls or impact from vehicles. As a general rule, long, thin objects, such as pipes and pool cues, tend to produce linear lacerations, while objects with flat surfaces tend to produce irregular, ragged or Y-shaped lacerations. However, the appearance of the laceration may not accurately reflect the instrument that produced it. Thus, a steel rod might produce not only a linear laceration of the scalp, but also a Y-shaped one. Just as with contusions, determining the age of lacerations is difficult.

Lacerations occur most commonly over bony prominences, such as in the head, where the skin is fixed and can more easily be stretched and torn. Since different components of soft tissue have different strengths, there is usually incomplete separation of the stronger elements, such as blood vessels and nerves, so that when one looks into the depth of the laceration, one sees "bridges" of tissue running from side to side (Figure 5.12).

The presence of bridging proves decisively that one is not dealing with an incised wound. The depths of the laceration should be explored for the presence of foreign material that could have been deposited there by the weapon or surface that caused the laceration.

If the blow or impact that causes a laceration is delivered at an angle, rather than perpendicular to the surface of the body, one will find undermining of the tissue on one side, which indicates the direction that the blow was delivered (Figure 5.13).

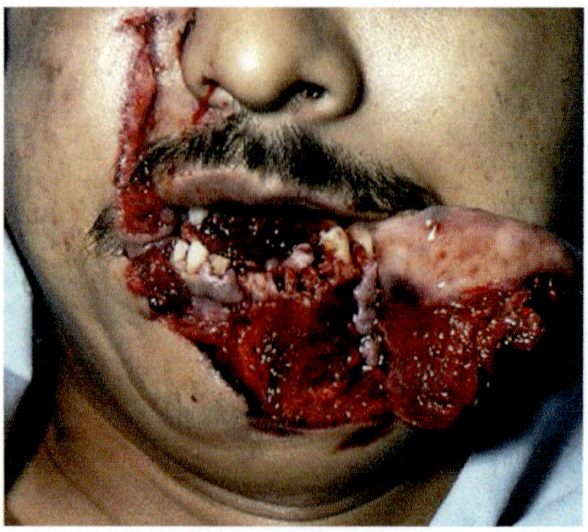

Figure 5.13 Laceration with avulsion of skin. Blow delivered from deceased's left to right.

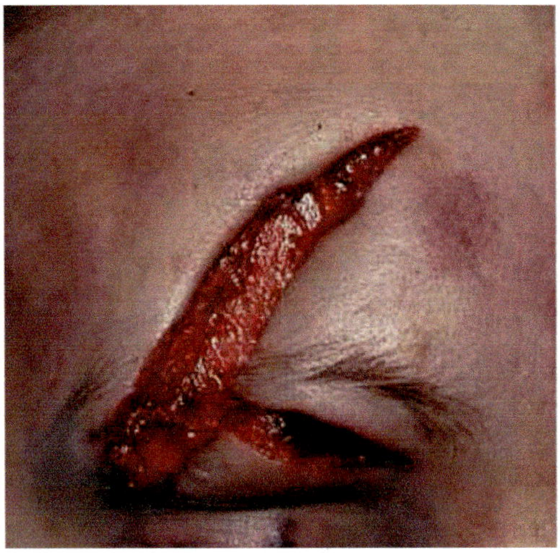

Figure 5.14 Laceration with sharp, almost incised margins.

The other side of the laceration, the side from which the blow was coming, will be abraded and beveled.

While most lacerations have irregular, abraded, even contused margins, if an individual is struck with a heavy object having a relatively sharp edge along the impacting surface, the wound produced may greatly resemble an incised wound (Figure 5.14).

Careful examination of the wound, however, will usually reveal at least some abrasion of the margin, plus bridging in the depths of the wound. Occasionally, a very dull knife may produce an incised wound with abraded margins. Again, careful observation of the edges and base of the wound with a dissecting microscope usually makes differentiation between an incised wound and a laceration relatively easy. In some instances, however, differentiation is not possible. Differentiation of a laceration from an incised wound of the head in a decomposed body is often not possible.

An **avulsion** or **avulsive injury** to the outside of a body is a form of laceration where the force impacting the body does so at an oblique or tangential angle to the skin, ripping skin and soft tissue off the underlying fascia or bone. Thus, tires passing over an extremity may avulse soft tissue off the bone. In a case of extreme avulsion, an extremity or even the head can be torn off the body. Internally, organs can be avulsed or torn off in part or *in toto* from their attachments.

A variation of an avulsive laceration is one produced by shearing forces, where the skin shows no signs of injury but the underlying soft tissue has been avulsed from the underlying fascia or connective tissue, creating a pocket that may be filled with a large quantity of blood. This injury is occasionally encountered on the backs of the thighs of pedestrians struck by motor vehicles. As the hood of the car impacts the back of the thigh and lifts up the pedestrian, it imparts a shearing force to this region, avulsing the skin and subcutaneous tissue off the fascia and creating pockets where blood can accumulate.

Fractures

Fractures of the bones can be produced by either the **direct** or **indirect** application of force to the bone.[10]

Fractures from Direct Application of Force

When a blunt object impacts a long bone, it tends to bend the bone, producing disruption or cracking of the bone on the side opposite the impact that is, the convex or tension side of the bone. With significant impact, however, there is crushing on the side of the bone to which the force is applied (the concave side), prior to the bone's cracking. In comminuted fractures, the bone is broken into more than two pieces.

Fractures caused by direct application of force to a bone site can be divided into penetrating, focal or crush fractures, depending on the amount of force applied to the bone and the size of the area to which it is applied. **Penetrating fractures** are caused by a large force acting on a small area. Because, for all practical purposes, this category is synonymous with gunshot wounds, they will be discussed in Chapter 7.

In **focal fractures**, a small force is applied to a small area and the resultant fracture is usually transverse. Overlying soft-tissue injury is relatively minor, for example, an abrasion, contusion or small laceration. In areas where two bones are adjacent to each other, such as in the forearm or calf region, typically only one bone is fractured. Focal fractures, produced by weapons such as a bat or pipe, are seen in forearms when an individual has tried to ward off blows from such instruments (Figure 5.15A).

In **crush fractures**, a large force is applied over a large area, with resultant extensive soft-tissue injuries and, often, comminuted fractures of the bone. In the forearm and lower legs, there is usually fracture of both bones at the same level. Most crush fractures of the extremities involve the legs, with motor vehicle-pedestrian accidents the most common etiology. The fractures produced are called **bumper fractures** (Figure 5.16).

In severe impact injuries of the legs, a number of possible fracture patterns can be produced (transverse; oblique; spiral; segmental; comminuted; longitudinal split; tension

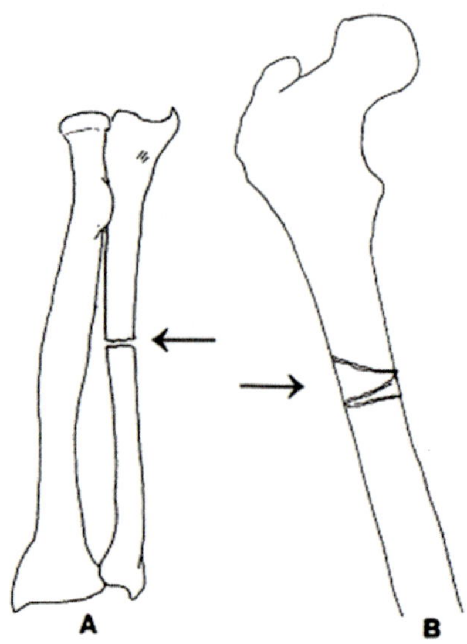

Figure 5.15 Direct fractures: (A) focal and (B) crushing. Arrow indicates direction of force.

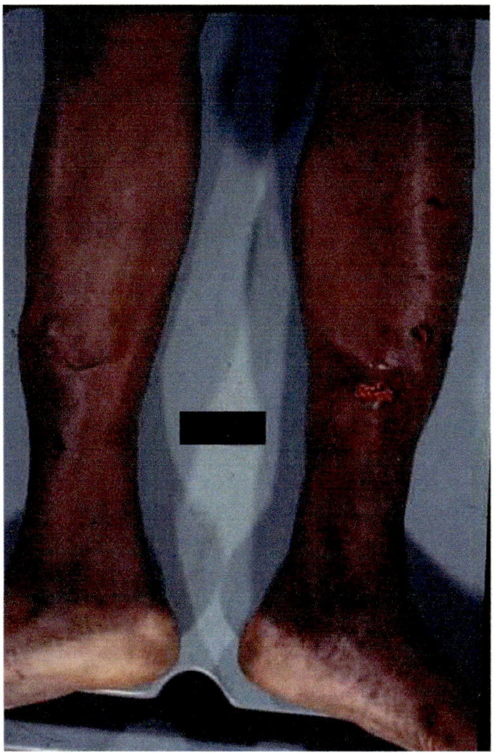

Figure 5.16 "Bumper" fractures of lower legs.

wedge; compression wedge).[11] The two most common patterns are tension wedge and oblique (Figure 5.17).

Tension wedge fractures can be used as an indicator of the direction of impact. In tension wedge fractures, the fractures begin opposite to the point of impact and radiate back through the bone at a 90-angle, giving rise to a wedge of bone, the point of which is directed in the direction of the force and the base of which is at the point of impact. What appears to be an oblique fracture on X-ray may turn out to be a tensile wedge fracture on dissection. On occasion, one will see compressive wedge-type fractures. These are extremely rare and may be confused with the common tension wedge fracture.

Fractures Caused by Indirect Application of Force

Indirect fractures are produced by a force acting at a distance from the fracture site. In this regard, it should be noted that bone is weaker to tension (stretching) than compression. Indirect fractures can be classified into six types (Figure 5.17):

1. Traction
2. Angulation
3. Rotational
4. Vertical compression
5. Angulation and compression
6. Angulation, rotation and compression fractures

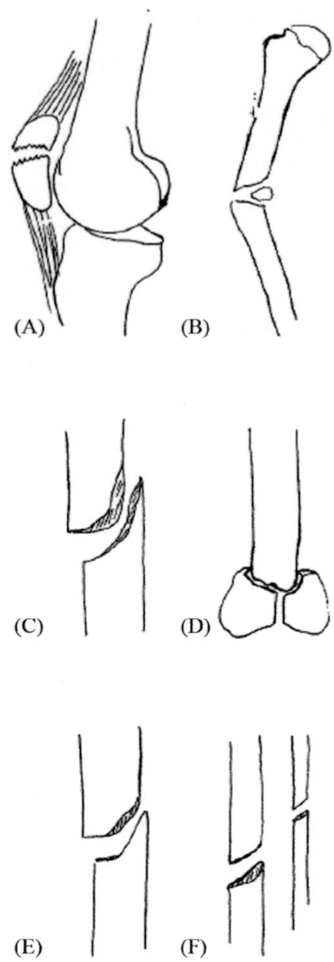

Figure 5.17 Indirect fractures: (A) traction; (B) angulation; (C) rotational; (D) vertical compression; (E) angulation and compression; (F) angulation, rotation and compression.

In **traction fractures**, the bone is pulled apart by traction. An example would be violent contraction of the quadriceps muscle with resultant transverse fracture of the patella. In **angulation fractures**, the bone is bent until it snaps. The concave surface is compressed and the convex surface is put under traction. This usually results in a transverse fracture.

In **rotational fractures**, the bone is twisted and a spiral fracture is produced. *Spiral fractures* occur only when the bone is subjected to torsional force. In the femur, most spiral fractures occur in the proximal third. The proximal and distant ends of a spiral fracture are connected by what Porta et al. call a "hinge."[12] The hinge distinguishes it from an oblique fracture. To determine in which direction a bone was twisted, ascertain the direction the spiral runs from the end twisted. This indicates the direction of torque.

Vertical compression fractures produce an oblique fracture of the body of long bones, with the hard shaft of the long bone driven into the cancellous end. In femurs, a T- or Y-shaped fracture is typically seen at the distal end of the femur. Such fractures may occur following impaction of the end of the femur into the instrument panel in motor vehicle crashes.

In **angulation** and **compression fractures**, the fracture line is curved, with an oblique component due to compression and a transverse component due to angulation. The last category is **angulation, rotation**, and **compression fractures**. The angulation plus rotation produces an oblique fracture, with the compression increasing the tendency toward fracture.

Pelvic Fractures

Fractures of the pelvis deserve special mention because of two unusual aspects. First, an immense amount of force is required to disrupt the pelvic ring. Second, because the pelvis is a ring, disruption of any portion of it is usually associated with disruption of another portion of the ring. Pelvic disruption or fractures are classified by the direction of the force.[13,14] There are four categories:

1. Anterior-posterior compression
2. Lateral compression
3. Shear
4. Complex fractures

In fractures due to anteroposterior compression, there is a direct blow to either the pubic symphysis or the posterior iliac spines, or violent external rotational forces applied to the femurs. Anteriorly, there is separation of the pubic symphysis. Posteriorly, there is bilateral separation of the sacroiliac joints anteriorly, with the posterior iliac ligaments generally intact.

In lateral compression, the force is applied either to the iliac crest directly or to the greater trochanter by the femoral head's being propelled into the acetabulum. Anteriorly, the pubic rami on the side of impact are usually fractured. However, there may be contralateral fracture of the pubic rami or, less commonly, fracture of all four pubic rami or even disruption of the pubic symphysis. Posteriorly, there is ipsilateral impaction of the sacroiliac joints with the posterior ligaments generally intact. If the femoral head produces lateral compression by being propelled into the acetabulum, there are usually ipsilateral fractures of the pelvic rami, disruption of the sacroiliac joints with impaction and fractures of the acetabulum.

Shearing injuries of the pelvis are due to extremely severe force. There is application of a shearing force to one or both of the sacroiliac joints. The force is perpendicular to the trabecular pattern of the posterior pelvic complex, which results in disruption of both the anterior and superior sacroiliac ligaments with gross disruption of the joints. With massive forces, the hemi-pelvis can be avulsed from the body. Anteriorly, there may be disruption of the pubic symphysis, two pubic rami or all four pubic rami.

In complex fractures, multiple forces from different angles have been exerted at the pelvis and one cannot simply classify the injuries as being due to the three aforementioned modes.

Dating Fractures

Healing of fractures depends on the ages of individuals and their nutritional status. After adulthood, age does not play an important role. Fractures of cancellous bone unite faster than those of cortical bone. In children, a callus is visible radiologically within 2 weeks of the fracture. The bone is consolidated in 4–6 weeks, though it usually takes 2–3 months to heal solidly. In adults, consolidation takes approximately 3 months, though in the case of the femur, it could take 4–5 months. These are only very general time periods.

In healing, fractures of the bone undergo a number of stages that end in repair of the bone. Initially, there is hemorrhage at the point of fracture secondary to rupture of vessels, with production of a fusiform hematoma surrounding and joining the ends of the bone. The periosteum is torn from the outer surface of the bone; the endosteum from the marrow. Fibrin is deposited in the hematoma. This is followed in 24–48 h by an inflammatory response with edema, continuing deposit of fibrin and the accumulation of large numbers of polymorphonuclear cells. As time passes, increasing numbers of macrophages appear.

The next stage begins 48 h after injury and is characterized by the appearance of fibroblast and mesenchymal cells with gradual development of granulation tissue. Necrosis of the bone adjacent to the fracture becomes evident, with empty lacunar spaces due to death of osteocytes. The line of demarcation between dead bone, with its empty lacunae, and live bone is evident. There is marked proliferation of the cells of the deep layer of the periosteum and, to a lesser degree, of the cells of the endosteum.

As the days pass, the periosteal proliferation results in the formation of a collar around what is becoming the callus. At the same time, the periosteal cells are proliferating, capillaries begin to grow out into the hematoma. Osteoblasts begin to appear and form new trabeculae. Approximately a week after injury, granulation tissue, fibroblasts, osteoblasts, chondroblasts and small islets of cartilage in the fibrous stroma appear. Osteoblasts produce a matrix of collagen and polysaccharide, which becomes impregnated with calcium to produce immature "woven" bone. The callus reaches its maximum size in 2–3 weeks. The next stage appears in 3–4 weeks and is marked by a hard bony callus, with the bone forming from periosteal and endochondral ossification. In the last stage, there is remodeling of the new bone from a woven appearance to mature bone.

Fat Embolism

Fat embolism is characterized by the presence of globules of fat in the lung and peripheral circulation. Fat embolization occurs in 90–100% of individuals with long-bone or pelvic fractures but is rare in children. Following trauma, fat droplets enter the circulation. The larger droplets are strained out by the lungs, where they lodge in the vasculature. The smaller fat globules travel through the pulmonary capillaries, enter the arterial circulation and are carried to the brain and other organs. In only a small percentage of individuals with fat emboli, however, does this condition become symptomatic. When this occurs, the individual is said to have the **fat embolism syndrome** (**FES**).[15–17]

FES was first described by Zenker in 1862 and diagnosed by von Bergmann in 1873.[18] This syndrome is characterized by progressive pulmonary insufficiency, mental deterioration, fever and a petechial rash.[19] Typically, symptoms do not appear for 24–72 h following injury. The petechiae are typically seen in the conjunctivae, as well as on the chest and the axillae. These major signs may be accompanied by tachycardia, thrombocytopenia and renal failure. Fat globules may be present in the urine, sputum and retina. Death occurs either because of a diminished oxygen uptake leading to hypoxemia or because of an increase of blood pressure in the pulmonary circulation leading to an acute fatal right heart failure.[20]

The etiology of pulmonary fat emboli is not completely understood. The most common theory suggested by Gossling and Pellegrini[21] states that fat is released into the venous system and becomes lodged in the pulmonary capillary bed causing mechanical obstruction of the pulmonary vasculature. Another theory is that the fat emboli cause direct toxic injury to the pneumocytes and endothelium, resulting in abnormalities in gas exchange. Baker et al.,[22] for example, claimed that local hydrolysis of fat emboli by pneumocytes generates free fatty acids that enter other organs and cause multi-organ dysfunction. This may explain why PFE seems to be also seen in nontraumatic cases.[23]

Microscopically, there are fat emboli in the pulmonary vasculature, with edema, transudate and exudate in the alveoli. Visualization of fat emboli within the pulmonary vasculature requires the use of frozen sections and fat stains. The presence of fat within the pulmonary circulation also proves that the deceased had a blood circulation when fat entered the vascular system and was, therefore, alive at the time the trauma was sustained. If the individual survives a few days, the brain will show small perivascular hemorrhages in the white matter around vessels containing fat emboli (Figure 5.18), however, in the early stages, the brain may appear grossly normal.

The most common cause of FES is long-bone fractures and the incidence increases with the number of fractures.[24] ten Duis noted that the syndrome developed in 3% of patients with a single fracture of the femur and 33% of patients with two fractured femora.[15] Other groups noted that PFE may also arise from crushed soft tissue even in the absence of fractures.[25,26] Mudd et al.[27] even stated that soft-tissue injury is the primary cause of PFE. While the FES is usually associated with long-bone or pelvic fractures, it can also be seen in association with acute pancreatitis, extensive burns, liposuction, decompression sickness and parenteral infusion of lipids.[16] It can also be precipitated by reaming and nailing procedures for long-bone fractures.

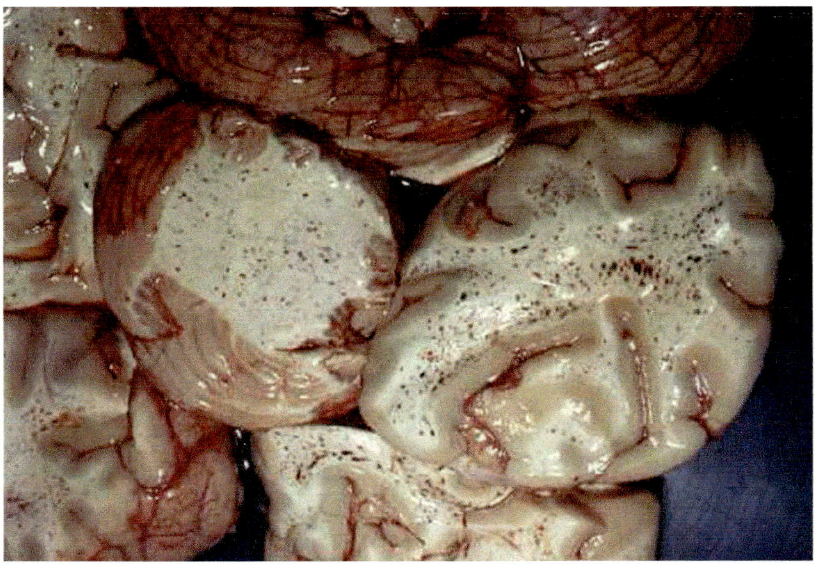

Figure 5.18 Petechial hemorrhages of brain caused by fat embolism in a 21-year-old female with a fracture of right femur.

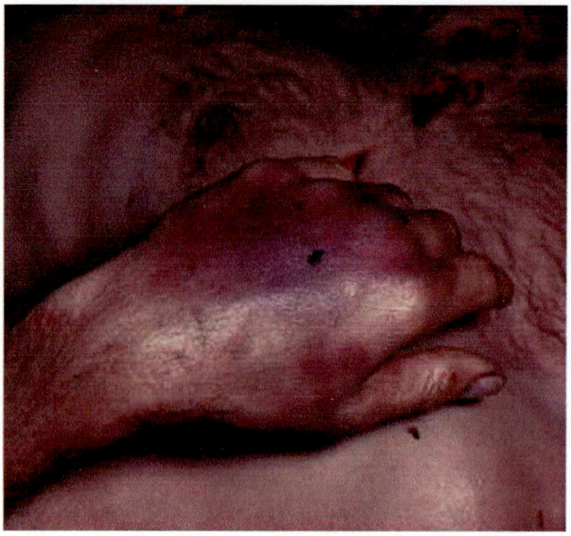

Figure 5.19 Abrasions and contusions on the back of a hand representing defense-type wounds.

Defense Wounds Due to Blunt Force

Just as one can have defense wounds from a knife attack, one can have defense wounds from an attack with a blunt object. There are generally abrasions and contusions on the back of the hands, wrists, forearms and arms (Figure 5.19).

Lacerations are less common and may contain embedded fragments of the weapon in the wounds. Even less common are fractures. When these occur, they generally involve the forearm and are incurred in attempts to ward off a blunt object.

Blunt Force Injuries of the Head and Neck

Injuries to the head and neck can be grouped into two broad categories based on the mechanism by which the injury is produced: **impact injuries** and/or **acceleration/deceleration injuries. Impact injuries** are caused when the head is struck with or against an object. These injuries consist of the local effects of contact between the head and the object and typically include:

- Soft-tissue injuries (lacerations, abrasions, contusions) of the scalp
- Fracture of the skull
- Contusions of the brain
- Subdural hematomas
- Epidural hematomas
- Intracerebral hemorrhages

Acceleration/deceleration injuries are due to sudden movement of the head the instant after injury, with resultant production of intracranial pressure gradients and the subjecting of the brain to both shearing and tensile forces. This mechanism of injuries typically produces **subdural hematomas** and **diffuse axonal injury** (**DAI**). While acceleration or deceleration injuries are often associated with impact, theoretically, impact is not necessary for the production of these injuries, just sudden angular rotation of the head. In most situations encountered by forensic pathologists, acceleration or deceleration injuries of the brain involve impact.

An impacting force to the head can produce linear acceleration, rotational (angular) acceleration or a combination of both. In **linear acceleration**, the force passes through the center of the head, accelerating the head in a straight line. In **rotational** or **angular acceleration**, the force does not pass through the center of the head and, thus, the head will rotate about its center. Impacts to the front and back of the head tend to produce linear acceleration while those to the side produce a combination of linear and angular. The combination of linear and angular acceleration of the head in the coronal plane, for example, side impact, is more injurious to the brain than similar acceleration in the sagittal plane (frontal impact) as angular acceleration sets up shear strains in the brain.[28–30]

Soft-Tissue Injuries

When the head is either struck with or against an object, including the ground, the initial injuries are incurred by the scalp and encompass the usual skin injuries previously discussed – lacerations, contusions or abrasions. Since the scalp is a very vascular, lacerations can produce profuse bleeding, which may, under the most unusual circumstances, be life-threatening.

Fractures

Fractures of the Face

Fractures of the mandible, maxilla, zygoma and zygomatic arch are produced predominantly by assaults and motor vehicle accidents. All can be fractured by a single blow. Maxillary fractures can be placed in five categories (Figure 5.20):

1. Dentoalveolar
2. LeFort I
3. LeFort II
4. LeFort III
5. Sagittal

In **dentoalveolar fractures**, direct force applied anteriorly or laterally causes separation of a fragment of the mandible. This fragment generally contains a number of teeth. The **LeFort I fracture** is a transverse fracture of the maxilla, above the apices of the teeth, through the nasal septum and maxillary sinuses, the palatine bone and the sphenoid bone. The **LeFort II** (the "pyramidal") fracture has the same path posteriorly. As it proceeds anteriorly, however, it curves upward near the zygomatic-maxillary suture, through the inferior orbit rim onto the orbital floor, through the medial orbital wall and across the nasal bones and septum. The **LeFort III** is a high transverse fracture of the maxilla that goes through the nasofrontal suture, through the medial orbital wall and frontozygomatic suture, across the arch and through the sphenoid. **Sagittal fractures** run in a sagittal plane through the maxilla.

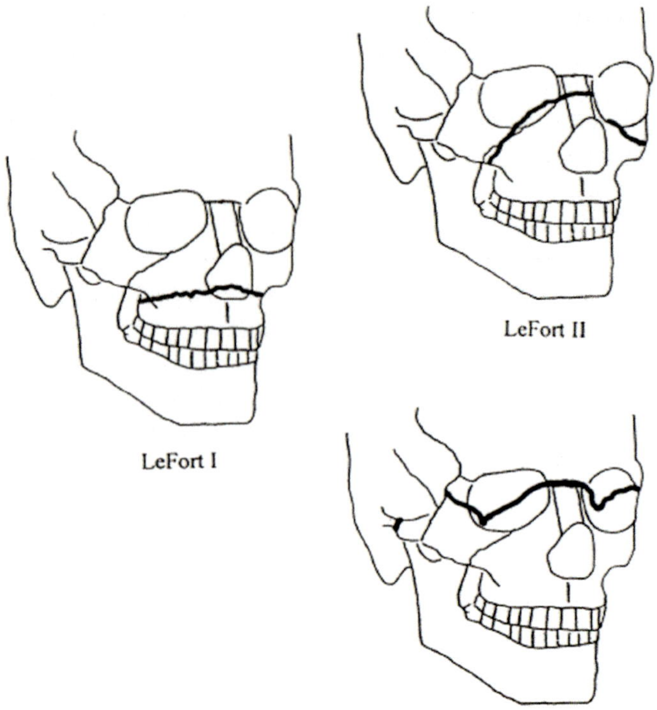

Figure 5.20 Fractures of the face: LeFort I, LeFort II and LeFort III.

Skull Fractures

In any fall or blow to the head, the degree of deformation of the skull, the generation of a fracture and the extent of any fracture produced are dependent on a number of factors:

- The amount of hair
- The thickness of the scalp
- The configuration and thickness of the skull
- The elasticity of the bone at the point of impact
- The shape, weight and consistency of the object impacting or impacted by the head
- The velocity at which either the blow was delivered or the head strikes the object

The amount of energy required for production of a single linear fracture from a low-velocity blow or fall depends on whether the head strikes a hard unyielding surface or a relatively soft yielding surface. With a yielding surface, a large proportion of the impacting energy is transferred to the surface by way of the deformation of the surface, thus decreasing the amount of energy available to cause head injury. In the case of a hard unyielding surface, for example, a steel plate, in which there is essentially no energy transferred to the impacted surface, it takes approximately 33.3–75 ft. lb of energy to produce a single linear fracture.[31,32] This energy is absorbed in 0.0012 s. The first 0.0006 s is used in deforming and compressing the scalp and the residual 0.0006 s is used in deforming the bone.[31] The amount of energy necessary to produce multiple linear fractures or stellate fractures is almost identical to that needed to produce a single linear fracture, with only a slight increase required.[31] In fact, the same amount of force necessary to produce a single linear fracture could produce a stellate fracture in another area of the skull. That skull fractures commonly occur when individuals fall on the back of the head becomes obvious when one realizes that a free fall of 6 ft. for a head weighing 10 lb gives an available energy of 60 ft. lb, well within the range necessary to produce a linear fracture of the skull if it impacts an unyielding surface. The velocity of the head at the time of impact is approximately 20 ft./s or 13.5 mph.[31]

If a head strikes or is struck by a deformable object, not all the energy possessed by either the object or head will be available for deformation of the skull. At impact, the object will tend to indent and deform so as to wrap itself around the head. Thus, the energy delivered is no longer in a localized focus but is dispersed over a considerable area, reducing the possibility of a skull fracture. Linear or comminuted fractures of the skull produced by impaction of a head and a relatively soft and flexible object, such as the instrument panel of a motor vehicle, require kinetic energy levels at impact of between 268 and 581 ft. lb.[32] Impact velocities are from 43 ft./s (29 mph) to 65 ft./s (45 mph). In one test, a human head impacting at 577 ft. lb of energy did not fracture.[32] The fractures produced with a head impacting an unyielding surface (in which 33.3–75 ft. lb of energy is needed to fracture the skull) are essentially identical to fractures produced with heads impacting a yielding surface and requiring 268–581 ft. lb to fracture.[32] Thus, the magnitude of energy necessary to produce a skull fracture is approximately 33.3–75 ft. lb, with other energy being utilized to deform and dent objects it impacts.

One point that has been stressed by numerous authors and should be repeated is that there is no absolute correlation between the severity of brain injury and the production of a linear skull fracture. Skull fractures can occur without any significant or detectable brain injury or any impairment of consciousness. Conversely, death may result from extensive brain injury without a skull fracture.

Simple linear fractures are typically seen in low-velocity impacts with a large area of contact between the head and impacting object. A fall to the pavement is the best example. With the increased velocity and, thus, greater force, one may have a series of complete or incomplete **circular fractures** encircling the impact point (Figure 5.21).

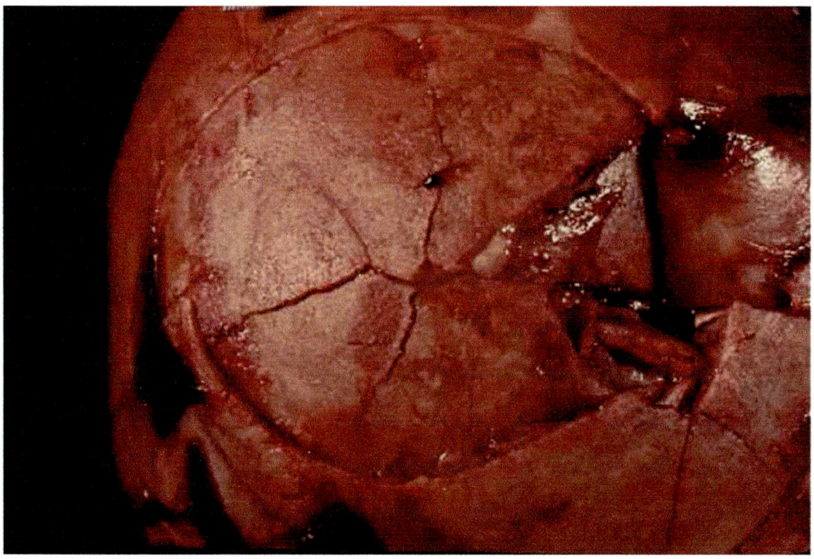

Figure 5.21 Circular fracture of cranial vault from fall on to top of head.

These fractures result from failure of the external surface of the bone at the edge of the in-bent area, due to extreme inbending at the time of impact.[33] If the velocity and energy of impact are increased even more, one gets **stellate fractures**, where there is depression of the bone at the point of impact. The severe inbending about the impact site produces fractures on the inner surface that radiate out from the site of the blow.[33] The concentric or circular fracture lines may be incomplete in that they stop at a linear fracture, indicating that the linear fracture preceded the concentric fracture. The opposite may also occur with the linear fractures stopping at the concentric fracture lines, which indicates that the latter preceded the former.

A **depressed skull fracture** occurs when the skull is struck with an object having a relatively large amount of kinetic energy but a small surface area, or when an object with a large amount of kinetic energy impacts only a small area of the skull. The scalp does not significantly affect the nature of the injuries to the skull. Large deformations occurring at a distance from the point of impact are no longer present.[31,33] At the point of impact, there is a depressed fracture, possibly with fragmentation. The fractures are due to failure of the inner surface of the skull secondary to the inbending. An example of this type of fracture is the circular depressed fracture of a hammer blow (Figure 5.22).

Here there are no linear fractures radiating to or from the circular depression in the skull. If there is insufficient energy to produce fractures of both the outer and inner tables of the skull, there will be a depressed fracture in the outer table, with the inner table intact. The fracture of the outer table is almost always larger than the fracture of the inner table. Most depressed fractures are compound in that there is an associated laceration of the scalp. Seizures can be a complication in a small percentage of depressed fractures.

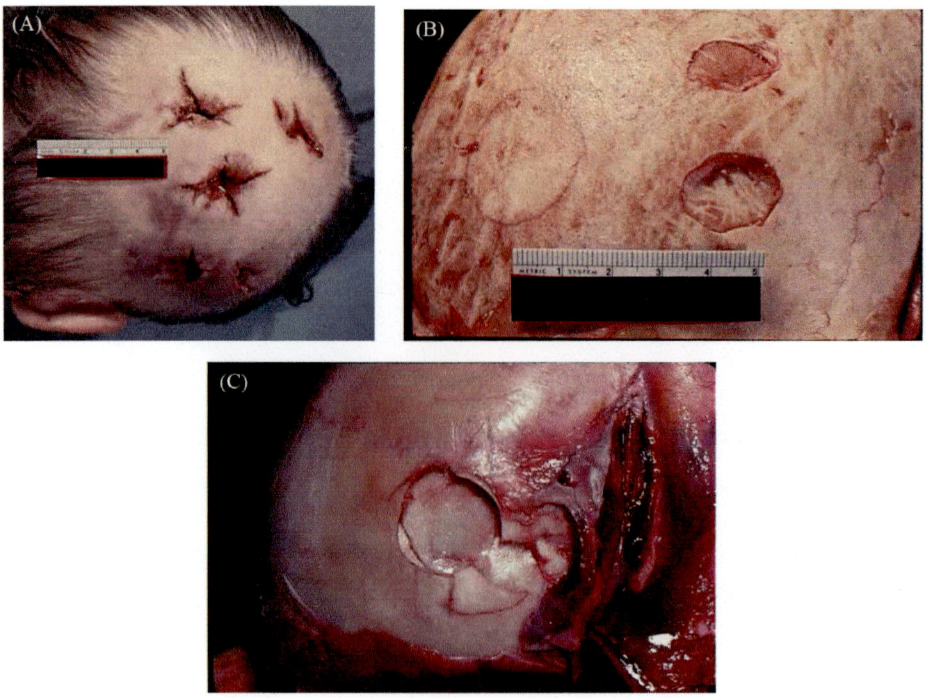

Figure 5.22 Blows to head with a hammer, with a (A) stellate lacerations of scalp and (B and C) depressed circular skull fractures.

Basilar skull fractures are quite common in forensic medicine. The base of the skull, by virtue of its construction and irregular shape, is weak. Almost any diffuse impact to the vertex of the skull will produce basilar fractures. Basilar skull fractures can occur from blows anywhere along the circumference of the skull below the cranial vault. They can run anterior-posteriorly, posterior-anteriorly, side to side or any combination of these three. Basilar skull fractures may be missed on X-rays of the skull. With a basilar fracture, intracranial passage of a nasogastric tube or nasopharyngeal airway can occur.[34]

Hinge fractures are transverse fractures of the base of the skull that completely bisects the base of the skull, creating a "hinge." The authors divide them into three categories as shown in Figure 5.23.

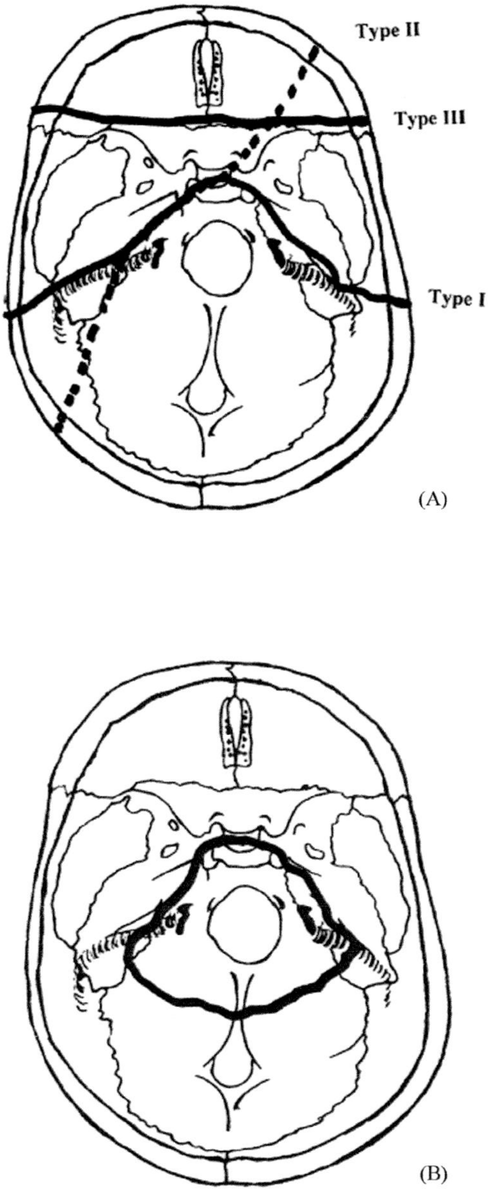

Figure 5.23 (A) Hinge fractures: types I, II and III; and (B) ring fracture.

Type I hinge fractures run in the coronal plane, extending from the lateral end of one petrous ridge, through the sella turcica, to the lateral end of the contralateral petrous ridge. Type II hinge fractures run from front to the contralateral back, passing through the sella turcica. Type III hinge fractures run from side to side in the coronal plane but do not pass through the sella turcica. *Type I hinge fractures are the most common form of transverse fractures of the base of the skull.* They have traditionally been ascribed to impacts on the side of the head and, less commonly, to impacts on the tip of the chin. In the latter instance, one would expect a laceration of the tip of the chin, though not necessarily fracture of the mandible.

Ring fractures are circular fractures of the base of the skull that surround the foramen magnum. Typically, they run from the sella turcica partly down the petrous ridges, before turning posteriorly, and then medially, joining in the posterior fossa, enclosing the foramen magnum (Figure 6.4B). They may be due to impacts on the top of the head that drive the skull downward onto the vertebral column, falls on the buttocks that drive the spine into the base of the skull and impacts to the tip of the chin. In ring fractures from impacts to the tip of the chin, almost invariably there is a laceration of the chin. Even though the force of impact is transmitted through the mandible to the base of the skull, in most instances, fractures of the mandible are not present. Experiments have revealed that more force is needed to fracture the mandible than to produce a basilar fracture.[35]

Contrecoup fractures of the anterior cranial fossae are isolated fractures of the anterior cranial fossae associated with contrecoup injuries of the brain, with the impact point on the opposite side of the skull. In a study of 171 deaths from craniocerebral trauma due to falls, Hein and Schulz found that contrecoup fractures of the anterior cranial fossae occurred in 12% of the cases.[36] All cases had fractures at the impact site, which was the occipital region. If one considered only falls where there was occipital impact, then 24% of the cases had contrecoup fractures.

It is important to understand that blows in different areas of the head can have different effects. A blow to the top of the head tends to produce a cranial vault fracture that might or might not extend into the temporal region or base of the skull. A blow in the occipital region generally produces a linear fracture of the posterior fossa; a blow to the temporoparietal region fractures through the temporal bone to the base of the skull; and a midfrontal blow produces fractures running to the orbits and sometimes into the maxilla.[31] One of the authors (VJMD) reviewed 86 cases of basilar skull fractures and found no correlation between the site of impact and generation of a hinge or ring fracture indicating that *hinge and ring fractures of the base of the skull can be produced by impacts anywhere on the circumference of the head.*

In skulls in which the sutures are not completely fused, suture lines represent areas of weakness and fractures may travel along them (**diastatic fractures**). Rarely, in infants and young children, diastatic fractures can be produced by severe cerebral edema. Thus, the authors had a case of an 18-month-old male admitted to a burn unit with burns over most of his body. He was never conscious and died a week after admission. At autopsy, there was separation of the coronal, sagittal and lambdoidal sutures due to the edema (Figure 5.24).

Fracture Dynamics

Whenever a head is either struck with or strikes an object having a broad flat surface area, the skull at the point of impact flattens out to conform to the shape of the surface against

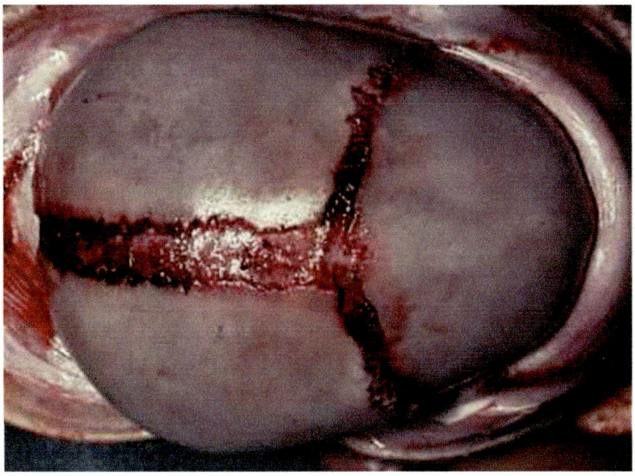

Figure 5.24 An 18-month-old child with separation of sutures due to severe cerebral edema.

which it impacts. As the skull is flattened and bent inward, adjacent to, but more distant areas are bent outward by a wave of deformation consisting of the central area of in bending and the peripheral area of out bending (Figure 5.25).[31,33]

This out bending can occur at a considerable distance from the point of impact. If a fracture of the skull occurs, the fracture begins at the point of impact and radiates to the point of out bending.

Gurdjian and coauthors conducted a number of studies on blunt force fracture propagation concluding that fractures began at the point of out bending and ran to the point of initial impact, the point of in bending.[33] Gurdjian's results are used to suggest that the point of impact was at a location other than the point of impact fracture epicenter. However, this

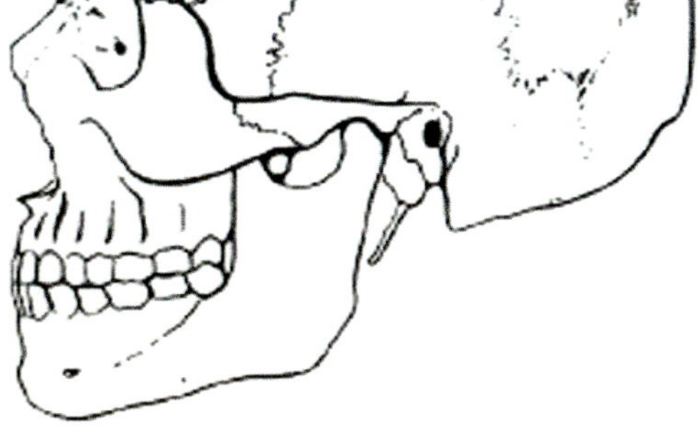

Figure 5.25 Indenting of skull at point of impact with outward bending at periphery.

theory has been disproven by Kroman et al.'s follow-up study[37] using current biomechanics research and technology. Specifically, the relationship of impact site and fracture patterning was tested using cadaver heads. Their results demonstrated that fractures radiate from the point of impact.

Fracture pattern recognition and interpretation are essential components of forensic pathology and antropology. In many cases, accurate interpretation of skeletal fractures may be the only objective means of determining cause and manner of death. In postmortem trauma assessment, fracture interpretation aids in identifying impact site location, sequencing blows and establishing the characteristics of the object responsible for injury. Blunt force trauma is one of the most common and complex areas of skeletal trauma. The cranium is often affected in blunt force trauma, and injury patterns can be complicated and difficult to understand. Correct cranial fracture interpretation provides information regarding the number of blows to the head, exact location of impact and size or type of object used to inflict the destructive force.

Neck Fractures

Cervical spine fractures are not uncommon in high-energy traumatic events such as motor vehicle collisions or falls from a height. Cervical spine injuries occur in approximately 3% of blunt force injury patients and are often lethal due to their high association with underlying spinal cord injury. Ninety percent of injuries to the cervical spine result in spinal cord trauma.[38]

The cervical vertebrae are divided into the upper, C1–C2, and the lower, C3–C7, vertebrae. The occiput, C1 and C2 form a functional unit bound together by ligamentous bands. There is no intervertebral disk between the occiput and C1, and C1 and C2. The vertebral arteries pass through the foramina of the transverse processes from C1 to C6 and are, thus, subject to injury from lateral fractures.

Atlanto-occipital (occipito-cervical) dislocation due to craniocervical ligamentous separation is an extremely severe injury commonly associated with death. Dislocation may be anterior, posterior, vertical and lateral. This injury is commonly seen in pedestrians struck by motor vehicles and in the occupants of motor vehicles involved in crashes. In a study of 100 consecutive deaths from motor vehicle accidents, 24 had cervical spinal injuries, with 8 having atlanto-occipital dislocation.[39] The other injuries involved the first cervical vertebra in three cases; the second in nine cases; the third to the seventh in four cases. Of the eight individuals with atlanto-occipital dislocation, only three had osseous injury (two involved a condyle, one a fracture of C1). Adams studied 12 cases of atlanto-occipital dislocation occurring secondary to traffic accidents.[40] Five had osseous injuries (two of the occipital condyles; three of C1). Nine of the 12 cases had pontomedullary brainstem lacerations, four had midbrain lacerations.

The atlas (C1) is a ring-like structure between the occipital condyles and the axis (C2). Isolated fractures are usually not associated with neurological injury. Fractures can be classified based on the location and stability of the fractures. Anterior arch injuries are usually due to hyperextension and may vary in severity from minimally displaced to comminuted to unstable; lateral mass fractures are due to lateral loading; posterior arch fractures are caused by hyperextension together with axial loading; burst fractures by axial loading.[41]

Fractures of the axis (C2) involve the dens, the neural arch or the body of the vertebra. Neurological injury from fractures of the dens is rare. If there is injury, it can vary from minor to fatal. Odontoid fractures are the most frequent spinal fracture in children below

8 years of age and adults above 70 years. They may be caused by falls on the head. Excluding the dens, the most common fracture is that of the neural arch between the superior and inferior articular processes, the "hangman's fracture." The most common mechanism is axial loading with extension or flexion. It is seen commonly in motor vehicle accidents and falls.

Less dramatic, and more difficult to detect than atlanto-occipital dislocations, are atlantoaxial (C1–C2) dislocations. Adams studied 14 traffic fatalities with C1–C2 dislocation.[42] Thirteen had sprains of the atlantoaxial facet joints; one a healed C1 fracture. Six of the 13 (2 children and 4 older individuals) had odontoid fractures. In sharp contrast to atlanto-occipital dislocations, there was only one pontomedullary laceration and two lacerations of the brainstem.

Approximately 50% of cervical spine injuries occur between C3 and C7[43] and these fractures can be divided into five types (Figure 5.26).[41] They vary in severity from mild to severe and all can cause spinal cord injury.

Flexion-distraction: a flexion injury characterized by disruption of the posterior ligaments with anterior displacement of a vertebra.

Flexion-compression: a more severe version of the flexion-distraction injury. There is disruption of the posterior ligaments with anterior and inferior displacement of a vertebra with compression and fracturing of the adjacent vertebra.

Extension-distraction: extension injuries that are the opposite of flexion-distraction injuries. There are no fractures of the vertebrae, but rather anterior disruption at the discs as they are pulled apart with posterior displacement of vertebrae.

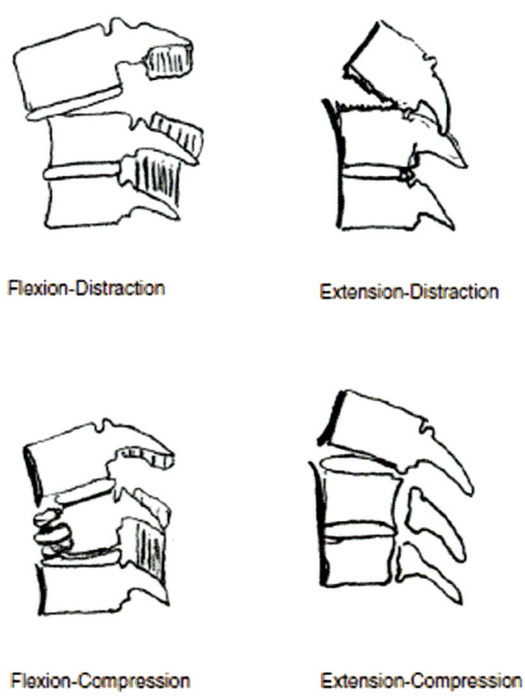

Figure 5.26 Fractures of lower cervical vertebrae.

Extension-compression: a more severe form of extension-distraction with fracture of the posterior elements of the vertebral bodies and increased anterior separation at the disk space.

Vertical compression: involves compression and fracturing of a vertebra.

Direct Brain Injury – Contusions and Lacerations

Contusions

Contusions are the most frequently encountered traumatic lesion of the brain. Contusions are more severe when associated with skull fractures and are less severe in brains with DAI.[42] Cortical contusions consist of areas of hemorrhage and necrosis that originate at the moment of impact. Occasionally, hemorrhage may be present without necrosis or necrosis with little or no hemorrhage.[42] The contusion hemorrhages are located at or near the crest of a gyrus, sparing the sulci.[42] They are usually multiple in number, streak-like and densely arranged (Figure 5.27) though occasionally solitary. If the hemorrhage is close to the surface of the cortex, there may be overlying focal subarachnoid hemorrhage (SAH).

If death is not immediate, the bleeding into the contusion may continue. The amount of bleeding depends on the type (small artery, capillary, vein) and caliber of the vessel injured as well as if there is any adjacent necrosis. If necrosis is present, the contusions develop a wedge-shaped appearance with the base of the wedge at the crest and the point toward the white matter. The area of necrosis is usually delineated by the hemorrhage, though the exact extent of the necrosis may not become clear for 10–12 h. If there is profuse

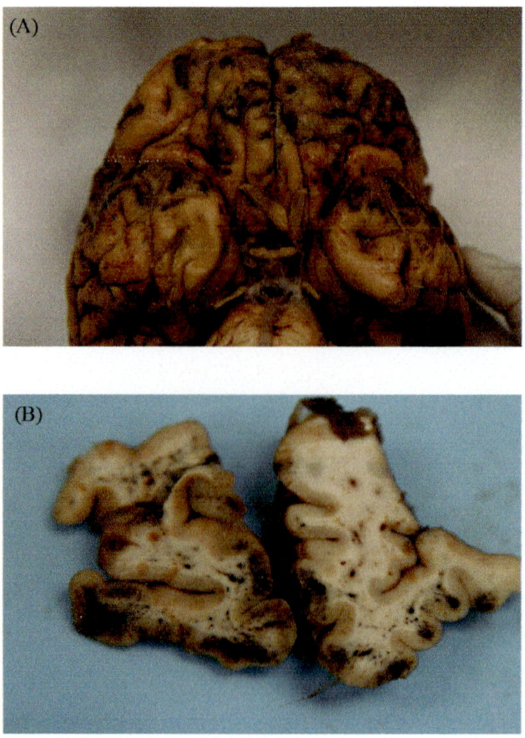

Figure 5.27 Contusions of cerebral cortex (A and B).

bleeding, the areas of hemorrhage may expand into the white matter or subarachnoid space, essentially forming an area of intracerebral hemorrhage. If the necrosis is purely ischemic, without hemorrhage, the lesion becomes visible grossly 10–12 h after the injury as an area of swollen gelantinous parenchyma.[44,45] Microscopically, it becomes visible at 3–5 h. Over time, contusions are reabsorbed with resultant golden-brown areas of gliosis.

Contusions are most often found in the frontal and temporal lobes of the brain. Less commonly, contusions are present on the lateral and ventral surfaces of the cerebral hemispheres. Contusions are not usually seen in infants. Rather, one sees lacerations involving the white matter, most commonly in the frontal and temporal lobes.[44,46] *Contusions may be absent in severe open fractures of the skull, with massive lacerations or even evisceration of the brain.* Thus, in jumps and falls from great heights, massive lacerations of the brain are often unaccompanied by contusions.

There are six types of contusions.[44] The first three are the coup-type of contusions:

1. **Coup contusions** occur at the site of impact and are due to the inbending bone snapping back (rebounding), inflicting tensile force injuries to the brain.[48] Coup contusions are less common than the second type of contusion.
2. **Contrecoup contusions** occur in the brain at locations directly opposite to the point of impact (Figure 5.28).

   They are tensile force injuries due to the brain rebounding backward from the skull following impact.[47] They are seen most commonly in the frontal poles, orbital gyri and temporal lobes. Contrecoup contusions are classically associated with falls. As their name indicates (*contre* being French for opposite), they develop opposite to the point of impact. Thus, an individual falling on the left side of the back of his head will have contrecoup contusions of the right frontal and temporal lobes. A fall onto the top of the head would result in contusions of the ventral surface of the cerebral hemispheres. Contrecoup contusions are virtually never seen in the occipital lobes, in spite of the frequent occurrence of individuals' falling on their faces. While usually, one has only contrecoup injuries following a fall, and no coup injuries, on occasion, an individual might have both coup and contrecoup contusions. When this occurs, the contrecoup contusions will always be much more extensive and severe than the coup contusions.

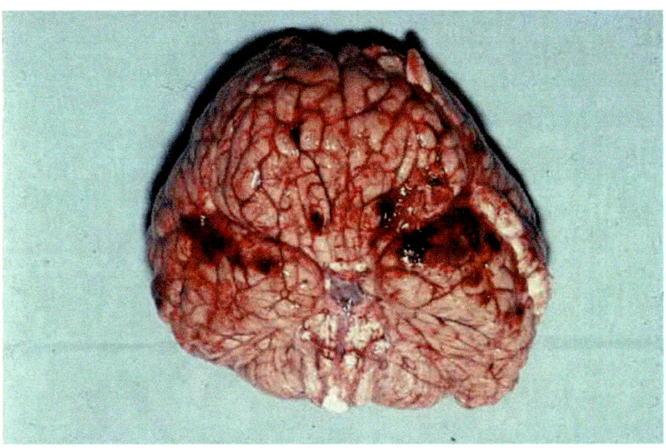

Figure 5.28 Contrecoup contusions of temporal poles due to fall on back of head.

3. **Intermediary coup contusions** are hemorrhagic contusions in the deep structures of the brain, for example, the white matter, basal ganglia, corpus callosum, brainstem and along the line of impact – that is, between the location of the coup and contrecoup points. They are said to be seen only in falls.[44] Intermediary contusions should not be mistaken for gliding contusions.

With blows to the head, if contusions are produced, they should be only coup contusions. Occasionally, however, the coup contusions are accompanied by contrecoup contusions (Figure 5.29). In these instances, the contrecoup contusions will be less extensive and less severe than the coup contusions.

The usual teaching is that, with blows to the head, if there are no coup contusions, there are no contrecoup contusions. This may not be completely correct. The authors have seen rare cases in which individuals have been struck on the head and there were small contrecoup contusions, but no coup contusions. There is always the possibility in these cases that, after such individuals were struck, they collapsed, striking their heads and incurring a contrecoup contusion from the fall.

The most important fact to remember about contusions is the relation of coup and contrecoup contusions to falls and blows. A fall on the head will produce contrecoup contusions opposite the point of impact and no or very minor coup contusions at the point of impact. A blow to the head may result in coup contusions and no or minor contrecoup contusions.

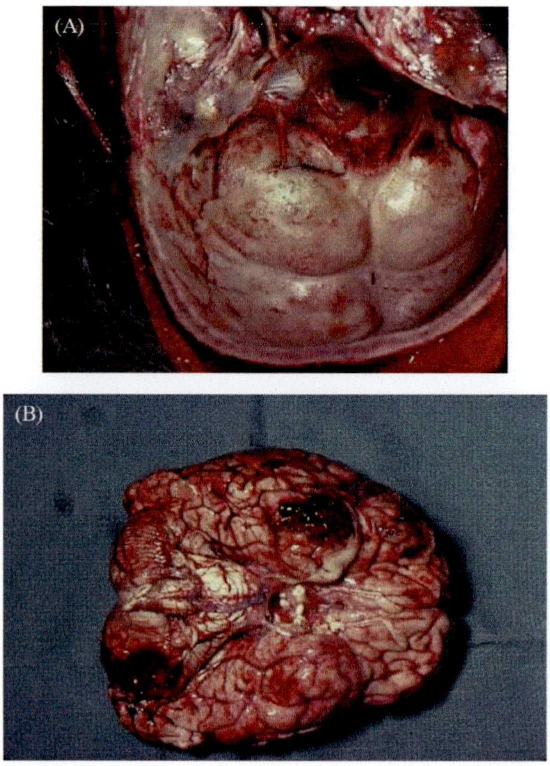

Figure 5.29 (A) Fracture of skull in the left posterior fossa with, (B) coup contusions of left cerebellar hemisphere and contrecoup contusions of right temporal pole. Eight-day survival.

The last three contusion types are as follows:

4. **Fracture contusions** are associated with fractures of the skull. They do not necessarily bear any relation to the point of impact, as the fracture line can be some distance from this point.
5. **Gliding contusions** are focal hemorrhages located in the cortex and underlying white matter of the dorsal surfaces of the cerebral hemispheres, principally in the frontal region. They are seen in falls and motor vehicle accidents.[44,48] They are independent of the site and direction of impact and are often found in association with DAI.[48]
6. **Herniation contusions** are caused by impaction of the medial portion of the temporal lobes against the edge of the tentorium, or the cerebellar tonsils against the foramen magnum. These are also independent of the site and direction of impact.

Traumatic intracerebral hematomas are discrete collections of blood within the cerebral parenchyma that are not in contact with the surface of the brain.[49] They are principally located in the white matter of the frontotemporal lobes and are caused by impact. They are said to differ from hemorrhagic intermediary coup contusions in that they are well demarcated, homogeneous collections of blood, in contrast to contusions that are blood and contused cerebral parenchyma. In the authors' opinion, this distinction is artifactual and may just reflect a longer survival time by the intracerebral hematomas with continued bleeding. One of the most interesting aspects of intracerebral hematomas is that they can appear hours to days after the injury.[50–52] There have been numerous cases where a computerized tomography (CT) scan on admission has shown no intracerebral hematomas, but subsequent CT scans, taken several hours to several days after admission, revealed some. In some instances, their development has been followed by successive CT scans. Primary intracerebral hemorrhages involving the basal ganglia are found in approximately 10% of fatal head injuries. They are caused by deceleration/acceleration forces and are commonly found in association with DAI and gliding contusions.[49] In 90% of the cases, the cause of the injury was either a motor vehicle accident or a fall. In the study by Adams et al., 43 of 63 patients had small (less than 20 mm) hematomas.[48]

Lacerations

Lacerating and penetrating wounds of the brain are most commonly due to fractures of the skull and may occur even in the presence of an intact scalp. Lacerations of the corpus callosum or septum pellucidum may occur due to blunt trauma to the head without any fractures of the skull (Figure 5.30).

This latter phenomenon appears to be more common in younger individuals, who have more elastic bone. Lacerations of the brain may show little and even no bleeding around them. This is apparently due to vasospasm of arteries, which can maintain a bloodless field for as long as 1 h.[44]

In contrast to adults, *impact trauma in infants (5 months or younger) does not produce cortical contusions,* but rather, grossly visible lacerations in the cerebral white matter and microscopic lacerations of the outermost layer of the cortex, which run parallel to the surface of the brain.[46] The lacerations of the cerebral white matter occasionally extend through the cortex or wall of the ventricles or both. They are most often present in the orbital

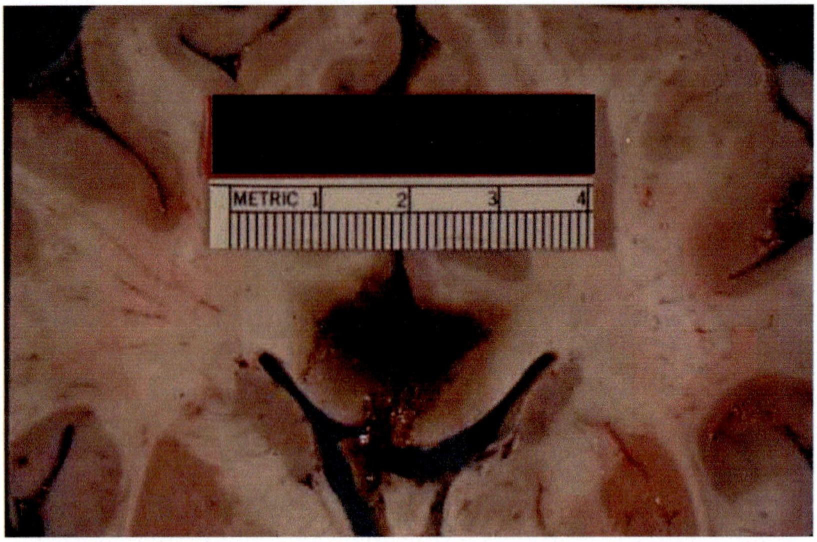

Figure 5.30 A 33-year-old male with transaction of corpus callosum. Impact to top of head. No skull fracture.

and temporal lobes and in the first and second frontal convolutions. Minimal bleeding is present in the lacerations and sometimes in the adjacent white matter. The earliest cellular reaction is seen at 36 h and is obvious by 72 h. Unlike contusions in the adult brain, the location and distribution of the white matter lacerations cannot be used to indicate whether the injuries were from a fall or a blow.

Violent hyperextension of the head and neck can cause laceration at the junction of the pons and medulla (Figure 5.31).[53,54]

These injuries can range from tears and hemorrhages in the pyramids at the junction of the medulla oblongata and pons to avulsion of the brainstem at the pontomedullary junction.[53] They are commonly associated with fractures of the base of the skull and fractures of the upper cervical vertebrae.[40,54] Occasionally, the only evidence of injury may be SAH present over the brainstem. While death is almost always immediate, partial laceration is sometimes associated with survival of a few hours. While generally ascribed only to hyperextension, some individuals feel that these injuries can be a form of DAI due to angular acceleration of the head.[54]

Intracranial Hemorrhage

Intracranial hemorrhage has a high mortality rate with the majority of the deaths occurring within the first 24 h.[55] It is a general term that refers to any hemorrhage within the cranial vault, including epidural, subdural, subarachnoid and intraparenchymal hemorrhage.

The dura is a gray membrane of connective tissue firmly adherent to the inner surface of the skull. Arteries run along the inner surface of the dura at its point of attachment with the skull. The space between the skull and dura is the epidural space and that beneath the dura the subdural space. It is important to note that these "spaces" are actually only potential spaces as the dura is usually tightly adherent to the underlying skull and the brain abuts the undersurface of the dura. The brain, in turn, is enclosed in two thin, transparent

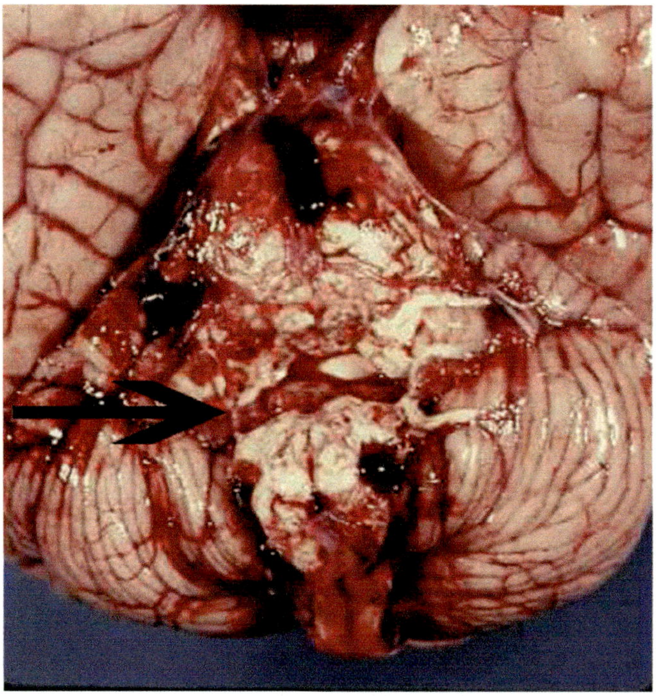

Figure 5.31 Complete avulsion of brainstem at pontomedullary junction.

membranes: the inner pia and the outer arachnoid. The subarachnoid space is between the arachnoid and pial membranes and contains the cerebrospinal fluid (CSF). CSF is produced by the choroid plexus that reaches the subarachnoid space through the foramen of Magendie of the fourth ventricle.

Each type of hemorrhage has different etiologies, including some natural causes; thus, it is recommended that the general term of "Intracranial hemorrhage" be avoided in the forensic setting. Hemorrhage should be described using the more specific terminology for each, as this assists in the understanding of the mechanisms involved and in delineating traumatic from nontraumatic etiology.

Epidural Hemorrhage

Epidural hematomas are primary impact injuries. They are relatively infrequent and are seen most commonly in falls and traffic accidents. They are infrequent in the elderly and the very young (less than 2 years of age) due to strong adherence of the dura to the skull in both these age groups. Epidural hematomas are caused by trauma to the skull and the meningeal vessels (principally the arteries) at the point of impact. At impact, the skull is bent inward, with stripping of the dura and laceration of meningeal vessels. A fracture is virtually always present at this point (90–95% of the time) in association with the epidural hematoma.

The area of avulsion from the dura is extended by arterial bleeding that strips the dura from the bone, permitting accumulation of blood. The inability of the venous system to generate sufficient pressure to strip dura from bone accounts for the infrequency of epidural hematomas following venous injury. Epidural hematomas unassociated with fractures are uncommon. These usually occur in children who have very elastic bones, such that the dura can be avulsed from the bone without fracture. In most such cases, bleeding is minor.[44,56]

Epidural hematomas usually have a thick, disk-shaped appearance (Figure 5.32B, C).

They are virtually always unilateral. Most epidural hematomas result from fractures of the squamous-temporal bone, with laceration of the middle meningeal artery (Figure 5.32A). Thus, most epidural hematomas are in the temporal region. Less commonly, there are lacerations of the anterior and posterior meningeal arteries with frontotemporal and parieto-occipital hematomas, respectively. Epidural hematomas caused by venous bleeding are the result of injury to the diploic veins, middle meningeal veins and dural sinuses.

Symptoms from an epidural hematoma usually occur 4–8 h after injury. There is a lucid interval prior to the development of severe symptoms in approximately one-third of patients. Occasionally, an individual will develop an epidural hematoma so rapidly that death will occur in as little as 30 min.[53] Death is caused by displacement of the brain with compression of the brainstem. With large fractures, there may be decompression of the epidural hematoma and survival.

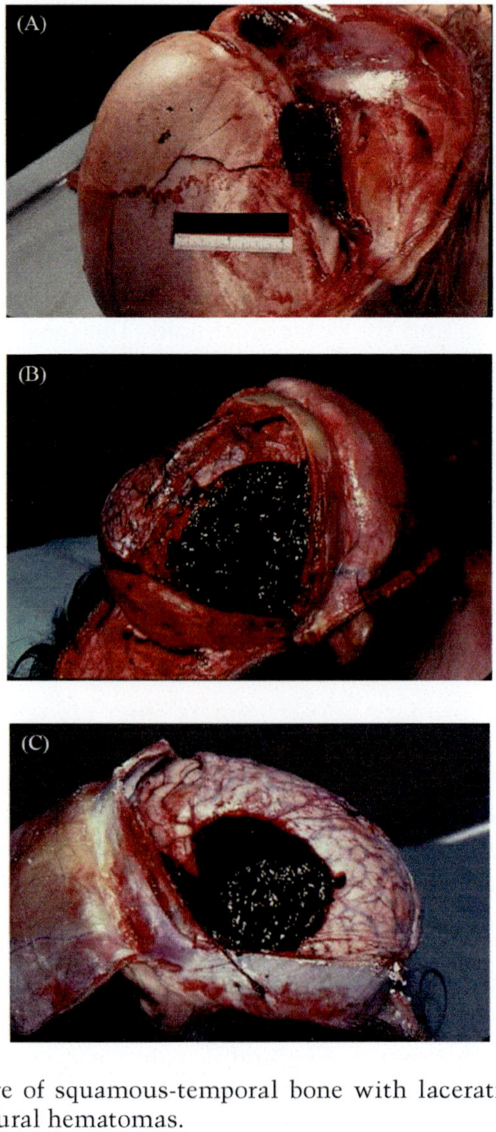

Figure 5.32 (A) Fracture of squamous-temporal bone with laceration of middle meningeal artery and (B and C) epidural hematomas.

Chronic epidural hematomas are rare.[57] They produce their signs and symptoms over a lengthy period of time. These lesions might lie quiescent for many days and then suddenly bring about death. It is hypothesized that chronic epidurals are more commonly associated with tears of venous rather than arterial structures. However, in some cases, tears in meningeal arteries have been demonstrated. Frequently, however, no point of bleeding is found. Symptoms are usually present from the time of the trauma, though they may be very minor in nature, such as headache or nausea. Drowsiness may or may not be present. Chronic epidural hematomas may or may not be associated with fractures of the skull. They are seen most commonly in older children and young adults. This is thought to be due to the ease with which the dura can be stripped from the skull in such individuals. Generally, an epidural hematoma is considered chronic when more than 48–72 h passes from injury to identification. In some individuals, the interval has been as long as 18 days.

In fire-related deaths, one can often see a postmortem epidural hematoma that is not related to trauma. In these cases, the epidural hematoma seen is a heat-induced artifact. The heat causes the dura to contract resulting in blood exudation from the venous sinuses.[58] The exuded blood then coagulates in the heat. These hematomas typically have a deep dark red color and are friable in nature.

Subdural Hematomas

The subdural hematoma is the most common lethal injury associated with head trauma (Figure 5.33).

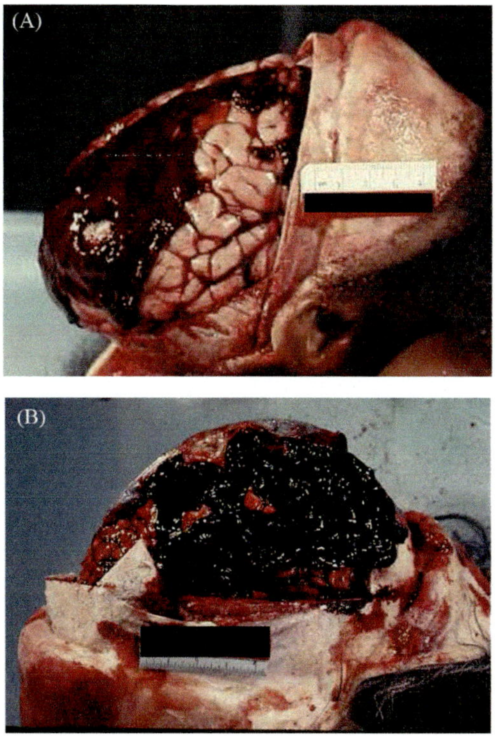

Figure 5.33 (A and B) Subdural hematoma.

The high mortality associated with subdural hematomas is due in part to associated brain damage.[49] Since a large number of subdural hematomas are caused by falls, it is not uncommon to find contrecoup contusions in association with subdural hematomas. Unlike epidural hematomas, subdural hematomas are often not associated with a fracture of the skull and can occur in the absence of cerebral contusions or any other visible brain injuries. Subdural hematomas are more common in the elderly and alcoholics.

Clinically, approximately 72% of all subdural hematomas are due to falls and homicidal assaults, with motor vehicle accidents accounting for about 24%.[59] This is in contrast to DAI, where approximately 89% of cases are due to motor vehicle accidents and only 10% to falls and assaults.

Subdural hematomas can be acute, subacute or chronic. Acute subdural hematomas manifest themselves clinically within 72 h of injury; subacute between 3 days and 2–3 weeks and chronic more than 3 weeks after injury. Subdural hematomas are caused by the stretching and tearing of the parasagittal bridging veins that drain the surface of the cerebral hemispheres into the dural venous sinuses. Large hematomas are able to form because the central venous pressure is usually greater than the intracranial pressure, allowing the veins to continue to bleed.[60] Bleeding will eventually stop when the blood coagulates and the pressure of the hematoma cavity equalizes with the venous pressure.

These injuries occur after the head impacts a hard surface and the brain is accelerated. This rapid acceleration causes the tearing of the bridging veins. The more rapid the acceleration or deceleration, and the shorter the time of acceleration or deceleration, the more likely one will have a subdural hematoma rather than DAI.[30,49,59] The reason that subdural hematomas are less common in motor vehicle accidents, in contrast to DAI, is that in a motor vehicle accident, the head typically strikes a yielding or energy-absorbing surface, thus extending the time interval in which the acceleration or deceleration occurs. This reduces the probability of a subdural hematoma's occurring, because it requires a large acceleration or deceleration over a short time. It does, however, predispose the brain to DAI.

Part of the lethality associated with subdural hematomas is because of injury to the cerebral parenchyma by the same acceleration/deceleration force that produces the acute subdural hematoma.[49] This acceleration or deceleration force may also induce brain injury of the DAI type. The severity of this injury would vary from totally recoverable to such that, regardless of the subdural hematoma, death would occur.

There is no consistent relation between the presence or location of skull fractures and the presence of subdural hematomas. A fracture might be either on the same or contralateral side to the hematoma or may not even be present (which is more common in elderly individuals). Subdural hematomas may be on the same or contralateral side as the point of impact or bilateral.[44] Subdural hematomas can occur without apparent head injury or with very minor injury in the elderly and in individuals on anticoagulants or who have bleeding dyscrasias. Occasionally, a cerebral aneurysm or intracerebral hemorrhage will rupture into the subdural space, producing a subdural hematoma.

In subdural hematomas, the onset of symptoms is usually rapid. In elderly individuals, however, symptoms may develop over days. There may be a relapse of symptoms secondary to recurrent hemorrhage. In an adult, a rapidly developing (acute) subdural hematoma becomes life-threatening when it reaches approximately 50 mL in size. With slow bleeding, a considerably larger subdural hematoma can be tolerated without symptoms or serious side effects. In infants, a smaller volume is life-threatening. Renewed bleeding into an old subdural hematoma can occur. It can be either "spontaneous" or the result of new trauma to the head. It originates from the sinusoidal vessels in the outer neo-membrane formed during the organization of the initial hematoma. The rapid development of a subdural hematoma with mass displacement of the brain with or without generalized cerebral edema may result in compression of the brainstem and development of secondary (Duret) hemorrhage. These may develop in as little as 30 min after trauma.

In subdural hematomas, the blood presses on both the crests and depths of the gyri so that the cerebral convolutions retain their normal contours. The hematoma, however, causes displacement of the cerebral hemispheres with flattening of the convolutions of the opposite hemisphere as they are pressed against the dura and bone. If rebleeding occurs within the sac formed by an organized subdural hematoma, the convolutions on the side of bleeding will become flattened as the fibrous membrane presses on the crests of the gyri.

If a person does not immediately die from a subdural hematoma, the hematoma will gradually become encapsulated by cells from the dura. The arachnoid does not participate in this encapsulation. Therefore, the capsule is attached to the dura and not the arachnoid. When formed, this sac of blood will press on the underlying gyri, flattening them, deforming the surface of the brain immediately underneath this sac. There is, however, no shifting of the hemisphere toward the other side, which is seen in the acute non-organized subdural hematoma.

Organization of a subdural hematoma follows a protracted course.[44] The subdural space has only a limited absorptive capacity; thus, a subdural hematoma is removed by a process of organization initiated by the dura. For the first few days immediately following a subdural bleed, the clot is not adherent to the dura. At about 4–5 days, the clot begins to become adherent at multiple sites.

About 24 h after the formation of the subdural hematoma, a layer of fibrin is deposited on the dura beneath the subdural hematoma. Fibroblastic activity starts at the junction with the dura by 36 h with a layer of fibroblasts 2–5 cells thick present after 4–5 days.[44] Invasion of the subdural hematoma by capillaries and fibroblasts is evident by 5–10 days. Hemosiderin-laden macrophages are obvious. Erythrocytes begin to lake. By 8 days, a membrane 12–14-cell thick is present on the dura. The neocapillaries in the membrane are the source for rebleeding into the subdural hematoma. The arachnoid surface of the subdural hematoma is initially coated only by fibrin. The membrane enclosing the arachnoid surface of the hematoma begins to form in about 14 days, at which time the dural membrane is one-third to one-half the thickness of the dura. By 3–4 weeks after injury, the hematoma is covered by a membrane of fibrous tissue that grows inward from the edges of the clot. By 4–5 weeks, the arachnoid membrane has half the thickness of the dura, with the dural surface equal in thickness to the dura. The clot is completely liquefied and hemosiderin-laden macrophages are present in the membranes. At 1–3 months, the membrane is hyalinized on both its inner and outer aspects, with large capillaries invading the clot. This goes on to eventual complete resorption, with only a residual gold-colored membrane adherent to the dura.

Some individuals do not develop significant symptoms of a subdural hematoma for weeks to months after head injury. The resultant hematoma is a **chronic subdural hematoma**. In this entity, instead of the initial acute subdural hematoma's becoming organized and then smaller as it is reabsorbed, it begins to enlarge. This continues until the chronic subdural hematoma produces sufficient symptomology.

The victims of chronic subdural hematomas tend to be either infants younger than 6 months of age or the elderly.[49,59] Both have cranial cavities that can accommodate the slow accumulation of large quantities of blood. In the case of infants, this is due to incomplete fusion of bony plates; in the elderly, increased intracranial space due to brain atrophy. In infants, chronic subdural hematomas may result in enlargement of the head. Adults with chronic subdurals often tend to be alcoholics. Because of the prolonged time between trauma and symptoms, in a significant percentage of individuals with chronic subdural hematomas, no history of trauma can be elicited. Chronic subdural hematomas are rarely seen in medicolegal offices.

The etiology of chronic subdural hematomas is generally thought to be rebleeding from thin-walled sinusoidal blood vessels in the neo-membrane of a resolving acute subdural hematoma. Lee et al., however, feel that most chronic subdurals originate as subdural hygromas.[61] A **subdural hygroma** is an accumulation of spinal fluid in the subdural space.[49,61] Trauma to the brain causes effusion of spinal fluid through the arachnoid, with the development of a hygroma. A small amount of bleeding may also be present, giving the fluid a xanthochromic color. Hygromas can also develop secondary to meningitis. If the hygroma, instead of being reabsorbed, continues to grow, it can produce the same space-occupying effects as a subdural hematoma.

The appearance of chronic subdural hematomas can vary with age. Most consist of an outer, gelatinous, membrane covering red-brown thick hemolyzed blood, often described as having a "motor oil" appearance. Over time, the blood will eventually completely resorb leaving a yellow, rust-colored stain of the overlying firm, fibrotic membrane.

Subarachnoid Hemorrhage

SAH may occur due to natural, accidental, homicidal, suicidal and/or undetermined causes. As discussed in Chapter 3, the majority of nontraumatic SAH is due to ruptured cerebral aneurysms, though hypertension, cocaine use and heavy alcohol use are all risk factors. However, SAH is also the most common indicator of traumatic brain injury (TBI).[62]

SAH can be focal or diffuse, minor or severe. In very rapid deaths, SAH tends to be multifocal. In most cases, it is of a diffuse nature, overlying the cerebral hemispheres, with minimal pooling on the ventral surface of the brain. Large collections of blood in the subarachnoid space of the base of the brain are more common in natural diseases than trauma, for example, a ruptured berry aneurysm.

In some instances, SAH may be the only visible sign of trauma to the brain. Such was the case of an individual struck repeatedly about the head with the barrel of a rifle, with resultant multiple lacerations of the scalp, but no fractures of the skull. The brain showed massive SAH, but no contusions or lacerations. That SAH in itself can cause death is illustrated by deaths following rupture of a berry aneurysm or laceration of a vertebral artery. While most SAH is of venous origin, occasional cases are caused by lacerations of the vertebral artery or one of the basilar arteries of the brain.

It is possible to have massive injury to the brain with minor focal SAH, especially if death is rapid. This is seen most commonly in cases with massive mutilating injuries of the head, such as when an individual jumps several stories to the ground. There are massive, gaping, compound fractures of the skull, with partial or even complete avulsion of the brain. The brain may show spotty SAH and no contusions. The absence of contusions in such cases is common. In one case, an individual had his head caved in with a baseball bat in front of a number of witnesses. The brain showed virtually no SAH and no contusions, though there were extensive lacerations. The absence of hemorrhage following lacerations to the brain has been reported as much as 1 h after injury and is presumably due to prolonged spasm of vessels.[44] SAH may cause subsequent development of communicative hydrocephalus because of a lack of reabsorption of CSF relative to production. This is due to SAH causing scarring of the arachnoid villi, such that it impedes their ability to reabsorb CSF.

SAH is characterized by a red discoloration (blood) under the leptomeninges, which gradually changes over a period of days to a purplish-black color due to the presence of methemoglobin.[63,64] At approximately 1 week after the event, the SAH has a brownish color, though the time needed to see this color change varies with the amount of SAH, with a purplish-black color persisting longer in larger SAH. With a survival time of many weeks to months, a gradual change to rust discoloration is noted. At 6–12 months survival, unless there is an associated cortical contusion, discoloration may no longer be present after a single prior SAH event.

Microscopically, intact red blood cells are seen in the subarachnoid space in an acute SAH. Neutrophils become apparent within 1–3 days of survival, with a peak in neutrophil presence at 3 days.[65] Gradually, neutrophils are replaced by lymphocytes and macrophages and erythrophagocytosis is seen.[66,67] The first appearance of hemosiderin-laden macrophages is at approximately 6–7 days post-event.[68] Fibrin and progressive connective tissue organization is noted within a post-survival period of approximately 2 weeks to 1 month and at approximately 2 months, the leptomeninges are thickened (10–15 layers, compared with normal range of 3–5 layers), with some neovascularization.[69] Macrophages and iron-positive pigment may persist in the subarachnoid space for years after the event.[70]

SAH can be produced postmortem secondary to decomposition, with lysis of blood cells, loss of vascular integrity and leakage of blood into the subarachnoid space. In addition, minimal SAH may be produced during the process of removing the brain. In this case, in the process of removing the skull cap, cerebral veins and the arachnoid are torn, with subsequent diffusion of blood into the subarachnoid space in the posterior aspect (dependent portion) of the cerebral hemispheres and cerebellum. While this hemorrhage is usually very minor, if the brain is not removed from the cranial cavity immediately but rather left to sit for a while, a considerable quantity of SAH may accumulate.

Subarachnoid Injury Due to Vascular Injuries

Traumatic SAH, particularly when located over the base of the brain, can be caused by vascular injuries. These injuries can be almost immediately fatal. Hyperextension can cause bleeding because of lacerations of the basal or vertebral arteries. Blows to the face might produce lacerations of the internal carotid artery or a vessel of the circle of Willis. Blows to the neck can cause lacerations of a vertebral artery with dissection of blood superiorly into the subarachnoid space.

Vertebral Artery Injury

Blunt trauma to the neck can cause severe injury to the vertebral arteries. The upper third of the cervical region is the area where the vertebral artery is most susceptible to trauma. Two types of trauma can result. In the most common form, there is a traumatically induced dissection in the vessel wall, along a length of vertebral artery, with rupture into the subarachnoid space at the base of the brain (Figure 5.34).

The second type of injury also involves dissection but, instead of rupture of the vessel wall, there is thrombosis of the lumen with infarction of brain tissue. Opeskin and Burke

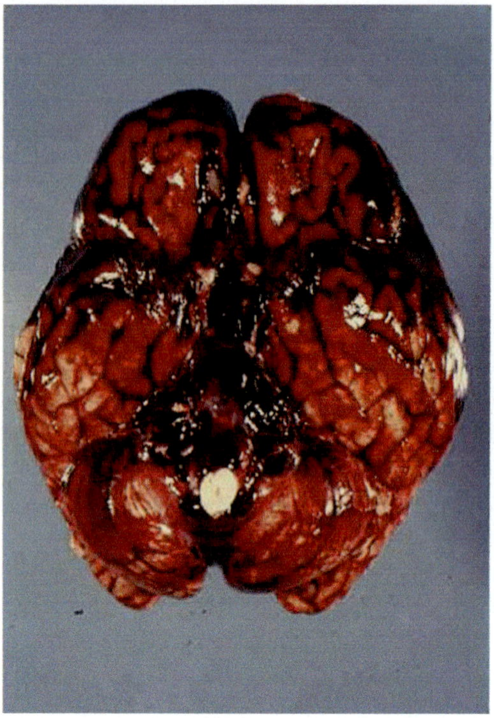

Figure 5.34 Massive subarachnoid hemorrhage secondary to laceration of vertebral artery.

reported on 25 cases of vertebral artery trauma.[71] In 19 cases, there was rupture with SAH, while in 4, there was thrombosis with ischemia. The remaining two cases had rupture, but death was too rapid for SAH.

The most common causes of vertebral artery trauma are blows to the neck, motor vehicle accidents, falls and cervical spine manipulation. In most of Opeskin and Burke's cases, considerable force was involved.[71] Chiropractic manipulation with resultant vertebral artery injury was the cause for two of their deaths. Injury of the vertebral artery should be suspected when an individual collapses and dies almost immediately after receiving a blow to the neck. In cases caused by rupture of the artery, an autopsy reveals SAH primarily concentrated on the ventral surface of the brain and around the brainstem.

In rupture of the artery due to blunt trauma, Opeskin and Burke noted bruising and abrasions below and behind the ear in 50% of 18 cases.[71] Fractures of the cervical spines were present in 10 of 25 cases. Demonstration of the vertebral artery injury is easiest by injection of radio-opaque dye into the vertebral arteries with radiological demonstration of the injury. Only after such demonstration, should there be dissection of the neck, because dissection is extremely difficult and, if not done correctly, may produce artifactual defects in the vessels.

Of 19 individuals with rupture and SAH in the study of Opeskin and Burke, 14 died immediately and 5 in 10 h to 3 days.[71] Four of the five delayed deaths were unconscious from the time of trauma. In the fifth case, rupture occurred 2–3 days after neck manipulation. Of the four individuals who died secondary to vertebral artery thrombosis, symptoms did not appear for 1 d to 4 weeks, with survival time of 3 days to 7 weeks.

Carotid Artery Injury

Carotid artery injuries can either be intracranial or extracranial and are probably more common than realized.[72,73] It occurs mostly in motor vehicle accidents, where it is often missed because of other injuries to the head. Intracranial injury is commonly associated with a fracture of the skull and SAH, though ischemic injury can also occur. In the neck, it may be found in association with hyperextension injury or spinal fracture. Injuries to the vessel can be caused by intimal lacerations with development of a thrombus resulting in ischemic injury; intimal laceration with subsequent dissection into the media in the presence of an intact adventitia, with development of a true aneurysm; and/or rupture of the wall of the artery resulting in subarachnoid or soft-tissue hemorrhage (depending on the location).

Injuries to the carotid often result in delayed neurological symptoms. In 29% of patients seen by Cogbill et al., significant neurological deficits developed more than 12 h after a normal admission neurological examination.[73] One of the authors reviewed a case of a thrombosis of the internal carotid artery just distal to the bifurcation of the common carotid artery. The injury was incurred in a low-speed motor vehicle collision and was due to the deployment of an airbag.

Traumatic Dissection or Aneurysm Formation of Intracranial Arteries

Dissection of intracranial arteries due to trauma is relatively uncommon.[74] If it does occur, however, it can cause cerebral infarction. It is caused by subintimal dissection of the intracranial anterior circulation arteries. Unlike other areas of the body where dissection is in the media, here it occurs subintimal, with resultant occlusion of the lumen by mechanical effects and the production of infarction.

Traumatic intracranial aneurysms are relatively uncommon as well, with approximately 100 or so reported in the literature.[75,76] Most occur in association with fractures of the base of the skull and involve the extracranial portion of the internal carotid artery. When the aneurysms occur intracranially, they most commonly involve the anterior aspect of the circle of Willis. Traumatic aneurysms might be either true or false aneurysms. Those involving the cerebral arteries are true aneurysms, as they are formed due to the lack of an external elastic lamina in the cerebral vessels.

Cerebral Edema

Following significant head injury, whether clinically mild or severe, swelling of the brain can occur. Brain swelling may be focal, adjacent to an area of brain injury; or diffuse, involving one or both cerebral hemispheres. Brain swelling is due to an increase in intravascular cerebral blood volume secondary to vasodilatation (congestive brain swelling), or an absolute increase in the water content of the brain tissue, or a combination of the two. An increase in tissue water content, or cerebral edema, is often incorrectly considered synonymous with brain swelling. If continued long enough, brain swelling caused by an increase in the intravascular cerebral blood volume progresses to cerebral edema, presumably due to increased vascular permeability. The magnitude of the brain swelling does not necessarily correspond to the severity of the injury. Massive cerebral (congestive) swelling can occur within 20 min following head trauma.[77]

Swelling of one cerebral hemisphere is seen most commonly with an ipsilateral subdural hematoma. The secondary swelling may, in fact, cause a more serious mass effect than the hematoma. The rapid onset of the swelling suggests that the etiology is congestive.

With severe brain injury, diffuse brain swelling of a severe degree may occur immediately without the individual regaining consciousness. Brain swelling, however, might not occur immediately after an injury, but rather develop minutes to hours later. Delayed brain swelling of a significant degree is rare. It is usually diffuse and more often associated with the less severe forms of brain injury. Typically, the patient receives a concussion, regains consciousness, only to become stuporous and lapse into coma minutes to hours later. Until recently, it was felt that children were more susceptible than adults to developing diffuse swelling, even after minor trauma.[78,79] Recent studies have challenged this contention. Lang et al. found that, while diffuse swelling might occur more readily in children, it is more benign.[80] Thus, in their study, 75% of children with diffuse swelling had a benign course, while two-thirds of adults had a poor outcome The researchers believed that a number of the previous studies had problems in that they were not able to adequately study changes in the brain in children because the studies were performed without CT scans.

If brain swelling develops to a severe degree and continues over a sufficient time, there can be herniation of the brain or secondary brainstem hemorrhage. A rapidly expanding intracranial mass or severe brain swelling can produce tonsillar, transtentorial or subfalcine herniation of the brain, with resultant necrosis, secondary infarction and Duret hemorrhages (Figure 5.35).

Herniation may be either symmetrical, due to brain swelling, or asymmetrical, due to a mass in one side of the brain or subdural space, for example, a subdural hematoma or intracerebral hemorrhage. In the case of diffuse brain swelling, there is usually symmetrical herniation of the cerebellar tonsils without brainstem hemorrhage. The brainstem and cerebellar tonsils are forced into the foramen magnum, with resultant dysfunction or even infarction of the brainstem. The individual becomes unconscious and develops respiratory difficulty that proceeds to arrest and death. Severe herniation of the cerebellar tonsils can result in infarction. In some individuals with prolonged survival, the authors have seen

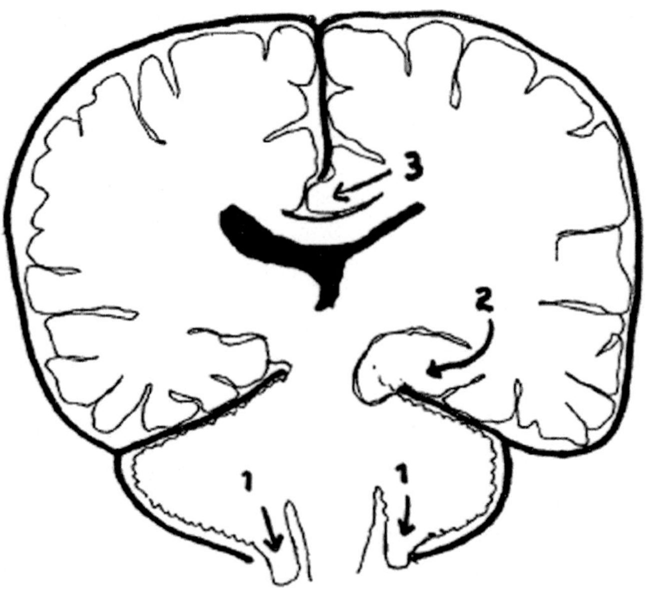

Figure 5.35 (1) Tonsillar, (2) transtentorial and (3) subfalcine herniation of brain.

the upper spinal cord encased in necrotic cerebellar tissues shed into the CSF. In dealing with an asymmetrical herniation caused by a subdural hematoma, in addition to ipsilateral cerebellar tonsil herniation, one often has a secondary brainstem hemorrhage (a Duret hemorrhage) involving the midbrain and pons.

Transtentorial or uncal herniation is due to a rapidly expanding supratentorial mass lesion. It may be either unilateral or bilateral, though unilateral herniation is more common because rapidly expanding lesions are usually unilateral. A rapidly expanding mass in a cerebral hemisphere means that ipsilateral uncal herniation can be expected. If severe enough, there will be displacement of the brainstem against the contralateral tentorial edge with injury to the brainstem and production of Kernohan's notch.

The third type of herniation is subfalcine or transfalcine herniation. This occurs when there is a rapidly expanding mass in one cerebral hemisphere or at least in the subdural space on one side. This causes herniation of the cerebral hemisphere across the midline below the edge of the falx. The herniating tissue is most often the cingulate or supracingulate gyrus.

As previously noted, herniation with compression of the brainstem can result in Duret hemorrhages. These are secondary herniation hemorrhages of the midbrain and pons. They might range from small streaks to massive confluent hemorrhage. They are in the midline and are most commonly associated with asymmetrical herniation of the brainstem. Duret hemorrhages may develop in only 30 min.

Axonal Injury

Axonal injuries are injuries to the neurons themselves and can be either focal or diffuse. Concussion and DAI while often considered as separate entities, both represent axonal injury along a spectrum, ranging from mild to severe. Chronic axonal injury can also occur, particularly in boxers or other professional athletes who sustain multiple concussions, such as football and hockey players.

It is believed that axonal injury occurs due to stretching of the axons usually resulting from rapid acceleration-deceleration and/or rotational (angular) forces, which causes injury to the neuronal cytoskeleton.[81] This results in alterations in the sodium and calcium channels and activation of phospholipases and proteolytic enzymes that further damage the cell. Axons are normally elastic, but on injury, can become brittle and broken. Transport of intracellular elements cannot proceed past the area of injury, leading to buildup and local swelling and the creation of the classic "retraction ball" seen on microscopy.[82] The retraction ball is considered the hallmark lesion of DAI, but can also be seen with other entities that result in neuronal damage, such as ischemia.

When the axon is injured, axonal or Wallerian degeneration, occurs, usually beginning 1–2 days after injury.[83] The axon and surrounding myelin degrade in a retrograde fashion.[83,84] and phagocytic cells are activated.[85] There is a dysregulation of the cell, with intracellular calcium and sodium increasing the potassium decreasing.[81,83] This results in damage to the mitochondria cytoskeleton and the axoplasm.[83,86] It can also lead to cerebral edema and disruption of the blood-brain barrier.[87]

Evidence of axonal injury becomes visible after approximately 12–24 h using hematoxylin and eosin stains and 15–18 h with silver stains. If one employs immunohistochemical techniques, injury is within 3 h or less with B-amyloid precursor protein (B-APP). Injury to axons has been detected as early as 40 min to 2 h with B-APP. These axonal changes by

B-APP are not specific for trauma, however, as similar changes have been seen in nontraumatic cases with cerebral hypoxia.[63,88,89] As time passes, the extent and degree of axonal injury increase.

At low levels of acceleration or deceleration, there is no anatomical disruption of the axons, only physiological dysfunction. This may lead to either complete recovery of an axon or its degeneration. As the physical force increases, there will be a progressive increase in the extent of irreversible physiological injury to axons (thus making it more likely that they will subsequently undergo degeneration). With mild trauma, the injury is predominantly physiological. Some axons, however, may show immediate physical disruption with cessation of functions. In other axons, the physiological disruption will eventually lead to degeneration. As the acceleration or deceleration force increases, the proportion in each category changes, until the predominant injury is shearing of axons and immediate cessation of functioning.

Concussion

Concussion is defined by Kelley et al. as "a trauma-induced alteration in mental status that may or may not involve loss of consciousness."[90] In **mild concussion**, there is confusion and disorientation, but no loss of consciousness. Retrograde amnesia may or may not develop. If it does, it develops 5 or 10 min after the trauma and, while it might subsequently decrease, there will always be some residue.[30] In **cerebral concussion**, there is immediate loss of consciousness, which usually returns within minutes but can persist for hours (<6 h) as confusion and retrograde, or posttraumatic, amnesia. What is clinically called concussion is thought to be a manifestation of diffuse brain injury, with no or insignificant irreparable physical injury to the brain. Blumberg et al. reported on autopsy findings of five individuals who died from other causes after incurring cerebral concussion.[91] Using B-APP, they found multifocal axon injury.

Death due to concussion usually involves two different mechanisms: second impact syndrome or post-concussive apnea. In **second-impact syndrome**, individuals incur a minor head injury to be followed by a second head injury before the symptoms of the first have disappeared.[92] These individuals then appear dazed but may complete the activity they were performing at the time of second impact, but then collapse into coma. This is seen virtually exclusively in sports. Mortality is approximately 50%. There is, however, controversy concerning the syndrome.

Post-concussive apnea occurs in individuals who, while acutely intoxicated with alcohol, sustain a significant head trauma, usually an assault (Figure 5.36).

These individuals are witnessed sustaining the head trauma then collapsing dead. At autopsy, the face and scalp may show soft-tissue injury but there is no intracranial hemorrhage (epidural, subdural, subarachnoid or intraparenchymal), and no skull fractures; though fractures of the nose may be present. Anterior and posterior dissection of the neck is unremarkable. The blood alcohol is elevated, though not lethal. DiMaio in two papers with Milovanovic[93] and Molina[94] reported a total of 11 deaths due to a combination of concussion and acute alcohol intoxication. In all of these cases, the individuals died after sustaining head trauma while intoxicated. Each of them became immediately unresponsive after the trauma, demonstrated no significant anatomic abnormalities at autopsy and had blood ethanol concentrations ranging from 0.168 to 0.33 g/dL.

It is believed that the cause of death in these cases was apnea due to a combination of concussion and acute alcohol intoxication.[93,94] Concussion alone or in combination with

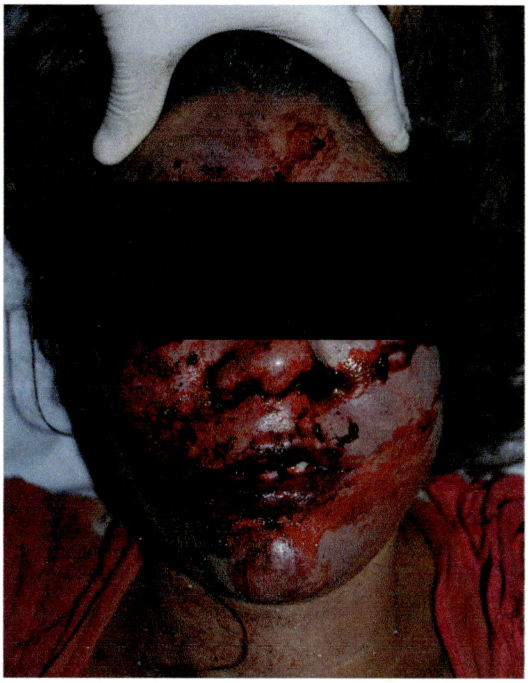

Figure 5.36 A 23 year old female involved in a motor vehicle collision without significant internal injuries. Blood alcohol 188 g/dL.

alcohol can produce posttraumatic apnea. With concussion alone, however, posttraumatic apnea is rare, brief, relatively mild and not life-threatening. Concussion in combination with alcohol produces apnea that can cause death. This was demonstrated by Zinc and Feustel in animal experiments.[95] They concluded that alcohol augments the effects of concussive brain injury with resultant posttraumatic apnea.

Diffuse Axonal Injury

Like concussion, DAI is a continuum, varying from mild brain injury and dysfunction to severe irreversible dysfunction. DAI has been associated with causing a persistent vegetative state or death. It has been shown that up to 72% of patients with moderate-to-severe head injuries have DAI.[96] Injury results from the effects of head motion on the brain. While it is considered an acceleration or deceleration injury, impact of the head on a hard object usually also occurs. While, in theory, impaction of the head is not necessary, in reality, brain injury in humans requires contact, not just acceleration or deceleration. In DAI, experiments have revealed that it *is not only the magnitude of acceleration that produces the injury, but the time over which the acceleration occurs.* Severe angular accelerations over a short time period result in subdural hematomas; acceleration over a long period of time, DAI.[28–30,97] This agrees with the observation that DAI is more common in vehicular accidents, where the time of impact may be prolonged due to absorbing materials, but rare in falls, where there is no absorption of impact. When DAI has been documented following falls, these have been falls from a considerable height.[98] It is extremely unlikely for DAI to occur from a fall from a person's own height.

DAI was first described in 1956 and is characterized by disruption of the axons in the white matter of the cerebral hemispheres, the corpus callosum and upper brainstem, as these areas, along with other midline structure and along the gray-white matter junction, are most susceptible to shearing forces.[96] Focal microhemorrhages are usually grossly visible in the corpus callosum and dorsolateral quadrant of the rostral brainstem due to injury of the small vessels as well as the axons. Occasionally, laceration or even transection of the corpus callosum can occur. Gliding contusions of the gray matter of the cerebral hemispheres and hippocampi may be present.

As discussed earlier, the histologic hallmark of DAI is axonal swelling or "retraction balls."[63,89,98,99] In DAI, the axons first appear dilated, like sausage links and then club shaped and finally (in 18–24 h) as round balls known as "retraction balls." They are seen in the cerebral white matter, corpus callosum and upper brainstem. The number of retraction balls increases during the first week after injury. This is because, while the initial trauma causes transection of some axons with the formation of retraction balls, other axons are irreversibly injured but continue functioning for a while prior to cessation of function and degeneration. Two to three weeks after injury, the number of axon retraction balls begins to decrease and clusters of microglial cells, the most prominent lesion, appear. This will be followed by astrocytes and demyelinization.[59]

The microhemorrhages within the white matter can often be seen on CT scans and are considered the clinical hallmark of DAI.[96] However, MRI is considered superior to CT for diagnosing DAI clinically as it can also detect the white matter lesions and associated edema.

DAI can be graded clinically or pathologically. Clinically, DAI is based on the time of coma or unconsciousness.[30] In mild DAI, there is a period of unconsciousness or coma of less than 24 h; in moderate, the coma lasts more than 24 h but there are no signs of brainstem involvement. In severe clinical cases, the coma is more than 24 h with signs of brainstem involvement or death. The pathological grading of DAI depends on the regions of the brain that demonstrate injury. In grade 1, the axonal damage is confined to the white matter of the cerebral hemispheres; in grade 2, the corpus callosum is also involved; and in grade 3, there is brainstem involvement.[96]

The authors have seen a number of deaths following blunt trauma to the head in which no, or at least insignificant, anatomical injury to the brain could be documented. They fall into two categories. The first is illustrated by the case of an 8-year-old boy riding in the back seat of a motor vehicle that was involved in a head-on collision with another vehicle. The boy was propelled over the back seat, striking the top of his head against the windshield. He was dead at the scene within minutes of the accident. At autopsy, there was no evidence of any injury to the scalp, skull, brain or neck (anterior and posterior dissection). A complete autopsy and toxicological screen were negative. A second, similar case involved a 20-year-old man who fell 20 ft. to the ground from a ladder. Death was immediate. At autopsy, there was a small laceration of the scalp in the temporal region without fracture of the skull or gross evidence of injury to the brain. A number of small perivascular hemorrhages were identified in the brainstem. There was no other evidence of injury. The neck was examined anteriorly and posteriorly. Death in these cases was presumably due to DAI.

G Forces and Roller Coasters

A side note should be made here about G forces and roller coasters. In recent years, much has been made about G-force tolerance and in particular the potential for injury on roller coasters. Gravitational force, called G force, is a directionless measure of linear acceleration. G force is often, incorrectly, used as the sole force measure for the development of head injury.[100] When assessing head trauma, all forces must be considered, including the velocity and direction of movement and the time frame over which the acceleration/deceleration occurs.[100] As just discussed earlier, linear forces usually result in more direct injuries such as skull fractures and cerebral contusions while rotational forces result in axonal and vascular injuries.

Studies have shown that humans can withstand large G forces occurring over a short period of time. For example, a human sneeze generates approximately 10 Gs but occurs for only a fraction (0.002) of a second. A boxer can also withstand a 3 ms punch of 100 Gs or more without acute injury.[101] However, a pilot exposed to force on the magnitude of 5–9 Gs will lose consciousness is those forces or sustained for more than 30 seconds, most likely due to the effects on cerebral blood flow.

In 2009, Pfister et al. studied G forces and roller coasters.[100] They found that the G forces sustained on roller coasters averaged 7.3 G, as compared to the force a male adult can generate in a pillow fight (10 G) or that are sustained in a car crash (29 G). They also measured the rotational forces and compared those as well, determining that roller coasters are no more detrimental than a pillow fight or heading a soccer ball.

Chronic Axonal Injuries

The theory that chronic, repetitive head injuries can result in brain damage was first reported in 1928 when Martland described the "punch drunk syndrome" in boxers.[101] This syndrome, in its final form, is characterized by slurred speech, ataxia, impaired memory, dementia, a broad-based gait and a Parkinsonian-like facial appearance.[101,102] These brain injuries result from the cumulative effect of multiple subconcussive blows. Strikes to the head can produce linear acceleration of the brain with resultant focal ischemic lesions, especially in the cerebellum.[103] These develop a few days after trauma. Straight blows to the face can also produce hyperextension of the neck, with resultant damage to the axons in medullopontine angle and the reticular substance of the brain, as well as retinal detachment.

This chronic brain injury is apparently irreversible and, in some cases, progresses even after the fighter stops boxing. In 1973, Corsellis et al. described a unique neuropathological pattern of injuries in such boxers.[104] He described a fenestrated cavum septi pellucidi; scarring of the cerebellum and cerebral hemispheres, with marked loss of Purkinje cells and loss of neurons with subsequent gliosis in the cerebral hemispheres and with resultant reduction in brain weight and enlargement of the lateral and third ventricles; degeneration and loss of the pigmented cells of the substantia nigra; and neurofibrillary tangles throughout the cerebral cortex and brainstem, most commonly in the medial temporal gray matter and the laterally placed temporal, insular and frontal cortex.

Along with the dementia found in such patients, other mood and psychological neuroses were also described. The syndrome also came to be known as post-concussive syndrome or chronic traumatic encephalopathy (CTE).[105] CTE is considered one of the tau protein neurodegenerative disorders, similar to Alzheimer's disease, however, it seems to show a unique pattern of p-tau accumulation. In CTE, the neurofibrillary tangles are mainly perivascular in location and involve the depths of the cerebral sulci, spreading to adjacent superficial layers.[105] There is also marked degeneration of the medial temporal and frontal lobes with involvement of the diencephalon and brainstem in later stages. This particular distribution of p-tau accumulation is unique from other neurodegenerative diseases, including Alzheimer's disease, chronic ethanol use and aging.

Individuals with CTE present with a wide spectrum of cognitive, behavioral, mood and motor disturbances. These patients will often die due to dementia or other dementia-related causes and most often do not fall under the jurisdiction of a forensic pathologist. However, in recent years, CTE has been blamed for violent deaths, such as homicide or suicide. While the presence of CTE does not change the underlying cause and manner of death in these cases, its presence at autopsy has been used by some to hypothesize about the motivations of such occurrences.

Blunt Force Injuries of the Chest

The thorax, or chest, is a bony-cartilaginous cage containing and protecting the heart, the lungs and their major blood vessels. The posterior surface (the back) is formed by the 12 thoracic vertebrae and posterior aspect of the ribs. The sides are formed by the ribs, separated from each other by the intercostal spaces, 11 in number, which are occupied by the intercostal muscles. The sternum and the ribs make up the front. The diaphragm forms the floor of the chest cavities and separates the thoracic from the abdominal cavities.

The heart lies between the two lungs in the middle of the chest, enclosed within a sac, the pericardium; each lung is enclosed by a serous membrane, the pleura. The heart is placed obliquely in the chest behind the body of the sternum and adjoining parts of the ribs. It projects farther into the left chest cavity than the right, such that about one-third of it is situated to the right and two-thirds to the left of the midline.

Nonpenetrating blunt force injuries of the chest organs can occur with or without external evidence of injury to the chest wall. In some cases, the absence of external injury is attributed to the clothing worn by the victims. Children and young adults, whose chests are pliable and elastic, may sustain severe injuries to the intrathoracic viscera without fractures of the sternum and ribs, whereas in older people, fractures of the ribs and sternum are frequent.

The Ribs and Sternum

There are four general types of rib fractures:

1. **Pathologic (spontaneous) rib fractures** occur in primary bone disease and tumors of bone.
2. **Iatrogenic (therapeutic) rib fractures**. During CPR, the patient may sustain multiple rib or sternal fractures, mediastinal hemorrhage and pneumothorax. These fractures usually involve the first six ribs, tend to be more left sided than right and are either anterolateral or anterior in a linear pattern. When terminal CPR is administered, these fractures may be accompanied by little to no hemorrhage. In the elderly, and in chronically debilitated or malnourished individuals, the ribs are fragile and easily broken when minimal pressure or violence is applied to the chest.

3. **Rib fractures caused by direct localized violence.** Depending on where the force is applied, one or more of the underlying ribs might be fractured. If severe localized direct force is applied to the chest, the fractured ribs can contuse the underlying lung parenchyma or the sharp, pointed fragments of rib can be driven into the pleural cavity, lacerating the pleura, lung or heart, resulting in pneumothorax or hemopneumothorax. Fractures of the first three ribs may be associated with injuries to the tracheobronchial airway and great vessels of the upper anterior chest, whereas fractures of ribs 10–12 can be associated with injuries to the diaphragm, liver and spleen.
4. **Rib fractures caused by indirect violence.** In indirect violence, severe anteroposterior (front-to-back) compression of the chest, such as would be caused by a fall from a height or a car rolling over the chest, may fracture the ribs, most often on their curved lateral portions. If the compressing force is from behind toward the front, the ribs tend to be fractured near the spine; if from the sides of the chest, the ribs fracture near the spine and the sternum. The sharp, pointed fragments of the fractured ribs can lacerate the underlying pleura, lungs and heart.

Regardless of the cause, fractured ribs can result in:

- Lacerations of the intercostal blood vessels with hemothorax
- Laceration of the lung with pneumothorax and/or hemopneumothorax
- Impaling wounds of the heart
- Pleurisy, empyema and pneumonia

Multiple rib fractures, usually resulting from trauma, can also lead to flail chest. A flail chest is usually defined as having three or more rib fractures in to or more locations.[106] This can result in significant pulmonary dysfunction due to either underlying lung injury or loss of mechanical function. In some instances, inspiratory effort resulting from diaphragmatic descent is associated with inward motion of the injured thoracic wall, with little or no ensuing ventilatory exchange. The increased work of breathing creates only increased negative intrapleural pressure changes, which in turn cause more paradoxical motion of the chest wall. This, combined with reduced pulmonary ventilatory efficiency caused by trauma to lung parenchyma, leads quickly to hypoxia.

Injuries of the sternum can be either iatrogenic, for example, during CPR, or the result of direct violence. Fractures are usually transverse and occur most frequently in the body of the sternum. They are caused by a violent impact on the anterior chest, for example, impacting a steering wheel, someone's jumping on a chest, or from severe anteroposterior compression of the chest, such as might be caused by a car's running over the victim. Fractures secondary to CPR usually occur at the level of the third or fourth interspace.

The Heart

Any massive crushing force applied to the anterior chest can cause bursting lacerations of the pericardium. These lacerations are almost invariably associated with injury to the heart or major blood vessels. The heart, protected in front by the sternum and ribs, is suspended in the pericardial sac by the aorta, pulmonary artery and vena cava. The front or anterior surface of the heart is formed chiefly by the right ventricle and, to a lesser extent, the left ventricle. Traumatic injuries of the heart are caused by severe direct violence to the anterior chest. The nature of the injuries depends on the severity of the localized violence, whether the impact is inflicted while the heart is filled with blood, and whether the force applied is sufficient to compress or crush the heart between the sternum and vertebral column. Injuries to the heart are usually associated with injury to other structures of the chest. Blunt chest trauma is frequently caused by automobile accidents. The driver sustains this trauma when the chest forcibly strikes the steering wheel, the front-seat passenger when the chest strikes the dashboard. Airbags and a lap belt combined with a good shoulder belt or harness can prevent or minimize this injury.

A localized force applied directly to the chest might be sufficient to cause a contusion of the anterior wall of either ventricle or the interventricular septum. Hemorrhage can occur in the conduction system with resultant arrhythmias.[107] Grossly, recent contusions appear as dark red, hemorrhagic areas. They must not be confused with an acute myocardial infarct. If the localized impact drives the heart against the vertebral column, a contusion of the posterior wall of either ventricle or the interventricular septum could result. A posterior cardiac contusion must not be confused with postmortem lividity, a change frequently found on the posterior ventricular surfaces of the heart. Microscopic study of the antemortem contusion will reveal localized interstitial hemorrhage and injured myocardial fibers. With cellular injury, there are EKG changes and release of cellular enzymes (e.g., troponin). Primary trauma to the heart must, but cannot always, be differentiated from iatrogenic injury due to CPR, open cardiac massage or intracardiac injections, especially if resuscitation is prolonged. The contused myocardium usually heals without any *sequelae* or residual injury. Rarely, it may undergo necrosis with rupture into the pericardial sac several days after the injury. It may also heal with fibrotic replacement of the contused myocardium and, rarely, form an aneurysm. Killen et al. reported a case of a posttraumatic pseudoaneurysm of the left ventricle.[108] They collected 12 more cases from a review of the literature. Complications were arrhythmia, cardiac failure and embolism.

Lacerations of the heart occur primarily when a very severe crushing force is applied to the anterior chest. Cardiac lacerations have an extremely high mortality rate and are most often fatal.[109] They can involve one or more areas of the heart, that is, atria, interatrial septum, ventricles, interventricular septum, papillary muscles, chordae tendinae or cardiac valves. Cardiac lacerations infrequently occur as isolated injuries (Figure 5.37).

Most often, they occur with other severe chest injuries, such as a motor vehicle collision. However, Ebert reported a case of a lethal cardiac laceration following chest trauma due to a kick from a horse.[109] Rapid cardiac failure occurs whenever a cardiac valve, chordae tendinae or papillary muscle is lacerated. Bolooki et al., while reporting two cases of ventricular septal defects produced by penetrating chest injuries, noted that defects caused by blunt trauma have been reported more frequently in the literature than defects from penetrating trauma.[110]

In 1971, Simson described the *chin-sternum-heart syndrome*.[111] This syndrome is known to occur in parachutists wearing protective helmets when there is incomplete deployment or partial failure of a parachute. The pattern of cardiac injury, multiple atrial, endocardial and myocardial lacerations, is associated with sternal compression by the chin with laceration of the chin. A similar syndrome can occur in individuals who have fallen down stairs, sustaining severe flexion injury to the neck. There is injury to the chin, compression or

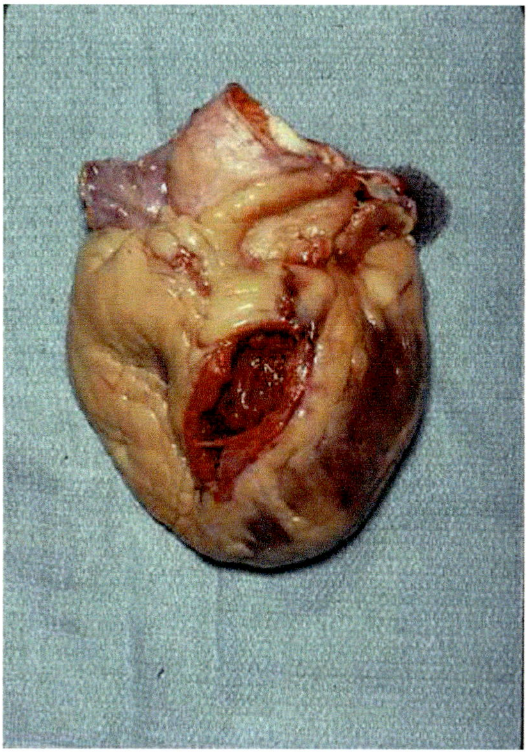

Figure 5.37 A 62-year-old male with a rupture of the right ventricle of the heart at the interventricular septum due to impact of chest on steering wheel. No external injuries present.

fracture of the sternum, cardiac injury and cervical spine fracture with injury to the spinal cord. In some cases of blunt trauma to the chest, the ribs are fractured, with the fractured ends puncturing the heart.

If the pericardial sac is not torn, a laceration of the heart will result in rapid death due to cardiac tamponade. As little as 150–200 mL of blood can cause death. The resultant increase in the intrapericardial pressure due to cardiac tamponade interferes with the entry of blood into the right heart and produces mechanical interference with the contractility of the ventricular myocardium. If the pericardial sac is lacerated, bleeding will occur into the pleural cavities.

On rare occasions, blunt force trauma to the anterior chest causes direct *injury to a coronary artery,* almost invariably the left anterior descending branch. Atherosclerotic vessels are more susceptible to trauma. Injury to coronary arteries can produce coronary occlusion from an intraluminal thrombus, hemorrhage into an atherosclerotic plaque, intimal laceration or a traumatic dissecting aneurysm.[112,113] Because of its medicolegal implication, the diagnosis of traumatic coronary thrombosis must be made with caution. Objective evidence supportive of this diagnosis is as follows:

- Injury to the chest wall and/or heart (fracture of the sternum and/or ribs overlying the thrombosed coronary artery, and/or injury to the myocardium adjacent to the thrombosed coronary artery)

- An incomplete tear of the wall of the thrombosed coronary artery, especially if survival is greater than 8–12 h and a myocardial infarction is present
- Finding the age of the infarct, when observed microscopically, to be consistent with the time interval between alleged coronary artery injury and death

In addition, serial electrocardiograph studies and cardiac enzyme determinations consistent with the time interval from trauma to testing support the hypothesis of injury to a coronary artery. It must not be forgotten, however, that posttraumatic coronary artery thrombosis may occur not as a primary complication of trauma but secondary to shock and intravascular stasis of blood, factors that are conducive to thrombus formation in victims with coronary atherosclerosis. Additionally, it should be noted that elevated troponin concentrations can be seen in cardiac injury of all types, whether traumatic or ischemic.

Commotio Cordis

Sudden death from cardiac arrest following a sudden, blunt, nonpenetrating impact to the chest in an individual with a normal heart and unassociated with structural injury to the heart occurs, though rarely. It is most often reported in association with sports activities and young athletes.[114,115] The usual description of the event is of a stationary individual struck in the chest by a baseball, a hockey puck, karate kick, etc., who then collapses virtually instantaneously or after a brief delay.[116] The blow does not appear to be of sufficient magnitude to cause cardiac arrest. Evidence of impact is not present in a substantial number of cases (approximately half). Impact points appear to be mainly over the left ventricle. These deaths are believed to be caused by a primary ventricular dysrhythmia induced by an abrupt, blunt, pre-cordial blow incurred at an electrically vulnerable phase of ventricular excitability, for example, the upstroke or peak of the T wave. CPR, even if performed immediately or in a timely period, appears to be ineffectual. This event has been reproduced in experiments where baseballs were propelled at high speed at animals' chests.[117]

The Aorta

The heart is suspended in the pericardial sac by the aorta, pulmonary artery and superior vena cava. Any force that violently compresses the anterior chest and forces the heart downward may exert sufficient traction on the aorta to tear it transversely. The superior vena cava and the pulmonary artery are rarely torn, though tears to the inferior vena cava along the base of the heart are not uncommon. Aortic lacerations are most often seen in automobile accidents, less commonly in falls. In automobile accidents, aortic lacerations occur in both head-on and side-impact crashes.

Virtually all lacerations of the thoracic aorta involve the descending portion, immediately distal to the origin of the left subclavian artery. The arch of the aorta is anchored by the great vessels arising from the aortic arch, that is, the right innominate, left common carotid and subclavian arteries, and the ligamentum arteriosum (which connects the left pulmonary artery to the arch of the aorta). Partial or complete lacerations of the descending aorta occur at almost precisely the same location – just distal to the origin of the left subclavian artery, at the junction of the aortic arch and the descending aorta (Figure 5.38).

The precise mechanism of this injury is not known. The relatively constant location of aortic lacerations, the relative fixation of the descending aorta just below the aortic isthmus, the relative fixation of the aortic arch by the vessels and the constant association of

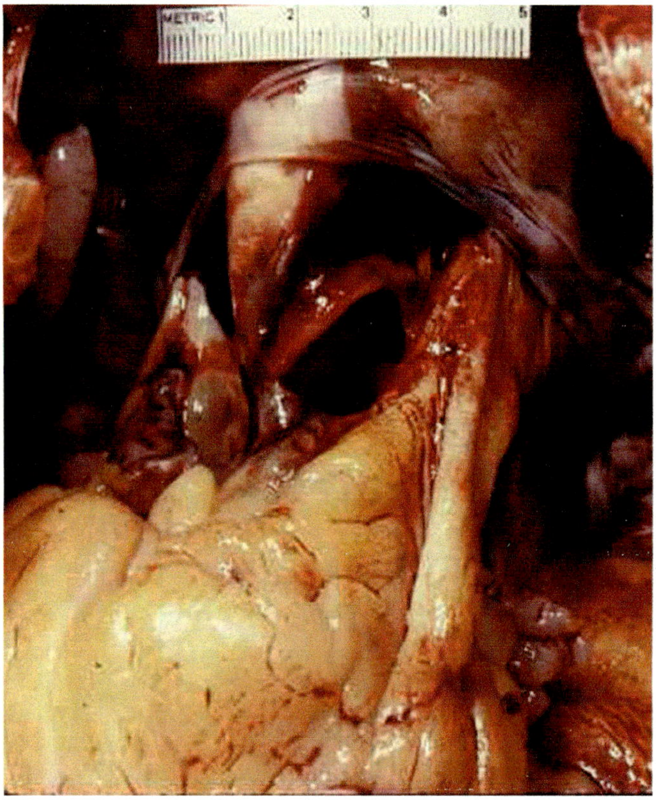

Figure 5.38 Motor vehicle accident with compression of chest and laceration of ascending aorta.

the aortic laceration with deceleration injuries, such as automobile collisions, suggest that the abrupt deceleration of the body and resulting forceful compression of the anterior chest and underlying mediastinal structures cause the heart and great vessels to be jerked away from the posterior chest wall to which the thoracic aorta is attached. This traction on the ligament ductus arteriosus and descending aorta at its point of fixation is sufficient to lacerate the aorta immediately below the origin of the left subclavian artery.

Rarely, a periaortic hematoma due to an aortic laceration may evolve into a false aneurysm. The blood at the periphery of the hematoma, which is contained by the periaortic and mediastinal soft tissue, undergoes organization until a restraining fibrous connective tissue wall is formed – the false aneurysm. This outer wall becomes adherent to the surrounding mediastinal structures, for example, the tracheobronchial tree and esophagus, incorporating them into the wall. Ultimately, the lining of the aneurysmal sac becomes continuous with the endothelium lining the aortic lumen. Because the false aneurysmal wall is composed of fibrous tissue without elastic tissue, continued aneurysmal enlargement is inevitable.

Bursting rupture of the ascending portion and arch of the aorta occur when a violent force compresses the heart and intrapericardial portion of the ascending aorta, producing a sudden rise in intracardiac and intraluminal pressure that results in a transverse tear of the aorta immediately above the cusps of the aortic valve (Figure 5.39).[118,119]

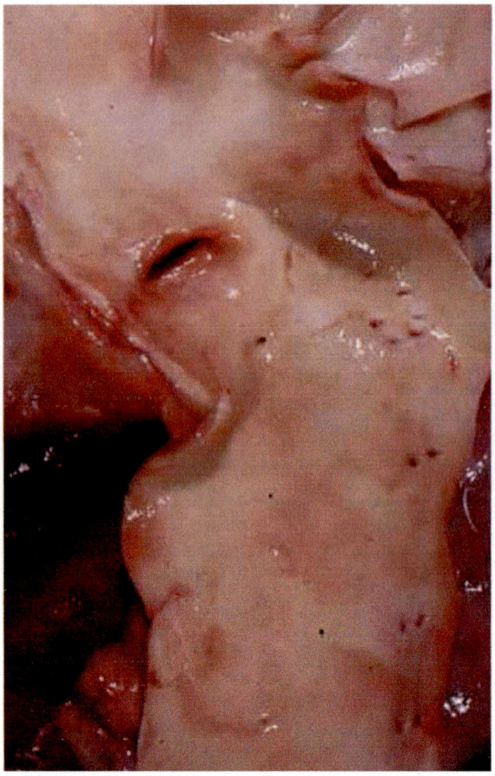

Figure 5.39 Small laceration of aorta, distal to origin of left subclavian artery.

This usually involves only a portion of the aorta's circumference. Death rapidly ensues from severe hemorrhage. These injuries are associated with fractures of the upper ribs and sternum.

While transmural rupture of the aorta due to trauma is common, traumatic dissection of the aorta is relatively rare.[120] Even rarer is a traumatic dissecting aneurysm of the ascending and arch of the aorta.[121,122] With regard to traumatic dissecting aortic aneurysms, Papadopoulos et al. reported the case of a 50-year-old hypertensive male who had sustained a steering wheel injury 4 years prior to admission to the hospital for sudden onset of pain in the lower back and left lower extremity.[123] The pain subsided rapidly, but the patient developed severe intermittent claudication. A translumbar aortogram revealed a dilated aorta with complete occlusion of the left common iliac artery. At surgery, a huge dissecting aneurysm of the descending thoracic aorta was found, with the intimal tear starting just distal to the left subclavian artery. The true lumen of the distal thoracic aorta was very narrow. A review of the literature up to October 1975 by these authors revealed 138 cases of chronic traumatic aneurysmal lesions of the thoracic aorta.[123]

Traumatic rupture of the ascending aorta must not be confused with spontaneous ruptures associated with cystic medial necrosis, which frequently occur in this area. Grossly, the lesions might resemble each other. However, the absence of injuries and the microscopic characteristics of cystic medial necrosis will differentiate the nontraumatic from the traumatic rupture. In cases of suspected traumatic laceration of the aorta, all natural diseases that might cause spontaneous rupture or aneurysmal formation, for example, atherosclerosis, syphilis or cystic medical necrosis, must be sought. It must be realized, however, that even if these conditions do exist, rupture could still be due to trauma.

Heggtveit et al. reported two cases of innominate artery aneurysms occurring after blunt trauma following a motor vehicle accident.[124] In such a case, the victim sustains injury to the chest just to the right of the sternum. This impact may produce nonpenetrating injury to the innominate artery and development of an aneurysm.

Traumatic rupture of the abdominal aorta, either partial or complete, is relatively uncommon, if not rare. Most but not all are caused by automobile accidents.[125] Rupture is commonly associated with fracture-dislocation of the underlying vertebrae.

Lungs and Airway

Traumatic rupture of the intrathoracic trachea and bronchus is usually the result of severe compressive injury of the chest. The most frequent site of rupture of the tracheobronchial tree is within 2.5 cm of the carina, especially in the main bronchi. Cases of combined injury to the trachea and bronchus occur infrequently. Approximately 30% of the victims have anterior fractures of the second and third ribs. Winter and Baum[126] reviewed the various mechanisms that have been suggested as being responsible for these injuries:

- Compression of a main bronchus against the vertebral column
- Direct compression by the sternum against a closed glottis
- Sudden rise in intraluminal pressure during forced expiration against a closed glottis with explosive effect
- Shearing forces that cut across the hilar areas
- Deceleration of the pendulous lungs moving forward against the relatively more fixed trachea and proximal bronchi

Most likely, there are several causative mechanisms with any one or a combination of these mechanisms producing bronchial or tracheal injury.

Like the heart, the lungs can be contused or lacerated. Pulmonary contusions can result as a consequence of either direct or indirect force on the lungs. Osborn refers to contusions of the posterior surface of the lungs as *contrecoup* contusions.[127] He found them to be in an almost constant position corresponding to the angle of the ribs. He further stated that the thorax is typically compressed from the front and sides, the posterior parts near the spine being relatively fixed; hence, the typical contrecoup lesion is posterior. If the alveoli under the site of impact fail to absorb the force of the striking rib, the anterior alveoli transmit the force to the posterior alveoli, causing the contusion of the posterior surface of the lung. Resolution of a pure pulmonary contusion is rapid and complete without residual scarring. Generally, improvement occurs within 48 h and clearing is complete a few days later.

A grinding force will produce multiple fractures of the ribs, costal cartilages and sternum, with mangling of the lungs. Intrapulmonary tears (lacerations) occur when the crushing force drives the chest inward, compressing the intrathoracic organs and exerting downward traction on the lung tissue. The intrapulmonary tears may be small and multiple, or single and large beneath an intact pleura.

Usually, a simple fracture of the rib will neither contuse nor lacerate the underlying lung. However, if the impact to the chest is forceful enough to cause inward displacement of the fractured ends of the ribs, they may puncture and lacerate the underlying pleura and lung. During postmortem examination, the inwardly driven broken ends of the fractured ribs may not be evident because they may have rebounded, giving the appearance of a simple fracture.

If a person is run over by an automobile or crushed beneath an overturned car or falling debris, the resulting injuries to the lung may consist of bursting ruptures. These occur most often when the glottis is closed and a severe compressive force is applied to the chest. The compressed intra-alveolar and intrabronchial air is trapped because it is unable to escape via the normal air passages, which are occluded. The intrabronchial and intra-alveolar air pressure will progressively increase, causing marked dilatation of the alveoli, which ultimately rupture, resulting in intrapulmonary hemorrhage and possibly a pneumothorax. In adults, the crushing force applied to the anterior chest will fracture the ribs, costal cartilages and sternum, whereas the same force applied to the posterior chest will drive the fractured ribs and vertebrae into the chest cavities.

In children, adolescents and young adults, severe trauma to the chest may cause the flexible thoracic cage to be markedly compressed without fracturing the sternum, ribs and costal cartilages. A normal lung, because of its elastic structures, is capable of withstanding gradual compression without injury. However, a sudden forcible blow to the chest could be sufficient to cause a contusion of the lung secondary to an inward bending of the rib(s). In children, it is not unusual to see a distinct subpleural hemorrhage corresponding to the width of the impacting rib. A localized blow to the chest compresses air within the alveoli that normally escapes via the air passages. If the air is trapped within the alveoli because the air passages are obstructed, the intra-alveolar air pressure will increase until it exceeds the limits of alveolar elasticity, at which time the alveoli rupture, resulting in intra-alveolar hemorrhage.

Complications of Lung Injuries

Hemothorax may result from lacerations of the lungs. Bleeding into the pleural cavity is not significant if the laceration is small because of the contractility of the elastic lungs and compression of the laceration by the expanding hemothorax. Massive intrapleural bleeding occurs, however, if the laceration is large and involves large blood vessels. Hemothorax might be augmented by bleeding from lacerations of the mediastinal tissues, diaphragm and internal mammary or intercostal arteries following fractures of the sternum and/or ribs. Blunt chest trauma can overstretch and lacerate old pleural adhesions, producing intrapleural bleeding. The amount of bleeding is dependent on the degree of vascularization of the pleural adhesions. During therapeutic or diagnostic thoracentesis, the needle may puncture and lacerate the intercostal artery, causing bleeding into the pleural cavity. Perforation of a pulmonary artery by a Swan-Ganz catheter may occur with a resultant hemothorax (Figure 5.40).

If the blood in a pleural cavity is not removed, it will gradually break down, undergoing a series of color changes, red to brown, with the ultimate formation of a chocolate brown pigment deposit and turbid brown fluid. Intrapleural blood may be diluted by serous effusion. The lacerated lung, hemothorax and diluting serous fluid are vulnerable to bacterial infection with production of pneumonia, lung abscesses, pleurisy and empyema.

Lacerated wounds of the lung can also result in leakage of air into the pleural cavity, producing a pneumothorax. When the pneumothorax is associated with intrapleural bleeding, it is called a pneumohemothorax. Pneumothoraces may be due to natural disease, medical procedures or trauma. A spontaneous pneumothorax may occur following rupture of an emphysematous bulla. Iatrogenic pneumothorax can be caused by external

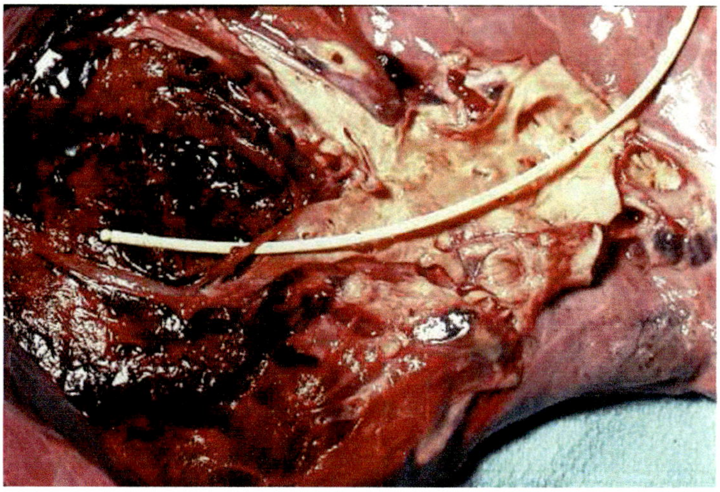

Figure 5.40 Perforation of pulmonary artery by a Swan-Ganz catheter with massive dissecting hemorrhage into pulmonary parenchyma and rupture into the chest cavity.

cardiac massage, percutaneously inserted subclavian catheters and continuous ventilatory support.[128,129] In 168 cases of pneumothorax, 54 occurred during or immediately following closed chest cardiac massage (49 on the left side and 5 on the right).[128] There were associated ipsilateral anterolateral rib fractures in 43 of these patients. Of the 54 patients, 45 had also received intracardiac medication administered percutaneous through the left side of the chest. Whether this contributed to the pneumothorax was unknown. In 51 patients, pneumothorax occurred following percutaneous insertion of a catheter in the subclavian vein. In addition, 61 patients developed pneumothorax during continuous ventilatory support, and 2 patients during tracheostomy. In 1982, Newman et al. noted the increased frequency of catheter complications involving the subclavian and internal jugular veins secondary to total parenteral nutrition.[129]

A tension pneumothorax can develop if a pulmonary laceration penetrates deep into the lung and severs a large bronchus. With each inspiration, air entering the bronchus escapes into the pleural cavity. On expiration, the lacerated edges of the bronchus act as a valve to prevent the air from passing out of the pleural cavity through the bronchus. With each inspiration, the volume and pressure of the trapped air increases until the air pressure is high enough to collapse the lung and displace the mediastinum and heart to the opposite side. At autopsy, the pleural cavity contains a collapsed lung with air under pressure, a concave depressed diaphragm and displacement of the heart and mediastinum to the opposite side. When a lacerated wound of the lung involves a pulmonary vein and adjacent bronchus, air exiting the bronchus may enter the pulmonary vein and be conveyed to the left atrium and ventricle, with resultant cardiac and cerebral air embolus.

Diaphragm

Traumatic rupture of the diaphragm is most often caused by severe blunt trauma to the lower anterior chest. It is frequently associated with fractures of the ribs and thoracoabdominal injuries. Violent compressive force applied to the lower anterior chest will cause overstretching and twisting of the diaphragmatic leaf, which ultimately ruptures. Forcible upward displacement of the abdominal viscera against the undersurface of the diaphragm may also create sufficient pressure to rupture the diaphragm. The severe crushing force applied to the lower chest-upper abdomen may produce a large hemidiaphragmatic defect with ragged hemorrhagic edges. The defect is usually large enough for protrusion of the abdominal viscera into the thoracic cavity. Traumatic rupture of the diaphragm is more common on the left. This is allegedly thanks to the protection afforded the right diaphragmatic leaf by the liver.

Rupture of the left hemidiaphragmatic leaf permits the stomach, intestine, omentum or spleen to herniate into the left pleural cavity. The left lung is compressed and the heart displaced to the right. Herniation occurs because of the difference between the positive pressure cavity of the abdomen and the negative pressure cavity of the thorax. The presence of the liver on the right side acts as a plug if an opening is made. Rarely, a part of the liver can pass through and become tightly constricted at the margin of the rent like a strangulated hernia. Rupture of the right hemidiaphragm is almost always associated with significant hepatic injury.

Blunt Force Injuries of the Abdomen and Pelvis

The abdominal organs are vulnerable to a variety of injuries from blunt trauma because the lax and compressible abdominal walls, composed of skin, fascia and muscle, readily transmit the force applied to the abdominal viscera. If the victim anticipates the blow and tightens the abdominal muscles, this will disperse the force of impact and thereby reduce the probability of internal injuries. Thus, the boxer who has conditioned his abdominal muscles and is prepared to receive such blows will sustain no injury to his abdominal organs.

The type of injury an abdominal organ will sustain depends on the organ involved. The soft, compact, vascular liver and spleen may be lacerated or crushed; a distended hollow organ, such as the stomach or intestines, will burst due to the rapid increase in intraluminal pressure produced by the force of impact. The severity of trauma is relative to the size of the blunt object, the force of impact, the organ traumatized and its condition at the time of impact. It cannot be overemphasized that the absence of external injury (contusions or abrasions) to the abdominal walls does not exclude injury, even massive injury, to one or more of the internal abdominal organs (Figure 5.41).

The lack of external injuries is attributable to the lax and compressible abdominal walls and protection afforded by clothing. If a traumatized victim complains of abdominal pains, but lacks visible signs of injury to the abdomen, the emergency room physician or surgeon may fail to clinically detect the early signs of intra-abdominal injury, and thus delay a lifesaving operation. This is especially true of intoxicated victims and individuals on high doses of tranquilizer whose condition renders them insensible to pain and obscures the signs of peritoneal irritation. The authors have also seen it with obese patients, where the usual palpable abdominal rigidity often present with such injuries may be masked by the overlying adipose tissues.

Trauma to the abdomen may be generalized, involving the abdomen as a whole, as exemplified by an individual run over by a vehicle, or localized, such as would occur if an individual was kicked in the abdomen. Most homicides resulting from blunt force involve localized injuries to the abdomen. Possibly only through a thorough investigation of the circumstances surrounding the victim's death will one be able to determine whether the blunt force injury was of a homicidal or accidental nature.

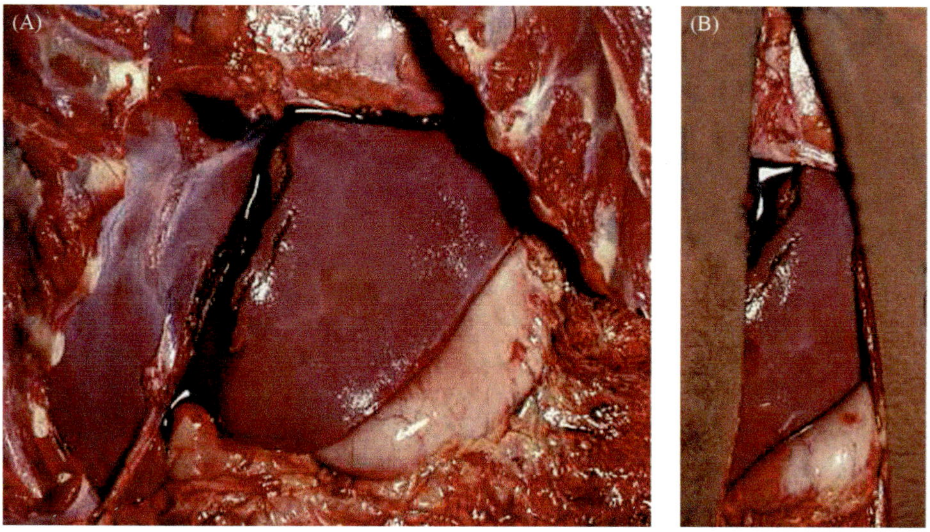

Figure 5.41 (A) Complete transection of liver (B) without any evidence of external trauma to anterior abdominal wall.

Since many individuals receive CPR nowadays, it is extremely important to differentiate iatrogenic injuries of the abdominal organs from those due primarily to trauma. Thus, with vigorous, slightly misplaced CPR, the authors have seen lacerations of the liver where it overlies the vertebral column. Several hundred milliliters of blood may be present in the abdominal cavity in these cases, even though these injuries were, in a sense, postmortem.

In 1983, Ducatman et al. described three cases of fatal rectus sheath hematoma.[130] This entity is characterized by apparent spontaneous nontraumatic hemorrhage into the rectus sheath, usually occurring after anticoagulant therapy. It may be either an immediate or contributory cause of death.

Liver

The liver lies in the upper right quadrant of the abdominal cavity. It is partly protected by the lower ribs and the xiphoid process of the sternum. It is the largest of the solid abdominal organs and is the one most frequently injured by blunt trauma to the abdomen. Severe localized blunt trauma applied to the right upper quadrant will often lacerate only the liver, whereas generalized blunt trauma tends to injure not only the liver, but the other abdominal organs, though with less frequency. Fractures of the adjacent ribs may or may not be present, depending on the age of the individual and the calcification of the ribs.

The liver is susceptible to trauma because of its large size, its anatomic position in the upper abdomen, its inability to give with trauma and the solid nature of its tissue. Injuries of the liver can be classified as **transcapsular lacerations**, in which both capsule and parenchyma are torn, and **subcapsular lacerations**, in which the capsule is still intact and the injury is either beneath an intact capsule or intraparenchymal. The right lobe is injured five times as frequently as the left, with the lesions occurring more commonly on the convex surface. Any severe localized force applied directly to the front of the liver will drive the liver in a posterior direction, crushing it against the posterior vertebral column, and producing a transcapsular laceration at the junction between the right and left lobes, immediately beneath the site of external impact (Figure 5.6). A variation of this is the contrecoup laceration of the liver where the laceration occurs on the posterior surface of the right lobe, at the point where it rests against the vertebral column. The same localized force that can produce transcapsular lacerations, if violent enough and directed to the front of the liver, may compress the liver, not only in a backward direction, but also in a lateral direction, causing an internal (subcapsular) laceration of the parenchyma.

Blunt trauma applied directly to the front of the liver may strip the capsule from its parenchymal attachment at the point of impact, resulting in the development of a subcapsular hematoma. Either the hematoma will undergo complete organization and be replaced by a thick fibrous connective tissue capsule or continuous subcapsular bleeding may create sufficient pressure to rupture with a resultant fatal intraperitoneal hemorrhage. Rupture of the subcapsular hematoma may occur days after the time of impact.

If the force impacting the front of the liver is directed upward, it may lacerate the inferior (under) surface of the liver, whereas, if the force is directed downward and backward, there is deformation of the dome of the liver with lacerations of the superior surface. Multiple superficial capsular lacerations of the diaphragmatic or superior surface of the right lobe of the liver are common in motor vehicle accidents.

If the force is directed straight at the liver, along its anterior margin, there can be lacerations of both the concave and convex surfaces. With severe crushing force applied over the front of the liver, such as might occur in a severe automobile accident or a brutal kick to the abdomen, there could be complete amputation of the left lobe of the liver when it is crushed between the anterior abdominal wall and the vertebral column.

In addition to injuries to the parenchyma of the liver itself, there may also be injuries to the portal vein, hepatic artery, and inferior vena cava. Isolated injuries to these vessels themselves are extremely rare, since any force sufficient to injure them would also produce extensive injuries to the liver.

Mays, in an experimental study, attempted to determine the amount of energy necessary to produce injuries to the liver.[131] He found that, in the energy range of 27–34 ft. lb, there were tears and lacerations of the capsule, but intrahepatic damage to the vascular and biliary trees was absent. If the energy was increased to 106–134 ft. lb, there was crevicing of the liver externally, but only an occasional disruption of a small bile duct or hepatic artery. There was no disruption of the major vascular or biliary trees. Increasing the energy to 285–360 ft. lb caused extensive pulpefaction of the liver, bursting injuries and severe disruption of the tributaries of the hepatic artery, portal vein and bile ducts, though the major divisions themselves remained intact.

As previously noted, not all injuries to the liver are of a primary traumatic basis. Thus, one can have injuries caused by CPR, liver biopsy, angiographic vascular studies and introduction of chemotherapeutic agents via the hepatic arteries. The authors have seen cases in which needle biopsies were performed only to have the patient exsanguinate a number of hours later due to massive intra-abdominal hemorrhage from the biopsy site. Intraperitoneal hemorrhage may also be due to rupture of a hepatic tumor.

Isolated traumatic rupture of the gallbladder due to blunt trauma is uncommon. Bursting rupture of the gallbladder, if present, is usually associated with massive injury to the liver. Isolated rupture of the gallbladder is said to be more common in children and young adults, possibly because their chests are more easily compressed. Leakage of bile into the abdominal cavity would cause chemical peritonitis.

Pancreas

The pancreas is located retroperitoneally, closely applied to the posterior abdominal wall. It is composed of a head, neck, body and tail, with the head lodged in the curve of the duodenum. The neck and body are in proximity to the portal vein, inferior vena cava and aorta, overlying the body of the second lumbar vertebra. The tail crosses the upper pole of the left kidney, terminating in the gastric surface of the spleen, in contact with the left flexure of the colon. Blunt force injuries to the pancreas are not common because of its posterior location and considerable distance from the anterior abdominal wall. If a severe localized force were applied to the epigastric region of the abdomen and injury to the pancreas incurred, it would generally be at the point where the pancreas overlies the second lumbar vertebra. Contusions, lacerations and transections can occur at this point. With lacerations of the pancreas, there is associated injury to the pancreatic ducts, with loss of pancreatic secretions into the abdominal cavity and chemical peritonitis.

Trauma to the pancreas can result in residual pseudocysts, either peripancreatic or intrapancreatic. In the peripancreatic cyst, blood and pancreatic secretions accumulate around the pancreas, beneath the intact peritoneum, forming a peripancreatic hematoma. Resolution leads to the formation of a cyst filled with clear fluid. The cyst wall is devoid of epithelial lining but does contain hemosiderin-laden macrophages and hemosiderin deposits in the fibrous connective tissue wall. In an intrapancreatic cyst, there is intrapancreatic bleeding, resulting in the formation of hematoma. With resolution, there is a cyst whose wall, again, is devoid of epithelial lining but contains hemosiderin. In contrast, neoplastic or congenital cysts have a distinct epithelial lining. Most pseudocysts of the pancreas are not caused by trauma, but rather are a result of pancreatitis.

Spleen

The spleen lies in the left upper quadrant of the abdomen, extending to the epigastric region and lying between the fundus of the stomach and the diaphragm. It is not as frequently injured as the liver because of its well-protected position in the left upper quadrant of the abdomen. Spontaneous rupture of the spleen, unassociated with any significant trauma, is associated with any condition that produces splenomegaly and an increased fragility of the parenchyma. The most common of such conditions are infectious mononucleosis, malaria and leukemia. While this rupture is said to be spontaneous, it may actually be due to a trivial, perhaps unrecalled, traumatic episode that would have absolutely no significance in a normal individual.

Severe trauma to the left upper quadrant of the abdomen can produce lacerations or bursting ruptures of the spleen. The extent of injury depends on the severity of the force and whether it is localized or generalized. Injuries can range from a small superficial capsular laceration up to virtual disintegration of the spleen. In some instances, the force delivered to the spleen is sufficient to lacerate the splenic parenchyma, but not to injure the capsule. If internal bleeding continues, a subcapsular hematoma could form. This may stop enlarging after a time and resolve, resulting in an area of scarring. If the bleeding continues, there will be a progressive increase in subcapsular pressure with rupture of the capsule and resultant intraperitoneal hemorrhage. The rupture of the capsule may occur hours or even days after the trauma. It might be due just to the buildup in pressure or be precipitated by another incident of trauma, even if it is minor. Microscopic sections will show that one is dealing with a delayed rupture of a subcapsular hematoma. During the period of development of the subcapsular hematoma and prior to its rupture, the patient may be either asymptomatic or complain of vague abdominal pain. Iatrogenic splenic rupture during CPR is extremely uncommon. If it does occur, it is probable that the spleen was not normal to begin with, but enlarged.

Gastrointestinal Tract

The gastrointestinal tract, including the mesentery, can be contused due to blunt trauma, but this is rarely a significant injury. The most significant injury of the gastrointestinal tract is rupture. While this is relatively uncommon due to the mobility of the individual segments, which enables them to be easily displaced by the full impact of a blow, when it does occur, death can result due to peritonitis that resulted from the spillage of intestinal contents into the peritoneal cavity.

Esophagus

Traumatic injuries of the esophagus secondary to blunt trauma are rare and of little interest to the forensic pathologist, because they rarely result in death. Repeated violent vomiting can produce lacerations of the esophagus, even perforations, at its lower end, where it meets the stomach. These lacerations are usually single in number, longitudinal and on the lateral or posterior wall. They can range from superficial, involving only the mucosa, to complete lacerations of the wall with perforation. Lacerations of the esophagus in this area are most frequently seen in alcoholics, following prolonged bouts of violent and excessive vomiting (Mallory-Weiss syndrome). Normally, in vomiting, the pyloric sphincter contracts and the lower and upper esophageal sphincters relax prior to contracture of the gastric musculature. It is postulated that, during violent spasmodic vomiting, if the upper esophageal sphincter fails to relax, the powerful contractions of the gastric musculature, aided by abdominal wall contractions, will propel the gastric contents into the esophagus. There is sufficient violence to cause a rapid rise in intraesophageal pressure, with rupture of the esophagus at its weakest point, the posterior lateral wall. This could result in mediastinal emphysema, bilateral hydrothorax, hydropneumothorax or massive hemorrhage, which is the terminal event in the Mallory-Weiss syndrome.

Stomach

The stomach lies in the left upper quadrant of the abdomen, extending to the epigastric and umbilical region. The greater part of the stomach, the fundus and body, is protected by the ribs. Injuries to the stomach are virtually all caused by localized blunt force applied to the epigastric or left upper quadrant, for example, a kick or a blow with the fist. This crushes the stomach between the anterior abdominal wall and the posterior vertebral column. Depending on the severity of the injury, there might be a contusion or actual perforation of the wall of the stomach. While injury to the stomach may be a solitary traumatic lesion, more often it occurs in association with other major abdominal trauma. The stomach may perforate immediately or the contusion may progress to a point of necrosis with subsequent perforation due to the digestive action of the gastric acids.

In most cases of rupture of the stomach, the stomach is distended with food or drink.[132] The more distended, the more vulnerable the stomach is to blunt force injury. An impact on the anterior abdominal wall compresses the stomach between the abdominal wall and the vertebral column, creating a sudden increase in intragastric pressure that is distributed uniformly over the entire stomach. If the pyloric sphincter and cardiac orifice are relaxed, the compressing force displaces the stomach contents into the duodenum and esophagus and the stomach is partially protected from the injury. If, however, the stomach contents are not evacuated, the rapid increase in intragastric pressure will overcome the resistance of the gastric wall, with resultant rupture. Rupture can occur in any portion of the stomach, but the anterior wall seems to be most often involved. There is usually a circular defect with ragged ecchymotic edges. In addition to the aforementioned causes of perforation, the stomach can also be perforated during endoscopic examination or biopsy, or by a feeding tube.

The Duodenum

Immediately distal to the stomach is the duodenum. It is situated in the umbilical region. Beginning at the pylorus, it is divided into four regions: the superior, descending, horizontal and ascending portions. The first three portions encircle the head of the pancreas. The ascending fourth portion overlies the vertebral column from the fourth to the second lumbar vertebrae where it becomes the jejunum. The ascending portion of the duodenum and the duodenojejunal flexure are fixed by the ligament of Treitz. Severe blunt force trauma to the abdomen may injure the duodenum, with the most common site of injury in the vicinity of the ligament of Treitz.

The fixed distal portion of the duodenum is compressed between the anterior abdominal wall and the lumbar vertebrae. Injury may range from a contusion to perforation to transection. The contusion may subsequently evolve into a perforation if it is severe enough to devitalize the wall by hemorrhage. In such a case, the duodenal perforation might occur hours or days after the injury was sustained. If the duodenum is distended at the time of impact, there could be a bursting rupture at the duodenojejunal flexure. The points of rupture are usually small and ovoid, with ragged ecchymotic edges.

The Small Intestines

There are three possible mechanisms for rupture of the bowel: compression between the anterior abdominal wall and the vertebral column or pelvis; deceleration at points of fixation (usually the ligament of Treitz or the ileocecal junction) or a local area of increased intraluminal pressure.

The jejunal portion of the small bowel principally occupies the umbilical and left iliac region, while the ileal portion chiefly occupies the umbilical, hypogastric, right iliac and pelvic regions. The terminal portion of the ileum usually lies in the pelvis in the right iliac region, where it opens into the cecum. The jejunum and ileum are attached to the posterior abdominal wall by a fold of peritoneum, the mesentery, which allows free movement of the jejunum and ileum. Blood vessels and nerves run through the mesentery. There is an increased incidence of injury to the jejunum and ileum in comparison with the stomach and duodenum, with the jejunum injured more often than the ileum.[133]

In most instances of severe abdominal impact, the small intestine is crushed between the anterior abdominal wall and the vertebral column or pelvis. The resultant lesion, a contusion, perforation or transection, depends on the severity of the blunt force and the area over which it is applied. A severe contusion can progress to a delayed perforation several hours or days after injury. Transection of the jejunum usually occurs just distal to the ligament of Treitz, where the jejunum is firmly attached to the posterior abdominal wall. In transection of the small bowel, there is usually associated injury to the mesentery. Spontaneous rupture of the small bowel may occur due to infarctions secondary to incarceration, strangulation, various ulcerative diseases of the mucosa and thrombosis of the mesenteric vasculature.

With severe blunt trauma to the abdomen and injury to internal organs, the mesentery of the small intestine is often contused or torn. There can be either single or multiple lacerations. The mesentery appears to be torn most often by a tangential blow to the abdomen that exerts traction on the membrane. Death could occur solely from injury to the mesentery if there is laceration of one of the large blood vessels coursing through the mesentery.

The Large Intestines

The large intestine, or colon, differs from the small intestine in its larger caliber, more fixed position and less vulnerability to trauma. The midportion or transverse colon is the most open to trauma because of its relation to the vertebral column and its exposed position in the mid abdominal cavity. A severe impact to the anterior abdominal wall may crush the midportion of the transverse colon between the anterior abdominal wall and the lumbar vertebrae. The resulting traumatic lesion depends on the severity of the blunt force and might range from a contusion to a laceration to transection. Rupture of the colon may also occur following insertion of foreign objects, hands or animals for sexual stimulation.[134] Iatrogenic rupture of the colon can occur during sigmoidoscopy, proctoscopy or a high colonic enema. Occasionally, a barium enema will result in perforation of the colon.

Kidneys

The kidneys are situated in the posterior part of the abdomen, termed the retroperitoneum, on either side of the vertebral column. The right kidney is usually slightly lower than the left. The posterior surface and upper portion of the right kidney rest on the 12th rib; the left kidney usually rests on the 11th and 12th ribs. The anterior surface of the right kidney is in contact with the right adrenal gland, liver and the right colic flexure. The anterior surface of the left kidney is in contact with the left adrenal gland, stomach, spleen, jejunum, colon and, medially, the pancreas.

Spontaneous rupture of the normal kidney does not occur. Blunt force injuries to the kidney are uncommon. They are usually seen following motor vehicle accidents or falls from great heights when there is massive blunt force trauma to the abdominal cavity. Blunt force applied to the flank may crush the kidney between the abdominal wall and the lumbar vertebrae. The most common injury to a kidney is a contusion. Aside from contusions, the majority of injuries to the kidney are small transverse lacerations beneath an intact capsule with minimal hemorrhage. Injuries producing massive lacerations of the kidneys up to fragmentation are uncommon and are associated with massive injury to the other abdominal organs. Blunt force can also cause injury of the renal vasculature resulting in the retroperitoneal bleeding.

Urinary Bladder

In adults, the empty urinary bladder is placed entirely within the pelvis, behind the pubic symphysis. When distended, the bladder may extend into the abdominal cavity. In children, the anterior surface of the bladder is in contact with the lower two-thirds of the abdominal wall between the symphysis pubis and the umbilicus. Beginning at puberty, it slowly begins to descend to its final position in the pelvis. Iatrogenic rupture of the urinary bladder may occur during instrumentation for diagnostic or therapeutic purposes. More commonly, severe blunt trauma to the pelvis and lower abdomen causes rupture. The degree and type of injury that occurs usually depends on the volume of urine in the bladder.

There are two types of rupture: **extraperitoneal** and **intraperitoneal**. Extraperitoneal occurs when the bladder is empty or contains only a small amount of urine. In extraperitoneal rupture, the bladder lies within the pelvis and is protected by the strong bony pelvis. Here lacerations of the urinary bladder are associated with fractures of the pelvis. Only rarely will extraperitoneal rupture occur without pelvic fractures. This is when blunt force is applied to the lower abdominal wall in a downward direction.

Intraperitoneal rupture of the urinary bladder occurs when the bladder is markedly distended by urine. At this time, a kick, a blow or any blunt force to the lower abdominal wall can compress the posterior wall of the bladder against the sacrum, raising the pressure within the bladder lumen and rupturing it, with urine entering the abdominal cavity.

Internal Genitalia

Injuries of the nonpregnant uterus are extremely rare. When they do occur, they are usually associated with extensive fractures of the pelvis. Blunt trauma injuries to the pregnant uterus and/or fetus are usually caused by automobile accidents, with falls and assaults accounting for a significantly smaller number of cases.[135,136] Placental separation is the leading cause of fetal death. Separation occurs at the moment of trauma but may not become evident for a few hours. This is probably due to a small separation at the edge of the placenta, with the development of a retroplacental hematoma that takes a while to grow and kill the fetus. In the absence of any direct trauma, the cause for the separation is severe distortion of the uterus that can occur with violent motion. Following the death of the fetus, labor usually begins within 48 h, though it may be delayed up to a few weeks. During this time, the mother may develop a disseminated intravascular coagulopathy. With fractures of the pelvis, there may be not only placental separation but direct fetal injury, for example, fracture of the fetal skull and/or internal injuries to the fetus.

Blunt Force Injuries of the Extremities

These injuries may be limited to the skin and subcutaneous tissues or extend to muscles, blood vessels, nerves, bones and joints.

Injury to upper extremities occurs in association with motor vehicle accidents, falls and assaults. In the case of homicide, the upper extremities should be closely scrutinized for defensive and offensive injuries. The fingernails, fingers, hands and forearms should be carefully examined for abrasions, contusions and lacerations. Broken or avulsed fingernails in a rape victim may indicate that the victim tried to protect herself. Fractured fingers and forearms are sustained by victims when they attempt to ward off a blunt instrument. Contusions, abrasions and superficial lacerations over the knuckles may corroborate a perpetrator's contention of self-defense. The absence of injuries to the hand, however, does not exclude the possibility that blows were struck with the fists. Injuries to the back of the arms may indicate the victim was attempting to ward off blows.

Avulsive wounds of the lower extremities are most frequently seen in automobile-pedestrian accidents. If an automobile wheel passes over the lower extremities, it can exert tangential pressure on the skin and subcutaneous tissues, separating them from the underlying muscles. The pocket created is soon filled with blood and liquefied fat. In other instances, the skin and subcutaneous tissue are also torn, forming a large flap of skin (Figure 5.42).

A blood-filled pocket may also be produced in the back and/or lateral (outer) aspect of the thigh in pedestrians impacted by the front of the hood. The tangential force of the hood impacting the thigh strips the skin and subcutaneous tissue from the muscle, creating a blood-filled pocket (Figure 5.43).

Crush injuries can also occur involving both the upper and lower extremities. In this entity, there is traumatic or ischemic muscle necrosis in persons pinned by beams and falling debris. This causes myoglobin release with resultant acute tubular necrosis (kidney damage).

Injuries of the extremities can also result in severe systemic alterations and death. Shock can result from severe crushing, soft-tissue injuries and/or compound fractures. Significant hemorrhage may occur from traumatic amputations, compound fracture with severing of a large vessel, multiple lacerations or severe avulsive wounds of the skin and

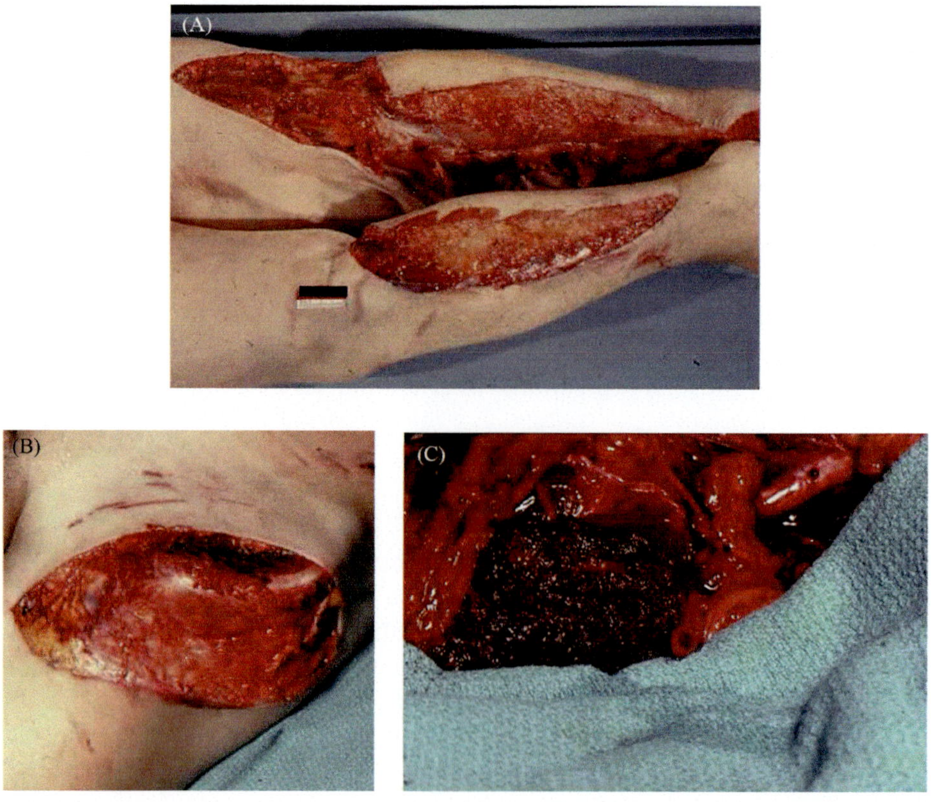

Figure 5.42 (A) Bilateral avulsion injuries of lower extremities caused by truck wheel passing over legs. (B) Avulsive injury of left thigh with (C) transection of femoral artery.

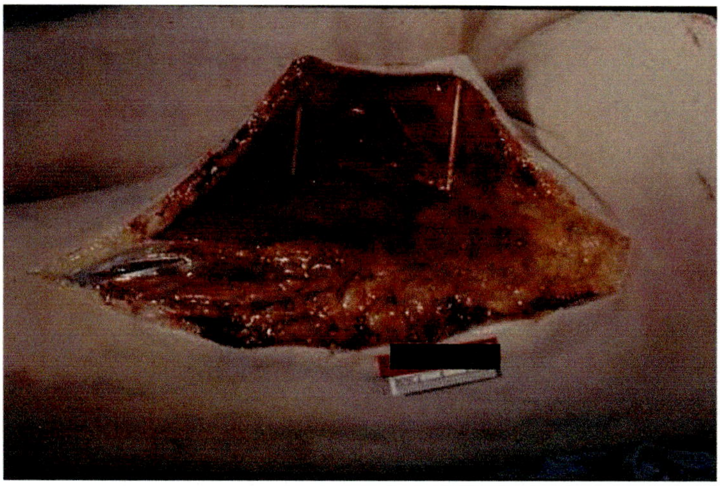

Figure 5.43 Blood-filled cavity (incised) in back of thigh caused by impact with front of automobile hood, with skin and subcutaneous tissue avulsed from muscle.

subcutaneous and underlying tissues, with tearing of numerous small vessels. Additionally, venous thrombosis leading to pulmonary emboli (discussed in Chapter 3), may occur after lower extremity venous injury. Thrombosis may also be secondary to venous stasis following prolonged immobilization of the lower extremity when the patient is confined to bed with a fractured extremity. There may be crushing injuries rather than fractures of the lower extremity with either direct injury to the veins or stasis by compressing hemorrhage and edema resulting from the leg injury. Fat embolism can also occur, see abovementioned discussion, after mechanical trauma to the extremities. Death can also result from infections that develop days to weeks after the traumatic event. Compound fractures are frequently contaminated with bacteria carried into the wound and lodged in the devitalized traumatized tissues. Depending on the virulence of the bacteria and immediateness and extent of surgical attention and cleansing of the wound, the infection may be limited to the skin or soft tissue or extend to the bone (osteomyelitis). A combination of aerobic and anaerobic organisms may cause gangrene of the lower extremity, a terminal hemolytic anemia, hemoglobinuric nephrosis, uremia and septicemia. Wounds contaminated with soil are occasionally infected with tetanus.

Additional Issues

Animal Bites

Animal bites are usually a combination of sharp and blunt force injuries. Perforations from the teeth are sharp in nature; however, the animal will usually then tear the tissues in an effort to subdue their prey and feed. Depending upon the animal, wounds may show paired perforations consistent with the cuspids (canine or fangs) teeth of the animal while the other teeth produce the lacerations as the animal shakes or pulls its victim. Thus, animal wounds are usually complex, consisting of lacerations, abrasions and fractures.

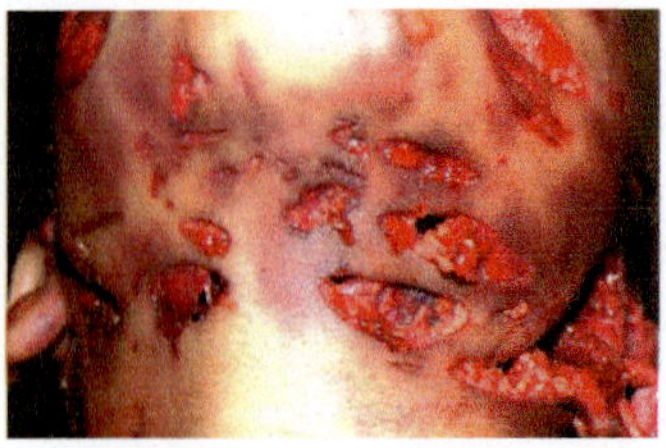

Figure 5.44 Bites of the face and neck in a dog-related fatality. (Photo courtesy of Dr. Norma J. Farley.)

In shark-related fatalities, these bites are typically to the extremities resulting in massive soft tissue and vascular damage, and even traumatic amputation. Death is usually due to either exsanguination or drowning.

Dog-related fatalities usually occur in individuals who are unable to adequately protect themselves, such as the young and old. Typically, multiple bite wounds are present and there is extensive damage of the underlying tissues resulting injuries of the blood vessels, musculature and organs (Figure 5.44).

In a review of 11 dog-related fatalities, Shields et al. found 10 of the deaths to show features of blunt and sharp force injuries, multiple wounds on various body locations and extensive craniofacial trauma with the ultimate cause of death being either exsanguination or nonsurvivable injuries of vital organs.[137]

Rocks and Stones

While just about any blunt implement can result in blunt force injuries – the ground, a wall, a chair, a motor vehicle – the classic implement has always been the rock. Even back in Biblical times, it was documented that David killed Goliath which nothing but a single stone and a sling. In fact, research has shown that in prehistoric times, throwing or slinging stones was as effective as using weapons when hunting animals even at distances up to 25 m.[138] Man soon learned that some stones were more deadly than others – they needed to be heavy and round – and learned to fabricate such from carving natural occurring stones of baking clay. They also learned to design weapons to increase the velocity and accuracy of such stones, namely, the sling and later the catapult.

While we may consider stone and rock throwing to be weapons of the past, there are still reports of thrown stones causing death. In 2004, Bhootra et al. reported a case of a stone throw by a sling shot resulting in death.[139] The decedent died 9 days after the assault and was found to have a skull fracture, subdural and SAH, purulent meningitis and a black stone embedded within the cerebral tissue.

References

1. Robertson I and Hodge PR, Histopathology of healing abrasions. *Forensic Sci* 1972; 1:17–25.
2. Hankey GJ, Eikelboom JW. Antiplatelet drugs. *Med J Aust* 2003;178:568–74.
3. Langlois NEI and Gresham GA, The aging of bruises: a review and study of the color changes with time. *Forensic Sci Int* 1991; 50:227–238.
4. Maguire S, et al., Can you age bruises accurately in children? A systematic review. *Arch Dis Child* 2005; 90(2):187–189.

5. Vanezis P, Interpreting bruises at necropsy. *J Clin Pathol* 2001; 54:348–355.
6. Betz P, Histological and enzyme histochemical parameters for the age estimation of human skin wounds. *Int J Legal Med* 1994; 107:60–68.
7. Byard RW, Wick R, Gilbert JD, and Donald T, Histologic dating of bruises in moribund infants and young children. *Forensic Sci Med Pathol* 2008; 4(3):187–192.
8. Robertson I, Antemortem and postmortem bruises of the skin: their differentiation. *J Forensic Med* 1957; 4:2–10.
9. Hernandez-Cueto C, Girela E, and Sweet DJ, Advances in the diagnosis of wound vitality: a review. *Am J Forensic Med Path* 2000; 21(1):21–31.
10. Harkness JW, Ramsey WC, and Ahmadi B, Principles of fractures and dislocations, in Rockwood CA, Green DP (Eds) *Fractures in Adults* Vol 1. JP Lippincott, Philadelphia, PA, 1984.
11. Kress TA, Porta DJ, Snider JN, et al., Fracture pattern of human cadaver long bones. Presented 1995 International IRCOBI Conference on the Biomechanics of Impact. Sept 13–15, 1995. Brunnen, Switzerland.
12. Porta DJ, Kress TA, Fuller PM, et al., Spiral fractures — definition and determination of torsional direction from radiographs. Presented at the Annual Meeting of the American Academy of Forensic Science, Nashville, February 19–24, 1996.
13. Pennal GF, Tile M, Waddell JP, et al., Pelvic disruption. *Clin Orthoped Related Res* 1980; 151:12–21.
14. Tile M, *Fractures of the Pelvis and Acetabulum*. Williams & Wilkins, Baltimore, MD, 1984.
15. ten Duis HJ, The fat embolism syndrome: review. *Injury* 1997; 28(2):77–85.(80)
16. Fabian TC, Unraveling the fat embolus syndrome (editorial). *NEJM* 1993; 329(13):961–963. (81)
17. Bulger EM, et al., Fat embolism syndrome: a 10-year review. *Arch Surg* 1997; 132(4):435–439.(82)
18. von Bergmann E, Ein Fall von todlicher Fettembolie. *Berl Klin Wochenschr* 1873; 10:385.
19. Gurd AR and Wilson RI, The fat embolism syndrome. *J Bone Joint Surg Br* 1974; 56:408–416.
20. Fracasso T, Karger B, Pfeiffer H, et al., Immunohistochemical identification of prevalent right ventricular ischemia causing right heart failure in cases of pulmonary fat embolism. *Int J Legal Med* 2010; 124:537–542.
21. Gossling HR and Pellegrini VD Jr, Fat embolism syndrome: a review of the pathophysiology and physiological basis of treatment. *Clin Orthop Relat Res* 1982; 165:68–82.
22. Baker PL, Pazell JA, and Peltier LF, Free fatty acids, catecholamines, and arterial hypoxia in patients with fat embolism. *J Trauma* 1971; 11:1026–1030.
23. Shapiro MP and Hayes JA, Fat embolism in sickle cell disease. Report of a case with brief review of the literature. *Arch Intern Med* 1984; 144:181–182.20
24. Falzi G, Henn R, and Spann W, On pulmonary fat embolism after injuries with different periods of survival. *Munch Med Wochenschr* 1964; 106:978–981.
25. Hiss J, Kahana T, and Kugel C, Beaten to death: why do they die? *J Trauma* 1996; 40:27–30.
26. Nichols GR 2nd, Corey TS, and Davis GJ, Nonfracture-associated fatal fat embolism in a case of child abuse. *J Forensic Sci* 1990; 35:493–499.
27. Mudd KL, Hunt A, Matherly RC, et al., Analysis of pulmonary fat embolism in blunt force fatalities. *J Trauma* 2000;48:711–715.
28. Gennarelli TA, et al., Diffuse axonal injury and traumatic coma in the primate. *Ann Neurol* 1982; 12:564–574.
29. Adams IH, Graham DI, and Gennarelli TA, Head injury in man and experimental animals: neuropathology. *Acta Neurochirugica Suppl* 1983; 32:15–30.
30. Le Roux PD, Choudhri H, and Andrews BT, Cerebral concussion and diffuse brain injury. In Cooper PR and Golfinos TA (Eds) *Head Injury* 4th ed. McGraw-Hill, New York, NY, 2000, Chap 7.
31. Lissner HR and Evans FG, Engineering aspects of fractures. *Clin Orthoped* 1958; 8:310–322.
32. Evans FG, Lissner HR, and Lebow M, The relation of energy, velocity and acceleration to skull deformation and fracture. *Surg Gynecol Obstet* 1958; 107:593–601.

33. Gurdjian ES, Webster JE, and Lissner HR, The mechanism of skull fractures. *Radiology* 1950; 54:313–338.
34. Castiglione AG, et al., Intracranial insertion of a nasogastric tube in a case of homicidal head trauma. *Am J Forens Med Path* 1998; 19(4):329–334.
35. Hopper RH, McElhaney JH, and Myers BS, Mandibular and basilar skull tolerance. Experiments Carried Out under the Auspices of Duke University.
36. Hein PM and Schulz E, Contrecoup fractures of the anterior cranial fossae as a consequence of blunt force caused by a fall. *Acta Neurochir* 1990; 105:24–29.
37. Kroman A, Kress T, Porta d, Fracture propagation in the human cranium: a re-testing of popular theories. *Clin Anat* 2011; 24:309–318.
38. Chan-Seng E, et al., Cervical spine injuries from diving accident: a 10-year retrospective descriptive study on 64 patients. *Orthop Traumatol: Surg Res* 2013; 99(5):507–508.
39. Bucholz RW, et al., Occult cervical spine injuries in fatal traffic accidents. *J Trauma* 1979; 19(10):768–771.
40. Adams VI, Neck injuries, I occipitoatlantal dislocations – a pathologic study of 12 traffic fatalities. *J Forensic Sci* 1992; 37(2):556–564.
41. Chapman JR and Anderson PA, Chapter 60: cervical spine trauma P1245–1295, in Frymoyer JW (Ed) *The Adult Spine: Principles and Practice* 2nd ed. Lippincott-Raven, 1997.
42. Adams VI, Neck injuries, II atlantoaxial dislocations: a pathologic study of 14 traffic fatalities. *J Forensic Sci* Philadelphia, 1992; 37(2):565–573.
43. Oshlag B, Ray T, and Boswell B, Neck injuries. *Prim Care*. 2020; 47(1):165–176.
44. Lindenberg R, Trauma of meninges and brain, in Minckler J (Ed) *Pathology of the Nervous System* Vol 2. McGraw-Hill, 1971.
45. Lindenberg R and Freytag E, Morphology of cortical contusions. *Arch Pathol* New York, 1957; 63:23–42.
46. Linderberg R and Freytag E, Morphology of brain lesions from blunt trauma in early infancy. *Arch Pathol* 1969; 87:298–305.
47. Gennarelli TA, Mechanisms of cerebral injury. Presented at the 34th Annual Meeting of the National Association of Medical Examiners. Indianapolis, September 14–19, 2000.
48. Adams JH, et al., Deep intracerebral (basal ganglia) haematomas in fatal nonmissile head injury in man. *J Neurol Neurosurg Psych* 1986; 49(9):1039–1043.
49. Cooper PR, Posttraumatic intracranial mass lesions, in Cooper PR and Golfinos JG (Eds) *Head Injury* 4th ed. McGraw-Hill, New York, NY, 2000.
50. Ninchoji T, et al., Traumatic intracerebral haematomas of delayed onset. *Acta Neurochirugica* 1984; 71:69–90.
51. Young HA, et al., Delayed traumatic intracerebral haematoma: report of 15 cases operatively treated. *Neurosurgery* 1984; 14:22–25.
52. Gentleman D, Nath F, and MacPhersen P, Diagnosis and management of delayed traumatic intracerebral hematoma. *Br J Neurosurg* 1989; 3:367–372.
53. Linderberg R and Freytag E, Brainstem lesions characteristic of traumatic hyperextension of the head. *Arch Pathol* 1970; 90:509–515.
54. Ezzat W, Lee CA, and Nyssen J, Pontomedullary rent: a specific type of primary brainstem traumatic injury. *Am J Forensic Med* 1995; 16(4):336–339.
55. Caceres JA and Goldstein JN, Intracranial hemorrhage. *Emerg Med Clin North Am* 2012; 30(3):771–794.
56. Mealey J, Acute extradural hematomas without demonstrable skull fractures. *J Neurosurg* 1960; 1(7):27–34.
57. Iwakuma T and Brunngraber CV, Chronic extradural hematomas: a study of 21 cases. *J Neurosurg* 1973; 38:488–493.
58. Kawasumi Y, et al., Heat haematoma: post-mortem computed tomography findings. *Clin Radiol* 2013; 68(2):e95–e97.

59. Graham DI and Gennarelli TA, Pathology of brain damage after injury, in Cooper PR and Golfinos JG (Eds) *Head of Injury* 4th ed. McGraw-Hill, New York, NY, 2000.
60. Miller JD and Nader R, Acute subdural hematoma from bridging vein rupture: a potential mechanism for growth. *J Neurosurg* 2014; 120(6):1378–1384.
61. Lee KS, et al., Origin of chronic subdural haematoma and relation to traumatic subdural lesions (review). *Brain Injury* 1998; 12(11):901–910.
62. Ross JL, et al., Forensic evaluation of subarachnoid hemorrhage. *Academic Forensic Pathology.* 2012; 2(1): 30–35.
63. Geddes JF, What's new in the diagnosis of head injury? *J Clin Path* 1997; 50(4):271–274.
64. Fishman RA, *Cerebrospinal Fluid in Diseases of the Nervous System* 2nd ed. WB Saunders, Philadelphia, PA, 1992, p 431
65. Toole JF, Robinson MK, and Mercuri M, Primary subarachnoid hemorrhage, in Toole JF (Ed) *Handbook of Clinical Neurology. Vascular Diseases, Part III.* Elsevier Science, New York, NY, 1989, pp 1–39.
66. Hardman JM, Cerebrospinal trauma, in Davis RL and Robertson DM (Eds) *Textbook of Neuropathology* 3rd ed. Williams & Williams, Baltimore, MD, 1997, p. 1179–1232.
67. Hammes EM, Reaction of the meninges to blood. *Arch Neurol Psychiatry* 1944; 52:505–514.
68. Adams RD and Sidman RL, *Introduction to Neuropathology.* McGraw-Hill, New York, NY, 1968, p 629.
69. Alpers BJ and Forster FM, The reparative processes in subarachnoid hemorrhage. *J Neuropathol Exp Neurol* 1945; 4:262–268.
70. Lindenberg R, Trauma of the meninges and brain, in Minckler J (Ed) *Pathology of the Nervous System.* McGraw-Hill, New York, NY, 1971, p 1705–1765.
71. Opeskin K and Burke MP, Vertebral artery trauma. *Am J Forens Med Path* 1998; 19(3):206–217.
72. Martin RF, et al., Blunt trauma to the carotid arteries. *J Vasc Surg* 1991; 14(6): 789–793.
73. Cogbill TH, et al., The spectrum of blunt injury to the carotid artery: a multicenter prospective. *J Trauma* 1994; 37(3):473–479.
74. Rutherfoord GS, Dada MA, and Nel JP, Cerebral infarction and intracranial dissection in closed head injuries. *Am J Forensic Med Path* 1996; 17(1):53–57.
75. Opeskin K, Traumatic pericallosal artery aneurysms. *Am J Forensic Med Path* 1995; 16(1):11–16.
76. Soria ED, Paroski MW, and Schamann ME, Traumatic aneurysms of cerebral vessels: a case study and review of the literature. *Angiology* 1988; 39:690–615.
77. Kobrine AI, et al., Demonstration of massive traumatic brain swelling within 20 minutes after injury. Case report. *J Neurosurg* 1977; 46(2):256–258.
78. Bruce DA, et al., Diffuse cerebral swelling in children: the syndrome of "malignant brain edema" *J Neurosurg* 1981; 54:170–178.
79. Snoek IW, et al., Delayed deterioration following mild head injury in children. *Brain* 1984;107:15–36.
80. Lang DA, et al., Diffuse brain swelling after injury: more often malignant in adults than children. *J Neurosurg* 1994; 80: 675–680.
81. Wolf JA, Stys PK, Lusardi T, Meaney D, and Smith DH, Traumatic axonal injury induces calcium influx modulated by tetrodotoxin-sensitive sodium channels. *J Neurosci* 2001; 21(6):1923–1930.
82. Smith DH and Meaney DF, Axonal damage in traumatic brain injury. *Neuroscientist* 2000; 6(6):483–495.
83. LoPachin RM and Lehning EJ, Mechanism of calcium entry during axon injury and degeneration. *Toxicol Appl Pharmacol* 1997; 143(2):233–244.
84. Cowie RJ and Stanton GB, *Axoplasmic Transport and Neuronal Responses to Injury Archived 2005-10-29.* Howard University College of Medicine 2005, Retrieved on 2008-01-17.
85. Hughes PM, Wells GMA, Perry VH, Brown MC, and Miller KM, Comparison of matrix metalloproteinase expression during Wallerian degeneration in the central and peripheral nervous systems. *Neuroscience* 2002; 113(2):273–287.

86. Castillo MR and Babson JR, Ca^{2}+-dependent mechanisms of cell injury in cultured cortical neurons. *Neuroscience* 1998; 86(4):1133–1144.
87. Zhou F, Xiang Z, Feng WX, and Zhen LX, Neuronal free Ca^{2}+ and BBB permeability and ultrastructure in head injury with secondary insult. *J Clin Neurosci* 2001; 8(6):561–563.
88. Oehmichen M, et al., Axonal injury — a diagnostic tool in forensic neuropathology? (Review). *Forensic Sci Int* 1998; 95(1):67–83.
89. Oehmichen M, et al., Pontine axonal injury after brain trauma and nontraumatic hypoxic-ischemic brain damage. *Int J Legal Med* 1999; 112:261–267.
90. Kelley JP, et al., Concussion in sports: guidelines for the prevention of catastrophic outcome. *JAMA* 1991; 226:2867–2869
91. Blumberg PC, et al., Staining of amyloid precursor protein to study axonal damage in mild head injury. *Lancet* 1994; 344:1055–1056.
92. Cantu RC, Second-impact syndrome. *Clin Sport Med* 1998; 17:37–60.
93. Milovanovic A and Di Maio VJM, Death due to concussion and alcohol. *Am J Forensic Med Path* 1999; 20(1):6–9.
94. Molina DK and DiMaio VJ, Head trauma and alcohol: a lethal combination. *Am J Forensic Med Pathol* 2015; 36(4):290–292.
95. Zink BJ and Feustel PJ, Effects of ethanol on respiratory function in traumatic brain injury. *J Neurosurg* 1995; 82:822–828.
96. Moenninghoff C, et al., Diffuse axonal injury at ultra-high field MRI. *PLoS ONE* 2015: 10(3): e0122329
97. Gennarelli TA and Thibault LE, Biomechanics of acute subdural hematoma. *J Trauma* 1982; 22(8):680–686.
98. Adams JH, et al., Diffuse axonal injury in head injuries caused by a fall. *Lancet* 1984;324: 1420–1422.
99. Gultekin SH and Smith TW, Diffuse axonal injury in craniocerebral trauma. *Arch Path Lab Med* 1994; 118:168–171.
100. Pfister BJ, Chickola L, and Smith DH, Head motions while riding roller coasters: implications for brain injury. *Am J Forensic Med Pathol* 2009; 30(4):339–345.
101. Martland HS, Punch drunk. *JAMA* 1928; 91:1003–1007.
102. Morrison RG, Medical and public health aspects of boxing. *JAMA* 1986; 255:2475–2480.
103. Lampert PW and Hardman JM, Morphological changes in brains of boxers. *JAMA* 1984; 251:2676–2679.
104. Corsellis J, Burton CJ, and Freeman-Browne D, The aftermath of boxing. *Psychol Med* 1973; 3:270–303.
105. Montenigro PH, Corp DT, and Cantu RC, Stern RA chronic traumatic encephalopathy: historical origins and current perspective. *Annu Rev Clin Psychol* 2015; 11:309–330.
106. Majercik S and Pieracci FM, Chest wall trauma. *Thorac Surg Clin* 2017; 27(2):113–121.
107. Bharati S and Levi M, The pathology of sudden death, in Josephson ME (Ed) *Sudden Cardiac Death (Cardiovascular Clinics) 15/3*. FA Davis Co, Philadelphia, PA, 1985, pp 1–27.
108. Killen DA, et al., Posttraumatic aneurysm of left ventricle. *Circulation* 1969; 39:101–108.
109. Ebert LC, et al., Fatal left ventricular rupture and pericardial tamponade following a horse kick to the chest. *Am J Forensic Med Pathol* 2011; 1(1):167–169.
110. Bolooki H, Karlson KE, Garzon AA, et al., Ventricular septal defects produced by penetrating chest injuries. *NY State J Med* 1969; 69:24712474
111. Simson LR Jr, Chin-sternum-heart syndrome: cardiac injury associated with parachute mishaps. *Aerospace Med* 1971; 42:1214–1218.
112. Suzuki I, Sato M, Hoshi N, and Manjo H, Coronary arterial laceration after blunt chest trauma. *NEJM* 2000; 343(10):742–743.
113. Cherng WJ, Bullard MJ, Chang HJ, et al., Diagnosis of coronary artery dissection following blunt chest trauma by transesophageal echocardiography. *J Trauma* 1995; 39:772–774.

114. Maron BJ, Poliac LC, Kaplan JA, and Mueller FO, Blunt impact to the chest leading to sudden death from cardiac arrest during sports activities. *NEJM* 1995; 333:337–342.
115. Viano DC, Andrzejak DV, Polley TZ, and King AI, Mechanism of fatal chest injury in baseball impact: development of an experimental model. *Clin J Sport Med* 1992; 2:166–171.
116. Marshall DT, Gilbert JD, and Byard RW, The spectrum of findings in cases of sudden death due to blunt cardiac trauma–'commotio cordis'. *Am J Forensic Med Pathol* 2008; 29(1):1–4.
117. Link MS, Wang PJ, Natesa GP, Bharati S., et al., An experimental model of sudden death due to low-energy chest-wall impact (commotio cordis). *NEJM* 1998 338:1805–1811.
118. Arajarvi E, Santavirta S, and Tolonen J, Aortic ruptures in seat belt wearers. *J Thorac Cardiovasc Surg* 1989; 98:355–361.
119. Symbas PJ, Horsley WS, and Symbas PN, Rupture of the ascending aorta caused by blunt trauma (review). *Ann Thorac Surg* 1998; 66(1):113–117.
120. Rogers F, Osler TM, and Shackford SR, Aortic dissection after trauma: case report and review of the literature. *J Trauma* 1996; 41(5):906–908.
121. Ono M, Yagyu K, Furuse A, Kotsuka Y, and Kubota H, A case of Stanford Type A acute aortic dissection caused by blunt chest trauma. *J Trauma* 1998; 44(3):543–544.
122. Gammie JS, Katz WE, Swanson ER, and Peitzman AB, Acute aortic dissection after blunt chest trauma. *J Trauma* 1996; 40(1):126–127.
123. Papadopoulos CD, Potter RT, Manoli AN, et al., Chronic traumatic dissecting aortic aneurysms. *NY State J Med* 1975; 75:2181–2184.
124. Heggtveit HL, Campbell JS, and Hooper GD, Innominate arterial aneurysms occurring after blunt trauma. *Am J Clin Pathol* 1964; 42:69–74.
125. Harkin DW, Kirk G, and Clements WDB, Abdominal aortic rupture in a child after blunt trauma on a soccer field. *Injury* 1999; 30:303–304.
126. Winter B and Baum R, Complete traumatic rupture of the bronchus with minimal trauma. *JAMA* 1968; 206:370–372.
127. Osborn GR, Findings in 252 fatal accidents. *Lancet* 1943; 2:277–284.
128. Steier M, Ching N, Bonfils-Roberts E, et al., Iatrogenic causes of pneumothorax: increasing incidence with advances in medical care. *NY State J Med* 1973; 73:1296–1298.
129. Newman LL, San Filippo JA, Halata MS, et al., Pneumothorax and hydrothorax following placement of central catheter. *NY State J Med* 1982; 82:341–343.
130. Ducatman BS, Ludwig J, and Hurt RD, Fatal rectus sheath hematoma. *JAMA* 1983; 249:924–925.
131. Mays ET, Bursting injuries of the liver. *Arch Surg* 1966; 93:92–106.
132. Semel L and Frittelli G, Gastric rupture from blunt abdominal trauma. *NY State J Med* 1981; 81:938–939.
133. Vance BM, Subcutaneous injuries of the abdominal viscera. *Arch Surg* 1928; 16:631–679.
134. Reay DT, Sexual abuse and death of an elderly lady by "fisting. *Am J Forensic Med Path* 1983; 4:347–349.
135. Rothenberger D, Quattlebaum FW, Perry JF, et al., Blunt maternal trauma: a review of 103 cases. *J Trauma* 1978; 18:173–179.
136. Crosby WM, Traumatic injuries during pregnancy. *Clin Obstet Gynecol* 1983; 26:902–912.
137. Shields LBE, Bernstein ML, Hunsaker JC, and Stewart DM, Dog bite-related fatalities: a 15-year review of Kentucky medical examiner cases. *Am J Forensic Med Pathol* 2009; 30(3):223–230.
138. Wilson AD, Zhu Q, Barham L, et al., A dynamical analysis of the suitability of prehistoric spheroids from the cave of hearths as thrown projectiles. *Sci Rep* 2016; 6: 30614.
139. Bhootra BL and Bhana BD, An unusual missile-type head injury caused by a stone: case report and medicolegal perspectives. *Am J Forensic Med Pathol* 2004; 25(4):355–357.

Sharp Force Wounds

6

One, two! One, two! And through and through
The vorpal blade went snicker-snack!

—Lewis Carroll, Jabberwocky

In general, wounds caused by pointed and sharp-edged weapons can be divided into four categories:

1. Stab wounds
2. Incised wounds (cuts)
3. Chop wounds
4. Therapeutic/diagnostic wounds

Stab Wounds

Stab wounds are sharp injuries that are *deeper than they are long*. They are produced by pointed instruments. In stab wounds, the edges of the wound in the skin are typically sharp, without abrasion or contusion (Figure 6.1).

The most commonly used weapon to produce a stab wound is a knife, which, by virtue of its cutting edge, can also produce incised wounds. The typical weapon is a flat-bladed, single-edged kitchen, pocket or folding knife with a 4- to 5-in. blade. Other devices, such as ice picks, scissors, screwdrivers, broken glass, forks, pens and pencils, have been used to inflict stab wounds.

The force needed to create a stab wound is discussed in more detail below, but the force needed for a knife to perforate the skin depends on the configuration and sharpness of the tip of the knife. The sharper, more needle-like the tip, the more readily it will perforate the skin.[1] Once the tip has perforated the skin, the rest of the blade will slide into the body with ease. As long as it does not contact a bone, a knife can readily pass through organs with very little force. Thus, even if a knife blade is driven its complete length into the body, this does not necessarily mean that the stab wound was inflicted with great force.

Stab Wound Dimensions

In stab wounds, the length of the wound in the skin can be equal, less or greater than the width of the knife. It may be greater if, as the knife perforates the skin, the cutting edge of the blade is drawn against the skin, slicing through it, enlarging the wound. The elasticity or laxness of the skin can also change the dimensions of the wound in the skin, increasing or decreasing it by a millimeter or two beyond the actual dimensions of the knife.

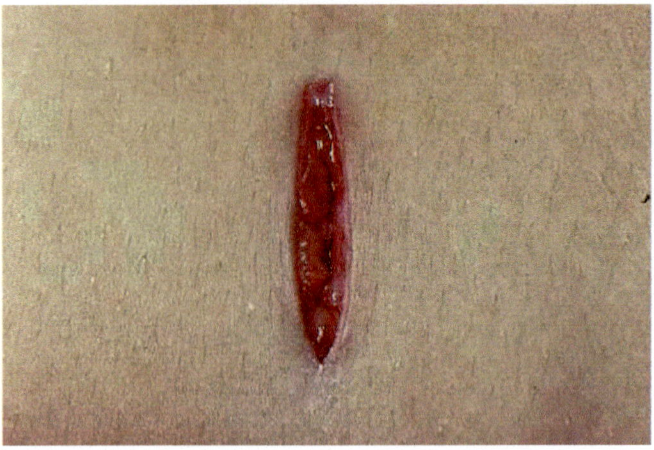

Figure 6.1 Stab wound by single-edged knife. Top squared off, lower end V-shaped.

The depth of the stab wound can be equal to, less than or greater than the length of the knife blade. If the knife is not inserted all the way, the wound track is less than the length of the blade. Or the knife may be plunged deeply into the body with such force as to indent the abdominal or chest wall, so that the length of the knife track exceeds the length of the knife blade. If there are numerous stab wounds in the body, one can usually get an approximation of the length and the width of the knife blade by examining them all and comparing the depths of each wound.

The depth a stab wound needs to achieve to produce a life-threatening or fatal wound depends on the area of the body stabbed. Minimum skin-to-organ distances for various organs have been determined by Connor et al. using computer tomography (CT).[2] There was no significant difference between the minimum skin-to-organ distances for males (44 cases) and females (27 cases). Table 6.1 gives the minimum, maximum and mean skin-to-organ distances for various organs. These distances may overstate the distance a knife needs to penetrate to reach an organ in that in real-life situations, the skin and subcutaneous tissue may be compressed by the force of the thrust.

Appearance of Stab Wounds in Skin

The size and shape of a stab wound in the skin depends on the nature of the blade, the direction of the thrust, the movement of the blade in the wound, the movement of the

Table 6.1 Distance from Skin to Organs (mm)

	Pleura	Pericardium	Liver	Spleen	Kidney	Thoracic Aorta	Abdominal Aorta	Femoral Artery
Minimum	10	15	9	12	19	31	65	13
Maximum	48	45	36	39	79	93	102	25
Mean standard	22	31	19	23	37	64	87	18
Deviation	7.9	7.1	6.3	7.0	13	15.1	10.3	3.9

individual stabbed and the state of relaxation or tension of the skin. The sharpness of a weapon will determine the appearance of the margins of the wound: sharp and regular; abraded and bruised; or jagged and contused. With a blunt cutting edge, the edges of the wound may be abraded. If an individual is stabbed such that the flat surface of the knife blade is at an oblique angle to the skin, the stab wound will have a beveled margin on one side with undermining on the other, indicating the direction from which the knife entered.

The parts of a single-edged knife (Figure 6.2) are as follows:

- Grip
- Guard
- Ricasso
- Back
- Spine
- Edge
- Point

The appearance of a stab wound can be influenced by how deep the knife is thrust in and what portion of the shaft penetrates or contacts the skin. If the knife is thrust with great force into the body up to the guard, then the imprint of the guard could be on the skin. If the knife is thrust in up to the ricasso, the wound can be squared at both ends.

In addition, the shape of a stab wound in the skin is determined not only by the shape of the blade, but also by the properties of the skin. If a stab wound is inflicted when the skin is stretched, the resulting long, thin wound will assume a shorter, broader appearance when the skin relaxes. Langer's lines can also influence the appearance of a wound. Langer's lines are a pattern of elastic fibers in the dermis of the skin, which is approximately the same from individual to individual. Plastic surgeons take advantage of this pattern of fibers to conceal scars. If one is stabbed across these lines, that is, perpendicular to the fibers, the fibers will pull apart the edges of the wound, creating a gaping wound (Figure 6.3).

Stab wounds parallel to Langer's lines produce narrow slit-like wounds. Between the two extremes are oblique wounds. Here, depending on the pattern of the fibers, the wounds may be asymmetrical or semicircular. If the edges of a gaping wound are drawn together, the size of the restored wound approximates the maximum possible width of the knife blade.

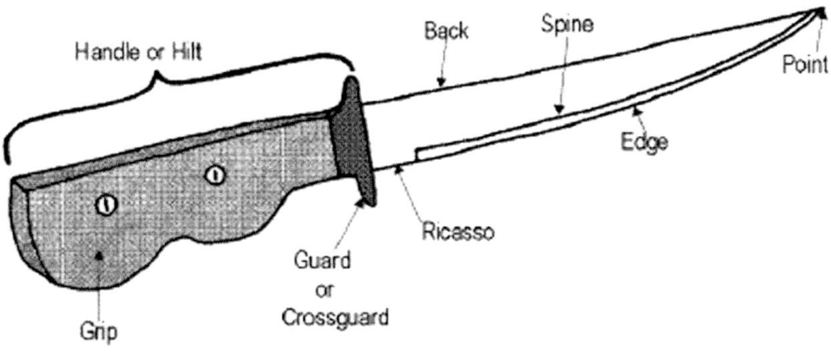

Figure 6.2 Parts of single-edged knife.

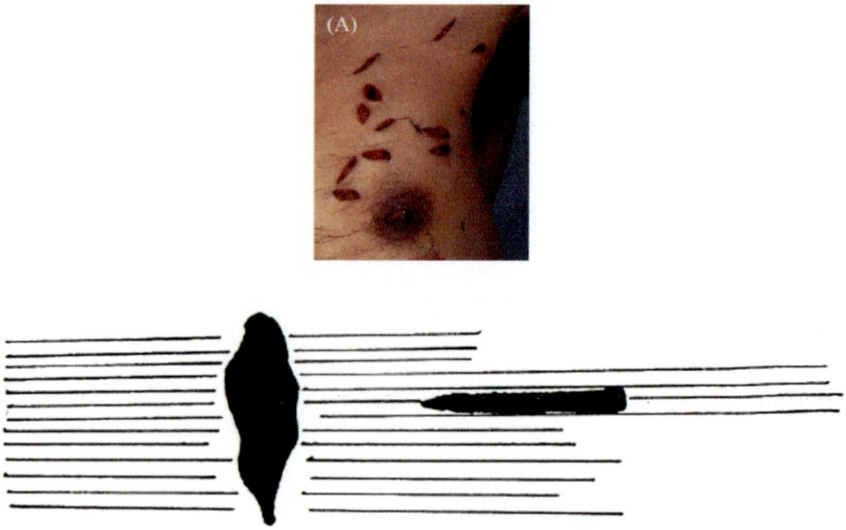

Figure 6.3 (A) Multiple stab wounds with same knife. Varied shapes to wounds due to Langer's lines. Effect of Langer's lines on stab wound perpendicular to (B) and parallel to (C) lines.

If a double-edged weapon is used to stab an individual, the wound produced may show bilateral pointed ends. If a single-edged weapon is used, theoretically, one end of the stab wound is pointed, and the other is squared off or blunted (Figure 6.1). However, stab wounds with double-edged weapons are uncommon in the United States. Virtually all stab wounds seen are made with single-edged weapons. When actual wounds are examined, it becomes obvious that a number of stab wounds caused by single-edged weapons have bilateral pointed ends like those made with double-edged weapons. There are two explanations for this. First, as the tip of the knife perforates the skin, it is pulled down, with the cutting edge slicing through the skin and the squared-off back of the knife not imparting its configuration to the skin because it does not contact it. Second, many single-edged knives have a cutting edge on the back of the knife at the tip. Thus, the initial plunge into the skin will produce a double-pointed wound. Then, as the rest of the knife goes through the skin, if it is pulled down slightly, the back or squared-off portion of the knife will never contact the skin. Thus, while in theory one can look at a stab wound and say the weapon was single- or double-edged, in reality, it is not always possible through examination of a single wound. If an individual is stabbed multiple times with a single-edged knife, examination of the wounds will usually disclose the typical single-edged configuration.

As a knife is withdrawn from the body, it may be twisted or the person stabbed may move. In such a case, the knife might produce a Y- or L-shaped wound (Figure 6.4).

There will be a primary stab wound with an extension caused by the knife's edge cutting a secondary path as it exits. A variation of this can be seen when the knife is only slightly rotated or the individual moves only slightly, such that one end (the cutting end) of the stab wound will have an inverted V-shaped notch or "fork" in it (Figure 6.5).

Thus, in this situation with a single-edged knife, one end of the stab wound will be squared or blunted and the other will be forked.

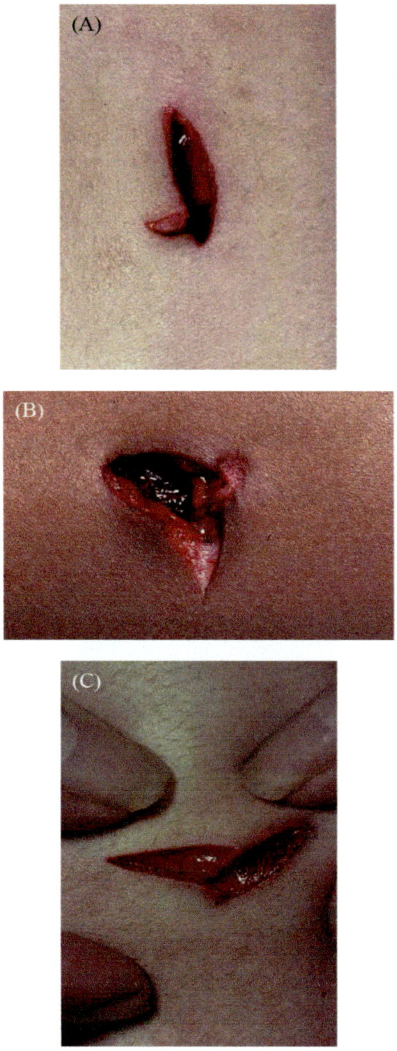

Figure 6.4 (A–C) Irregular configuration of stab wounds caused by knife being twisted or movement of victim as blade is withdrawn.

A fork at one end of a stab wound caused by the cutting edge of the knife can be confused with tears in the skin at the squared-off end of the stab wound produced by the back of the blade (the ricasso) lacerating the skin as the blade is plunged in. These tears can usually be differentiated from the fork cuts in that they are not as sharp and clean and are often confined to the superficial layers of the skin (Figure 6.6).

The most common reason for a large, irregular knife wound is movement of the victim as the weapon is withdrawn. Prosecutors, however, often contend that this is due to the perpetrator's twisting the knife in the body after stabbing the individual.

If a knife is plunged into the body with such great force that the full length of the blade enters, a patterned abrasion around the stab wound can be caused by the guard (Figure 6.7), which is a metal piece between the blade and handle originally designed to

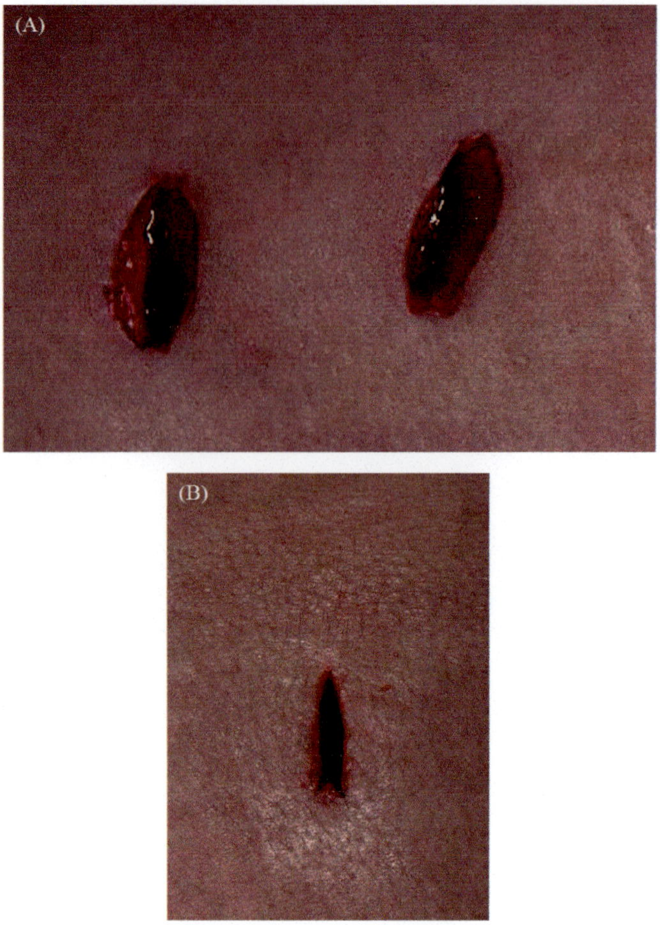

Figure 6.5 (A) Stab wounds from a single-edged knife with small forks at the cutting-edge end caused by the knife being withdrawn. (B) Double-edged stab wound with fork at one end.

keep the user's hand on the handle. Use of the term "hilt" is technically incorrect, because that term refers to swords. A mark from a guard will be symmetrical if the knife is plunged straight in (Figure 6.7A).

If the knife is plunged in a downward angle, then the guard mark will be prominent above the stab wound; if the knife is plunged upward, the guard mark will be below the stab wound. In oblique stab wounds, a knife plunged in from the right will have a guard mark on the right (Figure 6.7B, D).

In some stab wounds, examination of the wound will reveal both ends to have a squared-off or blunt appearance. This is caused by the knife's being plunged in the full length up to the guard. In most weapons, between the true edge of the knife and the guard, there is a short, unsharpened section of blade called the ricasso. This generally has a squared-off configuration that is identical on both the back and the cutting edge of the knife. Thus, if the knife goes in all the way, one end of the stab wound will be squared off by the back of the knife, and the other by the ricasso.

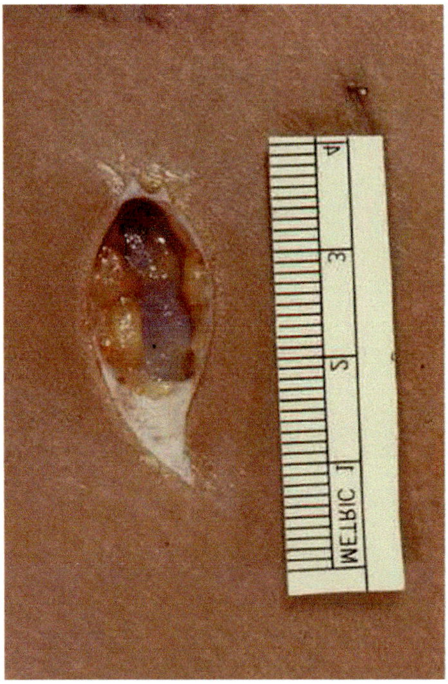

Figure 6.6 Tearing at squared-off margin of stab wound from single-edged knife produced by back of blade lacerating the skin.

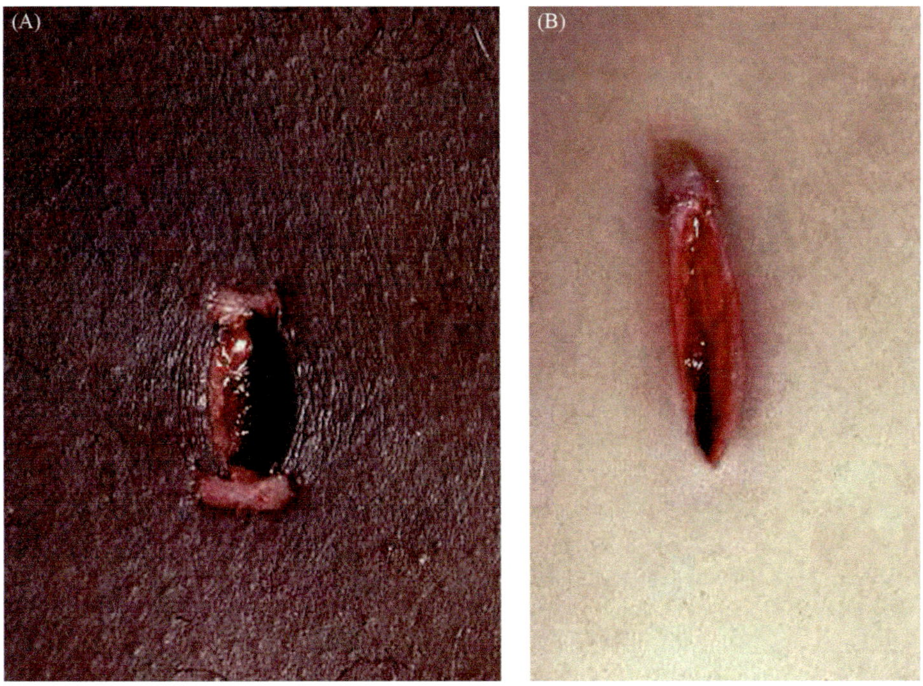

Figure 6.7 Patterned abrasions around stab wounds due to single-edged knife with guard. (A) Symmetrical marking at superior and inferior margins. (B) Knife plunged in a downward angle with guard mark at squared-off margin (*continued*).

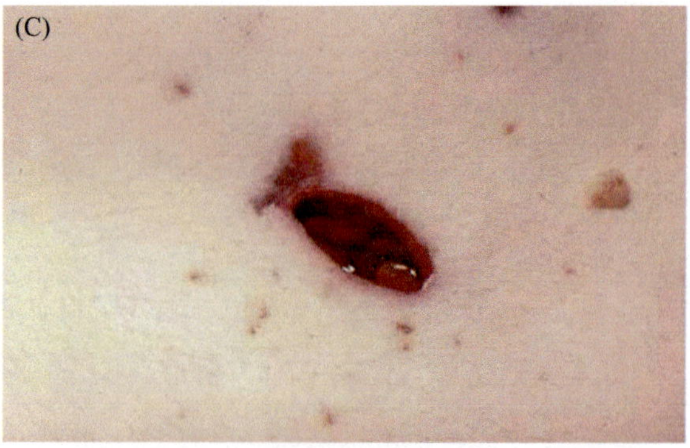

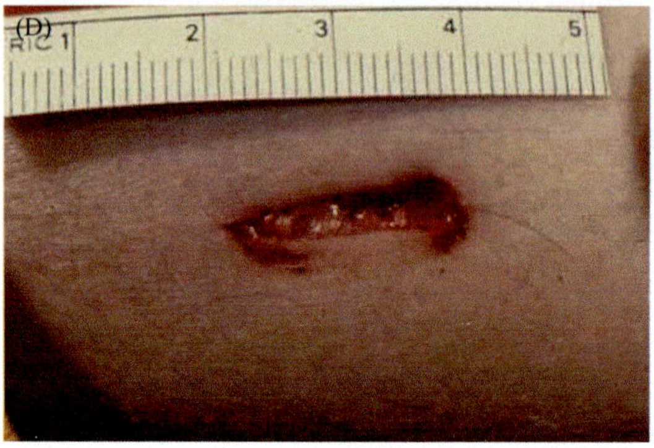

Figure 6.7 (*continued*) Patterned abrasions around stab wounds due to single-edged knife with guard. (C) Knife plunged upward with guard mark on inferior margin of stab wound. (D) Oblique stab wound with guard mark on inferior margin.

Stab Wounds from Weapons Other Than Knives

When an individual is stabbed with an implement other than a knife, the stab wound may have a characteristic appearance because of the unusual nature of the weapon. Because ice picks are no longer common household objects, ice pick wounds are rarely seen nowadays. Ice picks produce small, round or slit-like wounds that can be easily missed or confused with wounds caused by 0.22-caliber bullets or shotgun pellets (Figure 6.8).

An ice pick wound might be missed on a cursory examination of a body, especially if there is little or no external bleeding (Figure 6.9).

If a victim is stabbed with a barbecue fork, there will be clusters of two or three wounds, depending on the number of prongs on the fork (Figure 6.10A).

Each of the stab wounds will be equally spaced, as are the prongs of the fork. Perforation of the skin with a kitchen fork is generally not possible. The authors have seen only one death due to a stab wound with a kitchen fork (through the chest wall into a lung), though they have seen numerous attempts. What one sees is a pattern of three or four (depending on the number of prongs) abrasions or superficial penetrating wounds of the skin caused by the prongs of the fork (Figure 6.10B, C).

The authors have seen fatal stab wounds inflicted with pens, pencils, broken pool cues, etc. In one case, an individual was stabbed on the left side of the neck with a ballpoint pen.

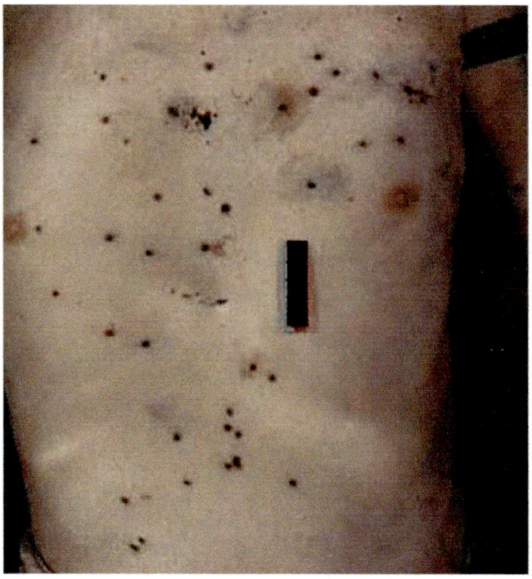

Figure 6.8 Elderly individual with multiple ice pick wounds of chest originally believed to be shotgun pellet wounds.

The pen perforated skin, muscle and ligaments; penetrating into the spinal column at the atlanto-occipital junction, and perforating the spinal cord (Figure 6.11).

The appearance of stab wounds made with scissors depends on whether the scissors were open or closed at the time of stabbing (Figure 6.12).

If closed, the tip of the scissors splits rather than cuts the skin, producing a linear stab wound with abraded margins. If the screw holding the two blades is not flush but protrudes, it can produce an angular laceration in the mid portion of one of the skin margins. If the two blades are separated, two stab wounds will be produced with each stab.

Figure 6.9 Inconspicuous ice pick wounds. (Photo courtesy of Dr. Norma J. Farley.)

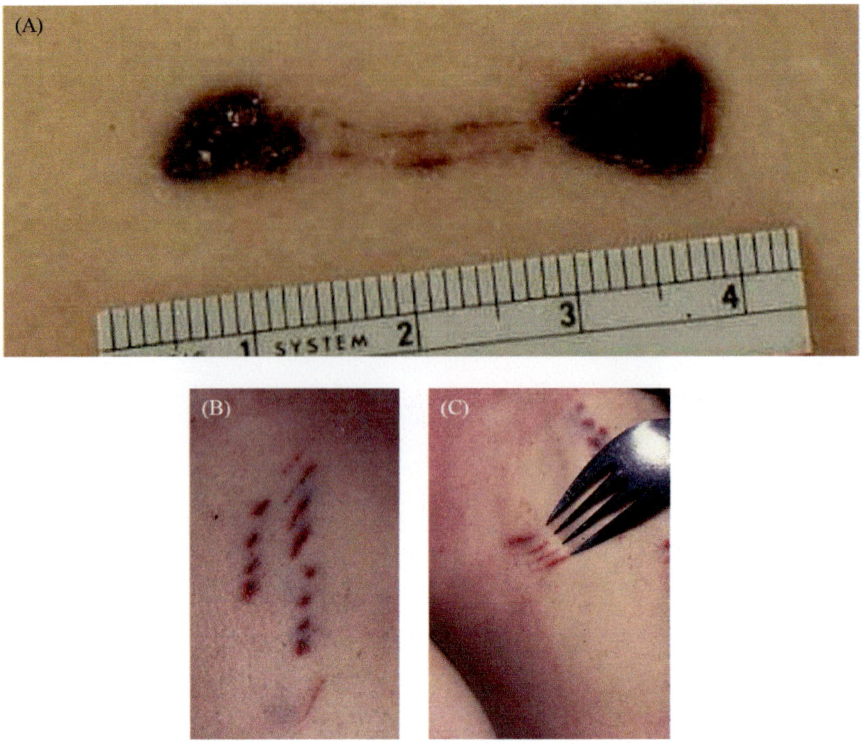

Figure 6.10 (A) Stab wound with barbeque fork. (B and C) Superficial stab wounds caused by kitchen fork.

Stab wounds with screwdrivers may show very characteristic configuration if the weapon is a Phillips screwdriver. In such instances, the X-shaped point of the blade will cause a circular wound with four equally spaced cuts and an abraded margin (Figure 6.13A, B).

A standard-blade screwdriver will produce a slit-like stab wound with squared ends and abraded margins (Figure 6.13C). Thus, one cannot be absolutely sure whether a wound has been produced by a screwdriver or by a knife with a narrow, dull blade, plunged in up to the guard.

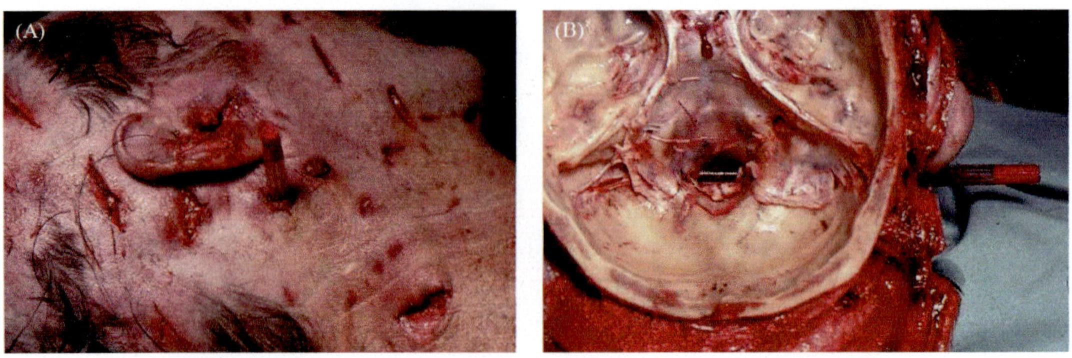

Figure 6.11 Stab wound of neck from a ballpoint pen (A). Stab wound of neck from a ballpoint pen with perforation of the spinal cord at the atlanto-occipital junction (B).

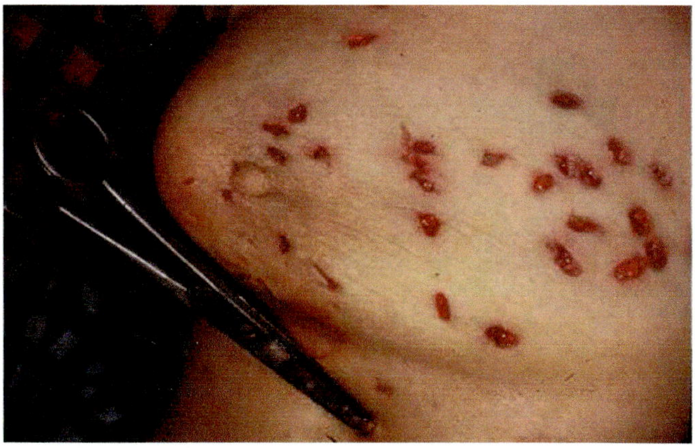

Figure 6.12 Suicide. Multiple stab wounds with scissors.

Stab wounds inflicted with a broken bottle tend to occur as clusters of wounds of different sizes, shapes and depths (Figure 6.14A, B).

The stab wounds are sharp edged but ragged, and there are differences in the depth of penetration for the individual wounds. Most fatal stab wounds with broken bottles are homicides, occasionally suicides and, rarely, accidents (Figure 6.14C). In one case, an individual died when he fell on a broken bottle. The broken end penetrated into the right side of the neck, severing a major vessel.

Stab wounds caused by swords and lances are virtually unheard of in the United States. The authors have encountered only one, a sword wound. Occasionally, one sees deaths caused by arrows or crossbow bolts. These are, in a way, stab wounds. The appearance of the wound depends on the arrowhead. Target arrows have pointed conical ends. They produce circular entrance wounds in the skin similar in appearance to bullet wounds. Hunting arrows have from two to five knife-like edges (four or five are the most common). The wounds produced are cross-like or X-shaped with the four-edged arrowhead. The margins of the wound appear incised, without abrasions (Figure 6.15).

Identifying the Weapon

The pathologist is often asked to give an opinion as to the characteristics of the implement used in a killing. Was the knife single- or double-edged? What was the length of the knife blade? The width of the blade? Was the blade serrated? Was more than one knife used?

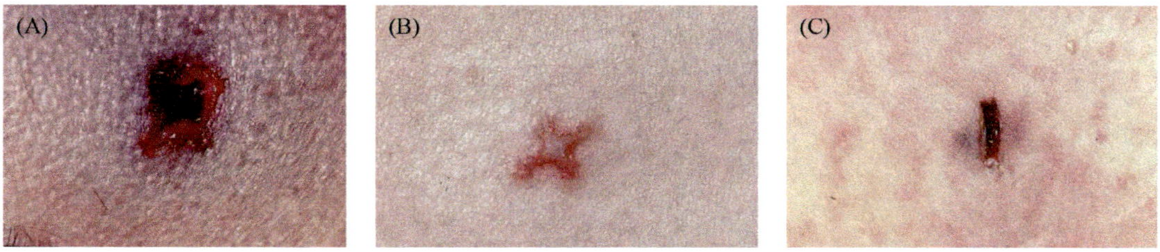

Figure 6.13 (A and B) Stab wounds with Phillips screwdriver. (C) Stab wounds from traditional screwdriver.

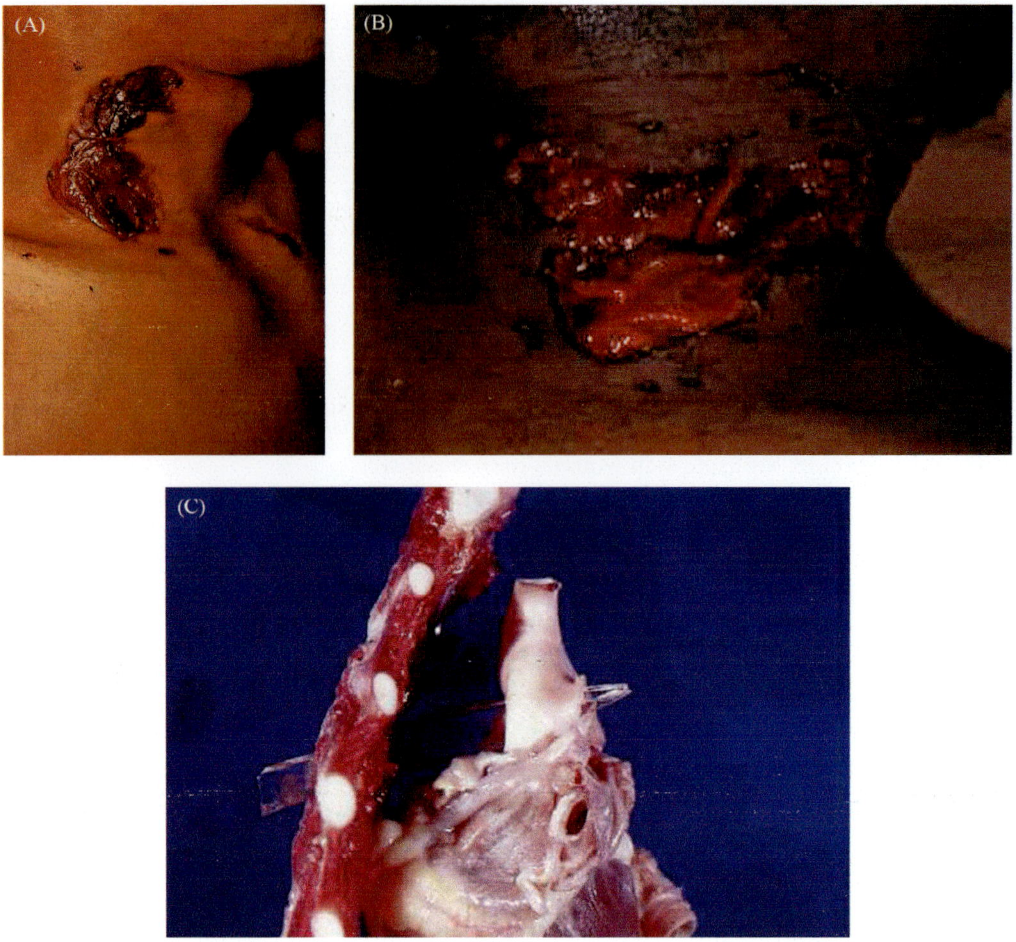

Figure 6.14 (A and B) Stab wounds from a broken bottle. (C) Sliver of glass perforating the sternum and aorta. Deceased fell through glass door.

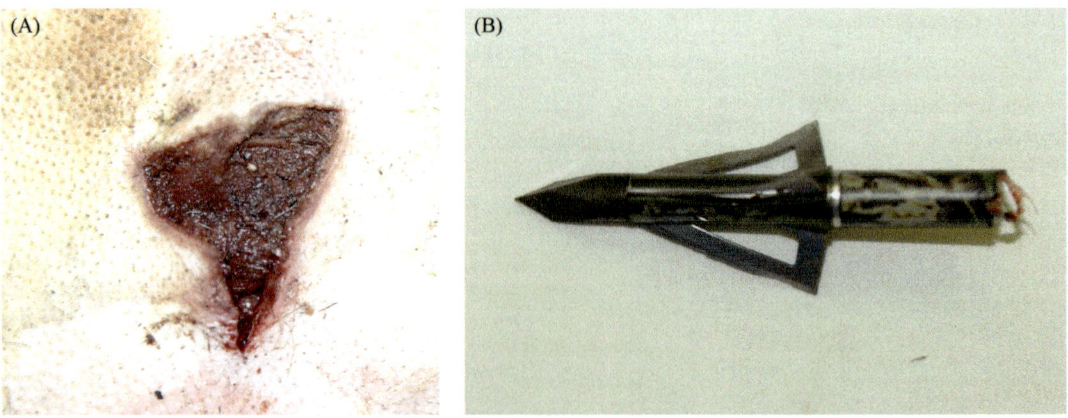

Figure 6.15 (A) Head wound from a three-pointed crossbow broadhead; (B) crossbow broadhead used to create wound in (A).

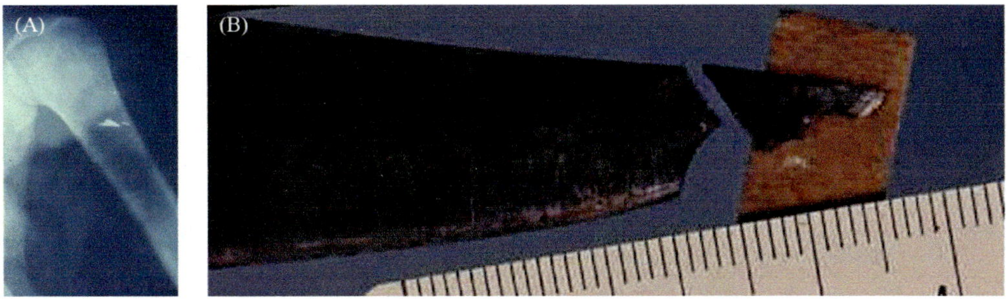

Figure 6.16 (A) Broken knife blade embedded in humerus. (B) Match made with murder weapon.

One should be extremely cautious in giving answers to these questions. In most cases, on examining a wound, the most information that can be deduced is the maximum width of the blade, an approximation of the length of the blade, whether it is single-edged or if it appears more than one implement was used. However, one can never definitely link a knife to a wound unless the tip of the knife has imbedded itself in the body and broken off (Figure 6.16).

If the knife is recovered, this tip can be matched to the knife by tool mark comparison. A physical match in such a case is as valid as a ballistics match of a bullet. In most instances, the most that one can do when presented with a knife and asked if it was the weapon that produced a specific wound is state that it could have been. The determination that the knife was serrated from the appearance of the wound is also rare (Figure 6.17).

All knives thought to have injured or killed an individual should be examined for the presence of blood or tissue. Any blood or tissue present can be typed by DNA techniques so as to link the weapon to the victim. It is possible for a knife or similar weapon to not show microscopic blood staining after it has been used to stab an individual. In stab wounds of solid organs, bleeding occurs only after the knife is withdrawn because pressure of the knife *in situ* prevents bleeding. During withdrawal of the knife, the muscular and elastic

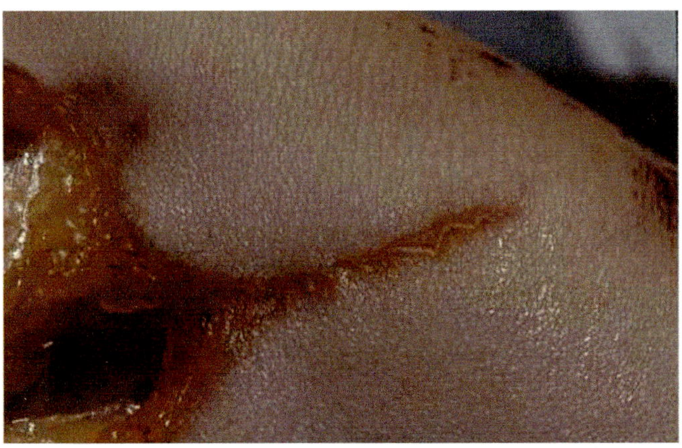

Figure 6.17 Stab wound from blade with serrated edge.

tissue of the solid organs stabbed or the elastic tissue of the skin may contract about the knife and wipe off the blood present on the blade of the knife. During its withdrawal from the body, the knife may also be wiped clean by the clothing. If a knife appears to be free of blood, the handles should be removed to see if any blood is there. With folding knives, the recess for the blade should also be tested for blood. Even though the blade or recess may appear to be free of blood or tissue, analysis of a wiping of the blade might still yield sufficient tissue to perform at least limited DNA analysis and typing. This may be sufficient to link a weapon to a victim. Additionally, external bleeding from a stab wound victim may not be copious, as the wound may close behind the knife as it is removed, allowing for minimal external blood loss.

On rare occasions, a knife is found embedded in the body. To remove it, the thumb and index finger should grasp the sides of the handle immediately adjacent to the skin. This will enable the examiner to avoid touching that portion of the knife handle that was in contact with the assailant's hand, where fingerprints may have been left.

Rarely, the weapon is found firmly clenched in the deceased's hand (see Figure 2.4). Cadaveric spasm, an intense muscular contraction of the hand, which occurs at the moment of death, indicates that the person had the weapon in his hand at the time of death.

Usually, following a suicidal stabbing, the weapon is found immediately adjacent to or a short distance from the body. Absence of blood on the hand is likely inconsistent with a suicidal cutting of the throat but may occur with suicidal stab wounds of the chest or abdomen. The absence of a weapon at the scene of a death suggests a homicide because an assailant usually does not leave the weapon at the scene of death. Rarely, a suicide victim survives long enough to clean the weapon and replace it in its usual storage area or hide it. It is also possible for a perpetrator to leave the weapon near the body to suggest a suicide.

Manner of Death

Most deaths due to stab wounds are homicides.[3] In such killings, multiple wounds are usually widely scattered over the body. Most of the wounds often fail to penetrate deeply and, thus, are not life threatening. Most life-threatening wounds involve the chest and neck, with injuries of the heart, lungs and vasculature.[3] Death is usually fairly rapid and due to exsanguination. Defensive-type injuries, usually located on the hands and forearms, are seen in approximately one-third of sharp force injury homicides.[3]

Suicide by stabbing is uncommon. When individuals decide to stab themselves, they will often unbutton or pull aside their clothing to expose the area that they intend to stab. Most suicidal stab wounds involve the chest and are single in number, though additional superficial hesitant wounds with minimal penetration (1 to 2 mm deep) or that just barely breaking the skin may also be present around the fatal wound. (Figure 6.18A)

These latter wounds are "hesitation" stab wounds. These hesitation, or tentative, injuries are present in approximately one-third of suicidal sharp force injury deaths.[3] Occasionally, a knife will be plunged into the body without any evidence of hesitancy (Figure 6.18B). In some instances, the knife is left *in situ*. In one case of which the authors are aware, an individual stabbed himself with two knives and left them embedded in his abdomen.

Once connected with the traditions of Japanese Samurai warriors, *seppuku* (commonly called *hara-kiri*) is an unusual form of suicide involving an abdominal stab

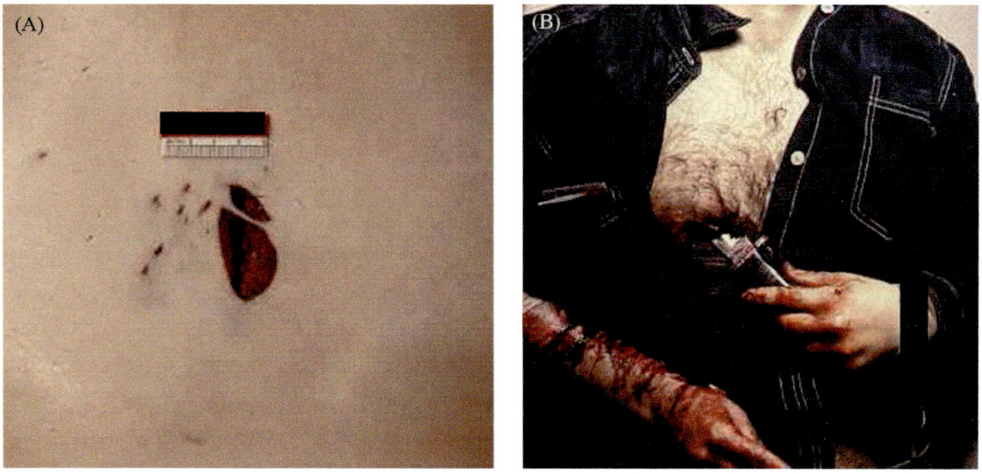

Figure 6.18 (A) Multiple suicidal stab wounds of chest with only one penetrating into chest cavity. (B) Single stab wound to the left chest with knife embedded in chest.

wound. A single large wound is inflicted in the abdomen. The sudden evisceration of the internal organs results in an immediate decrease of intra-abdominal pressure and cardiac return, which results in sudden cardiac collapse. The proper method for performing seppuku involves plunging a short sword into the left side of the abdomen, drawing the blade across to the right side of the abdomen and then turning it upward, producing an L-shaped cut.

Impaling injuries are very uncommon. When they do occur, they are usually caused by falls and traffic accidents. Rarely, one encounters deliberate sexually motivated impalement, usually involving the anus and genital area. Occasionally, individuals fall on an object that they are carrying, for example, a pencil. More commonly, individuals fall or jump from a structure onto a pointed object such as a fence.[4] Falling pipes and metal rods have also impaled individuals. In traffic accidents, a vehicle might crash into an obstacle, for example, a fence, which, in part or in whole, is driven into the car (usually the windshield), impaling the driver or a passenger (Figure 6.19); or shifting cargo,

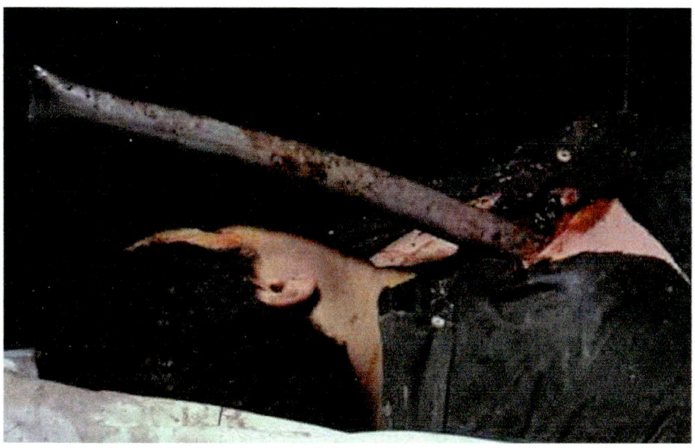

Figure 6.19 Impaling injury from a pipe.

for example, metal pipes in the back of a vehicle can slide forward and impale the driver or passenger if the vehicle abruptly stops. Rare cases have been reported involving wood splinters in a tornado.

Stab Wounds by Anatomical Location

In a stab wound death, all wounds should be located anatomically with the path and depth of wound delineated, including the organs injured. Probing of stab wounds is usually of very little benefit, in that the probe, with very little force, will produce multiple erroneous wound tracks. Thus, probing is not recommended.

Most fatal stab wounds are located in the chest, particularly the left chest. Among a number of explanations is that most people are right handed and, when facing a victim, will tend to stab the left chest. In addition, if the intention is to kill someone, one would stab in the left chest where the heart is thought to be.

Most fatal stab wounds of the chest involve injury to the heart, lungs or aorta. Fatal stab wounds of the right chest usually involve injury to the right ventricle, aorta or right atrium. Stab wounds of the left chest usually injure the right ventricle when parasternal, and the left ventricle as the stab wounds become more lateral and inferior.[5] While hemopericardium is common, death caused solely by cardiac tamponade is not. In cardiac tamponade, once a victim acutely accumulates more than 150 mL of blood in the pericardial sac, death can occur at any time. Rather than this scenario, however, most deaths are due to a combination of hemothorax, external blood loss and hemopericardium.

Stab wounds of the heart with severing of the left anterior descending coronary artery are rapidly fatal. In stab wounds, damage to the atria or great vessels leading to and from the heart are more serious than those of the ventricles because the ventricular muscle can contract, thus slowing or terminating bleeding; thus, some individuals survive stab wounds of the heart. Stab wounds of the heart are typically inflicted over the front of the chest, occasionally the sides and least commonly the back. The majority of the stab wounds of the left chest also perforate the lungs.

Stab wounds of the lungs, like those of the heart, typically occur from wounds over the front of the chest, less commonly the sides and only occasionally the back. Most such wounds are associated with wounds of the heart. Deaths from stab wounds of the lungs alone are usually due to exsanguination with massive hemothorax. Pneumothorax may also occur.

Stab wounds of the lower chest can produce injuries to not only the heart and lungs but also to the abdominal viscera. Fatal stab wounds of the abdomen usually involve injury to the liver or a major blood vessel, for example, the aorta, vena cava, iliac or mesenteric vessels. Occasionally, in wounds of the abdomen, death is not immediate. Rather, the victim develops peritonitis because of a wound of the bowel. The forensic pathologist, by virtue of his work, sees a biased sampling of cases – only those individuals who die of their injuries. Thus, in regard to all stab wounds of the abdomen, less than 10% involve the abdominal cavity and less than half of these inflict significant injury to the viscera.[3]

Stab wounds to the neck are also fairly common, occurring in just under 20% of sharp force injury deaths.[3] Stab wounds of the neck can produce rapid death by exsanguination; air embolism or asphyxia due to massive soft tissue hemorrhage with compression of the trachea and vessels in the neck. Delayed deaths might be due to cellulitis, or arterial thrombosis with cerebral emboli and infarction. In cases in which there are stab wounds of the neck, postmortem CT scan is recommended to rule out air embolus, though an X-rays of the chest may also be suggestive. Occasionally, in a stab wound of the neck, the knife will sever not only a major blood vessel, but also the trachea, with resultant massive hemorrhaging into the pulmonary tree.

Less common are stab wounds of the head. Stab wounds of the brain occur through the eye or the temporal region because of the thinness of the bone in these areas. Often, single stab wounds of the brain are not immediately fatal, and the victim may walk or run away from the assailant. In some instances, victims may not realize that they have been stabbed.[6,7] Rarely, stab wounds of the brain are not discovered until years after the assault. Sometimes, the knife blade might still be present. Victims of stab wounds of the brain have, on occasion, been hospitalized and the knife's entry into the brain not discovered because the wound was concealed by hair; in the fold of the eye or under the eyelid.[6] Death in such cases was due to either continuing intracranial bleeding or infection. At autopsy, the skull defect produced by the weapon will match the width and thickness of the knife blade or screwdriver or the diameter of an ice pick. Bleeding from a stab wound of the brain may be subdural, subarachnoid, intracerebral or a combination of all three.

Stab wounds of the spine are also uncommon. Like stab wounds of the head, the knife blade may break off and be found in the spinal column. Injury to the cord will produce either complete or partial paralysis below the level of injury. Delayed presentation is rare, but occurred as long as 30 years after the stabbing in one case.[8]

While most lethal stab wounds involve the trunk or neck, occasionally one will have a lethal stab wound of an extremity. Most commonly, the vessel involved is the femoral artery. In virtually all these cases, the individuals stabbed are intoxicated and do not realize the lethality of their injury. Instead, they keep walking around bleeding copiously before they collapse and die.

Most stab wounds of the upper extremities are sustained by victims as they try to defend or protect themselves from assailants. Defense wounds of the lower extremities occur but are uncommon.

In rare instances, the weapon used to inflict a stab wound, for example, an ice pick, may produce an inconspicuous external wound, with minimal or no external bleeding. This stab wound can be overlooked in examination of the body at the scene, where conditions for ideal examination are lacking (Figure 6.20).

Combination Incised-Stab Wounds

A combination incised-stab wound is a stab wound that is converted to an incised (slashing) wound. The wound starts out as a stab wound with the knife plunged into the body. The knife, instead of being immediately withdrawn, slices through the tissue, extending the length of the wound in the skin such that the wound is now longer than deep. This is accomplished in one continuous flowing movement. In Figure 6.21, the deceased was stabbed on the right side of the neck with the tip of the knife penetrating into the third cervical vertebra. The knife was then pulled anteriorly, slicing through skin, muscle and the jugular veins.

Usually, one cannot tell the direction the knife was drawn through the tissue from examination of the wound alone. The only way a differentiation can be made is if there is a nick or forked configuration to one end of the wound. If present, this indicates that the blade was drawn toward this end.

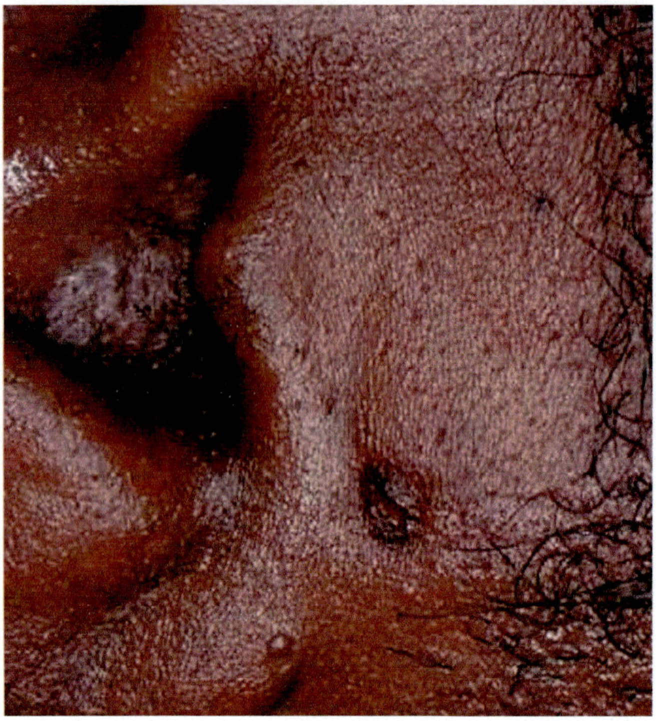

Figure 6.20 Inconspicuous single ice pick wound in front of ear. Ice pick perforated vertebral artery.

Incised Wounds

Incised wounds, or cutting wounds, are sharp force injuries that are *longer than they are deep*. A knife is the classical example of a weapon used to inflict an incised wound, though, in fact, any instrument with a sharp edge can do so, for example, a piece of glass, metal or paper. The sharp edge of the instrument is pressed into and drawn along the surface of the skin, producing a wound whose length is greater than its depth.

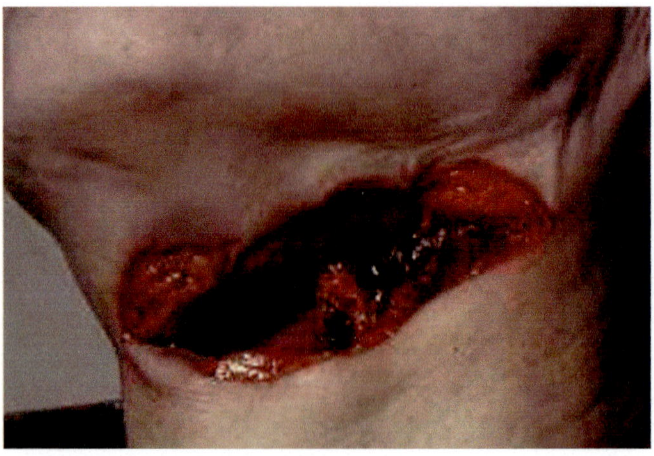

Figure 6.21 Incised-stab wound of right side of neck. The assailant was facing the deceased at the time the wound was inflicted.

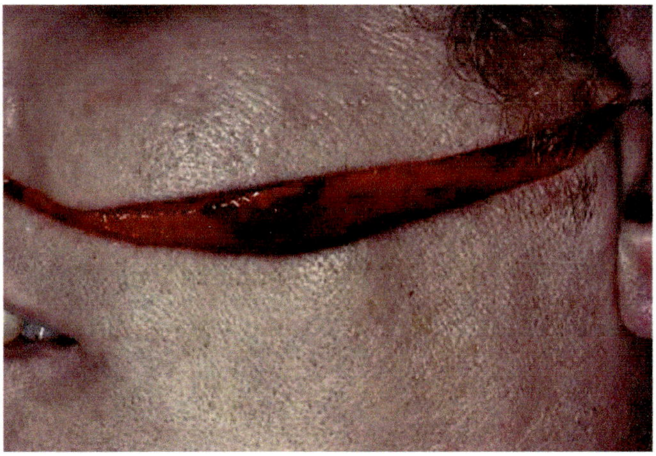

Figure 6.22 Incised wound of face caused by razor. Note the sharp, clean margins.

In incised wounds, the length and depth of the wound will not provide information as to the weapon. A 3-in.-long incised wound could have been produced by a 6-in. blade, a 2-in. blade, a razor or even a piece of glass. Incised wounds should not be confused with lacerations. Incised wounds have clean-cut straight edges are usually free of abrasion or contusion (Figure 6.22).

There is no bridging in the depth of the wound. Lacerations, which are tears in the skin caused by blunt force, generally have ragged, abraded margins with bridging of the base. One must realize, however, that a dull, irregular-edged or nicked cutting edge can produce an incised wound with irregular, contused or abraded margins because the wound is caused more by the pressure applied by the weapon than by the cutting edge. No bridging in the depth of the wound will occur, however.

Wounds of the scalp produced by heavy, usually metallic, objects with sharp edges can produce lacerations with sharp, non-abraded margins that can be confused with incised wounds. Careful examination of the base of the wound usually produces evidence of bridging, thus indicating a laceration. In some instances, however, just by examining a wound alone, it will not be possible to determine if it is an incised wound or a laceration. Other wounds on the body will often suggest the etiology of the ambiguous wound.

Incised wounds often begin very superficially, deepen and then become superficial again. If the blade is held at an oblique angle to the skin, the wound will present a beveled or undermined edge. If the angle is extreme, a skin flap will be produced. *On occasion, a single slash with a sharp, edged weapon might produce more than one incised wound.* These are **wrinkle wounds**, which occur when the skin is not flat, but "wrinkled," that is, in folds. Here, the cutting edge skips from crest to crest of the skin, leaving a string of cuts, all of which have resulted from a single slash (Figure 6.23).

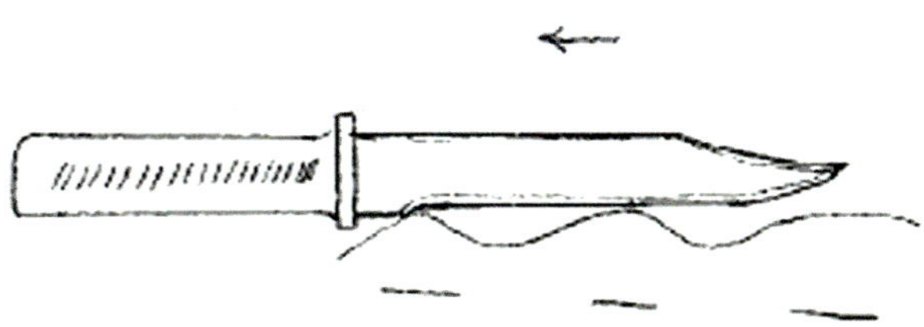

Figure 6.23 Incised "wrinkle" wound caused by knife drawn across skin from crest to crest.

Usually, these lie in a straight line and it is fairly simple to deduce what has occurred. If the skin is thrown into irregular folds, an irregular zigzag wound may be produced by a single swipe of the blade. In such a case, the blade rolls up the skin before cutting through it.

The edges of an incised wound tend to separate or gap. The extent to which the wound gaps and the shape it subsequently assumes depend on whether it is parallel, transverse or oblique to the direction of the elastic fibers in the skin (Langer's lines). Thus, an incised wound parallel to the contractile fibers will gape less than one made at a right angle or obliquely across the fibers because the fibers will pull the skin apart and evert the edges.

Incised wounds are usually not fatal. Most are seen in emergency rooms, where they are treated with a few sutures and the victims released. Incised wounds are most frequently inflicted on the exposed portions of the body: the head, neck and arms. If the victim survives, the wounds usually heal by primary intention, leaving a thin, linear scar. Fatal incised wounds generally involve the arms and neck.

Suicidal incised wounds are generally inflicted on those parts of the body most accessible to the victim. The victim may expose the portion of the body to be incised. For example, he may open his collar before cutting his throat, or pull up his shirt before cutting his chest or abdomen.

In self-inflicted incised wounds, **hesitation marks** (Figure 6.24) are present in approximately one-third of the cases.[3] These are superficial incised wounds adjacent to, a continuation of or overlying the fatal incised wound. They are very superficial and often do not go through the skin. One has the impression that the deceased attempted to cut the skin, but either because of pain or hesitancy, did not initially cut deep, but rather made multiple, very superficial cuts, almost like paper cuts, until finally, he built up enough courage to actually cut through the skin. Very superficial incised wounds identical to hesitation

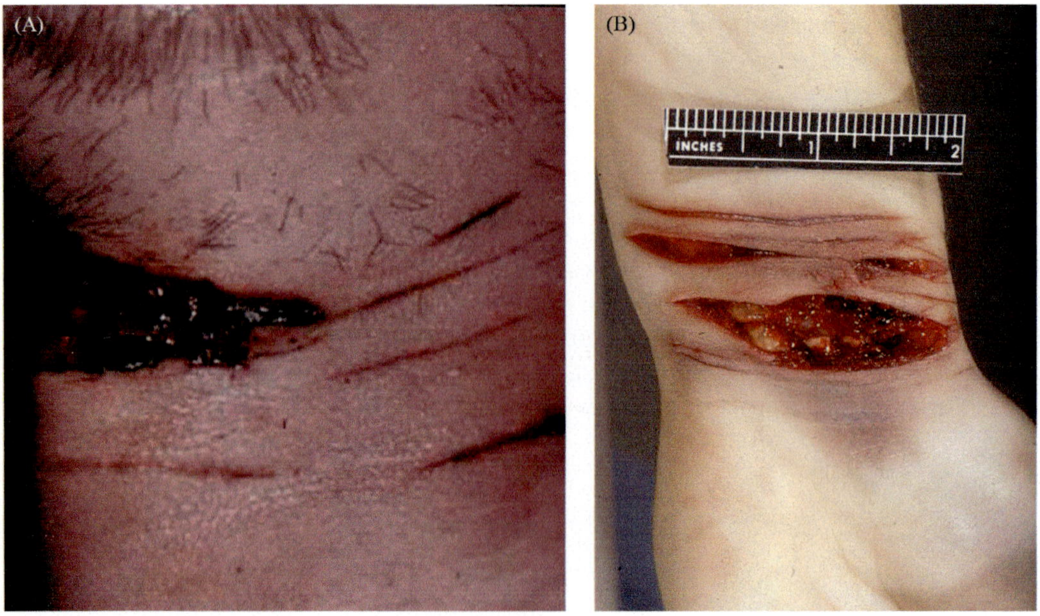

Figure 6.24 Incised wounds with hesitation marks (A) of neck (B) of the wrist. (B courtesy of Dr. Norma J. Farley.)

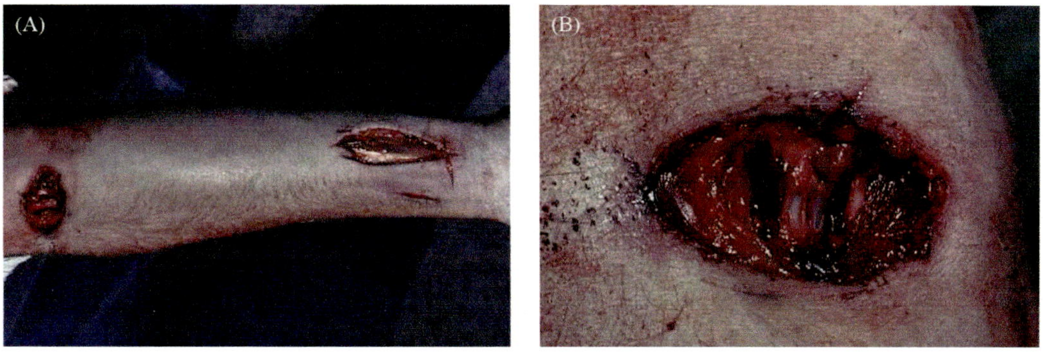

Figure 6.25 (A) Three self-inflicted incised wounds of flexor surface of left forearm, the two in the wrist, vertical in orientation (B) Detail of wound of antecubital fossa showing partial severing of artery and vein.

marks occasionally can be seen in homicidal incised wounds of the neck. This could be caused by either struggling of the individual prior to the infliction of the fatal wound or perhaps the perpetrator's initial hesitancy to cut the victim's throat.

Fatal incised wounds of the arms are most commonly suicidal. As a means of attempting suicide, cutting one's wrists is a poor method. Most people have a vague knowledge of anatomy and do not know where to sever a major vessel. In addition, they usually do not cut deep enough. Some individuals cut their forearms vertically, rather than horizontally, due to an ignorance of anatomy (Figure 6.25A).

One individual who did so had this fact explained to him by his physician. When the patient cut his wrist again later in the week, he cut the radial artery correctly and bled to death.

In self-inflicted incised wounds of the extremities, right-handed individuals usually cut the left wrist or forearm; left-handed individuals, the right wrist or forearm. These incised wounds are typically found on the flexor surface and radial aspect of the forearm (Figure 6.26A and B).

Thus, the presence of linear scars on the flexor surface in these areas suggests that an individual has attempted suicide in the past.

Defense wounds are wounds of the extremities incurred when an individual attempts to ward off a pointed or sharp-edged weapon and are found in approximately one-third of

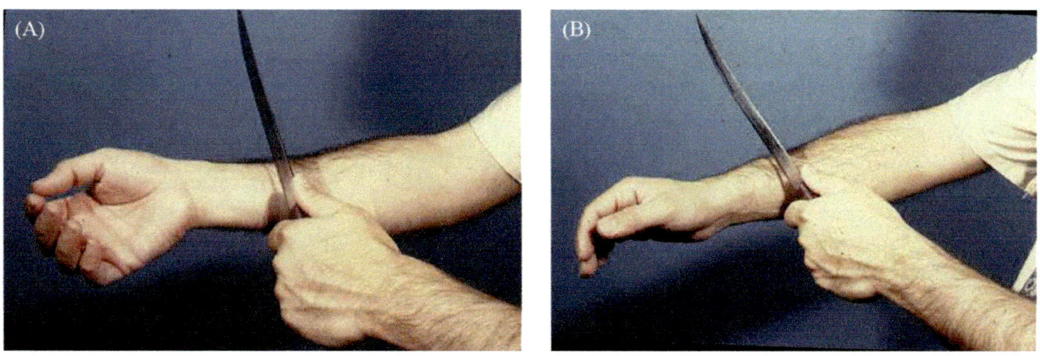

Figure 6.26 Demonstration of (A) self-inflicted incised wound of flexor surface of wrist and (B) self-inflicted incised wound of radial aspect of forearm.

sharp force injury homicides.[3] They are most commonly found on the palms of the hands, due to attempts to grasp or ward off the knife; the back (extensor surface) of the forearms and upper arms and on the ulnar aspect of the forearms (Figures 6.27).

Rarely, defense wounds will be found on the feet or legs. In such a case, the individual might have kicked out at the knife to try to ward it off, or he might have curled up and tried to cover his vital areas with the legs. Sometimes, the blade will often cut the fingers of the hand holding it. If individuals are using a knife and there is a lot of blood, there is a possibility that their hands could slip from the handle onto the blade, incurring an injury. In such an instance, the wounds produced may simulate defense wounds.

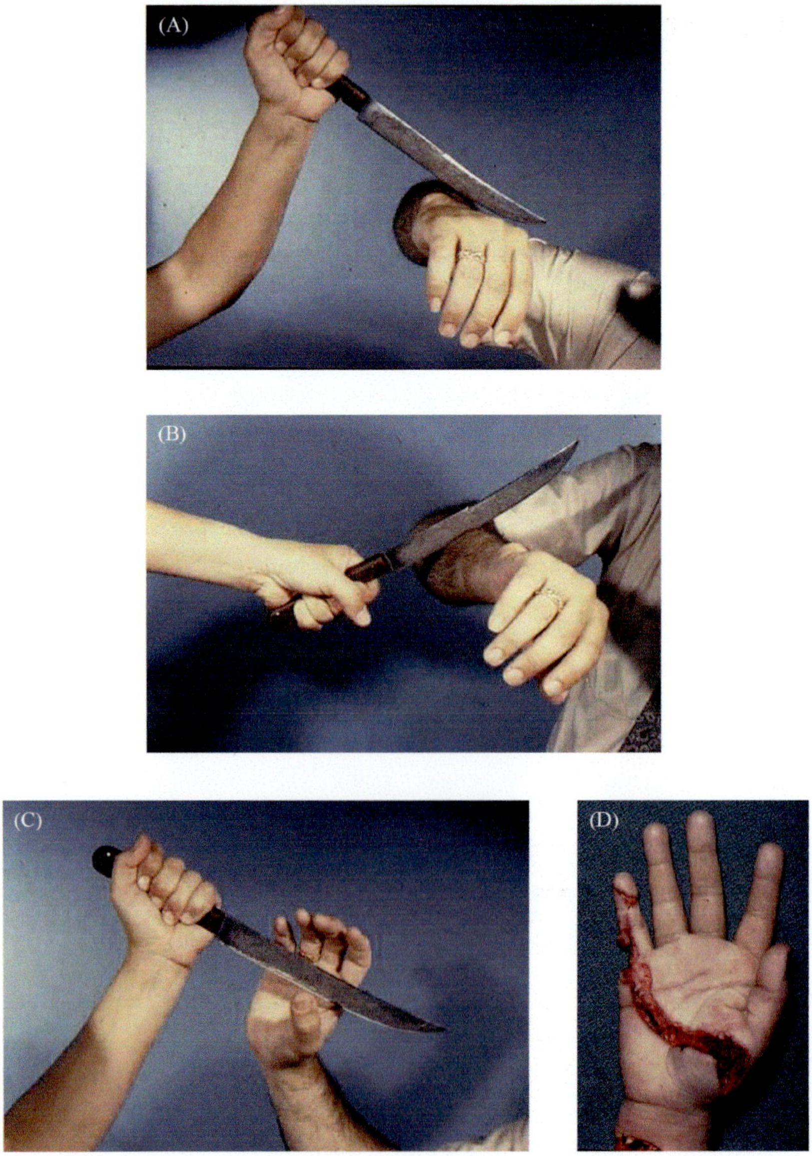

Figure 6.27 Demonstration of defense wounds of the (A) back of forearm, (B) ulnar aspect of forearm, (C) palm of hand and (D) actual palm wound incurred in attempt to grasp knife.

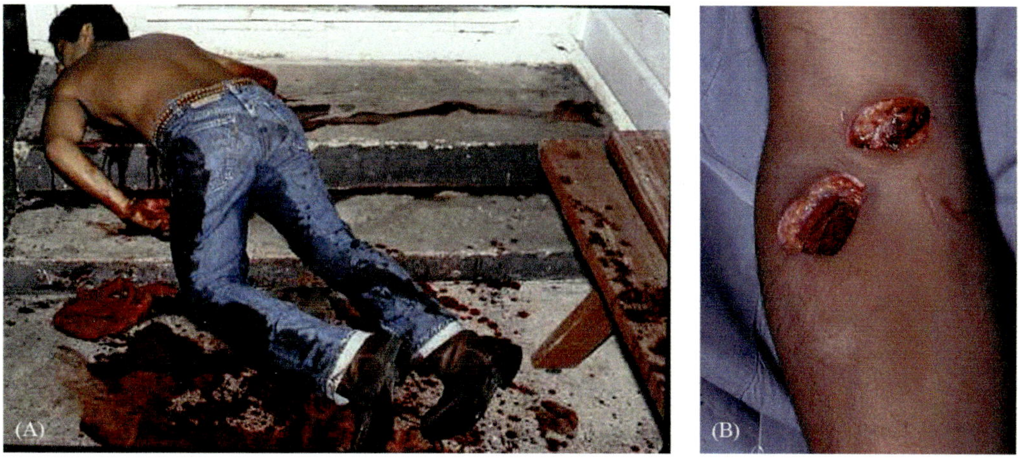

Figure 6.28 (A and B) While intoxicated, the deceased attempted to break a window and enter. He incurred wounds of the left arm, with severing of major vessels and exsanguination.

Pieces of glass have been used to cut wrists and throats and to slash people. They have been used in both homicides and suicides. Occasionally, an accidental death will be caused by glass. The authors have seen a number of cases in which an intoxicated individual knocked out a pane of glass with a hand or fist. In the process, as the arm went through the glass, or when it was pulled back, a jagged projection of glass cut the arm, inflicting a deep wound and severing a major vessel, with resultant exsanguination (Figure 6.28).

Incised Wounds of the Neck

Incised wounds of the neck can be accidental, homicidal or suicidal. Accidental wounds are extremely rare, usually seen only when an individual goes through a sheet of glass or is struck in the neck by a flying fragment of glass or some other sharp-edged projectile. Thus, in one case, a 13-year-old male was struck by flying glass when a bottle containing dry ice exploded. The fragment of glass severed his left jugular vein, causing exsanguination.

Homicidal incised wounds of the neck present two different pictures, depending on whether they are produced from the back or the front. Most commonly, a person's throat is cut from behind. The head is pulled back, exposing the neck, and the knife is then drawn across it. Often, the victim is face down on the floor or ground at the time the wound is inflicted. The perpetrator usually starts the incision high up on the side of the neck opposite to the hand they are using. The knife is drawn across the neck, from left to right by a right-handed assailant and from right to left by a left handed individual. The wound inflicted is first shallow, then deeper and then shallow again, terminating on the opposite side of the neck. The wound generally starts below the ear; runs downward and medially at an angle, then straight across the midline of the neck, and then upward, ending on the opposite side of the neck, lower than its point of initiation (Figure 6.29).

Homicidal incised wounds of the neck inflicted from the front tend to be short and angled (Figure 6.30).

A right-handed individual typically inflicts incised wounds on the left side of the victim's neck, with the slashes running downward and medially at an oblique angle. If the

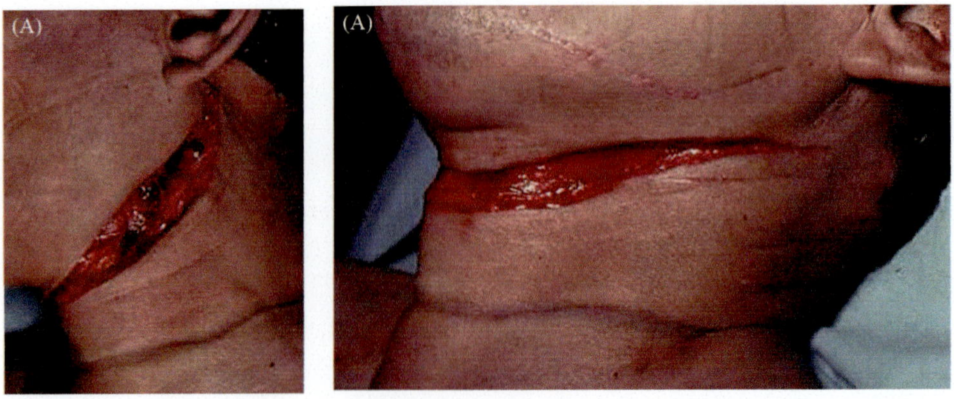

Figure 6.29 Homicidal incised wound of neck inflicted from back beginning below left ear (A) running downward and medially across the midline of the neck and upward on the opposite side of the neck, ending lower than its point of initiation (B).

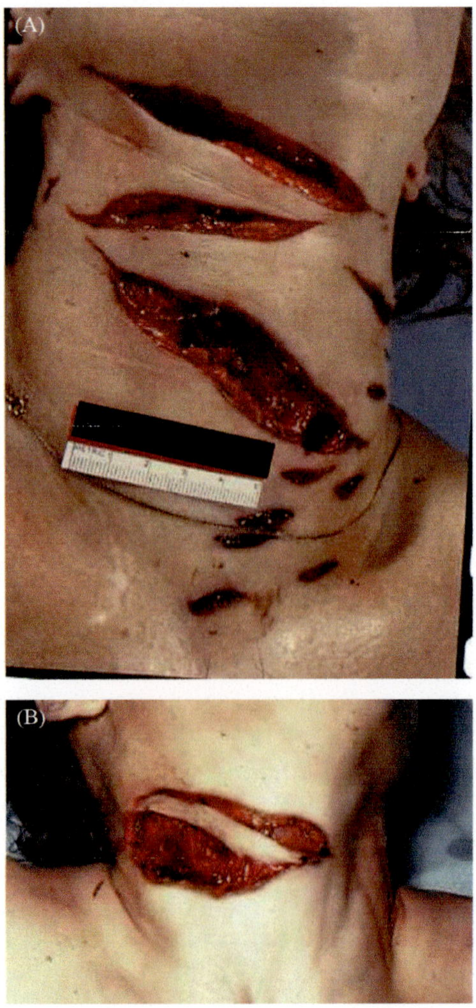

Figure 6.30 (A and B) Homicidal incised wounds of the neck inflicted from the front. Note short slashing nature of wounds.

wounds are inflicted on the right side, they tend to be fewer in number. Wounds across the front of the neck tend to be horizontal and short, extending a short distance to the right or left of the midline. Horizontally incised wounds inflicted from the front of the neck are the least common. The characteristics of the wounds produced by a frontal attack are obvious with an understanding of the etiology. Instead of the neck's being cut with one long, continuous motion, these wounds are inflicted by "swipes" or slashes made while facing the individual.

In self-inflicted wounds of the neck, the same general pattern holds as for a homicidal assault from the rear. The wound usually begins higher on the neck on the side opposite to where it terminates. Suicidal incised wounds of the neck are usually, but not always, accompanied by hesitation marks (Figure 6.31).

In rare instances, a fatal self-inflicted incised wound of the neck may be accompanied by cadaveric spasm (instantaneous rigor mortis) with the knife or razor found firmly clenched in the victim's hand. In some suicides, the weapon might not be present at the scene. Another person may have altered the scene, or, if the initial wound was not immediately incapacitating, the suicide victim was allowed time to conceal the weapon prior to death.

Incised wounds of the neck may be extremely deep and extend completely to the vertebral column. This is most common in homicidal wounds inflicted from the rear.

Death from incised wounds of the neck may be due not only to exsanguination, but to massive air embolus (see Chapter 20 for further discussion on air emboli). Air enters an open vein whenever there is a negative pressure gradient between the vein and the right atrium. This is facilitated by the negative intrathoracic pressure generated during inspiration. The higher the open vein is above the right atrium, the greater the pressure gradient and the more likely air is to enter the vessel. Thus, in individuals incurring stab or incised wounds of the neck with injury to the veins, the prosector may want to explore the possibilities of air embolism at the time of autopsy. A postmortem computed tomography scan (CT) or X-ray of the chest for the detection of air in the venous system and heart is recommended. Subsequently, the heart should be examined for air emboli. The length of time it takes to die following an incised wound of the neck depends on whether the venous or arterial systems are severed and whether there is air embolism.

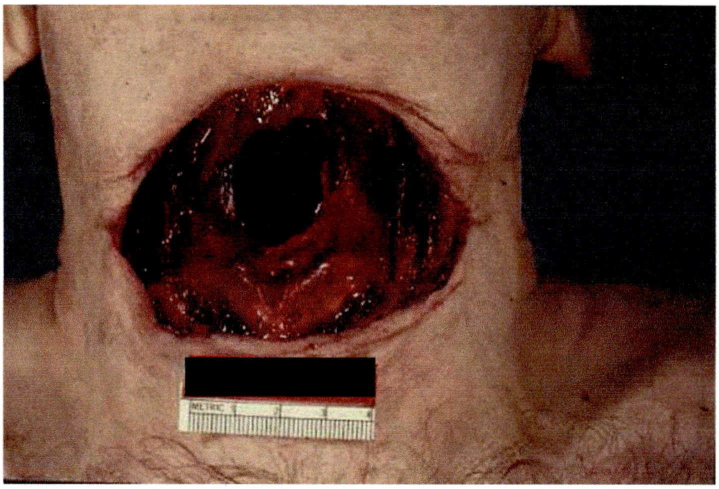

Figure 6.31 Self-inflicted incised wound of neck with hesitation marks.

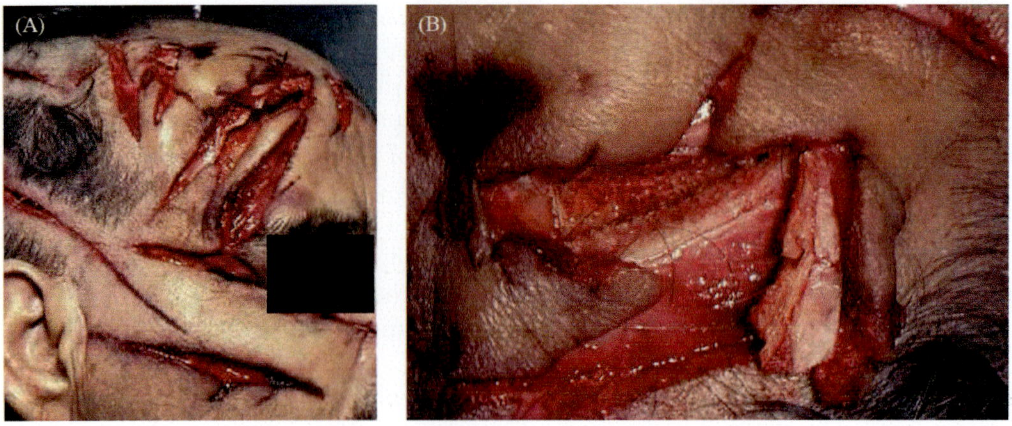

Figure 6.32 (A and B) Chopping wounds of head from machete. Note incised-like nature of wounds with cutting of underlying bone.

Chop Wounds

Chop wounds are produced by heavy instruments with a cutting edge, for example, axes, machetes and meat cleavers. The presence of an incised wound of the skin, with an underlying comminuted fracture or deep groove in the bone, indicates that one is dealing with a chopping weapon (Figure 6.32).

When the perpetrator pulls out a weapon that has embedded itself in the bone, they might give it a sharp twist, fracturing or breaking off the adjacent bone. In tangential wounds of the skull, chopping instruments may cut off disks of bone.

While most chop wounds appear incised, when there is a combination of cutting and crushing, they can have both incised and lacerated characteristics.

Therapeutic or Diagnostic Wounds

These are wounds produced by medical personnel during the treatment of a patient. Common examples are thoracotomy incisions; surgical stab wounds of the chest or abdomen for insertion of tubes and drains; laparotomy incisions; incisions for peritoneal lavage; cutdowns of the wrists, antecubital fossae and ankles; and tracheostomy incisions (Figure 6.33).

Some of these surgical wounds may be mistaken for primary traumatic injury; for example, a surgical stab wound of the chest for a drain could be interpreted as a homicidal stab wound. In other instances, the traumatic wounds are obliterated by the surgical procedure; for example, a stab wound of the left chest might be incorporated into a thoracotomy incision. Occasionally, a homicidal stab wound is converted to a therapeutic use, for example, a surgical drain might be placed into the chest cavity through a stab wound of the chest. If the individual dies and the drain tube is left in the stab wound, the wound could be misinterpreted at autopsy.

To avoid misinterpretation of therapeutic wounds, therapeutic tubing should never be removed prior to sending a body to the medical examiner; the chart should be reviewed prior to autopsy and, if any questions arise, the treating physicians should be consulted.

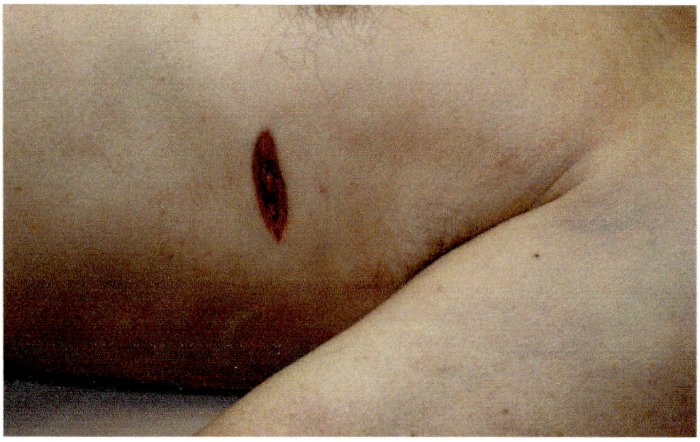

Figure 6.33 Finger thoracostomy incision in the lateral chest; could be confused with stab wounds.

Additional Issues

Clothing

For all sharp force injuries, one should always examine the clothing to see if there are defects corresponding to the wounds. This is to rule out an individual's being stabbed or cut and then the body dressed.

Bodies in Water

In bodies in which there is prolonged immersion in water, the water can leach out the blood in both stab and incised wounds, giving an almost postmortem appearance to these wounds, suggesting that they were inflicted after death rather than before (Figure 6.34).

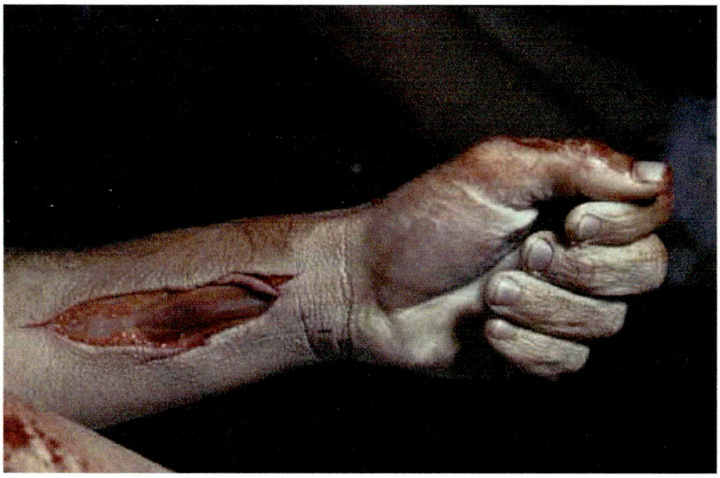

Figure 6.34 Antemortem incised wound of right forearm with blood leached out following prolonged immersion in water.

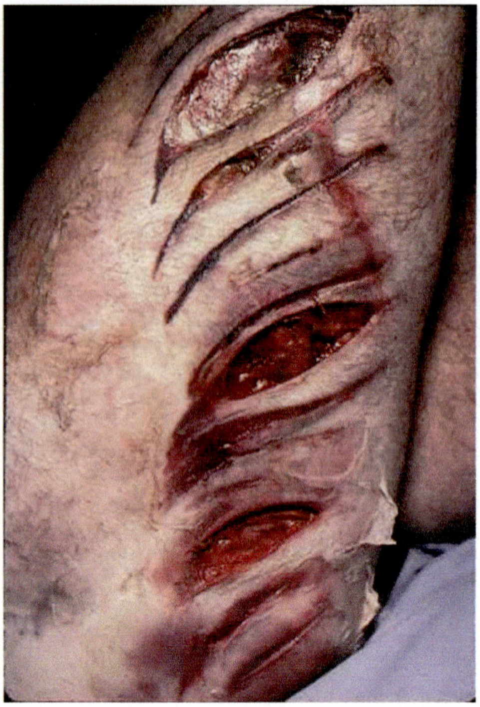

Figure 6.35 Body pulled from water; wounds caused by boat propeller.

Boat or airplane propellers can produce chop-like wounds of the body. On occasion, a body will be pulled from the water with multiple chop wounds (Figure 6.35).

The question then arises as to whether these are ante-or postmortem. If, on examination of the site of injury, there is hemorrhage in the soft tissue, one can be fairly sure that this is an antemortem injury. Absence of bleeding into a chop wound does not prove that the injury was postmortem, because prolonged immersion in water might result in the leaching out of the blood from the wound, giving the appearance of a postmortem injury.

Physical Activity Following a Fatal Sharp Force Injury

The question of whether an individual is capable of physical activity, that is, able to walk or run away from the assailant after receiving a fatal wound, depends on the organ(s) injured, the extent of the injury, the amount of blood lost and the rapidity with which the blood is lost. With profuse bleeding, physical activity is limited or lost rapidly; with slow bleeding, the victim is capable of walking away from the assailant. Not infrequently, a trail of blood will mark the path of escape. A wound that will disable one victim will not necessarily affect the physical activity of another. The authors have seen prolonged survival (several hours) following stab wounds of major vessels.

Karger et al. evaluated 12 cases of suicide from sharp pointed weapons in order to estimate the potential for physical activity following injury.[9] In all cases, the suicidal action and the subsequent behavior were witnessed. Seven of the victims had stab wounds of the heart. These latter deaths fell into three categories, based on time of survival and physical activity: immediate incapacitation (one case), short-term survival (two cases) and long-term survival (four cases). The short-term group collapsed in approximately 10 s; the long-term 2–10 min.

The individual who collapsed immediately had a 15 mm wound of the heart and a 450 mL hemopericardium. In the short-term group, both individuals collapsed in 10 s and had injuries to the right ventricle, ranging from 14 to 20 mm; both had a hemopericardium, one 250 mL with the other not specified. In the long-term group, the wounds ranged from 7 to 10 mm long and three of the four had wounds of the left ventricle; in only two cases was a hemopericardium mentioned, measuring 300 and 400 mL. The individual with the 400 mL tamponade lived the longest – 10 min.

An eighth case involved a stab wound of the heart with a cannula. This individual survived 2 h and was found to have a 600 mL tamponade. In another case, an individual stabbed himself in the right chest, injuring his lung and liver. He survived 2 h and was found to have a 2200 right hemothorax and a 700 mL hemoperitoneum.

Force Necessary to Inflict Fatal Stab Wounds

It is impossible to exactly quantitate the force exerted by an assailant in inflicting a fatal stab wound. After comparing and correlating the relation of each of the following four variables with those of the fatal stab wound, it is possible, however, to state in comparative terms the force required to inflict the fatal stab wound:

1. *The condition of the knife.* A sharp point; a dull point; a sharp or dull cutting edge; a thin or thick blade; double-edged or single-edged cutting blade. A sharp, pointed, double-edged, thin knife requires less force or effort to penetrate tissues or organs than a single-edged, blunt, pointed, dull blade.
2. *The resistance offered by the different tissues or organs penetrated.* Penetration of skin, cartilage and bone, which are tough structures, requires greater force than that required for penetration of soft tissue, such as fat. Therefore, the tissue or organs penetrated by the knife will indicate the amount of force exerted by the assailant.
3. *The depth and length of the stab wound.* A 2-in. blade causing a 4-in. deep stab wound must be inflicted with great force.
4. *The amount of clothing and its composition* will also determine the amount of force to be exerted. For example, leather belts, thick leather jackets, fur coats and so on will require a greater force for penetration than scant, soft clothing.

In regard to the second item above, O'Callaghan et al. measured the force necessary for a knife to penetrate different tissues.[10] They inflicted a series of stab wounds to a depth of 10 cm in cadaveric tissue and amputated specimens. They determined that the mean force to penetrate skin, subcutaneous fat and muscle was 11.1 lb (49.5 N) with a range of 7.9–12.4 lb; for subcutaneous fat and muscle 7.8 lb (35 N); for muscle 8.4 lb (37.5 N) and for fat 0.5 lb (2 N).

Postmortem Bleeding

Drainage from a postmortem incised or stab wound is usually minimal due to the small quantity of blood present in the severed blood vessel. However, should a large blood vessel be severed after death and the vessel be located in a dependent area of the body, the quantity of blood lost could be considerable. The dependent position enables the network of blood vessels communicating with the severed vessel to drain or "bleed" through the severed vascular wall. In postmortem experiments, one of the authors severed large blood vessels in the chest and abdominal cavities to determine the quantity of blood that could be lost in each body cavity; 300–500 mL of blood leaked out into the cavities. This quantity of blood is small in comparison with the usual amount of blood that accumulates during antemortem wounding.

When a victim is stabbed multiple times and bleeds heavily, the last stab wound inflicted may appear bloodless. In such cases, the medical examiner may experience difficulty in deciding whether this stab wound was inflicted before, during or soon after death.

During movement or transportation of a body, blood may escape from the wounds and stain the clothing. Thus, blood stains on the clothing at the time of autopsy may have occurred during movement and transportation of the victim's body. Blood stains or bloodstain patterns initially present on the clothing may be enlarged, increased in number or obliterated by the flow of postmortem blood during transportation.

Mutilation

Psychotic individuals may use edged weapons to mutilate either themselves or others. Mutilation usually involves the genitalia, ears or nose. Non-psychotic individuals may mutilate as a warning, in revenge or to collect souvenirs (usually ears). Husbands occasionally mutilate the genitalia of cheating wives. Sexual mutilation of prostitutes occurs, though rarely.

Tool Marks

Sharp implements, when they strike bone and cartilage, may impart characteristics of the implement, called Kerf marks. These marks may indicate the type of weapon used and in some cases identify the actual weapon. Kerf marks are usually due to knives as these are the most common sharp-edged weapons used. The cutting edge of the knife may leave striations on cartilage and bone that can be used for identifying purposes; thus, these surfaces should be collected at autopsy for later comparison. See Chapter 22 for a full discussion on tool mark identification.

References

1. Knight B, The dynamics of stab wounds. *Forensic Sci* 1975; 6:249–255.
2. Connor SEJ, Bleetman A, and Duddy MJ, Safety standards from stab-resistant body armour: a computer tomographic assessment of organ to skin distances. *Injury* 1998; 29(4):297–299.
3. Kemal CJ, Patterson T, and Molina DK, Deaths due to sharp force injuries in Bexar County, Texas, with respect to manner of death. *Am J Forensic Med Pathol* 2013; 34(3):253–259.

4. Missliwetz J, Fatal impalement injuries after falls at construction sites. *Am J Forensic Med Pathol* 1995; 16(1):81–3.
5. Wilson RF and Bassett JS, Penetrating wounds of the pericardium or its contents. *JAMA* 1966; 195:513–518.
6. DiMaio VJM and DiMaio DJ, An unsuspected stab wound of the brain. *Mil Med* 1972; 137:434–435.
7. Deb S, et al., Stab wounds to the head with intracranial penetration. *J Trauma* 2000; 48(6):1159–1162.
8. Kulkani AV, et al., Delayed presentation of spinal stab wounds: case report and review of the literature. *J Emerg Med* 2000; 18(2):209–213.
9. Karger B, Niemeyer J, and Brinkmann B, Physical activity following fatal injury from sharp pointed weapons. *Int J Legal Med* 1999; 112:188–191.
10. O'Callaghan PT, et al., Dynamics of stab wounds: force required for penetration of various cadaveric human tissues. *Forensic Sci Int* 1999; 104:173–178.

Ballistic Wounds

7

Whoever said the pen is mightier than the sword, obviously never encountered automatic weapons.

—General Douglas MacArthur

Firearm Basics

All firearms are designed in a similar manner, though the specifics vary, creating the different types of firearms. Essentially, every firearm consists of a grip or stock, a trigger, a hammer and a barrel (Figure 7.1).

When the trigger is pulled, the hammer strikes the firing pin against the base of the cartridge, igniting the primer followed by the main powder charge that then propels the bullet down the barrel. The primer is located at the base of the cartridge. When struck by the firing pin, it ignites, igniting the main powder charge in the cartridge case. Cartridges for rifles and handguns are said to be either **rimfire or center-fire**. This refers to the location and nature of the primer. In **rimfire ammunition**, the rim along the base of the cartridge is filled during manufacture with an impact-sensitive primer. When the rim is then crushed by the hammer or firing pin, the primer detonates and ignites the powder charge. In **center-fire ammunition**, the primer is a small brass or copper cup, located in the center of the base of the cartridge case. It contains a stable but shock-sensitive explosive mixture. When the hammer or firing pin strikes the primer, it detonates this material igniting the gunpowder.

In order to stabilize the bullet as it exits the muzzle, handguns and rifles have rifled barrels. **Rifling** imparts a rotational spin on the bullet as it travels down the barrel, which stabilizes its flight through the air, preventing it from tumbling, much like a quarterback puts a spin on the football. The spin, however, does not stabilize the bullet in the body. Upon entering the body, a bullet begins to yaw or rotate off its axis. If the wound path is long enough, the bullet may flip 180 degrees and travel base forward.

Rifling consists of a series of parallel spiral grooves that cut the length of the bore; the metal left between the grooves is called the "lands" (Figure 7.2).

The number of lands can vary between 2 and 20 depending upon the firearm and manufacturer. The lands and grooves create characteristic marks upon the bullets when fired, which can be used for bullet and firearm identification (Figure 7.3).

In firearms with polygonal rifling, the bore of the weapon has a rounded rectangular profile. Ballistic comparison of bullets fired from weapons with polygonal boring may be very difficult.

The bore of the barrel measured from land to land determines the **caliber**; however, this method is not always followed. For example, the .38 Special is .357 and the .30-06

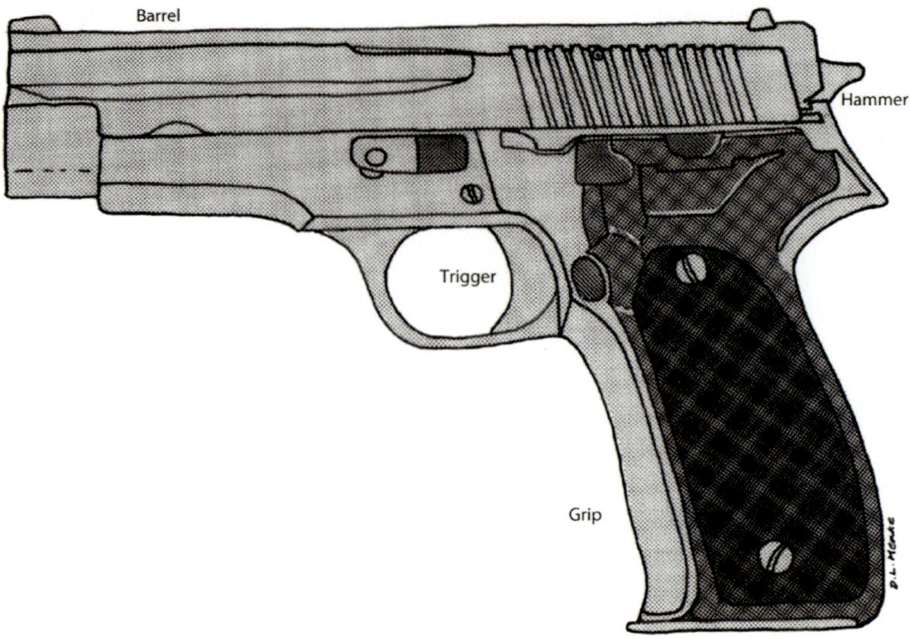

Figure 7.1 Diagram of a firearm.

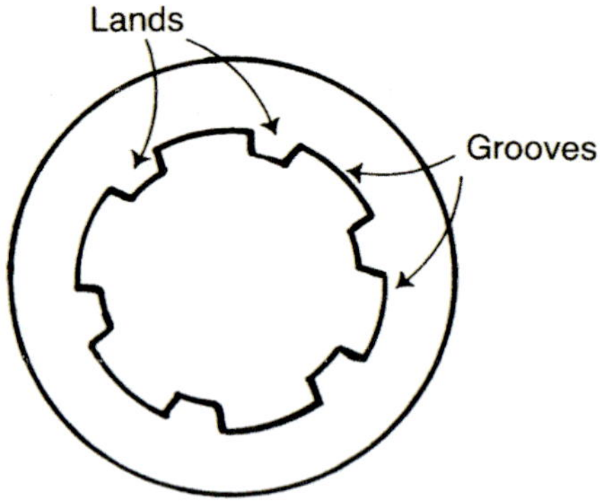

Figure 7.2 Illustration of lands and grooves (rifling) within the muzzle barrel.

Figure 7.3 Rifling marks on bullets.

refers to the year of adoption – 1906. In Europe, caliber is often designated by the bullet diameter and length of the cartridge case, such as with the 7.62 × 39 rifle cartridge. In shotguns, instead of caliber, **gauge** is used to designate barrel diameter. The gauge of a firearm refers to the number of lead balls the diameter of which adds up to 1 lb. The use of the term "magnum" actually has no relation to the caliber of the weapon. It actually denotes there is an extra powerful loading in rifles and handguns or an increase in the weight of the pellets in shotguns.

Common Types of Ammunition

Firearm ammunition usually refers to the type of cartridge used in a particular weapon. It is determined by the caliber, type of primer, type of propellant (i.e., ball powder, flake powder) and the bullet. The cartridge, often referred to as a "round," consists of the projectile or bullet, propellant (powder), primer and casing (Figure 7.4).

Projectiles vary depending upon the type of weapon and caliber and may include lead bullets, semi-jacketed or hollow-point bullets and full metal jacket bullets (Figure 7.5).

Lead bullets were originally round balls that were very unstable in flight. Nowadays, most lead bullets can be classified as round nose, wadcutter or semiwadcutter depending upon their design. Semi-jacketed bullets are usually lead tipped (soft point) or hollow point and are designed to deform upon impact, therefore imparting all its kinetic energy to its target and causing more damage. Full metal jacket bullets are designed to pass directly through their target and are used by most militaries since the passage of the

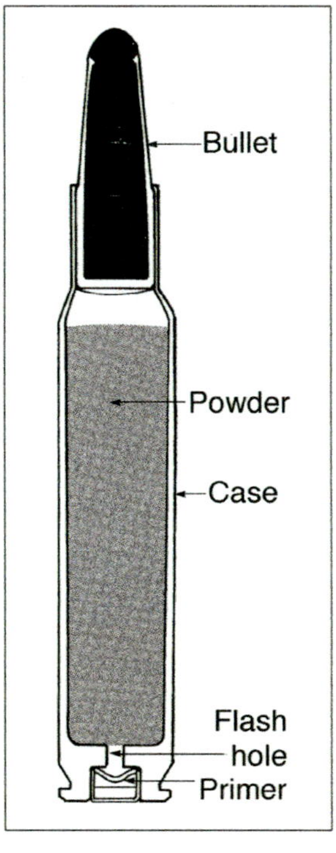

Figure 7.4 Anatomy of a round.

Figure 7.5 Different types of bullets; from left to right – full metal jacket, hollow point and lead.

Hague convention that prohibits the use of bullets that are designed to expand or flatten within its target.

Specialized ammunition also exists. Some handguns, such as the .38 Special, can fire specially designed shotshells ("rat shot"). Frangible bullets are designed to break apart upon impact. Flechette ammunition fires small elongated pointed projectiles similar to an arrow.

Main Types of Common Firearms

There are three main types of firearms:

- Handguns
- Rifles
- Shotguns

Handguns are smaller firearms with rifled barrels. They are considered low-velocity, low-energy weapons and typically have muzzle velocities between 750 and 1400 f/s and can impart between 64 and 550 ft lb of kinetic energy. Handguns can be further divided into revolvers and pistols (Figure 7.6A and B).

Revolvers hold their cartridges in a cylinder that is rotated by pulling the trigger. Most revolvers can only hold five to six rounds. Semiautomatic pistols have removable magazines within the grip that can hold 7–15 rounds. Bullets for revolvers and pistols can be lead, semi-jacketed or full metal jacket.

Rifles have long, rifled barrels and can be divided into center- and rimfire (Figure 7.7A).

Center-fire rifles are high-velocity, high-energy firearms, producing muzzle velocities >3000 f/s and imparting 1050–2500 ft lbs of kinetic energy. Center-fire rifle bullets are semi-jacketed or jacketed due to the higher muzzle velocities. Assault rifles are center-fire rifles that are autoloading, have a large capacity (usually 20 rounds or more), a detachable magazine and are capable of full-automatic fire (Figure 7.7B).

Figure 7.6 (A) Revolver and (B) semiautomatic pistol.

Rimfire rifles are considered low-velocity firearms and impart a similar wounding pattern as handguns. They generate muzzle velocities from 830 to 1750 f/s and impart 44–200 ft lbs of kinetic energy. Rimfire rifles tend to be smaller caliber, normally consisting of .22 caliber short, longrifle and magnum ammunition with bullet weights between 30 and 40 or 40 and 50 g with magnum loads.

Figure 7.7 (A) Center-fire rifle and (B) assault rifle.

Figure 7.8 Shotgun.

Shotguns have a long smooth bore barrel and typically fire multiple projectiles, called pellets, at a time (Figure 7.8). They are considered low-velocity firearms with muzzle velocities usually less than 1400 f/s. The lethal effect of a shotgun blast is usually due to multiple pellet perforations or the concussive effect of the blast itself, usually from close range. Shotguns' pellets are usually round lead balls, though they can also be manufactured from steel or other metals. Shotguns can also fire single projectiles, termed slugs, which can produce wounds similar in severity to center-fire rifles.

Wound Ballistics

The ability of a bullet to inflict damage is dependent upon how much kinetic energy it can impart to its target. Although bullets are small, their energy derives from their speed:

$$\text{Kinetic Energy} = \frac{1}{2}\,\text{mass} \cdot \text{velocity}^2$$

Thus, the factors that affect the seriousness of the wound are those factors that can affect a bullet's speed, such as the amount of yaw, the type of firearm, the type of ammunition and the presence of intermediary targets. In addition, the type of organ or tissue struck also plays a factor.

A bullet courses through a body like a boat on a lake. Since organs and tissues are of different densities and fluid composition, as the bullet passes through, it creates a wake, or a "temporary cavity," much like the wake of a boat (Figure 7.9).

Thus, the extent of injury from a bullet is due to the following:

1. The mechanical **shredding and crushing of tissue** by the bullet as it perforates the tissue
2. The shearing, compression and stretching injuries to the tissue due **to temporary cavity** formation
3. Secondary injuries due to **breakup of the bullet**

The location, size and the shape of the temporary cavity in a body depend on the nature of the bullet, the amount of kinetic energy lost by the bullet in its path through the tissue, how rapidly the energy is lost and the elasticity and cohesiveness of the tissue. The maximum diameter of the cavity occurs at the point at which the maximum rate of loss of kinetic energy occurs. This occurs at the point where the bullet is at maximum yaw, that is, turned sideways (at a 90-degree angle to the path) and/or when it fragments. Firearms

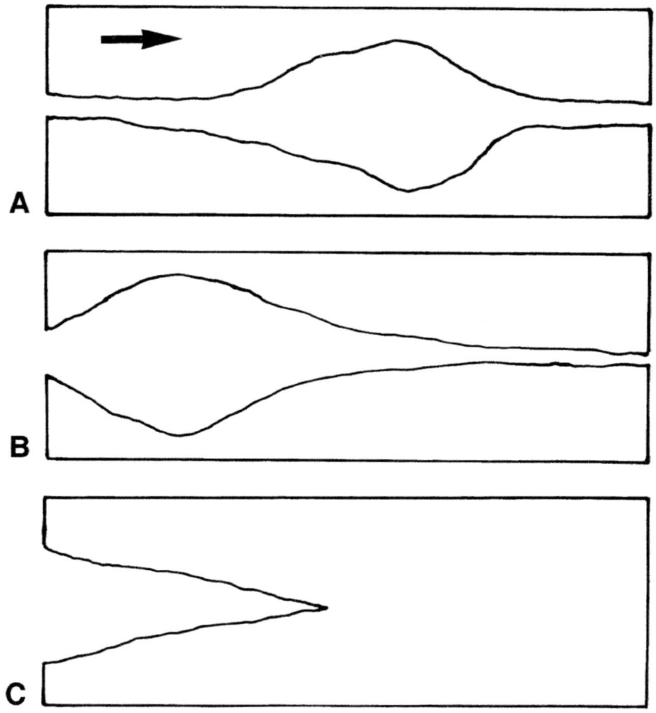

Figure 7.9 Illustration of temporary cavities.

with greater muzzle velocities generate more kinetic energy and create larger temporary cavities than lower velocity firearms.

The temporary cavity will undulate for 5–10 ms before coming to rest as a permanent track. Positive and negative pressures alternate in the wound track, with resultant sucking of foreign material and bacteria into the track from both entrance and exit and ejection of blood and tissue. The expanding walls of the temporary cavity are capable of doing severe damage. There is compression, stretching and shearing of the displaced tissue. Injuries to blood vessels, nerves or organs not struck by the bullet, and a distance from the path, can occur, as can fractures of bones (rarely).

The size of both the temporary and the permanent cavities is determined not only by the amount of kinetic energy deposited in the tissue but also by the density and elastic cohesiveness of the tissue. Maximum expansion of the cavity does not occur until after the bullet has passed through the target. In the case of handgun bullets, the bullet produces a direct path of destruction with very little lateral extension within the surrounding tissues, that is, only a small temporary cavity is produced. As a general rule, the temporary cavity plays little or no role in the extent of wounding, neither does breakup of the bullet.

In the case of center-fire rifle bullets, the two most important factors in determining the extent of injury are the temporary cavity and breakup of the bullet. Rifle bullets fall into two general categories: hunting bullets and military bullets. Hunting bullets are designed to expand and, in that process, at least some fragmentation of the bullet occurs. Thus, with this type of bullet, wounding is due to the combination of the crushed and shredded tissue generated by the bullet perforating tissue, the effects of the temporary cavity on tissue adjacent to the bullet path (shearing, compression and stretching) and secondary injuries due to fragmentation of the bullet. In the case of full metal jacket, nondeforming, bullets, such as those in military ammunition, wounding is due to the combination of the crushed and shredded tissue generated by the bullet perforating tissue, and the effects of the temporary cavity on tissue adjacent to the bullet path (shearing, compression and stretching). Injury due to breakup of the bullet does not ordinarily occur. The exception is the 5.56 × 45 mm, (.223) M-16 round. The maximum disruption of tissue with military bullets occurring at the point yawing of the bullet causes the maximum presentation of the surface area of the bullet to the tissue, that is, at 90 degrees yaw.

Range of Fire

When a firearm is discharged, heat and flame exit from the muzzle along with the bullet and a plume of gunshot residues consisting of soot, burnt and unburnt powder particles, vaporized metal from the bullet and cartridge case, and primer residues (Figure 7.10).

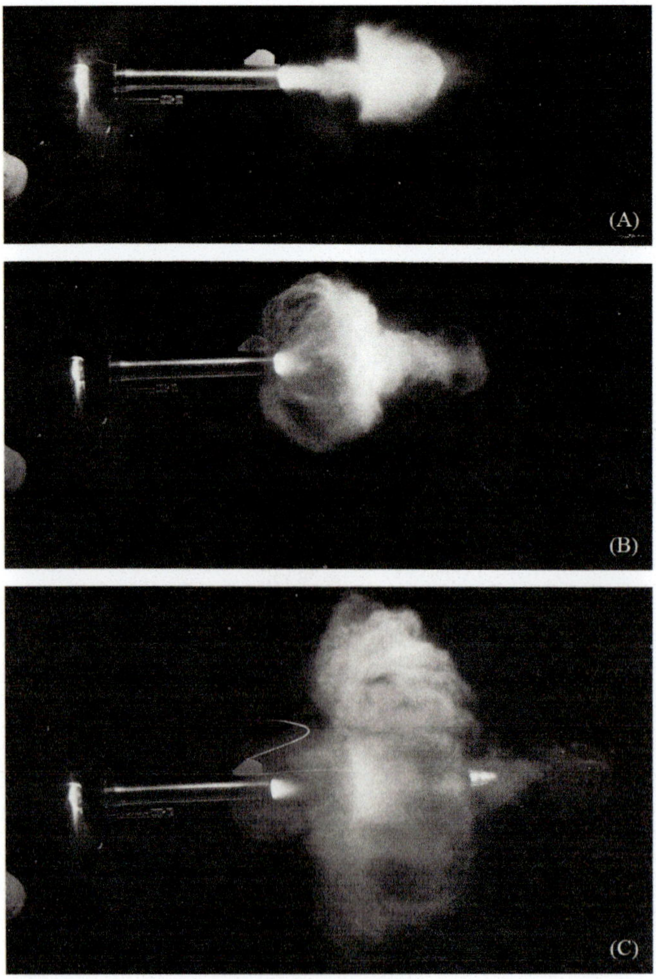

Figure 7.10 Photographs of a firearm being discharged illustrating the flame and gunshot residues that emanate from the muzzle along with the bullet.

These substances can mark the skin and clothing assisting the forensic pathologist in determining the range of fire. Gunshot entry wounds can be classified as close range, which includes contact, near-contact and intermediate-range wounds, or as having no evidence of close-range firing. Diagnosing a "distant" shot is impossible as distant shots simply show an absence of close-range features, which may occur if the firearm is discharged from a distance greater than the drop-off point (the point after which soot and powder fail to travel) for that firearm and ammunition or if there is an intermediary target, such as a pillow, thick clothing or other items between the firearm and the body.

Contact Wounds

A **contact wound** is one in which the muzzle of the weapon is held against the body at the time of discharge. In contact wounds, gas, soot and metallic particles avulsed from the bullet by the rifling, vaporized metal from the bullet and cartridge case, primer residue and powder particles, are all driven into the wound track along with the bullet. In **hard-contact wounds**, the muzzle of the weapon is held very tightly against the skin, indenting it so that the skin envelopes the muzzle at the time of discharge. All the materials emerging from the muzzle will be driven into the wound, often leaving very little external evidence that one is dealing with a contact wound. Inspection of the entrance, however, will usually disclose searing and powder blackening (soot) of the immediate edge of the wound (Figure 7.11).

A **loose-contact wound** is produced when the muzzle of the weapon is held in light contact with the skin at the time of discharge. The skin is not indented by the muzzle. Gas preceding the bullet and the bullet itself can indent the skin, creating a temporary gap between the skin and the muzzle through which gas can escape. Soot carried by the gas is deposited in a band around the entrance (Figure 7.12). This soot can easily be wiped away.

Contact wounds in regions of the body where only a thin layer of skin and subcutaneous tissue overlies bone usually have a **stellate** or cruciform appearance that is totally unlike the round or oval perforating wounds seen in other areas (Figure 7.13).

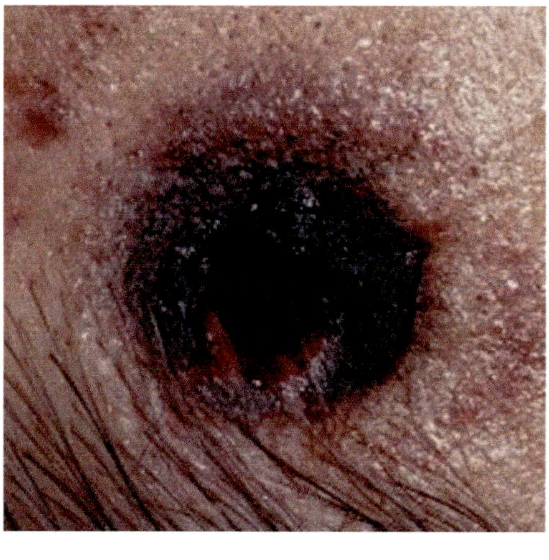

Figure 7.11 Hard-contact wound.

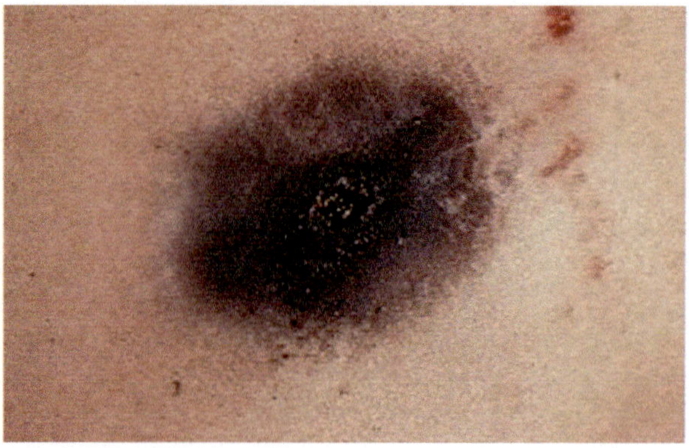

Figure 7.12 Loose-contact wound.

The most common area in which stellate wounds occur is the head. The unusual appearance of contact wounds over bone is due to the effects of the gas of discharge. When a weapon is fired, the gases produced by the combustion of the propellant emerge from the barrel in a highly compressed state. In hard-contact wounds, they follow the bullet through the skin into the subcutaneous tissue where they immediately begin to expand. Where a thin layer of skin overlies bone, as in the head, these gases expand between the skin and the outer table of the skull, lifting up and ballooning out the skin. If the stretching exceeds the elasticity of the skin, it will tear. These tears radiate from the entrance, producing a stellate or cruciform-appearing wound of entrance. The presence of tearing of the skin as well as its extent depends on the caliber of the weapon, the amount of gas produced by the combustion of the propellant, the firmness with which the gun is held against the body and the elasticity of the skin. In some contact wounds over bone, instead of the classical stellate or cruciform wound, one finds a very large circular wound with ragged, blackened and seared margins. In contact wounds of the trunk, stellate or cruciform entrances in the skin usually do not occur, even when the weapon and ammunition used to produce large volumes of gas, because the gas is able to expand into the abdominal cavity, chest cavity or soft tissue.

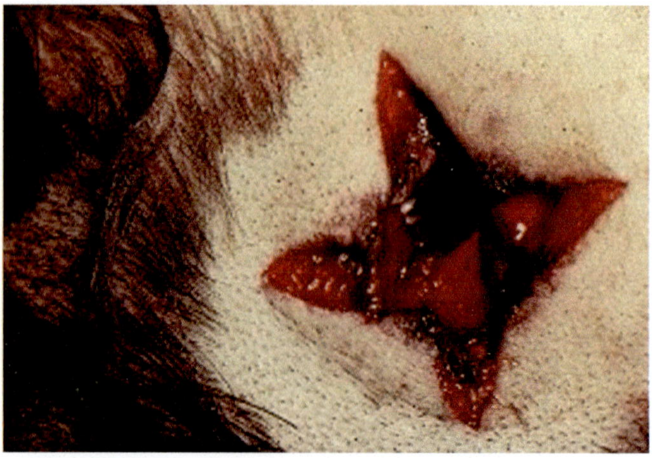

Figure 7.13 Stellate contact wound of the head.

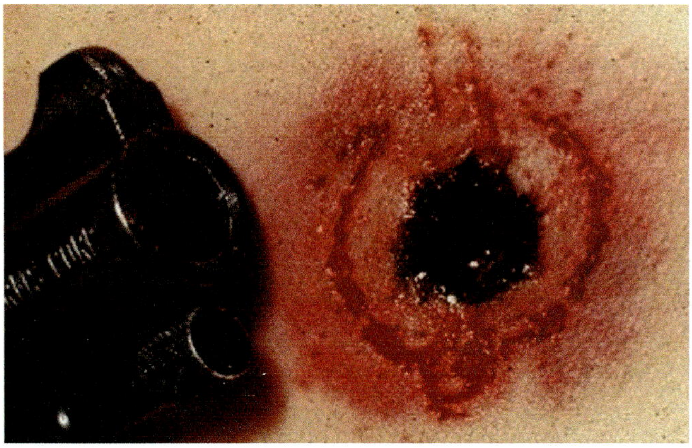

Figure 7.14 Muzzle imprint.

Additionally, in contact gunshot wounds, the gas expanding in the subcutaneous tissue may produce effects other than tearing of the skin. The ballooned-out skin may slam against the muzzle of the weapon with enough force to imprint an outline of the muzzle on the skin (Figure 7.14).

Such imprints may be extremely detailed or only focally apparent. Imprints of the muzzle of the weapon occur not only in regions where a thin layer of skin overlies bone but also in the chest and abdomen. The muscle beneath the entrance wound may also have a cherry-red hue, due to carboxyhemoglobin and carboxymyoglobin formed from the carbon monoxide in the muzzle gas.

Near-Contact Wounds

A near-contact wound is in a gray zone between contact and intermediate-range wounds. There is an overlap between the appearance of near- and loose-contact wounds making it difficult to differentiate the two. In near-contact wounds, the muzzle of the weapon is not in contact with the skin, being held at a very short distance away. The distance, however, is so small that the powder grains emerging from the muzzle do not have a chance to disperse and mark the skin, producing the powder tattooing that is the *sine qua non* of intermediate-range wounds. In near-contact wounds, there is an entrance wound, surrounded by a wide zone of powder soot overlying seared, blackened skin. The zone of searing is wider than that seen in a loose-contact wound. The soot in the seared zone is baked into the skin and cannot be completely wiped away. Small clumps of unburned powder may be present in the seared zones.

Intermediate Range

An **intermediate-range gunshot wound** is one in which the muzzle of the weapon is away from the body at the time of discharge yet is sufficiently close so that powder grains emerging from the muzzle strike the skin producing powder tattooing; this is the *sine qua non* of intermediate-range gunshot wounds (Figure 7.15).

While there may be blackening of the skin or material around the entrance site from soot produced by combustion of the propellant, this soot can usually be wiped away either

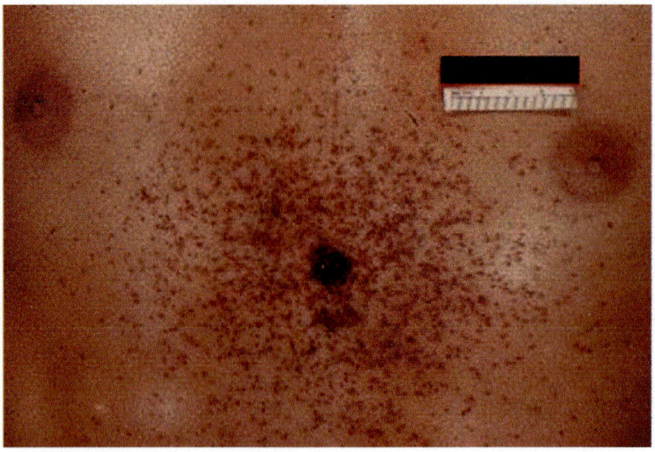

Figure 7.15 Powder tattooing.

by copious bleeding or intentional wiping, powder tattooing cannot. Tattooing consists of numerous reddish-brown to orange-red, punctate lesions surrounding the wound of entrance. Powder tattooing is due to the impact of unburned, partially burned or burning powder grains onto and into the skin. Unlike stippling, powder tattooing refers directly to this effect. "Stippling" is a more generic term that can refer to any marks surrounding an entrance wound, such as from glass or wood or other projectiles, which may strike the skin along with the projectile. Stippling is better used to describe shrapnel or blast injuries, while powder tattooing applies exclusively to gunshot wounds.

The size and density of the area of powder blackening vary with the caliber of the weapon, the barrel length, the type of propellant powder and the distance from muzzle to target. As the range increases, the intensity and density of powder blackening decreases and the size of the soot pattern area increases. For virtually all handgun cartridges, soot is absent beyond 30 cm (12 in.). In general for center-fire handgun cartridges, flake powder produces powder tattooing out to 18–24 in. (45–60 cm); cartridges loaded with flattened ball out to 30–36 in. (75 to 90 cm) and cartridges loaded with true or spherical powder out to 36–42 in. (90–105 cm). In contrast, .22 long rifle cartridges produce powder tattooing out to 18–24 in. (45–60 cm) with flake powder and 12–18 in. (30–45 cm) with ball powder. The maximum range at which tattooing occurs, as well as the size and density of the powder tattoo pattern, depends not only on the form of the powder but also on a number of other variables, including the barrel length, the caliber, the individual weapon and the presence of intermediary objects such as hair or clothing that will absorb some or all of the powder grains. The greater the range, the larger and less dense the powder tattoo pattern.

Distant Wounds

In **distant gunshot wounds**, the muzzle of the weapon is sufficiently far from the body so that there is neither deposition of soot nor powder tattooing (Figure 7.16). As discussed earlier, for center-fire handguns, distant gunshot wounds begin beyond 24–42 in. (60 cm) depending upon the type of ammunition used. The exact range depends on the particular weapon and ammunition and can be determined exactly only by experimentation

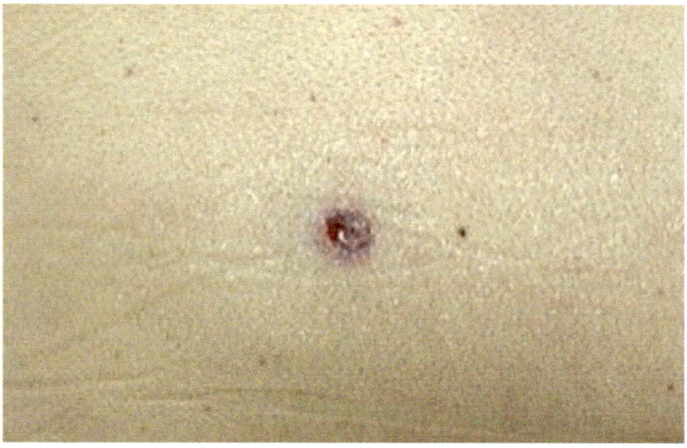

Figure 7.16 Distant wound.

with the specific weapon and ammunition. Distant wounds fail to demonstrate any of the characteristics described earlier. However, it should not be concluded that a wound represents a distant range of fire without first ruling out the presence of an intermediary target. Intermediary targets can filter out soot and powder before they reach the skin and can, therefore, create the appearance of a distant wound even at close range.

Irregular, cruciform or stellate entrance wounds can also occur in individuals shot at distant range, even where gas plays no role in the production of a wound. These occur when the bullet perforates the skin over a bony prominence or curved area of bone covered by a thin layer of tightly stretched skin. The head is the most common site for such wounds (Figure 7.17).

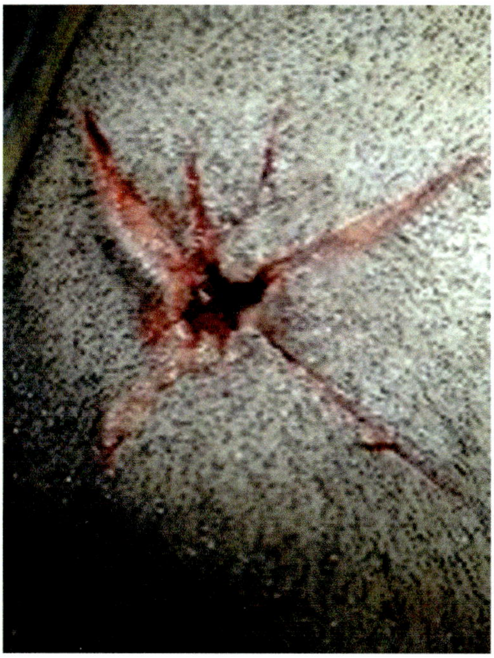

Figure 7.17 Stellate wound on the top of the head from a distant range of fire.

The forehead as it slopes back at the hairline, the top and back of the head, the supraorbital ridges and the cheekbone are also common sites.

Entrance and Exit Wounds

Entrance Wounds

Generally, entrance wounds are round to oval defects surrounded by a red to reddish-brown margin of abraded skin – **the abrasion ring** (Figure 7.18). The reddish-brown appearance of the abrasion ring is an artifact due to drying. Initially, an entrance hole is usually surrounded by a circumferential margin of absent epidermis that appears initially as a moist, white or reddish zone. After prolonged exposure to air, this zone assumes a brownish color due to the drying of the exposed dermis. Contrary to some theories, the abrasion ring is not due in any way to the temperature of the bullet. While bullets may easily attain a surface temperature of over 100°C after leaving the muzzle, the contact time between the bullet and skin is extremely short, insufficient to cause a burn

Abrasion rings can vary in width, depending on the caliber of the weapon, the angle at which the bullet entered and the anatomic site of entrance. Entrance wounds in the skin overlying the clavicle generally have a wider abrasion ring than those in other parts of the body, possibly due to the reinforcement of a thin layer of skin by curved bone. The abrasion ring around the entrance hole can be concentric or eccentric, depending on the angle between the bullet and the skin. A bullet striking perpendicular to the skin should produce a concentric abrasion ring (Figure 7.19).

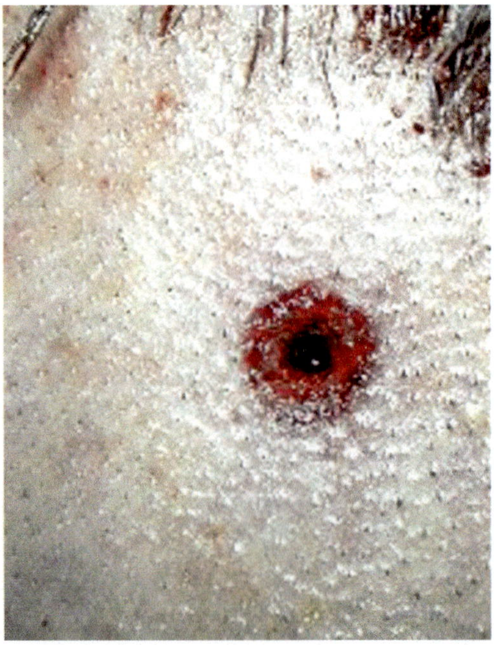

Figure 7.18 Classic entry wound.

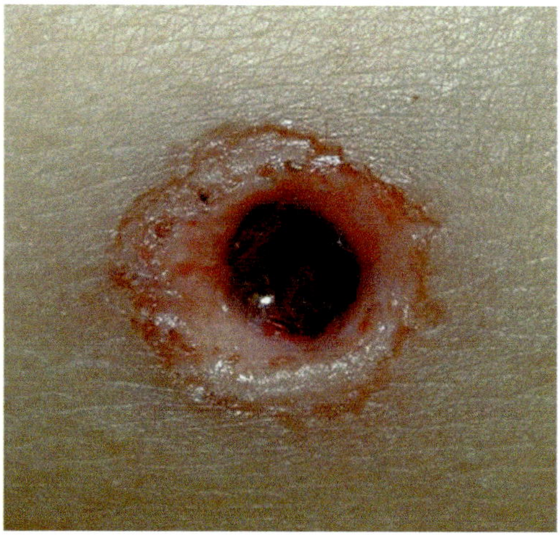

Figure 7.19 Entrance wound with a concentric abrasion ring.

If the bullet penetrates at an oblique angle, the zone of abrasion in the skin will be eccentric, with the zone wider on the side from which the bullet comes (Figure 7.20).

This, however, assumes that the skin is flat. People, however, are three-dimensional, with curves, depressions and projections. Thus, the bullet may be fired perpendicular to the body but strike a projecting surface, for example, the breast so that an eccentric abrasion ring wound is produced even though the bullet is going straight into the body. Thus, it is never possible to say with certainty in which direction a bullet has traveled through the body from examination of the entrance wound alone.

In fact, the appearance of an entrance wound is much more varied. A fresh wound may have a punched-out appearance with no abrasion ring, with immediate transition from normal-appearing skin to shiny pale dermis. The edge of the entrance will be sharp – as if a circular disk of skin had been cut out by a knife. The wound then bevels inward from this margin. Another wound may have a similar appearance but on close examination

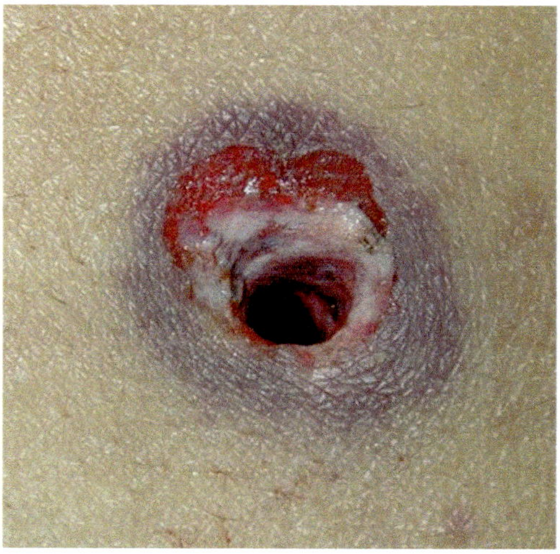

Figure 7.20 Entrance wound with an eccentric rim ring.

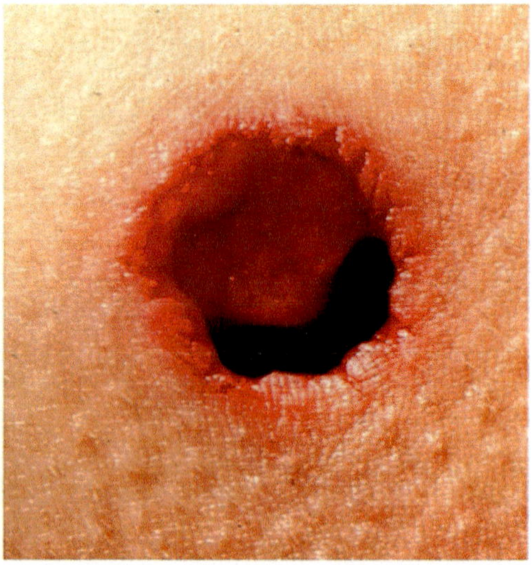

Figure 7.21 Entrance wound with circumferential micro-tears.

will show an inner zone to the punched-out edge consisting of remnants of epidermis. An entrance wound may show micro-tears of the edge of the peroration (Figure 7.21).

These may be distributed symmetrically or in oval wounds be asymmetrical. Most wounds with micro-tears show the absence of an abrasion ring.

The traditional explanation for the *abrasion ring* was that as the bullet indents and pierces the skin, the bullet abrades ("rubs raw") the edges of the hole. High-speed photography, however, has demonstrated that the abrasion ring was not caused by friction but by superficial tissue particles being thrown back against the direction of the fire, that is, the material from the edge of the entrance wound is ejected backward against the line of fire. As the bullet enters the skin, the skin is radially accelerated and displaced centrifugally, so that for a short time the wound is larger than the caliber of the bullet creating a temporary cone-shaped entrance, the tip of which is directed internally.[1]

Exit Wounds

Exit wounds are typically larger and more irregular than entrance wounds and, with rare exception, do not possess an abrasion ring. Exit wounds can be stellate, slit-like, crescent, circular or completely irregular (Figure 7.22).

The larger but more irregular nature of exit wounds is due to two factors. First, the spin that stabilized the bullet in the air is not effective in tissue because of the greater density of the tissue. Thus, as the missile travels through the body, its natural yaw is accentuated; if it travels through enough tissue, it will eventually tumble ending up traveling base first. Second, the bullet may be deformed in its passage through the body. Both the factors result in the presentation of a larger area of bullet at the site of the exit, with resultant larger and more irregular exit wounds.

In unusual circumstances, exit wounds will have abraded margins. These are called **shored exit wounds**. They are characterized by a broad, irregular band of abrasion of the skin around the exit (Figure 7.23).

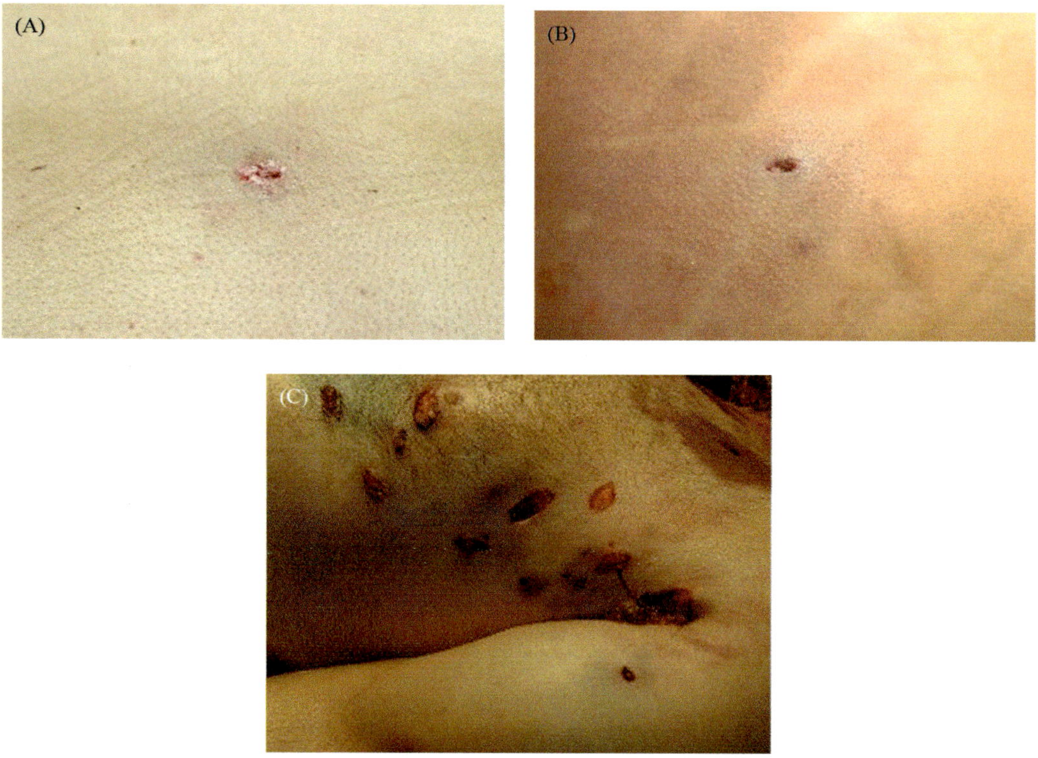

Figure 7.22 (A and B) Solitary exit wounds and (C) multiple exit wounds.

In such wounds, the skin is reinforced, or "shored," by a firm surface at the instant the bullet exits. Thus, individuals shot while lying on the floor, leaning against a wall or sitting back in a chair may have shored exit wounds. As it exits, the bullet everts the skin, with the everted margin impacting against the wall, floor or back of a chair, thus being abraded or "rubbed raw." Shored exit wounds can also occur from tight supportive garments, such as girdles, brassieres and belts, or even tight clothing.

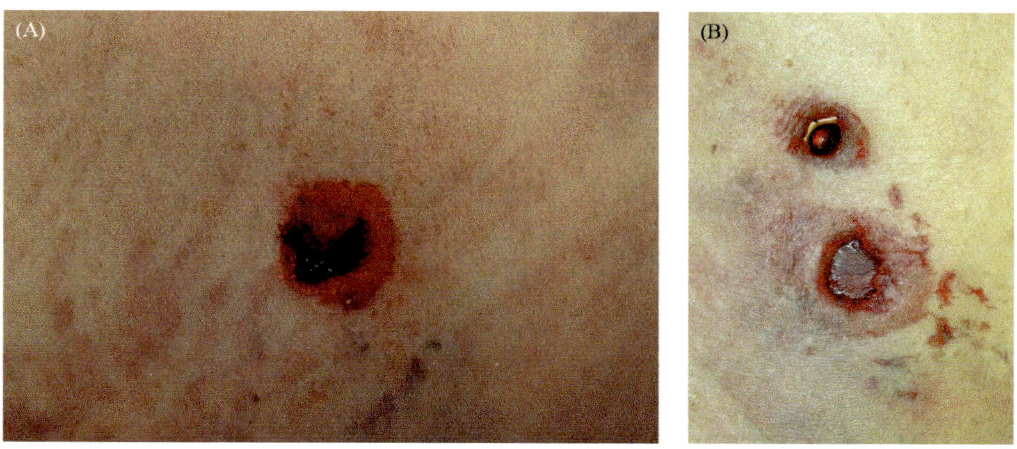

Figure 7.23 (A and B) Shored exit wounds.

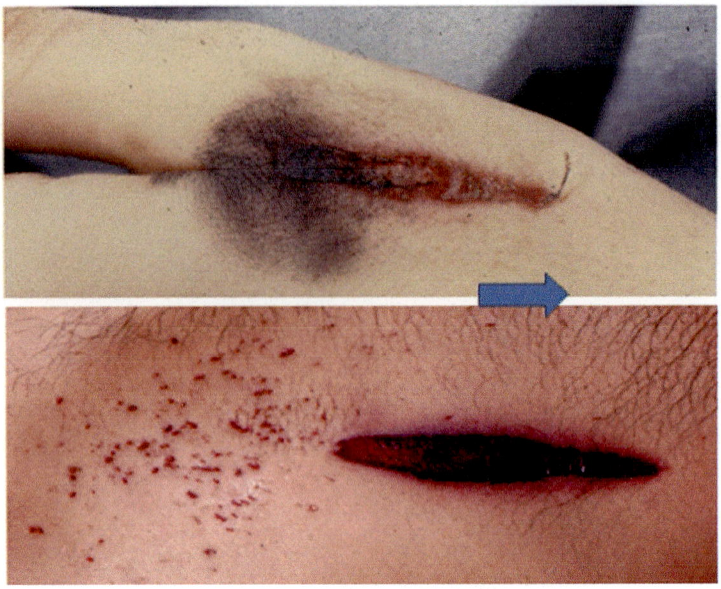

Figure 7.24 Graze wound (arrow shows the direction of travel).

Other Wound Types

A **graze** wound occurs when a bullet strikes the skin at a shallow angle, producing an elongated area of abrasion without actual perforation or tearing of the skin (Figure 7.24).

In a **tangential wound**, the injury extends down to the subcutaneous tissue. The skin is torn, or "lacerated," by the bullet (Figure 7.25).

It is often difficult to determine the direction of a graze wound; however, for a tangential wound, the skin tears often point in the direction from which the projectile came.

Superficial perforating wounds are shallow through-and-through wounds where the bullet passes just under the skin and in which the entrance and exit are close together (Figure 7.26).

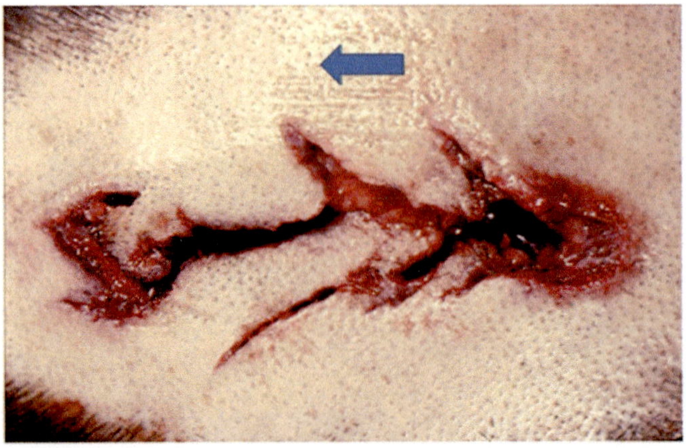

Figure 7.25 Tangential wound with the direction of fire.

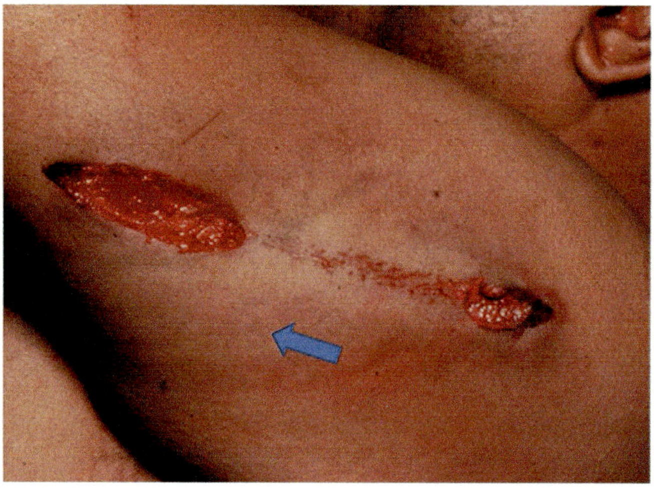

Figure 7.26 Superficial perforating wound with the direction of fire.

Reentry wounds occur when a bullet has passed through one part of the body and then reentered another part. The portion of the body initially perforated serves as an intermediary target. Most commonly, this occurs when a bullet perforates an arm and enters the thorax (Figure 7.27).

The reentry wound is usually characterized by a large irregular entrance hole, the edges of which are ragged and a wide, irregular abrasion ring. Occasionally, the exit and reentry wounds can be re-approximated to show mirror contusions or abrasions, which can occur when the skin of each is in close proximity to the other when the wound is sustained. This is most often seen along the axillae.

Rifle Wounds

In the case of center-fire rifle bullets, the two most important factors in determining the extent of injury are the temporary cavity and breakup of the bullet. As discussed previously

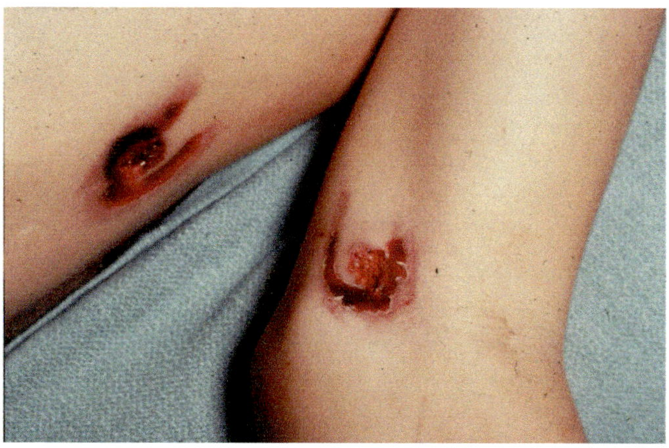

Figure 7.27 Exit wound of the arm with the reentry wound on the chest.

with wound ballistics, rifle bullets are often categorized as either hunting or military. Hunting bullets are usually semi-jacketed or hollow point and are designed to expand and, in the process, at least some fragmentation of the bullet occurs. X-rays of individuals shot with hunting ammunition usually show a characteristic radiologic picture that is seen almost exclusively with this form of rifle ammunition – the so-called **lead snowstorm** (Figure 7.28).

As the expanding hunting bullet moves through the body, fragments of lead break off the lead core and are hurled out into the surrounding tissues. An X-ray shows scores, if not hundreds, of small radiopaque bullet fragments scattered along the wound track (the lead snowstorm). These fragments vary from dust-like to large irregular pieces of metal. A rifle bullet does not have to hit bone for this phenomenon to occur. The absence of such a picture does not absolutely rule out the possibility as the lead snowstorm from hunting ammunition is dependent on the velocity of the bullet.

In the case of full metal jacket, nondeforming, bullets, such as those in military ammunition, wounding is due to the combination of the crushed and shredded tissue generated by the bullet perforating tissue, and the effects of the temporary cavity on tissue adjacent to the bullet path (shearing, compression and stretching). Military bullets, by virtue of their full metal jackets, tend to pass through the body intact, thus producing less extensive injuries than hunting ammunition. Military bullets also usually do not fragment in the body or shed fragments of lead in their paths and do not result in the "lead snowstorm" phenomenon. Because of the high velocity of such military rounds as well as their tough construction, it is possible for such bullets to pass through more than one individual before coming to rest.

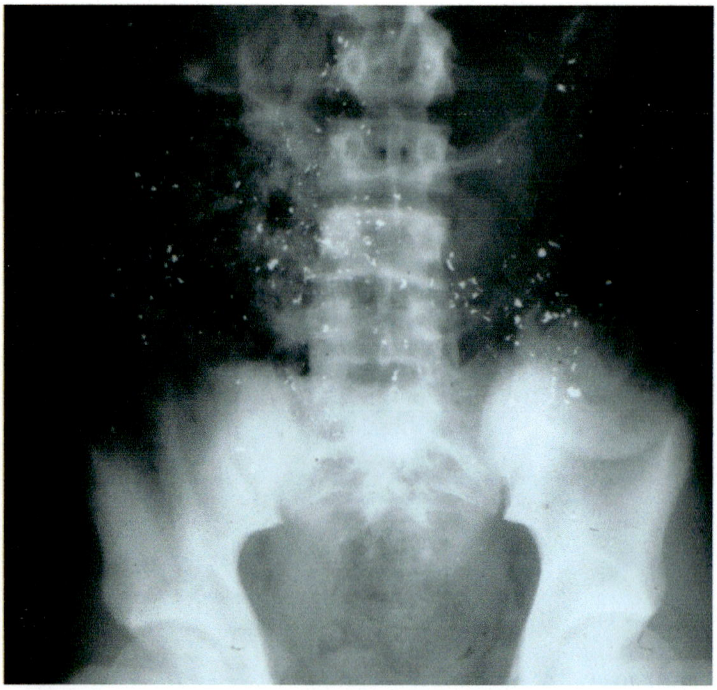

Figure 7.28 X-ray showing scattered lead fragments or "lead snowstorm."

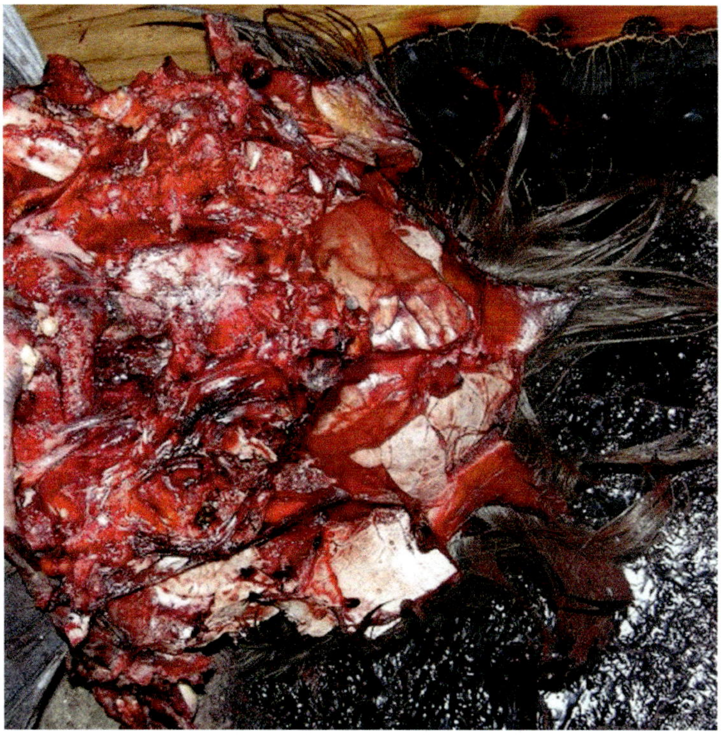

Figure 7.29 Contact rifle wound of the head.

Range of Fire

In some contact rifle wounds of the head, the entrance may be difficult to locate because of the massive destruction (Figure 7.29).

Contact wounds of the chest and abdomen often do not have the dramatic external appearance of such wounds in the head. The wound of entrance is typically circular in shape and usually larger in diameter than those due to pistol bullets. There is almost never tearing of the skin due to gas though the edges of the wound are seared from the effect of the expelled heat. Soot may be deposited in and around the wound though the amount of soot is usually less than that seen with most handguns. The imprint of the muzzle of the weapon is commonly present. In contrast to their benign external appearance, contact center-fire rifle wounds of the chest and abdomen produce massive internal injuries due to the temporary cavity effect rifle wounds create.

In intermediate-range gunshot wounds, powder tattooing may be present around the wound of entrance. The range out to which powder tattooing occurs from center-fire rifles depends on the physical form of powder in the cartridge cases. Two forms of powder are used in center-fire rifles' cartridges manufactured in the United States: ball and cylindrical powder. Cartridges loaded with cylindrical powder produce tattooing out to 12–18 in. Powder tattooing caused by ball powder extends to 2–3 ft.

Intermediate-range and distant head wounds show a wide degree of severity, depending on the style of bullet and the entrance site. Distant entrance wounds of the trunk inflicted by center-fire rifle bullets often appear similar to those produced by handgun bullets.

Shotgun Wounds

Rifles and handguns fire a single projectile down a rifled barrel. Shotguns have a smooth bore. Although they can fire a single projectile, they are usually employed to fire multiple pellets. The archaic term "gauge" is used to describe the caliber of the shotgun. This term refers to the number of lead balls of the given bore diameter that make up a pound. In 12-gauge, for example, it would take 12 of the lead balls to make 1 lb.

Gauge	Bore diameter (in.)
10	0.775
12	0.729
16	0.662
20	0.615
28	0.550
.410	0.410

Most shotgun barrels have some degree of "choke," that is, a partial constriction of the bore of a shotgun barrel at its muzzle so as to control shot patterns. The choke may be permanent and built into the barrel or the barrel may accept choke tubes that when screwed into the muzzle determine the choke of the barrel.

Shotgun shells consist of a plastic body (the tube); a thin brass or brass-coated steel head; a primer; powder; shot and wading. The wading can be either paper/composite or plastic (Figure 7.30).

Shotgun slugs produce massive internal injuries comparable in severity to those produced by a center-fire rifle hunting bullet (Figure 7.31).

Shotgun pellets fall into two general categories: birdshot and buckshot. Birdshot is used for birds and small game; buckshot is used for large game such as deer. Shot size generally ranges from no.12 to 000 buck; the smaller the shot number, the greater the pellet diameter. Lead birdshot ranges from no.12 (0.05 in. in diameter) to BB (0.18 in.). Buckshot is usually manufactured in seven sizes, ranging from no. 4 (0.24 in.) to 000 (0.360 in.). The buckshot in a shell is usually packed in granular white polyethylene filler (Figure 7.32).

Figure 7.30 Winchester, Federal and Remington wads.

Figure 7.31 Foster, Brenneke and Sabot shotgun slugs.

This filler cushions the shot pellets on firing, reducing shot distortion and improving the shot pattern. The granulated filler is of interest to the forensic pathologist in that it can produce stipple marks on the skin identical in appearance to powder tattoo marks.

For both birdshot and buckshot loads, the severity and lethality of a shotgun wound depend on the number of pellets that enter the body, the organs struck by the pellets and the amount of tissue destruction. The extent of tissue destruction from each individual pellet is limited to that tissue they physically shred; temporary cavities play no significant role in injury in shotgun injuries.

Shotgun slugs are used for deer and bear hunting in heavily populated areas where the slug's rapid loss of velocity allegedly affords greater protection from shooting mishaps. The wound of entrance from a shotgun slug is circular in shape with an abraded margin.

Range of Fire

At close range, the shotgun is the most formidable and destructive of all small arms. The severity of the injuries in contact wounds is due to two factors: the charge of shot and the gas from combustion of the propellant (also termed "blast effect"). Most contact shotgun wounds are suicidal in origin. Intermediate-range and close-range shotgun

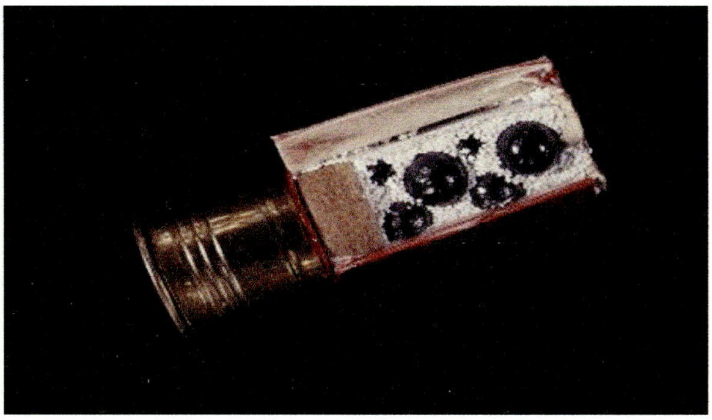

Figure 7.32 An opened shotgun cartridge showing the filler.

wounds are almost as mutilating as contact wounds because the pellets are still traveling in a single mass.

Contact shotgun wounds of the head are among the most mutilating of firearm wounds. Extensive destruction of bone and soft tissue structures with bursting ruptures of the head are the rule rather than the exception. Contact wounds of the trunk appear relatively innocuous when compared with the massive destruction produced by such wounds in the head. The wound of entrance will be circular in shape and will have a diameter approximately equal to that of the bore of the weapon. In hard-contact wounds, no soot surrounds the entrance site, but the edges of the wound will be seared and blackened by the hot gases.

As the range increases beyond 1–2 cm from the muzzle to target, powder tattooing will occur. Powder tattooing from a shotgun is less dense than the tattooing a handgun produces at the same range due to more complete consumption of powder caused by the greater barrel length. The maximum range out to which powder tattooing occurs from a shotgun depends to a great degree on the type of powder, that is, ball or flake. In shotgun shells loaded with flake powder, powder tattooing was present out to 24 in. (60 cm) but disappeared by 30 in. (75 cm). Using the same weapon and firing cartridges loaded with ball powder, definite tattooing was present at 30 in. (75 cm), with a very few marks present at 36 in. (90 cm) but absent by 40 in. (125 cm).

As the muzzle of the shotgun is moved farther from the body, tattooing disappears and the diameter of the circular wound of entrance increases in size until a point is reached where individual pellets begin to separate from the main mass. From contact to 2 ft, birdshot fired from a shotgun, generally, produces a single-round entrance wound (Figure 7.33A).

By 3 ft, the wound widens and the edges of the wounds will have scalloped margins (Figure 7.33B). By 4 ft, scattered satellite pellet holes are present around the main entrance (Figure 7.33C). By 6–7 ft, there is a definite cuff of satellite pellet holes around a slightly irregular wound of entrance (Figure 7.33D, E). Beyond 10 ft, there is a great variation in the size of the pellet pattern depending on the ammunition used, the choke of the gun and, most important, the range (Figure 7.33F, G).

At the same range, the pattern of different guns and brands of ammunition may vary from a central irregular perforation with numerous satellite wounds to a pattern of multiple individual pellet wounds. In all deaths from shotgun wounds, the size of the shot pattern on the body should be measured so that the range can be determined accurately. The range determinations by size and appearance of pattern given should be used only as a rough guide in estimating range. The only reliable method of determining range is to obtain the actual weapon and the same brand of ammunition used and then conduct a series of test shots so as to reproduce on paper the pattern of the fatal wound on the body.

At close range, when there is only a single large wound of entrance, the wad from a shotgun shell will be found inside the body. Depending upon the range of fire, as the wad enters the body, the individual arms or "petals" that have peeled back in flight may produce a patterned abrasion around the wound of entrance. These petal marks can occur even if the entrance site is covered with clothing. In 12, 16 and 20 ga, one will have a circular wound of entrance in the center of a Maltese cross abrasion (Figure 7.34A).

In .410 ga, shot cups have only three petals; thus, three equally spaced rectangular abrasions radiate from the entrance rather than four (Figure 7.34B). Petal marks are seen at ranges between 1 and 3 ft for 12-, 16- and 20-ga shotguns. Before 1 ft of range, the petals usually have not opened up sufficiently to mark the skin. By 1 ft, the petals are usually open enough to mark the skin. By 3 ft, the increasing air resistance bends the petals back so that

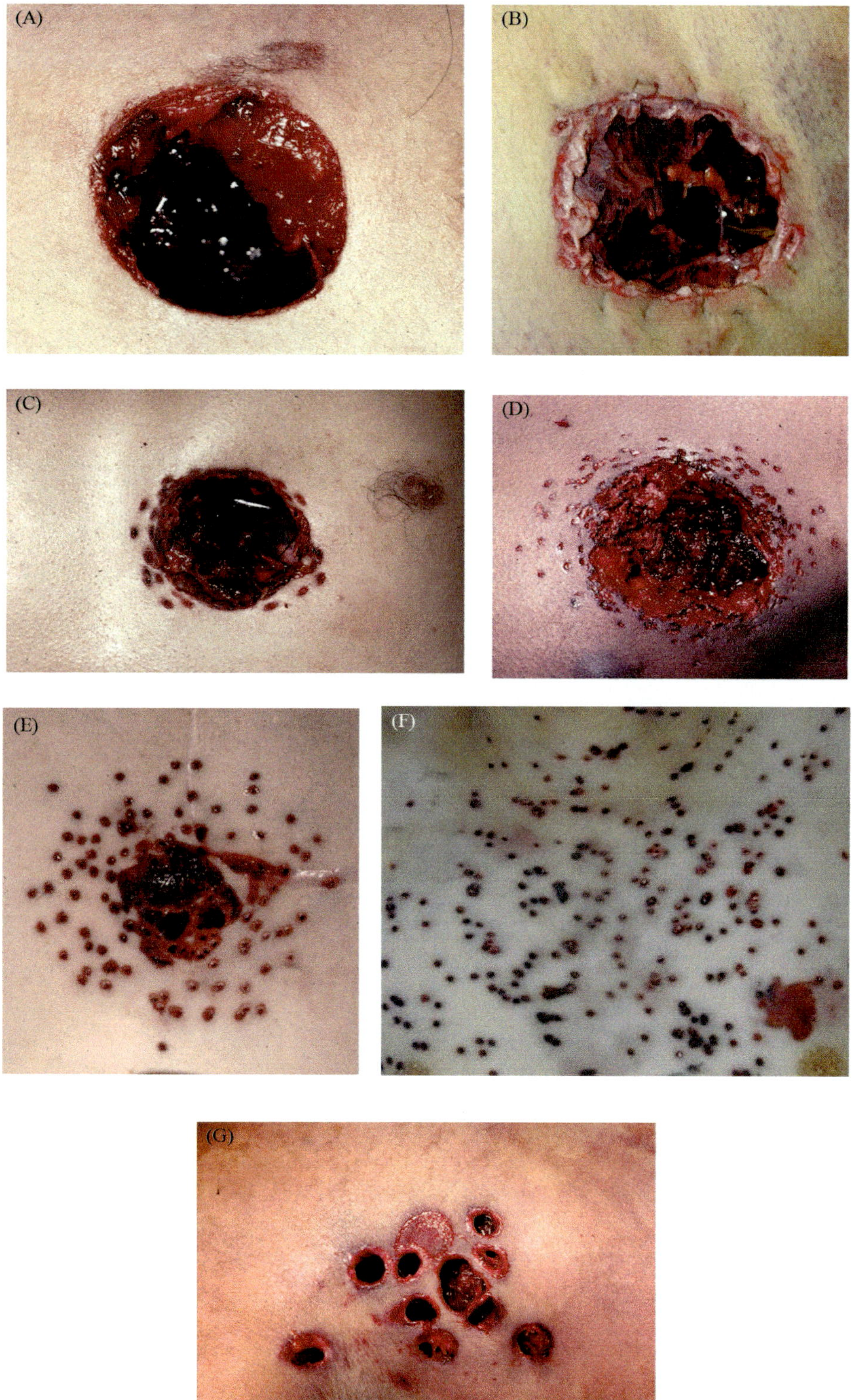

Figure 7.33 The spread of pellets after shotgun discharge: (A) single-round entrance wound, (B) entrance wound with scalloped margins, (C) scattered satellite pellet holes around the main entrance, (D and E) cuff of satellite pellet holes around irregular wound of entrance, (F) large spread of individual pellet defects and (G) spread of buckshot pellets.

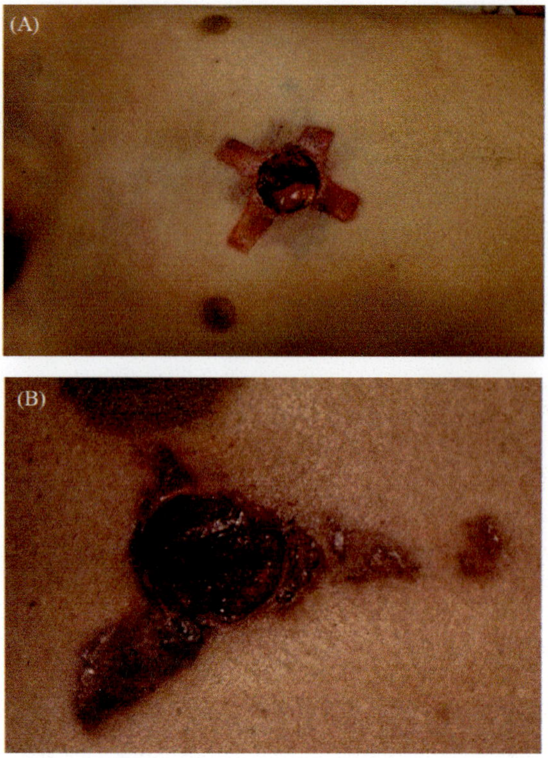

Figure 7.34 (A) Wadding mark from a 12-ga shotgun and (B) wadding mark from a .410 shotgun.

they are generally flush with the sides of the wad base and no petal marks are produced. Depending upon the shotgun, the wadding can travel up to 10 ft, and while it only enters the body at closer ranges, it can strike the body, leaving an irregular, often squared off, abrasion within dispersal area (Figure 7.35).

The presence of a wadding abrasion can also be of assistance when determining the range of fire.

If a shot charge strikes an intermediary target, this will result in an increase in the dispersion of the shot. This occurs secondary to the "billiard ball" effect. Here, the first pellets striking the intermediary target are delayed, allowing the following pellets to catch up and impact the first pellets, causing dispersion of the pellets. If an intermediary target is of sufficient thickness to cause dispersion of pellets prior to striking an individual, estimates of the range from the pattern on the body will be erroneous unless the effects of the dispersion are taken into account.

Other Issues

Caliber Determinations

The caliber of the bullet that enters the skin cannot be determined by the diameter of the entrance wound. The size of the hole is due not only to the diameter of the bullet but also to the elasticity of the skin and the location of the wound. An entrance wound in an area

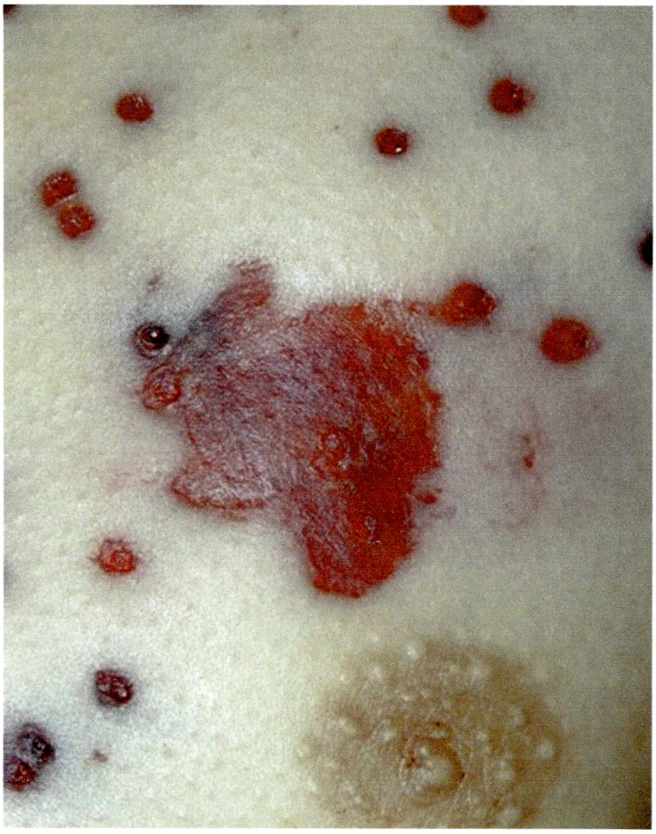

Figure 7.35 Wadding strike from a distant shotgun wound (same wound as Figure 7.33F).

where the skin is tightly stretched will have a diameter different from that of a wound in an area where the skin is lax. Similarly, the size of an entrance in bone cannot be used to determine the caliber of the bullet that perforated the bone though it can be used to eliminate bullet calibers.

Cylinder Gap

When a revolver is fired, gas, soot and powder emerge not only from the end of the muzzle but also from the gap between the cylinder and the barrel. This material emerges, fan-like, at an approximate right angle to the long axis of the weapon. If the revolver is in close proximity to the body at the time of discharge, there may be searing of the skin, deposition of soot or even powder tattooing from gas and powder escaping from the cylinder gap. The tattooing will be relatively scant. If the revolver is discharged by someone unfamiliar with the weapon, they may place their hand over the gap, resulting in searing of the skin and soot disposition in a characteristic pattern.

Ricochet Bullets

Entrance wounds due to ricocheting bullets tend to be atypical due to the fact that the bullet has been destabilized and is yawing, or tumbling, secondary to the act of ricocheting. This destabilized bullet then produces an irregular entrance wound. Ricocheting bullets are invariably destabilized and suffer a rapid loss of velocity, resulting in reduced ability to penetrate a body. The reduced penetration is due to a combination of reduced velocity at impact and premature/accelerated yawing in the body due to the fact that the bullet was yawing on entering. Ricochets occur when the bullet strikes a hard surface or fluid at a critical angle of impact (incidence) below which a bullet striking a hard surface will ricochet rather than penetrate. The critical angle of impact below which a bullet will ricochet off a hard surface is 10–30 degrees; for water, the critical angle is 3–8 degrees. The surface on which the bullet strikes the object is deformed by the ricochet, often imparting a characteristic, mirrored, flattened appearance to one side of bullet (Figure 7.36).

GSR Testing

As previously described, when a firearm is discharged, the firing pin strikes the primer located in the base of the cartridge, which ignites the flame propellant. Primers in the United States generally contain compounds of lead styphnate, barium nitrate and

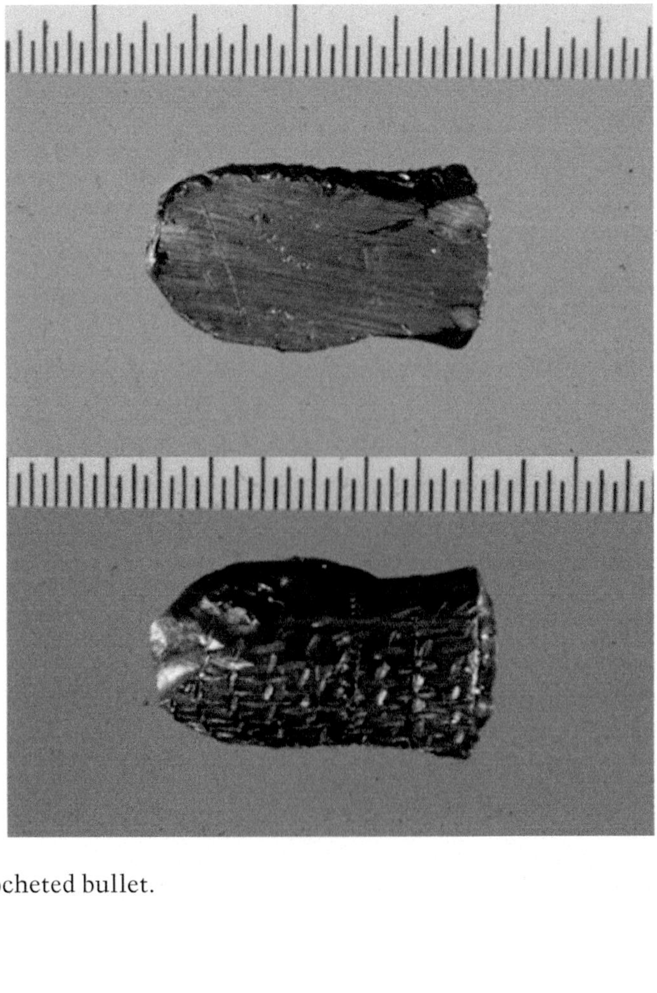

Figure 7.36 Ricocheted bullet.

antimony sulfide, though newer primers may lack one or all components. Heat generated by the resulting combustion vaporizes the metallic components of the primer mixture that are then expelled from the firearm through the muzzle, breech and/or cylinder gap. These ingredients can then recondense into metal droplets, which can deposit on the shooter, the victim, the gun and the surrounding environment.

Gunshot residue (GSR) testing is often performed on the hands of a living individual when they are suspected of discharging or handling a firearm. Detection of GSR on the hands of an individual having denied discharging a firearm is often useful for an investigator when interrogating such an individual or when trying to recreate the events of a shooting. Unfortunately, GSR is also often used to support or refute whether or not a wound was self-inflicted. However, interpreting GSR results from the hands of gunshot wound victims can be more complicated than that of someone who is merely suspected of having fired a weapon. Research has shown that gunshot residues can disperse circumferentially around a discharged firearm for several meters.[2] Thus, a positive result for GSR testing may indicate that a person discharged a firearm or was near a firearm as it was discharged. Unfortunately, in the case of firearm deaths, it is known that the decedent was near a firearm as it was discharged, as they sustained a gunshot wound, making a positive test irrelevant.

Furthermore, research has also shown that GSR testing performed on individuals known to have recently discharged a firearm varies from 10 to 70% positivity depending upon the firearm used.[3] In general, GSR is only positive in about 50% of such cases. Thus, a negative GSR test cannot be used to exclude that someone did not discharge a firearm.

For these reasons, GSR testing on the hands of gunshot wound victims is not recommended as the results cannot be interpreted.

Postmortem Imaging

Postmortem imaging either by radiographs or CT is invaluable in the evaluation of gunshot wounds. They should be taken in all gunshot wound cases, especially those in which there appears to be an exit wound. Imaging should always be performed while the deceased is fully clothed. This practice will reveal bullets that exited the body and are retained in the clothing.

Imaging is useful for a variety of reasons:

1. To see whether the bullet or any part of it is still in the body
2. To locate the bullet especially in cases of bullet emboli
3. To locate for retrieval small fragments deposited in the body by a bullet that has exited
4. To identify the type of ammunition or weapon used prior to autopsy or to make such an identification if it cannot be made at autopsy.
5. To document the path of the bullet

Postmortem imaging should be performed in all gunshot wound cases, even when there is an apparent exit wound, as an "exit wound" does not necessarily indicate that the bullet did, indeed, exit. Occasionally, an exiting bullet will have enough energy to create a

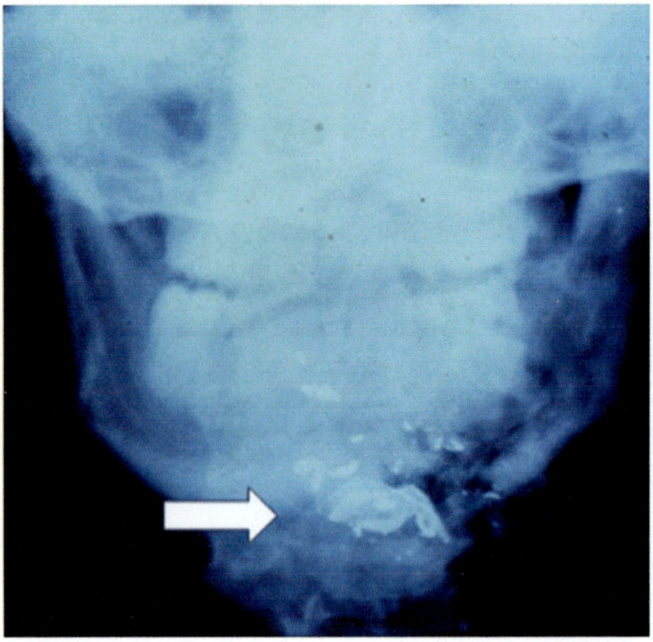

Figure 7.37 Radiograph showing retention of the copper jacket in the jaw; the lead core exited.

defect in the skin but will rebound back into the body. This may be due either to the elastic nature of the skin or to the resistance from overlying clothing. The "exit" can also be due to a fragment of bone being propelled through the skin ahead of the missile, with the bullet itself remaining in the body.

A special situation can arise with partial metal-jacketed bullets. Here, separation of the jacket and the core can occur as the missile moves through the body. The lead core may exit while the jacket remains (Figure 7.37).

The core is of no use for purposes of bullet comparison. Only the jacket possesses individual rifling characteristics. At autopsy, if one is unaware that the jacket is present in the body and that it was the core that exited rather than the whole bullet, the jacket can readily be missed. This is especially true if the jacket lodges in the muscle adjacent to the exit. To compound the problem, the core may be recovered at the scene by the police and then be mistaken for the complete bullet. The medical examiner may be informed that the "bullet" was recovered. Facilitating the misidentification of a lead core as a bullet is the fact that the core may have very faint "rifling" marks impressed on it through the jacket. These marks, however, are class characteristics, not individual characteristics; thus, ballistic comparison is not possible. Although in most instances the lead core exits and the jacket remains, sometimes the opposite situation occurs, with the jacket exiting the body.

Occasionally, the jacket and core will separate in the body, but neither will exit. The forensic pathologist may recover the core with "rifling" on it and assume it to be the complete bullet. They may then inadvertently leave the jacket in the body or discard it with the viscera. Such mistakes can be prevented by an X-ray of the body, which will reveal whether the separation of the core and jacket has occurred. With an X-ray, it is very easy to distinguish between the core and jacket by the different densities. However, it should also be remembered that not all jackets are radiodense, especially aluminum jackets, and can be missed even on X-ray.

In through-and-through gunshot wounds, small fragments of metal from the missile may be deposited along the wound track or in bone perforated by the bullet. These fragments are readily missed at autopsy, especially if only two or three are present. It may be important for investigative purposes, however, to recover such fragments as they can be analyzed for the presence of trace elements, for example, copper, antimony, arsenic, for comparison to a bullet recovered at the scene or bullets in a box of cartridges that is thought to have been the source of the fatal cartridge. [4]

Radiographs may also give a pathologist an idea of what type of weapon or ammunition they are dealing with before the autopsy. X-rays of shotgun wounds may reveal a slug or buckshot rather than birdshot. The complete absence of a missile on total body X-ray (thus excluding embolization) and lack of an exit wound would suggest a wound from a blank cartridge. The presence of small fragments of metal along the wound track virtually rules out full metal jacket ammunition, such as may be used in a semiautomatic pistol. The reverse is not true; however, the absence of lead on X-ray does not necessarily rule out a lead bullet. As discussed previously, radiographs of center-fire rifle wounds may have a "lead snowstorm."

High-velocity semi-jacketed pistol bullets (almost exclusively the .357 Magnum) may deposit fragments of bullet core as they perforate the skull. This picture may initially be confused with that of a "lead snowstorm" from a rifle bullet. Examination of the X-ray, however, will show that these fragments are larger, coarser and significantly fewer in number than those seen in the "lead snowstorm." X-rays of the head may also show evidence of internal ricochet. This is manifested by a trail of small lead fragments, which doubles back on itself.

Routine imaging in deaths from gunshot wounds may reveal old bullets, pellets or bullet fragments unrelated to the victim's death. There is usually no problem distinguishing them from new bullets when they are recovered, as the old bullets are encapsulated in fibrous scar tissue. These bullets usually have a black color as a result of oxidation (Figure 7.38).

Black discoloration can occur in a new bullet, however, if the bullet is exposed to the contents of the gastrointestinal tract.

It must be remembered that determination of range of fire in shotgun wounds cannot be made from the spread of the pellets on X-rays, however. A contact wound of the chest can produce an X-ray picture identical to that of an individual shot at 10 ft. This is due to the "billiard ball" effect.[5] Pellets entering the body in a mass strike one another, dispersing at random angles throughout the tissue. Also, in "explosive" contact shotgun wounds of the head with birdshot, virtually all the pellets may exit. This situation has caused confusion when no X-rays were taken of the head and the pathologist was unable to locate any pellets at autopsy. The pathologist then doubted the hypothesis that the individual had died of a shotgun wound. An X-ray in such cases should reveal at least a few pellets.

The exact caliber of a bullet cannot be determined with certainty on imaging. This is due to magnification of the bullet image depending on its distance from the source of

Figure 7.38 Discolored older bullet recovered at autopsy.

the radiation. Bullets close to the origin will appear larger and have fuzzier margins than those close to the detector. Radiographs can also show artifacts that can be misconstrued as bullets. The "stem" of a zipper often has the appearance of a slightly mushroomed bullet (Figure 7.39).

The dislodged crown from a tooth may appear as a flattened bullet (Figure 7.40).

In some cases, bullets carry fragments of an intermediary target, such as links from a necklace or a metal zipper, into the body and these can be visualized on imaging.

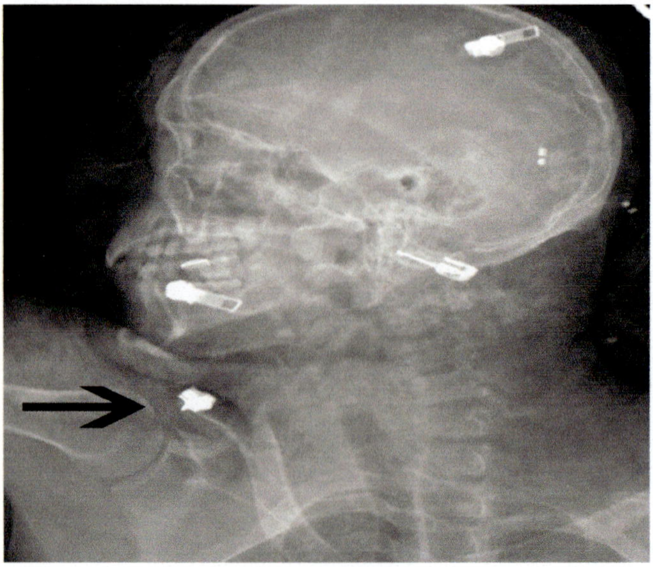

Figure 7.39 The arrow points to a zipper that may be confused with a bullet on radiograph.

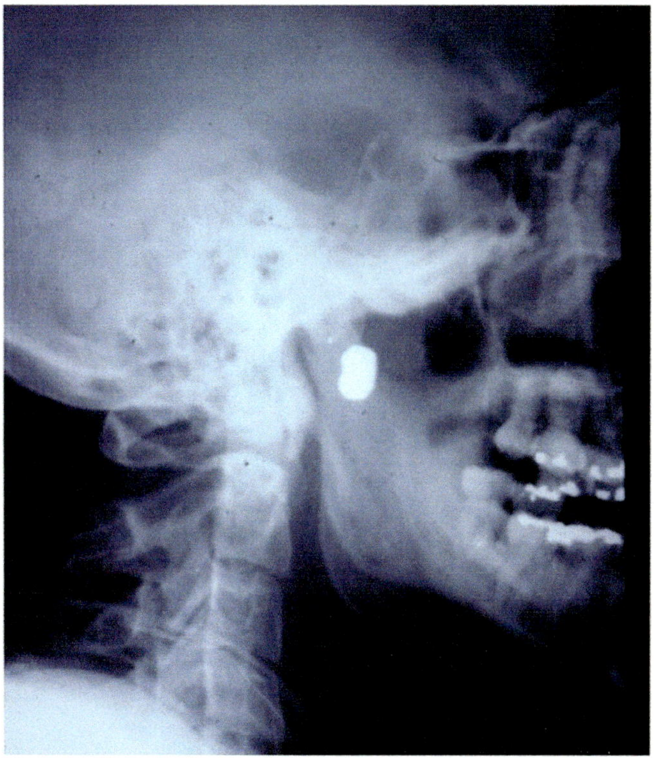

Figure 7.40 Flattened tooth in the posterior nasopharynx giving the appearance of a bullet.

References

1. Sellier K, Bullet entry studies of the skin. *Beitr Gerichtl Med* 1968; 25:265–270.
2. Blakey LS, Sharples GP, Chana K, and Birkett JW, Fate and behavior of gunshot residue—a review. *J Forensic Sci* 2018; 63(1):9–19.
3. Molina DK, Castorena J, and DiMaio VJ, Gunshot residue testing in suicides: part II analysis by ICP/. *Am J Forensic Med Pathol* 2007; 28(3):191–194.
4. Committee on Scientific Assessment.*National Research Council Forensic Analysis: Weighing Bullet Lead Evidence*. Washington DC National Academies Press, 2004.
5. Breitenecker R, Shotgun wound patterns. *Am J Clin Pathol* 1969; 52:269–285.

NOTE: For further information regarding all topics in this chapter, please see DiMaio, VJM *Gunshot Wounds: Practical Aspects of Firearms, Ballistics, and Forensic Techniques* 3rd ed. CRC Press, New York, NY, 2016.

Asphyxia

8

Another glorious day, the air as delicious to the lungs as nectar to the tongue.

—John Muir

Asphyxial deaths are caused by the failure of cells to receive or utilize oxygen. The deprivation of oxygen can be partial (hypoxia) or total (anoxia). The classical signs of asphyxia are visceral congestion, petechiae, cyanosis and fluidity of blood. These are nonspecific, however, and can occur in deaths from other causes. Visceral congestion is due to obstructed venous return and capillovenous congestion. The latter is a result of the susceptibility of these vessels to hypoxia, with resultant dilatation of the vessels and stasis of blood.

Petechiae are pinpoint hemorrhages produced by rupture of small vessels, predominantly small venules (Figure 8.1).

Rupture appears to be mechanical in etiology and is caused by sudden overdistention and rupture of the vessels following abrupt increases in intravascular pressure.[1,2] These are most common in the visceral pleura and epicardium. In asphyxial deaths from strangulation, petechiae are classically seen in the conjunctivae and sclerae. Petechiae, as nonspecific markers,[1,2] may be seen in the conjunctivae and sclerae in association with many different conditions, not all fatal, and not just in asphyxial deaths. They are routinely seen in the reflected scalp in all types of death and are of no diagnostic significance in this area. Petechiae of the epiglottis are also of no significance. Gordon and Mansfield documented the development of epicardial petechiae after death.[2]

Petechiae can develop after death in dependent areas of the body, for example, an arm hanging over the side of a bed. Here, gravity causes increased intravascular congestion and pressure with resultant mechanical rupture of small vessels.

Cyanosis is, of course, nonspecific and caused by an increase in the amount of reduced hemoglobin. It does not become observable until at least 5 g of reduced hemoglobin is present. Postmortem fluidity of blood is not characteristic of asphyxia or any cause of death, but rather the result of a high rate of fibrinolysis that occurs in rapid deaths, possibly by high agonal levels of catecholamines.[3]

Asphyxia results in a sequence of physiological events. First, the heart slows (bradycardia), followed by decreased respirations that progress to an eventual cessation of respiration. When blood oxygen concentrations fall sufficiently, there is eventually a slowing then a flattening of the electroencephalogram (EEG), resulting in brain death. The heart will continue to beat even after flattening of the EEG. In infants, bradycardia has been observed to start 30 s after the initiation of asphyxia, and flattening of the EEG at 90 s.[4] If, after cessation of respiration, the cause of the asphyxia is removed, respiration will not usually restart spontaneously, but the individual may be able to be resuscitated. Violent struggles with increased utilization of oxygen can speed up this sequence of events, just as natural disease could make the individual more susceptible to the effects of hypoxia.

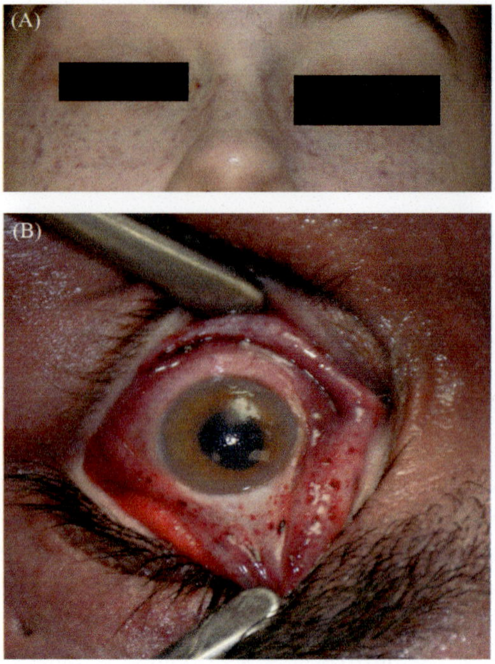

Figure 8.1 Petechial hemorrhages: (A) periorbital (B) subconjunctival.

Asphyxial deaths can be loosely grouped into three categories:

1. Suffocation
2. Strangulation
3. Chemical asphyxia

These deaths might be accidental, suicidal or homicidal in manner. Compared with other causes of homicide, homicides via asphyxia are relatively uncommon in the United States. They predominantly involve strangulation – manual and ligature strangulation. In the last 10 years, homicides ascribed to asphyxia have averaged approximately 500 cases per year.[5]

Suffocation

In deaths from suffocation, there is failure of oxygen to reach the blood. There are six general forms of suffocation:

1. Entrapment/environmental suffocation
2. Smothering
3. Choking
4. Mechanical asphyxia
5. Mechanical asphyxia combined with smothering
6. Suffocating gases

Entrapment/Environmental Suffocation

In suffocation by entrapment or environmental hazard, asphyxia is caused by inadequate oxygen in the environment. These deaths are almost exclusively accidental in nature. In **entrapment**, individuals find themselves trapped in an airtight or relatively airtight enclosure. Initially, there is sufficient oxygen to breathe. However, as respiration continues, they exhaust the oxygen and asphyxiate. The best example of this is a child trapped in a discarded refrigerator. Fortunately, this specific form of death by entrapment is becoming rare, as modern refrigerators do not have a latch system of locking and can be pushed open from the interior, though these can occur with other appliances as well (Figure 8.2).

Suicide and homicide by entrapment are rare, but do occur.

In **environmental suffocation**, an individual inadvertently enters an area where there is gross deficiency of oxygen. This deficiency is not due to displacement of the oxygen by suffocating gases, which will be discussed in another section, but rather that the oxygen has been depleted by some mechanism. For example, two deaths occurred due to a lack of oxygen in an underground chamber.[6] The normal percentage by volume of oxygen in the atmosphere is 20.946. In this particular case, the percentage by volume was 9.6. This lethal atmosphere was caused by fungus-like organisms and low forms of plant life present on the vault walls and in the sediment on the floor. The metabolic processes of the fungi and plant life resulted in depletion of oxygen by these organisms, with production of carbon dioxide. Thus, carbon dioxide, which is normally 0.033% in air, in this case, was 7.0%. The increased quantity of carbon dioxide, however, was insufficient in itself to have caused death by displacement of oxygen. It was the absolute lack of oxygen that caused death. At oxygen concentrations of 10–15%, there is impairment in judgment and coordination. Loss of consciousness occurs at 8–10%; death at 8% and less. At oxygen concentrations of 4–6%, there is loss of consciousness in 40 s and death within a few min.

In deaths due to **entrapment** or **environmental suffocation**, the cause of death cannot be determined by autopsy alone, *because there are no specific findings*. It is only by an analysis of the circumstances leading up to and surrounding death, and the exclusion of other causes, that one can make a determination as to the cause of death.

Figure 8.2 Discarded microwave where child hid during a game of hide and seek and became locked inside.

Smothering

Asphyxia by smothering is caused by the mechanical obstruction or occlusion of the external airways, that is, the nose and mouth. Deaths such as these are usually either homicide or suicide, very rarely accident (Figure 8.3A).

The most common form of suicidal smothering is the placing of a plastic bag over an individual's head (Figure 8.3B). If it is heavy plastic, it may be secured at the neck. More commonly, suicides employ the thin, filmy plastic bag. Here, there is often no necessity to secure the bag at the neck, because it clings to the face, occluding the airways. These filmy plastic bags also account for the rare accidental deaths by smothering when these bags are used to cover a mattress or pillow in a crib of a young child. The child becomes enmeshed in the bag and smothers. In all the deaths that the authors have seen in which plastic bags have been placed over the head, there have been no specific autopsy findings. Petechiae of the face, sclerae and conjunctivae were virtually always absent. Petechiae of the epicardium or pleural surfaces of the lung were sometimes present, but these are so nonspecific that the authors do not give any weight to them. If an individual commits suicide by use of a plastic bag and the bag is removed prior to notification of the authorities, a medical examiner cannot determine the cause of death by the autopsy.

Occasionally, an alcoholic is found face down on a pillow, dead. Circumferential oral and nasal pallor is noted and death is attributed to smothering. This pallor, however, can be caused postmortem by passive pressure of the dependent head on the pillow. Thus, the diagnosis cannot be made on this "evidence." The authors have grave reservations about this diagnosis. An individual would have to be in an alcoholic coma to smother this way.

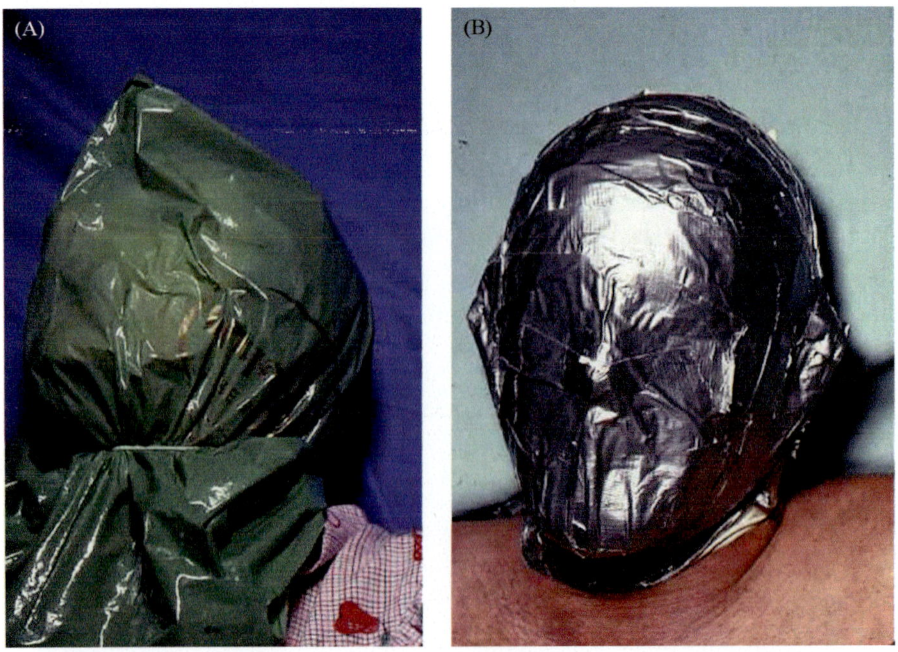

Figure 8.3 (A) Suicide of elderly female who secured plastic bag over head with tie around neck. (B) Accidental smothering in mentally retarded 43-year-old male who wrapped face in duct tape. Deceased had performed this act before.

Alcoholic coma, however, puts them in grave danger of death anyway and this is more likely the cause of death, rather than the alleged suffocation.

Accidental smotherings must often occur with infants. Occasionally, if an infant is sleeping in bed with an adult or older child, the other occupant can accidently occlude the nose and mouth of the infant while sleeping. The infant is unable to extricate him/herself from the position and ends up smothering, although, in these cases, the adult may also lie atop the infant accidentally, resulting not only in smothering but also in traumatic asphyxia. Accidental smothering deaths can also occur with infants sleeping in cribs if the infant becomes trapped either between a too-small mattress and the frame of the crib or between a defective crib and mattress, with the face wedged against the mattress (Figure 8.4).

The child is unable to move and smothers. Though, depending upon the position of the infant, there may be an element of positional asphyxia in these deaths as well.

Gags obstructing the nose and mouth can cause death by smothering. Such deaths, though unintentional, are still homicides if the victims die during the commission of a crime. Typically, a gag is placed around the face obstructing the mouth and nose (Figure 8.5).

Victims are usually elderly individuals who are either unable to struggle sufficiently to move the gag or who are unusually susceptible to the anoxia by virtue of natural disease. Mucus and fluids may accumulate in the nasal cavities and airways, contributing to asphyxia. In the elderly, there may be congestion of the face with scattered fine petechiae of the sclerae, conjunctivae and skin of the face. This has not been the case in young individuals in whom petechiae are usually absent. It is the discovery of the gag obstructing the airways that makes the diagnosis, not alleged signs of asphyxia.

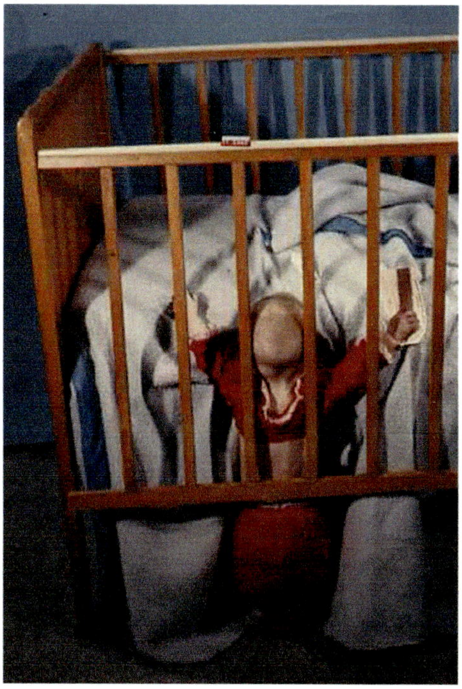

Figure 8.4 A 9-month-old child who slipped between frame and mattress of defective crib. Face wedged against mattress.

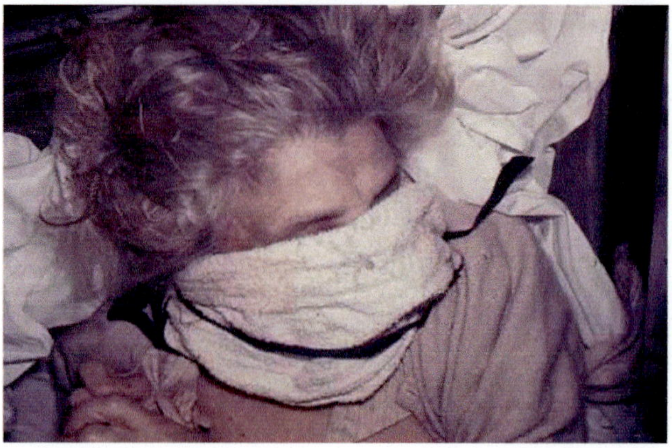

Figure 8.5 A 75-year-old woman, a victim of robbery. Asphyxiated from towel secured over mouth and nose.

In homicide by smothering, the implements used are usually pillows, bedding and the hands. Infants may be placed in plastic bags. The victims tend to be very young, very old, debilitated or incapacitated by restraints, disease or drugs. It is extremely difficult to smother adults in full control of their faculties, though the authors are aware of a homicidal smothering case where a young woman was smothered by binding her hands and placing a plastic bag over her head.

When a pillow is used, it is placed over the face and pushed down. This causes obstruction of the nose and mouth, asphyxia and death. There are usually no marks on the face. The face is not congested and there are no petechiae of the sclerae or conjunctivae (Figure 8.6).

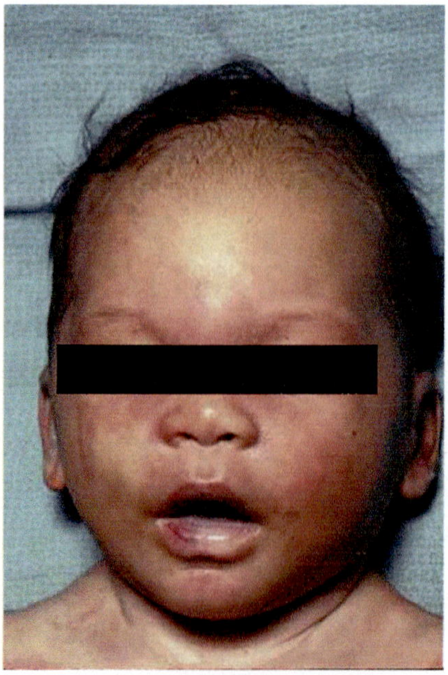

Figure 8.6 A 2-month-old infant smothered by parent. No petechiae of sclerae, conjunctivae or face.

Abrasion injuries of the face will occur only if the victim puts up a vigorous resistance. In a review of 15 smothering deaths involving children below the age of 2 years, of the 13 who could be evaluated for the presence of petechiae, only one had findings. This child had a single petechia of the conjunctiva and a single area of scleral hemorrhage. Because of the circumstances of this case, there was the possibility that the child might also have been choked. Pushing the face into the bedding will accomplish the same end as using a pillow.

Smothering can also be accomplished using the hands. The nose is pinched off with one hand, while the other hand is used to push the jaw closed. In small children, one hand can accomplish both these tasks. In infants and adults unable to put up any effective resistance, an autopsy will fail to disclose any injury due to this process. In adults, even those who can muster only a minimal struggle, there may be abrasions on the nose or chin from the fingernails, and contusions of the lips from pressure of the palm (Figure 8.7).

Choking

In choking, asphyxia is caused by obstruction within the air passages. The manner of death can be natural, suicide, homicide or accident. Natural deaths are not as common as they used to be, but can still occur. Acute fulminating epiglottitis can result in rapid death. In such cases, there is obstruction of the airway by the inflamed epiglottis and adjacent soft tissue; these individuals represent medical emergencies and can die literally in front of a physician. The individual develops a sore throat, hoarseness, respiratory difficulty, inability to speak and then suddenly collapses as the airway is completely obstructed. Inhalation of steam can cause a similar picture, with a markedly edematous, beefy-red mucosa in the larynx with obstruction (Figure 8.8).

Natural deaths can also be due to Ludwig's angina or idiopathic angioedema. In Ludwig's angina, there is an infection of the bilateral sublingual and submandibular spaces resulting in a posteriorly displaced tongue that can occlude the airway. In these cases, the patients usually present with cellulitis and submandibular induration and swelling of the tongue and floor of the mouth. Angioedema can occur with anaphylactic reactions or be drug-induced; however, hereditary angioedema can also occur, resulting from a deficiency of the C1 esterase inhibitor.

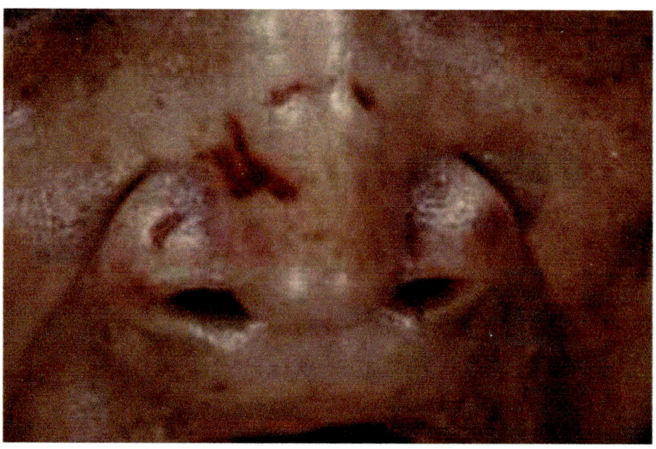

Figure 8.7 Elderly female smothered with hand. Fingernail marks on nose.

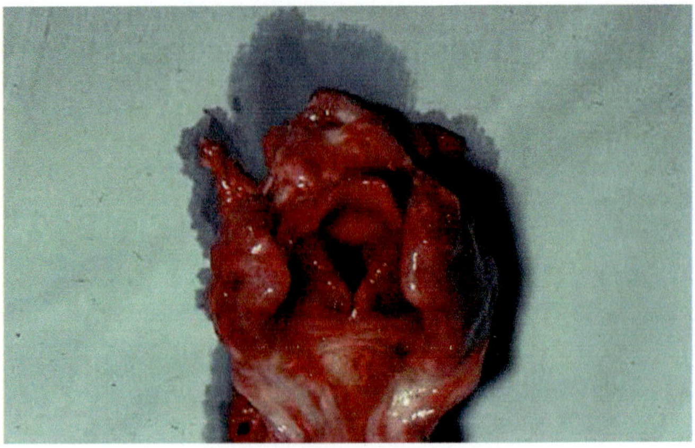

Figure 8.8 Massive laryngeal edema caused by inhalation of steam.

Homicidal deaths by choking are relatively uncommon. In infants, one occasionally sees a newborn murdered by stuffing toilet paper into its mouth. Figure 8.9A illustrates the case of an infant killed by her father by ramming a pacifier into her mouth.

In adults, individuals sometimes die during a robbery or burglary when a cloth or sock is rammed into the mouth to silence the individual. This is often done in conjunction with gagging (Figure 8.9B). This method of gagging individuals is shown quite frequently on television without any harmful consequences, but, unfortunately, in real life, the cloth can work its way backward, completely obstructing the posterior pharynx and causing the individual to asphyxiate. Suicidal choking deaths are rare, though the authors have seen one case of a mentally ill patient who died from choking after he intentionally crammed various materials, including cloth and tissues, down his throat.

Most choking deaths are accidental in manner. In 2017, there were approximately 5000 deaths ascribed to unintentional inhalation of food or other objects, resulting in obstruction of the respiratory passages.[7] In children, choking usually involves aspiration of a small object into the larynx with occlusion of the airway, for example, a small rubber ball or a balloon (Figure 8.10).

In adults, choking virtually always involves food (Figure 8.11).

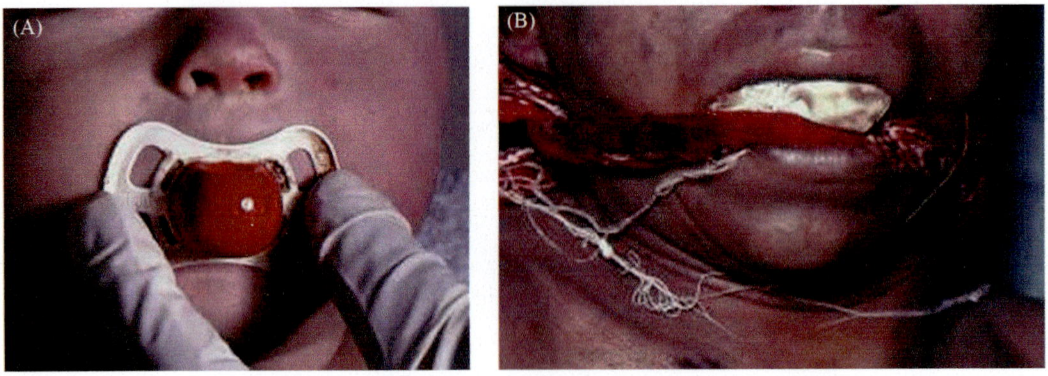

Figure 8.9 (A) Pacifier rammed into mouth by father. (B) Choked on gag that was secured by a bandana.

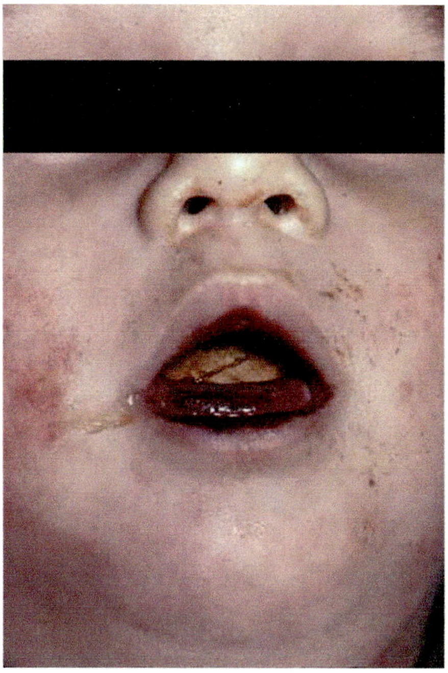

Figure 8.10 A 2-year-old choked to death on a wine cork.

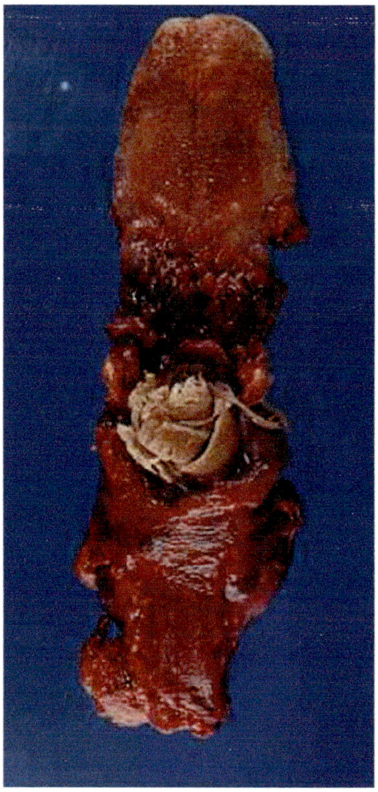

Figure 8.11 A 39-year-old male choked on a ham sandwich.

Though, occasionally, choking deaths occur when an individual falls into finely ground material, such as cornmeal or sawdust. There is involuntary inhalation and the airway is completely occluded by this material.

Choking on food is commonly associated with acute alcohol intoxication, bad-fitting dentures, neurological injury or senility. The piece of food will wedge in the laryngopharynx and larynx, completely obstructing the airway. Such deaths have acquired the name of "cafe coronary." The individual is eating, suddenly stops talking, stands up and collapses. Cardiopulmonary resuscitation is begun in the belief that the individual has suffered a heart attack. In fact, he has choked on food and his airway is completely occluded. Thus, cardiopulmonary resuscitation is ineffective. If the individuals giving mouth-to-mouth resuscitation are observant, they will see that the chest is not rising when they blow into the airway, which indicates obstruction.

Coughing during a collapse suspected of being caused by choking rules out this diagnosis as one must have an open airway to cough. Coughing involves the inspiration of 2–2.5 L of air, followed by closing off of the epiglottis and the vocal cords, contraction of the abdominal muscles to force up the diaphragm, while, at the same time, the expiratory muscles contract. The epiglottis and vocal cords open up and the air is then expelled out of the lungs, under pressure, usually carrying with it any foreign material present in the bronchi and trachea.[8] The expelled air can reach velocities of 75–100 mi/h.

The finding of small amounts of food material in the airway at autopsy does not indicate that the individual choked to death. Approximately 20–25% of all individuals aspirate food agonally, independent of the cause of death.[9] One can attribute a death to aspiration only if the airway from the larynx down is completely occluded by food. Death caused by massive aspiration of food is rarely seen in a medical examiner's office. It is most common in comatose patients who have impaired functioning of the central nervous system.

The diagnosis of choking death is made at autopsy when the airway is found occluded. If the individual had an occluded airway and the object or food was removed during resuscitation, the only way to make the diagnosis would be by history. There are no specific autopsy findings indicative of choking except for occlusion of the airway.

Some medical personnel will ascribe a death to choking even though the airway was never completely occluded. They suggest that laryngospasm is the cause of death. There is, however, no objective evidence that this can occur. If laryngospasm did occur, one would expect relaxation of the larynx as the victim became agonal. This, in turn, would lead to opening up of the airway and recovery. Others hypothesize that a fatal "vagal reaction" or "reflex cardiac death," mediated through the parasympathetic nervous system, occurred through hypersensitivity of the larynx to aspirated food. Again, there is just no objective proof that this entity exists.

Mechanical Asphyxia

In mechanical asphyxia, pressure on the outside of the body prevents respiration. Mechanical asphyxia is almost always accidental in manner. It can be subdivided into three types:

1. Traumatic asphyxia (a term often used interchangeably with mechanical asphyxia)
2. Positional asphyxia
3. Riot-crush or "human pile" deaths

Mechanical asphyxia has also been invoked as an explanation for deaths during a struggle. For a full discussion of the factors involved in this type of asphyxia, refer to Chapter 19 "Sudden Death during or Immediately after a Struggle."

Traumatic Asphyxia

Traumatic asphyxia occurs when a heavy weight presses down on an individual's chest or upper abdomen, making respiration impossible. One common form of traumatic asphyxia is individuals under a car, repairing it, when the jack slips and the vehicle falls on top of them (Figure 8.12).

At autopsy, there is congestion of the head, neck and upper trunk with numerous petechiae in these areas, the sclerae, the conjunctivae and the periorbital skin. Retinal hemorrhages may also be present. Internally, there is often no evidence of trauma in spite of the heavy weight on the chest. An occasionally encountered form of accidental traumatic asphyxia involves individuals buried in cave-ins with their heads above the ground. Rarely, traumatic asphyxia is homicidal. In one instance, an individual was knocked to the ground and a refrigerator and stereo were piled on top of him.

The most unusual case of traumatic asphyxia seen by one of the authors was that of a 5-month-old infant killed by a python. The snake wrapped itself around the baby, tightening its coils whenever the child exhaled. At autopsy, the only marks on the child were teeth

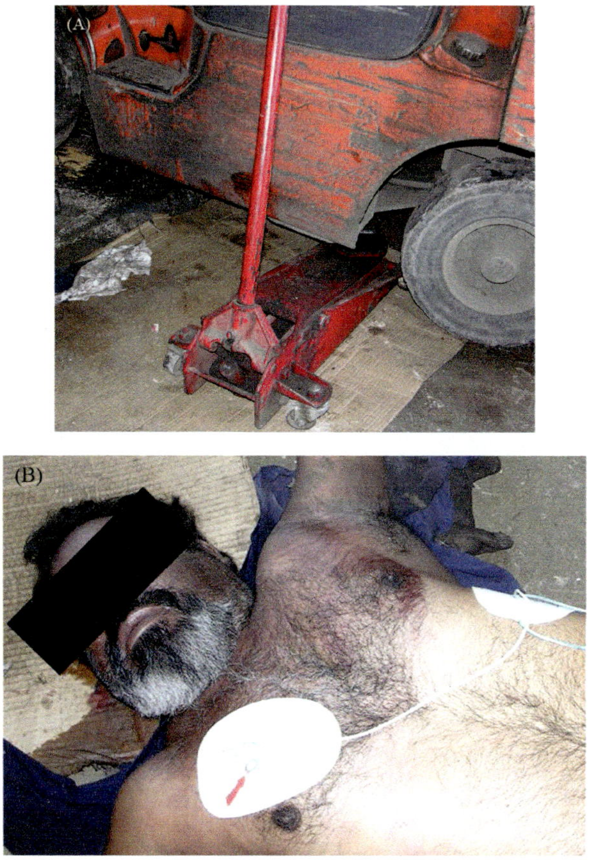

Figure 8.12 Traumatic asphyxia. (A) Deceased pinned under vehicle on which he was working. (B) Marked congestion of face and upper chest, above the level of compression.

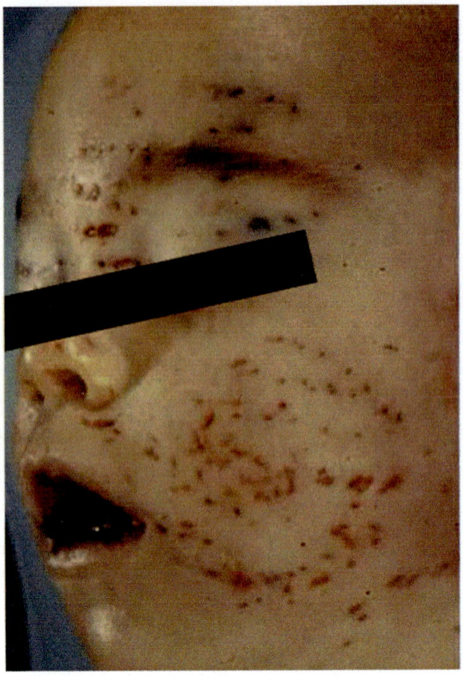

Figure 8.13 A 5-month-old infant killed by a python. No petechiae, hemorrhage or bruising of body. Puncture marks on face have a semicircular configuration and are caused by the needle-like teeth of the python.

marks on the face where the snake had tried to swallow the child whole (his head was too big for the snake's mouth) (Figure 8.13). There were no petechiae, hemorrhage or bruising.

Positional Asphyxia

Positional asphyxia is virtually always an accident and is commonly associated with alcohol or drug intoxication. In this entity, individuals become trapped in restricted spaces, where, because of the position of their bodies, they cannot move out of that area or position. This results in restriction of their ability to breathe, followed by death (Figure 8.14).

There is usually marked congestion, cyanosis and petechiae. Positional asphyxia might occur if individuals fall down a well and are wedged between the walls. Every time they exhale, they slip farther and farther down the well, preventing inhalation. It can also occur in elderly individuals due to bed rails, as discussed in Chapter 18.

One unusual, historical, form of positional asphyxia was crucifixion.[10] The victim was typically nailed to a cross with nails driven through the wrists into the crossbar and through the feet into the upright post. Death was caused by shock, both hypovolemic and secondary to the pain of nailing, plus dehydration and asphyxia. The weight of the body on the outstretched arms would interfere with exhalation by maintaining the intercostal muscles in an inhalation state. Exhalation would then become primarily diaphragmatic. Over a prolonged time, this would lead to impaired respiration and asphyxia.

Upside down suspension is another form of positional asphyxia. If an individual is suspended, upside down for a long enough period of time death can result. The mechanisms of death might be either acute cardiac or respiratory failure or a combination of both. The

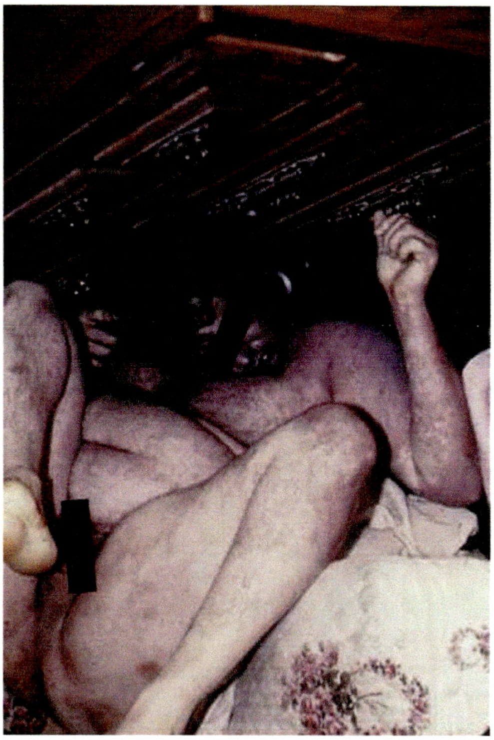

Figure 8.14 Positional asphyxia in acutely intoxicated individual.

length of time it takes for death to occur depends on the health of the individual. It could range from a few hours to a day, perhaps somewhat longer.

Riot-Crush

Riot-crush, as the name implies, occurs in riots, when the chest is compressed by stampeding people piling on top of each other. Respiratory movements are, thus, prohibited by this human pile. This is not due to the people trampling overreach other as reported by the news media. Rather the crowd creates forces that can reach levels almost impossible to resist or control. Evidence of bent steel railings after several crowd incidents show that forces of more than 4500 N (1000 lb) occurred. Forces are due to pushing, and the domino effect of people leaning against each other. Compressive asphyxia has occurred from people being stacked up vertically, one on top of the other, or horizontal pushing and leaning forces.[11]

Mechanical Asphyxia Combined with Smothering

Traumatic asphyxia combined with smothering is a combination of both these entities. It can be accidental or homicidal. An accidental form is **overlay**, where an infant is placed in bed for the night with either an adult or a larger child. Subsequently, the infant is found dead. During the night, the other individual rolled onto the infant, killing it by a combination of smothering and traumatic asphyxia. Other deaths in this category are individuals buried in cave-ins, grain or sand, etc. The physical findings at autopsy are generally absent. Rarely, a few fine petechiae of the facial skin, but not of the sclerae or conjunctivae, will be found.

Burking is a combination of suffocation and traumatic asphyxia developed (or at least perfected) by the "resurrectionists" Burke and Hare in the early 19th century.[12] These men made their living by digging up bodies from graveyards and supplying them to medical schools for dissection. They decided, however, to eliminate the chore of digging up bodies and go straight to the source. Victims, usually intoxicated, were brought to the ground, whereupon Burke knelt or sat on their chests, expelling the air and interfering with inspiratory efforts. He then put one hand over the victim's nose and mouth and used the other hand to press the lower jaw toward the upper. Visible injuries were virtually nonexistent. The two now had a fresh body for the schools.

Suffocating Gases

Deaths from suffocating gases are caused, not by the toxic nature of the gases, but rather by displacement of oxygen from the atmosphere. These gases, such as carbon dioxide (CO_2), nitrogen and methane (CH_4), physically displace oxygen in inspired air, thus preventing the cells from receiving oxygen. The atmosphere is composed of nitrogen (78%), oxygen (21%) and other gases. If an inert gas displaces oxygen in the air and reduces it to less than 25% of normal values (5–6% by volume of oxygen), this will cause unconsciousness in a few seconds and death in a few minutes.

Carbon dioxide and methane are the most commonly encountered suffocating gases. Both are essentially nontoxic and odorless. Both are found in sewers and mines. Methane is the principal constituent (94–96%) of natural gas that is used for cooking. It is odorless; the smell we detect from natural gas is an added ingredient to make leaks detectable. Toxicological analysis of the blood is of no help in the case of carbon dioxide, because it is a normal constituent of blood. Methane can be detected in the blood. Since the gas is not toxic, however, all that its identification would indicate is that the individual was exposed to an atmosphere containing methane, not that death was due to it; however, methane at concentrations higher than 6.0 μL/g is thought to be consistent with death due to asphyxia by oxygen displacement.

Determination of the cause of death in such cases is by knowledge of the circumstances surrounding the death and on the exclusion of other possible causes. "Typical" signs of asphyxia may be present, such as petechial hemorrhages, facial congestion, edema and cyanosis; however, these are nonspecific and can be seen in many types of deaths. In reality, there are no specific findings at autopsy for such asphyxial deaths.

Strangulation

Strangulation is a form of asphyxia characterized by occlusion of the blood vessels and air passages of the neck as a result of external pressure that leads to cerebral hypoxia. The external compression causes occlusion of the blood vessels supplying blood to the brain, namely, the internal carotid arteries and the vertebral arteries though the small spinal arteries and anastomotic connections of branches of the external carotid and subclavian arteries may also be affected.

The carotid arteries, by virtue of their location, are easily compressed by direct pressure to the front of the neck. In contrast, the vertebral arteries, being protected by a bony ring posteriorly, are resistant to direct pressure, but can be occluded by severe lateral flexion or rotation of the neck.[13] The amount of pressure necessary to occlude the carotid arteries is approximately 11 lb; for the vertebral arteries, it is 66 lb.[14] Pressure on the neck in the area of the carotid arteries causes unconsciousness in an average of 10 s.[15] If pressure is immediately released, consciousness is regained in 10–12 s. During this time, electrocardiographic (EKG) changes are minimal and EEGs show an increased amplitude of their waves, similar to the picture seen during an epileptic seizure. The pattern returns to normal in approximately 20 s.[16]

Rossen et al. conducted an extensive study involving occlusion of not only the carotid arteries but also the vertebral arteries and the anastomotic connections of branches of the external carotids and subclavian arteries.[17] This was accomplished using an inflatable pressure cuff placed on the lower third of the neck that produced 600 mm of mercury within one-eighth of a second of inflation. Only the small spinal arteries were not occluded. The subjects were 126 normal male volunteers between the ages of 17 and 31 years. Acute occlusion of the arterial circulation resulted in blurring of vision, constriction of visual fields, loss of consciousness and hypoxic convulsions. The pressure cuff was released upon loss of consciousness with a complete recovery within 1 or 2 min after the procedure and no subsequent *sequelae.* The convulsions occurred after loss of consciousness, were mild, generalized tonic and clonic and rarely continued more than 6–8 s. The EEG showed large, slow waves correlated with loss of consciousness. The EKG changes were minimal. Half the subjects lost consciousness in 6–6.5 s. The overall range was approximately 5–11 s.

Rossen et al. then studied the effects of prolonged occlusion of cerebral circulation on 11 individuals.[17] Complete occlusion of the cerebral blood flow was not achieved in every case, as in the other experiments. Cervical pressure was maintained for as long as 100 s in some tests. The subjects regained consciousness in 30–40 s and were able to walk from the room in 2 min. Convulsions, cyanosis, involuntary urination and defecation in some patients, bradycardia and dilatation of the pupils followed loss of consciousness. The convulsions were relatively mild, continuing during the whole period of unconsciousness in some individuals, lasting 30–40 s in others. Initially, after loss of consciousness, the heart rate was stable. Subsequently, bradycardia developed, with the heart rate dropping as much as 50%. Respiration continued throughout the test, increasing in rate.

Strangulation also causes occlusion of the blood vessels taking blood away from the brain (veins), resulting in an increase in intracranial pressure and CO_2 concentrations. Venous drainage of the head is by the jugular and vertebral venous systems. The vertebral venous system consists of an external plexus of veins in the deep muscles of the neck adjacent to the vertebral column and an internal vertebral plexus within the spinal canal. This internal vertebral plexus, though limited in its blood transport capacity, cannot be affected by pressure on the neck. In contrast, the amount of pressure necessary to occlude the jugular veins is 4.4 lb.[13]

Strangulation can also result in occlusion of the airways of the neck either through compression of the trachea or, when the noose is above the larynx, elevation and posterior displacement of the tongue and floor of the mouth. Compression of the trachea requires 33 lb of pressure.[14] However, blockage or compression of the air passages is not necessary to cause death in strangulations. This is evidenced by the fact that there have been a number of individuals who have hanged themselves with the noose above the larynx and a permanent tracheostomy opening below.

When investigating a possible asphyxia death, medical examiners must consider worth factors as well. The compression of the carotid arteries, with resultant decreased cerebral blood flow, can theoretically precipitate a stroke in an individual with atherosclerotic disease of the carotid or cerebral vasculature. The pressure can cause dislodgment of atherosclerotic material with a stroke caused by an embolus or if the vertebral arteries also have impaired blood flow due to atherosclerosis, then occlusion of the carotid arteries can threaten an already compromised circulation, resulting in thrombosis or stroke.

Autopsy findings in strangulation cases may be absent or minimal, as in most hanging deaths, or quite extensive, such as in manual strangulation deaths with a good deal of resistance on the part of the victim. The petechiae are caused by rupture of venules and capillaries secondary to increased intravascular pressure as a result of the obstructed venous return (the internal jugular veins) in conjunction with incomplete arterial obstruction, which permits the vertebral arteries to continue supplying blood to the brain. In the majority of ligature and manual strangulation, there are petechiae of the conjunctivae; however, the presence of petechiae does not indicate that death was due to strangulation, because they can be seen in a number of other conditions, including natural disease.[18] In severe vomiting or coughing, occasional petechiae might be seen. If the body remains in the prone position for a prolonged length of time, such that it is approaching decomposition, postmortem petechiae can form in the distribution of the livor mortis and be present on the skin, conjunctivae and sclerae. Petechiae may develop in victims of attempted strangulation who do not incur any life-threatening degree of asphyxia. Thus, in a study of 79 surviving victims of attempted strangulation (both ligature and manual), who showed stigmata of strangulation, conjunctival petechiae were observed in 14 victims, only 8 of whom became unconscious, and with only 4 experiencing sphincter incontinence.[19] This suggests that petechiae are not necessarily an indication of life-threatening asphyxia, but rather the effect of local venous congestion.

Hemorrhage over the back of the larynx and in soft tissue overlying the cervical spine can also be seen in strangulation deaths but should be interpreted as traumatic in etiology only with great care. In the majority of cases, it is not due to trauma to the neck, but rather is an artifact produced by overdistention and rupture of the venous sinuses, forming the pharyngolaryngeal plexus.[13] Such hemorrhage can and does occur in deaths from natural causes and might be either peri- or early postmortem in origin.

In general, there are three main forms of strangulation:

1. Hanging
2. Ligature strangulation
3. Manual strangulation

Most hangings are suicides and manual strangulations are homicides; however, ligature strangulations can be homicides, suicides or accidents.

In strangulation deaths, the neck must be carefully examined for evidence of trauma. The best way to examine the interior of the neck is to remove the viscera from the chest and abdominal cavities and then remove the brain. After there has been drainage through the cranial and chest cavities, the neck can be dissected in a relatively blood-free field. An *in situ*, layer-wise dissection of the neck musculature should then be performed, documenting any hemorrhages and fractures. Fractures of the thyroid cartilage, the cricoid cartilage or the hyoid bone can only be considered antemortem if there is blood at the fracture site. In the authors' opinion, blood detectable only microscopically at a fracture site is insufficient to prove that the fracture was antemortem.

Hanging

In hanging, asphyxia is secondary to compression or constriction of the neck structures by a noose or other constricting band tightened by the weight of the body. There may be either complete or incomplete suspension of the body (Figure 8.15A and B).

Incomplete suspension, with the toes or feet (less commonly the knees or buttocks) touching the ground, is extremely common. Hanging is the most common method of suicide worldwide[20] and virtually all hangings are suicidal; accidental hangings are uncommon

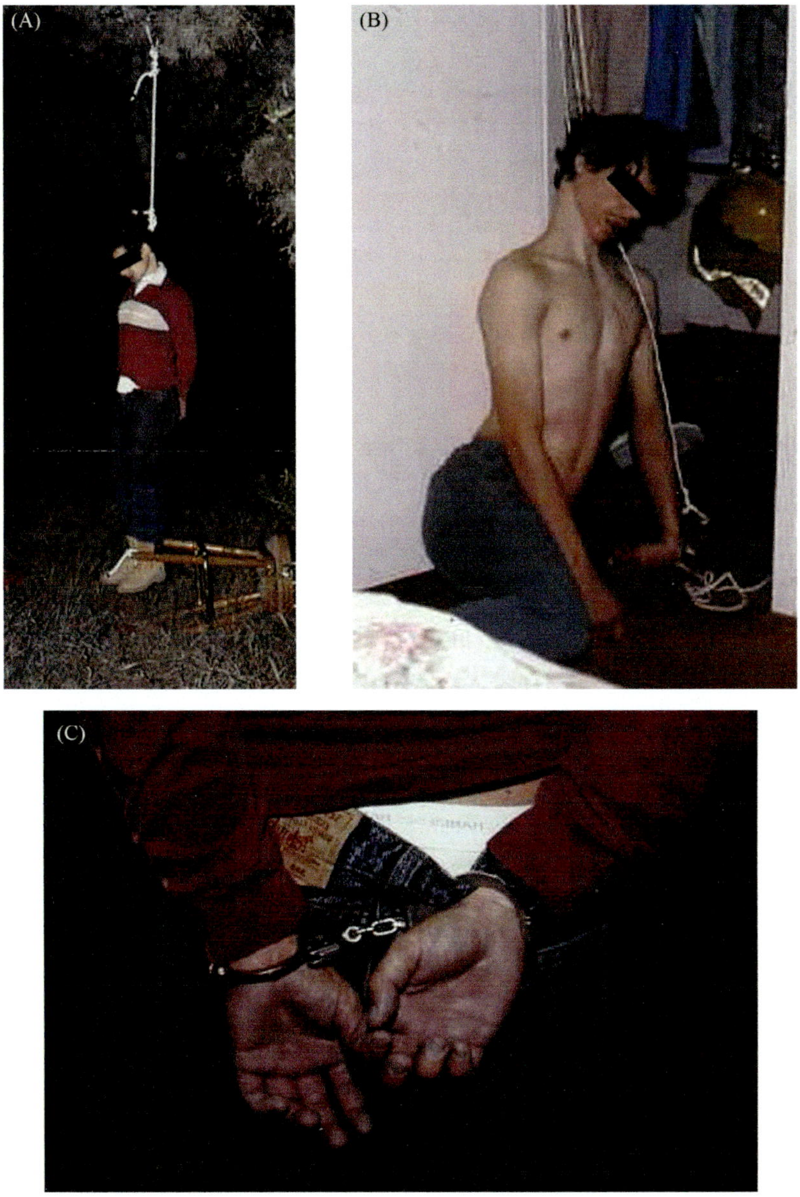

Figure 8.15 (A) Hanging with complete suspension. (B) Hanging with incomplete suspension. (C) Hanging with hands cuffed behind back.

and homicidal hangings very rare. Death is caused by compression of the blood vessels of the neck though obstruction of the airway can also occur. Fracture of the neck plays virtually no role in nonjudicial hangings. It is rare and, in our experience, is usually seen only in individuals with advanced degenerative disease of the cervical spine, such as osteoarthritis, in combination with complete suspension of the body, a sudden drop and, frequently, obesity.

Because of the small amount of pressure necessary to compress the jugular veins (4.4 lb) and carotid arteries (11 lb), one can hang oneself sitting, kneeling or lying down. The weight of the head (10–12 lb) against a noose is sufficient to occlude both the jugular veins and carotid arteries and cause death. The authors have seen cases where individuals have hanged themselves from a bedpost while lying in bed next to a sleeping spouse. Hangings in kneeling and sitting positions are also common.

The sequence of death in hangings is similar to that shown for other forms of strangulation. Sauvageau et al. reviewed 14 filmed hangings and found loss of consciousness to occur at approximately 13 s, "mild convulsions" at 15 s, decerebrate posturing at 19 s, loss of muscle tone at 1 min and complete loss of all movement by 4 min.[21]

In hangings, often a simple slipknot type of noose is used. The noose is constructed from anything that is handy. Most common are ropes, electrical cords and belts. In jails and prisons, convicts typically tear sheets into strips as well as using T-shirts, undershorts, trousers or even socks. Rarely, scratch marks will be seen above and below the ligature mark, where the victim tried to undo the noose. Occasionally, to prevent a change of mind, the victim ties his hands together. The authors have seen a number of cases where the victims bound their hands behind themselves (Figure 8.15C).

The most common point of suspension is the side of the neck, followed by the back and the front. At the time of suspension, the noose typically slips above the larynx, catching under the chin (Figure 8.16).

Present on the neck will be a furrow. This furrow generally does not completely encircle the neck, but rather slants upward toward the knot, fading out at the point of suspension – the knot (Figure 8.17).

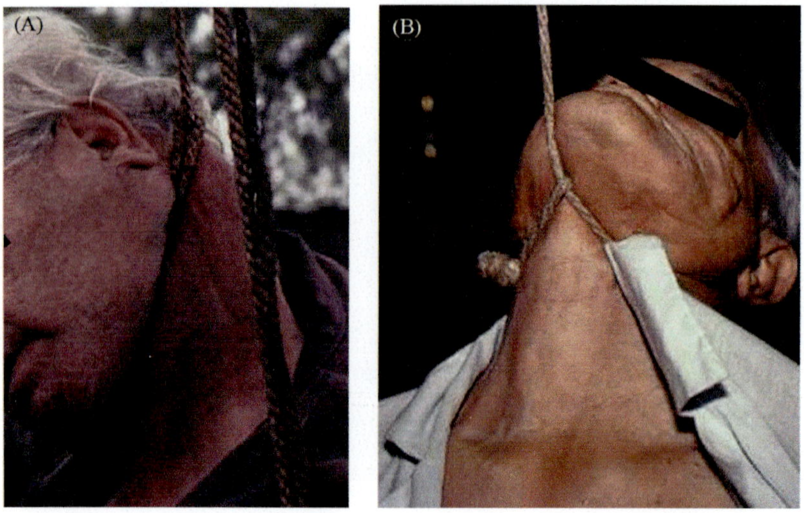

Figure 8.16 Hanging with point of suspension on (A) side of neck and (B) front of neck.

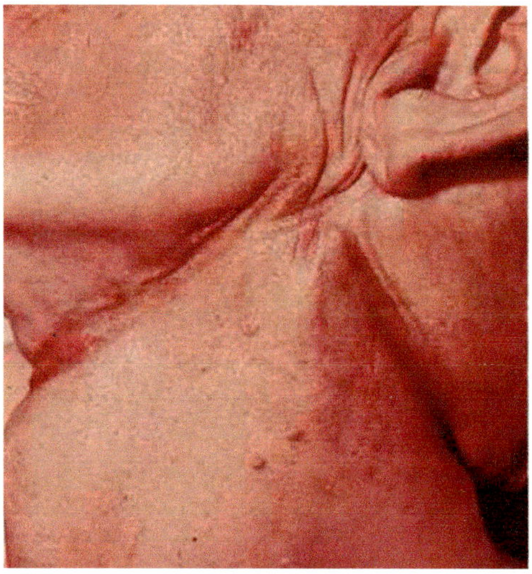

Figure 8.17 Furrow from noose slanting upward toward point of suspension.

If the knot is under the chin, its site might be indicated by an abrasion or indentation beneath the chin. Additionally, the clarity and configuration of the furrow depends on the material used. With a thin, hard ligature, the groove will be narrow, deep and distinct. A rope will often impart a mirror-image impression of the twist of the rope on the skin (Figure 8.18A).

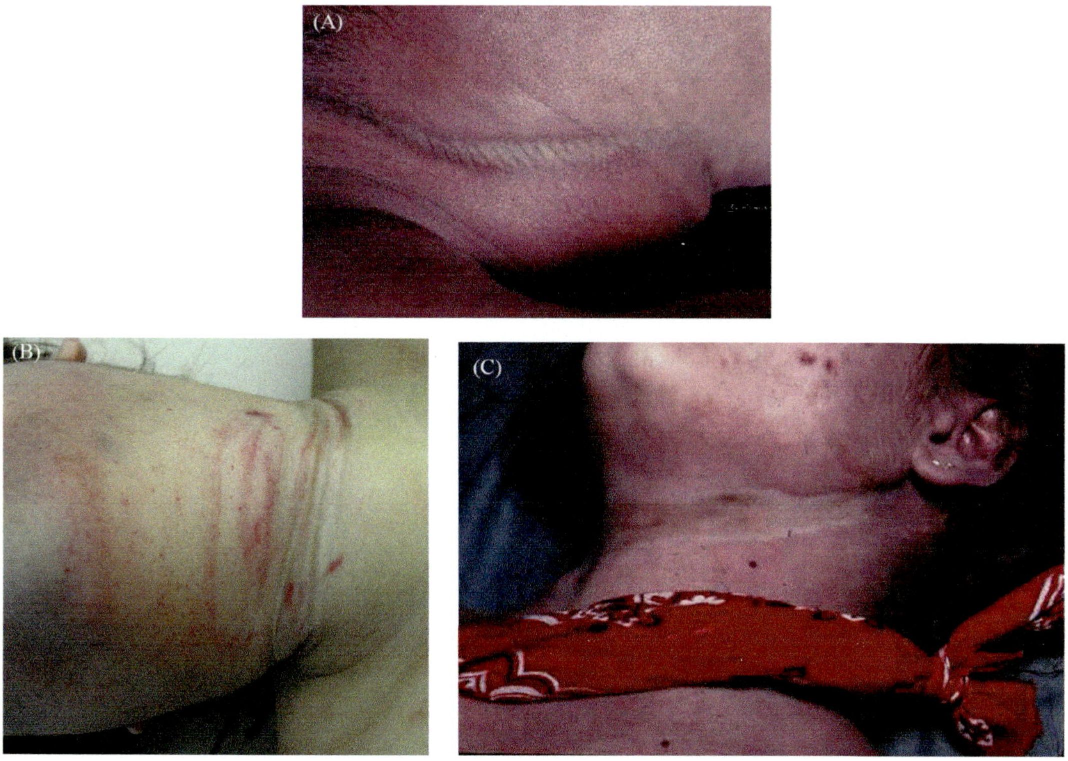

Figure 8.18 (A) Noose mark with pale yellow base and congested rim. (B) A broad indistinct furrow due to a folded sheet ligature. (C) Broad pale furrow due to a rolled cloth ligature.

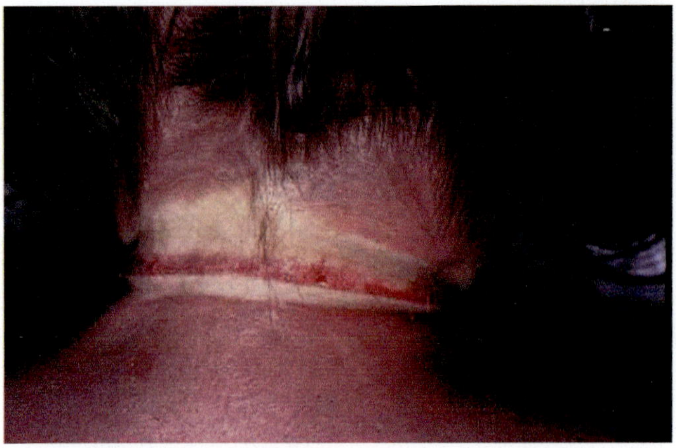

Figure 8.19 Suicide with double loops pinching skin.

This furrow initially has a pale yellow parchment appearance, with a congested rim. With time, the furrow dries out and becomes dark brown. If a soft noose, such as a towel, is used and the body is cut down shortly after death, no marks may be present on the neck (Figure 8.18B). A soft noose may also simply leave a poorly defined, pale, groove or blanching devoid of bruises and abrasions (Figure 8.18C). In some cases, the lower margin of the groove is pale, with the upper margin red, caused by postmortem congestion of vessels. The longer the body remains suspended, the more prominent the mark. The ligature mark is deepest opposite the point of suspension.

In the majority of suicidal hangings, the noose consists of a single loop. Less commonly, there are two loops. This results in two furrows that may be parallel, overlap at points, or follow two completely different paths, for example, one oblique and the other horizontal. The two loops might pinch the skin between them, producing a hemorrhagic strip of skin (Figure 8.19).

If the noose is a belt, there are usually two parallel ligature marks on the neck where the upper and lower edges of the belt dig into the skin (Figure 8.20).

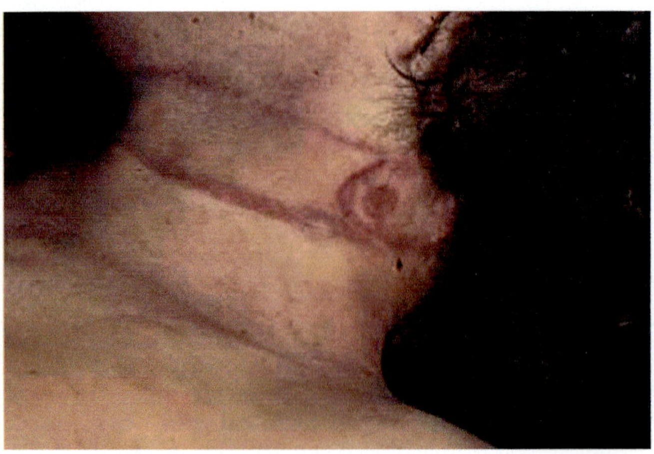

Figure 8.20 Suicide with belt.

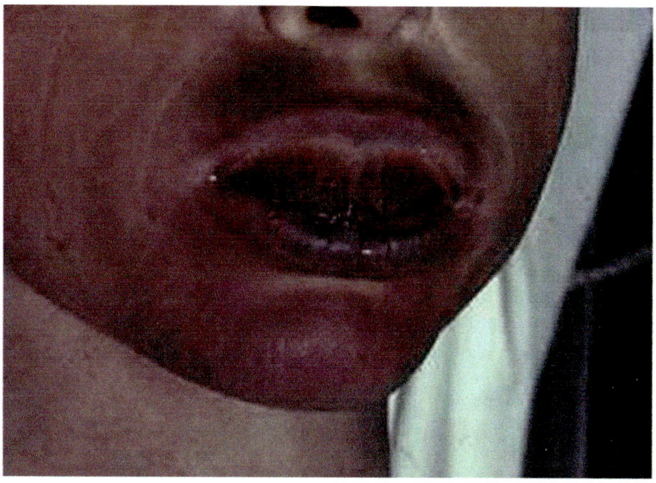

Figure 8.21 Suicidal hanging with protrusion of tongue and drying.

Despite decomposition, ligature marks tend to be well preserved and recognizable. The marks resist decomposition presumably because the ligature has compressed the underlying blood vessels, restricting access to the area by the putrefying bacteria.

In most hangings, the face is pale and the tongue is protruding and "black" from drying (Figure 8.21).

Facial congestion/petechiae are rarely seen in cases of complete suspension where there is complete occlusion of the cervical arteries and veins. However, in partial suspension hangings where the carotid arteries and venous drainage are completely occluded, the vertebral arteries continue to supply blood to the head, producing congestion of the face and petechiae. Thus, facial congestion and petechiae are commonly seen in these cases.

In hangings, blood will pool in the dependent areas of the body, usually the forearms, hands and lower legs, secondary to gravity. With time, punctate hemorrhages and Tardieu spots, caused by hydrostatic rupture of vessels, will be seen (Figure 8.22).

Prior to the removal of the noose from the neck, its nature and composition, width, mode of application, location and type of knot should be described in detail. After removal, the ligature mark on the neck should also be minutely described. One should describe the direction of the furrow (obliquely upward, horizontal, etc.), whether it is continuous or interrupted, its color, its dimensions (depth and width), whether there is a distinct imprint to the ligature pattern, the areas of the neck involved and its relation to local landmarks.

Usually, except for ligature marks, there are no other external marks (injuries) on the body. If some are present, the medical examiner must decide whether they are self-induced, occurred during the convulsive phase preceding death, were produced when the body was cut down or during attempted resuscitation, occurred when a swinging body contacted other objects, or were produced by a second party, making the case a homicide.

Internal neck injuries are rare in hangings. In their study of 75 hanging deaths, Hlavaty et al. found internal cervical injuries in only 7 cases (9%).[22] These injuries consisted of strap muscle hemorrhage in all seven, one with a fracture of the hyoid bone and one with a fracture of the thyroid cartilage. This is consistent with the findings of one of the authors who reviewed 83 consecutive hangings and found that only 10 (12%) had fractures; 9 showed fractures of the thyroid cartilage, specifically the superior horns; none showed fractures of

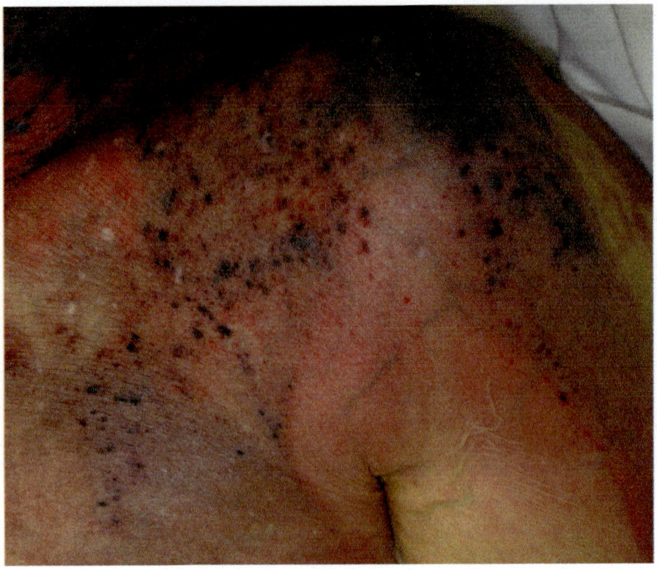

Figure 8.22 Tardieu spots.

the hyoid, and 1 a fracture of the cervical spine. This last case involved an obese woman with arthritic changes of the cervical vertebrae who stepped off a ladder, dropping a short distance before being fully suspended. Of the nine cases with fracture of the superior horns of the thyroid cartilage, seven were unilateral and two bilateral. Seventeen (20.5%) of the 83 cases, excluding those with fractures, showed hemorrhage in the strap muscles of the neck. The low incidence of fractures of the neck was also observed by Feigin.[23] In a retrospective study of 307 suicidal and accidental hangings, fractures of the neck organs were present in only 9.5% (29) of cases. In 3 cases, there were fractures of the cervical spine, C1–2, C3–4 and C6–7 (one in association with a fracture of the thyroid cartilage), 14 cases with fractures confined to the thyroid cartilage, 9 fractures of the hyoid and 3 fractures of the hyoid and thyroid cartilage. No individual had more than two fractures of the neck organs. Fractures were not associated with height of suspension, sex or the width of the ligature, though the likelihood of fractures did increase with age.

Homicidal hanging is very rare. It is virtually impossible for one of two healthy adults, equally matched physically, to hang the other unless the victim was beaten unconscious or rendered helpless by alcohol or drugs. In the first instance, one would suspect homicide by virtue of the injuries on the victim. In the second scenario, or if the victim was rapidly subdued by two or more stronger assailants, there might be no marks on the body except the noose mark or possible contusions of the arms, inflicted while being forcibly restrained by the assailants. If there is also a marked disproportion in strength between the assailant and victim, for example, an adult and a child or a large man and a small woman, it would also be possible to hang an individual without marks of violence. A person might also be ligature strangled and then strung up. But in this instance, the neck markings would not have the classic inverted-V configuration of a hanging. The authors, however, have seen suicidal hangings involving incomplete suspension where the noose mark overlaid the larynx and was horizontal, not sweeping upward to the point of suspension in an inverted-V configuration. To rule out any violence that might not be visible and to make sure the individual was not drugged, in all alleged suicidal hangings, a complete toxicologic screen should be performed and, in most instances, a complete autopsy.

Accidental hangings usually involve children who are playing at hanging or get entangled in a rope, or adults engaging in the practice of sexual (erotic) asphyxia. Rarely, infants will accidentally hang themselves from a pacifier suspended around their neck on a cord or get entangled in a toy or mobile placed above their cribs.[23] Accidental hangings of infants and toddlers have also been reported with pacifiers on strings, venetian-blind cords and drawstrings on clothing.[24-26]

Autoerotic asphyxial deaths are principally caused by hanging, in which transitory anoxia is intentionally induced to enhance sexual arousement produced by masturbation.[27] Such deaths are rare and the victim is virtually always a male. Only a few cases involving females have been reported.[28] The victim is typically found in a private area, nude or partially nude, sometimes wearing female clothing. There may be erotic literature, sexual paraphernalia or a mirror opposite the individual so that he can observe his actions. Typically, the deceased is found hanging by the neck, with a towel or some article of clothing interposed between the noose and the skin to prevent rope burns or marks on the neck (Figure 8.23).

This pattern of behavior is repetitive and there may be evidence that the individual has performed this act numerous times over many years. While the individual is typically found with a simple noose around the neck, there may be elaborate binding with multiple turns of the rope around the body, or the hands bound either in front of or behind the body. Analysis of the binding will reveal that the individual was capable of binding himself. In some instances, rather than a noose, a ligature or some other device capable of applying pressure to the neck is used. There is always some self-rescue device so that the individual can relieve pressure before losing consciousness. Unfortunately, because of equipment failure, a flaw in design or construction of the device or loss of control by the individual, accidental deaths occur.

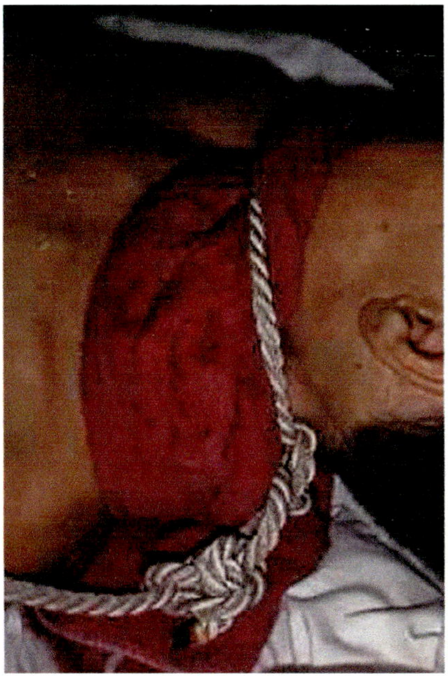

Figure 8.23 A 21-year-old male. Sexual asphyxia. Placed towel between noose and skin.

In all deaths from hanging, the police agency involved should notify the medical examiner's office immediately. If the victim is obviously dead, the body should not be cut down, so that proper photographic documentation and investigation of the scene can be made. The noose should never be cut from the body but left intact for transport with the body to the morgue. When the medical examiner removes the noose from the neck, the knot should not be untied. The noose should either be slipped off the head or cut opposite to the knot and the cut ends secured together with tape.

Research has long been performed on the hanging of dead bodies. Between 1817 and 1855, Casper performed 23 experiments to determine the effect of hanging on a dead body.[29] He concluded that the noose marks seen on the neck in hanging during life could be produced by a ligature applied to a neck within 2 h or if not later after death. Thus, noose marks on the neck do not necessarily mean that an individual was alive when he was hanged.

In **judicial hangings**, death is caused by fracture-dislocation of the upper cervical vertebrae with transection of the cord. The knot is placed under the left ear or, less commonly, under the chin. A trapdoor is sprung and the prisoner falls a specific distance determined by their weight. If they fall an insufficient distance, they strangle rather than breaking their neck; if they fall too far, they are decapitated. In properly performed judicial hangings, the victim abruptly stops at the end of their fall when their head is jerked suddenly and violently backward, fracturing his spine. Ideally, one then has the classical hangman's fracture – fracture through the pedicles of C2 with the posterior arch remaining fixed to C3. C1, the odontoid process and the anterior arch of C2 remain in articulation with the base of the skull. This injury pattern is caused by hyperextension and distraction and results in injury of the cord at C2–3. This classic fracture does not always occur in hangings. Thus, in an anthropologic study of six judicial hangings by Spence et al., there were fractures of the hyoid, the styloid processes and occipital bones as well as the cervical body of C2 and the transverse processes of C1–3 and C5.[30]

In a report by Hartshorne and Reay on two recent hangings, they found bilateral vertebral artery lacerations with associated basilar subarachnoid hemorrhage; fractures of the hyoid and thyroid cartilage and hemorrhage into the cervical muscle.[31] In one of the cases, there was also a fracture or separation at C2 and C3 with complete transection of the cord, bilateral carotid intimal tears and a subdural hematoma. In this latter case, the fall was 5.5 ft, with the knot slipping to the subaural area. In the other case, the fall was 7 ft, with the knot secured in the subauricular area.

In judicial hangings, consciousness is lost immediately, though the heart may continue to beat for 8–20 min and there may be muscular contractions of the facial muscles, twitching and convulsions of the limbs and trunk, and violent respiratory movements of the chest. In nonjudicial hangings, where the mechanism of death is strangulation, if there is complete suspension with occlusion of both the carotid and vertebral arteries, based on the experiments of Rossen et al., the victim should lose consciousness in 5–11 s, with half losing consciousness in 6–6.5 s. If the suspension results only in occlusion of the carotid arteries, unconsciousness may not occur for 10–15 s.

Ligature Strangulation

In ligature strangulation, the pressure on the neck is applied by a constricting band that is tightened by a force other than the body weight. In a study of 133 homicides caused by asphyxia, ligature strangulation accounted for 48 of the deaths; manual strangulation for 41.[32] In ligature strangulation, females predominate as victims, though not as much as in the case of manual strangulation. Of the 48 victims of ligature strangulation, 27 were females and 21 males. Though less common, both suicides and accidents can also occur.

In contrast to hanging deaths, the face and neck above the ligature mark appear markedly congested, with confluent scleral hemorrhage and petechiae of the conjunctivae. Fine petechiae might also be present on the skin of the face, especially in the periorbital regions. Petechiae are present in 86% of the cases of ligature strangulation.[32] The presence of a congested face, petechiae and scleral hemorrhage in ligature strangulation occurs because, unlike in hanging, there is no complete occlusion of the anterior vasculature. Blood continues to go into the head from the vertebral arteries. It cannot escape, however, because of the compressed venous system. This results in increased intravascular pressure, congestion and rupture of the vessels.

Ligatures used range from electrical cords, neckties, ropes and telephone cords to sheets and hoses. The appearance of a ligature mark on the neck is subject to considerable variation, depending on the nature of the ligature, the amount of the resistance offered by the victim and the amount of force used by the assailant. The ligature mark might be faint, barely visible or absent in young children or incapacitated adults, especially if the ligature is soft, for example, a towel, and removed immediately after death (Figure 8.24A–E).

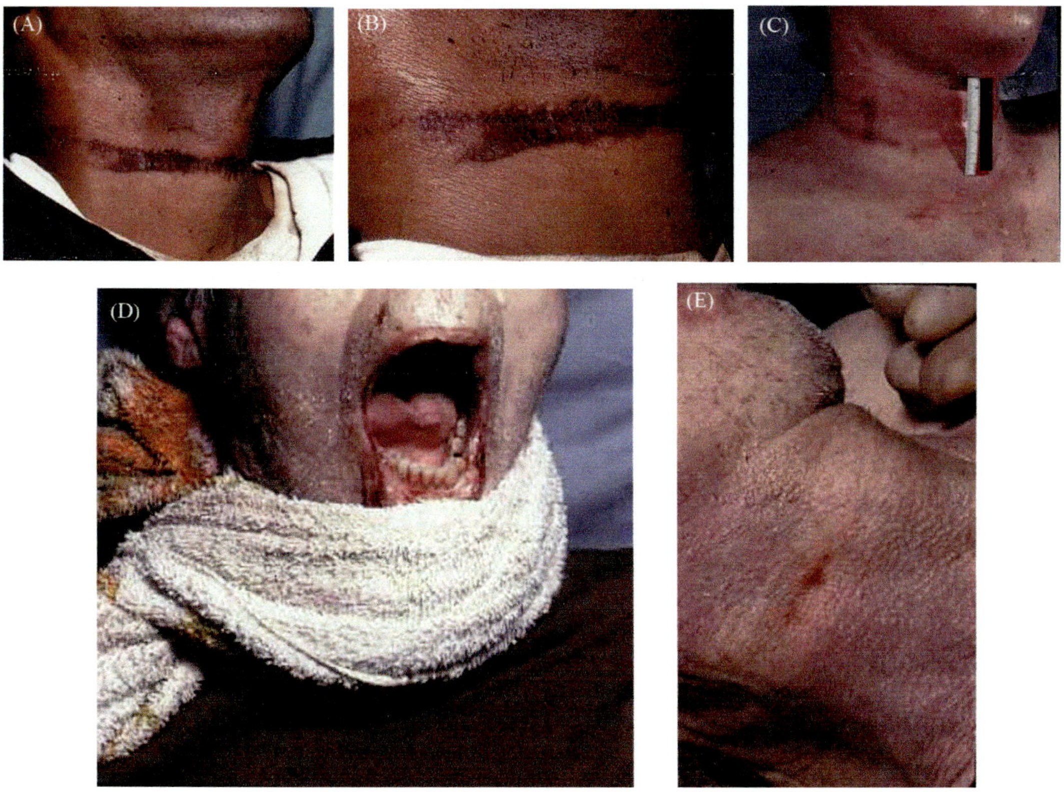

Figure 8.24 (A) Ligature strangulation with cloth band. Ligature marks on anterior and lateral aspects of neck. (B) Close-up showing vertically oriented pattern of cloth. (C) Poorly defined ligature marks on a young girl strangled with T-shirt. (D and E) Elderly man strangled with towel.

If a thin tough ligature is used, there will be a very prominent deep mark encircling the neck. Initially, it has a yellow parchment-like appearance that turns dark brown.

In ligature strangulation, in contrast to hangings, the ligature mark usually encircles the neck in a horizontal plane often overlying the larynx or upper trachea (Figure 8.25).

When a wire or cord is used, it often completely encircles the neck. There might be a break in the furrow, however, usually in the back of the neck, where a hand has grasped the ligature and tightened it at this point. Aside from the ligature mark, abrasions and contusions of the skin of the neck are usually not present. They can occur, however, if the assailant places his hands beneath and around the ligature and twists it, tightening it around the neck, or if the victim claws at his neck in an attempt to remove the ligature or relieve the pressure. If there is more than one loop of the ligature around the neck, there could be bruising of the skin if the ligature pinches the skin between two loops.

Injury to the internal structures of the neck is the exception rather than the rule. In a study of 48 ligature strangulation deaths, fractures of the hyoid or thyroid cartilage were present in only six cases (12.5% of the total cases) – five of the males (23.8%) and one (3.7%) of the females.[32] Altogether, there were 12 fractures in the six cases, 7 of the hyoid and 5

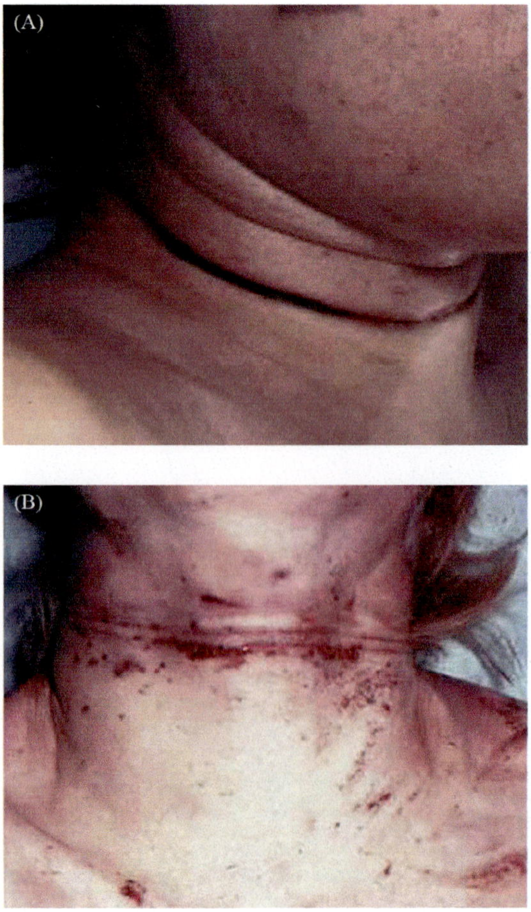

Figure 8.25 Victim strangled with (A) telephone cord and (B) bootlace. Face congested with numerous petechiae. Horizontally oriented ligature mark overlying larynx, encircling neck.

of the thyroid cartilage. Four of the victims had fractures of both the thyroid and hyoid; two, only the hyoid. The fractures of the thyroid cartilage all involved the superior horns.

Suicide using a ligature is rare. In such cases, the victim usually ties a ligature tightly around the neck (Figure 8.26A).

Because some individuals remain conscious for 10–15 s after complete occlusion of the carotid arteries, they have sufficient time to tie at least one, if not more, knots. Instead of tying a knot, some individuals tightly wrap a ligature several times around the neck, securing it in place by the overlapping loops. Other individuals use a tourniquet method: a ligature is loosely wrapped around the neck, knotted and then tightened by a stick inserted beneath the ligature and twisted multiple times. Clothing or the individual's own weight on the stick holds it in place, maintaining the "tourniquet." The authors have also seen cases where individuals used plastic lock-ties (zip-ties) to strangle themselves (Figure 8.26B).

Accidental ligature strangulation is rare. It is most often seen when clothing, such as a tie, scarf or shirt gets entangled in a moving machine. Isadora Duncan, the dancer, died of accidental strangulation when a scarf she was wearing became entangled in an automobile wheel.[33] Other deaths have involved motorcycles, snowmobiles, ski lifts and massage devices.[33]

In infants, the elderly and decomposing bodies, there can be pseudo-ligature marks that suggest strangulation. In infants, pale crease marks between overlapping folds (rolls) of neck skin can be mistaken for ligature marks. This can be further complicated in newborns by the presence of petechiae, which can be normally present in newborns delivered vaginally because of compression of the chest. A similar picture of pseudo-ligature marks can be seen in the elderly – pale crease marks caused by overlapping rolls of skin, petechiae of the sclerae and conjunctivae (caused by cardiac failure) – with the addition of retropharyngeal hemorrhage. Petechiae are often seen in acute cardiac failure, not uncommonly the cause or mechanism of death in elderly individuals. The case that comes to mind is that of an elderly woman found dead in bed with a pillow propping up her head, such that her chin was against her chest. There was a long history of cardiac disease. When the body was examined at the medical examiner's office, there was a horizontal mark across the front of her neck that simulated a ligature. The face above the mark was congested and there were fine petechiae

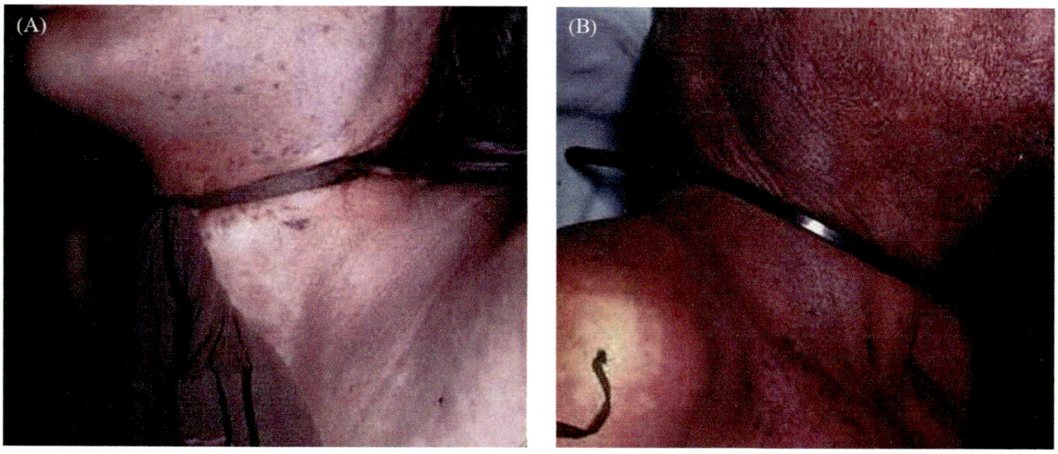

Figure 8.26 (A) Suicidal ligature strangulation using stocking. Six previous attempts at suicide. (B) Suicidal strangulation using plastic lock-tie.

of the sclerae, conjunctivae and periorbital skin, as well as retropharyngeal hemorrhage. At the time the body was initially autopsied, a full account of the circumstances and scene surrounding the death was unknown. For example, it was not known that the head had been propped up, that there was a long history of cardiac failure and that the woman died in a room with no windows and with a single entrance that was blocked by a bed in which her bedridden husband slept. Death was, in fact, caused by her long-standing coronary artery disease. The "ligature mark" was just an artifact – a crease caused by the positioning of the head. Pseudo-ligature marks can also be seen in decomposing bodies with tight collars or other clothing around the neck. The body, as it decomposes, swells around the tight-fitting garment that produces a deep furrow that simulates a ligature mark.

As with hangings, the ligatures, if present, and marks should be described in detail, as well as any other injuries on the body. In victims of homicidal ligature strangulation, hair is often found clutched in the hands. This should be recovered and retained along with a control sample of the victim's hair for comparison; often the hair present is found to be that of the victim. Fingernail cuttings should be taken to look for tissue of the perpetrator under the nails.

Manual Strangulation

Manual strangulation is produced by pressure of the hand, forearm or other limbs against the neck, compressing the internal structures of the neck. The mechanism of death is occlusion of the blood vessels supplying blood to the brain, that is, the carotid arteries. Occlusion of the airway probably plays a minor role, if any, in causing death. Virtually, all cases of manual strangulation are homicide. One cannot commit suicide by manual strangulation because, as soon as consciousness is lost, pressure is released and consciousness regained.

Occasionally, it is claimed that the death of a healthy individual ascribed to manual strangulation is unintentional and caused by a vasovagal reaction (reflex cardiac death) brought on by touching, grasping or striking the neck. This is an interesting theory, but unproven by objective evidence. The mechanism of death in such a case would be an arrhythmia produced by stimulation of the carotid sinuses. The carotid sinus is a focal area of enlargement of the common carotid artery where it bifurcates into the external and internal carotid arteries. Compression or stimulation of the carotid sinuses causes an increase in blood pressure in these sinuses with resultant slowing of the heart rate (bradycardia), dilatation of blood vessels (vasodilation) and a fall in blood pressure. In normal individuals, pressure on the carotid sinus causes minimal effects with a decrease in heart rate of less than six beats per minute and only a slight reduction in blood pressure (less than 10 mm Hg).[34] Some individuals, however, show extreme hypersensitivity to stimulation of the carotid sinuses. In such individuals, there is slowing of the heart and cardiac arrhythmias ranging from ventricular arrhythmias to cardiac standstill and hypotension. There are cases reported in which turning of the neck in varying positions or a high or tight collar has produced dizziness and fainting.[34,35] Some articles refer to cases of stimulation of the carotid sinus, which have allegedly produced bradycardia, progressing to cardiac arrest and death.[35] Review of the original case reports almost invariably indicates that these individuals were elderly suffering from some severe cardiovascular disease that in itself was capable of causing sudden death.

However, pressure on the common carotid artery below the sinuses reduces the blood pressure within the sinus by reducing the amount of blood flowing into it. This mimics hypotension or decreased blood supply from hemorrhage or shock, causing the heart to beat faster (tachycardia), the blood vessels to constrict (vasoconstriction) and a rise in blood pressure. This explains the fact that, while in most cases of manual strangulation, there is bradycardia, vasodilation and fall in blood pressure, in some cases, if the hands are lower down on the neck, there might instead be tachycardia, vasoconstriction and a rise in blood pressure.

In manual strangulation, the face usually appears congested and cyanotic, with petechiae of the conjunctivae and sclerae. Di Maio found petechiae present in the conjunctivae or the sclerae in 89% of his cases.[32] Fine petechiae might also be present on the skin of the face. The petechiae are most noticeable on the bulbar conjunctivae and conjunctival sac, the skin of the upper and lower eyelids, the bridge of the nose, the brows and the cheeks. Conjunctival hemorrhages will be larger if the victim struggles and the assailant responds with increased pressure about the neck. The characteristic signs of asphyxia – cyanosis and multiple petechiae – are most striking above the site of manual compression of the neck.

In most cases of manual strangulation, the assailant uses more force than is necessary to subdue and kill his victim. Hence, marks of violence are frequently present on the skin of the neck. Typically, there are abrasions, contusions and fingernail marks on the skin (Figures 8.27 and 8.28).

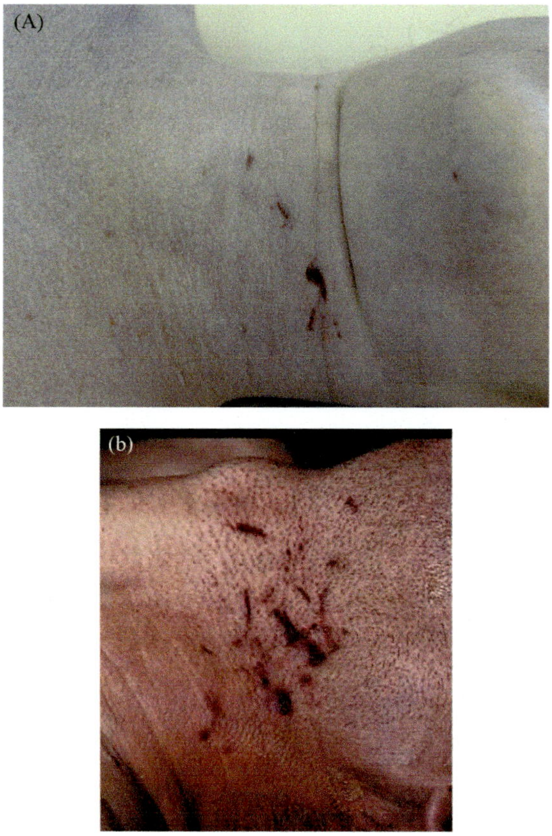

Figure 8.27 (A and B) Manual strangulation with fingernail marks and scratches on sides of neck.

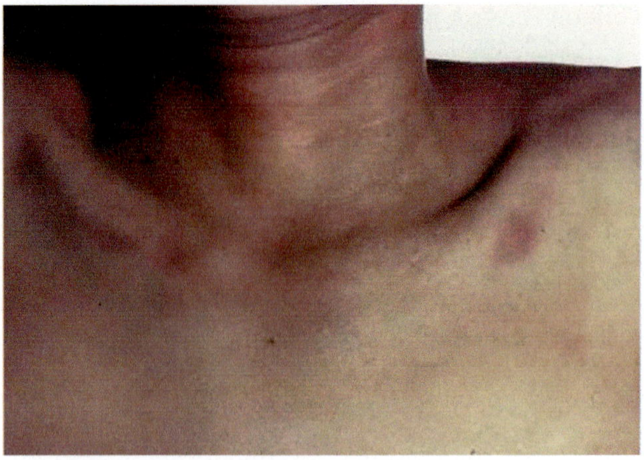

Figure 8.28 A 38-year-old female manually strangled. Bilateral fractures of superior horns of thyroid cartilage and fracture of cricoid cartilage. No external evidence of manual strangulation. Horizontal mark on neck is a surgical scar.

Rarely, no marks are present. Dissection of the throat usually reveals hemorrhage, often extensive, into the musculature (Figure 8.29).

Depending on the age of the victim and the amount of force used, there might be fractures of the hyoid bone or thyroid cartilage (Figure 8.30).

As age increases, so does calcification of these structures and the tendency to have fractures. Thus, these fractures are less common in individuals in their teens and late 20s

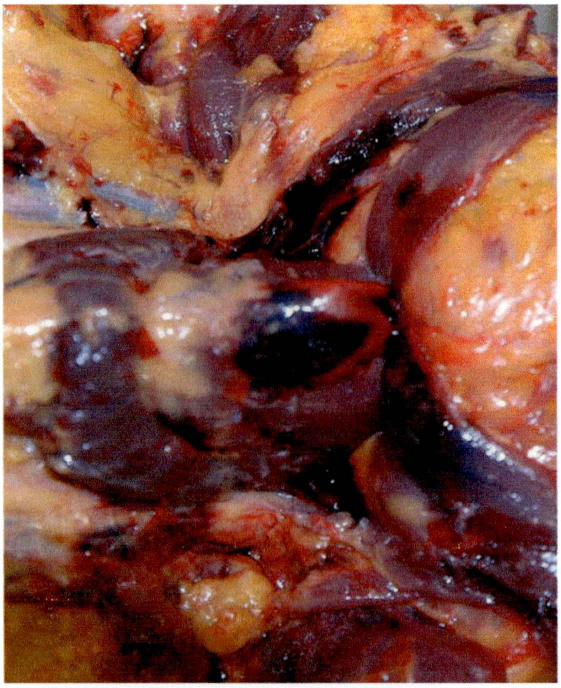

Figure 8.29 Hemorrhage within the cervical musculature in a manual strangulation.

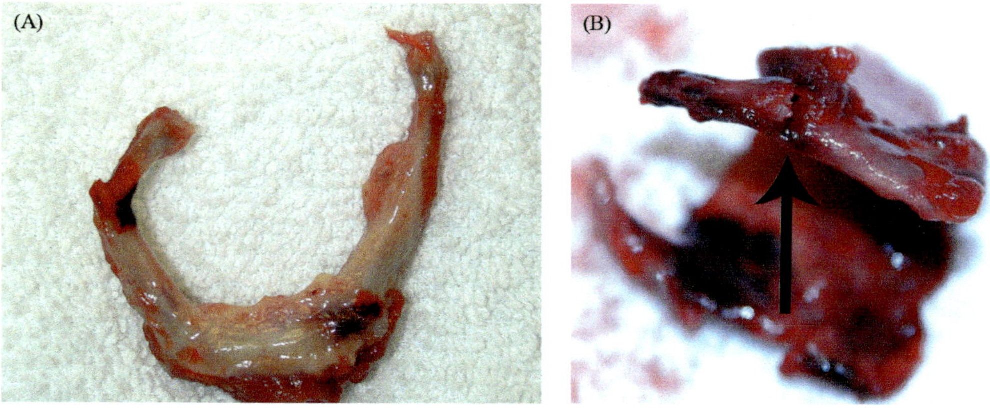

Figure 8.30 Fractures of the (A) hyoid bone and (B) thyroid cartilage.

than in individuals over 30 years of age. One must be careful not to mistake the cartilaginous separations between the greater horns of the hyoid and its body and the superior horns of the thyroid cartilage and thyroid plates for fractures. Hemorrhage must always be present at an alleged fracture site before it can be called an antemortem fracture.

The incidence of fractures in manual strangulation is high if a careful dissection of the neck is conducted. In the 41 cases of manual strangulation studied by DiMaio, the incidence of fractures was 68.1% (28 cases) involving 100% of the males (14 of 14 cases) and 52% (14 of 27 cases) of the females.[32] Harm and Rajs reported an incidence of 70% of their 20 cases; Simpson and Knight 92% of 25 cases.[19,36] Unilateral fractures of the hyoid predominated over bilateral fractures 3 to 1; with unilateral fractures of the hyoid, fractures of the left side dominated 11 to 7.[32] All the fractures of the thyroid cartilage involved the superior horns rather than the body of the thyroid. The latter fractures tend to be vertical and are usually caused by a blow to the thyroid cartilage.

Because of its location high up in the neck, the hyoid bone is relatively safe from injury by direct blows unless the neck is arched. In direct blows to the neck, fractures of the hyoid are generally seen only in association with a fracture of the mandible. The U shape of the hyoid does make it susceptible to fracture by compression. Thus, fractures of the hyoid are common in manual strangulation where a compressive force is applied to the structure.

The larynx, lying in front of the fourth through sixth cervical vertebrae, is protected in the midline only by skin and two layers of fascia. It is, therefore, susceptible to direct neck trauma, that is, blows to the neck. Thus, fractures of the body of the thyroid cartilage can be seen in blows to the neck. Lateral compression of the larynx, as might be expected in manual strangulation, causes fractures of the cornu (horns) of the thyroid. Fractures of the cricoid cartilage occur most frequently when the cartilage is compressed in an anteroposterior direction against the vertebral column. These fractures, which are usually vertical, might occur in the midline or laterally.

In manual strangulation, there is usually trauma to both the external and internal aspects of the neck. Because of the way the neck is usually grasped, the tips of the four fingers with their associated fingernails dig into the neck. Depending on the length, sharpness and regularity of the nails, they can produce linear or semilinear abrasions, scratches and scrapes (Figure 8.27B). The tips of the fingers can produce contusions or erythematous marks. Pressure as applied by the thumb tends not to be at the tip, but on the pad. Therefore, nail marks are less common from the thumb, though a contusion may be present.

Various methods of manual strangulation are used. The simplest involves using one hand and attacking the victim from the front. In this method of attack, one sees small contusions and erythematous marks in association with nail marks on one side of the front of the neck caused by the fingers. An erythematous mark or contusion and, less commonly, a nail mark caused by the thumb might be present on the opposite side of the neck. If the right hand is used, this thumb mark is on the right side of the neck. If two hands are used and the victim is attacked from the front, there are usually erythematous marks and contusions or nail marks on both sides of the front of the neck, usually posterior to the sternocleidomastoid muscles. A variation of a two-handed attack to the front of the neck involves using pressure applied by two thumbs on the central aspect of the neck. Here, the assailant presses both thumbs directly against or along the sides of the larynx and trachea. This results in erythematous markings or contusions of the anterior aspect of the neck. The area of hemorrhage can be either in a bilateral parasagittal plane or confluent across the midline. Fingernail marks, contusions and erythematous marks caused by the fingers will be on the lateral aspects of the neck.

If either one or two hands are used and the victim is attacked from the back, erythematous marks or contusions from the fingertips, as well as nail marks, are generally found on the front of the neck between the larynx and sternocleidomastoid. With one hand, the marks would be on only one side of the neck; with two hands, on both sides. Bruises from the thumbs will be present on the back of the neck.

A less common method of strangulation is an assault from the front using the palm of the hand to apply pressure to the neck without using the fingertips. The authors have seen this in a number of instances, all of which involved adults who were unconscious through acute alcohol intoxication, or young children. There was no evidence of trauma externally that could be related to either the fingertips or fingernails. In all but one instance, there was congestion of the face and petechiae of the conjunctivae and sclerae, as well as periorbital petechiae of the skin. No hemorrhage was noted internally and there was no injury to the internal structures of the neck.

Nail marks can be classified into three types using the classification of Harm and Rajs: impression marks, claw marks and scratch marks. Impression marks are "regularly curved, comma-like, exclamation mark-like, dash-like, or oval, triangular, rectangular epidermal injuries measuring 10–15 mm in length and up to a few millimeters in breadth."[19] They are produced when the fingertip digs into the skin at a right angle to it with the fingernails penetrating through the epidermis to the dermis. In the case of curved imprints, the concave surface does not necessarily correspond to the concave surface of the nail, but might just as easily be a mirror image.

Claw marks are U-shaped injuries of both the epidermis and dermis, varying in length from 3 to 4 mm to a few cm. In claw marks, the fingernails dig into the skin at a tangential angle, cutting the epidermis and dermis tangentially and undermining it. Scratch marks are parallel linear abrasions or erythematous bands in the epidermis up to 1.0-cm wide, produced when the fingernails dig into the epidermis at a vertical angle and then are drawn across the skin, producing an elongated injury.

While, in most manual strangulations, there is evidence of both external and internal injury to the neck, in some cases, there is no injury, either externally or internally. One of the authors (VJMD), over a period of 3 months, saw three women who had been manually strangled. The first showed absolutely no evidence, either externally or internally; the second showed congestion of the face with fine petechiae of the conjunctivae and skin of the face, but no evidence of injury to the neck, either externally or internally; and the third victim had abrasions and scratches of the skin with extensive hemorrhage into the muscles of the neck. All three women were killed by the same individual. All three had blood alcohols above 0.300 g/dL. The *modus operandi* of the perpetrator was to meet a woman in a bar, buy her liquor until she was extremely intoxicated and then go off with her and have sexual intercourse. He would then strangle her. At the time of strangulation, the women were unconscious through acute alcohol intoxication, so a very minimal amount of pressure was necessary. He would place his hand over their necks and push downward, compressing the vessels of the neck. In the last case, the individual regained consciousness and struggled, with the resultant injuries. The perpetrator admitted having killed a number of other women the same way over the past years in a number of states.

In manual strangulation, the victims are usually female. When they are male, they are often highly intoxicated. It is suggested that, in all manual strangulations, a complete toxicological screen be performed.

Sphincter incontinence is thought to be quite characteristic in strangulation. Harm and Rajs addressed this question in a study of 37 dead and 79 surviving victims of strangulation.[19] Of the 37 dead victims, 60% (22) had an empty urinary bladder, compared with 14% of 54 control autopsies whose causes of death were other than violence. Of the 79 surviving victims of asphyxia, 5% (4) had sphincter incontinence. Thus, sphincter incontinence, while more common in strangulation, is not an absolute finding.

In cases of strangulation, the presence of fractures of the larynx or hyoid indicates only that pressure or force has been applied to the neck. These fractures by themselves do not cause death. They are just markers of neck trauma. The authors have seen cases where someone has attempted to strangle an individual, causing fractures of the thyroid cartilage or hyoid, only to give up and stab or beat the victim to death.

Choke or Carotid Holds

Rarely, one may encounter a death alleged to have occurred due to application of either a choke hold or a carotid sleeper hold.[37–40] These terms are often used interchangeably, but, in fact, refer to two different holds whose purpose is to produce transient cerebral ischemia and unconsciousness. The arm and forearm are used to compress the neck, producing cerebral ischemia and unconsciousness. Occasionally, a baton, large metal flashlight, or some other device, will be used to compress the neck. The authors have seen a number of deaths involving the use of such instruments. In such cases, there is usually extensive hemorrhage in the neck and fractures of the hyoid or larynx.

With **choke (bar arm) holds** (see Figure 19.2), the forearm is placed straight across the front of the neck. The free hand grips the wrist, pulling it back, collapsing the airway and displacing the tongue rearward, which occludes the hypopharynx. Incapacitation is caused by collapse of the airway and the carotid arteries with resultant decrease in the supply of oxygen to the brain. Compression of the carotid arteries is the prime mechanism for loss of consciousness. If too much force is used, there could be fracture of the larynx or hyoid. Reay and Eisele reported two such cases with unilateral fractures of the greater cornu of the thyroid cartilage.[37] Following loss of consciousness, the chokehold is released and the victim should regain consciousness within 30 s. There should be no permanent *sequelae*.

Obviously, if the choke hold is maintained for too long, death will ensue, and one now has a case of manual strangulation.

In the **carotid sleeper hold** (see Figure 19.3), symmetrical force is applied by the forearm and upper arm to the front of the neck such that there is compression of only the carotid arteries and jugular veins and not the trachea. The arm is placed about the neck with the antecubital fossa or crook of the arm centered at the midline of the neck. The free hand grips the wrist of the other arm and pulls it backward, creating a pincher effect. This produces transient cerebral ischemia. The carotid sleeper hold impedes blood flow in the carotid arteries by pressure exerted on both sides of the neck by the pincher effect of the arm and forearm. If properly applied, the compression of the carotid arteries will cause loss of consciousness in approximately 10–15 s. On relaxation of the hold, cerebral blood flow will be restored and consciousness will return in approximately 10–20 s, without any serious side effects. Experiments by Reay and Holloway demonstrated that, during application of the carotid sleeper hold, blood flow is decreased an average of 85% to the head with a range in the five subjects of 82–96%.[38] The time to minimum blood flow averaged 6 s (range 3.2–7.2 s).

In theory, the carotid sleeper hold will cause rapid unconsciousness without injury to the individual. Unfortunately, in violently struggling individuals, a carotid sleeper hold can easily and unintentionally be converted into a choke hold, as the individual twists and turns to break the hold. Additionally, if the pressure is maintained after the loss of consciousness, it becomes manual strangulation and, if continued long enough, will cause death.

Both choke and carotid sleeper holds are safe if properly used, though the latter is the safer of the two, and are often used by law enforcement to subdue subjects. In weighing how much force is acceptable in a situation, one must realize that any action involving force always has the potential of producing severe injury and death.

Injuries of the Pharynx and Larynx Produced by Resuscitative Intubation

Resuscitative injuries of the pharynx and larynx secondary to intubation can mimic injuries caused by strangulation and neck holds. In a study of 50 individuals who had endotracheal intubation prior to reaching an emergency room, in an unsuccessful attempt at resuscitation, 37 (74%) had injuries of the airway following the intubation.[41] Injuries to the mouth consisted of focal contusions, lacerations, and focal abrasions of the lips and buccal mucosa. Injuries of the posterior oropharynx and laryngopharynx were contusions of the base of the tongue, contusions of the epiglottis, petechiae of the epiglottis, contusions of the piriform recesses and laceration of the epiglottis (one case). Injuries to the larynx (32 cases) included contusions and petechiae of the mucosa as well as 7 cases in which there were hemorrhages in the superficial and deep muscles of the larynx. Thus, petechiae of the epiglottis, larynx and trachea are of no diagnostic significance. Externally, the individuals had cutaneous neck abrasions in two cases; facial petechiae in three and conjunctival petechiae in 10.

Injuries to Perpetrators of Strangulation

Harm and Rajs, in their study on strangulation, also documented injuries in the assailant.[19] Twenty perpetrators of strangulation were examined for injuries. Of these, 13 (65%)

showed a total of 98 injuries. Interestingly, the presence or absence of defense injuries on the victims did not correlate with the presence of injuries on the perpetrator. Thus, of the victims killed by the 13 assailants who showed evidence of injury, 6 showed defensive injuries of the hands and arms, while 7 showed no injuries indicative of a struggle even though the injuries on the assailant indicated that a struggle did occur.

Nail marks (impressions, claw marks and scratches) constituted 82% of the injuries incurred by the 13 assailants. The other 18% of injuries were nonspecific in nature. Eleven (85%) of the assailants had from 2 to 26 nail marks. Seventy percent of these nail marks on 10 of the 11 assailants were on the backs of the hands and forearms and were predominantly impressions. Most of the nail marks were concentrated on the back of the index finger and thumb. The face and right shoulder were secondary sites of injury.

Chemical Asphyxia

In chemical asphyxia, inhalation of a gaseous compound prevents utilization of oxygen at the cellular level. The most common asphyxiants are carbon monoxide, cyanide and hydrogen sulfide.

Carbon Monoxide

Carbon monoxide (CO) is a colorless, odorless, tasteless, nonirritating gas, the relative density of which is a little less than that of air. The most common sources of carbon monoxide in deaths are fires, automobile exhaust, defective heaters and incomplete combustion of burning products, such as charcoal briquettes. Carbon monoxide is produced whenever organic materials are burned with an inadequate supply of oxygen necessary to produce complete combustion. Excluding deaths during fires and a very small number of homicides, there are approximately 1500 deaths caused by carbon monoxide poisoning annually in the United States, consisting of approximately 400 accidents and 1100 suicides per year.[42] The majority of both the suicides and accidents involve automobile exhaust; however, these deaths are declining due to reduced CO emission in automobile exhaust.

Carbon monoxide produces tissue hypoxia by competing with oxygen for binding sites on the oxygen-carrying hemeproteins (hemoglobin, myoglobin, cytochrome c oxidase, cytochrome P-450).[43] The affinity of carbon monoxide for hemeproteins varies from 30 to 500 times as much as oxygen, depending on the hemeproteins.[43,44] For hemoglobin, it is from 250 to 300 times greater than that for oxygen. Thus, even when atmospheric oxygen is resumed, the displacement of carbon monoxide by oxygen is slow. In addition to the greater affinity of hemoglobin for carbon monoxide, the presence of carboxyhemoglobin alters the oxygen affinity of the hemoglobin by shifting the oxyhemoglobin dissociation curve to the left, decreasing the release of oxygen to tissue. This results in a hypoxia of the tissue greater than what would be produced by an equivalent degree of anemia. It is believed that carbon monoxide also has a direct toxic effect at the cellular level by impairing mitochondrial respiration, caused by carbon monoxide's binding to the cytochrome oxidase complex.[45] Unlike hemoglobin, the affinity of cytochrome oxidase is much greater for oxygen; however, during cellular anoxia, carbon monoxide might bind. Carbon monoxide can also bind in intracellular myoglobin, impairing the oxygen supply to the heart muscle; this may exacerbate underlying cardiac conditions, increasing the risk for arrythmias or fatal heart attacks.

The percent saturation of carbon monoxide is defined as the percentage of hemoglobin combined with carbon monoxide in the form of carboxyhemoglobin. Because of the greater affinity of hemoglobin for carbon monoxide, extremely low concentrations in the atmosphere can produce very high blood saturation. For example, a concentration of 0.5–1% (5–10,000 parts per million) CO in the atmosphere can produce carboxyhemoglobin saturation levels of 80% in 2–15 min, while concentrations of 0.2–0.3 would take 30–45 min and concentrations of 0.02–0.06 would take 4–6 h.[46]

Humidity, high environmental temperature, high altitude and physical activity all increase the respiratory rate and, thus, the absorption of carbon monoxide. The Occupational Safety and Health Administration (OSHA) recommended maximum allowable exposure limit is 35 ppm over 8 h.[47] For safety purposes, workers exposed to carbon monoxide should never have a blood carboxyhemoglobin level above 5%. In practice, this is not always possible. While nonsmokers have blood carboxyhemoglobin levels of 1–3%, smokers often have "normal" levels of carboxyhemoglobin of 5–6%, commonly reach 10% and may even exceed 15%.[48] Blood carboxyhemoglobin levels of 10–14% have been observed in firefighters after a blaze[49] and cases of hemolytic anemia.[50] Elevated levels of carboxyhemoglobin (up to 13%) can also be found in police officers working in tunnels or workers in garages where motor vehicles are running, if the individuals are also smokers.

Automobile Exhaust

After fires, the second most common source of carbon monoxide in fatalities is inhalation of the exhaust fumes of automobiles. Most such deaths are suicide, but accidental deaths do occur. Accidental deaths have occurred due to faulty vehicles or even while vehicle was in motion, and some with partly open (2- to 4-in.) windows.[51] Accidental deaths occur when a car is started and left running in a garage to warm up while the driver goes back to the house. Carbon monoxide from the exhaust then leaks into the house, killing the residents. This may also occur with newer push-button cars where the driver inadvertently leaves the car running without turning it off upon returning home.

The quantity of CO produced by a gasoline engine depends on a number of factors, including idling speed, air-fuel ratio, compression ratio and the presence of a catalytic converter. Prior to the introduction of catalytic converters, an idling engine could produce 7% CO, while the same engine in a vehicle traveling at 60 mph, with the carburetor adjusted for efficient operation, produced less than 0.5% CO.[52] Diesel engines have traditionally produced smaller quantities of carbon monoxide than gasoline engines.

By 1975, most new cars were equipped with catalytic converters designed to convert CO to CO_2 via an oxidation and a reduction reaction. The 1980s saw the introduction of even more sophisticated converters, oxygen sensors and computers to increase the efficiency of the converters. Catalytic converters, if properly adjusted, eliminate most of the carbon monoxide, meaning that idling engines can produce exhaust with less than 0.1% CO.[53] Because of this, forensic pathologists have begun to see occasional deaths caused by inhalation of exhaust fumes in which the CO level is in the normal range.[54] Such deaths are thought to be caused by displacement of oxygen by CO_2, the toxic effects of CO_2, and possibly the actions of other compounds in the exhaust.

Catalytic converters have limitations. They do not become fully operational until they and the engine reach a certain temperature. Thus, there is an initial rise in CO exhaust to a high level with a subsequent decline to a constant lower level. The warmer the engine, and, thus, the converter, prior to starting, the lower the maximum CO level.[53] If the catalytic converter becomes overheated, it becomes less efficient.

If the automobile is left running in an enclosed space, not only is there a buildup of CO, but there will also be a raise in the temperatures. A 26-year-old female was found dead in a small van with a hose running from the exhaust to the left side door window.[52] The exhaust gases caused a gradual rise in cabin temperature from 21.6 to 40.50°C in the front of the cabin and to 34.9°C at the rear. This elevation in cabin temperature is consistent with the observation that many individuals found dead of carbon monoxide poisoning in automobiles show postmortem slippage of the skin, though they have been dead only a short time.

DiMaio and Dana reported three deaths as a result of inhalation of carbon monoxide from automobile exhaust fumes while outdoors.[55] Blood carboxyhemoglobin concentrations ranged from 58 (in a decomposing body) to 81%. All individuals were found lying adjacent to the exhaust pipe of an automobile. Two deaths were suicides. These cases illustrate the fact that, even in the outdoors, deaths from carbon monoxide inhalation can occur if the individual is in proximity to a rich source of carbon monoxide for a prolonged time.

Non-Motor Vehicle Deaths

Charcoal briquettes are made to smolder, not burn with a flame and this incomplete burning produces carbon monoxide. Thus, if these grills are used in an unventilated environment such as a residence, garage, trailer, tent or even a porch, death can be caused by the large amount of carbon monoxide produced. Occasionally, individuals camping out will use charcoal briquettes to keep warm. This has resulted in a number of fatal CO poisonings. Carbon monoxide poisoning has also occurred with natural and butane gas heaters following buildup of carbon deposits, with resultant incomplete combustion of gas. The authors are familiar with the deaths of three family members residing in a house without electricity who were using a gas generator placed inside the home to power the air conditioner.

Carbon monoxide can also get into the air tanks of scuba divers. Here, carbon monoxide emitted by gasoline-driven compressors might be accidentally sucked up and mixed with the air being pumped into the scuba air tanks.

Findings in Carbon Monoxide Poisoning

Haldane and Killick studied the effects of exposure to carbon monoxide (CO).[56,57] The symptoms, when they appear, are progressive, roughly paralleling the blood levels of CO. Initially, the signs and symptoms are often subtle. At levels of 0–10% carboxyhemoglobin saturation, there are generally no symptoms. In individuals at rest, CO levels from 10 to 20% are often symptomless, except for a headache. If tested, however, these individuals will show impairment in the execution of complex tasks. Haldane experienced no ill effects at levels up to 18–23%. Killick's symptoms were negligible below 30%, though, between 30 and 35%, she had a headache with throbbing and fullness of the head.[56] Between 30 and 40% CO, there was a throbbing headache, nausea, vomiting, faintness and drowsiness. As levels approach 40%, the slightest exertion caused faintness. Pulse and respiration are rapid. Blood pressure falls. Between 40 and 60% CO, there is mental confusion, weakness and loss of coordination. Haldane at 56% was unable to walk unaided.[57] At 60% CO and beyond, individuals lose consciousness, develop Cheyne-Stokes respiration, have intermittent convulsions, depressed heart action and respiratory failure, and die.

Autopsy findings in CO deaths can be nonspecific. In Caucasians, there may be a prominent pink complexion caused by coloration of the tissue by carboxyhemoglobin, which has a characteristic cherry-red or bright-pink appearance that can be seen in the tissue. Cherry-red livor mortis may also be present. However, this coloration can also occur with prolonged exposure of the body to a cold environment (either at the scene of death or in a morgue "cooler") or cyanide poisoning. In darker pigmented individuals, this discoloration may be more prominent in the conjunctivae, nail beds and mucosa of the lips.

Internally, the musculature and the internal viscera may also have a bright cherry-red coloration. This coloration of the viscera will persist even if tissue is removed and placed in formaldehyde; embalming also does not change the color of the viscera. Blood withdrawn from the vessels may also have this characteristic color. This is not invariable, however. One of the authors autopsied an individual with a carboxyhemoglobin level of 45% in whom the characteristic coloration was not present. The death was a result a defective heating unit in the home.

The brain is the organ most sensitive to the actions of carbon monoxide. Brain damage is characteristically localized to certain selective areas. If death does not occur immediately, the injury to these areas may increase over hours and days. Carbon monoxide produces selective injury to the cerebral gray matter. Bilateral necrosis of the globus pallidus is the most characteristic lesion, though other affected areas include the cerebral cortex, particularly the second and third layers; the white matter, the hippocampus, the Purkinje cells of the cerebellum and substantia nigra. The lesions in the globus pallidus, however, are nonspecific and can be seen in drug overdoses as well. It has been demonstrated that some cells, for example, CAI pyramidal cells in the hippocampus, may resume their functioning after exposure to the carbon monoxide only to die days later.[58] It has been hypothesized that this delayed injury is caused by postischemic reperfusion injury and the effects of CO on vascular endothelium and oxygen radical–mediated brain oxygen reoxygenation.

Neurological *sequelae* caused by CO poisoning can develop during the acute phase of poisoning or postexposure from 3 to 240 days after exposure without overt symptoms.[59–62] In this situation, after an asymptomatic interval, the patient can develop subtle abnormalities such as personality changes or mild cognitive deficits to severe dementia or psychosis.[59,60] Transitory cortical blindness and memory defects are common. In addition, there can be aphasia, apathy, disorientation, hallucinations, incontinence, slow movements and muscular rigidity. CO encephalopathy may cause a number of behavioral and functional impairments, including alterations in attention, executive functioning, verbal fluency, motor abilities, visual-spatial skills, learning, short-term memory and mood and social adjustment.

The delayed neurological syndrome in carbon monoxide intoxication is associated with lesions of the cerebral white matter. These lesions are nonspecific, however, and are found in other conditions associated with hypoxia and hypotension. It appears that a combination of hypotension and hypoxia is necessary to produce these lesions.

Carboxyhemoglobin Concentrations

The carboxyhemoglobin levels of individuals who die of CO poisoning can vary greatly, depending on the source of the CO, the circumstances surrounding the death and the health of the individual. In elderly individuals, and those suffering severe diseases, such as coronary artery disease or chronic obstructive pulmonary disease, saturations as low as 20–30% can be fatal. Carboxyhemoglobin concentration in house fires average 57%, with concentrations of 30 or 40% common. In contrast, in individuals dying from the inhalation of exhaust fumes, concentrations are mostly over 70%, averaging 79%. Low levels in individuals dying of inhalation of exhaust fumes might be found if the car stops running after the victims are in an irreversible coma but continue breathing, gradually decreasing their carboxyhemoglobin concentration in spite of irreversible hypoxic injury to the brain. The half-life of carbon monoxide, breathing room air at sea level, is approximately 4–6 h. Oxygen therapy reduces the half-life elimination, depending on the concentration of oxygen. Half-life elimination with oxygen therapy is shortened to 40–80 min breathing 100% oxygen at 1 atm, and 15–30 min breathing hyperbaric oxygen.[49] If an individual reaches an emergency room alive, a pulse oximeter cannot be relied on to accurately determine oxygenation levels as it cannot distinguish carboxyhemoglobin from oxyhemoglobin at the usual wavelengths employed.[63,64]

While elevated CO levels are virtually the rule in house fires, there might be no elevation of CO in a death from a flash fire that occurs in an open environment. Individuals who die in motor vehicle accidents in which a gas tank explodes, theoretically, might not show an elevated carbon monoxide. This latter occurrence is very rare, usually involving unusual circumstances.

Carbon monoxide can pass from the maternal to the fetal blood. The carboxyhemoglobin (COHB) concentration of the fetus is dependent on the percent saturation of the mother's hemoglobin with CO. Saturation of fetal hemoglobin with CO lags behind saturation of the maternal hemoglobin because of the slow dissociation of maternal carboxyhemoglobin. After a time, however, equilibrium will be reached and the final COHB may be up to 10% higher than maternal COHB.[65] Carbon monoxide can produce intrauterine death of the infant even though the mother may survive.

Carboxyhemoglobin concentrations in blood and body cavity fluids of decomposed bodies are dependent on the carbon monoxide level of the blood prior to the death. Carbon monoxide is not produced postmortem through the decomposition of hemoglobin, myoglobin and other substances. Dominguez et al. found that carboxyhemoglobin saturation in blood was not markedly altered during postmortem decomposition, with values of not more than 6% determined in dogs submerged in seawater for 4 days.[68] They also found that carboxyhemoglobin saturation in blood was not significantly different from that in the fluids of the thoracic cavities. Additionally, Kunsman et al. showed that carboxyhemoglobin concentrations are stable for up to 2 years if kept refrigerated in sealed EDTA or sodium fluoride tubes.[69]

In some individuals, death from carbon monoxide poisoning is not immediate. In such cases, if the production of the carboxyhemoglobin ceases after the onset of irreversible coma, the individual will gradually eliminate the carbon monoxide from the body, even though irreversible injury has occurred. Thus, the authors have seen individuals who died from carbon monoxide poisoning register low or even negative carboxyhemoglobin levels at autopsy. Such a diagnosis is made on the basis of scene investigation. For example, a man is found dead in a parked car. The ignition is on and the gas tank is empty. An autopsy and complete toxicological analysis fail to reveal a cause of death. Examination of the car, however, reveals defects in the exhaust system such that high concentrations of CO built up in the car while it was running.

Suicide or Accident

In suicides from CO, the diagnosis is often immediately apparent at the scene. A victim will usually be found either in a garage or a car with the ignition on. The car may be running, but more commonly is not. Pipes or hoses connected to the exhaust might lead into the compartment of the vehicle (Figure 8.31).

Accidental deaths caused by carbon monoxide can be subtle in their presentation. A person might be found dead in a parked car with the ignition on and the motor either running or stalled. Death is caused by carbon monoxide entering a defect in the vehicle. An investigator, however, could mistakenly ascribe the cause of death to heart disease. When more than one individual is found dead in a car, the ignition of which is on, almost inevitably, death is caused by CO. If more than one person is found dead in a residence, or one individual dead and others comatose, without any evidence of trauma, the first agent one should suspect is carbon monoxide poisoning often caused by a defective heating unit.

Sometimes, people will try to make a suicide look like an accident. They will be found in a garage, with the door closed, the ignition of the car on, the hood open and tools on the fender. The expected conclusion is that such individuals were overcome by exhaust fumes while repairing the vehicle. Such cases, however, are invariably suicide. This is because, if one were to run a car in a closed garage, within 2–3 min the atmosphere would be so noxious, so irritating to the respiratory system, that one could not affect any repair at all. It would be necessary to turn the car off and open the garage door to let the fumes escape.

Figure 8.31 Elaborate hose setup from the exhaust in an intentional CO poisoning.

Cyanide

Hydrogen cyanide and its salts, potassium and sodium cyanide, are potent, rapidly acting poisons. Cyanide produces cellular hypoxia by inhibiting intracellular cytochrome oxidase. Specifically, cyanide binds to the iron in cytochrome a_3, a component of the cytochrome c oxidase complex in mitochondria, preventing electron transport and the utilization of oxygen. This results in cellular hypoxia and anaerobic metabolism causing lactic acid production and metabolic acidosis. In massive acute cyanide poisoning, the mechanism of toxicity may involve other enzyme systems as well. Signs and symptoms of acute systemic cyanide poisoning may develop rapidly within minutes, depending on the route and extent of cyanide exposure. Cyanide toxicity can be treated with hydroxocobalamin, a synthetic vitamin B12 injection.[70] Hydroxocobalamin combines with cyanide, preventing the cyanide from binding to cytochrome a_3. The cyanide and hydroxocobalamin combine to form cyanocobalamin, which is then excreted in the urine.

There is no cumulative effect from ingestion or inhalation of cyanide. One either dies or survives. Cyanide salts are used in photography, engraving, electroplating and chemical laboratories. Most deaths caused by ingestion of cyanide are suicide and involve individuals who work in laboratories in which cyanide is used.

Cyanide salts are harmless until they come into contact with acid, at which time there is production of hydrogen cyanide gas. Inhalation of this gas in a small room, in very high concentrations, such as a gas chamber, can produce almost immediate collapse and death. This, however, is the exception. In most instances, it takes minutes to die following inhalation of cyanide gases. Even in the Nazi death chambers, where pure cyanide gas in large quantities was pumped into a closed chamber, it took minutes to cause death. Ingestion of cyanide salts can produce rapid death if the salts contact gastric acid and the stomach is empty. With a full stomach, there might be a delay of several minutes to an hour before death occurs. According to Baselt[71] and J. Garriott (personal communication), the minimum adult lethal dose is approximately 200 mg for either sodium or potassium cyanide. Cyanide can also be created during fires particularly if the fire burns at high temperatures and if plastics, such as polyurethane, or synthetic fabrics, wool or silk are involved.

At the autopsy of an individual who ingests a cyanide salt, the mouth and stomach give off the distinct smell of bitter almonds. Unfortunately, the ability to smell cyanide is governed by a genetic trait and a significant percentage of the population cannot smell it. The gastric mucosa and blood may have a bright red color and livor mortis is often bright pink, similar to that seen in CO poisoning. This coloration is caused by cyanide's inhibition of the cytochrome oxidase system, which prevents the utilization of circulating oxyhemoglobin. It is oxyhemoglobin that gives the bright pink color to the blood, not cyanohemoglobin, which is not formed in any significant quantity in life. If a strong solution of potassium or sodium cyanide was ingested, there may be some alkaline burns of the gastric mucosa. If there was some vomiting of this material, these burns might be seen in the skin adjacent to the mouth. If hydrogen cyanide is inhaled, the only changes at autopsy are a bright pink color to the blood and livor mortis.

The detection and quantitation of cyanide in the blood is beset with difficulty. Analysis of the blood for the presence of cyanide should be conducted as soon as possible. Not only can cyanide degrade over time, but it can be produced postmortem in blood in both the body or a test tube, through the process of decomposition. In addition, if the method of analysis is not absolutely specific, other substances in the blood (sulfides) can react like cyanide, giving falsely elevated results.[72] One extensively quoted study ascribing numerous deaths to cyanide is suspect because of its methodology.[73]

Cyanide is detoxified by the liver into thiocyanate. Normal thiocyanate concentrations in the blood range from 1 to 4 mg/L in nonsmokers and from 3 to 12 mg/L in smokers. Blood cyanide levels in healthy subjects range from 0.016 to 0.041 mg/L. Toxic levels of cyanide range from 0.1 to 5 mg/L, with fatal levels generally greater than 1 mg/L. Individuals in industries exposed to cyanide on a chronic basis may have a mean level of 0.232 mg/L for smokers and 0.183 mg/L for nonsmokers. One worker, a smoker, had a level of 2.2 mg/L, which would ordinarily be considered a lethal level.[74]

In fire victims, cyanide concentrations have been found to range from 0.1 to 8.0 mg/L, usually in the presence of elevated concentrations of carboxyhemoglobin as well (mean 40%).[75] However, cyanide has been hypothesized to be a possible toxin in fire deaths, particularly in deaths where the CO concentration is low.

Hydrogen Sulfide

Hydrogen sulfide (H_2S) is produced by the fermentation of organic matter. It is found in sewers, sewage plants and cesspools, as well as in the oil, chemical and textile industries. Hydrogen sulfide, in conjunction with CO_2 and methane formed in sewers, is known as sewer gas. Just like cyanide, there is no cumulative effect to the inhalation of H_2S. It is thought that the toxic effects of H_2S are mediated by an inhibition of cytochrome oxidase.

Hydrogen sulfide is often detected by pungent, rotten-egg odor that is noticeably at concentrations as low as 0.005 ppm. In low concentrations (<100 ppm), H_2S is a local irritant resulting in headaches, nausea and irritation of the mucus membranes. At concentrations greater the 150 ppm, pulmonary edema and paralysis of the olfactory nerves can occur, numbing the ability to detect the harmful gas. With concentrations of 500 ppm, unconscious and death can occur after 30–60 min of exposure; concentrations of >700 ppm can lead to collapse of the central nervous system resulting in rapid loss of consciousness, coma and death.

At autopsy, the deceased appears cyanotic with dark-colored blood and mucus membranes. This is caused by the reduction of oxyhemoglobin and the formation of methemoglobin. Additionally, H_2S reacts with metals to form darkly colored metal sulfides, often resulting in a black discoloration of coins in the pockets of victims dying from H_2S exposure (Figure 8.32).

Laboratory measurement of H_2S usually involves measuring both the sulfide and thiosulfate concentrations; thiosulfate being formed by the oxidation of H_2S by the liver. Blood sulfide concentrations as high as 0.05 mg/L have been detected in nonlethal cases of H_2S exposure with lethal concentrations ranging from 5 to 29 mg/L.[76,77] However, the determination of H_2S toxicity can be difficult as sulfide can be created during decomposition and concentrations as high as 33 mg/L have been detected as a result.[76]

Investigation of H_2S deaths can be difficult. Since toxicological analysis may not be of assistance given the overlap in concentrations created with decomposition and lethal concentrations, a thorough scene examination is extremely important. H_2S is also dangerous to those responding to the toxicity, though, so extreme caution must be undertaken when extricating victims from such situations. While in the past, most H_2S toxicities were accidental, suicides have been increasing in incidence.[78] H_2S suicides were first reported in

Figure 8.32 Coins corroded in a hydrogen sulfide death.

Japan though a number have also been described in the United States. Incidences of H_2S suicides are thought to be increasing because of the Internet dissemination of instructions regarding how to create hydrogen sulfide gas using common household chemicals, usually hydrochloric acid (found in commercial pool cleaners) and lime sulfur (calcium polysulfide) found in common pesticides. Templates for warning signs for loved ones and first responders are also available over the Internet as well as reports that H_2S is a painless method for suicide in that victims lose consciousness with a single intake of breath and die immediately.

References

1. Ely SF and Hirsch CS, Asphyxial deaths and petechiae: a review. *J Forensic Sci* 2000; 45(6):1274–1277.
2. Gordon I and Mansfield RA, Subpleural, subpericardial and subendocardial hemorrhages. *J Forensic Med*1955; 2:31–50.
3. Gilg T, et al., Investigations on postmortem coagulation and fibrinolytic reactions in blood. *Beitr Gerichtl Med* 1986; 44:399–405.
4. Rossen CL, et al., Two siblings and recurrent cardiorespiratory arrest: Munchausen syndrome by proxy or child abuse? *Pediatrics* 1983; 71:715–720.
5. CDC's WISQARS™ (Web-based Injury Statistics Query and Reporting System) https://www.cdc.gov/injury/wisqars/index.html accessed 6 Sept 2019.
6. DiMaio DJ and DiMaio VJM, Two deaths caused by a lack of oxygen in a water vault. *J Forensic Sci* 1974; 19:398.40 1.

7. National Safety Council, *Injury Facts 2017.* National Safety Council. https://www.nsc.org/home-safety/safety-topics/choking-suffocation accessed 6 Sept 2019.
8. Guyton AC and Hall JE, *Textbook of Medical Physiology* 10th ed. W.B. Saunders, Philadelphia, PA, 2000.
9. Knight BH, The significance of the postmortem discovery of gastric contents in the air passages. *J Forensic Sci* 1975; 6:229–234.
10. Edwards WD, Gabel WJ, and Hosmer FE, On the physical death of Jesus Christ. *JAMA* 1986; 255:1455–1463.
11. Fruin JJ, The Causes of Prevention of Crowd Disasters. Presented at the First International Conference on Engineering for Crowd Safety, London, England, 1993.
12. Roughead W, *Burke and Hare* 3rd ed. Edinburgh, Cited in Polson C, Gee DJ, Knight B, *The Essentials of Forensic Medicine.* Pergamon Press, New York, NY, 1985.
13. Camps FE and Hunt AC, Pressure on the neck. *J Forensic Med* 1959; 6:116–135.
14. Brouardel P, Cited in Polson CJ, Gee DJ, Knight B, *The Essentials of Forensic Medicine.* Pergamon Press, New York, NY, 1985.
15. Ikai M, et al., Physiological studies on choking in judo, in *Bulletin of the Association for the Scientific Studies on Judo, Part 1, Studies in General.* 1958; pp 1–12.
16. Suzuki E, Medical studies on choking in judo, with special reference to electroencephalographic investigation, in *Bulletin of the Association for the Scientific Studies on Judo.* 1958; pp 23–48.
17. Rossen R, Kabat H, and Anderson JP, Acute arrest of cerebral circulation in man. *Arch Neurol Psychiatry* 1943; 50:510–528.
18. Rao V and Weti CV, The forensic significance of conjunctival petechiae. *Am J Forensic Med Pathol* 1988; 9:32–34.
19. Harm T and Rajs J, Types of injuries and interrelated conditions of victims and assailants in attempted and homicide strangulations. *Forensic Sci Int* 1981; 18:101–123.
20. Ajdacic-Gross V, Weiss MG, Ring M, et al., Methods of suicide: international suicide patterns derived from the WHO mortality database. *Bull World Health Organ* 2008; 86(9):726–732.
21. Sauvageau A, Laharpe R, King D, et al., Agonal sequences in 14 filmed hangings with comments on the role of the type of suspension, ischemic habituation, and ethanol intoxication on the timing of agonal responses. *Am J Forensic Med Pathol* 2011; 32(2):104–107.
22. Hlavaty L, Kasper W, and Sung L, Current analysis of hangings that deviates from recently published studies. *Am J Forensic Med Pathol* 2016; 37:299–305.
23. Feigin G, Frequency of neck organ fractures in hanging. *Am J Forensic Med Pathol* 1999; 20(2):128–130.
24. DiMaio VJM, Accidental hangings due to pacifiers. *JAMA* 1973; 226:790.
25. Rauchschwalbe R and Mann NC, Pediatric window-cord strangulations in the United States, 1981–1995. *JAMA* 1997; 277:1696–1698.
26. Petruk J, et al., Fatal asphyxiations in children involving drawstrings on clothing. *Can Med Assoc J* 1996; 155(10):1417–1419.
27. Uva JL, Review: autoerotic asphyxiation in the United States. *J Forensic Sci* 1995; 40(4):574–581.
28. Byard RW, Hucker SJ, and Hazelwood RR, Fatal and near-fatal autoerotic asphyxial episodes in women. *Am J Forensic Med Pathol* 1993; 14(1):70–73.
29. Casper JL, *Handbook of the Practice of Forensic Medicine*, vol 2, 3rd ed., GW Balfour (trans). New Syndenham Society, London, 1982, pp 169–182.
30. Spence MW, et al., Craniocervical injuries in judicial hangings: an anthropologic analysis of six cases. *Am J Forensic Med Pathol* 1999; 20(4):309–322.
31. Hartshorne NJ and Reay DT, Judicial hanging (letter). *Am J Forensic Med Pathol* 1995; 16(1):87.
32. DiMaio VJM, Homicidal asphyxia. *Am J Forensic Med Pathol* 2000; 21(1):1–4.
33. Habal M, Meguid MM, and Murray JE, The long scarf syndrome—a potentially fatal and preventable hazard. *JAMA* 1972; 221:1269,1270.
34. Weiss S and Baker JP, The carotid sinus reflex in health and disease. *Medicine (Baltimore)* 1933; 12:297–354.

35. Thomas JE, Hyperactive carotid sinus reflex and carotid sinus syncope. *Mayo Clin Proc* 1969; 44:127–139.
36. Simpson K and Knight B, *Forensic Medicine*, 9th ed. Edward Arnold, Baltimore, MD, 1985.
37. Reay DT and Eisele JW, Death from law enforcement neck holds. *Am J Forensic Med Pathol* 1982; 3:253–258.
38. Reay DT and Holloway GA, Changes in carotid blood flow produced by neck compression. *Am J Forensic Med Pathol* 1982; 3:199–202.
39. Koiwai EK, Deaths allegedly caused by use of "choke holds" (ShimeWazal). *J Forensic Sci* 1987; 32:419–432.
40. Kornblum RN, Medical analysis of police choke holds and general neck trauma: I, II. *Trauma*, February 1986; 27(51:7–60; June 1986; 28(l):13–64.
41. Raven KP, Reay DT, and Harruff RC, Artifactual injuries of the larynx produced by resuscitative intubation. *Am J Forensic Med Pathol* 1999; 20(1):31–36.
42. Hampson NB, U.S. mortality due to carbon monoxide poisoning, 1999–2014. Accidental and Intentional Deaths. *Ann Am Thorac Soc* 2016; 13(10):1768–1774.
43. Caughey WS, Carbon monoxide bonding in hemeproteins. *Ann NY Acad Sci* 1970; 174:148–153.
44. Wald G and Allen DW, The equilibrium between cytochrome oxidase and carbon monoxide. *J Gen Physiol* 1957; 40:593–608.
45. Dolan MC, Carbon monoxide poisoning. *Can Med Assoc* 11985; 133:392399.
46. Von Oettingen WF, *Carbon Monoxide: Its Hazards and the Mechanism of Its Action*, U.S. Public Health Service, Bulletin, vol 290. U.S. Government Printing Office, 1944 Washington, DC.
47. Occupational Safety and Health Administration, *Occupational Safety and Health Guideline for Carbon Monoxide*. http:/www.oshaslc.gov/SLTC/healthguidelines/carbonmonoxide/recognition.html.
48. Ernst A and Zibrak JD, Carbon monoxide poisoning (current concepts). *NEJM* 1998; 339(22):1603–1608.
49. Radford EP and Levine MS, Occupational exposure to carbon monoxide in Baltimore firefighters. *J Occup Med* 1976; 18:628–632.
50. Hampson NB, Carboxyhemoglobin elevation due to hemolytic anemia. *J Emerg Med* 2007; 33(1):17–19.
51. Baker SP, et al., Fatal unintentional carbon monoxide poisoning in motor vehicles. *Am J Public Health* 1972; 62:1463–1467.
52. Tsunenari S, et al., Suicidal carbon monoxide inhalation of exhaust fumes. *Am J Forensic Med Pathol* 1985; 6:233–239.
53. Morgen C, et al., Automobile exhaust as a means of suicide: an experimental study with a proposed model. *J Forensic Sci* 1998; 43(4):827–836.
54. Atkinson P, et al., Suicide, carbon dioxide and suffocation. *Lancet* 1994; 344:192–193.
55. DiMaio VJM and Dana SE, Deaths caused by carbon monoxide poisoning in an open environment (outdoors). *J Forensic Sci* 1987; 32:1794–1795.
56. Killick EM, The acclimatization of the human subject to atmospheres containing low concentration of carbon monoxide. *J Physiol* 1936; 87:41–55.
57. Haldane J, Carbon monoxide poisoning. *Br Med J* 1930; ii 16–18.
58. Seisjo BK, Oxygen deficiency and brain damage: localization, evaluation in time and mechanisms of damage. *J Toxicol Clin Toxicol* 1985; 23(46):267–280.
59. Choi HS, Delayed neurologic *sequelae* in carbon monoxide intoxication. *Arch Neurol* 1983; 4:433–435.
60. Mimura K, Harada M, Sumiyoshi S, et al., Long-term follow-up study on sequelae of carbon monoxide poisoning; serial investigation 33 years after poisoning. *Seishin Shinkeigaku Zasshi* 1999; 101(7):592–618.
61. Ginsberg MD, Carbon monoxide intoxication: clinical features, neuropathology and mechanisms of injury. *J Toxicol Clin Toxicol* 1985; 23(46):281–288.
62. Werner B, et al., Two cases of acute carbon monoxide poisoning with delayed neurological *sequelae* after a "free" interval. *J Toxicol Clin Toxicol* 1985; 23(4–6):249–265.

63. Buckley RG, et al., The pulse oximetry gap in carbon monoxide intoxication. *Ann Emerg Med* 1994; 24:252–255.
64. Vegfors M and Lennmarken C, Carboxyhe-moglobinaemia and pulse oximetry. *Br J Anaesth* 1991; 66:625–626.
65. Farrow JR, et al., Fetal death caused by nonlethal maternal carbon monoxide poisoning. *J Forensic Sci*, 1990; 35(6):1448–1452.
68. Dominguez A, Halstead JR, and Domanski TJ, The effect of postmortem changes on carboxyhe-moglobin results. *J Forensic Sci* 1964; 9:330–341.
69. Kunsman GW, Presses CL, and Rodriguez P, Carbon monoxide stability in stored postmortem blood samples. *J Anal Toxicol* 2000; 24(7):572–578.
70. Houeto P, Hoffman JR, Imbert M, et al., Relation of blood cyanide to plasma cyanocobalamin concentration after a fixed dose of hydroxocobalamin in cyanide poisoning. *Lancet* 1995; 346(8975):605–608.
71. Baselt RC (Ed), *Disposition of Toxic Drugs and Chemicals in Man* 5th. Chemical Toxicology Institute, Foster City, CA, 2000.
72. McAnnalley BH, et al., Determination of inorganic sulfide and cyanide in blood using specific ion electrodes: application to the investigation of hydrogen sulfide and cyanide poisoning. *J Anal Toxicol* 1979; 3:111–114.
73. Silverman SH, et al., Cyanide toxicity in burned patients. *J Trauma* 1988; 28:171–176.
74. Chandra H, et al., Chronic cyanide exposure—a biochemical and industrial hygiene study. *J Anal Toxicol* 1980; 4:161–165.
75. Stoll S, Roider G, and Keil W, Concentrations of cyanide in blood samples of corpses after smoke inhalation of varying origin. *Int J Legal Med* 2017; 131(1):123–129.
76. Barbera N, Montana A, Indorato F, et al., Evaluation of the role of toxicological data in discriminating between H_2S femoral blood concentration secondary to lethal poisoning and endogenous H_2S putrefactive production. *J Forensic Sci* 2017; 62(2):390–394.
77. Spagnolo EV, Romano G, Zuccarello P, et al., Toxicological investigations in a fatal and nonfatal accident due to hydrogen sulphide (H_2S) poisoning. *Forensic Sci Int* 2019; 300:e4–e8.
78. Sams RN, Carver HW, Catanese C, and Gilson T, Suicide with hydrogen sulfide. *Am J Forensic Med Pathol* 2013; 34(2):81–82.

Sudden Death in Infancy

9

Of all things in life, there should be nothing so preventable, as there is nothing on the face of it so unnatural, as the death of a little child, yet it is of all things in life the commonest, the only thing we really make, as a community, the least effort to prevent.

—Charles Dickens

Infants most commonly die from natural disease processes, though accident and homicides also occur (see Chapter 10 "Neonaticide, Infanticide and Child Homicide"). Natural deaths more commonly occur in younger children, while accidental deaths increase with increasing age. The most common etiology of natural deaths includes infectious processes, tumors, congenital heart disease and other congenital abnormalities. Common accidental modalities include motor vehicle collisions, drownings and suffocation. This chapter will focus mainly on the forensic issues of sudden infant deaths and the necessary investigation.

Diagnosis of Intrauterine Deaths (Stillbirth)

Intrauterine fetal demise (IUFD) refers to the death of an infant prior to delivery. This can be due to placental or umbilical cord issues such as placental insufficiency, placental abruption, cord prolapse or nuchal cords; fetal issues such as infection or congenital or genetic abnormalities; or maternal issues such as hemorrhage, maternal infection or even maternal death.

The hallmark of an IUFD is delivery of a severely macerated infant indicating that the child has been dead in utero for a prolonged time. Presentation to an emergency room, EMS crew or police agency of a full-term child born without a physician present and showing very early or minimal signs of maceration can be misinterpreted as evidence of trauma during or immediately after delivery. Even physicians may misinterpret an IUFD as trauma. For example, a full-term infant was delivered at home by a midwife and was placed in warm water for "stimulation" and scrubbed to remove the vernix caseosa. The child did not respond and "died." The child was brought to an emergency room to be pronounced dead. The emergency room physician saw the child and called the police, stating that there were scalding burns of almost the complete body. On examination of the body by one of the authors (VJMD), there was slippage of the skin of the trunk, extremities and lower half of the face, with sparing only of the palms and soles of the feet (Figure 9.1), consistent with maceration, not thermal injury. Internal examination showed early autolysis, further illustrating that the infant had been deceased prior to birth.

Delivery of a macerated infant is absolute evidence of an intrauterine death. When a fetus dies in utero, it is suspended in sterile fluid within an intact amniotic sac. There it undergoes aseptic autolytic changes, that is, maceration, due to the infant's tissue and cellular enzymes aided by the favorable body temperature. The earliest sign of maceration in a stillborn is skin slippage (separation of the epidermis from the dermis). This may be present as early as 6 h after death

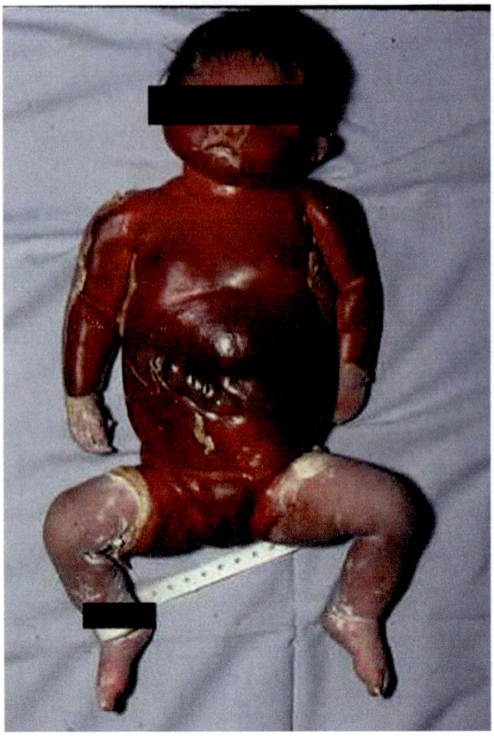

Figure 9.1 A stillborn showing evidence of intrauterine decomposition. Incorrectly diagnosed as scalding injuries following a live birth.

in utero and is expected after more than 12 h.[1,2] As intrauterine decomposition proceeds, bullae may form under the skin. On rupture, the exposed skin dries out, becoming reddish brown. The tissue will develop a reddish coloration caused by hemolysis. Serosanguinous fluid will accumulate in the thoracic and abdominal cavities. The internal organs will undergo autolysis, becoming diffluent. If the fetus is retained several days intrauterine, the skull will collapse and the brain will become semi-liquefied. If the IUFD is diagnosed prior to delivery, often labor is induced to expel the fetus. If care is not taken during delivery, the fetal tissues may separate, resulting in amputation of limbs or even decapitation, which again should not be misinterpreted as trauma.

Birth-Related Deaths

Birth is traumatic to both the mother and child. Depending on the ease of delivery, the amount of trauma that the child may incur can vary from minor to fatal. Significant birth injuries occur in less than 2% of births in the United States, with fatal injuries representing even less. Traumatic injuries usually occur in larger infants, breech presentations or those births that require instrumentation such as forceps.

Craniofacial injuries are the most commonly encountered birth injuries. A small amount of hemorrhage into the scalp is normal. It is not rare for children to present with caput succedaneum, a hemorrhagic edema of the scalp and superficial fascia caused by the trauma of delivery. Subperiosteal and epidural hemorrhages are rare. Epidural hemorrhage is usually associated with a skull fracture, tends to be small in extent and is usually not a cause of death.

The cranial vault of an infant is formed of poorly mineralized plates of bone with membranous sutures. This results in the child being able to withstand considerable cranial distortion without fracture of the bone. Fractures, when they occur, usually involve the parietal bone and are linear, extending along the lines of cleavage.[3] Such fractures in themselves are probably not life-threatening but indicate that significant force has been exerted on the head. They are seen in difficult extractions most often where forceps are used. A more significant form of cranial injury is separation of the squamous and lateral parts of the occipital bone. These do not fuse until the second year of life. In difficult deliveries, the squamous and lateral portion of the occipital bone may be displaced forward, tearing the dura and occipital sinuses, with resultant subdural hemorrhage in the posterior fossa and laceration of the cerebellum. This injury is seen most commonly in occipital posterior presentations and is commonly missed at autopsy.

Subdural hemorrhage can also occur during traumatic deliveries from tearing of the bridging veins and, rarely, of the dural folds, which would require significant deformation of the head. It has been estimated that approximately 15–20% of infants will have birth-related subdural hematomas (SDH).[4] However, these SDHs are usually asymptomatic and require no medical intervention.

In unwitnessed births outside the hospital in which the infant is brought in with fractures of the skull, the mother may state that the injury was caused by precipitous delivery in the erect position with the infant's head striking the ground. Such an occurrence would, in theory, be more common in a multiparous woman with a large birth canal, a small child and vigorous labor. Klein, however, felt such fractures to be rare.[5] He reported 183 cases of precipitous delivery in women kneeling, sitting or standing with the infant falling to the ground. Only one child died, and there were no instances in which a skull fracture could be detected externally. It must be remembered that when the child is delivered, the umbilical cord is still attached. The cord (average length, 20 in.) will tend to pull the child short, thus preventing the head from hitting the ground with full force.

Other injuries can occur during birth as well, including spinal cord injuries and intra-abdominal bleeding; however, these are uncommon and mostly considered in the setting of the birth history. Investigation of such injures is often easier if the birth occurred in a hospital setting, than if the birth occurred at home and in the absence of medical professionals.

Sudden Unexplained Infant Death (SUID)

Sudden unexplained deaths have occurred during infancy since the dawn of time. In the first century BCE, in Babylon, such deaths were believed to be due to the action of the demon Larbatu. While Hebrew folklore taught that Lilith, Adam's first wife, was doomed to haunt the earth as *La Broosha*, a vampire cat who fed on infants. These days we have our own folk tales, from toxic gases in mattresses to critical diaphragm failure. Yet the truth is that we still do not know what causes these deaths.

The term sudden infant death syndrome (SIDS) rose to widespread acceptance in the 1969–1970s. The definition of SIDS evolved over the years until it became solidified as the sudden, unexpected death of an apparently healthy infant who is of less than 12 months of age, where, after a comprehensive autopsy examination and review of all medical history and the scene and circumstances of death, a cause of death cannot be ascertained. In recent years, the National Association of Medical Examiners has recommended the term SUID (sudden unexpected infant death) to be used instead of SIDS, as has the International Congress on Unexplained Deaths in Infants and Children.[6]

SUID accounts for between 3000 and 4000 deaths per year in the United States. The national incidence has been dropping since 1990 when the American Academy of Pediatrics started issuing safe sleep recommendations, including the back to sleep program and other safe sleep initiatives.[7] In 2018, the incidence of SUID in the United States was 90.9 per 100,000 live births.[7]

While SIDS is presumed to be composed of a heterogeneous group of disease processes not due to a single entity, it is a **diagnosis of exclusion** and is **not** a single disease. These facts are often misunderstood by both the public and the medical profession. While the majority of the cases are likely due to natural etiology, some are also due to trauma, most likely suffocation. The term SUID encompasses all possible natural etiologies of SIDS as well as possible environmental factors such as the sleeping environment, including unsafe bedding and co-sleeping, which may lead to asphyxia events.

Epidemiology

Premature infants seem to be at a greater risk for SUID. However, the vast majority of SUID deaths involve full-term infants. As in most disease entities, males outnumber females. Race does not appear to be a factor, but the socioeconomic status of the family does. SUID deaths appear to vary with the environmental temperature. As the temperature decreases, there tends to be more SUID deaths. This could, in part, be because overlay cases and increased co-sleeping during the winter months, or to a "cold" (more common in cold weather), which triggers a mechanism causing death.

SUID deaths occur almost invariably while the child is asleep. Most children are found dead in their cribs in the morning when their parents go to feed them. The peak incidence for crib deaths appears to be between midnight and breakfast. SUID deaths, however, occur throughout the day and not only in cribs and beds, but also in baby carriages, the backs of autos and even while the child is being carried by a parent. However, the child always appears to be asleep at the time of death.

SUID deaths appear to occur in families at random. There is no evidence of a genetic etiology. Siblings of SUID victims have the same risk as the general population. There is a small number of reports of more than one SIDS death in a family and of SIDS deaths in twins.[8,9] Some of these cases can probably be attributed to pure random chance; some to undetected environmental hazards. The majority, however, probably represent infanticide. It is the general policy of the authors to ascribe the first death in a family presenting as SIDS to SUID. The second death by the same mother is labeled undetermined or possible SUID, and a more intensive investigation of the circumstances surrounding the death is conducted. The police are usually asked to interview the family, though in a discreet fashion. A third death with the same mother and father is thought by the authors to be homicide until proven otherwise possibly infanticide by smothering and are discussed elsewhere in the book. It is the authors' opinion that, while a second SUID death with the one mother is improbable, it is remotely possible and she should be given the benefit of the doubt under most, but not all, circumstances. A third case, in our opinion, is probably not possible. Such a case should be labeled undetermined and probable homicide; in such cases, a complete autopsy should be performed by microscopy, toxicology and genetic screening.

Etiology

The etiology of SUID is presumably multifocal and includes not only natural causes, but also accidents and, rarely, homicides. New theories as to etiology seem to arise every few years and then disappear only to be resurrected in future years. Syndromes such as thymo-lymphaticus, manifested by an "enlarged" thymus; viral inflammation of the midbrain; immunopathogenesis; unstable homeostatic control; and various other hypotheses have all been proposed.

One hypothesis claimed that SIDS deaths could be produced by DPT (diphtheria-pertussis-tetanus) inoculations. A study by the National Institute of Child Health and Human Development shows that of 757 cases of SIDS, 40% had received DPT vaccine.[10] In a control group matched by age, race and birth weight, 53% of the children had been immunized. Thus, no link has ever been found between DPT inoculation, or any other vaccination and SIDS.

Another theory was that of hereditary idiopathic apnea. In 1972, Steinschneider described five infants suffering from multiple cyanotic and apneic episodes of unknown etiology during sleep.[11] Two of these children, siblings, subsequently died. Steinschneider hypothesized that prolonged sleep apnea was a cause of SIDS. There then arose an extensive literature on this subject. Brought into prominence were "near-miss" SIDS cases. These were characterized by infants who were successfully resuscitated after being brought into the emergency room with episodes of apnea and cyanosis. In some children, there was repeated admission for this entity. In most, however, nothing subsequently developed. It must be realized that the initial observation of the apnea and cyanosis was often at home by nonmedical observers, and the validity of their observations is open to question. In other instances, there is absolutely no doubt that these near-miss episodes represented multiple episodes of assault on the child by smothering, thus constituting what some call Munchausen syndrome by proxy.[12–14] In 1995, the deaths described in Steinschneider's paper were found to be homicide by smothering.[15]

After many years of study, there is still absolutely no proof that apneic spells commonly seen in premature infants and SIDS are related.[16,17] However, because of this theory, the use of apnea monitors came into fashion. However, Southall et al. studied the breathing patterns of 6914 full-term and 2337 premature infants over 24-h periods prior to hospital discharge in an attempt to see if they could detect SIDS cases.[18] Sudden death occurred in 29 of the infants studied. None of these had had prolonged apneic episodes while they were studied. None of the infants who had had prolonged apnea during the test period died. Additionally, there is no proof that the use of apnea monitors has prevented any deaths from SUID, and since the underlying rationale for them has been discredited, there is no valid reason for their use.[16,17]

Several other hypotheses have endured as potential etiologies for SUID. One involves serotonergic abnormalities in the brainstem resulting in dysregulation of neurological cardiorespiratory control during sleep.[19] Another hypothesis involves prolongation of the QT interval or other cardiac rhythm disturbances leading some experts to recommend genetic testing of all infants dying from SUID.[20] However, many gene mutations are not completely understood, leading to the possibility that an infant died *with* a genetic mutation rather than *from* that mutation. Additionally, misdiagnosis of such may have substantial implications for family members and future family planning. Thus, the appropriate use of such testing must be carefully considered.[21]

SUID deaths may also include asphyxial deaths, either unintentional due to unsafe sleep practices or intentional smothering. Gafafer was the first to propose the importance

Figure 9.2 Scene re-enactment with a teddy bear indicting the terminal position of an infant who was sleeping on the couch beside their parent.

of the sleep environment in possibly causing death, claiming that children could suffocate in there bedclothes or bedding.[22] Though Wooley, in 1945, was critical of this concept, he proposed that complete autopsy examinations should be performed in any unexplained death of an infant and, when no cause of death was determined, the medical profession should admit that it is ignorant of the cause of death rather than alleging that the child had smothered in its bedclothes.[23] Today, we recognize the risk of both the sleep environment as well as the presence of others in the same bed as pertinent risk factors for death and include those as part of the investigation process (Figures 9.2 and 9.3).

SUID Investigation

In any sudden infant death, just as in any death investigated by the medical examiner's office, there are three components to the investigation: the scene investigation, the autopsy and the laboratory studies. Regardless of whether or not the body has been moved, investigators should go to the scene and document it. The parents or caretakers of the child should be questioned as to the circumstances leading up to and surrounding the death: the last time the child was seen alive, the last time it was fed and when it was put to bed. It should be determined in what position the child was found, face down or face up. Was the

Figure 9.3 A crib filled with blankets, stuffed animals and pillows could lead to unintentional asphyxia of an infant. (Photo courtesy of Alexandra Ramirez.)

infant's head covered by a blanket or wedged between the mattress and slats? If the body has been moved prior to the investigation, the individuals who moved the body should be questioned to obtain this information. If possible, a stuffed animal or other suitable model should be used to re-create the sleeping environment or other circumstances (Figure 9.4).

Figure 9.4 Scene reenactment with a teddy bear indicating the terminal position of an infant – face down in a chair.

Questioning of the parents should be done with a sensitive, sympathetic and compassionate approach. The parents of a dead infant are subjected to severe psychological trauma with, not infrequently, feelings of guilt that they did something to cause the death. Attempts should be made to ease the grief and prevent a guilt-ridden reaction. Investigators, in addition to investigating the scene, should do their best to convince the parents that they are in no way at fault or to blame for the infant's death and that there was no way to know for certain if a death could have been prevented. If, subsequently, the case turns out not to be a SUID, or there is something that the parents could have done to prevent the death, no harm has been done by this approach.

At the scene, investigators should approach the parents in a non-accusatory manner and should interview, not interrogate. The parents should be permitted to tell their story without interruption. They should be allowed as much time as they need to describe the circumstances surrounding their infant's death. Most frequently, the bulk of the information needed will be ascertained by simply listening to the distressed parents. If some circumstances preceding or surrounding the infant's death need clarification, the examiners' questions should be neither inflammatory nor accusatory. Otherwise, they will reinforce the guilt feelings frequently present in the parents and cause them to become resentful and uncooperative.

A thorough history should also be obtained, including questions such as the follows:

- Age, date of birth, birth weight if known, race and sex.
- Who was the last person to see the infant alive (date and time)?
- Who discovered the dead infant (date and time)?
- What was the place of death (the child's crib or bed, the parent's bed or elsewhere)?
- What was the position of the infant when found dead?
- Was the infant's original position changed (why and by whom)?
- If resuscitation was attempted, give the method and the name of the person who attempted the resuscitation.
- Had the infant been sick lately? Had a cold or sniffles? Any other minor illnesses?
- Was a physician consulted? Who?
- What treatment had been prescribed?
- Was the child on any medication? What type?
- When was the child last seen by a physician? Why and by whom?
- Was the infant exposed to any illnesses recently?
- Had there been any illnesses in the family recently?
- Was the child breast-fed or bottle-fed? When was the time of the last feeding? What was fed?
- Had there been a difference in the appearance or behavior of the child within the last few days?
- Have there been any other SIDS deaths in the family?
- If someone other than the parent was caring for the child, have any other children died in his or her custody?

The list above offers an outline of the types of questions to be asked but should not be considered all-inclusive. The United States Centers for Disease Control and Prevention offers a comprehensive manual regarding the investigation of infant deaths from which individual jurisdictions may base their protocols.[24]

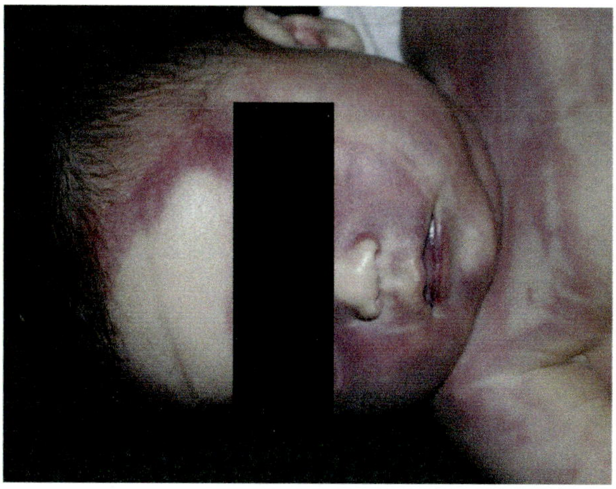

Figure 9.5 Anterior lividity in an infant who was placed face down to sleep.

After the scene investigation, a complete autopsy should then be performed, including microscopic evaluation of the major organs. Occasionally, postmortem lividity is mistaken by medical or police personnel for bruising or blood-tinged froth from the mouth and nose mistaken for blood. While nontraumatic, lividity can assist the forensic pathologist in determining terminal position (Figure 9.5).

Diaper rash is also on occasion mistaken for trauma. All of these factors should be considered and evaluated. Full radiographs should also be performed to rule out trauma, whether acute or remote. A full toxicology panel should also be performed, including vitreous electrolyte analysis. Microbiology testing, as well as metabolic and genetic screening, may be warranted on a case by case basis.

Certification of SUIDs

The certification of SUIDs is an evolving process and is inconsistent over different jurisdictions.[6] It is recommended that all SUID deaths be certified as "undetermined" manner since the cause of death is not actually known. A SUID death with no known risk factors may be certified simply as SUID. However, if known risk factors are present, such as co-sleeping or sleeping in an unsafe environment, such as on a couch or in an adult bed surrounded by pillows, this should be indicated as well. For example, the cause of death may read "sudden unexplained infant death with co-sleeping" or "sudden unexplained infant death in an unsafe sleep environment" as this provides a more accurate understanding regarding the death.

References

1. Wigglesworth JS, The macerated stillborn fetus, in *Perinatal Pathology* 2nd ed. WB Saunders Co, Philadelphia, PA, 1996, pp 78–86.
2. Strachan GI, The pathology of fetal maceration. *Br Med J* 1922; 2:80–82.
3. Wigglesworth JS, Intrapartum and early neonatal death: the interaction of asphyxia and trauma, in *Perinatal Pathology* 2nd ed. WB Saunders Co, Philadelphia, PA, 1996, pp 87–103.
4. Högberg U, Andersson J, Squier W, et al., Epidemiology of subdural haemorrhage during infancy: a population-based register study. PLoS One 2018;13(10):e0206340.

5. Klein cited by Taylor AS, *Medical Jurisprudence* 7th ed. Blanchard and Lea London, 1961.
6. Goldstein RD, Blair PS, Sens MA, et al., Inconsistent classification of unexplained sudden deaths in infants and children hinders surveillance, prevention and research: recommendations from the 3rd International congress on sudden infant and child death. *Forensic Sci Med Pathol* 2019; 15(4):622–628.
7. Centers for Disease Control and Prevention Sudden Unexpected Infant Death and Sudden Infant Death Syndrome: Data and Statistics.. Available at: https://www.cdc.gov/sids/data.htm. Accessed 4 January 2020.
8. Oren J, Kelly DH, and Shannon DC, Familial occurrence of sudden infant death syndrome and apnea of infancy. *Pediatrics* 1987; 80:355–358.
9. Ramos V, Hernandez AF, and Villanueva E, Simultaneous death of twins: an environmental hazard or SIDS. *Am J Forensic Med Pathol* 1997; 18(1):75–78.
10. Hoffman HJ, et al Diphtheria-tetanus-pertussis immunization and sudden infant death: results of the National Institute of Child Health and Human Development Cooperative Epidemiological Study of Sudden Infant Death Syndrome risk factors *Pediatrics* 1987;79(4):598–611
11. Steinschneider A, Prolonged apnea and the sudden infant death syndrome: clinical and laboratory observations. *Pediatrics* 1972; 50:646–654.
12. Berger D, Child abuse simulating "near miss" sudden infant death syndrome. *J Pediatr* 1979; 95:554–556.
13. Minford AMB, Child abuse presenting as apparent "near miss" sudden infant death syndrome. *Br Med* 11981; 282:521.
14. Rosen CL, et al., Two siblings with recurrent cardiorespiratory arrest: Munchausen syndrome by proxy or child abuse. *Pediatrics* 1983;71:715–720.
15. Firstman R and Talan J, *The Death of Innocents*. Bantam Books, New York, NY, 1997.
16. Milner AD, Apnea monitors and sudden infant death. *Arch Dis Childhood* 1985; 60:76–80.
17. Avery ME and Frantz ID, To breathe or not to breathe: what have we learned about apneic spells and sudden infant death? (Editorial retrospective). *NEJM* 1983; 309:107–108.
18. Southall DP, et al., Identification of infants destined to die unexpectedly during infancy: evaluation of predictive importance of prolonged apnoea and disorders of cardiac rhythm or conduction. *Br Med J* 1983; 286:1092–1096.
19. Kinney HC, The serotonin brainstem hypothesis for the sudden infant death syndrome. *J Neuropathol Exp Neurol* 2019; 78(9):765–779.
20. Ackerman MJ, Prior SG, Willems S, et al., HRS/EHRA expert consensus statement on the state of genetic testing for the channelopathies. *Heart Rhythm* 2011;8:1308–1339.
21. Tang Y, Williams N, and Sampson BA, Genetic testing in sudden unexpected natural death in the young: New York City office of the chief medical Examiner's experience and perspective. *Forensic Sci Med Pathol* 2019; 15(3):481–484.
22. Gafafer WM, Time changes in mortality from accidental mechanical suffocation among infants under one year in different geographical regions of the United States, 1925–32; Studies on fatal accidents of children. *Public Health Rep* 1936; 51:1641–1646.
23. Wooley PV, Mechanical suffocation during infancy. *J Pediatr* 1945; 26:572575.
24. Hanzlick R, Jentzen J, and Clark S, Sudden, Unexplained Infant Death Investigation: Guidelines for the Scene Investigator, Centers for Disease Control and Prevention. 2007. Available at: https://www.cdc.gov/sids/pdf/508SUIDIGuidelinesSingles_tag508.pdf. Accessed 4 January 2020.

Neonaticide, Infanticide and Child Homicide

10

Speak roughly to your little boy,
And beat him when he sneezes.

—**Louis Carroll,** ***Alice's Adventures in Wonderland***

The number of children murdered each year in the United States is relatively small in relation to the total number of murders. This fact has been obscured by the media, which (report) thousands of children being murdered each year. This dramatic pronouncement is obtained by considering any individual at or below the age of 18 years as a child. Table 10.1 shows the data for 2017 as to number of homicides by age.[1]

Most child murders occur in the first 2 years of life, with most of these in the first year. The deliberate killing of a child in the first year of life by either act or omission is infanticide. Many such cases represent filicide, the killing of a child by its parent.

Neonaticide

This can be defined as the deliberate killing of a child within 24 h of its birth. The perpetrator is usually the mother. She delivers the child and kills it. Occasionally, she is assisted by a relative or a friend, but usually neonaticide is an act committed by a single individual with no witnesses. Most of the perpetrators are young and unmarried. Some claim not to have realized they were pregnant until they went into labor. Their goal is either to conceal the fact that they gave birth to a child or to dispose of an unwanted child.

Finding dead infants in sewers, trash dumps and public bathrooms is not uncommon in large metropolitan areas. These infants are either victims of neonaticide or are stillborn. The mother is usually the individual who abandoned the child. If apprehended, her defense is usually that the child was stillborn; she panicked and disposed of the body. Thus, in cases of suspected neonaticide, the first fact to establish is whether the child was alive at the time of birth. This is often one of the most difficult things to do. The presence of intrauterine maceration may indicate an intrauterine demise while the presence of milk or any food material in the stomach would indicate that the child was alive. Unfortunately, in cases of neonaticide, the killing usually occurs immediately after birth and one does not find milk or food material in the stomach.

The standard test to determine if a child has breathed has traditionally been the hydrostatic test. This consists of determining whether the lungs float in water. If they sink, the child is presumed to have been stillborn, and if they float, the child is presumed to have been born alive. There are problems with this test. If putrefaction has taken place, then, even in the stillborn, the lungs might float. Second, some children who are delivered alive take only a few breaths and do not aerate their lungs enough to float. Because of this,

Table 10.1 Data for 2017 Showing Breakdown of Child Homicides by Age

Ages	Total murders
Infants (under 1 year)	302
1–4 years	303
5–9 years	154
10–14 years	178
15–19 years	1835

physicians have resorted to microscopic examination of the lungs. If the alveoli were collapsed, then it was presumed that the children had not breathed. If they were completely and uniformly distended (presumably by air), then the child obviously had breathed. Unfortunately, microscopic examination is even more inaccurate than the hydrostatic test. If there has been attempted resuscitation, there may be distention of the air passages and alveoli by air, and it will not be possible to determine whether the child was alive or stillborn. One of the authors had a case of a child dead 10 h intrauterine who, on microscopic examination of the lungs, showed uniform distention of all alveoli, which is consistent with a child who has breathed for several hours. The lungs did not float, however.

At the present time, the authors place most reliance on the hydrostatic test. We determine if both lungs float *in toto* and then we attempt to float sections of the lungs. If all float, then in our opinion, the child most likely breathed and was, therefore, most likely alive. This, of course, assumes that there has been no attempt at resuscitation and that there is no decomposition. The liver can be used as a marker for putrefaction as well, as the liver should sink; if the liver floats, the results of the lung float test should be negated. Other findings used to determine whether a child was alive include petechiae of the lungs or heart and air in the stomach on radiological examination. Neither of these criteria is valid. Petechiae are nonspecific and can occur from intrauterine stress, and gas in the stomach can be due to labored respiratory efforts as the infant is in transit through the birth canal.

Once it has been established that a child was born alive, one has to determine how it was killed. The simplest, most convenient and probably the most common method of killing infants of this age is by suffocation. This can be accomplished by the direct application of a hand over the face, by obstructing the nose and mouth with an object such as a pillow or by placing the child in a plastic bag. Less common methods are strangulation, stuffing the mouth with rags or toilet paper, drowning the child in a toilet or bathtub, throwing the child off a building and abandonment, with death caused by exposure or lack of care.

Deaths following abandonment may be unintentional in that the mother places the child in an area where she expects it to be found, but for some reason it is not, or environmental conditions (such as temperature) change radically. Given moderate temperatures, newborns can survive 7–10 days without food or water. This was illustrated in the Mexico City earthquake of September 1985 where 44 newborns were buried beneath tons of debris when a hospital collapsed.[2]

The more violent methods of homicide used on older children are rarely used in neonates. People generally do not beat or stomp neonates. Unfortunately, suffocation of a neonate usually leaves no physical signs. Thus, the pathologist can make this diagnosis only if the mother leaves the baby in a plastic bag, leaves toilet tissue in the mouth or confesses. If none of these occur, then one can only speculate as to the cause of death.

If the body of a newborn is placed in a warm dry atmosphere, it will frequently undergo mummification. This may be aided by the relatively bacteria-free condition of a newborn. Mummified infants are occasionally found in trunks in attics and beneath floorboards of old houses.

Infanticide

Once past the first few days of life, the methods used to commit homicide change radically. In addition, the mother is joined by the husband, boyfriend or babysitter as possible perpetrators. Most child homicides occur in the first 2 years of life, the majority in the first year, with a steep decline after the second year. In 2017, 303 children between the ages of 1 and 4 years were murdered in the United States.[1]

The murders of young children can be placed in a number of categories. There is the classical battered child, with its variant the neglected or starved child; the "impulse" or "angry" homicide, with its variant the "punished" child (often a scalded child); and the "gentle" homicide, smothering, with its variant the lethal form of Munchausen's syndrome by proxy. There is also a miscellaneous category for deaths that do not fit into any of these categories.

Contrary to what one would conclude from reading the clinical medical literature and the popular press, deaths of children do not usually involve the classical battered baby syndrome, but rather are more likely "impulse" or "angry" homicides. In the authors' experience, most child homicides fall in this category.

In a series of 101 homicides of children aged 5 years or younger who died of blunt force injuries, approximately one-third of the children showed absolutely no external evidence of injury.[3] In others, external injuries were relatively mild and tended to be about the head and neck. In the study, the majority 49.5% were 12 months of age or less, with the incidence of injury and death decreasing per year with age. Craniocerebral injuries accounted for death in 72% of the children, 21% were thoracoabdominal injuries and 7% had both head and thoracoabdominal injuries. Review also found that, as the age of the child increases, abdominal injuries become more common as a cause of death.

In children dying of head injuries, the most common finding is a subdural hematoma with or without a skull fracture. The authors reviewed a series of deaths of young children in which there was epidural, subdural or subarachnoid hemorrhage or a combination of these. The five cases of epidural hematoma all showed fractures. In four children with only subarachnoid hemorrhage, one showed no fractures. In 39 children dying with subdural hematoma, (in four cases bilateral), 17 (43.6%) did not show skull fractures. The four cases with bilateral subdural hematomas had skull fractures. Fractures of the skull seem to be more commonly associated with bilateral subdural hematoma and subarachnoid hemorrhage than single-sided subdural hematomas.

In the children dying of abdominal injuries, 76% had injuries of the intestine, pancreas or mesentery, 14% had liver injuries and 2% injuries to both the liver and intestines.[3]

In children dying of blunt force injuries, there are usually multiple contusions and abrasions of the body, recent and healing, most commonly about the head. Lacerations, burns and patterned injuries caused by belts, coat hangers and sticks might also be present. Parallel rows of linear contusions with intervening pale skin suggest a belt or stick; loop-shaped marks suggest a coat hanger or electric cord (Figure 10.1).

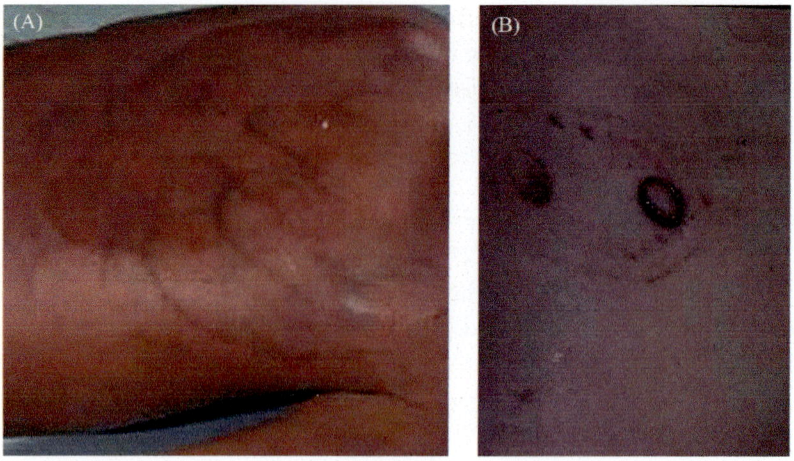

Figure 10.1 (A) Loop-shaped contusions caused by coat hanger. (B) Imprint of belt.

Contusions may be very difficult to see, especially in dark-skinned children. Therefore, it is suggested that long cuts be made down the back, buttocks and extremities to look for soft-tissue hemorrhage (Figure 10.2).

The interior of the mouth should always be examined for lacerations and contusions of the frenulum, gums and lips, as well as for dislodged teeth that might have been caused by blows to the mouth (Figure 10.3).

Often perpetrators may try to explain injuries found on an infant as resulting from cardiopulmonary resuscitation (CPR). Injuries to the face, lips and gums may be ascribed to attempted resuscitation. While some minor injuries of the lips can occur with resuscitation, multiple abrasions and contusions of the face do not. Rib fractures are also often ascribed to CPR. Dolinak studied the presence of rib fractures after removal of the parietal pleura in 70 infants, aged 2 weeks to 8 months, without known trauma who received CPR prior to death.[4] In the eight infants with fractures, all were anterolateral, five were bilateral, seven had multiple fractures and all had subtle fractures with little associated hemorrhage located. Posterior rib fractures are not associated with CPR and are often indicative of inflicted injury.

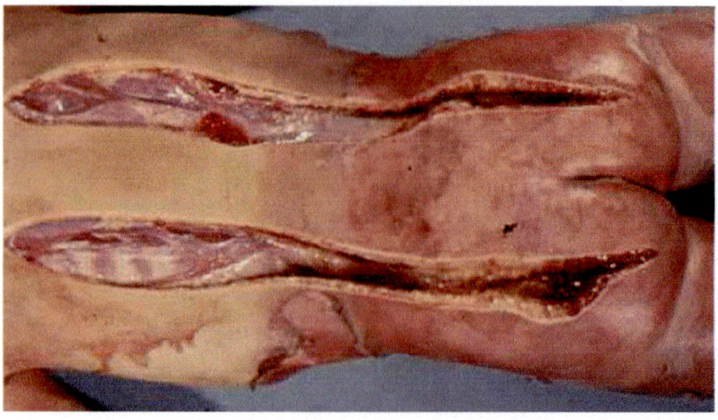

Figure 10.2 Long incisions made down back in search of soft-tissue hemorrhage.

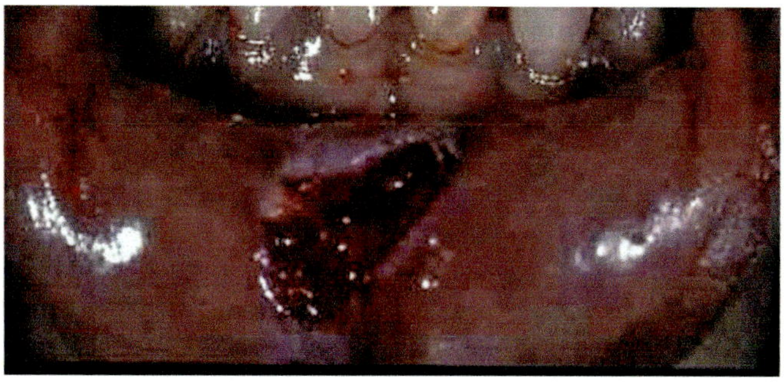

Figure 10.3 Laceration of mucosa of lip caused by blow to mouth.

While infant homicides are most often due to blunt force, infants can also be shot, stabbed and poisoned, just as older children. Poisoning is very easy in infants since they are often bottle fed. The authors have had a number of apparent Sudden Death in Infancy (SIDS) cases in which toxicological analysis revealed the deaths to be caused by drug toxicity.

Battered Child Syndrome

The battered child syndrome refers to a condition characterized by repeated intentional acts of trauma to a young child inflicted at the slightest or most trivial provocation. Deprivation of food and water is a variant of this trauma. Classically, the child presents to a physician or an emergency room with an acute injury accompanied by evidence of both old and recent bruises, fractures and other injuries. There might be skull or extremity fractures, ruptured viscera, subdural hematomas or burns. There is often a delay in bringing the child to the hospital, with an explanation by the parents that they did not realize that the child was so ill. There is usually a significant discrepancy between the history given by the parents and the clinical findings. The explanation as to how the recent trauma occurred is vague, inconsistent or contradictory with the injuries. Multiple bruises are ascribed to the fact that the child "bruises easily" or is "always falling down." Head injuries are said to have occurred when the child fell from the arms of the parent, fell out of a high chair or rolled off a table or bed. In the case of burns, children are alleged to have put their hands in boiling water, pulled a pot of hot water on themselves, climbed into a tub and turned on the hot water (or it may be alleged that a sibling turned on the hot water). If a child is starved and dehydrated, they are described as a "fussy eater" who seems to "spit everything up." There is often severe diaper rash, which is said to be because the child has "very tender skin" and seems to be "allergic to everything."

Prior to 1962, the battered child syndrome was unrecognized. In 1946, John Caffey, a Pittsburgh radiologist, wrote an article entitled "Multiple Fractures in the Long Bones of Infants Suffering from Chronic Subdural Hematoma."[5] Dr. Caffey described in detail the history of six infants aged 2 weeks to 12 months with chronic subdural hematomas and a total among them of 23 fractures of the long bones. In retrospect, these are classic textbook examples of repeated assaults on infants. Caffey, however, failed to recognize the true nature of the cases; he did not comprehend the etiology of this trauma, even after he had systematically eliminated all possible disease processes.

In 1953, Silverman determined that, in children presenting this way, a history of trauma could be obtained, even if the initial history was negative, provided the family was carefully interviewed.[6] The history he obtained from the parents is the usual one given by individuals who batter children: the baby fell from the arms; the parent fell down the stairs with the baby; the baby's arms and legs got caught in the crib slabs; the parent grabbed the child to save it from a collapsing bassinet; the parent was throwing the child in the air, playing a game, and missed; and so forth. Silverman did not realize the inadequacy and incompatibility of the history to the injury and felt that there was possibly an individual factor that predisposed some children to injury more than others.

It was left to Kempe et al. in 1962 in their article "The Battered Child Syndrome" to give widespread recognition to this syndrome.[7] The authors detailed the etiology of the trauma in infants and charged physicians with the duty to see that repetition of such injuries did not occur. Since then, there has been a tremendous amount of literature on child abuse, such that it has become almost a trendy social issue in certain circles. Thus, one sees bumper stickers stating "It Shouldn't Hurt to Be a Child." The popularity of this entity in certain sociological circles has led to an underdiagnosis of other forms of child abuse and murder. This is because everyone is looking for the classic battered baby syndrome, which is often not the presentation of a murdered child.

At autopsy, the battered child will present with multiple bruises of various ages over the body, especially about the head and chest. Most children, when they incur bruises accidentally, as in falls while playing, receive them on the lower legs or the forearms. Battered children tend to have injuries to the head. There may be patterned bruises of the extremities caused by the child's being gripped firmly with the fingers or patterned bruises of the trunk caused by the child's being hit with a belt or coat hanger. In some instances, however, the bruises are not visible in spite of beatings. Thus, again, in cases of deaths following suspected child abuse, long incisions should be made down the back, buttocks and extremities to reveal underlying soft-tissue hemorrhage. One must be careful not to confuse the Mongolian spot, an area of hyperpigmented skin in the lumbosacral region in some young children, with a bruise. Rarely, death will be due solely to exsanguination from massive bleeding into the soft tissue, caused by a beating.

Blows to the face may cause tears of the frenulum and dislodge teeth. There may be cuts on the inner surface of the lips in older children from the lips being driven against the teeth. There might be cigarette burns on the body (Figure 10.4).

On occasion, the child might have been disciplined by having its hand plunged into hot water or held against a hot surface. Hot fluids might have been thrown onto the child. There may be trickle-like burns where the water has run down the body. X-rays might reveal fractures.

Most battered children die as a result of head trauma. There are subdural and subarachnoid hemorrhages with or without fractures of the skull. It is not at all uncommon to find brain injury without skull fractures. Occasionally, a fracture might lead to secondary meningitis. There may be evidence of old subdural hematomas, as well as recent ones. Fractures of the skull and injury to the brain may be present with no or only insignificant injury to the skin and soft tissue of the head. The absence of external trauma to the head does not rule out trauma (Figures 10.5 and 10.6); in fact, neither does the absence of

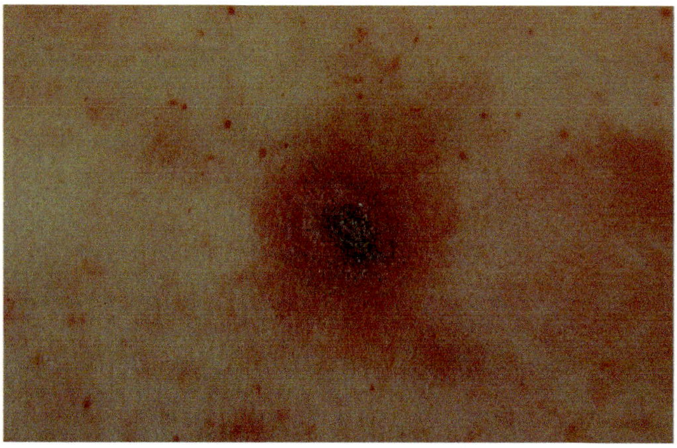

Figure 10.4 Healing cigarette burn on the chest of an infant.

internal scalp hemorrhage. A head might impact a flat, yielding surface with enough force to incur brain injuries but without incurring contusions of the scalp, either externally or internally.

While head trauma is the most frequent cause of death and morbidity in abused children, accidental trauma rarely causes intracranial injury in infants. Most (95%) of serious or life-threatening head injuries in young children and infants can be blamed on abuse; accidental trauma, such as motor vehicle accidents; falls from great heights; other less common, extremely traumatic situations account for the other cases.[8] An infant's falling from a bed, couch or high chair at most suffers a mild concussion. Trying to explain an intracranial injury with such a situation is not viable. This conclusion is consistent with a study by Helfer et al. of 85 children who fell from a crib, bed or examination table while in the hospital.[9] The height of the falls was approximately 36 in. (90 cm). The 85 falls resulted in

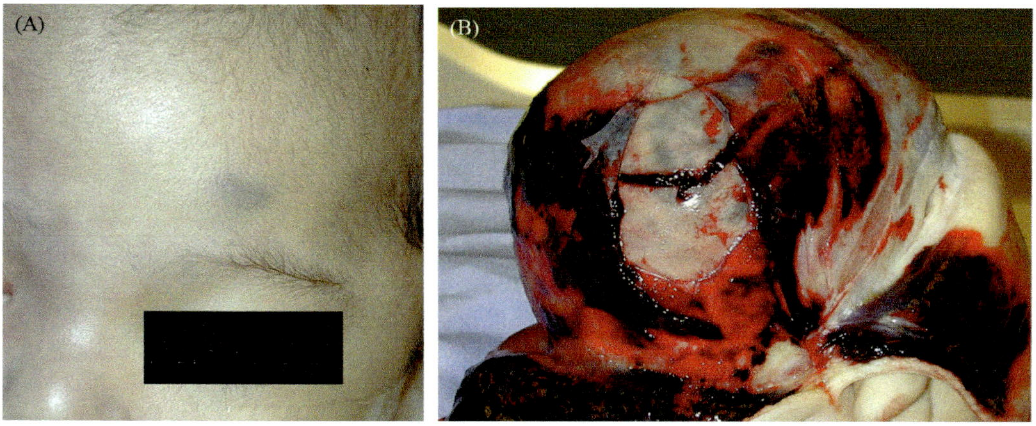

Figure 10.5 A 1-year-old child admitted to hospital in an unconscious state. (A) Only injury on the scalp was small forehead contusion, even after shaving scalp. (B) Retraction of scalp reveals massive scalp hemorrhage with skull fractures.

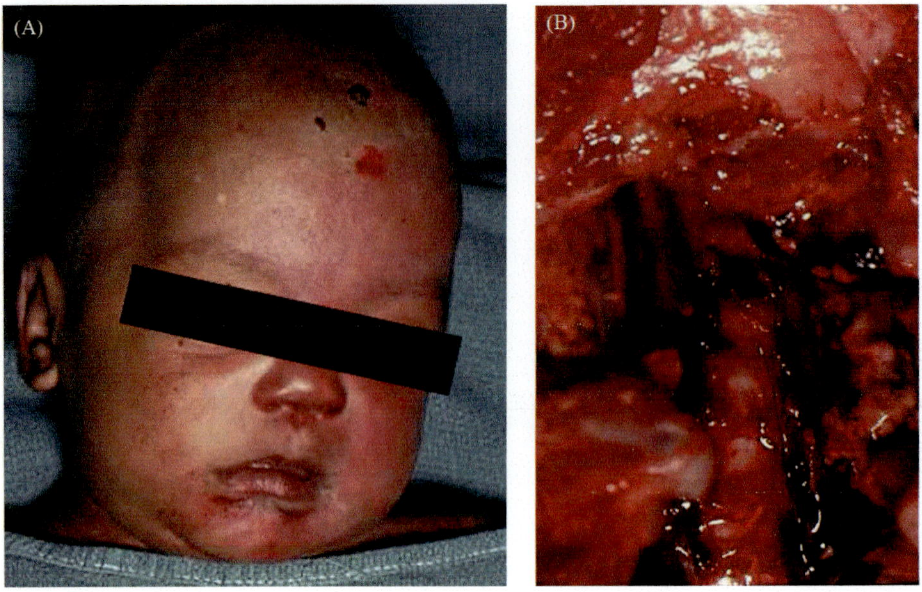

Figure 10.6 A 32-month-old child brought to medical examiner's office with diagnosis of SIDS. Externally, (A) three healing scabs of forehead and excoriation of chin. At autopsy, (B) fracture of neck at C6–7. Parent admitted slamming child's head against bed, face down.

57 cases in which there was no apparent injury, 20 children in which there was a bump or contusion, 17 cases in which there was a small cut, scratch or bloody nose and one instance in which there was a fracture of the skull. (The total number of findings adds up to more than 85 because there was more than one finding in some cases.) In the child with the fractured skull, there were neither serious nor apparent *sequelae*. There was, in fact, no sign of soft-tissue injury over the site of the fracture.

Severe head injuries are often associated with retinal hemorrhage. If the child survives, retinal scarring may result. Retinal hemorrhage can occur naturally from birth trauma, but in these instances, scarring usually does not occur.[10] While retinal hemorrhage is more common in homicides, it can occur in severe accidental head injuries. Retinal hemorrhages are also seen in bleeding disorders, sepsis, vasculopathies and increased intracranial hemorrhage. [11,12] Rarely cases have also been reported of retinal hemorrhage being caused by abrupt and severe compression of the chest, such as the effects of a shoulder harness in a car crash.[13]

After head injuries, the next most common cause of death in battered children is injuries to the abdomen. The child is either punched or kicked in the abdomen. There may be no external evidence of injury at all to the abdominal wall, yet, within the abdominal cavity, there may be lacerations of the liver, rupture of the spleen, tears in the mesentery, rupture of the bowel and a massive hemoperitoneum. A severe blow to the abdomen might cause transection of the liver, duodenum and/or pancreas at the point where it overlies the vertebral column. In cases of isolated bowel injury, death may be due to peritonitis.

Some attorneys have used as a defense that the abdominal injuries were caused by CPR. Price et al. reviewed 324 child fatalities caused by natural disease who were resuscitated.[14]

None had abdominal injuries regardless if CPR was performed by trained medical personnel or lay persons, including parents and bystanders. Bush et al. reviewed 211 child fatalities in children less than 12 years of age who died of nontraumatic causes, who had CPR.[15] Fifteen children had at least one injury; seven of which were considered medically significant. There were no injuries to the abdominal organs. Only three children had potentially life-threatening injuries: a pneumothorax; an epicardial hematoma, and pulmonary interstitial hemorrhage associated with hemoperitoneum.

The Neglected or Starved Child

Death due to neglect, including starvation, is a variant of the battered baby syndrome. Here, the child is fed insufficiently or sporadically and left to lie in its own feces and urine. The child presents with sunken, wizened features, a sunken abdomen, prominent ribs, wrinkled, loose skin with loss of turgor and an overall emaciated appearance (Figure 10.7) and often a severe, ulcerating diaper rash.

There are three possible explanations for a child presenting this way: criminal neglect, parental ignorance of the care and feeding of an infant or a congenital disease, for example, malformation of the gastrointestinal tract, or a malabsorption syndrome. Malnutrition can be the result of the mother's ignorance of proper feeding and care of the child if she is young, poor, uneducated or intellectually challenged. The child, in this instance, is often only marginally nourished. If it develops severe diarrhea, in a matter of several hours, its underlying malnutrition can be so exacerbated as to cause the child to present in a serious condition.

Most starved and neglected children are hospitalized at least once before they die. If their condition is not due to congenital disease, they rapidly gain weight in the hospital and are discharged in a healthy, well-nourished state. If such children are subsequently found dead in a starved condition, one then can conclude that this was a purposeful action and the case is a homicide. In cases where there are no prior admissions, one must first exclude any possible natural disease causing malnourishment.

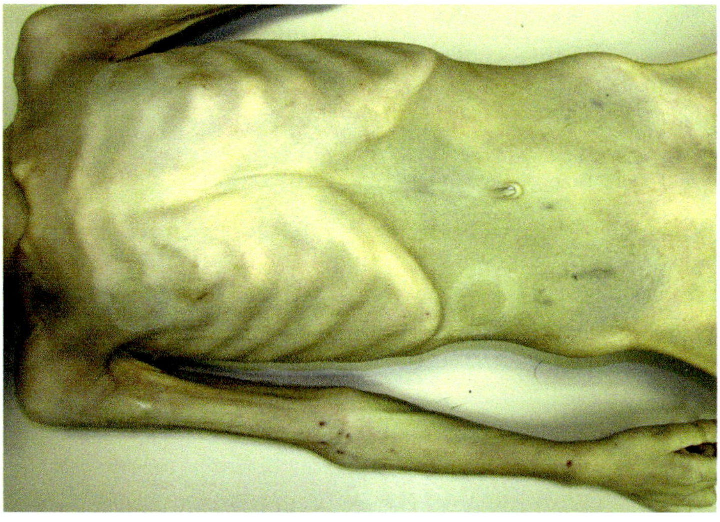

Figure 10.7 A starved child.

The "Impulse" or "Angry" Homicide

The majority of cases of infanticide or child murder fall into this category. These children are the victims of a sudden violent act brought on by a slight or trivial provocation. The perpetrator is often a husband, boyfriend or, less often, the mother. Children crying or dirtying their diapers give rise to a sudden venting of suppressed anger and frustration by the perpetrator. Typically, the child is picked up and thrown or slammed against an object, floor or wall. Aside from the fatal injuries, the child may be relatively well cared for and well nourished. Some might show a few minor old injuries but not the severe multiple injuries of different ages shown by children of the battered child syndrome. Death is usually caused by head trauma. Less commonly, there are severe abdominal injuries following a blow or kick to the abdomen. The severe nature of the internal injuries may not be visible externally. Occasionally, cases presenting as SUID have turned out to be impulse homicides with massive non-visible (at least externally) head or abdominal trauma. Explanations for the trauma usually are "He fell out of my arms"; "I was throwing him up in the air and catching him when I missed"; "He fell from his high chair"; "He rolled off the bed"; and so on.

Some individuals use immersion of a child in hot water as a disciplinary measure. Thus, an individual might plunge a child's hand or foot into boiling water to "teach" him not to perform a certain act. The forensic pathologist, however, more commonly sees the child who has been lowered into water up to his waist. Children who incur intentionally induced scalding burns are initially seen in the emergency rooms of hospitals, usually with a story that the child had been accidentally burned. Often, there will be a delay between the time of the injury and the child's being brought to the emergency room. Adults will usually ascribe this to their not having realized the severity of the injury. Yet, one will be presented with a child with second- or third-degree burns over half of the body with injuries so severe as to be obvious to even a layperson. The story of how the burns are incurred usually follows one of a few scenarios. The individual may say that they were bathing the child and did not realize the water was so hot until the child began to scream. Yet, these same adults show no evidence of any burns to their hands. With older children, they state that the child climbed into the bathtub and turned on the hot water and inexplicably was unable to get out. A variation of this is that the child was placed in the bathtub and a sibling turned on the hot water. A careful analysis of these stories shows they do not make sense, nor does the pattern of burns match the history.

In most cases of child abuse caused by scalding, adults intend to punish the child for some infraction such as dirtying a diaper. Typically, they will run water into a sink or bathtub, grasp the child underneath or by the arms and lower them into the water. What they fail to realize is that the water heater in many houses and apartments is set at around 140°F. At this temperature, full-thickness burns can be inflicted in a matter of several seconds following immersion.[16] As the temperature of the water decreases, the time needed to inflict full-thickness burns increases.

On lowering a child into the water, the child's feet contact the water first. This causes an involuntary withdrawal of the feet such that there is flexion at the knees and hips. Thus, the child is immersed in a squatting position. In most instances, the water is not very deep, somewhere between 6 and 12 in. Because of the position of the child as it is placed in the water, there will be a very characteristic distribution of burns (Figure 10.8).

The skin in the popliteal fossae and in the knee region is spared because the child flexes its legs such that the knees project above the water and the flexed thigh and calf protect the skin of the popliteal fossa. If the thigh is brought back hard against the abdomen, which is

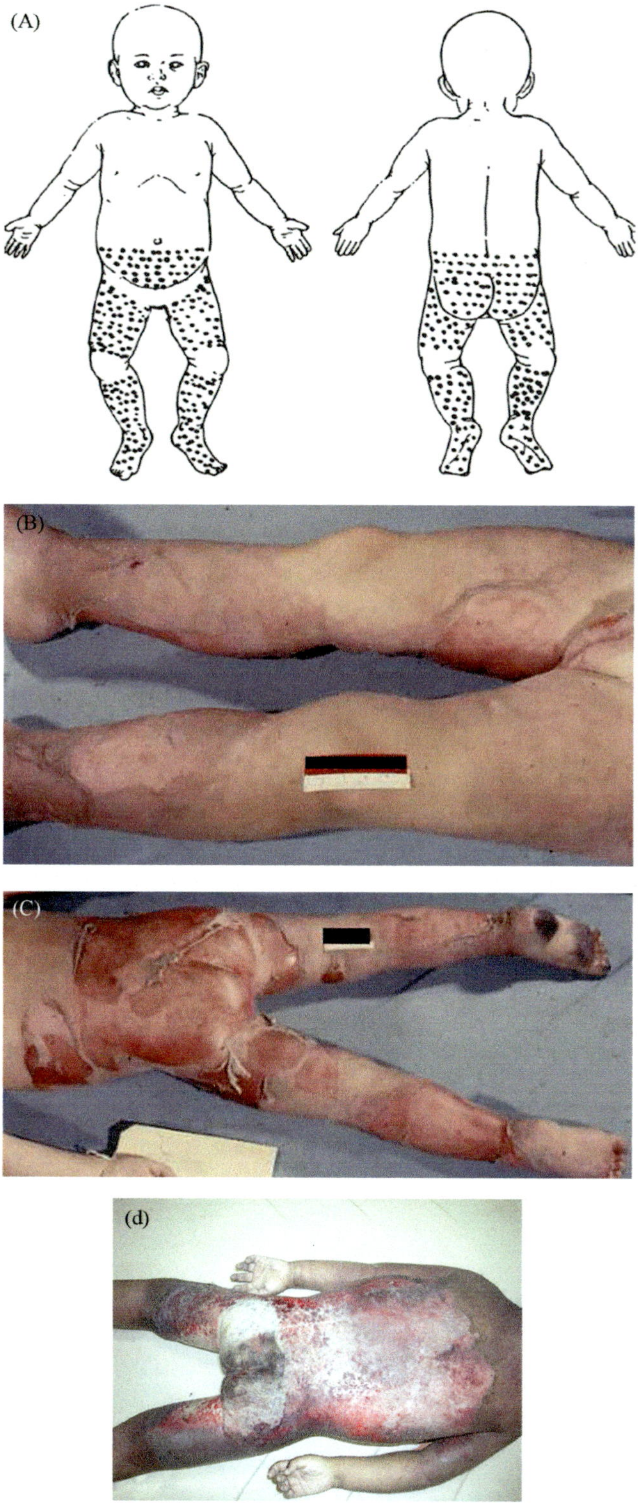

Figure 10.8 (A) Illustration of usual distribution of scalding burns with sparing of knees, popliteal fossae and inguinal regions. (B) Sparing of knees. (C) Sparing of popliteal fossa. (D) Sparing of the buttocks which was in contact with the tub.

often the case, there may also be sparing of the inguinal regions. If the child is wearing a diaper and immersion is not very long, there may be some sparing of the inguinal region by the diaper.

If a child is burned accidentally, such as may occur if they drop a hot liquid on themselves, a particular pattern of the burn can usually be seen. Usually, the burn shows irregular margins and is of a nonuniform depth. The burn will also show central larger area where the majority of the liquid first came into contact with the child, with smaller, satellite burns surrounding. Typically, fluids flow down from the initial contact and may show an "arrow down" pattern pointing downward on the body.[17] The presence of clothing or intermediary substances may also affect the pattern of the burn as well. The pattern of the burn most be considered as part of the burn investigation, as not all burns are intentional. Unfortunately, however, throwing a hot liquid on a child may resemble the pattern created if the child spilled the liquid on him/herself accidentally, so a thorough investigation including circumstantial information and physical findings must be undertaken.

Table 10.2 shows the correlation between water temperature and time necessary to cause epidermal damage and full-thickness burns. It is based on human experimentation.[16] Because the individuals involved were adults, it is probable that the times are actually shorter for young children since they have thinner, more delicate skin.

The Gentle Homicide

Probably the most commonly missed method of homicide in infants and young children is smothering. Based on the authors' experiences, smothering is, after impulse homicides, the second most common type of homicide in infants. In infants, smothering is very easily accomplished. One closes off the child's nose with two fingers, at the same time pushing up on the lower jaw with the palm to occlude the airway. Other methods have involved placing a pillow or towel over the child's face and pressing down; pushing the face down into bed clothing, or just covering the nose and mouth with one's hand. These descriptions are based on either confessions or witnessed homicides. In a few cases, attempted homicides have been videotaped.

The true number of smothering in infants is not known and can never be known until there is some scientific test to determine whether an individual has been smothered. The amount of force necessary to produce smothering is so minor in this age group that there is virtually never evidence of trauma. The amount of time necessary to smother an infant, such that their electroencephalogram (EEG) is flat and there is no spontaneous

Table 10.2 Water Temperature in Relation to Scalding Burn Times

Temperature (°F)	Threshold for epidermal injury (s*)	Full-thickness burns (s*)
120	290	600
125	50	120
130	15	30
140	2.6	~7
150	<1	2.3

* s = seconds.

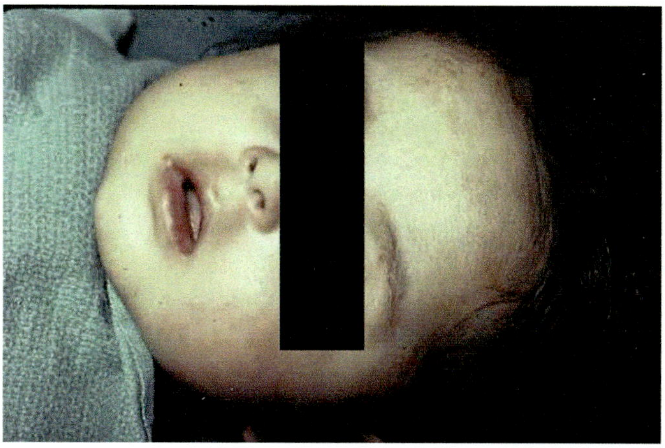

Figure 10.9 A 2-month-old child brought to medical examiner's office as a SIDS death. At autopsy, no injury and no petechiae. Mother subsequently admitted smothering child with a towel.

respiration, has been documented at 70–90 s.[18,19] Autopsy findings are essentially unremarkable, the same as those found in SUID deaths (Figure 10.9).

Undoubtedly, a small percentage of SUID deaths are due to smothering. This has been estimated as high as 10%. It has been the authors' opinion that this percentage was too high and smothering disguised as SUID probably accounted for only a few percent of alleged SUID cases.

While most homicidal suffocation of infants is sporadic, a small number of individuals, a small number of babies are smothered by individuals, virtually all of whom are mothers, practice a lethal form of Munchausen's syndrome by proxy, now known as *Factitious Disorder Imposed on Another.* In this condition, children are brought to physicians and hospitals for induced signs and symptoms of illnesses in conjunction with a fictitious history.[20] The child is usually subjected to multiple hospital admissions and extensive medical evaluations, treatments and procedures for these nonexistent medical conditions. With the more common forms of Munchausen's by proxy, the diagnosis is usually made after a number of admissions because the symptoms and signs usually do not make sense clinically and appear bizarre. Male and female children are affected equally and, in virtually every instance, the perpetrator is the mother.[20] The father is usually supportive of the mother, is unaware of what she is doing and usually stands by her after she is accused. Initially, multiple and varied tentative diagnoses are considered. The mother and child seem to be extremely close, and it is difficult for the physician or social worker to realize what the mother is doing.

The more lethal variant of Munchausen's syndrome by proxy was long unrecognized by pediatricians, though it was described in the forensic pathology literature, without resort to this terminology, by DiMaio and Bernstein in 1974.[21] In this variant, the perpetrator, usually the mother, repeatedly smothers the child into unconsciousness. Children are then either resuscitated by the parent or brought to an emergency room in a semi-moribund state, with a history of apnea, cyanosis and losing consciousness. This continues to recur until the children are admitted to the hospital. After admission, the children are worked up extensively, with no abnormal findings. Usually, these children never have these episodes of apnea and cyanosis while in the hospital. If they do, a careful history reveals that the parents who have witnessed these attacks outside the hospital are alone with the children in the hospital room at the time the attack occurs. After discharge from the hospital, the "attacks" continue until either the diagnosis is made or the children killed.

Rosen et al. were the first to describe two siblings with recurrent cardiorespiratory arrest caused by smothering by the mother, in which the act was documented on videotape.[19] The first child was a 5-month-old girl admitted for cardiorespiratory arrest. Her 4-year-old brother had had a similar medical history. The mother gave a history of almost daily episodes of apnea, cyanosis, bradycardia and loss of consciousness since 1 week of age. The attacks were very common, with the longest period between attacks only 72 h. These attacks occurred whether the child was asleep or awake. The child had been extensively worked up by computerized tomography, ECG and EEG and had been given multiple anticonvulsive medications. She had had multiple apneic episodes in the hospital and was found apneic, cyanotic, bradycardic and unresponsive. Ventilation with oxygen and closed chest massage always resuscitated the child. On this admission, however, the physicians became suspicious and, using video equipment, were able to document the mother smothering the child by placing the palm of her right hand over the baby's face. She kept the hand in position for 90 s. The heart rate began to fall 30 s after the obstruction of the airway. The EEG slowed and flattened at 90 s.

As awareness of this syndrome spread among pediatricians, and because of the availability of video cameras, other cases have been discovered and documented. Thus, Southall et al. reported two cases of apneic episodes induced by smothering that were documented by video cameras.[19] In one instance, the mother placed a T-shirt over the nose and mouth of a 22-month-old child and forced his head onto the mattress. In the second child, 6 months of age, the mother also placed a garment over the face of the child and forced its head onto the mattress. In a prior episode, which was not videotaped, but during which monitoring was being conducted, the child was found unconscious and cyanotic apparently after 2 min of smothering.

The videotapes showed that both the children struggled violently until they lost consciousness. Thus, the term "gentle" homicide is a misnomer. It took at least 70 s before electroencephalographic changes, probably associated with loss of consciousness, occurred. No marks were seen on the lips or nose. Southall et al. describe a series of physiological changes observed by their recording during the smothering.[20] Initially, there was the sudden onset of large body movements, apparently the child's violent struggling against the smothering. At 1 min, there was the appearance of a series of deep breaths occurring at a relatively slow rate with a prolonged expiratory phase, in other words, a "gasping" respiratory pattern. About this time, the EEG showed large slow waves progressing to an isoelectric baseline indicative of cerebral hypoxemia.

Deaths from the lethal form of Munchausen's syndrome by proxy may also be diagnosed as cases of "near-miss SIDS" (an entity which may not exist). Berger presented two cases of child abuse by suffocation presenting as near-miss SIDS.[22] Fortunately, both children survived. The perpetrator was the mother in both instances. She apparently put her hand over her child's nose and mouth. Minford also reported child abuse presenting as apparent near-miss SIDS.[23] Again, the child did not die. The mother admitted holding his nose, causing the child to become cyanotic and apneic.

Familial SIDS has also been invoked as a defense in Munchausen's syndrome by proxy death cases. In one instance, a mother was indicted by the grand jury for smothering two children, though she was never tried for either death, because the district attorney refused to try the case. He was advised by a pediatrician that the two deaths were examples of hereditary SIDS and was quoted the work of Steinschneider who argued a hereditary basis for SIDS, leading to the widespread use of apnea monitors for prevention.[24] Forensic pathologists were immediately skeptical about the article, strongly suspecting serial homicide, however, following the publication of Steinschneider's article, a number of additional articles appeared in the medical literature describing multiple cases of SIDS in families, thus appearing to confirm that SIDS was indeed hereditary. In March 1994, the mother cited in the Steinschneider's article confessed to smothering all five of her children because she could not stand their crying. She was subsequently tried and convicted of homicide.[18,20]

While such cases may be difficult to prove in court, without video evidence, United States v. Woods is a landmark case that set a precedent for allowing evidence during trial that a defendant may have committed similar crimes in order to prove corpus delicti, that a murder had in fact been committed. At trial evidence was allowed to show that over a 23-year period of time, eight other children, six of whom died, suffered similar medical arrests in the defendants care as did the child she was on trial for murdering. The defendant had not been previously charged or convicted with any crimes involving the eight other children. The court found that the extraneous evidence involving these other children showed the child, who she was on trial for murdering, was in fact a victim of murder and whose death was not result of some unknown medical illness. The admission of these repeated incidents were allowed into evidence under an argument, similar to the doctrine of chances, to show that repeated incidents of the same kind are unlikely to happen to the same person by accident. This case is especially important in the prosecution of child abuse cases where children, due to age and condition, are unable to give witness testimony against their abuser (Personal Communication Samantha DiMaio, J.D.).

Shaken Baby Syndrome

> The most notorious description of the sequela of violent shaking was published in 1871; it involved an incident in July 1862 and a young girl *"who grabbing her victim under the arms, began shaking her violently," "shook her backward and forward with all her might... as Alice went on shaking...{the victim} kept on growing shorter—and fatter—and softer—and rounder—and was a kitten, after all." "If any one of them an explain it" said Alice... "I'll give him sixpence. I don't believe there's an atom of meaning in it."* (As told in Louis Carroll's *Alice's Adventures in Wonderland.*)

The concept of the shaken baby injuries, that is, shaken baby syndrome (SBS), was introduced by John Caffey in 1972 to describe a clinical pathological entity in infants characterized by retinal, subdural or subarachnoid hemorrhages caused by violent shaking.[25] As described previously in the chapter, he had previously written a paper entitled "Multiple Fractures in the Long Bones of Infants Suffering from Chronic Subdural Hematoma"[5] in which he failed to recognize the true etiology the syndrome as being traumatic. Years later he then hypothesized that the syndrome was due to shaking a child causing a whiplash action of the child's relatively heavy head in association with weak neck muscles, an immature, partially membranous skull, a relatively large subarachnoid space and a soft, immature brain. In other words, these injuries were not caused by direct-impact injuries to the head, but rather by indirect acceleration-deceleration traction stresses caused by the head's whipping back and forth. Interestingly, many of the cases described in Caffey's original paper would not be classified as examples of SBS nowadays, as no brain injury was involved. Caffey's paper also suffered from a number of scientific issues and likely would not be published today. Most of his paper was conjecture without any scientific basis, such as over-vigorous "burping" might be fatal and breath-holding spells, body-rocking and head-rolling could be damaging to the brain, as well as 15 of the 27 cases presented being from *Newsweek* magazine.[25] In formulating SBS, Caffey took a number of diverse observations: intracranial bleeding and retinal hemorrhage and a lack of evidence of head impact to construct a unifying hypothesis.[25] A hypothesis, however, is not necessarily a truth. One is obligated to either prove or refute a hypothesis. The way to accomplish this is by experimentation and repeated objective observations to exclude other possible explanations.

In most of the original reports on SBS, the diagnosis was made on a clinical basis. If death occurred, autopsies were not always performed and scant mention was made of the findings. Following the initial description, as more cases of this "syndrome" were diagnosed and studied, injuries to the scalp and skull (contusions and fractures), explainable only by impact trauma, began to be detected in alleged cases. In Duhaime et al.'s case series of 48 infants and young children diagnosed as SBS, 13 of these children died.[26] Seven showed no evidence of blunt trauma to the head clinically (i.e., scalp contusions, subgaleal or subperiosteal hemorrhage or a skull fracture). At autopsy, however, all 13 children had evidence of blunt head trauma: 8 had soft-tissue contusions and 5 had contusions and skull fractures. Of the seven deaths in which blunt trauma to the head was missed clinically, four presented with the classical symptoms of retinal hemorrhage, subdural hematoma and subarachnoid hemorrhage. The other three, while having subdural hematoma and subarachnoid hemorrhage, did not have retinal hemorrhage.

Because of the detection of impact trauma in cases alleged to be due to SBS, some authors modified the terminology to the "shaken impact syndrome."[27] In this "revised" version of the syndrome, the child is shaken, presumably causing retinal hemorrhages and intracranial bleeding, and then the head is impacted against a hard surface, causing contusions and fractures and presumably additional intracranial hemorrhage. However, no differentiation between pre-impact intracranial trauma from postimpact is given. To many observers, the "shaken impact syndrome" appears to be an attempt to explain away inconvenient observations that call into question the existence of the SBS itself.

To prove the concept of SBS by observation, one must have objective evidence that excludes other etiologies. The original observations, in which head impact was "excluded," were almost all clinical and did not involve autopsies. By virtue of this, the quality of the observations is open to serious question. Cases where the child does not die and the absence of signs of impact are based on external and radiological examinations cannot be used to substantiate the existence of this entity, as there can be extensive impact injury, such as skull fractures, without either external or radiologic evidence of trauma. Absence of external or radiological evidence of injury, in cases where massive trauma is demonstrated at autopsy, is routinely seen by all experienced forensic pathologists. When alleged cases of SBS began coming to autopsy, evidence of impact (contusions, fractures) was observed. If there is a skull fracture, a subgaleal hematoma or scalp hemorrhage, one does not need to invoke shaking as an etiology, as an already proven etiology already exists – impact. There is no need for one to propose two causes for injuries in a case where one would be sufficient. Thus, one cannot use these cases to prove the existence of SBS since there is a plausible and accepted explanation for the injuries, namely, an impact of the head.

An attempt to validate SBS experimentally with a biomechanical study was made by Duhaime et al.[26] They subjected models of 1-month-old infants, implanted with an accelerometer, to repetitive violent shaking by adult males and females. After each shaking episode, the occipital area of the model was impacted against either a metal bar or padded surface. The results of 69 shaking tests were then compared with 60 impacts. The mean peak tangential acceleration was 9.29 g for the 69 shaking episodes and 428.18 g for the 60 impacts. Mean time intervals were 106.6 and 20.9 ms, respectively. Thus, acceleration due to impact exceeded acceleration due to shaking by a factor of nearly 50 times. As expected, impact against a padded surface was associated with significantly smaller acceleration (mean 380.6 g) and a longer time pause (mean 24.22 ms) than against a metal bar (489.5 g and 17.13 ms).

Both the magnitude of angular acceleration and the time interval of the acceleration are important biomechanical factors influencing the nature of the injuries. Large angular accelerations over short time intervals tend to result in subdural hematomas, while longer intervals are associated with diffuse axonal injury. Based on work by Thibault and Gennarelli on subhuman primates, the angular acceleration and velocity associated with shaking is below the injury range for concussion, subdural hematoma or diffuse axonal injury, while the results from the impacts are within the range.[28]

What about the rare case of traumatic intracranial bleeding in a child where there is no evidence of impact on the scalp or skull? Absence of trauma does not preclude impact. The authors have seen numerous cases of witnessed impact involving both adults and children who subsequently died of head trauma in which there was no evidence of impact in the scalp or skull at autopsy. This observation is explained nicely by Bernard Knight, in his book *Forensic Pathology,* stating "Although shaking presumably may cause subdural hematoma (SDH), it is likely that it is a relatively uncommon cause, compared with impact. This situation may well have arisen because a blunt impact upon the head of an infant, if spread over a wide area following contact with a flat surface, can leave no external scalp mark, no subscalp bleeding and no fracture of the skull — yet the transmitted forces can still be sufficient to cause high strain — shearing stresses within the cranial cavity leading to subdural bleeding."[29]

Some practitioners contend that retinal hemorrhages are pathognomonic of the SBS and make the diagnosis of this entity based on their presence alone. The problems with this assertion are twofold. First, the underlying premise (the existence of the SBS) is unproven. Second, retinal hemorrhage can occur with other etiologies as discussed previously. Thus, the mechanism(s) causing retinal hemorrhages are unknown though increased retinal venous pressure, extravasation of subarachnoid blood and traction of retinal vessels at the vitreoretinal interface due to angular deceleration have all been proposed.[30]

Another aspect of the shaken baby theory that appears to be ignored by proponents of this entity is the lack of neck and cervical spinal cord injuries. If the head is whipping back and forth with such velocity as to tear cerebral blood vessels and cause retinal hemorrhage, why are there no fractures of the cervical spinal column? Some argue that the suppleness (bendability) of the spine in small children prevents injury to the bony structures; however, this does not explain the lack of spinal cord injuries. The cord should be crushed, or at least stretched or torn, by the "supple" vertebrae shifting back and forth; however, such injury is not described in these cases.

Some advocates of SBS contend that the presence of epidural hemorrhage in the cervical spinal area confirms the diagnosis of shaking. Harris and Adelson studied 19 infants dying of natural disease or SIDS.[31] They found epidural hemorrhage of varying degrees in 18 cases. They concluded that the presence of epidural hemorrhage in the cervical cord area was not related to trauma, not damaging to the cord and probably due to hemodynamic forces. In fact, this is often seen in nontrauma cases as a result of lividity and rupture of the spinal vessels posteriorly. It can also be created artifactually if the spinal cord is opened via an anterior approach due to cutting through the vascular bone marrow in the process. The case, in a study of this phenomenon in 50 children below the age of 3 years, some of whom had been allegedly shaken, found no relationship between shaking and epidural hemorrhages.[12]

In recent years, some have argued that SBS occurs due to neck trauma, not head trauma;[31,32] however, this hypothesis still does not explain the injuries often ascribed to SBS – namely, the classic triad of subdural hemorrhage, retinal hemorrhage and encephalopathy. In fact, Lynøe et al. studied the evidence for SBS using a tool to assess bias in research (QUADAS).[33] They assessed 3773 abstracts and 30 full articles. Of the articles, 28 were found to have a high degree of bias, including methodological shortcomings and circular reasoning, and the other two were found to have moderate bias – no study was found to have a low risk of bias. The authors concluded that "…there is insufficient scientific evidence on which to assess the diagnostic accuracy of the triad in identifying traumatic shaking."[33]

Thus, the authors have grave reservations as to the existence of SBS as was expressed in the first edition of this book. Since then, there has not been a cause to change this opinion but rather to solidify it. There is just no conclusive evidence that this entity exists. However, the authors do feel that the injuries ascribed to shaking are indeed inflicted; they are simply due to impact of the head with or against an object rather than whiplash injuries due to shaking.

Non-Inflicted Causes of Intracranial Hemorrhage

While most children presenting in the first few years of life with intracranial bleeding and retinal hemorrhage are victims of child abuse, this is not absolute. Children do have accidents. Most such accidents, however, are clear-cut and involve significant violence, for example, a motor vehicle accident or a fall from a great height.

In rare instances, natural disease can present a picture resembling child abuse. One rare example is rupture of a cerebral aneurysm.[34] Another is late-form hemorrhagic disease of the newborn,[35] which is caused by vitamin K deficiency. Typically presenting 4–6 weeks after birth, it is manifested by intracranial bleeding (subdural, subarachnoid, intracerebral) as well as bleeding in the skin, gastrointestinal tract and urogenital tract. Rutty et al. described the case of a 9-week-old boy brought to the hospital unconscious, with a right subdural hematoma and bilateral retinal hemorrhage.[35] With such a presentation, the first thought is child abuse. In this case, because the child lived long enough to get to the hospital and survive 24 h, hematological tests could be performed revealing elevated levels of "protein-induced vitamin K absence" (PIVKA). Severe vitamin K deficiency results in production of this nonfunctioning protein. This and other tests confirmed the diagnosis of late-form hemorrhagic disease of the newborn. If the child had died at home or had been dead on arrival at the hospital, the diagnosis of a natural disease would not have been made and the case thought to be child abuse. As no impact points to the head would have been found, many individuals would have described the death as a classic case of SBS.

Child Homicides

Homicides in children is a very broad topic, encompassing a multitude of different causes including poisoning, stabbing, clubbing, drowning and shooting. Generally, the perpetrators fall into one of a number of types. There is the psychotic assailant, often a parent, who will shoot, stab or club the child for some delusional reason. These assailants usually make no attempt to conceal their actions. They might say that the child was possessed by the devil or is the devil. Such deaths present very little problem to either the medical examiner or the police agency, because the perpetrators are quite willing to describe in detail what they have done and the cause of death is quite obvious.

The second type of perpetrator is the sane individual who commits murder for reasons that might or might not be apparent. Such an individual might use obvious violence (e.g., stabbing), but claim that the assailant was another individual, or that the child was kidnapped. They might attempt to make a death appear to be an accident. Thus, the perpetrator will relate that a child accidentally drowned in the bathtub or fell into a river. The deaths may be more subtle, especially if poison is used. Poisoning is very easy in children, because they are often dependent on adults for feeding. The perpetrators are generally not psychotic, but just wish to dispose of a child for some reason or other. Because of this, it is a very good idea to perform complete toxicological analysis on young children in which no anatomical cause of death is apparent, just as with SIDS deaths. In one 2-year span, one homicide was obvious, one was an accident blamed on the mother's misinterpreting the dispensation of medication and a third undetermined as to manner, but most probably a homicide. In a fourth case, where a child died of asphyxia when cotton was wedged down its throat, there was also a toxic level of propyl alcohol in the blood.

Occasionally, infants and young children are killed by their siblings. They may beat them or even smother them. Sibling jealousy might be a motive.

Radiologic Evidence of Child Abuse

The radiological features of skeletal injury can play a significant role in the diagnosis of child abuse. Radiological evidence of skeletal trauma occurs in about a third of abused children, with most such injuries occurring in the first 2 years of life.[36] The location, nature and multifocal aspect of the skeletal injuries have to be considered. Thus, epiphyseal-metaphyseal fractures of the long bones of the arms and legs and rib fractures exclusive of the newborn period are considered specific for child abuse. Multiple repetitive fractures of other areas are only suggestive of child abuse, but are not specific.

The majority of battered children are young – a third less than 1 year old and half less than 2.[37] In nonfatal cases exhibiting skeletal trauma, the most frequent sites of injury are the extremities (77%), the skull (34%) and the rib cage (19%).[37] In the extremities, epiphyseal-metaphyseal injuries are considered by many to be diagnostic of child abuse.[37,38] This is because the forces necessary to produce these fractures do not generally occur in accidental trauma at this age. In this entity, there is partial or complete separation or fracture of the epiphysis, the physis and a thin layer of metaphyseal bone due to violent traction or torsion of the limb. Microscopically, there is a transmetaphyseal disruption (microfractures) in the subepiphyseal area.[38] The typical epiphyseal-metaphyseal fractures associated with abuse are said to be fracture-separation of one or both corners of the metaphysis ("corner fracture"), fracture-separation of an arc of the metaphysis (the "bucket-handle" fracture) and complete separation with displacement of the metaphyseal fragment.

In infants and children, the periosteum can be sheared off the bone by twisting and pulling. This results in subperiosteal bleeding, with accumulation of blood between the periosteum and the cortex of the bone. New bone formation takes place in the hematoma, with bone formation along the shaft of the bone. On X-ray, the subperiosteal calcification appears as a thin line paralleling the bone.[39] In some instances, the subperiosteal bone formation can be very extensive (Figure 10.10).

Diaphyseal injuries are four times as frequent as epiphyseal-metaphyseal fractures.[36,37] The type of fractures produced may be either spiral or transverse. **Spiral fractures** are caused by twisting of an extremity. Especially in the non-walking child, they are highly suggestive of abuse. Spiral fractures, however, can occur accidentally from a fall and are not diagnostic of child abuse. **Transverse fractures** are produced by either a direct blow to the bone or a bending of the bone. Again, these can be of an accidental nature. Transverse fractures caused by blows are much more common than spiral fractures in child abuse cases.

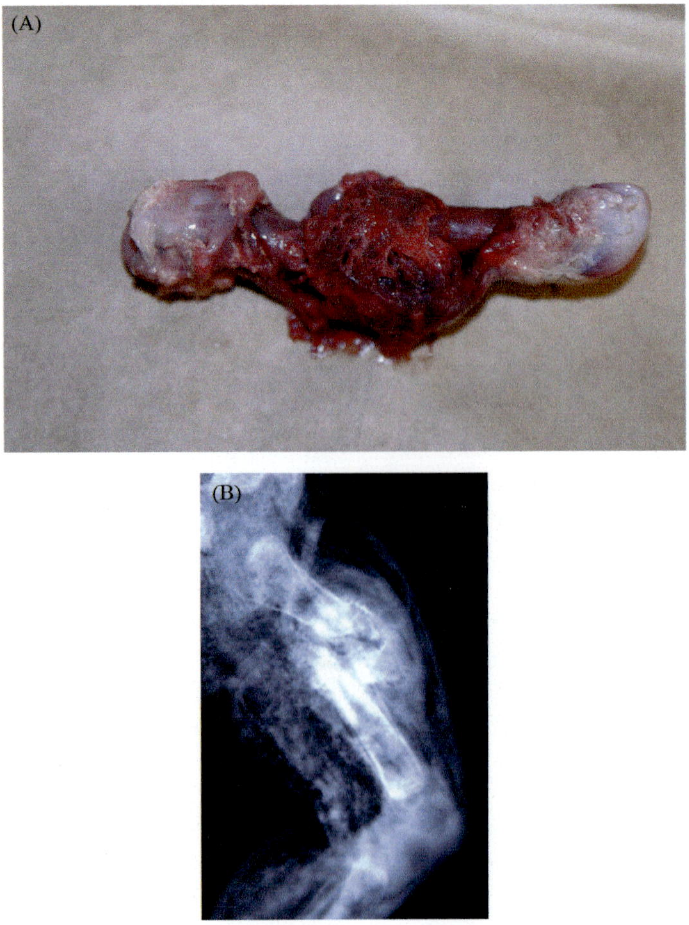

Figure 10.10 Healing fracture of femur in an infant with extensive callus formation (A) gross specimen; (B) radiograph.

A common type of injury seen in child abuse are rib fractures.[36,37] Rib fractures outside the neonatal period in a young child without an obvious history of trauma of an accidental nature, such as an automobile accident, and free of intrinsic bone disease are virtually specific for child abuse.[36,37,40] They are caused by sudden, violent compression of the chest. In battered children, they are often multiple in number, bilateral and most frequently posterior adjacent to the costovertebral junction. Most occur in children younger than 2 years of age. On X-ray and at examination, there might be evidence of healing fractures of different ages (Figure 10.11).

Posterior rib fractures in child abuse cases are believed to be due to squeezing or direct trauma to the ribs. Lateral fractures of the ribs would be due to violent anterior-posterior compression of the chest.

Occasionally, attempts have been made to explain rib fractures in young children as being caused by resuscitation. Feldman and Brewer studied 50 patients, ages newborn to 97 months (mean age 27 months), who received CPR.[41] Only one of these showed evidence of a rib fracture and this child was subsequently shown to have suffered child abuse. Betz and Liebhardt reviewed 94 cases of nontraumatic death in children of ages several days to 7 years who had CPR.[40] In two of the cases, there were rib fractures. The first was a 2-month-old with a diagnosis of SIDS. The child had bilateral, midclavicular fractures of ribs 2–5. The second child was 5 years old and had fractures of ribs 2–6 on the right in the midclavicular line. Both children had been resuscitated by physicians. Children resuscitated by nonmedical personnel had no fractures. Betz and Liebhardt point out that the fractures they observed were anterior, while most fractures from abuse are posterior. This is in agreement with the observations of Bush et al., who reviewed 211 nontraumatic fatalities of children below 12 years of age who received CPR.[15] In only one case were there rib fractures. This was a 3-month-old infant, dying of SIDS, who had bilateral fractures of the eighth and ninth ribs at the sterno-chondral junction. Thus, in children, especially infants, fractures from resuscitation are extremely rare and, when present, are anterior in location, at the sterno-chondral junction and midclavicular line.

Fractures of the clavicle are relatively uncommon in child abuse cases. Most occur in the midportion and are similar in location to those resulting from accidental trauma. Fractures of the distal ends of the clavicle are less common and are caused by sudden traction on the extremity.[38] These are more suggestive of child abuse.

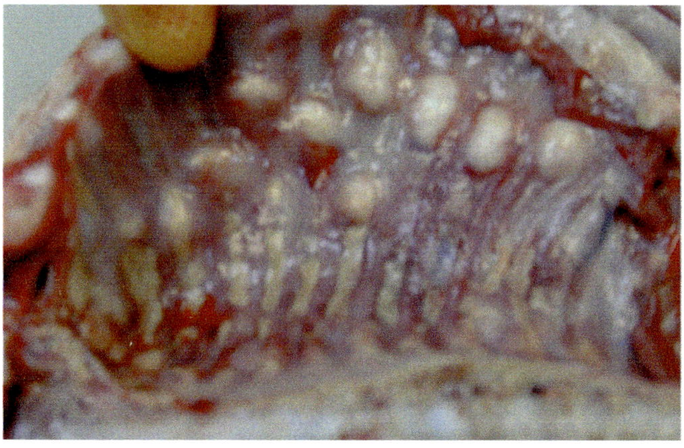

Figure 10.11 Multiple healing rib fractures in a child; several acute fractures were also present.

References

1. WISQARS Fatal Injury Database. Centers for Disease Control and Prevention. Available at: https://webappa.cdc.gov/sasweb/ncipc/mortrate.html; Accessed 11 January 2020.
2. Russell G, Mexico miracles amid the ruins. *TIME*, October 7, 1985; 126(14):38.
3. Molina DK, Clarkson A, Farley KL, and Farley NJ, A review of blunt force injury homicides of children aged 0 to 5 years in Bexar County, Texas, from 1988 to 2009. *Am J Forensic Med Pathol* 2012; 33(4):344–348.
4. Dolinak D, Rib fractures in infants due to cardiopulmonary resuscitation efforts. *Am J Forensic Med Pathol* 2007; 28(2):107–110.
5. Caffey J, Multiple fractures in the long bones of infants suffering from chronic subdural hematoma. *Am J Roentgenol Radiat Ther* 1946; 56:163173.
6. Silverman F, The roentgen manifestations of unrecognized skeletal trauma in infants. *Am J Roentgenol Radiat Ther* 1953; 69:413–426.
7. Kempe C, et al., The battered child syndrome. *JAMA* 1962; 181:17–24.
8. Billmire ME and Myers PA, Serious head injury in infants: accident or abuse. *Pediatrics* 1985; 75:340–342.
9. Helfer RE, Slovis TL, and Black M, Injuries resulting when small children fall out of bed. *Pediatrics* 1977; 60:533–535.
10. Sezen F, Retinal hemorrhage in newborn infants. *Br J Ophthalmol* 1970; 55:248–253.
11. Case MES, Neuropathology of head and neck injuries in young children. Presented at the AAFS 52nd Annual Meeting, February 21, 2000, Reno, NV.
12. Mattheij M, Venstermans C, de Veuster I, et al., Retinal haemorrhages in a university hospital: not always abusive head injury. *Acta Neurol Belg* 2017; 117(2):515–522.
13. Kelley JS, Purtscher's retinopathy related to chest compression by safety belts. *Am J Ophthalmol* 1972; 74:278–283.
14. Price EA, et al., Cardiopulmonary resuscitation—related injuries and homicidal blunt abdominal trauma in children. *Am J Forensic Med Pathol* 2000; 21(4):307–310.
15. Bush CM, et al., Pediatric injuries from cardiopulmonary resuscitation. *Ann Emerg Med* 1996; 28:40–44.
16. Moritz AR and Henriques FC, Studies of thermal injury: 11. The relative importance of time and surface temperature in the causation of cutaneous burns. *Am J Pathol* 1947; 23:695–720.
17. U.S. Department of Justice Office of Justice Programs Office of Juvenile Justice and Delinquency Prevention Burn Injuries in Child Abuse, June 2001 NCJ 162424.
18. Rosen CL, et al., Two siblings and recurrent cardiorespiratory arrest: Munchausen syndrome by proxy or child abuse? *Pediatrics* 1983; 71:715–720.
19. Southall DP, et al., Apneic episodes induced by smothering: two cases identified by covert video surveillance. *Br Med J* 1987; 294:1637–1641.
20. Zitelli BI, Seltman MF, and Shannon RM, Munchausen's syndrome by proxy and its professional participants. *Am J Dis Child* 1987; 141:1099–1102.
21. DiMaio VIM and Bernstein CG, A case of infanticide. *J Forensic Sci* 1974; 19:744–754.
22. Berger D, Child abuse simulating "near-miss" sudden infant death syndrome. *J Pediatr* 1979; 95:554–556.
23. Minford AMB, Child abuse presenting as apparent "near-miss" sudden infant death syndrome. *Br Med J* 1981; 282:521.
24. Steinschneider A, Prolonged apnea and the sudden infant death syndrome: clinical and laboratory observations. *Pediatrics* 1972; 50:646–653.
25. Caffey J, On the theory and practice of shaking infants. *Am Dis Child* 1972; 124:161–169.
26. Duhaime A, et al., The shaken baby syndrome: a clinical, pathological and biomechanical study. *J Neurosurg* 1987; 66:409–415.
27. Bruce DA and Zimmerman RA, Shaken impact syndrome. *Pediatr Ann* 1989; 18:48294.
28. Thibault LE and Gennarelli TA, Biomechanics of diffuse brain injury, in *Proc. 4th Exper Safety Vehicle Conf.* American Association of Automotive Engineers, New York, NY, 1985.

29. Knight B, *Forensic Pathology* 2nd ed. Hodder Headline Group, London, Oxford University Press, New York, 1996.
30. Duhaime A-C, et al., Nonaccidental head injury in infants—the "Shaken-baby syndrome". *N Engl J Med* 1998; 338(25):1822–1829.
31. Harris LS and Adelson L, Spinal injury and sudden infant death. *J Clin Pathol* 1969; 52:289–295.
32. Matshes EW, Evans RM, Pinckard JK, et al., Shaken infants die of neck trauma, not of brain trauma). *Acad For Path* 2011; 1(1):82–91.
33. Lynøe N, Elinder G, Hallberg B, et al., Insufficient evidence for 'shaken baby syndrome' – a systematic review. *Acta Paediatr* 2017; 106(7):1021–1027.
34. Plunkett J, Sudden death in an infant caused by rupture of a basilar artery aneurysm. *Am J Forensic Med Pathol* 1999; 20(2):211–214.
35. Rutty GN, Smith CM, and Malia RG, Late-form hemorrhagic disease of the newborn: a fatal case report with illustration of investigations that may assist in avoiding the mistaken diagnosis of child abuse. *Am J Forensic Med Pathol* 1999; 20(1):48–51.
36. Merten DF, Radkowski MA, and Leonidas JC, The abused child: a radiological reappraisal. *Radiology* 1983; 146:37–381.
37. Leonidas JC, Skeletal trauma in the child abuse syndrome. *Pediatr Ann* 1983; 12:875–881.
38. Kleinman PK, Marks SC, and Blackbourne B, The metaphyseal lesion in abused infants: a radiologic-histopathologic study. *Am J Radiol* 1986; 146:895–905.
39. Brogdon BG, *Forensic Radiology*. CRC Press, Boca Raton, FL, 1998.
40. Betz P and Liebhardt E, Rib fractures in children—resuscitation or child abuse? *Int J Legal Med* 1994; 106:215–218.
41. Feldman KW and Brewer DK, Child abuse, cardiopulmonary resuscitation and rib fractures. *Pediatrics* 1980; 73:339–342.

11 Deaths Caused by Motor Vehicle Incidents

Decisions can be like car accidents, sudden and full of consequences.

—Allison Glock

In 2018, there were nearly 40,000 deaths in the United States due to motor vehicle collisions.[1] Fatal motor vehicle crashes more commonly affect men than women and most crashes involve passenger cars or light trucks, including sports utility vehicles and vans, with approximately 10% of fatal crashes involving large trucks, including semitrucks. Drivers account for the majority of deaths in motor vehicle fatalities, accounting for about 50%, with passengers and pedestrians each representing just under 20% and motorcyclists approximately 10%.[1]

The most common cause of fatal motor vehicle collisions in the United States is driver impairment. As a general rule, approximately half of all motor vehicle operators killed in crashes are under the influence of alcohol. If one considers only drivers who cause the accidents, it would be safe to say that 65–75% are to some degree under the influence of alcohol or drugs.[2] Distracted driving, including mobile phone use and texting while driving, also accounts for approximately 10% of all fatal crashes.[3] Although texting and driving is banned in most states, the use of mobile phones while driving continues to be a major problem in the United States. It is estimated that cell phone use increases the risk of a crash by 4.5.[4]

Investigation of Motor Vehicle Deaths

Deaths due to motor vehicle crashes are dependent upon many factors, including the type of vehicle involved, the dynamics of the crash and the presence or absence of other factors, including underlying illnesses or intoxication status. Injuries can result from impaction of the individual on some portion of the interior or exterior of the car; violation of the integrity of the passenger compartment by intrusion of part of the car or of another object, for example, another vehicle or a lamppost, into the passenger compartment; ejection from the motor vehicle, either in part or entire; and subsequent fire.

It is recommended that autopsies be performed on all acute deaths in motor vehicle collisions. Autopsies are performed to:

- Determine the cause of death
- Confirm that death was caused by injuries suffered in the incident
- Determine the extent of these injuries
- Detect any disease or other factors, for example, drugs, that could have precipitated or contributed to the accident or death
- Detect any criminal activity associated with the death
- Document all findings for subsequent use in either criminal or civil actions
- Establish positive identification of the body, especially if it is burnt or severely mutilated

Crashes caused by natural disease are rare and do not represent a serious danger to the public. Sudden natural deaths at the wheel generally result in the death of only the driver, with the cause of death usually the natural disease. The driver is often able to stop the vehicle. When a collision does occur, there are usually only minor injuries with minor vehicular damage. Most commonly, these involve sudden cardiac deaths in older persons who may or may not have been actively driving at the time.

Motor Vehicle Collisions

Motor vehicle incidents can be divided into four categories, depending on how the accident occurred:

1. Front-impact crashes
2. Side-impact crashes
3. Rollovers
4. Rear-impact crashes

The probability of a fatality depends to a degree on the size and type of vehicle involved in a crash. Small vehicles, by virtue of their size, are less able to absorb crash energy. Thus, severe injury and fatalities are more common with such vehicles. Utility vehicles and pickups are generally heavier than are automobiles; therefore, the occupants of the former vehicles are more likely to survive crashes with cars. Pickups and sports utility vehicles, however, are more likely than cars to be involved in fatal single-vehicle crashes. In sports utilities, this is caused by their tendency to rollover.

Deaths are slightly more common in multiple-vehicle crashes than single-vehicle crashes. In fatal single-vehicle crashes involving a car, the frequency of the type of crash causing death, in descending order, is frontal impact, side impact, rollover and rear impact.[5] For utility vehicles and pickups, it is rollovers, frontal impacts, side impacts and rear impacts. In fatal multivehicle crashes involving a car, the frequency of type of crash in descending order is frontal and side impacts (approximately equal), followed by rear impacts and then rollovers. For pickups and utility vehicles, it is frontal impact, side impact, rear impact and finally rollover.

Front-Impact Crashes

Front-impact crashes are the type of crash that most people think of when talking about motor vehicle incidents. Textbooks tend to concentrate on this type of collision, because it is easy to explain and understand. When two vehicles crash head-on, or a vehicle crashes into a fixed object, unless the driver and passengers are restrained, they will continue their forward movement, even though the car has stopped. If unrestrained, the driver's knees will impact the instrument panel; the chest the steering wheel; and the head the windshield, sun visor region above the windshield or the frame (generally in this order). The same pattern of injuries would be true for unrestrained passengers, except they would impact the dashboard rather than the steering wheel. If the front impact is off-center, the driver or passenger might impact the A pillar with their head.

With the use of airbags and restraint devices, most injuries are due to cabin intrusion. If the drivers and passengers have restraint devices and if the passenger compartment retains its integrity, then the occupants of the vehicle should survive without any significant injury. The intrusion of part of the vehicle or another object into the passenger compartment may be transitory, with the portion of car or the object springing back. Thus, it might not at first be obvious that there has been violation of the integrity of the passenger compartment.

If the driver is restrained by belts, but without an airbag, the knees may still impact the instrument panel while the head flexes forward, with the chin impacting either the sternum or, in severe collisions, the steering wheel. Unrestrained individuals in the back seat will hit the back of the front seat, the passengers in the front seat come up against the windshield or the sun visor area. Objects protruding from the instrument panel, such as levers or knobs, can produce patterned abrasions on the victims.

If the head of the driver or front-seat passenger impacts the windshield, there will be abrasions and superficial cuts of the forehead, nose and face, with the injuries having a vertical orientation (Figure 11.1).

Thin slivers of windshield glass might be embedded in the wounds or be found loose on the clothing. The glass cuts, *per se,* are not serious, thanks to the construction of the windshield. Windshields are designed to prevent serious cuts and people going through them. The latter phenomenon, however, can still occur if the windshield pops out of the frame. Present-day windshields consist of thin outer and inner layers of glass with a thick core of plastic. Impaction of the head against the windshield with great force can cause the glass to shatter, but the plastic will only bulge.

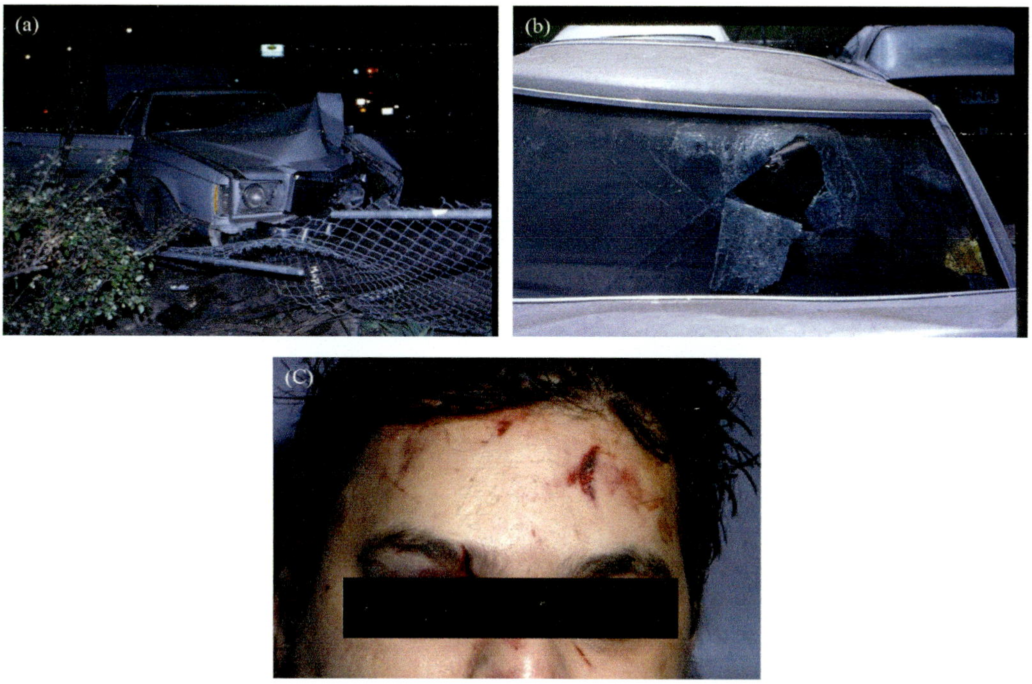

Figure 11.1 Abrasions and superficial cuts of the forehead (C) caused by impacting the windshield (A and B).

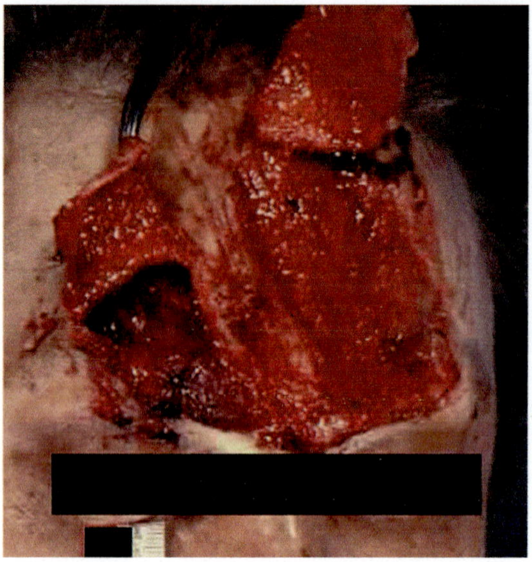

Figure 11.2 Avulsion of skin caused by impact with windshield.

Blunt force impact on the windshield, while not causing serious incised wounds, can, with enough force, produce fairly severe soft-tissue injuries. There can be partial avulsion of the skin with the avulsed skin anchored superiorly (Figure 11.2).

These wounds, because of their location, often bleed very heavily, appearing very dramatic and life-threatening. This has caused emergency room physicians to concentrate all their attention on these seemingly severe, but actually non-life-threatening, head injuries and to neglect chest and abdominal injuries that eventually caused death (Figure 11.3).

In addition to the external injuries, impaction of the head with the frame of the car above the windshield can cause basilar skull fractures, closed head injury and fractures of the neck. Basilar fractures tend to run along the length of the petrous ridges passing through the sella turcica ("hinge fractures"). Less common are ring fractures and multiple fracture lines of the base of the skull.

In neck injuries, the most common fatal injuries are upper cervical fractures or dislocation at the atlanto-occipital junction (Figure 11.4).

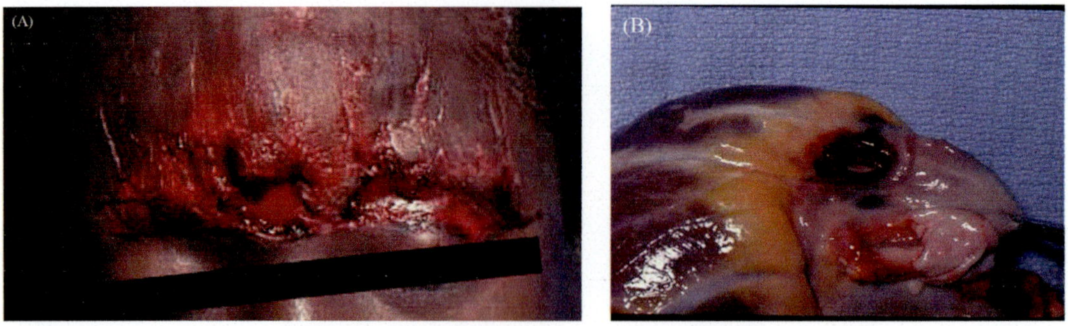

Figure 11.3 (A) A 24-year-old male with severe laceration of forehead caused by impact with windshield. Treated for nonexistent brain injuries. (B) Cause of death: a 1-cm laceration of the right atrium with hemopericardium (250 mL).

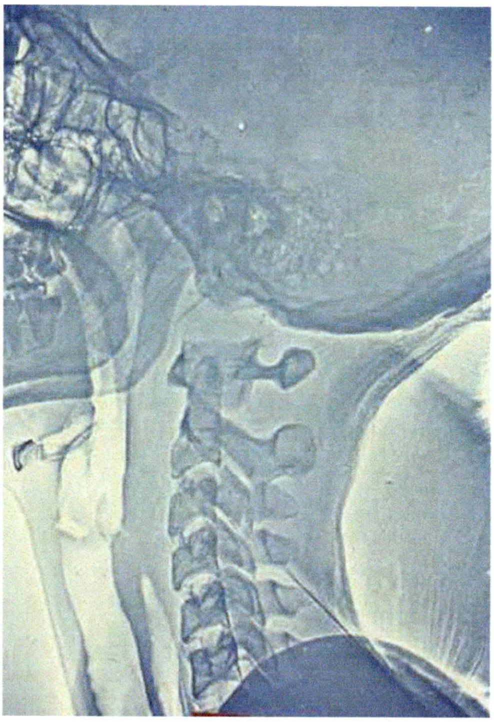

Figure 11.4 Fracture-dislocation of neck at atlanto-occipital joint.

This can result in either complete transection or crushing of the cord. In other instances, the cord is violently pulled down, with partial or complete avulsion of the brainstem, ventrally, at the ponto-medullary junction.

In the absence of airbags or belt restraints, the chest of the driver can impact the steering wheel and the chest of the passenger, the dashboard. Evidence of injury from such an impact varies from imprinted abrasions/contusions of the wheel or instrument panel to complete absence of any evidence of external injuries (Figure 11.5).

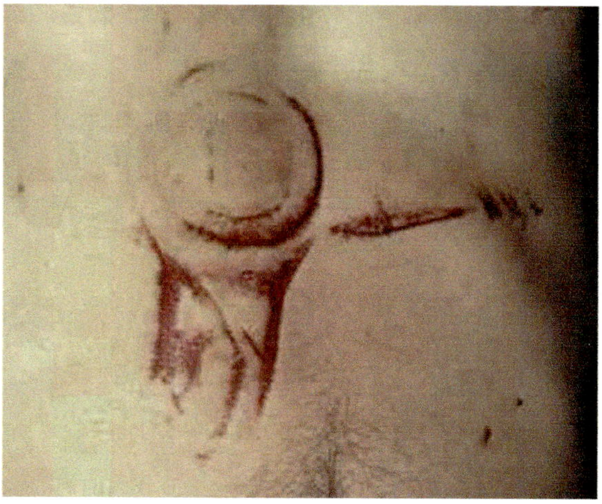

Figure 11.5 Imprint of steering wheel on chest.

The following internal injuries are fairly typical, depending on the amount of force and the age of the victim:

- Transverse fracture of the sternum (usually at the third intercostal space)
- Bilateral rib fractures
- Impaling injuries of the lung caused by fractured ribs
- Contusions, internal lacerations and rupture of the pulmonary parenchyma
- Rupture of the heart
- Transection of the aorta
- Lacerations of the liver and spleen

Because of the elastic nature of the sternum or ribs in young individuals, there can be extensive thoracic injuries without fracture. Serious chest injuries from impact against the steering wheel became less frequent with the introduction of energy-absorbing compressible steering wheel columns in the late 1960s. At the time, this was estimated to have reduced overall driver fatalities in frontal crashes 12%, with serious injury (including fatalities) reduced by 38%.[6]

One of the most common fatal thoracic injuries is transection of the aorta (Figure 11.6).

Typically, this occurs immediately distal to the origin of the left subclavian artery. Occasionally, one will see at autopsy individuals who have survived motor vehicle accidents in the past and died for other reasons. On opening the aorta, faint, horizontally oriented, linear scars on the intimal surface of the aorta distal to the left subclavian artery can be seen. These represent incomplete lacerations of the intima that subsequently healed. While the etiology of thoracic aortic lacerations has classically been ascribed to rapid deceleration, more recent work suggests that it is caused by chest compression.[7]

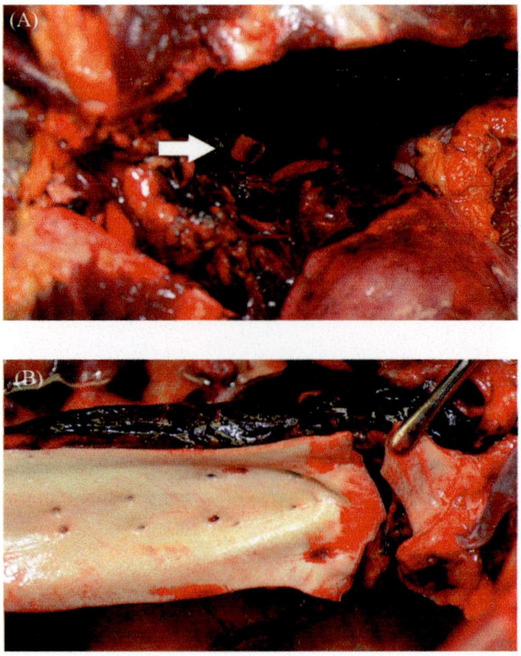

Figure 11.6 Aortic transection (A and B).

Injury to the heart is less common than aortic injuries. The most common injuries are myocardial contusion, laceration of the pericardial sac, rupture of the right atrium, rupture of the right ventricle anteriorly at the interventricular septum, rupture of the left atrium and laceration of the interatrial septum (Figure 11.7).

Occasionally, individuals die from intraparenchymal pulmonary hemorrhage caused by massive pulmonary contusions.

In addition to the chest injuries, there can be lacerations of the liver and spleen. The injuries of the liver range from superficial capsular lacerations to bursting rupture. With massive blunt trauma, there might be rupture of the left hemidiaphragm. With both splenic and hepatic injuries, the extent of the injuries may not be appreciated initially, especially in the case of subcapsular hematomas. The individual will be examined and thought to have only minor injuries. A peritoneal tap will reveal no blood. The patient will die hours, if not days, later when the subcapsular hepatic or splenic hematoma ruptures. The authors have seen deaths in individuals where the physicians were so concentrated on other injuries that they ignored the possibility of abdominal injuries. In one case, the patient was given an initial peritoneal tap with no blood found. Although the patient subsequently complained of abdominal pain and had a drop in hematocrit, the physicians were so concerned with the other injuries that they lost their patient to the liver injury.

Occasionally, there will be a motor vehicle accident in which the driver impacts the steering wheel and in which no anatomical cause of death presents after a complete autopsy and toxicological screen. There may be soft-tissue trauma to the chest and a fractured sternum or ribs, but insufficient injuries to explain death. Such deaths are caused by fatal cardiac arrhythmia secondary to a cardiac contusion. Examination of the heart might fail to

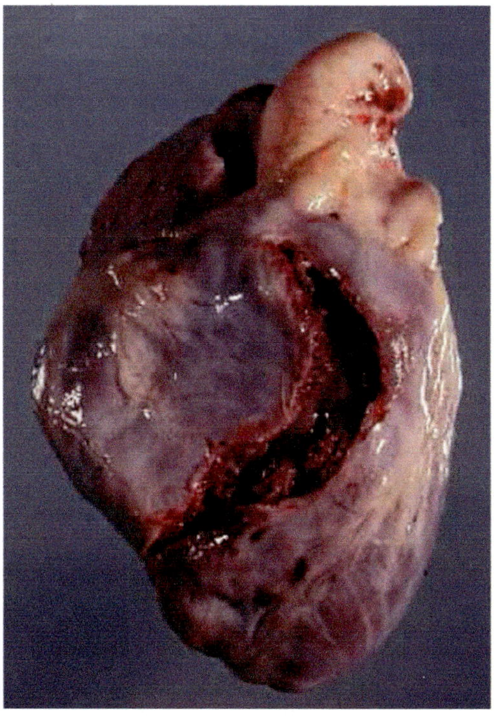

Figure 11.7 Rupture of heart caused by chest's impacting steering wheel.

reveal any evidence of impact because of the suddenness of the death. Some individuals do not develop cardiac arrhythmias until hospitalized. In these individuals, the presence of a cardiac contusion is confirmed by enzymatic tests and EKGs. The patients usually recover, though occasionally, they will die from an arrhythmia. Rarely, the authors have seen traumatic dissecting aneurysms of the left anterior descending coronary artery caused by blunt trauma to the chest.

Before death can be ascribed to cardiac contusion, positional or traumatic asphyxia (to be discussed) must first be ruled out. A careful dissection of the neck, both anteriorly and posteriorly, in the upper cervical region must also be performed. The authors have seen a number of deaths caused by posterior fracture or dislocation of the upper cervical region, while no hemorrhage was seen anteriorly or in the subarachnoid space of the brainstem. This injury would have been missed if the posterior aspect of the cervical spine had not been explored. These injuries are caused by hyperflexion of the head. In any automobile death in which no cause of death is found at autopsy, the back of the neck should be explored.

In elderly individuals, death can occur with injuries that a younger person might survive. Thus, rib fractures, minor cardiac contusions, pulmonary contusions and some minor intrathoracic or intra-abdominal injury might cause death in an elderly individual with an unstable cardiac status.

Seat belts and airbags, while effective in decreasing the incidence of death and injury, can, themselves, produce injuries and even death. Lap belts can produce tears of the mesentery and omentum and occasionally laceration of the bowel. Shoulder belt use may be reflected by a linear abrasion running downward and medially on the left side of the neck of the driver or the right side of the neck of the front passenger (Figure 11.8A).

A poorly defined area of abrasion and contusion indicating the distribution of the belt might be seen on the skin of the lower abdomen (Figure 11.8B). These injuries are also

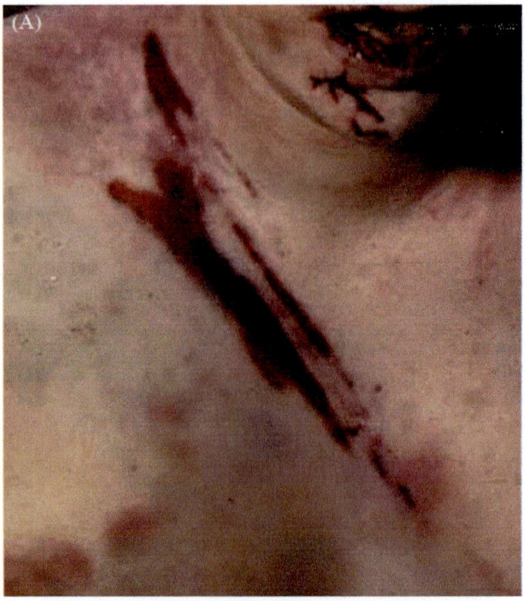

Figure 11.8 Abrasions and contusions caused by (A) shoulder belt (*continued*).

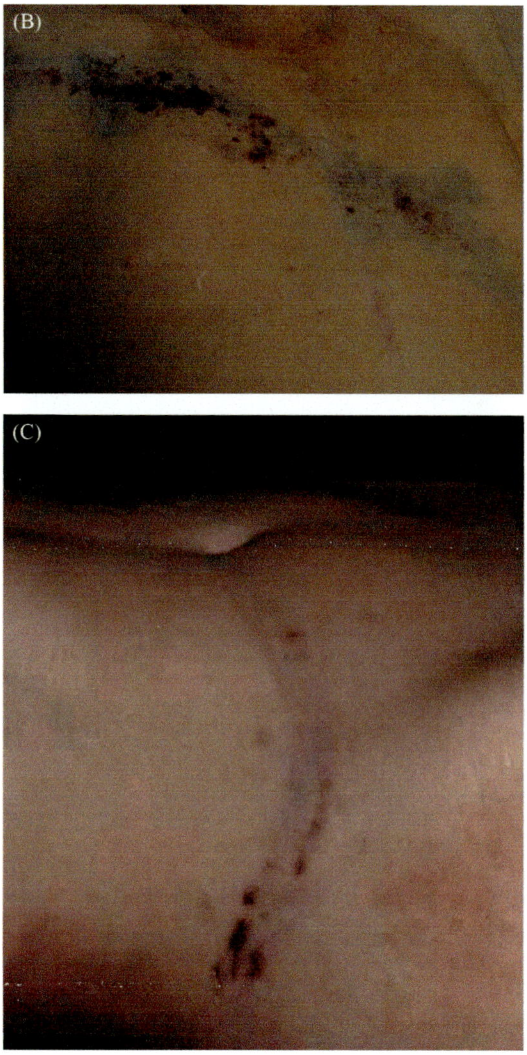

Figure 11.8 (*continued*) Abrasions and contusions caused by (B) shoulder belt and (C) lap belt.

associated with intestinal rupture, which may not be diagnosed initially. The authors have seen several cases, particularly in obese individuals, who died several days after automobile collisions with peritonitis due to undiagnosed intestinal injuries.

In addition to the aforementioned injuries, one also sees dicing injuries, which are superficial cuts of the skin caused by the fragments of glass produced when the side and back windows of a car shatter (Figure 11.9).

Glass used in these windows is tempered glass, which is designed to shatter into little glass cubes on violent impact. This is to prevent the individuals in the car from incurring serious cuts from slivers of glass. The marks produced by these little cubes of glass tend to be linear, right angled and very superficial. They are not life-threatening. Drivers typically have them on the left side of the face and forehead and the left arm; passengers on the right side of the face and forehead and right arm.

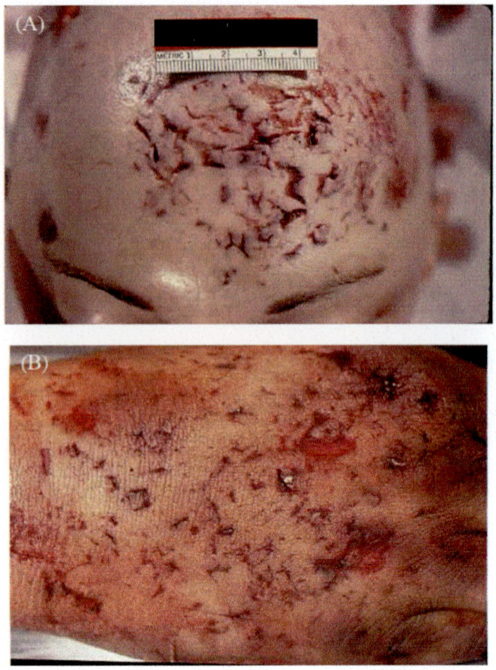

Figure 11.9 Dicing injuries of back of left hand (A) and forehead (B).

In head-on crashes, the floorboards can be driven upward and inward, twisting the foot on the ankle and causing a fracture. In other instances, if the seat goes forward, the foot can be trapped beneath the seat, breaking the ankle.

Side-Impact Crashes

The second type of collision is the side impact. In fatal crashes involving passenger cars, it is second in frequency to front impacts. These crashes usually occur at intersections when a car is struck broadside by another vehicle going through the intersection at right angles to the first. In such cases, dicing injuries can be found on either one or both sides of a driver, depending on whether the side glass is propelled into the driver; the driver into the glass, or both. Side-impact crashes can also occur when a car skids sideways, striking a fixed object such as a tree or pole with its side.

In car-to-car collisions, where the impact is to the driver's side, force is applied from the shoulder level downward. The head can flex laterally through the side window, striking the impacting vehicle. It might also impact the A or B pillars. If the impacting vehicle is a truck, the force is delivered from roof to floor level, and the intruding vehicle can make direct contact with the head. A seat belt or frontal airbag in this situation yields virtually no benefit. External injuries – abrasions, lacerations, dicing injuries and fractures – will tend to be on the left side of the body, and the left arm and leg may be fractured. Internally, fractures of the ribs tend to be predominantly on the left side. While textbooks always discuss transections of the aorta from head-on collisions, these injuries can result from a side impact as well. In addition, there might be rupture of the heart, with the same type of injuries as those in head-on collisions. Lacerations of the liver and, to a lesser degree, the spleen, can be present, as well as lacerations of the left kidney. Basilar fractures and fractures of the neck might occur. The overall impression with such cases, however, is that the injuries to the left side of the body are more severe than the right. In the case of passengers in this vehicle, the injuries will tend to be to the left side. Unrestrained front-seat passengers might be cushioned by the driver, reducing the severity of the injuries to some degree. The use of a seat belt by the passenger can reduce the severity of or even eliminate injuries by preventing the passenger from making contact with the driver, the impacting vehicle or structures in the passenger compartment.

If the impact is from the right (i.e., the passenger's) side, the injuries will tend to be more severe on the right side of the body. Transection of the aorta may occur, though it is less common than from front- or left-side impacts. Lacerations of the heart, liver and spleen; fractures of the neck; and basilar skull fractures can also occur.

As noted, seat belts tend to keep people in place rather than having them hurled from one side of the vehicle to the other. They are less effective in preventing injuries in side impacts than in head-on crashes, because the sides of motor vehicles are constructed of thin sheet metal.

When a side impact occurs, fatalities usually occur in the car impacted rather than the car impacting, because the engine protects the impacting driver and passengers. In side-impact collisions with fixed objects, that is, when a car slides sideways into a fixed object, the driver or a passenger if not restrained may partially pop out the window, impact the fixed object and then pop back into the vehicle.

Rollovers

Rollovers account for approximately 20% of all fatal motor vehicle accidents.[8] They represent approximately one-third of fatal crashes involving utility vehicles; 25% for pickups; 20% for vans and 10% for large trucks.[8] Rollover crashes are reportedly more lethal than either front-impact or side-impact crashes,[8] but only due to the higher ejection rates. If the occupants are restrained and not ejected during the crash, rollovers are generally less lethal than head-on and side-impact collisions. Anything that prevents ejection of an occupant increases the probability of survival. Because of better design, present-day car doors usually do not open in rollovers. Instead, the unrestrained individual is ejected out the window. Thus, the use of a seat belt is very beneficial in such accidents. If one is not wearing a seat belt, one may be thrown about the passenger compartment like a rag doll and not infrequently ejected from the vehicle. Ejection may be complete with the car rolling over the ejected individual, or just the head and upper trunk may protrude to be rolled over by the vehicle. The body may then pop back into the car. It is not uncommon in rollover accidents to see a blood-stained depression in the roof of the car adjacent to a window (Figure 11.10).

The head of one of the individuals in the vehicle protruded through the window as the car rolled over, with the head causing the depression as it was crushed. Paint from the roof is sometimes left on the head of the victim in such instances.

The injury patterns in rollover accidents in which an individual is not restrained are much more variable because the individual is thrown about, impacting various surfaces.

Figure 11.10 Blood-stained depression in roof of car adjacent to window where head popped out and was rolled over.

Thus, there is no specific injury pattern. If the individual is ejected and the car rolls over his trunk but not his head, there may be no external evidence of trauma (Figure 11.11).

Subsequent autopsy, however, can reveal massive ruptures of the lungs, heart, liver, spleen and mesentery.

In restrained individuals who die in rollover crashes, one will occasionally see cranio-cerebral injuries and neck fractures due to the head being forced downward by collapse of the roof of the car as it rolls over.

Most single-vehicle rollover accidents involve a vehicle's running off the roadway, followed by an abrupt attempt to steer it back onto the road. The attempted correction causes the vehicle to skid sideways. As it does, it begins to tip over toward the leading side. If there is sufficient lateral momentum, the tires will plow into the surface and the vehicle will roll over. If the momentum is insufficient, the vehicle will fall back onto its wheels. The point at which the vehicle begins to roll over is approximately where the tire marks stop. The propensity of the vehicle to tip is determined not only by the side momentum but also by the height of the vehicle's center of gravity (thus, the increased tendency of utility vehicles to roll over) as well as the nature of the ground surface. A vehicle is more likely to roll over on dirt than pavement.

As a vehicle begins to roll, it becomes airborne. With a low center of gravity, such as in automobiles, the rolling vehicle tends to land on the edge of the roof opposite to the side of the car that is leading the rollover. In vehicles with a high center of gravity, such as utility vehicles, the impact point is more likely to be the leading edge of the vehicle roof. After impact, the vehicle continues to roll, often coming to rest back on its wheels. When a vehicle rolls over, it usually does not do it more than once. By studying the scene and the vehicle, an accident reconstructionist can estimate the speed of the vehicle at the time of rollover, the number of rolls, the impact points on the vehicle and the direction of the roll.

Rear-Impact Crashes

Rear-impact crashes are the least common form of fatal accident. This is because the occupants of the front seat of the impacted car are protected by the trunk and rear passenger

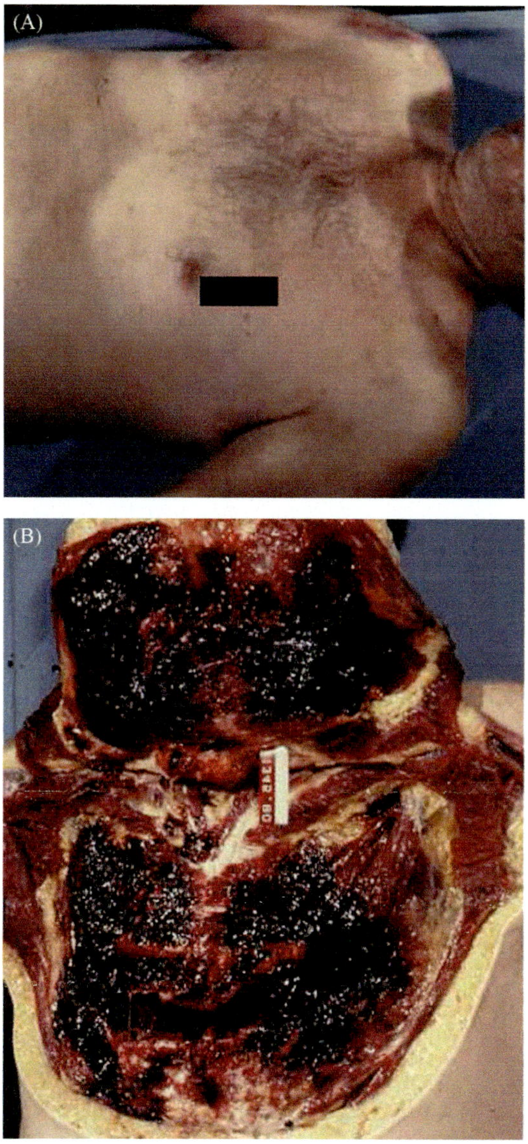

Figure 11.11 Tractor rolled over deceased with (A) no external evidence of injury but (B) massive internal injuries with fractures of ribs and sternum and rupture of internal organs.

portion of the vehicle. These usually decelerate the impacting vehicle sufficiently to protect individuals in the front seat. People in the impacting automobile are protected by their car's engine. Rear-impact crashes account for many civil suits involving whiplash syndrome. Although relatively uncommon, one of the potential dangers with the rear-impact crash is rupture of the gas tank, with ignition of the fuel. Rupture of the tank is, of course, proportional to the speed of impact. In the authors' experience, most fatal automobile fires begin under the hood of the car and are not related to rear impact.

In rear-impact collisions, there may be seatback failure such that the back of the front seat goes horizontal. At the same time, the occupant of the seat can go backward, impacting the rear seat or the roof, or even be ejected out the rear window. This can result in serious, if not fatal, head and/or neck injuries. This can occur even if the individual is wearing a seat belt. In one case seen by the authors, the seat partially failed after a rear impact, creating a ramp, with the driver propelled backward and upward. His head impacted the roof of the car with such force as to embed hair in the cloth lining. The impact fractured his neck, producing quadriplegia.

Positional Asphyxia

Occasionally, a fatally may occur in motor vehicle collision without any injuries to be body. In such cases, positional or traumatic asphyxia must be considered. Positional asphyxia occurs when a person cannot voluntarily change from an abnormal position that may interfere with ventilation; traumatic asphyxia occurs when a heavy weight presses down on an individual's chest or upper abdomen, making respiration impossible. Traumatic asphyxia may occur in the cases of cabin intrusion which trap the occupant and prevent respiration (Figure 11.12).

Positional asphyxia is more commonly associated with rollover crashes resulting in a prolonged inverted position. There are different explanations in the literature as to how fatal asphyxia occurs for persons in an inverted position. Death in this position may result not only because of the mechanical interference with breathing in an inverted position, but also due to the pathophysiologic effect of being upside down. One study proposed death occurred from respiratory muscle fatigue due to the abdominal organs pressing against the diaphragm. Some individuals suggest cardiac arrest occurs when there is severe hypoxia of the myocardium.

Asphyxial deaths are often associated with florid petechiae of the face and subconjunctiva as well as a history of prolonged extrication.

Additional Considerations

Multiple Crash Types

In the aforementioned discussion of injury patterns associated with different types of crashes, we have neatly divided all crashes into four categories: front impact, side impact,

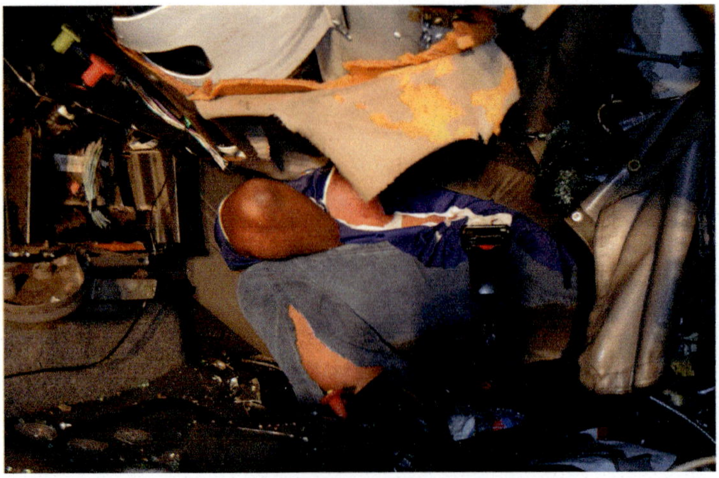

Figure 11.12 Traumatic asphyxia in a decedent who was trapped in a flexed position with his head between his knees. No injuries were present at autopsy.

rollover and rear impact. This is, of course, an artificial distribution. There can be a combination of the types. Thus, there might be a front impact where the car is deflected, rolls over and slams sideways into a tree.

Battery Injuries

One minor, infrequent, but interesting injury should be mentioned here. Occasionally, an individual is brought into the morgue with a gray-to-pale-green color, leathery texture to the skin (Figure 11.13) caused by the car battery rupturing and spraying the victim with acid.

Vehicle Fires

Fires can also occur secondary to a motor vehicle crash. The majority of vehicle fires occur in passenger vehicles (83%) with 66% occurring in standard passenger cars and less than 1% in buses.[9] Non-passenger vehicles account for approximately 10% of vehicle fires with 9% occurring in transport vehicles (i.e., freight). The majority (60%) of fatal vehicle fires were the result of a collision.[9]

When fires occur, most are confined to the engine compartment, which is protected from the passenger compartment by a fire wall. When fatalities or severe injuries occur with a vehicle fire, they almost invariably result in a major lawsuit against the automobile manufacturer. Because of this, in any motor vehicle accident where there is a fire and a burned body is removed from the vehicle, a complete and thorough autopsy should be

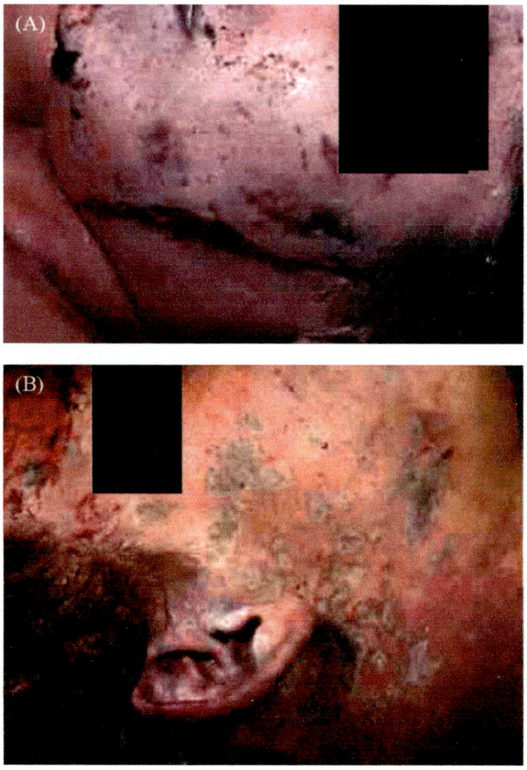

Figure 11.13 (A and B) Acid burns of face from ruptured battery.

performed. This should involve examination of the neck, both anteriorly and posteriorly, especially if there are no evident traumatic injuries to explain death.

Blood carboxyhemoglobin analysis should also be performed. If no blood can be obtained, spleen can also be used; if necessary, bone marrow, liver and muscle can all be used as alternative specimens. Carbon monoxide testing is often used to prove vitality at the time of fire; however, the authors have seen several cases of individuals who were alive during a motor vehicle fire who died without elevated concentrations of carboxyhemoglobin. This is presumably because the fire behaves as a flash fire in an open environment.

A number of experiments have been conducted involving burning vehicles. No propellants were used in these experiments. In one case, a fire was started in the passenger compartment of an automobile.[10] The four windows were left open and a 10-km/h wind blew steadily through the windows from the driver's to the passenger's side. Maximum temperatures in the compartment ranged from 867 to 1133°C. The maximum carbon monoxide level was 15,100 ppm; the carbon dioxide level 122,000 ppm. Oxygen concentration dipped down to 8.5%.

In a similar experiment, the same type of car was burned, again with the fire started in the passenger compartment, but with the windows closed.[11] After a period of smoldering and heavy smoke formation, the fire erupted with a flashover. It burned for less than 1 min before it went out, presumably because of lack of oxygen. The temperature rise away from the immediate vicinity of the fire was minimum (maximum of 30°C). At the time of flashover, the temperature rose to 29°C on the floor, 266°C at the driver's head level and 603°C at the headliner. After the flashover, the temperatures dropped to below 50°C. Prior to the flashover, the CO was from 110 to 260 ppm; the CO_2 levels 700 to 1000 ppm. Subsequently, CO rose to 24,800 ppm; CO_2 59,000 with O_2 falling to 8%.

Toxicology in Motor Vehicle Accidents

The majority of motor vehicle crashes involve a driver who is under the influence of drugs or alcohol. Every state has legal limits defined for intoxication with ethanol, most defining legal intoxication at a blood alcohol concentration of 0.08 g/dL. Approximately 60% of fatally injured drivers in the United States are test positive for alcohol with 20% of testing positive for two or more drugs.[12]Drugs affecting driving ability include both legal and illicit drugs. Sedative drugs such as alcohol, marijuana, benzodiazepines and other anxiolytics can impair judgment and motor coordination a slow reaction time; while stimulants such as cocaine and methamphetamine can also impair judgment and increase risk taking behavior and aggressive driving.

With the recent legalization of marijuana in several states, studies have shown an increased risk for motor vehicle collisions while under the influence of THC. It is estimated that the odds for being involved in a fatal motor vehicle collision increases 16-fold for alcohol only, 1.5-fold for THC only and 25-fold for both THC and alcohol.[13] In the same study, nearly 50% of drivers tested positive for alcohol and 12% for THC.

Thus, in all fatal motor vehicle accidents, a complete toxicologic screen for alcohol, acid, basic, and neutral drugs should be performed on both drivers and passengers. Tests for alcohol alone are not sufficient. In select cases, analysis for opiates, cocaine and certain circumstances carbon monoxide is indicated. Drug testing on passengers is recommended for two reasons – first, a "passenger" occasionally turns out to have been the driver; second, the presence of a drug or alcohol in a passenger often reflects the toxicologic status of the driver.

Often victims of motor vehicle accidents do not die immediately and are transported to a hospital. Here, intravenous fluids are started and massive blood transfusions begun. Prior to instituting a transfusion, blood is virtually always drawn for type and crossmatching. Unused blood for this purpose is usually retained in the blood bank for at least 7 days. Thus, it is often possible to obtain original, pre-transfusion blood for toxicologic analysis within 1 week of admission to a hospital.

If, in spite of the transfusions and medical attention, the victim dies within a few hours of admission, toxicologic screens should still be performed on blood and vitreous fluid removed at autopsy. In spite of massive transfusions, it is possible to document elevated concentrations of alcohol in the blood in many people. This is because alcohol, being water soluble, distributes itself throughout the body of a drinker. When they are then transfused, the alcohol diffuses back into the blood from water in the tissue in an attempt to equalize the concentrations. Vitreous is also valuable in that it reflects alcohol and drug levels 1–2 h prior to death and is essentially unaffected by the transfusions.

It is also recommended that carboxyhemoglobin concentrations be measured in most motor vehicle deaths, since occasionally death might be caused by, or the accident precipitated by, acute carbon monoxide poisoning. The source of the carbon monoxide is usually a defective exhaust system in the vehicle.[14]

Suicide by Motor Vehicles

A small number of single motor vehicle accidents are suicides. Typically, drivers crash their cars head-on into a fixed object such as a concrete bridge, an embankment or a utility pole. The individual turns off the road and drives a significant distance, straight into the object, without using the brakes. It is usually obvious from a study of the tire tracks that such individuals had sufficient time to turn back onto the road or avoid the obstacle if they had accidentally gone off the road. In addition, if the death was witnessed, no brake lights would have been observed. There are probably other such suicides that go undetected. The cause of the "accident" in such cases is attributed to drinking or falling asleep at the wheel.

In all suspected cases, one should examine the soles of the shoes of the driver to see if there has been transfer of the pedal pattern to the shoe sole. If the pattern is that of the gas pedal, then one may surmise that, at the time of impact, the individual was accelerating. This is often used as supporting evidence of a suicide.

Determination of Who Was Driving

Occasionally, accidents occur in which there are two or more occupants in a vehicle and it is not clear who the driver was. In some cases, all the people may be dead, or a survivor, although he might have been the driver, to avoid legal liability might claim that a deceased individual was driving. In such instances, examination of the body, car and clothing can be decisive in determining who actually was the driver. The pattern of injuries, for example, seat belt marks, dicing injuries or an imprint of a steering wheel, might identify the driver. In other instances, examination of the car might show fibers in the broken steering wheel or in the sun visor that correspond to the clothing of one of the individuals. Examination of the soles of shoes for a pedal pattern from an accelerator or brake might be of aid. There might be deposits of blood on the steering wheel, visor or windshield that can be typed by DNA to identify the driver.

In one case, a 20-year-old girl was suspected of driving a motor vehicle involved in a fatal collision. Her blood alcohol showed that she was intoxicated at the time of the collision. She

Figure 11.14 Brake pedal with imprint of sole of shoe.

claimed that the other individual in the car, who had been killed, was the driver. Her shoes and the pedals of the car were examined. There could be no transfer of the pedal pattern to the soles of her shoes because they were covered by fine parallel grooves that would not take an impression from the pedals. Examination of the pedals, however, revealed the pattern of the sole of the shoes indicating that she had been the driver of the motor vehicle (Figure 11.14).

Motor Vehicle-Train Accidents

Collisions between trains and motor vehicles are virtually all of the side impact-type, with the train impacting the side of a vehicle that is either trying to beat the train through the intersection or is stalled on the tracks. Less commonly, a speeding vehicle impacts the side of a train. The nature of the injuries varies from typical side- and front-impact automobile injuries to the more common nonspecific pattern of massive mutilating injuries. Since many of these cases evolve into civil suits, a complete autopsy and analysis for alcohol and drugs is mandatory. Many of the drivers are, in fact, under the influence of alcohol. Additionally, most train companies have cameras affixed to the front of the train and this video footage should be reviewed as part of the death investigation.

Motor Vehicle Restraints and Airbags

Vehicle restraint systems, namely seat belts, and airbags are designed to work together to prevent many of the injuries above. Of course, if there is significant cabin intrusion, even these devices may not prevent serious injury or death. Seat belts are designed to minimize the movement of the body during a collision and keep a person inside a car, preventing ejection, while airbags are designed to prevent injuries from the body impacting the rigid components of the vehicle itself, such as the steering wheel or instrument panel.

Seat Belts

Seat belts became standard in automobiles in 1964 and their use is required by law in every state with the exception of New Hampshire; however, it is estimated that only 69% of motor vehicle occupants use safety belts.[15] In 2016, more than half of the motor vehicle fatalities in persons aged 13–44 years of age were unrestrained.[16] There are three main forms of automobile belt-type restraints: lap belts, shoulder (diagonal) belts and three-point belts (lap plus shoulder belt).

Lap belts were the first form of restraint offered, becoming standard in automobiles in 1964. They are still found in older vehicles and in the back seats of some newer vehicles. Lap belts are effective in reducing mortality and morbidity, predominantly by preventing ejection of the driver and passengers at the time of a crash. They also prevent rear passengers from impacting or being propelled over the front seats. In frontal collisions, they prevent impact of the head of the driver or passenger with the windshield frame and reduce injuries that would be caused by impacting the steering wheel and dashboard. However, on frontal impact, the head and chest may jackknife over the belt such that the driver's head can impact the steering wheel and the front passenger's head on the dashboard. Both can incur serious and fatal injuries.

While successful in reducing mortality and injury, on occasion, a lap belt can also cause injury. If the belt is worn too high (above the pelvis), the body can violently jackknife, producing compression fractures of the lumbar vertebrae; transverse fractures of the vertebral bodies; as well as fractures of the pedicles, transverse processes and lamina of the lumbar vertebrae.[17–19] The vertebral injuries are caused by severe flexion combined with shearing forces. Soft-tissue injuries produced by lap belts consist of contusions and lacerations of the duodenum, jejunum and ileum and lacerations of the spleen and pancreas. In intestinal injuries, the lacerations are on the anti-mesenteric side of the bowel.

While all of the aforementioned injuries occur from wearing the lap belt too high, such injury can still take place if it is worn properly through a phenomenon called "**submarining**." Submarining occurs when, at high-speed frontal impact, the pelvis sinks down into the seat and slides under the belt. This can result in laceration of the liver and spleen, rupture of hollow viscera, such as the intestines and spinal injuries. Contusions and abrasions on the abdominal wall are often seen in association with this syndrome and caused by the belt and referred to as the "seat belt sign."[20]

Shoulder restraints were introduced in 1968 and, without concomitant use of a lap belt, can produce fractures of the cervical, thoracic and lumbar spine; fractures of the ribs and sternum and injuries of the larynx, liver, spleen and kidney.[19]

The combined lap and shoulder belts (three-point restraints) were introduced in 1974 and are now standard on all vehicles made in the United States. With the three-point restraint, the benefits of the lap belt are augmented by the benefits of the shoulder belt. Impaction with the steering wheel and dashboard are prevented. However, the three-point restraint still can produce injuries such as rib fractures, fractures of the clavicles and sternum and cervical spine fractures.[18,19] While lap-shoulder belts can produce injuries, such hazards are outweighed when one realizes that they reduce fatalities for drivers of passenger cars by 45%.[15] The part played by seat belts in saving lives is further evidenced in their ability to prevent individuals from being ejected from vehicles – 75% of occupants ejected from passenger cars are killed.[21] Only 1% of occupants who are restrained are ejected compared with 22% of unrestrained occupants.

Airbags

Airbags were introduced to reduce serious injuries and deaths in automobile crashes, especially in those individuals not using seat and lap belts; however, they are intended to be used in conjunction with seat belts. Compared with lap-shoulder belts, airbags are significantly less effective. Thus, airbags alone have an estimated effectiveness of 14% in reduction of fatalities in drivers in crashes of all types compared with 45% for lap-shoulder belts used alone. The estimated reduction in fatalities when used together is 50%.[15]

Airbags are essentially a cushion designed to fill with air quickly, then deflate, allowing the soft bag to absorb the impact and associated energy, instead of the rigid components of the vehicle. The use of airbags in passenger vehicles became standard in 1998. The first airbags were in the front of the vehicle, termed frontal airbags, and were intended to provide protection in frontal crashes from impacts against the steering wheel and dashboard. Side airbags were then developed to protect the occupants from side-impact collisions. These airbags are designed to protect the head and neck from impacting the windows or side frame of the vehicle. Modern vehicles may contain up to ten different airbags in various locations.

To perform their function, airbags should fill as much of the space as possible between the driver and the steering wheel or the passenger and the dashboard. In addition, the airbag must deploy as rapidly as possible. As with any lifesaving device or drug, there is the potential for adverse side effects. Thus, airbags can produce injury, and, on rare occasion, death.

Deployment of airbags depends on several factors, each being unique to the design of the vehicle. In general, these factors include the collision speed that triggers deployment, the speed of deployment, the distance of extension and the physical characteristics of the airbag. Deployment of airbags usually occurs when crash sensors detect an impact equivalent to hitting a solid barrier at least 10–15 mph.[15] There is some thought that the threshold for deployment is too low, and that there is no risk of severe injury or fatalities to drivers until impact speed is approximately 30 kph (18 mph). Some suggest that 18 mph should be used for the threshold for deployment, at least for belted individuals.[22] Some vehicles have a higher threshold than the 10–15 mph while others have dual thresholds. An example of dual-threshold deployment is found in Mercedes automobiles, where the threshold for deployment is 12 mph if the passenger is unbelted and 18 mph if belted.[22]

Inflation of the airbag is usually by a pyrotechnic device with production of gas. The velocity of deployment ranges from 100 to 200-plus mph, with older airbags deploying faster than newer. Deployment time is at least 30 ms. Airbags can be tethered or untethered. In the former, tethers control the excursion of the bag toward the occupant as well as the shape. The distance that the airbag can travel from wheel to driver can range from 12 to 20 in., with the untethered bags traveling farther. Newer airbags will be less powerful and able to modify the amount of inflation depending on the size of the driver or passenger. Side-impact airbags are smaller than front-impact bags and must inflate faster.

Just like seat belts, airbags can cause injuries, but, unlike seat belts, the injuries can be immediately lethal. Most injuries related to airbag deployment are caused by the occupant sitting too close to the airbag and being struck at high velocity by the airbag as it deploys, particularly drivers seated too close to the steering wheel (less than 10 in.). This usually occurs with women of small stature or shorter drivers are injured more frequently because they must sit closer to the steering wheel to reach the gas and brake pedals. Children below the age of 13 years, especially when the children are unrestrained or out of position, are also commonly injured by airbag deployment. Rear-facing infant or child restraints should never be used in front seats, as they place the child's head and body very close to the airbag

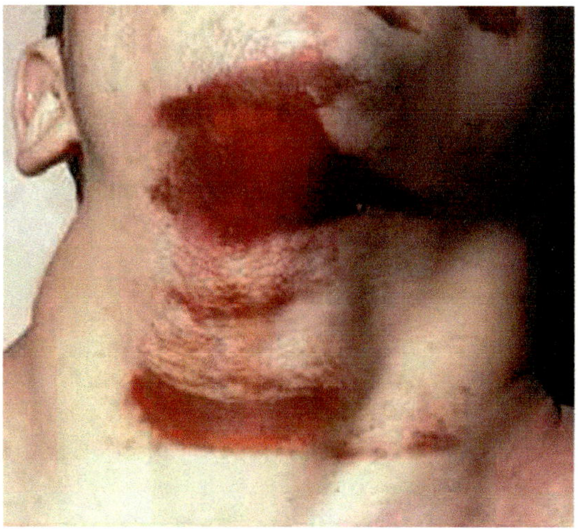

Figure 11.15 Abrasions on undersurface of chin and on neck caused by deploying airbag. Cause of death was fracture of cervical spine.

housing. In some vehicles, for example, Mercedes, there are "pretensioners" that are activated by the same sensor system that activates the airbag. Pretensioners pull the slack out of the shoulder strap before the airbag deploys, pulling wearers back in the seat before they begin to move forward, reducing the subsequent force of impact between the airbag and the person. This reduces the likelihood of airbag injury.

Fatal injuries ascribed to airbag deployment include cervical spine dislocations or fractures, basilar skull fractures and injuries to thoracic and abdominal viscera. The injured person may show characteristic abrasions of the anterior neck and under surface of the jaw (Figure 11.15).

Abrasions of the chest might also be present. In one relatively minor accident reviewed by one of the authors (VJMD), there was blunt trauma to the right internal carotid artery, just distal to the bifurcation of the common carotid artery. At the scene, the driver appeared somewhat disoriented. She was seen at a hospital and sent home, only to be readmitted 12 h later, with a history of convulsions. She was alert, oriented, and could speak but had left-sided hemiparesis. An angiograph showed complete occlusion of the right internal carotid artery caused by thrombosis. She gradually deteriorated over the next few days, dying of widespread infarction of her right cerebral hemisphere. The traumatic injury of the internal carotid artery was demonstrated at autopsy.

Effectiveness

Since airbags and seat belt restraints are both associated with significant injuries, one may wonder why we use them. We must not lose sight of the fact that while these safety features can cause injury, they also prevent even more injuries. There is also no guarantee that even if airbag or seat belt injuries occur, that equally or even more serious injury would not have occurred without their use. In a review conducted by the National Highway Traffic Safety Administration, airbags reduced the risk of fatality in 31% in front-impact crashes.[23] Additionally, it was estimated that airbags reduce the fatality risk by 9% when drivers are otherwise restrained (using a seat belt) without an airbag and by 13% in unrestrained drivers. Furthermore, when airbags and lap-shoulder belts are both used, it is estimated that fatalities can be used by 50%.

Sensing Diagnostic Modules ("Black Boxes")

In motor vehicle incidents resulting in death or serious injury, there are often civil suits. In such cases, there is often controversy as to the speed of the vehicle at the time of the collision, the force of impact, whether the driver was braking or taking evasive action, whether seat belts were being used and whether the airbags properly deployed. Were the injuries incurred consistent with the account of the accident, the use of seat belts and the result of a deploying airbag? The forensic pathologist might be asked to answer those questions pertaining to injuries. Unfortunately, in regard to seat belt use, more often than not, a lap or chest belt does not leave identifiable markings on the body.

Virtually all of the aforementioned questions regarding the vehicle, the actions of the driver, use of seat belts and deployment of airbags will no longer be speculative. Motor vehicles are now being equipped with Sensing Diagnostic Modules ("black boxes"). Some manufacturers have been equipping their cars with these devices for years (e.g., Mercedes) and, more recently, insurance companies have made similar devices available to their clients. These devices are continually monitoring a number of the vehicle functions (speed, throttle position, engine RPM, brake use, impact velocity, seat belt use, airbag deployment, etc.). On impact, the device stores all the recorded data collected over the past 5 s or so. This can then be played back to determine the events immediately preceding and at the time of crash.

Motorcycle Deaths

The classic quip of "Give your son a motorcycle for his last birthday," in a way, summarizes motorcycle incidents. The motorcycle, by its design, is intrinsically dangerous. A collision that might result in minor injuries with an automobile can result in death with a motorcycle. In 2018, there were just under 5,000 deaths of motorcyclists accounting for approximately 10% of all motor vehicle fatalities.[1] In a 2019 study of motorcycle deaths, it was shown that most fatalities occurred during daylight hours (54%) and at normal highway speeds (55 mph) without evidence of speeding (64%).[24] Deaths occurred mainly due to striking an object, including another vehicle (45%) or losing control of the vehicle (42%). Helmets were worn in the majority of the deaths (58%).

In incidents involving automobiles, the most dangerous thing that can happen to an individual is to be ejected from the vehicle. Motorcycles involved in collisions always eject their operators or passengers. Individuals dying in motorcycle accidents typically die of either head or neck injuries, with the former more common. There are usually extensive skull fractures, predominantly basilar. The injuries occur from impacting the ground or another object, for example, a curb or a lamppost. If the individuals are not wearing protective clothing, and even when they are, there can be extensive confluent scrape-like abrasions as they slide across the pavement. An incision into this area typically reveals no underlying subcutaneous hemorrhage because these injuries are very superficial and limited to the skin. Passengers falling off the backs of moving motorcycles typically have lacerations of the back of the head, fractures of the posterior fossa, contrecoup contusions of the frontal lobes of the brain and abrasions of the back and elbows. If the person tumbles forward, there will be abrasions of the face. While motorcycle helmets reduce the incidence of head trauma in low-speed accidents, at moderate and high speeds, they are of limited value.

The most common causes of motorcycle collisions are alcohol or drugs, speeding and reckless driving and failure of drivers of cars to see the motorcycle. The most common cause of a motorcycle fatality is running off the road. Approximately 30% of motorcycle operators involved in fatal crashes are positive for either ethanol or illicit drugs.[24]

The authors have seen a number of motorcycle operators beheaded or having arms avulsed due to cables or wires stretched across roads or used as supports to poles or towers (Figure 11.16A–C).

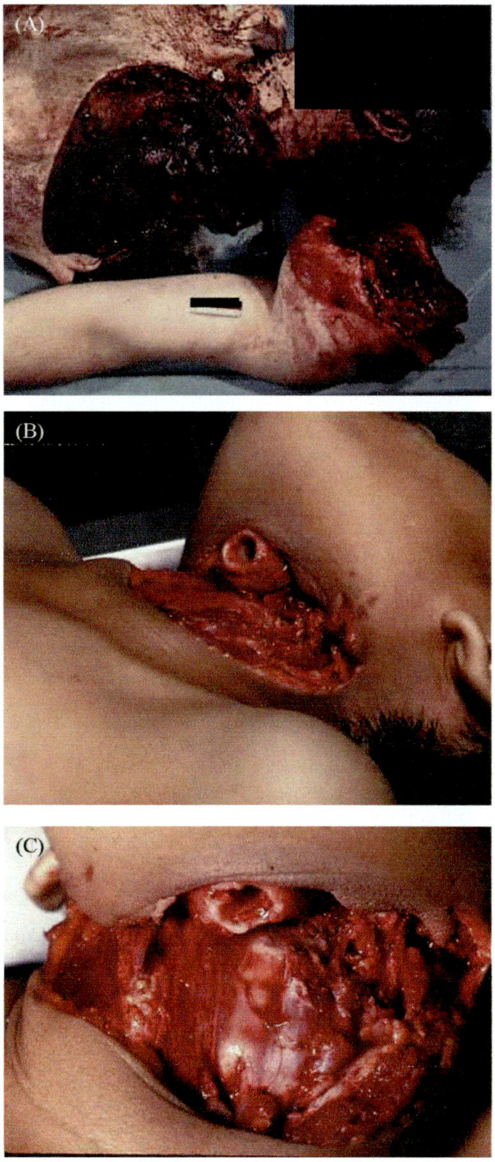

Figure 11.16 (A) Complete avulsion of right arm by guy wire. Note sharp margins. (B) Incomplete beheading due to wire. (C) Sharp margins to wound, almost as if neck had been cut with a knife.

Injury occurs when the operator does not see the cable or wire. Examination of the amputated heads and extremities shows the edges of the wounds to be sharp, almost as if they had been produced with a knife. If one found such a head and body without knowing the individual had been on a motorcycle and beheaded by a wire, one would think that the head had been cut off with a sharp, edged instrument, so sharp are the edges of the wound.

Occasionally, a motorcycle rider, seeing a car stop abruptly in front of him and knowing he will not be able to stop in time, will drop his motorcycle on its side and skid toward the vehicle in an attempt to prevent impacting it. The authors have seen a number of cases in which this was effective in preventing any serious damage to the motorcyclist. Unfortunately, in one case, the operator skidded beneath the car, hooking his chin on the bumper and dislocating his neck at the atlanto-occipital junction.

As mentioned previously, operators of automobiles often do not see motorcyclists, either because of their low profile or because auto drivers are not attuned to looking for motorcycles. Automobiles will turn in front of a motorcycle and the motorcycles will crash into the car. Automobiles going through an intersection will crash into a motorcycle, failing to see it. This may account for the high rate of fatalities due to motorcyclists crashing into another object, as discussed earlier.

All-Terrain Vehicles and Snowmobiles

The aforementioned discussion of motorcycles also applies to a degree to off-the-road, all-terrain vehicles (ATVs). These are now all four-wheeled vehicles. Three-wheeled vehicles are no longer sold in the United States because they are believed to be unsafe. Fatal injuries tend to involve the head and neck, with occasionally the ATV's turning over and landing on top of the operator. The operators who are killed often are children too young to legally operate motor vehicles or motorcycles.

Mention at this time can also be made of snowmobiles. One of the more common causes of death with these vehicles is drowning. This occurs when a driver attempts to cross a frozen lake and does not realize that the ice is not thick enough to support the vehicle.

Pedestrian Deaths

When a pedestrian is struck by a motor vehicle, the pattern and severity of the injuries, as well as their etiologic mechanisms, depend, for the most part, on four factors:

1. The speed of the vehicle
2. Its physical characteristics
3. Whether it was braking
4. Whether the victim was a child or an adult

Relationship between Speed at Impact and Injuries

The speed of the vehicle is probably the most important factor in the causation of severe injuries. Between 20 and 40 km/h (12 to 25 mph), the nature of the injuries produced changes, becoming severe. This is not to say, however, that severe, even fatal, injuries cannot occur at lower speeds.[25]

Karger et al. studied 47 pedestrian-passenger car fatalities in regard to impact velocity and injury.[25] They found that four types of injury appeared to be correlated with impact velocity:

1. Fracture of the spine
2. Rupture of the thoracic aorta
3. Inguinal skin rupture
4. Dismemberment

With regard to fractures of the spine, they found that almost half involved the cervical spine, first appeared at an impact velocity of 27.5 km/h (17 mph), were common above 45 km/h (28 mph) and were present in all cases with impact velocity above 67.5 km/h (42 mph). Ruptures of the thoracic aorta first appeared at 63 km/h (39mph), were always present above 85 km/h (53 mph) and were associated with corresponding fractures of the thoracic spine. Ruptures of the inguinal skin first occurred at 66 km/h (41 mph) and were always present at 95 km/h (59 mph) and above. Dismemberment first occurred at 98 km/h (61 mph). In regard to this last observation, Zivot and DiMaio reviewed 85 fatal motor vehicle-pedestrian deaths, and, in five cases, found amputation of a limb, and in two, transection of the torso. In all seven instances, the vehicles were going a minimum of 55 mph (88.5 km/h).[26]

Child Pedestrians

In children struck by non-braking or late-braking motor vehicles, impact with the front of the vehicle is above the body's center of gravity. The victim is impacted, slammed down and run over. If the vehicle is braking hard prior to the impact, the front of the vehicle dips below the child's center of gravity and the child may be thrown forward.

Adult Pedestrians

If an adult is struck by a truck with a high front, the situation is the same as with a child. With non-braking or late-braking, the impact to the adult is above the center of gravity and the individual is slammed down and run over. If the truck is braking hard prior to impact, the individual is thrown forward.

If adults are struck by an automobile or light truck, rather than a truck with a high front, a different pattern of injuries occurs because victims are impacted below the center of gravity. With non-braking or late-braking automobiles at very high speed, the pedestrian is picked up and thrown over the top of the car. Examination of the automobile reveals either scuff marks or dents on the bumper, as well as denting of the front of the hood in most instances. There may be dents on the roof or trunk of the car when the individual is hurled over it. The authors have seen this pattern in individuals struck at high speeds, that is, the high 60s and 70s mph range. In these cases, there is often mangling of the body with partial or complete amputation of a limb by the massive blunt trauma (Figure 11.17).

The skin in the groin area may also show traumatic striae (stretch marks) if it has been violently stretched by impact at the buttocks (Figure 11.18).

Striae might also be present on the neck because of violent bending with subsequent massive fracture of the cervical vertebrae.

If the motor vehicle is traveling at a moderate speed at the time of impact, the pedestrian will be picked up, land on the hood, impacting the windshield and sliding off. The automobile

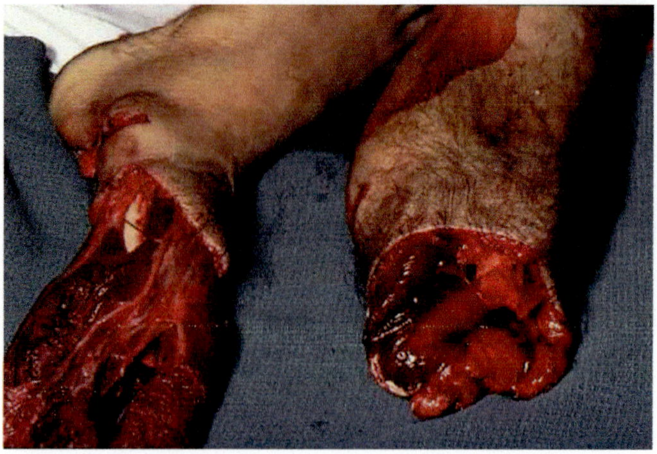

Figure 11.17 Traumatic amputation of lower extremities by motor vehicle moving at high rate of speed. Note the sharp edges of amputated limbs.

will then present the classic picture of a pedestrian impact: scuffing or dents on the bumper, indentation of the front and top of the hood and an impact site on the windshield (Figure 11.19).

Fragments of glass from the windshield may be found in the hair of the victim, because often it is the head that hits the windshield. In addition, hair might be found in the windshield. The authors have also seen the weave pattern of clothing imprinted on the hood. In some instances, threads have been caught by the deformed hood, which could be linked to clothing. As the body impacts the front of the hood and indents its top, paint smears can be imparted to the clothing. All of the aforementioned trace evidence can be used to link a victim and car in the cases of hit and run.

If the pedestrian is struck by the extreme lateral or outer portions of the front of the vehicle, that is, the headlight area, the individual will be picked up onto the fender and will roll off. Damage to the car will generally be confined to the headlight area and the fender, with no damage to the top of the hood or the windshield.

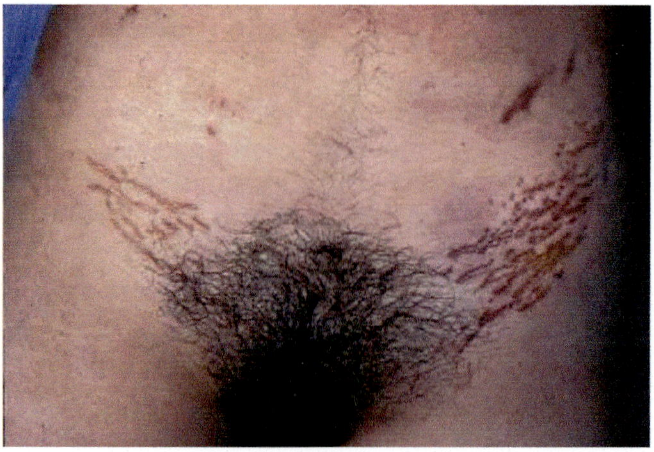

Figure 11.18 Striae in inguinal regions caused by overstretching of skin. Deceased pedestrian was struck in buttocks by speeding motor vehicle.

Figure 11.19 Typical pattern of damage to motor vehicle that has impacted a pedestrian. Dented hood and impact site on windshield.

If an automobile traveling at either high or moderate speed brakes hard prior to impact with an adult, there are two possibilities, in both of which the pedestrian is struck below the center of mass by a rapidly decelerating vehicle. In the first possibility, the pedestrian is thrown forward. In the second, the individual is struck by the vehicle, picked up, lands on the hood, and is then propelled forward, again coming to rest in front of the rapidly decelerating vehicle. In the latter case, there will be damage to the front and top of the hood.

Injury Dynamics

The first portion of a motor vehicle to impact a pedestrian is the bumper. If the automobile is not braking, in most present-day vehicles, the impact point in a male of average height would be the knee region or just below it. Obviously, with shorter individuals, it will be higher. Most drivers, however, are able to brake prior to hitting a pedestrian. Because of this, the bumper impacts the mid or lower aspect of the tibia and fibula, that is, the calf region. Depending on the speed of the vehicle and the strength of the bones, there might be fractures of either or both the tibia and fibula, with the fractures either closed or open. These are called "bumper fractures" (Figure 11.20).

Not uncommonly, bumper fractures are at different levels on the two legs. This suggests that the individual was either walking or running at the time of impact, with the higher placed injury indicating the leg that was in contact with the ground and supporting the body weight. If the individual was oriented sideways to the impacting vehicle, the "bumper fractures" might be confined to one leg. In some instances, there are no fractures,

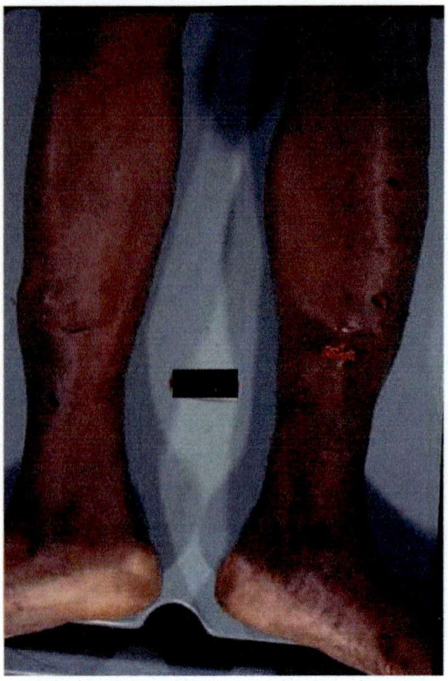

Figure 11.20 "Bumper" fractures of lower legs.

just abrasions of the skin and hemorrhage into the calves. In other cases, there might be no visible injuries and it is not until an incision is made in the calf that one sees internal hemorrhage. Occasionally, no injury is present. The long-bone fractures produced by impaction with the bumper are usually of two types – first, a wedge-shaped fracture with the apex of the wedge pointing in the direction of the force and, second, an oblique fracture.[27]

On impact, the pedestrian is picked up with the head and trunk impacting the hood and windshield. Often, the body pivots on impact such that the buttocks and upper thigh region strike the front of the hood. The tangential force directed by the hood to the buttock and thigh may cause stripping of the skin and subcutaneous tissue from the muscles, creating a pocket in the upper thigh-buttock region. There can be extensive bleeding into these pockets, with collection of 1–2 L of blood. These pockets are often not visible externally. They can be readily palpated and then exposed with an incision.

As the individual is picked up and thrown by the vehicle, they can literally be stripped of their clothing. The authors have seen cases in which bodies have been found on a highway dressed only in a shirt and undershorts. At first, it was thought that the individuals were intoxicated and were walking around half-dressed. Subsequent examination at the scene revealed their trousers, often turned inside out, with paint smears on the outer surface. In other words, these individuals were struck by the motor vehicle and, as they were thrown through the air, the trousers and shoes were stripped from the body. Horizontal linear marks on the ankles may represent the edges of shoes that were torn off the feet.

If an individual is run over by a wheel, there are often tire tread marks on one surface of the body with scrape-like abrasions on the opposite side, that is, the pavement side (Figure 11.21).

The abrasions are caused by the body's scraping along the ground as the spinning tire pushes it backward. Tire tread marks are not invariably present, but if they are, may be on the clothing as well as, or instead of, the skin (Figure 11.22).

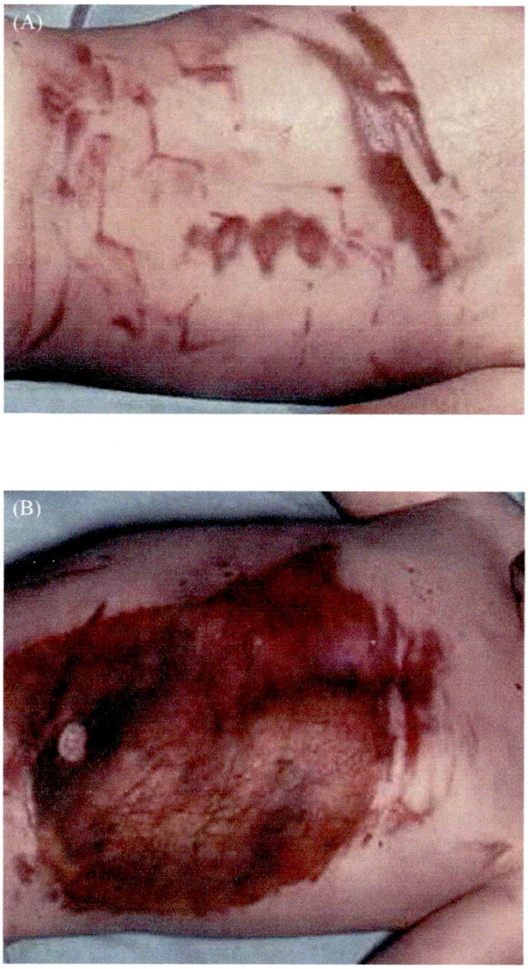

Figure 11.21 A 3-year-old child run over by a truck with (A) tire marks on the back and (B) scrape abrasions on chest, which was in contact with pavement.

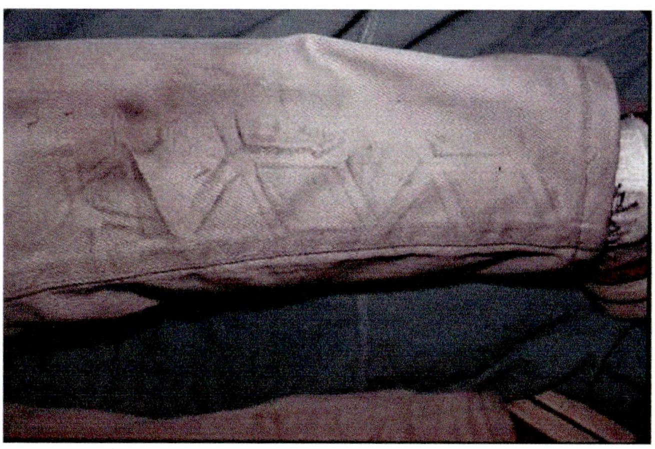

Figure 11.22 Tire tread marks on clothing in a hit-and-run death.

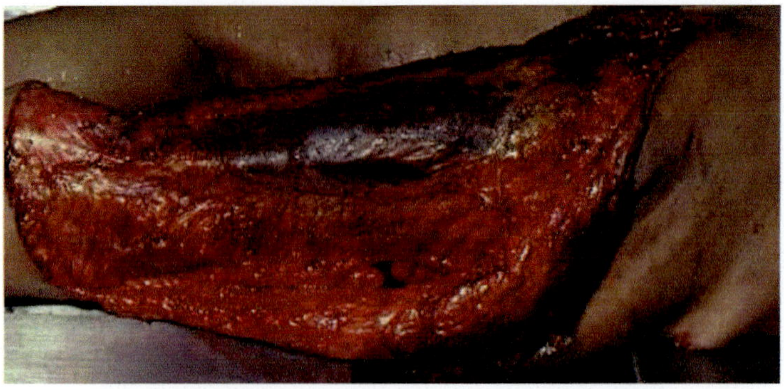

Figure 11.23 Skin avulsed from thigh by wheel running over leg.

If the wheel passes over a limb, the spinning movement of the tire may avulse skin and subcutaneous tissue from the fascia and muscle (Figure 11.23).

In hit-and-run deaths, photographs of the tread marks with a ruler in the field should be taken for subsequent comparison with a tire. In passing over a victim, grease or dirt from the undersurface of the car can be deposited on the body or clothing. Head hair, samples of grease from the body and the clothing should be retained. When a suspect vehicle is found, the undersurface should be examined for blood, hair and clothing fibers. Any material recovered can then be compared with material removed from the body.

In pedestrian incidents, the most common causes of death are head injuries and fracture-dislocations of the cervical spine, predominantly at the atlanto-occipital joint. In many motor vehicle-pedestrian incidents, injuries to the chest and abdomen are minimal or absent. The determining factor as to amount of injury appears to be the velocity of the vehicle and whether the individual was thrown into a fixed object. There are usually abrasions and lacerations of the face where the head has impacted the ground after the body is thrown. Extensive scrape-like abrasions may be present on the body where it has skidded across the pavement. If the individual was fully dressed in heavy material, there might be virtually no injuries on the outside of the body, except for some minor abrasions of the face and head.

Just as thoracic aorta lacerations occur in drivers and passengers, so can they also occur in pedestrians struck by a vehicle. Brundage et al. reported a 12.7% incidence of traumatic rupture of the thoracic aorta in a review of 220 pedestrian fatalities.[28] The predominant site of laceration was immediately distal to the origin of the left subclavian artery (15 of 28 cases, or 53.6%). Four (14.3%) were in the ascending aorta or arch of the aorta. In half the individuals with aortic injury, there was associated thoracic spinal injury.

Occasionally, an individual will be found on a road or a parking lot with crushing injuries of the body, tire tread marks on one surface and brush abrasions on the opposite side (Figure 11.24).

No evidence of an impact with the front of a motor vehicle will be seen. Toxicology virtually always will show acute alcohol intoxication. These are individuals who have gone to sleep or passed out on a road or in a parking lot, only to be subsequently run over by a vehicle whose driver did not see them.

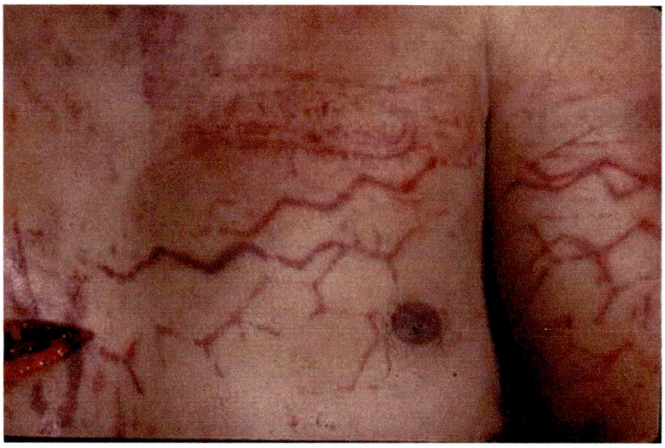

Figure 11.24 Tire tread marks across arm and chest in a 42-year-old male who, while asleep in a parking lot, was run over by a truck.

References

1. WISQARS Fatal Injury Data, Fatal Injury Reports, National, Regional and State, 1981–2018. Centers of Disease Control and Prevention. Available at: https://webappa.cdc.gov/sasweb/ncipc/mortrate.html; Accessed 21 April 2020.
2. Garriott JC, DiMaio VJM, and Rodriguez RG, Detection of cannabinoids in homicide victims and motor vehicle fatalities. *J Forensic Sci* 1986; 31:12741282.
3. Ascone D, Lindsey T, and Varghese C, *An Examination of Driver Distraction as Recorded in NHTSA Databases, DOT HS 811 216*. National Center for Statistics and Analysis (U.S.), 2009.
4. Klauer SG, Guo F, Simons-Morton BG, et al., Distracted driving and risk of road crashes among novice and experienced drivers. *N Engl J Med* 2013; 370:54–59.
5. National Highway Traffic Safety Administration, *Traffic Safety Facts 1998*. National Highway Traffic Safety Administration, Washington, DC.
6. Kahane CJ, *An Evaluation of Federal Motor Vehicle Safety Standards for Passenger Car Steering Assemblies, DOT HS 805 705*. National Highway Traffic Safety Administration, Washington, DC, January 1981.
7. Crass JR, et al., A proposed new mechanism of traumatic aortic rupture: the osseous pinch. *Radiology* 1990; 176:645–649.
8. Deutermann W, Characteristics of Fatal Rollover Crashes 6. Performing Organization Code NRD-31 7. U.S. Department of Transportation National Highway Traffic Safety Administration. Technical Report:HS8094382, 2002.
9. Highway Vehicle Fires (2014–2016) Topical Fire Report Series. National Fire Data Center, U.S. Fire Administration, 2018; 12(2).
10. Abu-Isa IA, Fleck LL, and Jacques CHM, Research Report PO-399, AN 87: Vehicle Combustion Experiments II. Electrical Ignition of Interior with Windows Opened. GMC Research Labs, March 1979.
11. Abu-Isa IA, Fleck LL and Jacques CHM, Research Report PO-363, AN 67: Vehicle Combustion Experiments I. Electrical Ignition of Interior with Windows Closed. GMC Research Labs, October 1977.
12. Brady JE, Li G. Prevalence of alcohol and other drugs in fatally injured drivers. *Addiction*. 2013;108(1):104–114.
13. Chihuri S, Li G and Chen Q, Interaction of marijuana and alcohol on fatal motor vehicle crash risk: a case-control study. *Inj Epidemiol* 2017; 4(1):8.

14. Baker SP, Fisher RS, Masemore WC, et al., Fatal unintentional carbon monoxide poisoning in motor vehicles. *Am J Public Health* 1972; 62:1463–1467.
15. National Highway Traffic Safety Administration, *Fourth Report to Congress: Effectiveness of Occupant Protection Systems and their Use*. National Highway Traffic Safety Administration, Washington, DC, May 1999.
16. National Highway Traffic Safety Administration, Traffic Safety Facts: 2016 Data: Occupant Protection. U.S. Department of Transportation, 2018. Publication no. DOT-HS-812-494. Available at: https://crashstats.nhtsa.dot.gov/Api/Public/ViewPublication/812494External; Accessed 4 June 2018.
17. Williams N and Ratliff DA, Gastrointestinal disruption and vertebral fracture associated with the use of seat belts. *Ann R Coll Surg* 1993; 75:129–132.
18. Hendey GW and Votey SR, Injuries in restrained motor vehicle accident victims. *Ann Emerg Med* 1994; 24:77–84.
19. Sims JK, et al., Automobile accident occupant injuries. *JACEP* 1976; 5:796–808.
20. Chandler CF, Lane JS, and Waxman KS, Seatbelt sign following blunt trauma is associated with increased incidence of abdominal injury. *Am Surg* 1997; 63:885–888.
21. National Highway Traffic Safety Administration, *Traffic Safety Facts 1999 - Overview*. National Highway Traffic Safety Administration, Washington, DC.
22. Kallina, Ingo (head of design and safety at Mercedes Benz), Testimony at NTSB Air Bag Public Forum, March 1997.
23. Third Report to Congress Effectiveness of Occupant Protection Systems and Their Use, National Highway Traffic Safety Administration, U. S. Department of Transportation Washington, D. C. 20590 December 1996.
24. Saunders RN, Dull MB, Witte AB, et al., The danger zone: injuries and conditions associated with immediately fatal motorcycle crashes in the state of Michigan. *Am J Surg* 2019; 217(3):552–555.
25. Karger B, Teige K, Buhren W, and DuChesne A, Relationship between impact velocities and injuries in fatal pedestrian-car collisions. *Int J Legal Med* 2000; 113:84–88.
26. Zivot U and DiMaio VJM, Motor vehicle–pedestrian accidents in adults: relationship between impact speed, injuries and distance thrown. *Am J Forensic Med Pathol* 1993; 14(3):185–186.
27. Kress TA, et al., Fracture patterns of human cadaver long bones. Presented at 1995 International IRCOBI Conference on the Biomechanics of Impact, September 13–15, 1995 - Brunnen, Switzerland.
28. Brundage SI, et al., The epidemiology of thoracic aortic injuries in pedestrians. *J Trauma* 1998; 45 (6):1010–1014.

Mass Fatality Incidents

12

What goes up, must come down.

—Isaac Newton

Unfortunately, in this day and age, mass fatality disasters, both natural and man-made, are increasing in frequency. Thus, planning and understanding are the key to a successful investigation and response. Every medical examiner's and coroner's office needs a mass fatality plan. It is best to formulate these plans along with the Office for Emergency Management for the jurisdiction. Plans need to include contingencies for not only large-scale mass disasters from natural events, such as hurricanes and tornados, but also transportation crashes (i.e., planes, trains), mass shootings, explosions and chemical, biological and radiologic (nuclear) disasters. While the investigation of every mass disaster is different, including the involved parties, whether it remains under local jurisdiction or becomes a federal event, the key is to know your resources and plan for such events ahead of time. Additionally, having a team of people already established, such as dentists and anthropologists, who can be called in for assistance should a disaster occur, is paramount.

A full discussion of mass disaster planning is beyond the scope of this book, as several resources exist for developing these plans. The injuries seen in mass fatalities due to natural events tend to involve blunt force injuries due to the destructive forces involved (such as in a tornado) or drowning due to the high waters (such as with hurricanes and floods). Mass shooting events create gunshot wounds as discussed in Chapter 7, "Ballistic Wounds." The findings in chemical, radiological and biological events depend completely on the type of agent involved, and numerous resources exist regarding these types of deaths and investigations.[1-3] Thus, this chapter will focus on the injuries seen in transportation events, mainly air vehicle crashes, and explosions.

Air Crashes

Air crashes may involve hot-air balloons, gliders, motorized gliders, hang gliders, helicopters, light aircraft, commercial aircraft or military aircraft. The role of the forensic pathologist in an air crash depends on the nature of the craft, the number of passengers or crew and the circumstances of the crash.

Lightplanes

In lightplane crashes, the forensic pathologist usually deals with only a few bodies that are generally in much better condition than those from the crash of a commercial aircraft (Figure 12.1).

If there is more than one individual involved, the forensic pathologist may have to determine who the pilot was by the pattern of injuries. Patterned abrasions and contusions from

Figure 12.1 Scene of a lightplane crash.

restraint belts, the console or controls might indicate who the pilot was. Swabs and/or recovery of tissue from these surfaces with subsequent DNA typing might also identify the pilot.

Differentiation of a pilot from a passenger is said to be possible by the finding of "control surface injuries." These are alleged to occur when the forces generated by the impact of the crash are transmitted to the pilot's arms and legs through the aircraft controls. Control surface injuries of the arms consist of lacerations of the palms, fractures of the carpal and metacarpal bones and fractures of the distal radius and ulna. In the legs, there are fractures of the tarsal and metatarsals and the distal tibia and fibula. In a review of 100 aircraft fatalities, however, Campman and Bexfield found a high incidence of these injuries in the passengers as well.[4] They concluded that the presence of these injuries lacked sufficient sensitivity and specificity to indicate that the individual who incurred them was the pilot in control of the aircraft.

As in all air crashes, the pathologist must identify charred and dismembered bodies, document injuries and determine whether natural disease, drugs or violence played a role. Because of the smaller number of bodies, identification is usually easy. Most identifications are based on fingerprints and dental records, occasionally on comparison of ante- and postmortem X-rays and, though rarely, the use of DNA.

Crashes of Commercial Aircraft

In crashes involving commercial planes, the main role of the forensic pathologist is to identify the bodies, as there is often fragmentation of remains (Figure 12.2).

Figure 12.2 Fragmented remains in an airplane crash.

Initially, identification should be attempted using fingerprinting, dental identification and comparison of ante- and postmortem X-rays. If these methods are unsatisfactory, one can use DNA typing. DNA identification procedures can be used not only for whole bodies but also for body fragments. As a last resort, it might be necessary to utilize nonscientific methods of identification, such as documents on the bodies, jewelry, exclusion (e.g., knowing that there is only one child on board), or use of nonspecific characteristics such as tattoos and scars.

In addition to identifying the passengers' remains, the forensic pathologist will autopsy the flight crew in attempting to determine whether natural disease or drugs might have contributed to the accident, although, because of the size of the flight crew and the sophisticated instrumentation of commercial planes, this is highly unlikely. The forensic pathologist will search for trauma unrelated to the crash that might explain why the crash occurred. Thus, one will look for gunshot wounds and evidence of an explosion. Bodies should be imaged to look for possible bomb fragments. Autopsies on passengers will usually be selective and intended to shed light on how the plane crashed, whether gases produced by fire played a part in the deaths, and whether there is evidence of explosive injuries.

Causes of Crashes

Whether in light or commercial plane crashes, the pilot (flight crew in commercial planes) should have a complete toxicological screen for the presence of any potentially intoxicated substances. Generally, one is looking for any drug or substances that could impair reflexes and thinking to a degree sufficient to contribute to or cause the accident. Because of this, very sensitive and specific methods of analysis must be utilized in the toxicological screen. However, only rarely will natural disease or drugs play a role in airplane crashes. When they do, virtually all instances involve lightplanes. For the most part, airplane crashes are due to pilot error, mechanical defects, weather or a combination of these factors.

Crash Scene

The majority of airplane accidents occur as planes are taking off and landing. Rutherford, in reviewing 473 civilian air crashes throughout the world, found that 34.9% occurred as the planes took off; 36.9% as they descended and landed; 26.4% in mid-flight and 1.8% while parked. The number of fatalities per crash was relatively few. Thus, in 50.7% of the crashes, there were fewer than 5 fatalities, and in 72.7%, fewer than 20.[5]

The most important initial act at a crash site is to secure the scene, document it and preserve any evidence for the team of investigators that will come. Body parts should not be indiscriminately moved, but should be left in place and documented as to where they were recovered in relation to other body parts and whatever is left of the plane (Figure 12.3).

Unfortunately, in commercial crashes, one is often dealing with parts, rather than with bodies. Also, unfortunately, airplane crashes bring out souvenir hunters and looters.

The actual handling of body identification and processing of the bodies will vary from area to area. One may set up a temporary morgue adjacent to the crash site with refrigerated trucks and a tent-like arrangement. Identification can then be made directly at the scene. In other instances, the bodies may be transported to a morgue. Again, the use of a refrigerated truck is usually necessary because of the large number of bodies involved and the convenience of using such a device. There also may be a combination of identification at the scene and at the morgue. If there is suspicion of bomb involvement, imaging of bodies should be performed and examination for explosive residue conducted.

The forensic pathologists should be realistic and realize that in a major commercial airplane disaster, they play a relatively minor role. Other investigators, including accident reconstruction specialists, human factor specialists, meteorologists, biomechanical experts, power plant engineers, metallurgists and aerodynamicists, play a greater role than the forensic pathologist. This is because the primary goal of airplane accidents is to determine why the accident occurred. These experts have three major areas of concern: the pilot (or flight crew), the aircraft and the environment (weather, mountain ranges, other planes).

Crash Patterns

There are six basic patterns of airplane crashes:[6]

1. The hole in the ground
2. The spin impact
3. The spiraling impact
4. The small angle of impact
5. In-flight disintegration
6. The wire strike

The hole-in-the-ground pattern is caused by a high-speed dive into the ground at a nose-down attitude of between 45 and 90°. The heavier components of the airplane, such as the engines, will be found at or buried in the bottom of the crater. In such accidents, the pilot was obviously not in control of the aircraft.

Figure 12.3 Fragmented human remains within the debris of a plane crash (A&B).

In the spin impact, the plane dives into the ground, usually at a nose-down attitude, while spinning. Because of the relatively low speed associated with spins, the crater produced is shallower than the hole-in-the-ground pattern (Figure 12.4).

The wings will have scarred the ground outside the impact crater. The inside wing of the spinning aircraft is usually the first to strike the ground, with the outside wing creating

Figure 12.4 A shallow crater formed by a spin impact of a small passenger plane. The engine and fuselage of the plane along with several occupants were buried under the crater.

a ground scar directly opposite the scar produced by the inside wing. The scars on the ground will indicate the direction of rotation. While most airplane crashes impacting in spin-type accidents do nose down, occasionally some will impact flat.

When a plane hits the ground while spiraling, the spiral impact pattern is created. Here, the inside wing strikes the ground first and then the outside wing. Unlike the pattern from the spin impact, however, wreckage is spread over a relatively large, fan-shaped area. The wings may be torn from the aircraft but come to rest some distance from the fuselage. The engines usually separate from their mounts when mounted on the wing and remain near the initial point of impact.

Small-angle-of-impact accidents may be either high or low speed. The low-speed, small-angle-of-impact accident is usually the result of a forced landing. Here, the aircraft damage is substantially less than that of a high-speed impact and individuals may survive. In the high-speed, small-angle-of-impact, there are long, fan-shaped debris patterns, with the aircraft breaking into many pieces, the heavier parts traveling the farthest forward in the pattern of debris. As the plane begins to impact, the first mark seen could be from the wheels if the landing gear is down, or the propellers, if the plane is a propeller aircraft. In wooded areas, the wings can be damaged by treetops long before contacting the ground. High-speed, small-angle-of-impact accidents are essentially caused by a controlled flight into the ground because of flying too low.

In in-flight disintegration, major parts of the aircraft are scattered over a wide area without an apparent logical pattern. This type of patternless scattering is seen in in-flight explosions, major structural failure and mid-air collisions. Mid-flight accidents account for 26.4% of all accidents.[5] If only one aircraft is involved, the case should be treated as an in-flight bombing. The bodies should be X-rayed for bomb fragments or fragments of the plane propelled into the body by an explosion. Burns caused by proximity to a detonating bomb should be sought. Clothing should be saved for analysis for explosive residue. Swabs of the skin should also be taken for such purposes.

Wire strikes usually involve low-level flights by helicopters and crop dusters. They occur when the low-flying vehicle strikes a wire.

In-Flight Fire

In-flight fires are indicated by elevated carbon monoxide levels in the passengers or crew, as well as the presence of soot downstream from the area of fire damage in the aircraft. Beads of molten aluminum will also be blown downwind along the fuselage from the area of fire damage. In postcrash fires, there is a widespread pattern of soot and fire damage without any specific distribution of soot and melted aluminum. Carbon monoxide levels are negative in the passengers.

Helicopter Crashes

These might involve a crash into a stationary object (e.g., a tower or an electrical line), as well as a mid-air explosion, a mid-air crash into another aircraft, sudden loss of power or impact into the ground. The only unusual aspect of these crashes, compared with those involving fixed-wing aircraft, is that if a helicopter loses power or is somehow incapacitated in flight (e.g., a mid-air crash), the helicopter might drop straight down. The resultant injuries might be more similar to those from falls rather than traditional aircraft crashes.

Hot-Air Balloons

Hot-air ballooning is popular in some areas of the United States. Fatalities are uncommon. Ballard et al.[7] recently reviewed hot-air balloon crashes over a 12-year period. They found 78 hot-air balloons crashed involving 518 occupants with 91 serious injuries and 5 fatalities; 83% of the crashes resulted in one of the more serious or fatal outcomes.[7] Of the serious injuries described, 56% were lower extremity fractures. Most crashes (81%) occurred during landing with 65% involving hard landings. During landing sequences, gondola dragging, tipping, bouncing and occupant ejection were associated with poor outcomes. Fixed object collisions contributed to 50% of serious injuries and all five fatalities. In an earlier study, Cowl et al. reviewed 495 hot-air balloon crashes that involved 1533 individuals, occurring over a 32-year period.[8] In their study, there were 92 fatalities and 384 serious injuries. Like Ballard et al., they found that most crashes occurred while approaching a landing zone (20.6%) or during landing (46%). Collision with a power line accounted for 27.7% of the crashes and 44.6% of the fatalities. Contact with a power line can cause the basket to overturn, or the basket cables to be severed by the wires or electrocution. The cause of the crashes was predominantly pilot error or incapacitation (85.1%). Equipment failure was responsible for 7.3%. Of the crashed resulting in serious or fatal outcomes, 20%

of balloons were significantly damaged or destroyed.[7] The incidence of injury and mortality is high among hot-air balloon tour crashes and the proportion of balloon crashes attributed to paid rides appears to be increasing.[7]

Lightning Strikes

Lightning-related aircraft accidents are very uncommon. Thus, Cherington and Mathys were able to identify only 40 such incidents from 1963 to 1989.[9] These resulted in 290 fatalities. Thirty of the accidents involved private planes and ten commercial aircraft. Lightning can cause an accident by (1) entering the fuel compartment and igniting the fuel, (2) temporarily blinding the pilot by the bright flash or (3) disrupting the electrical system. Because of upgrading of the fuel, electrical and automatic control systems, Cherington and Mathys felt that accidents caused by lightning should become even less common. The last confirmed commercial plane crash in the United States directly attributed to lightning occurred in 1967 when lightning caused a catastrophic fuel tank explosion.[10] Since then, much has been learned about how lightning can affect airplanes. As a result, protection techniques have improved. Today, airplanes receive a rigorous set of lightning certification tests to verify the safety of their designs. However, with the use of composite materials in airplane construction, another problem has arisen. These materials are not conductive. Thus, if they are struck by lightning, the lightning could burn a hole through the material. Manufacturers are developing methods to conduct electricity from lightning strike points.

Explosion and Blast Injuries

Explosions are complex events where there is rapid conversion of liquids or solids into gases. Explosions create gases that are under high temperature and pressure; the pressure is then promulgated radially as in a waveform outward from the center of the explosion. The resulting high power kinetic force is termed brisance, the shattering effect of an explosion.

Explosions can produce unique patterns of injuries. These injuries depend upon the type and strength of explosion and the materials involved, the environment in which it occurred (i.e., closed space or open field) and the distance between the victim and the blast, including any intervening protective barriers or environmental hazards. For example, underwater blast injuries are often more severe because the shock waves travel faster in water than in air.

Blast injuries occur as a result of the pressure wave generated in an explosion. Injuries caused by blast waves can be primary, secondary, tertiary and quaternary. Primary blast injuries are due to the direct effect of the blast wave hitting the body. If a body is close to a high power explosion, there may be complete body disruption and fragmentation.

Primary blast injuries are due to the energy of the shock wave dissipating at the interface between air and liquid because of the change in acoustic impedance.[11,12] Thus, hollow organs, such as the lungs, ears and gastrointestinal tract, are most susceptible to this type of injury as the rapid change in pressure leads to organ distortion and injury/rupture.[11] The tympanic membranes are most susceptible to these pressure changes and are almost always found in blast injuries where other organ injuries are present.

Pulmonary injuries may include lacerations and contusions. One might even see rib or intercostal markings along the lung surfaces due to the rapid expansion of the lungs striking against the overlying rigid rib cage combined with a brief compression of the rib cage onto the lungs from the pressure wave.[11] Pulmonary hemorrhage can also occur due to rupture of the alveolar septae and capillaries, which can also create direct communication between the air-filled alveoli and the vascular system allowing air embolism. Hemothoraces and pneumothoraces may also be present due to the pulmonary injuries.

Gastrointestinal injuries include lacerations and rupture, most commonly in the large intestine and cecum/distal small intestine. Bowel perforation may also occur as a delayed consequence of injury resulting from overexpansion of the bowel wall resulting in bowel ischemia and necrosis.

The brain is also susceptible to blast injury, from propagation of the pressure wave along the cerebrospinal fluid as well as acceleration-deceleration injury due to the shock wave itself, resulting in both shearing and concussive-type injuries of the parenchyma. During the wars in Iraq and Afghanistan, numerous soldiers sustained brain injuries due to blasts.[12]

Secondary blast injuries result from being struck by shrapnel, flying debris or secondary missiles and are most often penetrating injuries. Tertiary blast injury occurs when a person impacts against an object, usually the ground or a wall, due to the force of the blast, resulting in blunt force trauma. Quaternary injuries include injuries that are not directly due to the blast but are a result of the blast, such as burns or exposure to toxic chemicals or gases.

Crush Injuries

Crush injuries can occur in both natural and man-made disasters. Both earthquakes and explosions can result in structural collapse, entrapping individuals within the debris. This can lead to traumatic asphyxia due to the collapse of structures across the chest and/or abdomen impeding respiration as well as compression of extremities resulting in ischemia and tissue injury; the latter of which is termed crush injury. Crush injuries most often affect the lower extremities (74%) followed by the upper extremities (10%) and trunk (9%).[13] Crush injuries can result in traumatic rhabdomyolysis that can lead to systemic illness, termed crush syndrome, resulting acute renal failure, electrolyte disturbances and death. In earthquakes that cause major structural damage, the incidence of crush syndrome ranged from 2 to 15%.[13]

References

1. Centers for Disease Control and prevention, Medical examiners, coroners and biologic terrorism: a guidebook for surveillance and case management. *MMWR* 2004; 53:1–36.
2. Hanzlick R, Nolte K, deJong J; National Association of Medical Examiners Bioterrorism and Infectious Disease Committee. The Medical Examiner/Coroner's Guide for Contaminated Deceased Body Management. *Am J Forensic Med Pathol.* 2009 Dec;30(4):327–38
3. Wood CM, DePaolo F, and Whittaker RG, *Guidelines for Handling Decedents Contaminated with Radioactive Materials.* Centers for Disease Control and Prevention, 2007.

4. Campman SC and Bexfield KD, The sensitivity and specificity of control surface injuries in aircraft accident fatalities. Presented at the 34th Annual Meeting of NAME, Indianapolis, Sept. 16, 2000.
5. Rutherford WH, An analysis of civil air crash statistics 1977–1986 for the purposes of planning disaster exercises. *Injury* 1988; 19:384–388.
6. Horton NL, Cited by Schiff B: after the fall. *AOPA Pilot* 1988; 31:67–70.
7. Ballard SB, Beaty LP, and Baker SP, Hot-air balloon tours: crash epidemiology in the United States, 2000–2011. *Aviat Space Environ Med* 2013; 84(11):1172–1177.
8. Cowl CT, et al., Factors associated with fatalities from hot-air-balloon crashes. *JAMA* 1998; 79(13):1011–1014.
9. Cherington M and Mathys K, Deaths and injuries as a result of lightning strikes to aircraft. *Aviat Space Environ Med* 1995; 66(7):687–689.
10. Rupke EJ, What happens when lightning strikes an airplane? *Sci Am* 2001. Available at: https://www.scientificamerican.com/article/what-happens-when-lightni/; accessed 3 May 2019.
11. Sharpnack DD, Johnson AJ, and Phillips YY, The pathology of primary blast injury, in Zajtchuk R, Jenkins DP, and Bellamy RF (Eds) *Conventional Warfare: Ballistic, Blast, and Burn Injuries*. Office of the Surgeon General of the United States Army, Washington, DC, 1991, pp 271–294.
12. Ropper A, Brain injuries from blasts. *N Engl J Med* 2011; 364:2156–2157.
13. Centers for Disease Control and Prevention, Blast Injuries Crush Injury and Crush Syndrome. 2006. Available at: https://www.hsdl.org/?abstract&did=235885; accessed 22 Nov 2019.

Burns and Fire Deaths

13

I am Fire, I am Death.

—Smaug, *The Hobbit*, J.R.R. Tolkien

In 2017, there were approximately 1,319,500 fires in the United States resulting in approximately 3400 deaths and 14,670 injuries.[1] Approximately 73% of the fires occur in the home and are caused by smoking, defective electrical wiring, carelessness, cooking and other factors.[1]

Burns

Burns can be divided into five categories:

1. Flame
2. Contact
3. Radiant heat
4. Scalding
5. Chemical
6. Microwave

In **flame burns**, there is actual contact between a body and the flame, with scorching of the skin progressing to charring. **Flash burns** are a variant of flame burns. They are caused by the initial ignition (or "flash") from flash fires that result from the sudden ignition or explosion of gases, petrochemicals or fine particulate materials. Typically, the initial flash is of short duration, a few seconds at most. All exposed surfaces are burned uniformly. If the victim's clothing is ignited, a combination of flash and traditional flame burn occurs. Flash burns usually result in partial-thickness burns and singed hair (Figure 13.1).

If the heat pulse is very short, because the thermal conductivity of the skin is low, the burn is superficial.

Contact burns involve physical contact between the body and a hot object. At a surface temperature of 70°C and higher, trans-epidermal necrosis occurs in less than a second.[2] **Radiant heat burns** are caused by heat waves, a type of electromagnetic wave. There is no contact between body and flame or contact with a hot surface. Initially, the skin appears erythematous and blistered, with areas of skin slippage. With prolonged exposure to low heat, the skin will become light brown and leathery (Figure 13.2).

With most radiant heat burns, the hair remains intact, at least, initially. If the radiant heat continues long enough, there will be charring of the body. Three factors

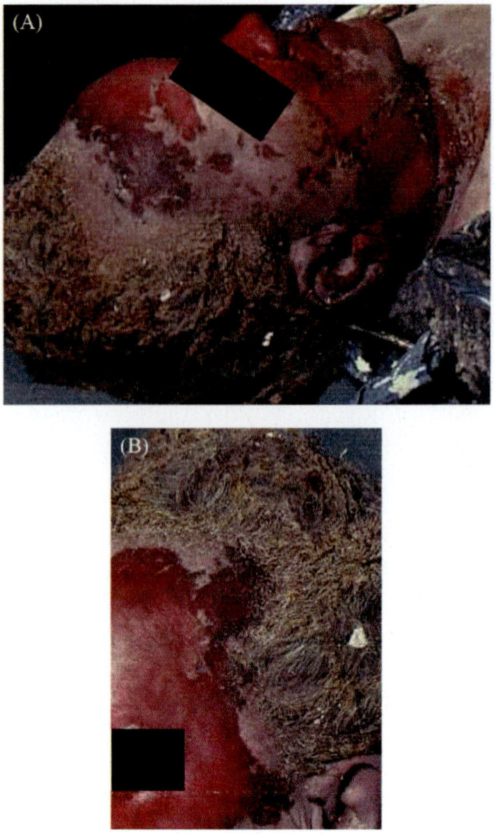

Figure 13.1 (A and B) Flash burns from methane explosion. Hair singed.

determine the occurrence of radiant heat burns, their extent and their severity. These are as follows:

1. Temperature of the heat wave contacting the skin
2. Time of exposure
3. Whether the skin is covered with clothing

Extremely high radiant heat temperatures can cause burns in seconds. Thus, Ripple et al. concluded that air temperatures above 1500°C will cause second-degree burns on bare skin in less than 10 ms.[3]

Scalding burns are caused by contact with hot liquids, most commonly water. Scalding burns generally occur on exposed skin, since even one layer of clothing can be sufficient to protect the body. The last two forms of burns are **chemical burns** and **microwave burns**.

Severity of Burn Injuries

The severity of a burn injury in an individual depends on the following:

- The extent of the burned area
- The severity of the burn

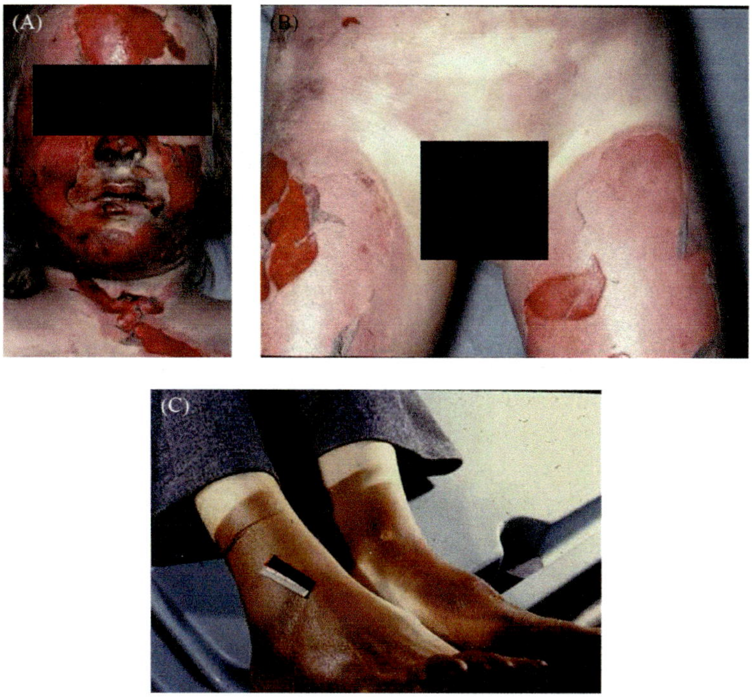

Figure 13.2 (A and B) Radiant heat burns with erythema, blistering of skin and skin slippage. (C) "Cooked" skin caused by prolonged exposure to low heat.

- The victim's age
- The presence of inhalation injuries

In living individuals, the extent of the burn is indicated as the percentage of total body surface area (TBSA) involved by the injury. This is determined by the "rule of nines." If one considers the total body surface as 100%, then the head is 9%, the upper extremities are 9% each, the front of the torso is 18%, the back is 18%, each lower extremity is 18% and the perineum is 1%.

Burns can be described as being: first-, second-, third- or fourth-degree; superficial, partial-thickness or full-thickness burns; or a combination of both the systems of nomenclature. In **first-degree (superficial) burns**, the skin is erythematous without blisters. Microscopically, there are dilated congested vessels in the dermis. The epidermis is intact, but there is some injury of the cells. There is subsequent desquamation of necrotic epidermal cells, for example, peeling in sunburns. First-degree burns can be caused by prolonged exposure to low-intensity heat or light (e.g., sunburn) or a short-duration exposure to high-intensity heat or light.

Second-degree (partial-thickness) burns are subdivided into superficial and deep. Classically, in second-degree burns, the external appearance is a moist, red and blistered lesion. In superficial second-degree (partial-thickness) burns, there is destruction of the striatum granulosum and corneum, with the basal layer not totally destroyed and edema at the dermal-epidermal junction. This injury heals without scarring. In deep second-degree (partial thickness) burns, there is complete disruption of the epidermis and destruction of most of the basal layer. There might be blistering. The dermal appendages (the hair and sweat glands) are spared and act as the source of regenerating epidermis. Second-degree burns usually heal without scarring.

In **third-degree burns (full-thickness) burns**, there is coagulation necrosis of the epidermis and the dermis with destruction of the dermal appendages. Externally, the lesions usually have a dry white leathery appearance. There are no blisters. The lesions might also be brown or black, caused by charring and eschar formation. This wound heals as a scar. In **fourth-degree burns**, there are incinerating injuries extending deeper than the skin.

It should be understood that the surface appearance of a burn does not necessarily indicate the depth of injury. The extent of necrosis or degree of burn can be diagnosed only in retrospect if the victim survives. Thus, a person who has been in contact with a hot surface might have a pale lesion with a white leathery appearance that seems to be a third-degree or full-thickness burn. It will subsequently be found, however, to be only a deep, second-degree (partial-thickness) burn.

The thickness of the skin in the area in which the injury is inflicted can have an effect on the appearance of the wound. Thus, in thick skin, such as that of the palm, what appears to be a third-degree burn may be only a second-degree (partial-thickness) one, while, in a thin area of skin, what appears to be a second-degree burn could turn out to be a third-degree (full-thickness) one.

Clothing

Accidental ignition of an individual's clothing causes approximately 150–200 deaths a year.[1] The victims tend to be either very young or very old. Flame burns in women very commonly occur during cooking when they reach across a stove while wearing a long-sleeved nightgown, robe or dress and the clothing is ignited by the flame of a gas burner.

Clothing can offer some protection from burns, especially from flash and radiant heat, by reflecting and absorbing it. Burns may be diminished in extent and depth. If the clothing gets ignited, however, flame burns are produced. The protective quality of clothing depends on the type of heat exposure (e.g., flame and flash), the physical properties of the fabric and the tightness of the fit. The severity of a burn may be decreased when the clothing is light colored or loose fitting, such that it provides an air space between the material and the skin; dry and multilayered. Burn severity is increased by dark clothing that is wet with perspiration and stretched tightly over the skin.

Deaths Caused by Fire

Deaths caused by fire might be either immediate or delayed. **Immediate deaths** are caused by either direct thermal injury to the body, that is, burns, or, more commonly, to a phenomenon called "smoke inhalation." **Delayed deaths** within the first 2 or 3 days are caused by shock, fluid loss or acute respiratory failure caused by inhalation of gases with injury to the respiratory tree. Deaths after this period are generally caused by sepsis or chronic respiratory insufficiency.

The Burned Body

At autopsy, burns should be described in detail, including their severity and distribution. In the case of children, >20% TBSA burns are considered to be life threatening, while in the case of adults, that percentage may increase to 40%. The TBSA of the burns can often be estimated using the rule of 9s:

Rule of 9s (Adult)	
Head	9%
Anterior thorax	18% (9 each chest and abdomen)
Back	18%
Arms	9% each
Anterior legs	9% each
Posterior legs	9% each

On gross examination, it is usually impossible to distinguish acute antemortem from postmortem burns. Microscopic examination of the burns is not helpful unless the victim has survived long enough to develop an inflammatory response. Lack of such a response, however, does not necessarily indicate that the burn was a postmortem one. One of the authors (VJMD) had an occasion to examine microscopic slides of third-degree burns incurred in Vietnam, with the patients subsequently evacuated to Japan where they died 2 or 3 days later. In some of these burns, there was no inflammatory reaction, presumably caused by heat thrombosis of dermal vessels such that inflammatory cells could not reach the area of burn and produce a reaction.

Not all bodies in a fire end up charred and disfigured. Some show no evidence of injury at all, while others demonstrate only searing burns. In the latter instance, the skin is of a light brown color with a stiff leathery consistency. Blisters may also be present. Blisters do not necessarily indicate that the deceased was alive at the time the burns were incurred, since they can be produced postmortem. A mistaken impression exists that an erythematous rim surrounding the blisters or burns indicates that the individual was alive at the time they were incurred (Figure 13.3).

This is incorrect. Blisters with a red rim have been produced on dead bodies. Heat applied to the skin causes contraction of dermal capillaries forcing liquid blood to the periphery of the blister or burn, simulating an antemortem hyperemic inflammatory response.

If a body is severely burned, the skin might split or be completely burned away, exposing muscle (Figure 13.4).

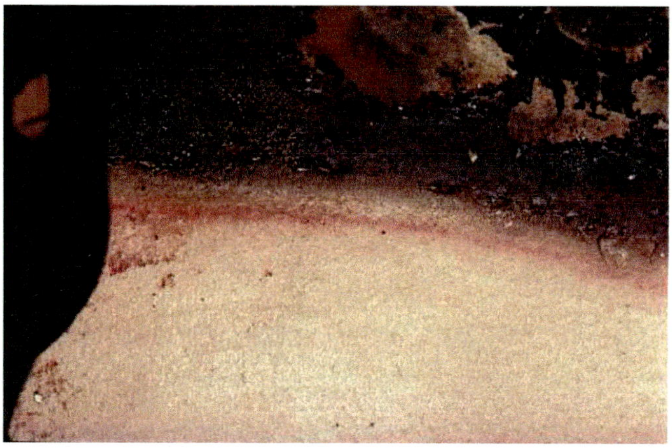

Figure 13.3 Postmortem burn with erythematous rim.

Figure 13.4 Charred body with skin burned away; muscle exposed and ruptured.

This muscle often shows rupture caused by heat. Any unburned skin will usually have a seared leathery consistency. If the victim was lying on a flat surface, while the body as a whole might be severely charred, the skin resting on the surface may be perfectly preserved. In the case of severely burned bodies, portions of the chest and abdominal walls might be burned away, exposing the viscera. The internal organs may appear seared or charred.

Burned bone has a gray-white color, often showing a fine superficial network of heat fractures on its cortical surface (Figure 13.5).

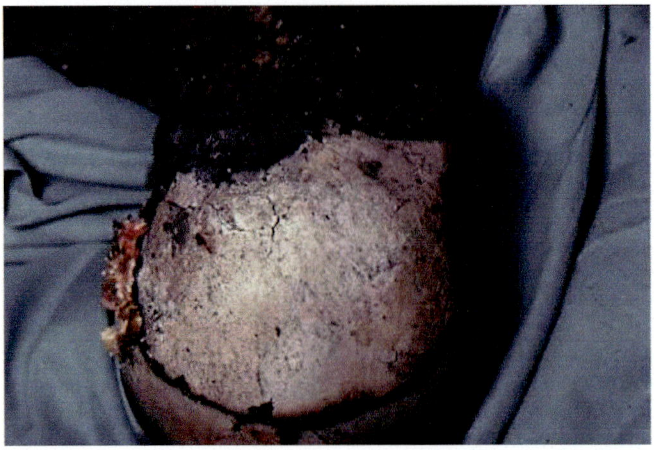

Figure 13.5 Scalp burned away exposing cranial vault. Linear heat fractures of gray, white, crumbling (calcined) bone.

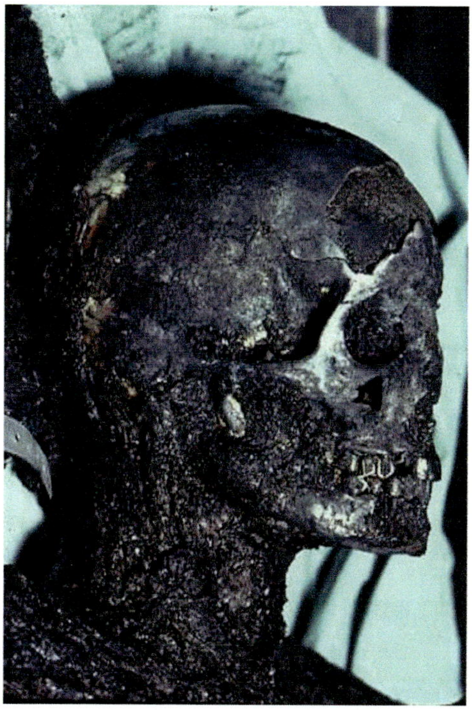

Figure 13.6 Partial skeletonization of face caused by soft tissue burned away. Portions of outer table of skull have fallen away in left frontal region.

It may crumble on handling. It is quite common for the soft tissue of the face to be burned away, revealing the skull (Figure 13.6).

The outer table of the exposed cranial vault may show a network of fine crisscrossing heat fractures. In some cases, the outer table can fragment and be absent. Bodies will often be brought in without hands and feet, which have been burned so badly that they are either unrecognizable at the scene or have become fragmented.

Burned bodies may present with a **pugilistic** attitude. Coagulation of the muscle due to heat causes contraction of muscle fibers with resultant flexion of limbs. Thus, the upper extremities assume the position of a boxer holding his hands up in front of him. Assumption of the pugilistic attitude is unrelated to whether the individual was alive or dead prior to the fire.

A common artifact in severely burned bodies with charring of the head is the presence of a **postmortem epidural hematoma** (Figure 13.7).

There should be no difficulty in distinguishing these from antemortem epidural hematomas. Postmortem fire epidurals are of chocolate brown color and have a crumbly or honeycomb-like appearance. They are large, fairly thick (up to 1.5 cm) and typically overlie the frontal, parietal and temporal areas, in some cases with extension to the occipital area.

Smoke Inhalation

For the victim of a fire whose body shows no or minimum evidence of thermal injuries, the cause of death is often attributed to "smoke inhalation." Though this is often used synonymously with carbon monoxide poisoning, smoke inhalation injuries can be more than just CO toxicity (see the "Inhalation Injuries" section).

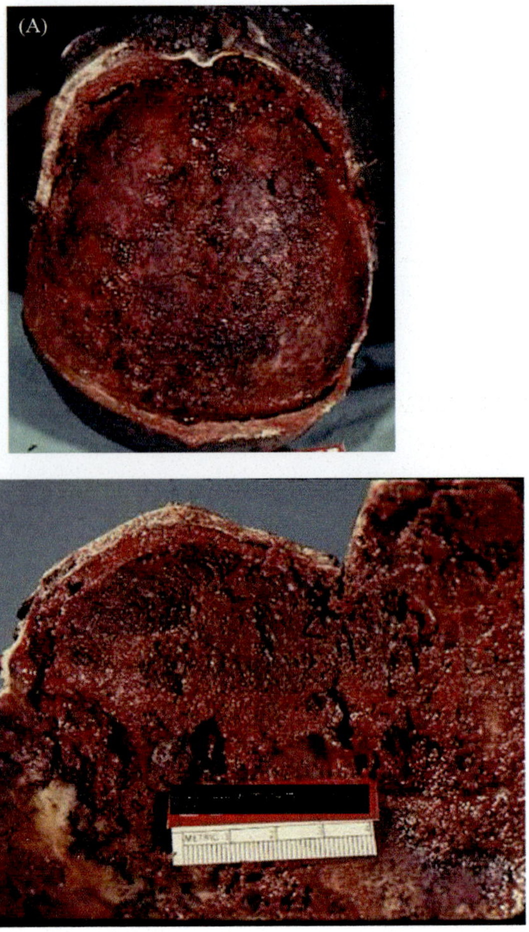

Figure 13.7 (A and B) Postmortem epidural thermal hematoma.

Examination of individuals overcome by smoke inhalation will usually reveal soot in the nostrils and mouth as well as coating in the larynx, trachea and bronchi (Figure 13.8).

The absence of soot, however, does not necessarily mean that the individual was dead prior to the start of the fire. The authors have seen numerous cases in which there was no soot in the larynx or trachea, yet the analysis of blood for carboxyhemoglobin (evidence of carbon monoxide) revealed lethal concentrations.

At autopsy, individuals dying from carbon monoxide intoxication often display a cherry-red coloration of livor mortis as well as of muscles, internal organs and blood. In spite of this coloration, a carbon monoxide determination on the blood is mandatory. The cherry-red coloration can also be produced by other factors (e.g., cyanide). A cherry-red coloration to livor mortis is also very common in bodies exposed to cold for long periods of time. In addition, an individual could have a fatal carbon monoxide level, yet a prominent cherry-red color could be absent.

Attributing the cause of death in smoke inhalation cases to carbon monoxide intoxication is a simplification of a complicated process. The actual mechanism of death in individuals dying of smoke inhalation is not always clear. In individuals who die during fires, actual carbon monoxide levels, while toxic, are often insufficiently high to have caused death.

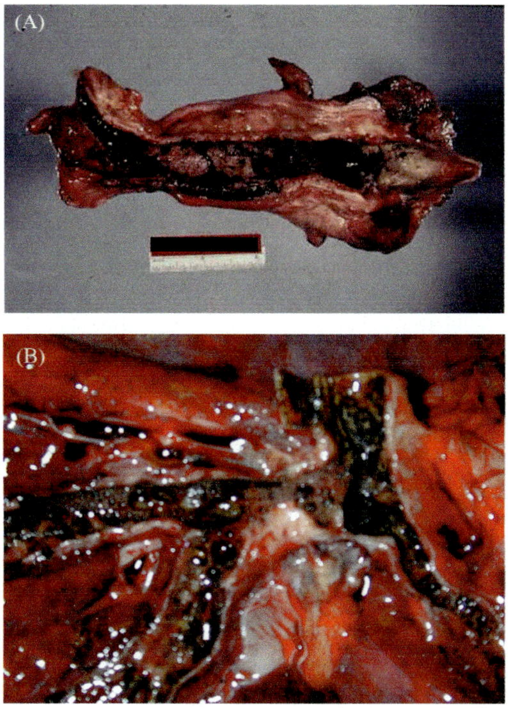

Figure 13.8 (A) Soot in larynx and trachea and (B) bronchi.

These concentrations are characteristically 20% lower than in deaths caused by inhalation of carbon monoxide exhaust fumes. Thus, in the authors' experience, in individuals whose deaths are caused by inhalation of automobile exhaust, the average carboxyhemoglobin concentration is 79%, with 82% of cases having concentrations of 70% or greater. In fires, the average carboxyhemoglobin concentration is 57%, with carboxyhemoglobin concentrations of 30 or 40% common, and with some levels in the 20% range. In some instances, this is aided by an underlying disease. Thus, an individual with severe coronary atherosclerosis could die at lower carboxyhemoglobin concentration than a healthy individual. In other cases, drugs or alcohol can act as contributory factors.

A number of factors other than carbon monoxide have been suggested as causing death in smoke inhalation cases. These are oxygen deprivation, cyanide, free radicals and non-specified toxic substances. Oxygen deprivation caused by the fire's consumption of oxygen is not realistic as a causation of death in house fires. If there were insufficient oxygen to maintain life, the fire would go out.

Cyanide is produced in the burning of many common synthetic substances. It may, in a few rare instances, be a contributory cause of death, but to ascribe most or even many deaths to cyanide poisoning is a mistake. Cyanide as a cause of death in fires is a favorite theory of attorneys in cases of civil litigation. They picture the deceased as having been rapidly overcome and succumbing to a cloud of cyanide produced by burning synthetics. In fact, the amount of cyanide produced in fires is relatively small, with actual concentrations in real-life situations being very low. Even in closed rooms with the introduction of pure gaseous cyanide in high concentrations, as occurred in the Nazi death chambers, incapacitation is not necessarily immediate and death may not occur for a number of minutes (see Chapter 8 for further discussion on cyanide).

Free radicals have also been proposed as one possibility in causing death, because they can inactivate surfactants, thus preventing oxygen from crossing the alveoli into the blood.[4]

Inhalation Injuries

Inhalation injuries are often ascribed to the inhalation of hot gases with "burning" of the air passages. As early as 1945, Moritz et al. found that inhalation of hot dry air sufficient to cause instantaneous burning of the skin had little or no effect on the lungs.[5] In their experiments, animals were made to inhale dry room air heated to 350 and 500°C. This dry air lost most of its heat before reaching the lungs such that there was no injury to either of the lungs or lower trachea. Injury to the upper trachea was described as mild. If the air was hot and moist, however, there were burns of the airways.

Thermal burns of the tracheobronchial tree are rare and most often caused by steam, which contains 4000 times more heat than air.[5,6] Hot air, whether dry or moist, can produce a rapidly fatal obstructive edema of the larynx. This, however, is very uncommon. The inhalation injuries of the lungs are usually chemical injuries caused by the byproducts of incomplete combustion.[6] These produce pulmonary edema due to injury at the endothelial-epithelial interface, alveolar collapse due to decreased production of surfactant and bronchociliary injury. The concept of laryngospasm caused by inhalation of extremely hot gases has been suggested. The laryngospasm is supposed to prevent inhalation of gases produced by the fire (e.g., carbon monoxide). This concept, however, is just a conjecture.

Identification of the Deceased

In many fire deaths, thermal injuries to the body are insignificant. If there are no distinct disfiguring burns, the establishment of identity is readily performed by personal identification, photographs or fingerprints. If a body is charred to such a degree that facial structures are mutilated and no fingerprints can be obtained, other methods of identification must be used. In all severely burned bodies where fingerprints are unobtainable, dental or DNA identification may be necessary (see Chapter 2).

Cremation

The most thorough study of the changes a body undergoes as it is burned is done by Bohnert et al., who observed the cremation of 15 bodies.[7] The 15 bodies, in either oak or fir coffins, were cremated at temperatures between 670 and 810°C. It took between 2 and 3 h to reduce the bodies to ash and pieces of calcined bone. Cremation of a body in a crematorium occurs under controlled conditions where the body is continuously exposed to a uniform heat source. This is not true in accidental fires, where exposure to the fire might be intermittent and the temperature of the fire might fluctuate, never reaching that of a crematorium. Thus, in the article by Bohnert et al., the time taken to go from one stage of cremation to another is not so important, but rather the sequence of the changes that occur as a body burns.

Bohnert et al. found that, being 10 min into the cremation, the scalp had burned away, exposing the cranial vault, which was not calcined. The soft tissue of the face was charred. After 20 min, the external table showed fissures or the coronal and sagittal sutures burst.

By 30 min, there were large gaping fractures in the cranial vault with the external table beginning to fragment. The facial bones were calcined with only sparse soft tissue, if any. By 40 min, the calvarium had burned away, exposing a shrunken and blackened brain. The facial bones were free of soft tissue, calcined and disintegrating. The soft tissue of the neck was absent in half the cases and charred in the rest. By 50 min, the base of the skull was visible and the facial bones disintegrating. By 60 min, only the core of the facial bones and the base of the skull were left.

As to the trunk, after 20 min, the skin of the anterior chest was burned away, exposing charred muscle. In slightly more than half the cases, the anterior aspect of the ribs was visible, with the sternum and costal cartilage burned away in three of these cases. By 30 min, the thoracic and abdominal cavities were exposed, with the internal organs blackened and shrunken except for the intestines, which, though blackened anteriorly, were moist posteriorly. The anterior aspect of the ribs was calcined. After 40 min, the ribs were exposed and calcined up to the posterior axillary lines. The thoracic and abdominal organs, which were shrunken with a sponge-like surface, were, with the exception of the liver, unrecognizable by 50 min and reduced to ash by 60 min.

In regard to the extremities, after 20 min, the skin of the arms and legs was burned away, with the exposed muscle charred and the radius and ulna partially visible. The bones of the hands were visible, calcined and connected by charred soft tissue, except in cases where they were completely destroyed. The forearms were generally reduced to their proximal portions by 30 min and absent by 40 min. The upper arms were largely devoid of soft tissue by 40 min, with the head of the humerus visible and the humeri calcined with extensive longitudinal fractures. As to the legs, by 30 min, the distal femurs and the tibiae were mostly free of soft tissue, with the exposed bones calcined with longitudinal fractures with rolled-up edges. By 50 min, the arms were gone and the femurs reduced to calcined stumps.

Causes of Fires

Smoking is a common cause of house fires. In some situations, one might not know whether the individual was a smoker and, if so, whether this was a possible cause of the fire. Postmortem samples can be analyzed for the presence of nicotine, which would suggest whether the deceased was a smoker, however, with the increase in vaping, nicotine does not always indicate the use of combustible tobacco products.

Children are often the initiators as well as the victims of fires. This is often associated with lack of supervision – either none for an extended time or inadequate quality of supervision. Often, children start the fires that kill them. When a fire does start, children tend to panic and hide in closets, under beds or in bathrooms. In urban areas, where there is extensive substandard housing, fires with the death of large numbers of children are not uncommon. The reaction of authorities is to arrest the parent for criminal negligent homicide and endangering the welfare of the dead children. This usually eases the conscience of the officials, who are often responsible for the social conditions that led to the situation that resulted in the fire and deaths.

Homicide by Fire

Deaths in fires are, for the most part, accidental. If, however, the fire is deliberately set, these deaths are properly classified as homicides. In cases where there is suspicion of arson, a ruling as to the manner of death should be delayed until a complete investigation by the fire department is carried out.

Fires are purposely set for a number of reasons. The most common is for profit, that is, insurance fraud. Fires might also be set for revenge, because of mental instability (pyromania) or to conceal a crime such as burglary or homicide. Arson in an attempt to burn a body or conceal the cause of death, while infrequent, occurs. Such attempts are usually in vain, as the first thing the medical examiner establishes is that the individual was dead prior to the fire. It is, in fact, extremely difficult to burn a body, because of its high water content. Thus, a body that on the outside shows extensive charring, with heat fractures and partial loss of the extremities, will often show perfect preservation of the internal viscera. Fires seldom generate a high enough temperature, over a long enough time, to cremate a body. The temperatures to which the body is exposed fluctuate widely, depending on the materials burning; how rapidly they are consumed; what new materials, if any, replace the burned materials and how rapidly firefighters intervene. Outside a crematorium, fires lack the intensity and the time to completely incinerate a human body. The only way to properly cremate a body outside a crematorium is to elevate it on a grill-like structure, so that as it burns, the melting fat will feed the fire and contribute to the consumption of the body.

Self-Immolation

Self-immolation is rare. Individuals usually douse themselves with a flammable liquid, generally gasoline, and set themselves on fire. The container and the matches (cigarette lighter) are usually present at the scene. These should be examined for fingerprints. Generally, individuals incur second- or third-degree burns over most of their bodies, with the burns more concentrated on the front. Death may not be immediate; rather, the individuals die of complications of their burns. In a study of 32 cases by Shkrum and Johnston, 56.25% of individuals were dead at the scene.[8] This corresponds almost exactly with the study of Leth and Hart-Madsen, who found that 56% of the deaths in their series of 43 cases occurred at the scene.[9]

The forensic pathologist should retain portions of clothing for the analysis of volatile substances. This clothing should be placed in a glass container with a screw-top cap. It should not be placed in a plastic bag, as the volatile material may escape through the plastic. Another way to preserve clothing for examination for volatile substances is to place it in a clean paint can and close the can. One might also want to pick up soil from beneath where the individuals initially ignited themselves to analyze the presence of volatile substances.

In deaths caused by self-immolation, comment is often made that blood carboxyhemoglobin concentrations may not be elevated but be in the normal range since these are "flash" fires. What is often not appreciated is that, in most deaths caused by self-immolation and in most deaths caused by flash fire, carboxyhemoglobin is elevated. It is when the self-immolation occurs outdoors or in a large enclosure (a large room) that one tends to get a low or negative carboxyhemoglobin concentrations. Even here, carboxyhemoglobin may be elevated. Shkrum and Johnston reviewed 32 cases of self-immolation, 18 of which involved individuals dead at the scene.[8] Eleven of the 18 died in motor vehicles. The accelerants used in these 11 cases were gasoline in 9 cases, kerosene in 1 and propane in 1. All 11 individuals had elevated carboxyhemoglobin concentration, ranging from 28 to 80% with an average of 58%.

Five individuals killed themselves in houses. Carboxyhemoglobin levels were 9, 11, 14, 33 and 38%. The average was 21%. Two individuals died outdoors. Their carboxyhemoglobin levels were 17 and 25%. In the review by Leth and Hart-Madsen, six of seven individuals testing negative for carbon monoxide committed suicide in the open air, with the seventh in a large room.[9] Only two of their cases occurred in a motor vehicle, and both of those had a carboxyhemoglobin of greater than 50%. Thus, it appears that, in small enclosures such as a motor vehicle, self-immolation can result in high carboxyhemoglobin concentrations. In larger enclosures or the outdoors, carboxyhemoglobin may range from "normal," to slightly elevated to moderately elevated.

This section would not be complete without mentioning spontaneous human combustion. This phenomenon or concept is absurd and warrants no further discussion.

Scalding Burns

Scalding burns are of three types: immersion burns following accidental or deliberate immersion in a hot liquid, usually water; splash or spill burns – usually accidental – and steam burns caused by exposure to superheated steam. Hot water accounts for most of the immersion, spill and splash burns (Figure 13.9A).

These may be homicidal or accidental. Scalding of children is a common form of child abuse (Figure 13.9B) (see Chapter 12). While most splash burns are accidents, the authors

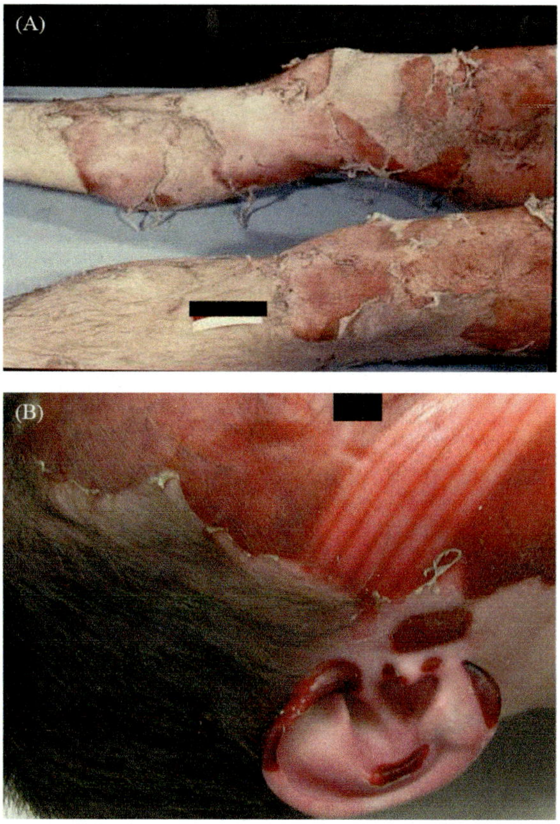

Figure 13.9 (A) Scalding burns of a decedent who fell into a vat of hot fluid (160°F). Hair did not burn. (B) Scalding burns of a child whose face was held under hot water flowing from a faucet; notice the splash burns on the ear.

have seen cases where individuals have boiled water and then intentionally thrown it on a victim. These are usually domestic homicides, with the victim the husband. The severe nature of burns from boiling water is appreciated when one realizes that water heated to 158°F can cause a full-thickness burn in adult skin in 1 s of contact.[2] Splash burns in accidents tend to be multiple and of varying depths.

Accidental spill burns typically involve children in kitchens, who pull a pot or a cup of hot tea, coffee or water down onto themselves. The burns are on face, neck, upper chest and arms. Clothing protects the skin from these burns. The hot fluid cools as it falls onto the skin and flows down the body, producing superficial scald burns with a red, moist surface. As the fluid moves down the body, the burns become progressively less severe.

An individual exposed to superheated steam sustains severe scald-like burns of the body. With inhalation, there are laryngeal, tracheal and respiratory burns. The latter may progress to adult respiratory distress syndrome. In some instances, there is massive edema of the larynx, with an asphyxial death.

Temp (°F)	Time to cause 2nd–3rd-degree burns
120	5–10 min
125	1–2 min
130	10–30 s
140	3–7 s
145	2–3 s
150	1–2 s

Chemical Burns

In chemical burns, the amount of tissue damaged depends on the agent, its strength and concentration, the quantity of the chemical, the duration of contact and the extent of penetration of the body by the chemical. Chemicals continue to act on tissue until they are either neutralized by another agent or inactivated by the tissue reaction.[10]

Chemicals coagulate protein by reduction, oxidation, salt formation, corrosion, protoplasmic poisoning, metabolic competition or inhibition, desiccation or as a result of the ischemic complication of vesicants. More simply, chemical burns are classified as caused by acids, alkali and vesicants (blister-producing substances).

Strong acids generally have a pH of less than 2. Alkaline agents usually need a pH of 11.5 or greater to injure tissues. The percentage of chemical in a solution will usually determine the degree of tissue damage. Alkalies produce more severe injury than acids because they tend to dissolve protein and saponify fat. They produce a liquefaction necrosis, permitting deeper invasion of tissue by chemicals, with deep burns and marked edema. In contrast, acids precipitate protein, producing a coagulation necrosis with a resultant hard eschar or scab. The burns produced by acid tend to be clearly demarcated, dry and hard. Edema is mild. The burns are often second-degree-deep partial-thickness. If there is prolonged contact, there can be third-degree burns, especially from concentrated sulfuric or nitric acid. In this case, the scab tends to be dark, leather-like and dry. Hydrofluoric acid gives much deeper burns than most acids. The color of the eschar depends to a degree on the acid. Nitric acid produces a yellow scab; sulfuric, black or brown; hydrochloric, white or gray; and phenol, light gray or light brown.

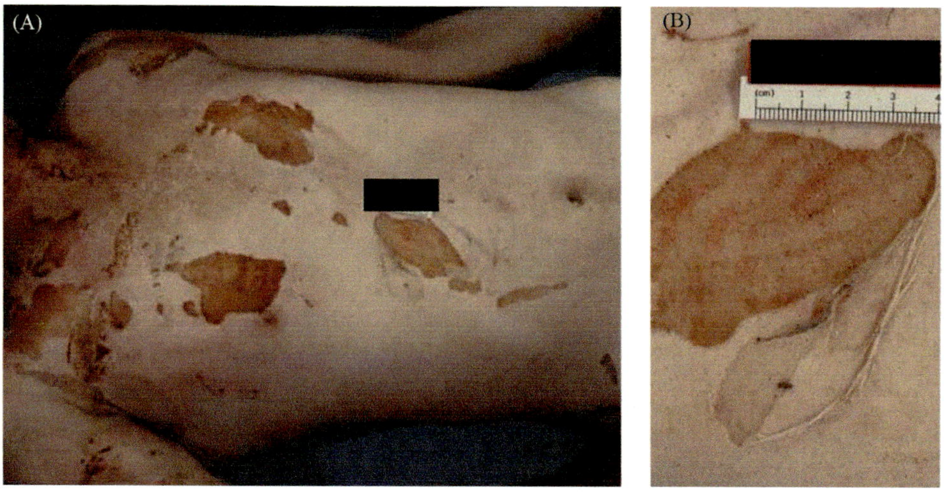

Figure 13.10 (A and B) Postmortem chemical burns caused by gasoline.

Some agents, such as phenol, yellow phosphorus and ammonium sulfide, cause not only chemical burns but also systemic poisoning. Thus, phenol is associated with acute tubular necrosis; phosphorus with liver and kidney necrosis.

Some very common compounds can produce chemical burns. Prolonged contact with gasoline or cement can result in chemical burns. Cement has a pH of 12.5–14 and thus is a very strong alkaline compound. Prolonged contact with hydrocarbons, such as gasoline, can cause chemical burns through their irritant effect and their high lipid solubility (Figure 13.10).

The latter permits dissolution of fatty tissue. Gasoline chemical burns are partial-thickness burns.

Chemical Eye Injuries

The degree of injury to the eye from either an acid or an alkaline compound depends on the pH of the compound, its concentration and the period of contact with the eye. The corneal epithelium is a barrier to injury from acid, because acid produces a coagulative necrosis that limits penetration through tissue. Alkali, on the other hand, produces a liquefaction necrosis enabling greater penetration of tissue. Animal experiments have revealed that damage to eyes is not always related to pH. The concept that acid solutions with a pH below 2.5 produce severe damage to the cornea is not always correct. Thus, hydrochloric acid with a pH of 1.28 produced no corneal opacity. Phenol with a pH of 7.7 and acetic acid with a pH of 2.7 produced opacities.[11]

Just as a pH below 2.5 was believed to always cause corneal damage to eyes, it is generally felt that alkali, with a pH value of 11.45 or greater, will produce severe ocular damage. This also is not absolutely correct. Sodium hydroxide solutions with pH values of 12.8 and 12.3 did not produce corneal opacities. If, however, the pH was elevated to 13.1, then opacities occurred. One must, therefore, conclude that the degree of eye damage cannot be based on pH alone and that pH values of 2.5 and 11.5 can be used only as general guidelines for the prediction of ocular injury. The concentration of the chemical and period of contact with the eye prior to washing must be taken into account.

Microwave Burns

Microwaves create heat through molecular agitation. The greater the water content of a particular tissue, the greater the heat produced. Thus, muscle, which has more water than fat, tends to be heated more than fat. While conventional ovens employing radiant heat cook from the outside in, microwaves directly heat the internal tissue. With radiant heat, the maximum injury occurs to the outside of the body, while with microwave ovens, the opposite may occur.

Burns caused by microwave ovens, as reported in the literature, tend to be indirect. These are usually the cases in which a microwave heats a liquid to a very high temperature and the person ingests the liquid without realizing how hot it is. Direct microwave injures are rare. Those having forensic relations are even rarer. Alexander et al. reported that two children incurred full- and partial-thickness burns caused by being placed in microwave ovens.[12] The burns were well demarcated without charring. Biopsies of the burns in one case showed sparing of different tissues, with a sandwich-type appearance of the burns. Thus, there were burns of the skin, sparing of the subcutaneous fat and burns of the muscle. The burns were based on the distribution of water in these tissues.

Miscellaneous

Flash Fires: Fires Involving Flammable Hydrocarbon Liquids

The flash point of hydrocarbons is the temperature at which sufficient fuel has evaporated to sustain a brief flash of fire. The flame, however, will not continue to burn until the hydrocarbon reaches a slightly higher temperature, the flame or fire point. Here, the flame will continue to burn until the fuel is consumed. With hydrocarbon fuels, it is the vapors from evaporation that burn, not the fuel. When the vapor ignites, it raises the temperature of the hydrocarbon, causing increased and rapid evaporation of fuel and thus sustaining the fire.

Hydrocarbon fuels have a characteristic range of concentrations over which they vaporize and will burn. This is their flammability range. For example, for natural gas (which is principally methane), it is between 4 and 15%. At vapor concentrations below 4%, there is not enough vaporized fuel to sustain combustion. Above 15%, there is not enough oxygen available to sustain combustion. Thus, natural gas will only burn when the vapor concentration is between 4 and 15%. The flame in a flash fire moves out in all directions from the point of ignition. After the initial flash, the ensuing fire causes evaporation of fuel that then sustains the fire.[13] The temperature in flash fires from hydrocarbon fuels is around 500–975°C.

In flash fires in rooms, within 45 s of ignition, the oxygen falls markedly and the CO_2 rises proportionately. CO production follows 15–30 s after the maximum temperature, occurring as oxygen is depleted. Oxygen can fall to 8.5% in 1.5–3 min, while CO_2 can increase up to 12–16% in less than 1.5 min. In the initial portion of the fires, the CO might reach a concentration of 9500 parts per million in a matter of 1.5–2 min. If the flash fire is confined to a limited space such as one room and there is no significant introduction of new air, the fire will go out through lack of sufficient oxygen.

Flashover

Fires in confined spaces such as in a room can produce a phenomenon called a **flashover**. Once a fire starts, even if it is initially small, it produces radiant heat, hot gases and smoke. The gases and smoke rise, forming a layer immediately below the ceiling. As the smoke and hot gases accumulate, this layer thickens, extending downward toward the floor. Initially, the hot gases heat the ceiling and the adjacent upper walls. Radiant heat from the fire and hot gases begin to heat objects in the lower portion of the room. The combustible materials in the room begin to give off flammable gases (this process is called pyrolysis). If the original fire burns out, or if sufficient oxygen cannot get into the room, the fire dies out. If, however, the fire continues to burn, at some point, the combustible objects in the room reach their ignition temperatures. If this occurs more or less simultaneously, flame sweeps over the room involving most combustible objects. This is called flashover. The pre-flashover period lasts for 5–20 min in most circumstances. Time to flashover cannot be predicted with certainty, as it depends on many factors (e.g., fuel, oxygen supply). The temperature in a room at time of flashover is between 500 and 600°C or 932 and 1112°F.

Surgical Fires

Surgical fires are a rare but serious preventable safety risk in modern hospitals. Data from the United States show that up to 650 surgical fires occur each year, with up to 5% causing death or serious harm.[14] Fires in the operating room are one of the most serious risks that can affect the safety of patients in a modern hospital. The whole surgical team has a role to play in minimizing risks. There are three risk factors: the first category is represented by an oxygen-rich environment, being generated by anesthetic gas use and tenting within the surgical drapes. The second is fuel from skin preparation fluids, flammable swabs and body hair; and the third is ignition sources from diathermy, lasers or high-speed drilling and cutting instruments.

References

1. U.S. Fire Statistics. U.S. Fire Administration. FEMA. Available at https://www.usfa.fema.gov/data/statistics/
2. Moritz AR and Henriques FC, Studies of thermal injury: II. The relative importance of time and surface temperature in the causation of cutaneous burns. *Am J Pathol* 1947; 23:695–720.
3. Ripple GR, Torrington KG, and Phillips YY, Predictive criteria for burns from brief thermal exposures. *J Occup Med* 1990; 32(3):215–219.
4. McAnnalley BH, et al., Determination of inorganic sulfide and cyanide in blood using specific ion electrodes: application to the investigation of hydrogen sulfide and cyanide poisoning. *J Anal Toxicol* 1979; 3:111–114.
5. Moritz AR, Henriques FC, and McLean R, The effects of inhaled heat on the air passages and lungs. *Am J Pathol* 1945; 21:311–331.
6. Bellamy RF and Zajtchuk R (Ed.) Textbook of military medicine, Part I, Volume 5, *Conventional Warfare: Ballistics, Blast and Burn Injuries*. U.S. Government Printing Office, Washington, DC, 1991.

7. Bohnert M, Rost T, and Pollak S, The degree of destruction of human bodies in relation to the duration of the fire. *Forensic Sci Intern* 1998; 95:11–21.
8. Shkrum MJ and Johnston KA, Fire and suicide: a three year study of self-immolation deaths. *J Forensic Sci* 1992; 37(1):208–221.
9. Leth P and Hart-Madsen M, Suicide by self-incineration. *Am J Forensic Med Path* 1997; 18(2):113–118.
10. Jelenko C, Chemicals that "burn.". *J Trauma* 1974; 14:65–72.
11. Murphy JC, et al., Ocular irritancy responses to various pHs of acid and bases with/without irrigation, *Toxicology* 1982; 23:281–291.
12. Alexander RC, Surrell JA, and Cohle SD, Microwave oven burns to children: an unusual manifestation of child abuse. *Pediatrics* 1987; 79:255–260.
13. Deltaan JD, The dynamics of flash fires involving flammable hydrocarbon liquids. *Am J Forensic Med Path* 1996; 17(1):24–31.
14. Roccos B and Donaldson LJ, Alcohol skin preparation cause surgical fires. *Ann R Coll Surg Engl* 2012; 94(2):87–89.

Deaths in Water

14

Water is the life-giver and the death-bringer

—Michael Scott

Drowning can be defined as death caused by submersion in a liquid. It often occurs not only in oceans, lakes, pools or even bathtubs but also in water as shallow as 6 in. in the case of infants, intoxicated individuals and epileptics.

Within the 5 years of 2013–2017, over 21,000 people died due to drowning in the United States.[1] In 2017 alone, there were 4508 fatal drownings with the majority of those being unintentional (82%).[1] Approximately three-quarters of people who die from drowning are male and about one in six people who die from drowning are children aged 14 and younger.[1]

The main factors associated with drowning risk are as follows:

1. Lack of swimming ability
2. Alcohol and or drug abuse
3. Lack of barriers to prevent unsupervised water access
4. Lack of close supervision while swimming (drownings can occur even in the presence of lifeguards)
5. Failure to wear life jackets when boating
6. Seizure disorders
7. Long QT syndrome
8. Other medical events

Physiology of Drowning

It is believed that there are typically five stages of drowning:

Surface struggle	10–20 s
Involuntary breath holding	20–90 s
Unconsciousness	60–120 s
Convulsions	90–120 s
Death	3–10 min

An actively drowning victim can ordinarily be recognized by being in a vertical or diagonal body position in the water, with the head back and face looking up, with an "O"-shaped mouth, either gasping for air or involuntary holding his breath.[2] They are typically unable to call for help. There is usually very little or no leg movement. The arms may be weakly grasping, as if trying to climb a nonexistent ladder out of the water. The victim often appears disoriented and may have a surprised look on his face. Eyes are either wide open or squeezed tightly shut. Surface struggle typically lasts no more than 10–20 s before the victim progresses to other stages of drowning. The length of each drowning stage is dependent on the victim's age, fitness level, exertion level and swimming ability as well as water temperature and whether other complications, such as seizures, shallow water blackout, medical or traumatic injuries, are involved.

After the surface struggle, people tend to sink beneath the surface of water, at which time their initial reaction is to hold their breath. This involuntary breath holding continues until the breaking point is reached, at which time the individual has to take a breath. The breaking point is determined by a combination of high carbon dioxide levels and low oxygen concentrations. According to Pearn, the breaking point occurs at PCO_2 levels below 55 mm Hg, when there is associated hypoxia, and at PAO_2 levels below 100 mm Hg, when the PCO_2 is high.[2]

Upon reaching the breaking point, the individual involuntarily inhales and may experience fear and may be aware that they are going to die. Unconsciousness will occur in 1–2 min. The involuntary gasping for air underwater will continue for several minutes, until respiration ceases. The developing cerebral hypoxia will continue until it is irreversible and death occurs. This takes several minutes.

Craig[3,4] studied the breath-holding breaking point (the point at which a breath would be taken involuntarily) in human volunteers during simulated underwater swimming. He found that at rest, the breath-holding breaking point was 87 s at which time the partial pressures of CO_2 and O_2 in alveolar air were 51 and 73 mm Hg, respectively. After hyperventilation, breath holding could be maintained for a full 146 s with a $PACO_2$ of 46 mm Hg and a PAO_2 of 58 mm Hg. When exercise followed hyperventilation, the breath-holding breaking point was only 85 s. In this instance, $PACO_2$ was 49 mm Hg and PAO_2 was 43 mm Hg. Craig concluded that exercise, such as swimming, increased metabolically produced carbon dioxide, and the arterial carbon dioxide tension was relatively low in his volunteers because stores had been depleted during hyperventilation; thus, the urge to breathe was delayed. With exercise after hyperventilation, the arterial oxygen tension decreased to levels incompatible with the maintenance of consciousness before the time the level of CO_2 had become unbearable. He surmised that the loss of consciousness during underwater swimming was the result of cerebral hypoxia rather than hypercarbia.[3,4]

If the person is not rescued, aspiration of water continues, and hypoxemia quickly leads to loss of consciousness and apnea. The sequence of cardiac rhythm deterioration is usually tachycardia followed by bradycardia, pulseless electrical activity and finally asystole.

The type of water that is inhaled, fresh versus salt, probably has very little influence on whether the individual will survive. In fresh water, large volumes of water can pass through the alveolar-capillary membranes. Fresh water alters or denatures pulmonary surfactant, while seawater dilutes or washes it away.[2,5] The presence of either chlorine or soap in fresh water apparently has no effect on this property.[2] The denaturation of surfactant can continue even after a person has been apparently successfully resuscitated. Loss or inactivation of pulmonary surfactant and alveolar collapse decreases lung compliance, resulting in profound ventilation perfusion mismatch with up to 75% of the blood perfusing non-ventilated areas.[6]

The point at which cerebral anoxia becomes irreversible is dependent on both the age of the individual and the temperature of the water. With warm water, this time is somewhere between 3 and 10 min.[2] Submersion of children in extremely cold or icy water has resulted in successful resuscitation with intact neurological outcome for as long as 66 min following drowning.[7] No matter what the time interval involved, consciousness is usually lost within 3 min of submersion.[2]

The mechanism of death in acute drowning is irreversible cerebral anoxia. Experiments in the late 1940s and early 1950s suggested that death was caused by electrolyte disturbances or cardiac arrhythmias produced by large volumes of water entering the circulation through the lungs.[8,9] However, even when large volumes of water are absorbed, there is no evidence that the increase in blood volume causes significant electrolyte irregularities or hemolysis, or that it is beyond the capacity of the heart or kidneys to compensate for the fluid overload.[2,10]

Survival after Prolonged Submersion

As previously mentioned, survival following prolonged underwater submersion in ice cold water may be for as long as 66 min in the case of children and infants.[7] The traditional explanations for this have been that immature brains are more resistant to anoxia and that the "diving reflex" is still present in children. The diving reflex refers to vasoconstriction in the vascular beds (except for the heart and brain), shunting of blood to the brain and heart and bradycardia, all triggered by immersion of the face in cold water. There is, however, some question as to whether the diving reflex exists in humans exactly as it does in animals.[11] Bradycardia does occur, but there has been no proof of the vasoconstriction in the vascular beds with shunting of blood to the heart and brain.

Some argue that these children survive because of the rapid development of hypothermia.[7,11] Because of the relatively large surface area and lack of adequate insulation in children, the body cools very rapidly. This is especially true in conjunction with the swallowing and aspiration of large quantities of cold fluid. There is rapid cooling of the body caused by immersion in cold water and aspiration of cold water with absorption of this water into the circulation. Thus, while in warm water, a submersion time of 3–10 min is thought to represent the maximum time prior to irreversible neurological injury, and in ice water, submersion times as long as 66 min have been reported with neurological recovery.[7]

Autopsy Findings

At autopsy, there are no pathognomonic findings to indicate the diagnosis of drowning. The diagnosis is based on the circumstances of the death, plus a variety of nonspecific anatomical findings. Chemical tests put forth to make the diagnosis are nonspecific and essentially unreliable. A diagnosis of drowning cannot be made without a complete autopsy, especially a complete toxicological screen, because this is a diagnosis of exclusion. If individuals are found in water and all other causes of death have been excluded, they are presumed to have drowned. It must be remembered, however, that people have fatal heart attacks and fall into water, and that victims of a fatal drug overdose are occasionally "dumped" into a body of water. Attachments of heavyweights to a body to keep it underwater is consistent with both homicidal and suicidal drownings, as is disposal of the body of an individual who has died from some other cause than drowning.

The hands and soles can often show water immersion "washerwoman" changes, i.e. moist wrinkling of the epidermis, if the deceased has been in the water for more than 1–2 h (Figure 14.1).

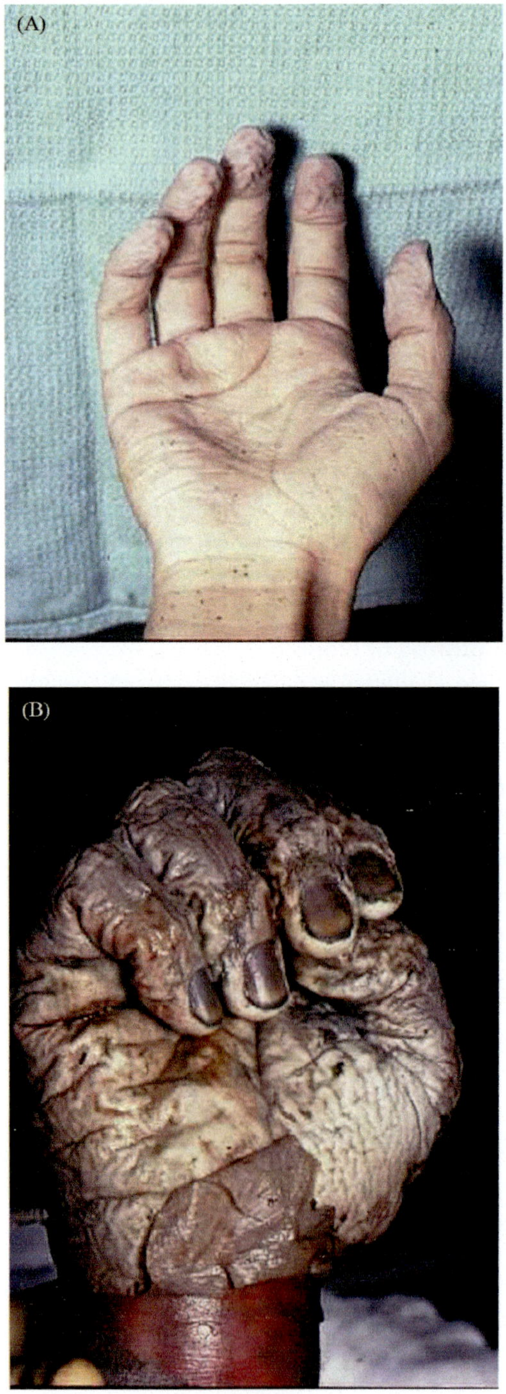

Figure 14.1 (A and B) Water immersion change ("washerwoman") of palms caused by prolonged immersion in the water.

Experiments have shown that if you place the hands of a corpse in water whose temperature ranges between 10 and 18°C, initial formation of water immersion change appears at the fingertips in 20–30 min (maximum of 100 min), with the whole finger involved at 50–60 min (maximum of 150 min).[12] This appearance of the hands and feet does not indicate that the deceased drowned, as it will develop whether they were alive or dead when they entered the water. The same is true for "goose flesh" (cutis anserina). This is a spasm of the erector pili muscles caused by rigor mortis and, again, does not indicate whether the person was alive or dead when entering the water.

When initially recovered from the water, the body might be in full rigor mortis, even though only a short time has passed from the time of the drowning. This is caused by violent struggling at the time of drowning, with a decrease in ATP and rapid development of rigor mortis. Bodies cool much more rapidly in water than air. Thus, the decomposition of bodies in water often takes longer.

The more "typical" findings in the autopsy of drowned individual may include pulmonary edema, pleural effusions and water within the stomach. Upon reaching the breaking point, the individual involuntarily inhales, taking in large volumes of water into the lungs. Some water is also swallowed and will be found in the stomach. During this interval of submersed breathing, the patient may also vomit and aspirate some gastric contents.

In the classic drowning, white or hemorrhagic edema fluid is present in the nostrils, mouth and airways. Compression of the chest can cause it to flow out. Pulmonary edema is, however, nonspecific. An individual dying of a drug overdose and disposed of in water can also have pulmonary edema. The lungs of the typical drowning victim are large and bulky, completely occupying their respective pleural cavities and a white or hemorrhagic frothy exudate or foam is commonly found in the trachea and bronchi. On cut section, the lungs usually have a brick-red appearance, with large quantities of edema fluid flowing from the cut surfaces (Figure 14.2).

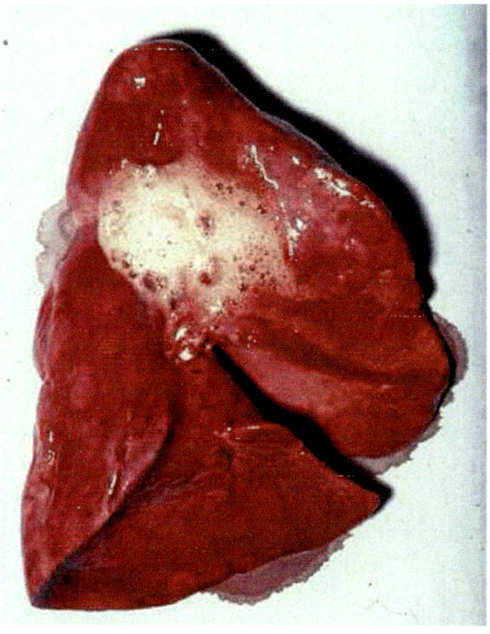

Figure 14.2 Hemorrhagic pulmonary edema.

Somers et al. studied the pathological findings of individuals, ages 9 months to 17 years, who drowned in fresh water (bathtub deaths excluded).[13] In individuals not resuscitated, the incidence of having a frothy exudate was 100%, pleural effusion was present in 40%, increased lung weight in 70% and all three in 40%.[13] In resuscitation with restoration of cardiac output, this dropped to 50, 33, 79 and 8%, respectively, while resuscitation with the successful restoration of cardiac output for a period of time, it was 16, 32, 84 and 4%, respectively.[13]

The mechanism of development of pulmonary edema and pleural effusions is thought to be transudation of inhaled fluid across the alveolar-capillary and capillary interstitial barriers, with gradual leakage of the fluid into the pleural space during and after the drowning episode. These findings, as well as frothy exudate in the airways, are not specific for the diagnosis of drowning and, in fact, may be absent in part or in whole. There is contradictory data as to the whether the amount of pleural fluid and pulmonary edema is different between saltwater and freshwater drowning.

Cerebral edema manifesting as a swollen brain with flattening of the gyri may also be found. Cerebral edema is a nonspecific finding consistent with cerebral hypoxia. Hemorrhage may appear in the petrous or mastoid bones. This, again, is nonspecific and, if sought, can be found in individuals dying of heart disease, drug overdose or other causes of death. Thus, the drug overdose victim dumped in water and the heart attack victim collapsing into water can have the water immersion change of the palms and soles, goose flesh, pulmonary edema and hemorrhage into the petrous and mastoid bones. However, the presence of vegetation and stones as would be found at the bottom of the body of water found clutched in the hands indicates that the cause of death was, in fact, drowning, because they imply that the deceased was alive when entering the water.

Decomposition, blunt force injuries and animal predation are also not uncommonly found in drownings. When a person drowns, the body sinks, assuming a position of head down, buttocks up and extremities dangling downward. Unless there are strong currents, the body will not move very far from its initial position. In relatively shallow water, the extremities or face may bump or drag against the bottom of the body of water, often causing postmortem injuries to the face, back of the hands, knees and toes. The crown of the head and the buttocks can be seen at water level. In deeper water, the body stays below the surface until decomposition begins and gas forms; the body then gradually rises to the surface. In very cold water, the body might stay submerged for months before decomposition creates enough gas to bring it to the surface. Depending on how long a body has been in the water, there might be evidence of animal activity, for example, fish, turtles, crabs or shrimp. The authors have seen bodies that appear relatively intact but, when opened up, reveal the complete absence of the thoracic and abdominal viscera. Examination of the exterior of the body will reveal a defect(s) in the trunk that communicates with the chest or abdominal cavity, through which water denizens have eaten their way inside, where they consume the internal viscera.

Immersion of a body in the water for several hours may cause leaching out of the blood from antemortem wounds. Thus, an individual might be found with a number of what appear to be bloodless postmortem wounds that are, in actual fact, antemortem and the cause of death. This can cause problems when a body is pulled out of the water exhibiting propeller cuts. There may be no bleeding around these injuries, initially leading to the conclusion that these were postmortem injuries when, in fact, they were antemortem, the blood having been leached out by the action of the water. The authors have seen leaching out of blood as early as 3–4 h following immersion.

Dry Drowning

Some individuals who drown are considered to be victims of "dry drowning." Here, the lungs do not have the heavy, boggy and edematous appearance typical of drowning lungs. Rather, the fatal cerebral hypoxia is alleged to be caused by laryngeal spasm. Dry drowning is said to occur in 10–15% of all drownings. What is theorized to occur is that when a small amount of water enters the larynx or trachea, there is a sudden laryngeal spasm mediated as a vagal reflex. Thick mucus, foam and froth may develop, producing an actual physical plug at this point. Thus, water never enters the lungs. The authors have never seen the physical plug said to occur in the larynx and the laryngospasm cannot be demonstrated at autopsy, as death causes relaxation of the musculature. While the aforementioned explanation for dry drowning is interesting, it is a hypothesis and not proven. Thus, the authors do not endorse the use of this term or concept. It is probable that dry drowning is just one end of a spectrum of changes seen in the lung produced by the occlusion of the airways by water, with the other end the heavy, boggy lung containing a massive amount of edema fluid.

Tests for Drowning

A number of tests have been developed over the years to determine whether a person has drowned. The most famous is the Gettler Chloride test,[14] in which the blood was analyzed from the right and left sides of the heart. If the chloride level was less on the right than on the left, the person was assumed to have drowned in saltwater. If it was elevated on the right side of the heart over the left, then one was thought to be dealing with a freshwater drowning. Tests have also been done for other elements in the blood, as well as comparing the specific gravity of blood in the right versus the left atria. All of the aforementioned tests are unreliable and of no help in diagnosing drowning.

A more exotic, though controversial, test involves the identification of diatoms in the tissue of drowning victims. Diatoms are microscopic unicellular algae varying in size from 5 to more than 500 μm. These organisms have a silica skeleton in the shape of two valves. They are found everywhere in all types of water (fresh, brackish and saltwater), on moist soil and in the atmosphere. Some authors contend that the identification of diatoms in human organs is a clear proof of drowning, while others say that it is not possible to come to this conclusion because of the widespread distribution of these organisms throughout the environment.[15,16] The whole question revolves around whether diatoms are normally present in human organs, their density if present, and what types are present. Lung, liver, kidney and bone marrow have been analyzed for diatoms and conclusions have been reached based on the presence or absence of these organisms. Some medical professionals have found diatoms in the organs of non-drownings, while others have not.

If diatoms are present in a body, there are three possible ways they could have gotten there. The first is by inhalation of airborne diatoms, the second is by ingestion of material containing diatoms and the third is by aspiration of water containing diatoms, with subsequent circulation of these throughout the body. Complicating all this is the fact that diatoms are so ubiquitous that some of the analyses may have been contaminated by the glassware and reagents used.

Today, people who use diatom analysis tend to deal with closed organ systems, such as femoral bone marrow or an encapsulated kidney from a non-decomposed body. Contact of the sample with water is limited to triple distilled water. The instruments are specially cleaned to prevent contamination with diatoms. The material, such as bone marrow, is digested in concentrated acid. The deposit is examined with a standard microscope for the presence of the diatoms. The water in which the individual has allegedly drowned is sampled to see what types of diatoms are present and a comparison is made between those found in the water and those found in the body. While a positive comparison is helpful, a negative result does not rule out drowning.

Rip Currents

As waves travel from deep to shallow water, they will break, or crest, as they approach the shore. Some waves crest more strongly, while others are weaker, which can create a circulation of the water, known as rip currents. Rip currents can be very powerful and usually extend from the shore out to sea. Rip currents can occur at any beach with breaking waves, including the Great Lakes. The United States Lifesaving Association estimates that there are over 100 deaths annually in the U.S. due to rip currents and that over 80% of beach rescues performed are due to such currents.[17] Rip currents should not be confused with undertow. Undertow is the flow of water back to the sea from the shoreline, while a rip current is a strong circulating channel of water – rip currents are much more dangerous.

Rip currents are dangerous for all beach goers, even the best swimmers. They have speeds typically around 1–2 ft/s; however, can get up to 8 ft/s. Rip currents are commonly found on all beaches, often around sea breaks, such as sandbars or other structures (i.e. piers) and are usually mild, with slow speeds. However, under certain conditions, the speeds can quickly and suddenly increase, resulting in dangerous conditions. Rip currents are not dangerous because they pull people underwater, but because they pull people out to sea. They also do not require that a person being swimming in deep water to be affected, as they can quickly pull a person standing in waist deep water along the shore out to sea.

Unexplained Drowning and Cardiac Channelopathies

Drownings of individuals, especially in pools, may be of unknown etiology. A complete autopsy may fail to reveal drugs, alcohol, trauma or natural disease to explain the drowning. Witnesses may state that there was no struggle during or preceding the drowning. An autopsy may be completely negative except for the signs of drowning. The drowning occurs even with adjacent individuals and no attempt to struggle or obvious impairment. The individual just seems to dive or slip under the water. Recent research has found that a significant number of these drownings may be secondary to a heritable and potentially lethal cardiac channelopathy,[18] such as congenital long QT syndrome (LQTS) (see Chapter 3 for more information).

This etiology in drowning cases was investigated by Tester et al.[18] They collected 35 unexplained drowning victims (23 males and 12 females; 17 ± 12 years of age [range 4–69 years]) referred for a cardiac channel molecular examination. Of these, 28 (20 males, 8 females) drowned while swimming, and 7 (3 males, 4 females) were bathtub submersions. Polymerase chain reaction, denaturing high-performance liquid chromatography and DNA sequencing were used for a comprehensive mutational analysis of the three major LQTS-susceptibility genes (KCNQ1, KCNH2 and SCN5A). Of the 28 victims of swimming-related drowning, 8 (28.6%) were mutation positive. Of additional note is that none of the bathtub victims were mutation positive. Although sudden death usually occurs in symptomatic patients, it can also happen with the first episode of syncope in about 30% of the patients. Their conclusion was that nearly 30% of the victims of unexplained swimming-related drowning hosted a cardiac channel mutation that could have caused death.[18]

Drownings in Bathtubs

Drownings in bathtubs are relatively uncommon, usually involving young children left unattended by a parent. Some undoubtedly are homicides. Adults in the throes of a seizure can also drown in a bathtub (Figure 14.3).

Less clear are instances where an individual found in a tub has toxic or lethal drug levels. Did they pass out and drown, die of the drugs and eventually slide underwater, or were they placed in the tub following an overdose in a futile attempt to revive them? Similar questions arise in regard to the individual with severe heart disease found in a bathtub underwater. Did they die of a heart attack and then slip under the water or did they have an incapacitating heart attack, slip under the water and drown? The presence of pulmonary edema is of no help, as it might be present in drug overdoses, heart failure or drowning.

Rarely, a case involving an adult dead in a bathtub will be homicide. Such was the case of George Joseph Smith who was convicted of murdering three women by drowning them in a bathtub, known as the Brides in the Bath Murders.

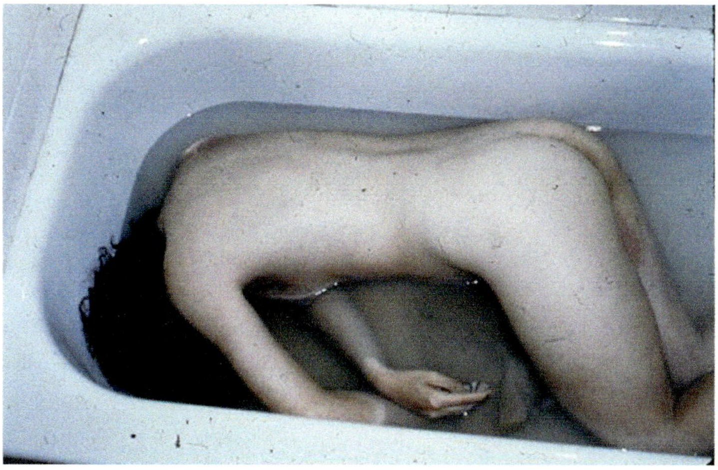

Figure 14.3 A 27-year-old epileptic drowned in the bathtub.

If, while taking a bath, one's feet are grasped and one is pulled underwater, there can be an involuntary inhalation of water as the water rushes into the nasopharynx. This, exacerbated by panic and being in a smooth-walled, wet, slippery container, could result in an inability to save oneself, with rapid loss of consciousness and death. Possibly, no injuries will be seen at autopsy. Rarely, the authors have seen well-documented cases where an individual slipped in the bathtub, struck his head and drowned.

Scuba Divers

Deaths occurring with the use of scuba (self-contained underwater breathing apparatus) equipment require in-depth investigation involving multiple experts. Most forensic pathologists do not have the necessary experience or expertise to invest such deaths and would be well-served by consulting someone who does. The investigation must include not only a complete autopsy examination, but also a review of the clinical and circumstantial information, including the dive information, any antecedent medical therapy and a complete analysis of the diving equipment by a diving technician.[19] In addition, scene reenactment may be considered as well. Scene reenactment may also be beneficial as just because equipment passes a functional test, there may be issues when used in the same manner as it was during the actual incident being investigated.[19] Scene reenactment should only be conducted by trained experts in the field.

In addition to a full review of the clinical and circumstantial information, forensic pathologists and dive experts may also review the dive computer records. Many divers now wear computers that track detailed information of their dive, including depth, duration, number of ascents and ascent rate, and this information may be instrumental in investigating a fatal dive.[19]

Deaths occurring during scuba diving are most often due to drowning, though they can also be the result of natural disease processes, an environmental hazard, defective equipment or as a consequence of being underwater at increased pressure resulting in decompression sickness or pulmonary barotrauma. Divers occasionally get trapped by underwater debris or in caves or are attacked by marine life. Equipment can be the cause of death if it is defective or if there is the contamination of the contained air by a substance such as carbon monoxide. Severe rusting of the interior of the tank could result in a tank atmosphere depleted of oxygen due to the formation of iron oxide. Too rapid an ascent to the surface can cause air embolism, pneumothorax or interstitial emphysema.

Autopsy of these cases requires expertise in the field to correctly interpret all findings. Tests for gas emboli and pneumothoraces should be performed, as well as a postmortem CT scan prior to examination. Postmortem CT has proven beneficial for identifying internal gas and is often more reliable than the autopsy findings. If gas is found to be present, however, it must be correctly interpreted as medical therapy (i.e., cardiopulmonary resuscitation), decomposition and postmortem decompression artifact can all lead to artifactual gas deposits.[19] However, the presence of a pneumothorax with pneumomediastinum and lung damage is highly suggestive of gas embolism.[19]

Both decompression sickness and gas embolism are due to the effects of increased pressure on the body. In decompression sickness, the elevated pressures found at depths (usually >100 ft) cause gases to go into solution, particularly nitrogen. If there is a too rapid an ascent from such depths, the gases may then "bubble" out of solution and into the body tissues. The most common symptom of decompression sickness is joint pain (aka "the bends"), though other symptoms include headache, fatigue and, rarely, respiratory difficulty (aka "the chokes"). With rapid ascent, these changes in pressure can result in barotrauma, most commonly affecting the ears and lungs. Pulmonary barotrauma can lead to fatal pneumothoraces and gas embolism. The lung injury can allow gases to pass directly into the pulmonary circulation.

Due to the myriad of possible etiologies of death, including drowning, natural disease, trauma- and pressure-related issues, the authors, again, recommend that such deaths be thoroughly and accurately investigated by a team of experts.

Neonaticide by Drowning

Neonaticide by a mother soon after the birth of a child occasionally occurs. Drowning is one method, commonly occurring in a toilet.[20] Homicidal drowning must be differentiated from the disposing of an already dead infant in water. Therefore, the question of whether an infant was alive after delivery is the most important question for the pathologist to answer. If the signs of a separate existence are absent, one is dealing with a stillbirth. If the signs of a separate existence are present, the possibility of infanticide has to be investigated (see Chapter 10 for a full discussion). Underwater births, which come in and out of fashion, can confuse the issues as under these circumstances, a negative hydrostatic lung test does not rule out the possibility of the child having been born alive.

References

1. Centers for Disease Control and Prevention, National Center for Injury Prevention and Control, Web-based Injury Statistics Query and Reporting System (WISQARS) [online]. Available from: http://www.cdc.gov/injury/wisqars; accessed 13 May 2019.
2. Pearn J, Pathophysiology of drowning. *Med J Aust* 1985; 142:586–588.
3. Craig AB, Causes of loss of consciousness during underwater swimming. *J Appl Physiol* 1961; 16:583–586.
4. Craig AB, Underwater swimming and loss of consciousness. *JAMA* 1961; 176:255–258.
5. Giammona ST and Modell JH, Drowning by total immersion: effects on pulmonary surfactant of distilled water, isotonic saline and sea water. *Am J Dis Child* 1967; 114:612–616.
6. Ornato JP, The resuscitation of near-drowning victims. *JAMA* 1986; 256:75–77.
7. Bolte RG, et al., The use of extracorporeal rewarming in a child submerged for 66 minutes. *JAMA* 1988; 260:377–379.
8. Swann HG and Spafford NR, Body salt and water changes during fresh and sea water drowning. *Tex Rep Biol Med* 1951; 9:356–382.
9. Swann HG, et al., Fresh- and sea-water drowning: a study of the terminal cardiac and biochemical events. *Tex Rep Biol Med* 1947; 5:423–437.
10. Modell JH and Davis JH, Electrolyte changes in human drowning victims. *Anesthesiology* 1969; 30:414–420.
11. Conn AW and Barker CA, Fresh water drowning and near-drowning – an update. *Can Anaesth Soc* 1984; 31:S38–S44.
12. Reh H, On the early postmortem course of "washerwoman's skin at the fingertips. *Z Rechtsmed* 1984; 92(31):183–188. (In German).

13. Somers GR, Chiasson DA, and Smith CR, Pediatric drowning: a 20 year review of autopsied cases: II. Pathologic features. *Am J Forensic Med Pathol* 2006; 27:20–24.
14. Gonzales TA, Vance M, and Helpern M, *Legal Medicine and Toxicology*. Appleton-Century Co, New York, NY, 1937.
15. Peabody AJ, Diatoms and drowning – a review. *Med Sci Law* 1980; 20(4):254–261.
16. Foged N, Diatoms and drowning – once more. *Forensic Sci Int* 1983; 21:153–159.
17. Rip Currents. United States Lifesaving Association. Available from: https://www.usla.org/page/ripcurrents#Survival; accessed 13 May 2019.
18. Tester DJ, Medeiros-Domingo A, Will ML, Ackerman MJ, Unexplained drowning and cardiac channelopathies: a molecular autopsy series. *Mayo Clin Proc* 2011; 86(10):941–947.
19. Edmunds C and Caruso J, Recent modifications to the investigation of diving related deaths. *Forensic Sci Med Pathol* 2014; 10:83–90.
20. Dressler J, Schmidt U, Hanisch U, et al., Neonatal freshwater drowning after birth in the bathroom. *Am J Forensic Med Pathol* 2011; 32: 119–123.

Electrocution 15

Electricity is really just organized lightning

—George Carlin

Deaths caused by electrocution are infrequent. Virtually all are accidents, with suicides rare and homicides even rarer. These deaths involve both low-voltage (<600 V) and high-voltage (>600–750 V) currents. They virtually always involve alternating currents, because direct current is used less. In addition, humans are four to six times as sensitive to alternating currents as to direct. Alternating currents between 39 and 150 cycles/s have the greatest lethality. In the United States, alternating current is generated at a 60-Hz frequency; in Europe at 50-Hz.

Amperage, or the amount of current flow, is the most important factor in electrocution. It is directly related to the voltage and inversely related to the resistance. Voltage is a measure of the electromotive force and ohms are the resistance to the conduction of electricity. This is expressed in the formula:

$$A = \frac{V}{R}$$

Residential voltage in the United States is approximately 110–120 V from line to ground. High-voltage lines in suburban and urban areas are approximately 7500–8000 V line to ground with transcontinental high-tension lines 100,000 V or greater. For electrocution from low-voltage (110–120 V) household current, there must be direct contact with the electrical circuit, with death primarily caused by ventricular fibrillation (VF). In high-voltage incidents, direct contact with the wire is not necessary. As the body approaches the high-voltage line, an electric current (arc) may jump from the line to the body. In addition, the temperature generated by an arc current can be as high as 40,000°C. Electrocution from these lines occurs when they break, fall to the ground and are touched, or when an intact or "live" line is touched by a tall metal object such as a ladder, pole or crane with which a person is in contact.

Resistance to electrocution in humans involves the skin. With 120 V, dry skin may have a resistance of 100,000 Ω; dry and calloused skin up to a million ohms; moist skin 1000 Ω or less, and moist, thin skin as low as 100 Ω.[2] With high-voltage currents, skin condition plays no significant role in resistance to electrocution.

Mechanism of Death

Amperage is the most important factor in electrocution. Since voltage is usually constant, the main factor in determining the amount of amperage that enters the body is

Table 15.1 The Distance an Electric Arc Can Jump*

Voltage	Distance Current Can Arc
1000	few mm
5000	1 cm
20,000	6 cm
40,000	13 cm
100,000	35 cm

*As reported by Somogyi and Tedeschi.[1]

the resistance, as expressed in ohms. The minimal amount of amperage perceptible to a human as a tingle is 1 mA (0.001 A). A current of 5 mA will produce tremors of the musculature while 15–17 mA will cause contracture of the muscles, which prevents release of the electrical source. This latter current is the "no-let-go" threshold. At 50 mA, there is contracture of all muscles, respiratory paralysis and death if the current is sustained. VF occurs at currents between 75 and 100 mA. Extremely high currents, ~1 A and higher, do not cause VF, but rather ventricular arrest. If the current is then turned off, and there is no significant electrothermal injury to the heart, the heart should begin to beat normally.

When electrical current enters the body, it runs from the point of contact to the point of grounding, following the shortest path. Most commonly, the path is from hand to foot or hand to hand. The time necessary for a current to cause death depends on the amperage. Thus, in very low-amperage electrocutions, where death is caused by paralysis of the muscles with secondary asphyxia, prolonged contact (i.e., several minutes) with the electrical current would be necessary. With household current, in which the mechanism of death is VF, the duration of contact necessary to produce fibrillation may be measured in seconds or tenths of seconds, depending on the amperage. This is, of course, determined by the resistance. Thus, with 120-V current and 1000 Ω of skin resistance, 120 mA reach the body. In such a case, contact for 5 s would be necessary to produce VF.[3] If the point of contact is thin moist skin, resistance may be as low as 100 Ω. In such cases, the current entering the body would be approximately 1200 mA (1.2 A) and VF could occur in 0.1 s. With high-voltage electrocution, cardiac arrest is essentially instantaneous.

Low-voltage electrocution usually does not produce systemic injuries. The electrical injury causing death in low-voltage electrocution is a lethal ventricular arrhythmia, usually VF. There are three established means for this.[4] The first is delivering a single strong electrical impulse at the initiation of the T wave, instantly causing VF. The second requires high rate cardiac capture (typically >450 BPM) that induces VF within a few seconds; this mechanism requires less current than "T-shock" induction but several pulses (usually at least 6). The last method requires less current than the first two, but longer duration (more pulses) and involves long-term high-rate cardiac capture causing sufficient ischemia to lower the VF threshold to allow for induction of VF. Additional mechanisms have also been proposed, including respiratory paralysis and arrest, inducing ventricular tachycardia or asystole and increasing the ventricular effective refractory period (VERP).

In low-voltage electrocution with VF, consciousness may not be lost immediately. In fact, it is very common for the individual receiving a fatal electric shock to not lose consciousness, but to yell out or state that he just "burned" himself prior to collapse. This is because the brain has approximately 10–15 s of oxygen reserve, irrespective of the heart. Thus, an individual can remain conscious for 10–15 s after cessation of the heart as a pumping organ. In cases of low-voltage electrocution, resuscitation and defibrillation may prevent death. It should be kept in mind that VF is occasionally self-reversible in that the heart will revert to spontaneous rhythm following a short time of fibrillation.

Death from high-voltage electrocution is usually caused by either the electrothermal injury produced by the current or respiratory arrest. High-voltage arcs can generate temperatures as high as 40,000°C resulting in severe thermal injury. The hyperthermic effects of high-voltage currents can be seen in judicial execution, where third-degree burns develop at the site of contact between the electrodes and skin, as well as in the observation by Werner that, following execution, the brain temperature was as high as 63°C.[5]

In addition, high-voltage electrical currents can cause the same cardiac rhythm disruptions described above; however, while the heart may start again spontaneously following cardiac arrest, respiration might not resume because of paralysis of the respiratory center. This is probably caused by damage to the respiratory center of the brainstem by the hyperthermic effects of the current.

Fractures Caused by Electrocution

When an individual contacts an electrified source having a current of 50 mA or greater, there is generalized muscular contraction. Whether the current is low- or high-voltage, these contractions can fracture bones. Tarquinio et al. reported bilateral scapular fractures from a 440-V, 60-Hz current; Dumas and Walker from exposure to a 220-V, 50Hz current.[6,7] Stueland et al. described a case of bilateral humeral fractures from contact with 110 V; Shaheen and Sabet bilateral fractures of the femoral necks secondary to contact with a 220-V current.[8,9] Fractures of T12 and L1 vertebrae have also been reported.[10] Tarquinio et al. mention that fractures were frequently seen as complications of electroconvulsive or "shock" therapy prior to the use of muscle relaxants in this therapy.[6]

Involuntary Movements Caused by Electricity-Induced Contraction of Muscle

Contact with current, especially high-voltage current, may produce violent muscle contractions. As previously noted, these can cause fractures. Wright et al. describe the following reactions that can result from electrically induced contraction of muscle:[11]

The back and neck arch backward.

The arms rotate inward the elbows flex and the hands form fists.

The hips and knees lock straight and the feet extend

If the individuals are grasping something, they will continue to do so.

Wright et al. feel that these muscular contractions, if violent enough, can propel an individual forward or backward, depending on the original position.

Autopsy Findings

In all cases of high-voltage electrocution but in only about half (50%) the cases of low-voltage electrocution, electrical burns will appear on the body. In low-voltage electrocution, these may occur at the point of entry or the point of exit, at both, or at neither. If the current enters over a broad surface area that offers minimal resistance, there may be no electrical burn. The best example of this is an individual electrocuted in a bathtub. Absence of burns in low-voltage electrocutions, however, can occur with only a small area of contact. Electrocution can produce accelerated onset of rigor mortis caused by the muscle contractions and depletion of adenosine triphosphate (ATP). If this does occur, it may be eccentric, reflecting the passage of the current through the body.

Electrical burns tend to be on the palms of the hands and tips of the fingers (entry sites) and soles of the feet (exit sites) (Figure 15.1A–D).

In low-voltage electrocutions, they may appear as either an erythematous area of blistering or as an irregular chalky white lesion, often with raised borders and a central crater. There may be some yellowish or black discoloration of the burn sites caused by heat. Generally, the burns are small in size, from a few millimeters up to 1–1.5 cm. Microscopically, the epidermis shows a Swiss cheese appearance. If there is only brief

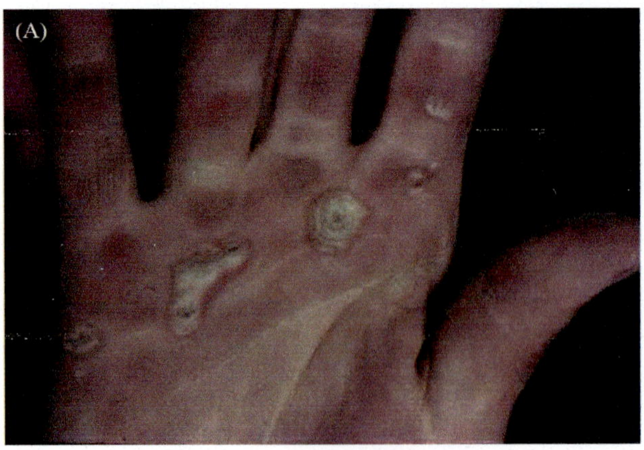

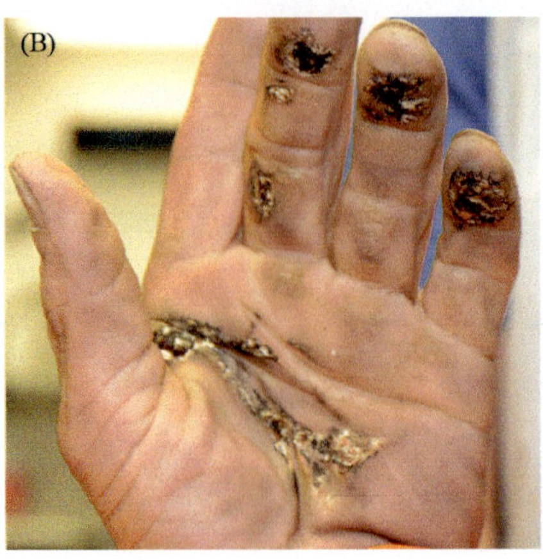

Figure 15.1 (A and B) Electrical burns of hands representing points of entry (*continued*).

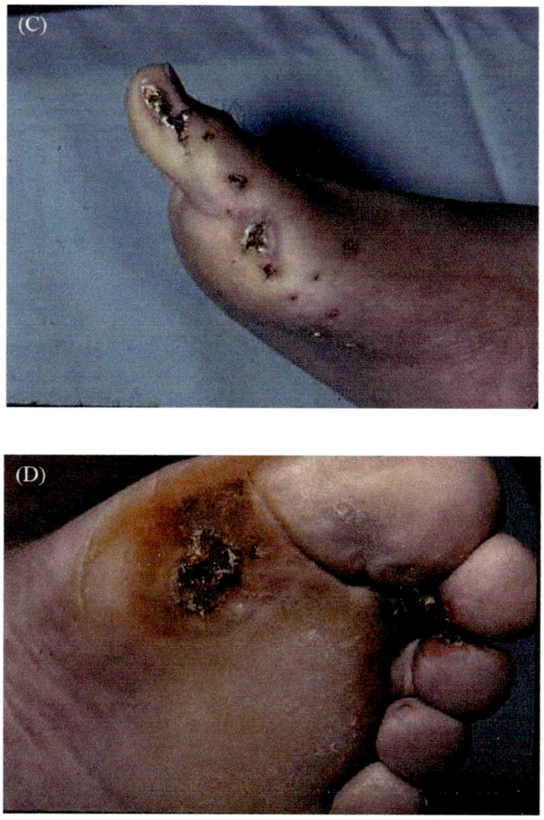

Figure 15.1 (*continued*) (C and D) Electrical burns of feet representing exit sites.

contact with a live wire, there may be no burns. The person may collapse from VF and fall away from the wire. When there is prolonged contact, there will be severe burns caused by the heat generated by the electrical current. One cannot differentiate antemortem from postmortem electrical burns. The burns indicate only that current has passed through the skin. Minute particles of metal from the conducting surface may be deposited in the burns, especially in high-voltage electrocutions. These can be located and identified by scanning electron microscopy.

In contrast to low-voltage burns, high-voltage burns may be extremely severe, with charring of the body. If the burns occur from contact or proximity to a high-voltage line, numerous individual and confluent areas of third-degree burns will present (Figure 15.2).

The multiple small burns are caused by arcing of the current. If the contact with the high-voltage current is not direct, but through current running through an intermediary object such as a ladder or pole, the burns are large and irregular, chalky white in color, often with raised borders and a central crater with yellowish or black discoloration of the burn sites caused by heat. If the individual is wearing shoes, and the exit site is a foot, there may be arcing exit burns. With very high voltage, there can be massive destruction of tissue with loss of extremities and rupture of organs.

In all cases of suspected electrocution, there should be an examination of the alleged source of the electrical current including electrical devices the individual was handling

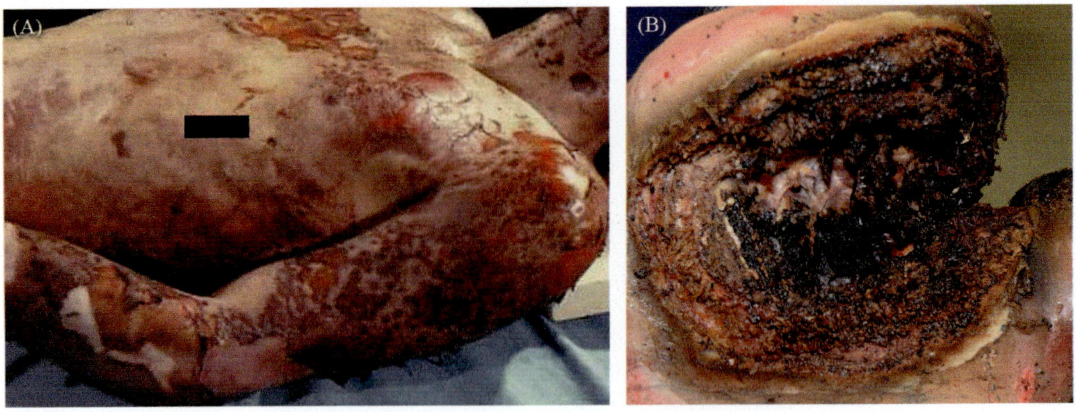

Figure 15.2 (A and B) High-voltage electrical burns with multiple individual and confluent burn areas.

at the time of death. In low-voltage electrocutions, examination of the device rather than examination of the body will often provide the cause of death, because burns may not be present. Thus, one can make a diagnosis of electrocution without an electrical burn, based on the circumstances of the death, negative autopsy findings and the examination of the electrical device in use. In high-voltage electrocution, tissue from the victim may be adherent at the point of contact with the source of the current (e.g., a metal ladder).

Manner of Death

Most deaths caused by electrocution are accidental in manner. Not infrequently, these can be blamed on defective tools or electrical appliances. Electrocutions caused by high-voltage wires occur secondary to inadvertent contact with a high-voltage line when operating or in contact with a device such as a "cherry picker." Other causes of electrocution are touching a downed electrical line or inadvertently making contact with a line via a radio antenna or kite. The authors have also seen cases of a sexual nature where electrodes have been found in the anus or attached to the penis.

Suicides are rare, although occasionally, individuals will build elaborate devices to electrocute themselves. Homicides are even rarer. The most common method of homicide with electrical current is to drop a plugged-in electrical device into a bathtub while an individual is taking a bath. There are usually no electrical burns in such a case and, if the electrical device is removed, the cause of death will be missed.

Bathtub electrocutions, both homicidal and accidental, are becoming less common, because of the fairly widespread use of low-voltage ground-fault current interrupters (GFCIs). These are now required in kitchens, bathrooms and outside outlets. This device monitors the current flow. If there is a greater than 5-mA difference, the circuit is broken, thus preventing electrocution. A normal circuit breaker does not function until a 15-A difference is detected. Thus, in most cases of electrocution, the house fuse is unaffected by the electrocution. Electrocution in water could also be caused by defective lights in a swimming pool. GFCIs prevent this type of accident.

Lightning

A lightning bolt is produced when the charged undersurface of a thundercloud sends its electrical charge to the ground. Since the undersurface is usually negatively charged, virtually all discharges are also negative. Approximately 5% of lightning flashes, however, are positive discharges. These are most frequent in mountainous regions.

A lightning bolt may injure or kill an individual by a direct strike, a side flash or conduction through another object. An example of the last instance would be a lightning bolt's hitting a crane, with the electricity flowing down the metal structure and striking a grounded worker who is touching the crane. The injuries produced would be the same as if the crane had hit a high-power electrical line, that is, burns at the entrance and exit sites, often multiple and severe.

In a side-flash strike, the bolt of lightning hits an object, such as a tree, and then ricochets, striking the individual. In a direct strike or a side-flash strike where the individual is relatively close to the object from which the bolt jumps, the current can either spread over the surface of the body or enter it, or it can follow both routes. In most cases seen by the forensic pathologist, the current has both flowed over the surface of the body and entered. In such cases, it is quite common to find the clothing torn, shoes burst, hair seared, burns on the skin caused by zippers and other metal objects heated by the lightning and burns caused by the entrance and exit of current. Cutaneous burns are not severe but always present.[12] On histological examination, the epidermis is separated from the papillary dermis. Rupture of the tympanic membrane is present in approximately 81% of cases.[12] Objects constructed of ferrous metal on the body may be magnetized. Other metal objects, such as coins, may show burns. The torn clothing and burst shoes sometimes have led to misinterpretation of the nature of the injuries. People struck by lightning and found next to a road have been thought to be hit-and-run victims. If one is inside a metal vehicle, such as a car or train, when it is struck by lightning, the probability of injury is extremely small. On rare occasions, death or injury has been reported when an individual was using a telephone and the line was hit by lightning.[13]

Deaths from lightning are caused by high-voltage direct current. Death is caused by cardiopulmonary arrest or electrothermal injuries. With a direct hit by lightning, death is probably inevitable, because of burns and injury to the respiratory center of the brain. Amperage in this case would be in the kiloampere range. If the electrocution is secondary to a close point of impaction, survival may be possible. In fact, most individuals injured by lightning do survive. One of the lesions considered pathognomonic for lightning injury is the "arborescent" or fern-like injury of the skin called Lichtenberg figures (Figure 15.3).

This lesion is a patterned area of transient erythema that appears within 1 h of the incident and then gradually fades within 24 h. The erythematous marks are not burns. ten Duis et al. believe that this lesion is caused by positive discharges over the skin.[14] They hypothesize that the lesion occurs when an individual struck by a negative lightning bolt is then hit by a secondary positive flashover from a nearby grounded object. Another possibility is that it represents an entrance point in an individual struck by a positively charged lightning bolt. Both explanations, neither of which are exclusive of the other, would explain the relative rarity of the arborescent lesion in individuals struck by lightning.

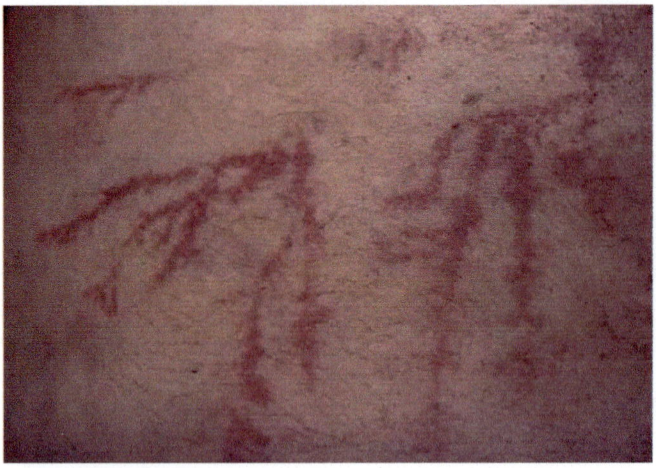

Figure 15.3 "Arborescent" burn of lightning.

References

1. Somogyi E and Tedeschi CG, Injury by electrical force, in Tedeschi CG, Eckert WG, and Tedeschi LG (Eds) *Forensic Medicine*. WB Saunders Co, Philadelphia, PA, 1977, pp 645–676.
2. Bruner JMR, Hazards of electrical apparatus. *Anesthesiology* 1967; 28:396–425.
3. Ferris LP, et al., Effect of electroshock and health. *AIEE Trans* 1936; 55:498.
4. Kroll MW, Fish RM, Dhanunjaya D, et al., Essentials of low-power electrocution: established and speculated mechanisms. 34th Annual International Conference of the IEEE EMBS, San Diego, CA, 2012.
5. Werner AH, Death by electricity. *NY Med J* 1923; 118:498–500.
6. Tarquinio T, Weinstein ME, and Virgilio RW, Bilateral scapular fractures from accidental electric shock. *J Trauma* 1979; 19(2):132–133.
7. Dumas JL and Walker N, Bilateral scapular fractures secondary to electrical shock. *Arch Orthop Trauma Surg* 1992; 111(5):287–288.
8. Stueland DT, et al., Bilateral humeral fractures from electrically induced muscular spasm. *J Emerg Med* 1989; 7(5):457–459.
9. Shaheen MA and Sabet NA, Bilateral simultaneous fracture of the femoral neck following electrical shock. *Injury* 1984; 16(1):13–14.
10. Rajam KH, et al., Fracture of vertebral bodies caused by accidental electric shock. *J Indian Med Assoc* 1976; 66:35.
11. Wright RK, Broisz HG, and Shuman M, The investigation of electrical injuries and deaths. *Presented at the Meeting of the American Academy of Forensic Science*, Reno, NV, February 2000.
12. Wetli CV, Keraunopathology: an analysis of 45 fatalities. *Am J Forensic Med Path* 1996; 17(2):89–98.
13. Johnstone BR, Harding DL, and Hocking B, Telephone-related lightning injury. *Med J Aust* 1986; 144:706–709.
14. ten Duis HJ, Klasen H1, Nijsten MWN, et al., Superficial lightning injuries—their "fractal" shape and origin. *Burns* 1987; 13:141–146.

Hyperthermia and Hypothermia: The Effects of Heat and Cold

16

That emperor, who sways the realm of sorrow, at mid breast from the ice, stood forth.

—**Dante Alighieri's *Inferno***

The Effects of Heat and Cold

Normal body temperature is generally considered to be 98.6°F (37°C) orally and approximately 1°F (0.6°C) higher rectally. Body temperature, however, can vary from individual to individual, by age, time of day, physical exertion, etc. Thus, newborns and the elderly have temperatures averaging 1°C higher. Cyclic changes in body temperature occur with decreases of 0.5°C early in the morning (approximately 1:00–2:00 a.m.) and slight elevations later in the morning and afternoon. Hard exercise can raise the rectal temperature up to 104°F.[1] Rectal temperatures of 39–40°C are common in marathoners after a race.[2]

To further complicate this matter, the normal oral temperature is based on 19th-century data. More recent work by Mackowiak et al. indicates that 98.2°F (36.8°C) is the mean normal oral temperature, with 99.9°F (37.7°C) as the upper limit.[3] Maximum temperatures varied with time of day with a low temperature in the early morning. They thought that 98.9°F (37.2°C) in the morning and 99.9°F (37.7°C) overall should be regarded as the upper limits of oral temperature in adults. Thus, we see that there is no exact "normal" temperature, but rather a range.

Maintenance of normal body temperature is a delicate balance between heat load and heat loss. Heat load is the sum of heat generated by oxidation of metabolic products and heat acquired from the environment. Heat is lost by three mechanisms: **conduction**, **radiation** and **evaporation**.[1]

Loss of heat by conduction is either by direct conduction from the surface of the body to another object or by conduction to air. Loss of heat by direct conduction to objects is relatively minor. For example, if an individual sits in a chair, heat conducted from the body will raise the temperature of the chair to that of the body. When this has occurred, heat loss will stop.

In contrast to limited heat loss by direct conduction, sizable quantities of heat can be lost by conduction to air. The molecules composing the skin transfer heat to contiguous air molecules, producing a thin zone of heated air adjacent to the skin. This zone usually remains relatively stationary. Once this layer of air absorbs heat until it is equal to the temperature of the body, heat loss ceases. If, however, this layer of heated air is continually removed and new air introduced (by a fan or wind), the loss of heat by conduction will continue. This movement of air around the body, with resultant continued loss of heat, is known as **convection**. Winds will blow away the layer of air immediately adjacent to the skin, thus accounting for the feeling of cold and increased heat loss when the wind blows.

There is, however, a limitation on this process. Once the wind has cooled the skin to a certain temperature, the rate at which heat flows from the core of the body to the skin is the limiting factor in heat loss, rather than the rate of conduction and convection.

The second method of heat loss is by **radiation**. Here, there is loss of heat in the form of infrared rays. These radiate from the body in all directions. Heat rays, however, radiate from all masses. Thus, walls, floors, ground, etc., all radiate infrared heat rays. If the environment becomes hotter than the body, radiant heat given up by the surroundings will exceed the loss of heat from the body by radiation.

The third method of heat loss is by **evaporation**. This is the *primary method of cooling the overheated body.* As water evaporates from the body, 0.58 cal of heat are lost for each gram of water that evaporates.[1] The two mechanisms of heat loss by evaporation are **insensible** heat loss and **sweating**. Insensible heat loss is loss of moisture from the non-sweating individual. This is the water that evaporates from the skin and lungs. It occurs at a rate of about 600 mL/day, that is, a continual heat loss of 12–16 cal/h.[1] Insensible heat loss is caused by continued diffusion of water molecules through the skin and respiratory surfaces regardless of the body temperature.

The more important of the two methods of evaporation that produce cooling of the body is sweating. In cold weather, the rate of sweat production is essentially zero. In hot weather, the maximum rate of sweat production varies from 700 mL/h in the unacclimatized person to 1.5–2 L/h in a person maximally acclimatized to heat.[1] In individuals sweating heavily, dehydration can rapidly develop. Dehydration, in turn, predisposes an individual to the development of hyperthermia and heatstroke. To prevent this, individuals exposed to high temperatures are urged to increase their fluid intake. This is especially necessary for those engaging in strenuous activities such as manual labor or jogging. Some people ingest too much fluid and develop hyponatremia.[4] The symptoms of this are nonspecific – nausea, vomiting, headache, muscle weakness, confusion and seizures. Symptoms occur when serum sodium levels decrease to <130 mmol/L, becoming severe at levels <125 mmol/L. When serum sodium drops below 120 mmol/L, it shows that more than 50% of individuals have seizures.

When people are exposed to hot weather for several weeks, they begin to progressively sweat more and more. First, they sweat 700 mL/h. This doubles within 10 days, increasing up to three times as much within 6 weeks. This is caused by increased sweat capability of the sweat glands. Sweat contains sodium chloride or salt. When the rate of sweat secretion is very low, the sodium chloride concentration of the sweat is also very low because sodium and chloride are reabsorbed before they reach the surface of the body. As the rate of secretion becomes progressively greater, the rate of sodium chloride reabsorption does not increase equally, so that the concentration of sodium in the sweat can rise almost to the level of the plasma. Extreme sweating can deplete the extracellular fluids of electrolytes, particularly sodium and chloride. Thus, extra sodium and chloride must usually be added to the diet in tropical climates. Persons who sweat profusely can lose as much as 15–30 g of sodium chloride each day until they become acclimatized.[1] After 4–6 weeks, the loss of sodium decreases and may be as little as 3–5 g/day. A person who has lived in the tropics since childhood actually has more active sweat glands in the body than an individual from a cold climate. People are born with an excess of sweat glands. When they live in a temperate zone, many of these become permanently inactive during childhood. If, however, they remain in the tropics, they remain functional throughout life.

The skin, subcutaneous tissues and fat act as heat insulators in the body. Fat is especially important because it conducts heat only one-third as readily as other tissues. When no blood is flowing from internal organs to the skin, the insulating properties of the male body are approximately equal to three-fourths of the insulating properties of the usual suit of clothes. In women, because of greater body fat, this insulation is even greater.

Increased loss of heat from the body can be caused by increased flow of blood to the skin. Immediately beneath the skin is a venous plexus that is supplied by an inflow of blood. Full dilatation of these vessels can increase the rate of heat transfer to the skin eight-fold. Such a high rate of blood flow causes heat to be conducted from the internal portions of the body to the skin with great efficiency. Reduction in the rate of blood flow decreases the efficiency in heat conduction. Thus, the skin is used as a radiator system, with the flow of blood to the skin the mechanism of heat transfer from the body core to the skin. As long as the body temperature is greater than that of the surroundings, heat is lost principally by radiation and conduction. Thus, a nude person sitting in a room at normal room temperature would lose approximately 3% of heat by conduction to objects, 15% by conduction to air, 60% by radiation and 22% by evaporation (insensible heat loss).[1]

When the temperature of the surroundings is greater than that of the skin, instead of losing heat, the body gains heat by radiation and conduction from the surroundings. In this situation, the only means by which the body can rid itself of heat is by evaporation. Any factor preventing adequate evaporation under such circumstances causes the body temperature to rise. If this continues long enough, the individual will develop heatstroke and die.

High humidity interferes with heat loss by sweating. With high humidity, the air holds almost as much moisture as possible. As a result, the rate of evaporation is greatly reduced or totally prevented so that the secreted sweat remains in a fluid state. Consequently, the body temperature approaches the temperature of the surroundings or rises above this temperature, even though sweat continues to pour forth.

It has already been mentioned that a thin zone of air adjacent to the skin usually remains relatively stationary and is not exchanged for new air at a rapid rate unless convection air currents are present. Such lack of air movement prevents effective evaporation in the same way that it prevents effective cooling by conduction of heat to the air. The local air becomes saturated with water vapors and further evaporation cannot occur. When convection currents occur, the saturated air is swept away from the skin and unsaturated air replaces it. Convection is of even more importance with heat loss from the body by evaporation than by conduction to air. This explains why fans are so helpful in keeping the body temperature down.

Clothing has the opposite effect. It traps the air around the body, decreasing the flow of convection air currents. Thus, the rate of heat loss from the body by convection and conduction is greatly decreased. Ordinarily, clothes decrease the rate of heat loss from the body to about half than that from a nude body.[5] Arctic clothing can decrease heat loss to as little as one-sixth of the nude state. When clothing becomes wet, the rate of heat transmission increases as much as 20-fold because of the high conductivity of heat by water. This is why wet clothing is so deadly in arctic regions.

In an individual who is clothed, the effectiveness of heat loss by evaporation is dependent upon the material. Fabric that is pervious to moisture, such as cotton, allows almost normal heat loss by the body by evaporation. This is because, when sweating occurs, the sweat dampens the clothing and evaporation then occurs on the surface of the clothing.

This cools the clothing, which, in turn, cools the skin. Thus, in tropical regions, light clothing that is pervious to sweat but impervious to radiant heat from the sun prevents the body from gaining radiant heat, while at the same time allowing it to lose heat by evaporation, almost as if one were not wearing clothing.

Hyperthermia

When individuals' ability to cool the body can no longer compensate for the heat load, they develop heatstroke. This is a life-threatening condition classically manifested by hyperthermia (a rectal temperature of 105–106°F or higher), hot, dry skin, altered sensorium, tachycardia, hypotension and hyperventilation. The very old and very young are more susceptible to heatstroke. Predisposing health conditions and individual susceptibility include alcoholism, dehydration, obesity, preexisting disease (cardiac and neurological) and the use of diuretics and major tranquilizers such as phenothiazines, tricyclic antidepressants and monoamine oxidase inhibitors. Relative humidity also plays a role. As humidity increases, the apparent temperature may be significantly higher than the actual recorded temperature (Table 16.1).

Obese individuals show a greater susceptibility to heatstroke. This is due to a number of factors: (1) increased adipose tissue creates greater demand on the heart; (2) the fat provides extra insulation for the body, preventing loss of heat; and (3) since metabolic heat is produced in proportion to the bulk of the tissue and is lost in proportion to the surface area, the larger bulk-to-area ratio in the obese reduces efficient heat loss.

While the classic definition of heatstroke requires a minimum rectal temperature of between 105 and 106°F, there is some variability in this, just as there is with the hot, dry skin. In individuals who develop heatstroke following extreme exertion (e.g., military recruits), there may initially be some sweating, though a hot, flushed, dry skin is more common. The skin may also appear blanched and relatively cool because of intense catecholamine release.[6] Individuals who develop heatstroke secondary to extreme exertion

Table 16.1 Heat Index Chart: Air Temperature and Relative Humidity versus Apparent Temperature

Temp.	Relative humidity (%)										
(°F)	50	55	60	65	70	75	80	85	90	95	100
110	**150**										
105	**135**	**142**	**149**								
100	*120*	*126*	**132**	**138**	**144**						
95	*107*	*110*	*114*	*119*	*124*	**130**	**136**				
90	96	98	100	102	*106*	*109*	*113*	*117*	*122*		
85	88	89	90	91	93	95	97	99	102	*105*	*108*
80	81	81	82	83	85	86	86	87	88	89	91
75	75	75	76	76	77	77	78	78	79	79	80
70	69	69	70	70	70	70	71	71	71	71	72

Note: Danger = Italic; Extreme danger = Bold.

Figure 16.1 Body of a man with an organic brain syndrome who became lost outside during the hot summer months.

have a greater tendency to develop rhabdomyolysis and disseminated intravascular coagulopathy than those individuals whose heatstroke is unrelated to exertion.

Heatstroke is generally seen in two settings. The first involves relatively young individuals exposed to high temperatures while undergoing extreme exertion – military recruits and football players in training are examples. Individuals working outside for long periods of time in the heat also fall into this category, as well as migrants walking into the United States through the southern territories during the hot summer months, and the elderly, particularly those with dementia, who may wander away from home or their facility, becoming lost outdoors (Figure 16.1).

The other setting for hyperthermia deaths is a prolonged heat wave. In this latter circumstance, affected individuals are generally over the age of 60. Deaths caused by heatstroke during heat waves usually do not present the first day or two of the heat wave, but appear toward the end of the first week, as the victims' heat-adaptive systems give out. Many also have preexisting cardiovascular disease.

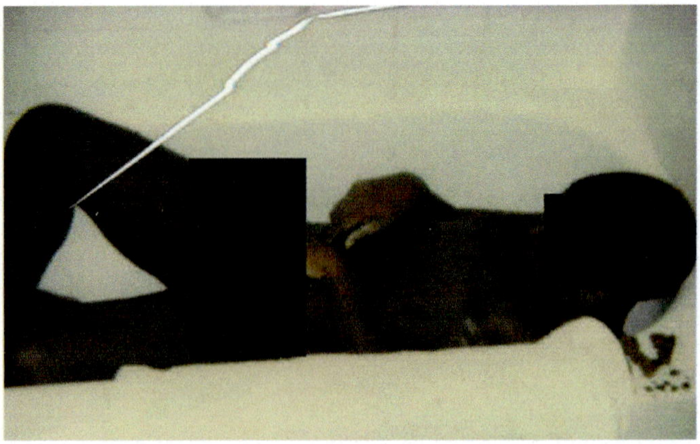

Figure 16.2 Young man with multiple sclerosis who died due to hyperthermia while bathing.

Other more rare causes of hyperthermia also occur, such as malignant hyperthermia related to anesthesia, or hyperthermia associated with Excited Delirium syndrome. Multiple sclerosis patients are also susceptible to paralysis due to hyperthermia and should exercise care while bathing or using hot tubs. One of the authors (VDM) has seen a case of hyperthermia in a young man with multiple sclerosis who died after prolonged immersion in hot water while bathing (Figure 16.2)

Symptoms of heatstroke may come on suddenly or be preceded by prodromic symptoms – nausea, vomiting, vertigo, muscle cramps, dyspnea and a feeling of warmth. Experiments have been carried out to determine the subjective impressions of individuals exposed to heat stress.[7] Initially, there is a loss of ability to concentrate and a vague feeling of impending physiologic deterioration is experienced. Awareness of body heat and profuse perspiration is replaced by the realization that sweating has diminished and then suddenly ceased. The face feels dry and hot, while, at the same time, the individual notes the feeling of a film of dried salt on the cheeks, forehead and corners of the mouth. Then comes the realization that the slightest movement of the body produces an increase in heart rate and a premonition of a fainting spell. Paresthesias develop in the hands, feet and ankles. The face, which until now was pinkish red, abruptly turns ashen gray, suggesting impending cardiocirculatory collapse. Exposure in volunteers ended at this point, to prevent their becoming stuporous and lapsing into the coma of heatstroke.

As the circulating blood temperature rises to a level higher than 42.4°C, there is generalized vasodilation, with resultant effective reduction in blood volume. Diminished peripheral resistance leads to increased and rapid venous return and increased cardiac output. The left side of the heart cannot keep pace with the right. The increase in venous return results in the elevation of venous pressure that triggers high-output cardiac failure and circulatory collapse.[7,8] The resulting tissue anoxia may explain the paresthesias. The same increase in venous pressure is ultimately thought to be responsible for the cessation of sweating seen at the peak of the heatstroke syndrome. Thus, it has been noted that if venous pressure increases, sweating begins to decrease; as venous pressure decreases, sweating is restored.

Diagnosis of heatstroke antemortem is relatively straightforward because of the characteristic symptoms and signs, as well as the elevated body temperature. The autopsy findings of heatstroke, however, are not specific and may include diffuse petechiae and hemorrhages of the serosal membranes.[9] Individuals surviving more than 24 h may show lobular pneumonia, acute tubular necrosis of the kidneys, adrenal hemorrhage or necrosis of the liver. Also noted are subendocardial hemorrhage, degeneration of myocardial fibers and disseminated intravascular coagulopathy. If the diagnosis of heatstroke has not been made prior to death, the diagnosis, if it can be made, is often circumstantial, based on history, exclusion of other causes of death and perhaps a rectal or core temperature. If an individual's time of death is known and if a rectal temperature taken shortly thereafter shows hyperthermia, a diagnosis of heatstroke can be made if, at autopsy, there is no other explanation for the hyperthermia. If the time of death is unknown, a rectal temperature may be of help in making the diagnosis of heatstroke. If an individual is found at 8 a.m., when the environmental temperature is 78°F and he has a rectal temperature of 103°F, and no medical explanation for the increased temperature is found at autopsy, the individual can be diagnosed as having had heatstroke. The same individual found dead at 3 p.m. with an environmental temperature of 105°F and a rectal temperature of 105°F cannot be diagnosed as dying of heatstroke, because the elevated body temperature may be caused by radiant heat and conduction from adjacent heated surfaces. Unfortunately, there are no diagnostic anatomical criteria at autopsy for heatstroke.

Kids in Cars

Deaths from heatstroke also occur in children left unattended in automobiles. Death may occur in such environments even after short periods of time, depending upon ambient internal temperatures. In the United States, 30–60 children die per year due to hyperthermia from being left unattended in a parked vehicle. Some may be forgotten or intentionally left in the car, while others may inadvertently lock themselves in while playing in the vehicle. The time it takes for death to occur depends on many factors, including the type of vehicle, time of day, solar exposure, ambient weather (i.e., temperature and humidity) and core temperature of the individual. Additionally, children are more at risk of hyperthermia due to their higher body surface area and less developed thermoregulation system, as compared to adults, though the elderly may also be at risk.

In a study by Zumwalt et al., thermometers with a temperature range of 100–320°F were placed out of direct sunlight on the backseats and in the trunks of two passenger cars, one white and the other light blue.[10] The cars were then left in direct sunlight. Readings were taken on 39 separate days at 12 noon, 3 p.m. and 5 p.m., with the outside ambient temperatures also recorded. Table 16.2 summarizes the results of the tests. Outside temperatures ranged from 82 to 97°F; corresponding passenger compartment temperatures

Table 16.2 Temperature Range in Two Test Cars (°F)

	Noon		3:00 p.m.		5:00 p.m.	
Location	Outside	Inside	Outside	Inside	Outside	Inside
Passenger compartment						
Blue car	82–92	104–128	87–96	115–132	89–97	117–136
White car	82–92	102–126	87–96	109–128	89–97	114–132
Trunk						
Blue car	89–92	102–126	87–96	112–131	89–97	112–128
White car	86–92	100–108	87–96	100–118	89–97	101–112

ranged from 82 to 136°F. There were no significant differences between the temperatures in the passenger compartments of the white and blue cars. The trunk temperature of the blue car was essentially identical to that in the passenger compartment, while the trunk temperatures in the white car were consistently lower than the compartment temperatures. It is speculated that, in the passenger compartments, radiant heat readily enters through the glass, with car color playing no role, while, in the trunks, the reflective qualities of the white car were responsible for the lower temperatures.

In a second study by Surpure, two cars, one large and one small, were parked in direct sunlight and shade.[11] In direct sunlight, the maximum temperatures in the small and large cars were 70 and 65°C, respectively. The smaller car heated up more rapidly than the larger car. Leaving the windows partially open was not particularly helpful. Thus, in the small car, with the front windows open 2 inches, the maximum temperature was 70°C. If, however, the front windows were left fully open, the maximum temperature in the sun reached 50°C. When the small car was parked in the shade, there was a significant difference, with a maximum temperature of only 44°C.

Additionally, King et al. found that 75% of the temperature increase occurred within the first 5 min of closing the vehicle doors and that the maximum temperature increase occurred within 15 min.[12] Like Surpure, they also found that opening the windows had minimal effect on the increasing temperatures or the maximum temperature rise.

Just like with children, animals, such as dogs and cats, should never be left in a closed or partially closed vehicle in moderate or hot temperatures, as a lethal temperature can rapidly arise killing the animals.

Malignant Hyperthermia

Malignant hyperthermia is an inherited disorder of the muscle-cell membrane predominantly associated with the administration of halogenated anesthetic agents and succinylcholine.[2,13] In this disorder, the triggering agent raises myoplasmic Ca (2+) levels, with resultant rise in body temperature and muscle rigidity. Three clinical myopathies that predispose to malignant hyperthermia are known. The most common is Evans myopathy that is inherited as a Mendelian dominant. Manifestation of this condition may be insidious or fulminant and may not occur every time anesthesia is administered. In its most dramatic presentation, following administration of succinylcholine or halogenated volatile anesthetics, there is a rapid sustained rise in temperature. There can be generalized muscle rigidity, tachycardia, cardiac arrhythmia or arrest. Complications include the following:

- Rhabdomyolysis (with elevated creatine kinase peaking the second or third day)
- Renal failure secondary to rhabdomyolysis
- Acidosis
- Electrolyte disturbances (especially hyperkalemia and hypocalcemia)
- Disseminated intravascular coagulopathy

While malignant hyperthermia typically occurs immediately after administration of the anesthetic agents, it can be delayed up to 11 h.[13]

In individuals with the genetic susceptibility to malignant hyperthermia, attacks can occur unassociated with anesthesia. Thus, vigorous exercise in a hot environment can precipitate an attack. Neuroleptic agents can trigger an attack by raising myoplasmic levels of

$Ca^{2}+$ (the neuroleptic malignant syndrome). This syndrome occurs in approximately 0.2% of patients receiving neuroleptic agents, usually within the first 30 days following institution of therapy.[2]

Miscellaneous Causes of Hyperthermia

Hyperthermia can be due to various other causes. Though body temperature may be normal or only slightly elevated in thyrotoxicosis, in thyrotoxic crisis, rectal temperatures of 40°C can occur. Severe dehydration with volume depletion can lead to cutaneous vasoconstriction with decreased sweating, impaired heat loss and hyperthermia. Cocaine, methamphetamine and aspirin intoxication can all cause hyperthermia through excess heat production. In severe salicylate intoxication, there is excess heat production as salicylates uncouple the bonds formed by oxidative phosphorylation in skeletal-muscle mitochondria.[2]

Saunas

In a sauna, there is exposure to an extremely hot and relatively dry environment with air temperatures ranging from 170 to 250°F (60–120°C).[14] The "bather" is usually able to remain in this environment for 10–30 min. Core temperature begins to rise in 1–3 min with a constant rate of increase after 3 min. Rectal temperatures, which are an approximate reflection of core temperature, rise from 37.6 to 40.0°C. Once outside the sauna and back at normal room temperature, the body's core temperature returns to normal in approximately 30 min. In hot, dry environments such as a sauna, sweating is the only means of cooling. Perspiration rates may increase to 0.8–2.0 kg/h. Individuals with severe heart disease are at risk in a sauna because of the strain on the cardiovascular system from the body's attempt to adapt to the high environmental temperatures and the potential risk of hyperthermia.

Exercise, Body Temperature, Humidity and Exhaustion

Individuals in a sauna are exposed to extremely high temperatures in a very dry environment. During this time, they do not engage in any significant physical activity. Thus, increase in body temperature is solely due to exposure to a hot environment. This is an artificial situation. In ordinary life, individuals are usually exposed to a hot environment, and possibly a high humidity, while undertaking physical activity.

Experiments have been conducted in which trained athletes have engaged in continuous and strenuous activity (on bicycle ergometers) to the point of complete exhaustion in a hot environment.[15,16] The humidity varied from dry (10% relative humidity) to humid (87%). The body temperature increased due to both the heat of the environment and the heat generated by the metabolism of work. The tests were continued over 8–13 consecutive days to evaluate heat acclimation.

In a **hot**, **dry environment** (40°C, 10% relative humidity), endurance increased from an initial 48 ± 1.9 to 80 ± 3.3 min.[15] Mean core (esophageal) temperatures were 39.8 ± 0.13°C on the first day; 39.7 ± 0.15°C on the last day.

In hot humid air (35°C; 87% relative humidity), exhaustion was reached in 44.6 ± 2.8 min.[16] After acclimation, the subjects reached exhaustion at 52.0 ± 1.9 min. The mean core temperature at exhaustion was 39.9 ± 0.1°C both before and after acclimation. Sweating increased with acclimatization with both tests.

In view of these studies, it appears that a high core temperature is the critical factor for exhaustion during exercise in a hot environment. With exposure to a hot environment, whether it be dry or humid, exhaustion sets in and physical exertion ceases with a core temperature of approximately 40°C. Even if there is no physical activity, when core temperature approaches 40°C, the body senses danger. Thus, the individuals in the sauna, exposed to a hot, dry environment without physical activity, leave the sauna when their core temperature is approximately 40°C.

Hypothermia

The term hypothermia is used when an individual's body temperature is below 95°F (35°C). This will occur when the loss of body heat exceeds heat production. The most common cause of hypothermia is exposure to low temperatures. Accidental hypothermia occurs in alcoholics going to sleep or passing out in a cold environment, individuals lost while hiking or skiing and those who have been immersed in ice-cold water. This last condition, immersion hypothermia, is extremely dangerous because of the more rapid loss of heat in water than in air. Body heat is lost three times faster in water than in dry, cold air of the same temperature, as water conducts heat 20–25 times faster than dry air.[17]

The elderly may die of hypothermia in their homes because of inadequate heating coupled with debilitating diseases or inadequate nutrition. The latter conditions impair the ability of the body to maintain normal temperature. Infants are much more susceptible to hypothermia than adults. This is because their surface area in relation to body mass is considerably greater than that of adults. In newborn infants, vasomotor reflexes are underdeveloped and the heat-regulating center is insufficient for at least several hours after birth. Thus, hypothermia is more frequent in the first few weeks of life and is associated with a very high mortality.

The body's defense against cold is vasoconstriction of blood vessels in the skin and muscles so as to conserve heat, combined with an increase in generation of heat. Heat production is increased in two ways: first, there is shivering. During maximum shivering, heat production can rise as high as five times normal. Second, there is chemical thermogenesis, that is, an immediate increase in the rate of cellular metabolism. The degree of thermogenesis that occurs is directly proportional to the amount of brown fat. In adults, who have almost no brown fat, it is rare that chemical thermogenesis increases the rate of heat production more than 10–15%. In infants, who have a large amount of brown fat, the increased heat production is as much as 100%. The thickness of an individual's subcutaneous fat also affects whether hypothermia will develop and how soon. Fat individuals tolerate cold better than skinny individuals. Because of the thicker layer of subcutaneous fat, women endure cold better than men.

Compensatory increases of heat production by the body, such as that caused by shivering, can maintain body temperature to about 90°F (32°C), where impairment of cerebral functioning, manifested by analgesia, clouding of consciousness, hallucinations and slowing of reflexes begins. Shivering ceases between 90 and 85°F. Respiration becomes less frequent and shallower, and there is a decrease in the pulse rate. Below 85°F, the ability of the hypothalamus to regulate temperature is completely lost. Cold narcosis appears at 85°F, and reflexes are abolished at 81°F. As hypothermia develops, electrocardiographs show prolongation of the PQRS waves with inverted T waves. At about 86°F, atrial fibrillation often appears. Between 82 and 77°F, death may occur from ventricular fibrillation.

Hypothermia can cause a hemoconcentration by two mechanisms. The first is cold diuresis.[18] Exposure to an environmental temperature of 59°F (15°C) is sufficient to trigger diuresis in an individual. The second mechanism is the leaking of plasma into the extracellular spaces. This is known as "cold edema." Hyperglycemia occurs in the early phases of hypothermia.[19] It is caused by the action of glucocorticoids and epinephrine on the liver, with resultant depletion of glycogen. With prolonged hypothermia, hypoglycemia may develop.[18,20,21] This is more common in alcoholics. The hypoglycemia may be accompanied by elevated levels of insulin.[19]

Many cases of hypothermia seen by the forensic pathologist involve individuals who die of exposure while under the influence of alcohol. Alcohol is said to contribute to the fatal outcome by causing cutaneous dilatation of peripheral vessels and thus loss of heat. This is the warm flush that an individual experiences when drinking alcohol. However, a number of individuals have been reported as surviving deep hypothermia because of alcohol intake. This survival is attributed to protection against cardiac fibrillation by the alcohol. This protective effect has been reproduced in dogs as well as individuals during surgery with body temperatures reduced to 25–26°C.[22] In these individuals, alcohol was administered to maintain a blood concentration of approximately 400 mg%. Increase in circulation and reduction of oxygen consumption in the brain might explain some of the protective effects of alcohol.

Hypothermia in Water

A fair amount of data concerning survival time in cold water is known from experiences in World War II, as well as from experiments carried out in concentration camps.[17,19,23] In concentration camps, it was found that it takes 70–90 min for a man to die when immersed in water at 4–9°C.[19] Data on shipwreck victims showed that survival time of these individuals, who were better nourished than the concentration camp victims, was 2 h.[17]

In immersion in cold water, the thickness of an individual's subcutaneous fat is the most important internal factor affecting the rate at which the body cools. In water at 15°C, obese individuals cool at a rate that may be hardly discernable, while a thin individual's body temperature can fall by 2.5°C in the first half hour.[24] In children, the ratio of skin surface area to body mass is greater than in adults; thus, the rate of body cooling is faster. Boys under 10 years of age, in water at 20.4°C, often showed falls in body temperature below 35°C after as little as 30 min.[25] Clothing retards body cooling in water, though not as effectively as in air. In very cold water, exercise accelerates the rate at which the body temperature falls, because increased flow of blood to exercising muscles carries away more heat than is produced by the exercise.[26]

Deaths have been reported within a half hour following immersion in water at 32°F (0°C). The individuals who die under these circumstances probably do not die primarily of hypothermia. Death is probably caused by cardiovascular etiology due to the effects on the heart of the sudden cooling of the skin, that is, constriction of blood vessels, and reflex stimulation of the heart, with increased blood pressure and cardiac output, with the resultant sudden increase in the work of the left ventricle. Both ventricular and atrial ectopic beats are common during the first few minutes of cold immersion.[27] They usually cease after a few minutes, as the temperature receptors in the skin adapt to the low temperature. Rarely, the arrhythmias progress to ventricular fibrillation, followed by sudden death. Ventricular fibrillation caused by these mechanisms probably accounts for the occasional case of a swimmer's diving into cold water only to float up or sink to the bottom, dead. Older individuals may be especially susceptible to a cardiovascular mechanism of death in cold water immersion.

Reflex disturbances of breathing could also account for some of the rapid deaths following immersion in cold water. Sudden cooling of the skin following immersion in water with a temperature approaching 0°C causes marked reflex stimulation of breathing for a few minutes such that breathing can often not be controlled voluntarily.[28] In instances where the water is choppy, waves breaking over the head of an individual can result in the inhalation of water and drowning before hypothermia causes death.

Post-immersion deaths can occur following the rescue from cold water of individuals who appear to be in no danger of dying. The individual may be conscious when taken out of the water, only to lose consciousness when taken into the warmth of the facility. This appears to be related to the "afterdrop phenomenon."[29] Following removal from cold water, an individual's body temperature continues to fall for a period of time before it starts to rise. This occurs even if the subject is rapidly rewarmed. The first graphic records of the afterdrop were in experiments at Dachau. These observations were subsequently reproduced in experiments, though the body cooling was restricted to safe limits. The exact mechanism causing death is not understood but appears to be manifested by cardiac arrest.

The critical temperature to maintain thermo-equilibrium in water was determined to be 35°C (95°F) by Burton and Bazett.[30]

Hypothermia on Land

Determination of survival time in dry cold on land is more complicated than in cold water because of the multiple factors that play a role in determining to what temperature the body is actually exposed. On land, the principal factors that determine whether an individual becomes hypothermic are the environmental temperature, wind speed and clothing. Wind, by dispersing the warm air surrounding the body, causes a chilling effect by magnifying the effects of the environmental temperature. This observation has led to the construction of the windchill index. This index computes the combined effects of air temperature and wind speed. Thus at 10°F, if the wind blows at 2 mph, an individual will feel cold; at 5, mph very cold; at 10, bitterly cold; and at 15 mph, exposed flesh will freeze. If the clothing an individual wears is soaked through with water, the air temperature used in the windchill index should be adjusted down to 6°C (11°F) from the measured temperature before using the index.[31] The critical temperature to maintain thermo-equilibrium in dry air was determined to be 25°C (77°F) by Wilkerson et al.[32]

Individuals suffering from hypothermia on land may show either red patches on the skin or pale areas of subcutaneous edema. Mental disorientation is common. They are often unconscious with a low or unrecordable blood pressure, a slow, irregular pulse and slow, shallow respiration. They may appear dead. Heart sounds may not be detected with a stethoscope at 86°F (30°C). The pupil reflex can vanish at 77°F (25°C).[33] If such individuals are found dead, at autopsy the livor mortis will have a cherry-red color. This is due to the increased amounts of oxyhemoglobin caused by antemortern binding of oxygen to the hemoglobin. In some cases, however, bodies have been reported as being totally white. Areas of bluish discoloration might also be seen on the hands, elbows, knees and feet, probably representing minor frostbite areas. Histologically, these lesions are characterized by edema and hyperemia of the dermis with occasional foci of inflammatory cell infiltrates.

In individuals who do not immediately die from hypothermia, but survive a while, there may be development of hemorrhagic pancreatitis; erosions and hemorrhages of the gastric mucosa, ileum and colon; bronchopneumonia; acute tubular necrosis; and cardiac muscle degeneration. Wischnewsky spots (Figure 16.3), small punctate submucosal hemorrhages seen along the gastric mucosa, are often touted as a diagnostic finding in hypothermia deaths, however, while their presence may support the diagnosis of hypothermia, they are a non-specific finding and can be seen in with other causes of death. Additionally, they are only present in approximately 50% of hypothermia deaths, so their absence does not exclude hypothermia.

In individuals who die of uncomplicated hypothermia, that is, are found "frozen," there are no specific lesions that can be attributable to the hypothermia. Victims of hypothermia are often found undressed (paradoxical undressing). This is explained by terminal hallucinations and feelings of warmth that are caused by paralysis of the thermal regulatory mechanism.[34]

In addition to hypothermic deaths, cold weather is often associated with sudden death in individuals with coronary artery disease. The lower the temperature, the greater the risk of a coronary attack. Individuals with angina pectoris almost invariably experience pain on exposure to air temperature of less than 15°F (–10°C).[35] This pain is caused by coronary spasm or increased stroke volume induced by breathing cold air.

Figure 16.3 Wischnewsky spots along the gastric mucosa of an 83-year-old man who died of hypothermia.

References

1. Guyton AC and Hall JE, *Textbook of Medical Physiology* 10th ed. WB Saunders, Philadelphia, PA, 2000.
2. Simon HB, Hyperthermia: review article. *NEJM* 1993; 329(7):483–487.
3. Mackowiak PA, Wasserman SS, and Levine MM, A critical appraisal of 98.6°F, the upper limit of the normal body temperature, and other legacies of Carl Reinhold August Wunderlich. *JAMA* 1992; 268:1578–1580.
4. Backer HD, Shopes E, and Barkan H, Exertional heat illness and hyponatremia in hikers. *Am J Emerg Med* 1999; 17:532–539.
5. Pugh LGC, Clothing insulation and accidental hypothermia in youth. *Nature* 1966; 209:1281–1286.
6. Knochel JP, Heat illness, in Callahan ML (Ed) *Current Therapy in Emergency Medicine*. BC Decker Inc, Philadelphia, PA, 1987.
7. Gold J, Development of heat pyrexia. *JAMA* 1960; 173:1175–1182.
8. Daily WM and Harrison TR, Study of mechanism and treatment of heat pyrexia. *Am J Med Sci* 1948; 215:42–55.
9. Adato B, Dubnov-Raz G, Gips H, Heled Y, and Epstein Y, Fatal heat stroke in children found in parked cars: autopsy findings. *Eur J Pediatr* 2016; 175(9):1249–1252.
10. Zumwalt RE, Petty CS, and Holman W, Temperature in closed automobiles in hot weather. *Forensic Sci Gaz* 1976; 7:7–8.
11. Surpure JS, Heat-related illness and the automobile. *Ann Emerg Med* 1982; 11:263–265.
12. King K, Negus K, and Vance JC, Heat stress in motor vehicles: a problem in infancy. *Pediatrics* 1981; 68:579–582.
13. Denborough M, Malignant hyperthermia: seminar. *Lancet* 1998; 352:1131–1136.
14. Hasan J, Karvonen MJ, and Piironen P, Special review. Part 1: Physiological effects of extreme heat, as studied in the Finnish "sauna" bath. *Am J Phys Med* 1966; 45:296–314.
15. Nielsen B, et al., Human circulatory and thermoregulatory adaptations with heat acclimation and exercise in a hot, dry environment. *J Physiol*, 1993; 460:467–485.
16. Nielsen B, et al., Acute and adaptive responses in humans to exercise in a warm, humid environment. *Eur J Physiol* 1997; 434:49–56.
17. Molnar GW, Survival of hypothermia by men immersed in the ocean. *JAMA* 1946; 131:1045–1050.
18. Paton BC, Accidental hypothermia. *Pharmacol Ther* 1983; 22:331–377.
19. Simpson K, Exposure to cold-starvation and neglect, in Simpson K (Ed) *Modem Trends in Forensic Medicine*. Mosby Co, St Louis, MO, 1953.
20. Fitzgerald FT, Hypoglycemia and accidental hypothermia in an alcoholic population. *West J Med* 1980; 133:105–107.
21. Stoner HB, et al., Metabolic aspects of hypothermia in the elderly. *Clin Sci* 1980; 59:19–27.
22. MacGregor DC, et al., The effects of ether, ethanol, propanol and butanol on tolerance to deep hypothermia. *Dis Chest* 1966; 50:523–529.
23. Cooper KE, Hunter AR, and Keatinge WR, Accidental hypothermia. *Int Anesth Clin* 1964; 2:999–1013.
24. Keatinge WR, The effects of subcutaneous fat and of previous exposure to cold on the body temperature, peripheral blood flow and metabolic rate of men in cold water. *J Physiol* 1960; 153:166–178.
25. Sloan REG and Keatinge WR, Cooling rates of young people swimming in cold water. *J Appl Physiol* 1973; 35:371–375.
26. Keatinge WR, Chapter 4: Role of cold and immersion accidents in Adam JM (Ed) *Hypothermia – Ashore and Afloat*. Aberdeen Univ. Press, Great Britain, 1981.
27. Keatinge WR and Evans M, The respiratory and cardiovascular responses to immersion in cold and warm water. *Q J Exp Physiol* 1961; 46:83–94.

28. Keatinge WR and Nadel JA, Immediate respiratory response to sudden cooling of the skin. *J Appl Physiol* 1965; 20:65–69.
29. Golden FStC and Hurvey GR, Chapter 5: The "After drop" and death after rescue from immersion in cold water in Adam JM (Ed) *Hypothermia – Ashore and Afloat*, Aberdeen Univ. Press, Great Britain, 1981.
30. Burton AC and Bazett HC, Study of average temperature of tissue, of exchange of heat and vasomotor responses in man by means of bath colorimeter. *Am J Physiol* 1936; 117:36–54.
31. Adam JM, Chapter 1: Cold weather: its characteristics, dangers and assessment, in Adam JM (Ed) *Hypothermia – Ashore and Afloat*, Aberdeen Univ. Press, Great Britain, 1981.
32. Wilkerson JE, Raven PB, Horvath SM. Critical temperature of unacclimatized male Caucasians. *J Appl Physiol.* 1972 Oct;33(4):451–5.
33. Stewart TM, Chapter 3: Mountain rescue and the exposure syndrome, some case reports and observations, in Adam JM (Ed) *Hypothermia – Ashore and Afloat*, Aberdeen Univ. Press, Great Britain, 1981.
34. Bedin B, Vangaard, L and Hirvonen J, Paradoxical undressing in fatal hypothermia. *J Forensic Sci* 1979; 24:543–553.
35. Kavanagh T, A cold-weather "jogging mask" for angina patients. *Can Med Assoc J* 1970; 103:1290–1291.

Sexual Assault

17

Sexually-based offenses are considered especially heinous.

—Law & Order: Special Victims Unit

Sexual assault is defined by three elements in a female: carnal knowledge, force and commission without consent. Carnal knowledge is the slightest penetration of the labia minora by a foreign body, most often the penis; hymenal penetration or ejaculation is not necessary. Force may involve the use of violence, threat of violence or coercion. The actual number of sexual assaults that occur each year is unknown, mostly due to a significant number of unreported cases.

The Living Victim

Sexual assault examinations present a unique problem to physician clinicians in that they often inherit the burden of not only treatment, but also proper collection of evidence. For the correct handling of rape cases, both medically and legally, there must be coordination between the physicians examining the victims and the police agency dealing with jurisdiction. Sexual assault examinations are very specialized examinations, with different requirements than the usual physician-patient interactions, for that reason, there are clinicians specially trained to conduct such examinations, as well as national protocols on their performance.[1]

It is preferable that victims of rape be examined at one central hospital by experienced clinicians trained in the handling and treatment of such patients and with the proper collection of evidence. In a number of areas, such examinations are conducted by specially trained forensic nurses. Often, these victims are examined at several different locations by clinicians not experienced with such examinations, and thus, the documentation of the assault and collection of the evidence may suffer. Additionally, these examinations should not be rushed and often take several hours to perform, given the issues involved. Thus, having a staff member dedicated for such a purpose who can take their time with the patient is preferable.

When the victim of a sexual assault is brought into the hospital, they should be triaged ahead and separately from the nonemergency patients. Written, witnessed consent should be obtained before the examination and interview. Hospitals and emergency rooms should have a "rape kit" at all times. Such kits contain the necessary materials for collection and packaging of the collected evidence as well as forms with pertinent questions to be asked and diagrams that can be used to illustrate injuries. During the examination, if the clinician is not female, a female chaperone should always be present. The name of the victim is recorded, along with the date and time of the alleged assault, the date and time of the examination and, if the police have been notified, the attending law officer's name and badge number. The law enforcement officer should not be present during the examination. The only people present should be the examiner and a nurse, one of whom should be female.

The examination should first focus on the treatment of life-threatening injuries. Once injuries are addressed, the examination can continue and should include collection of specimens as well as photographic documentation. After collection, the chain of evidence must be maintained. The examining physician should either hand over the evidence directly to a police officer or a representative of the crime laboratory, or place it in a secure storage area for subsequent transmittal.

If examination of victims is done by physicians, they should preferably be senior staff obstetrician/gynecologists and not residents. Senior staff members are more experienced and their testimony will carry greater weight in court. In addition, a resident might have moved out of the area by the time the case comes to court. In court, the physician or forensic nurse should never be expected to state whether the crime of rape has occurred. Rape is not a diagnosis, it is a matter of jurisprudence. The examiner should testify to their examination, including the presence or absence of any trauma, and any evidence that they collected.

The first step of the sexual assault examination is to obtain a history from the patient. This includes a medical history and a brief account of the alleged assault. Three important questions should be asked:

Did the assailant's penis penetrate the vulva?

Did the assailant experience ejaculation?

Did the assailant wear a condom?

Similar questions regarding anal and oral intercourse should also be asked. The victim is asked whether she douched, bathed, showered, defecated or urinated prior to the examination. All the aforementioned factors can influence whether the physical evidence needed to document sexual intercourse is present. Vertical drainage from the vagina is the worst enemy to the collection of evidence. Because of this, it is recommended that the examiner should retain the undergarment (i.e., panties) the victim was wearing. Thus, any drainage of semen into the undergarment can be documented.

After taking a history, the patient is examined. The physician or forensic nurse will conduct the examination in such a manner that objectively acquired evidence can be used to prosecute an assailant in an actual case of rape, or to disprove a false charge of sexual assault. The patient's general appearance and emotional state are noted, as well as whether she is under the influence of alcohol or drugs. The patient's emotional state does not necessarily reflect on the validity of her charges. Some rape victims will appear cold and detached, while others will be hysterical. To assess intoxication status, it is recommended that urine and blood samples be obtained for toxicological analysis.

All clothing should be examined for stains, tears, missing buttons, dirt, gravel, grease, leaves, etc. The patient herself is then examined. The examiner will look for bruises, bites and lacerations. The hands should be examined for broken fingernails. Is the pubic hair matted? Are there any foreign hairs mixed with the patient's pubic hair? Pubic hair combings should be obtained. The external genitalia are examined for abrasions, lacerations and hematomas (Figure 17.1). The vagina and cervix are then examined internally by the use of an unlubricated speculum and all injuries should be described and swabs should

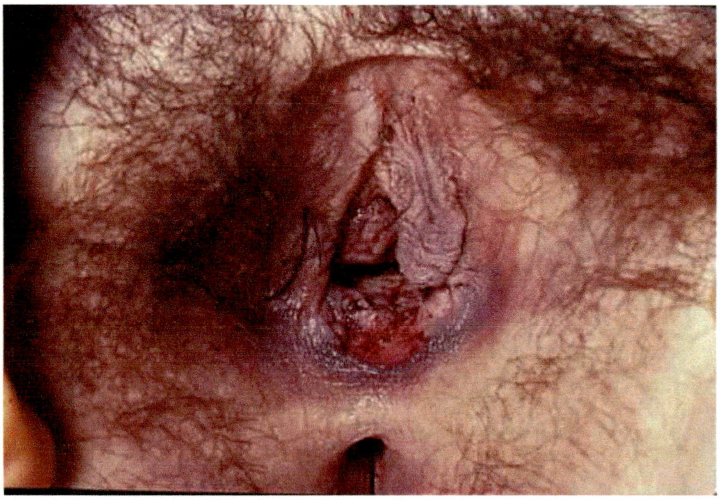

Figure 17.1 Rape-homicide with laceration of vagina at 6 o'clock position.

be obtained. The swabs should be analyzed for the presence of sperm and DNA of the perpetrator, see discussion below regarding sperm and Chapter 22 for a further information on DNA analysis.

If there is a bite mark on the patient or if the patient gives a history of the perpetrator's licking a portion of her body (e.g., the nipples), these areas should be swabbed in an attempt to recover saliva. These swabs can then be analyzed for DNA. Positive DNA identification has been made in a number of cases from saliva on the body of the victim. After the swabbing of the bite mark, photographs should be taken. A metric ruler should be included in the photographs. Ideally, one should have a forensic odontologist on call so that they can examine and document the bite mark. They might take casts of the bite mark in addition to photographing it.

During the physical examination, evidence will be collected to document the rape. The only significant differences in the collecting of evidence between the living rape victim and the dead individual are that, in the living individual, a culture will be made from the cervix to detect the presence of venereal disease, and swabs of the mouth and rectum may not be taken if there was no penetration of these orifices.

The absence of trauma to a rape victim does not negate the validity of her claim of rape. While up to 70% of female victims of sexual assault may have some sort of documented extragenital trauma, only 19% of those were found to be significant injuries.[2] In a study of 1266 sexually assaulted women, only 24% had documented genital injuries (i.e., abrasions, contusions or lacerations) with 27% of those who reported anal penetration having evidence of anal injuries.[3] Another study of 500 sexually assaulted women found 23% with genital trauma compared to 6% (n = 68) of consensual intercourse.[4] Some hospitals perform a wet prep slide from the vaginal vault to assess for sperm as part of the sexually assault examination in females. In a study of 501 cases, sperm was only identified in 23%; however, when examined by the crime laboratory, 45% were positive for sperm.[5]

Following the examination, the patient is treated for her injuries, as well as given drugs for prevention of pregnancy, if desired, and medication for prevention of venereal disease. The patient should be seen 2 weeks after the assault in a follow-up examination.

Repeated testing for sexually transmitted infectious diseases (i.e., HIV, Hep C) should be performed over the next few months.

For a male victim, much of the examination remains the same. The interview and documentation of injuries is identical; however, instead of taking vaginal swabs, penile swabs are usually obtained. Anoscopy may also be indicated, if anal penetration is reported. In addition, in the cases of male sexual assault, one of the examiners, either the examiner or assistant, should be male, if desired by the victim. Some male victims prefer female examiners, especially in the cases of homosexual rape.

Rape-Homicides

Rape-homicides are relatively uncommon. When they do occur, they are usually more vicious than routine homicides and generate more publicity and public outcry. They are often extremely difficult to solve because they frequently represent the purest form of stranger-to-stranger crime – that is, the victim and assailant are unknown to each other. There is usually only one assailant, so there is no one to "squeal" to the police. In addition, it is not the type of crime that most people brag about in bars.

In rape-homicides, the cause of death is usually strangulation, stabbing or blunt force injuries. Rape victims are rarely shot. Excessive force and unnecessary savagery are common in rape-homicides. Occasionally, there is mutilation of the body (Figure 17.2A and B).

In cases of rape-homicide, the medical examiner, in addition to determining the cause of death, has to document evidence of sexual assault and collect trace evidence that can be used subsequently in any criminal proceedings. In rape-homicides, as in all homicides, the medical examiners' involvement with the body should begin at the scene. This does not mean that they have to be present personally, but at least an investigator from their office should be present. At the scene, the body should be manipulated and touched as little

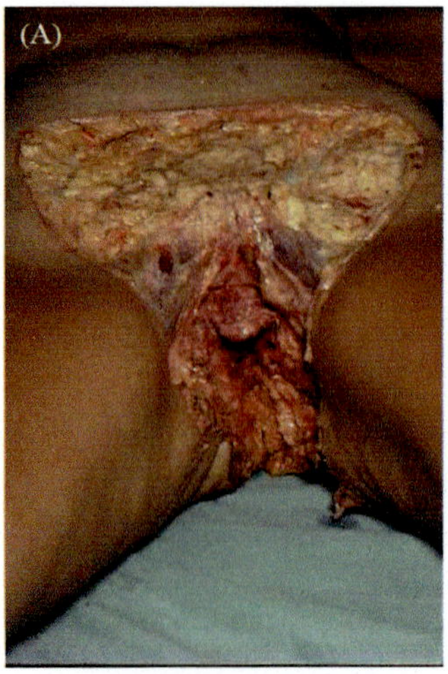

Figure 17.2 (A) A 39-year-old prostitute stabbed and beaten. Nipples cut off and "skinned" in pubic and perineal region (*continued*).

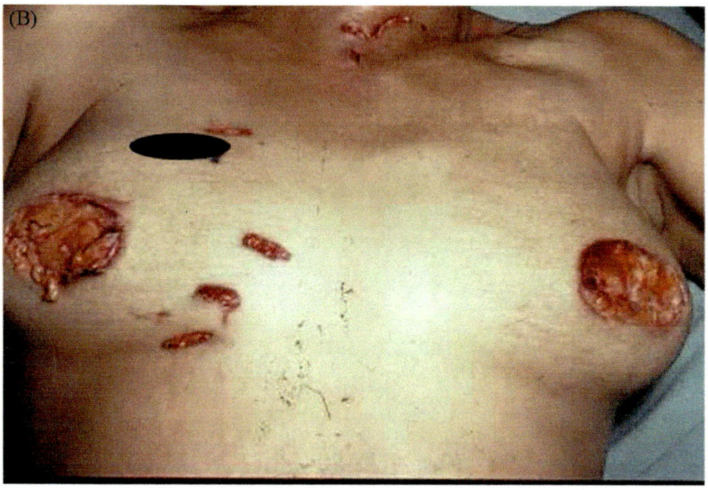

Figure 17.2 (B) A 39-year-old prostitute stabbed and beaten. Nipples cut off and "skinned" in pubic and perineal region.

as possible. The scene is not the place for examination of the body, either by a physician or an investigator. Manipulation of a body at the scene could result in destruction of trace evidence.

Transport of the Body

Prior to transporting the body from the scene, paper bags should be placed on the hands to preserve any trace evidence that might be clutched in them or beneath the fingernails. Paper bags should be used instead of plastic, because there will be condensation of moisture inside plastic bags as the body is shifted from cold to warm environments. In addition to covering the hands, the body should be wrapped in a clean white sheet or placed in a clean body bag. This serves two purposes: to prevent loss of trace evidence from the body in transporting it to the morgue and to prevent the body from picking up debris from the vehicle transporting the body that might subsequently be confused with legitimate trace evidence.

Examination of the Body

On arriving at the morgue, the body should never be undressed or fingerprinted prior to examination by the medical examiner. A number of authorities are now attempting to lift fingerprints from the skin of a body in which there has been close contact between the assailant and victim; however, such procedures are virtually always nonproductive and can interfere with more valuable testing such as the attainment of trace or DNA evidence.

Prior to the autopsy, the medical examiner should be thoroughly knowledgeable as to the circumstances surrounding the death, as well as any special tests the police may deem necessary. An autopsy should never be conducted until the medical examiner fully understands the circumstances surrounding the death.

Trace Evidence Recovery from the Hands

The first part of the autopsy consists of examining the hands for foreign material clutched in the hands or present under the fingernails. The body should never be fingerprinted prior to examination of the hands by the medical examiner. Any material removed from the hands, as well as nail clippings, should be put in labeled containers. It is not uncommon to find hair clutched in the hands of rape-homicide victims who have been strangled or beaten about the head. In most instances, however, this turns out to be their own head hair. Thus, it is necessary at the time of the examination to obtain head hair from the victim as a control standard.

After examining the hands for trace evidence, the fingernails are clipped and placed in marked containers. Clipping and retention of the fingernails is recommended over just scraping and retaining material under the nails. The fingernail clippings can subsequently be examined by a forensic scientist for foreign material that might have come from the assailant. The most important of the materials sought is tissue that might have been deposited under the nails if the deceased scratched her assailant. This tissue can be typed for DNA. A number of identifications of assailants have been made through DNA typing of tissue recovered from under the fingernails. A clean pair of scissors or nail clippers should be used to prevent contamination of the cuttings by DNA material from a nonassociated source.

Examination of the Clothing

After examining the hands, one should examine the clothing while it is still on the body. The medical examiner should carefully search for fibers, hair, glass, paint or any foreign material that might have been transferred to the deceased's body from the assailant, the surroundings or the vehicle used to transport the body of the victim. The medical examiner should note whether any defects in the clothing correspond to the wounds in the deceased to determine whether the individual was attacked with the clothing still on or whether the body was subsequently dressed. Any material removed from the clothing should be put into an envelope and labeled with the deceased's name, case number, date, what is present in the envelope, where it came from and who recovered it. Once the clothing has been examined while on the decedent, it can be removed and then reexamined for any additional trace evidence. The clothing should then be photographed and packaged for release and further testing, should it be needed.

The Body

The medical examiner can now begin the examination of the body, documenting any evidence of trauma by written notes, diagrams, X-rays or photography. At the same time, the medical examiner will begin to collect trace evidence from the body. Samples of head hair should be obtained and retained. These can be compared with hair found clutched in the hands; in a vehicle used to transport a body; on a suspected assailant or, if there was blunt trauma to the head, hair recovered from a suspected murder weapon. The pubic hair is combed to recover any foreign hair deposited there from the pubic hair of the assailant. The combings and the comb are placed in a labeled envelope. In the case of a deceased victim, 15–20 pubic hairs are pulled with forceps and placed in a separate envelope to serve as controls when examining the loose hair. In a living victim, an equal number of pubic hairs are cut, not pulled. Experiments have been conducted to determine the frequency of pubic hair transfer during sexual intercourse. Exline et al. determined that, under optimum conditions, there was transfer of pubic hair to males in 23.6% of cases and to females in 10.9%.[6] If the hairs contain roots, they can be analyzed by DNA so as to make absolute identification. If no root material is present, the hairs can then be analyzed by mitochondrial RNA. Visual examination of the hair of the suspected assailant as to its physical appearance should never be used to make a positive identification.

The next step is to obtain samples from the vaginal vault. If death was fairly recent, a hanging drop preparation for motile sperm can be made. Vaginal smears on glass slides are prepared and air-dried. Two cotton-tipped swabs soaked with material from the vaginal vault should be air-dried and placed in cardboard boxes (not test tubes). Oral and rectal smears and swabs should also be obtained and retained in all autopsy cases. The slides should be placed either in clean plastic slide holders or in new cardboard holders. The latter should not be reused to prevent carryover of vaginal or seminal material to a subsequent slide placed in the cardboard container.

Forensic scientists can review the vaginal, rectal and oral slides to identify any spermatozoa. One must be cautious in the identification of semen either by visual identification of sperm or by DNA in "rectal swabs". In women, if the body has been placed on its back, seminal fluid may leak from the vagina down between the buttocks into or around the anus giving a false positive for evidence of anal intercourse. To prevent this, one must carefully spread the buttocks before inserting the swab into the anus preventing contamination of the rectal swab by semen from the vagina. In males, semen can leak downward from the penis into the perianal area. In both cases, one must be careful not to contact the perianal skin that may also be contaminated by semen.

Survival Time of Sperm

The survival time of spermatozoa in the vagina of living individuals as reported in the medical literature is quite variable. This can be explained by two factors: where the sample was collected and what criteria are used to identify sperm. Swabs should be taken from the vaginal pool and not the cervix, because sperm can survive in cervical mucus much longer than in the vagina. Sperm seen on a cervical swab may remain 2–3 days and may represent a previous consensual sexual encounter in cases of alleged assault. Additionally, the criteria used to identify sperm also affect the timing. Some clinicians identify sperm only when they see a complete spermatozoon – one with a head and tail. Other individuals require only the head to be present. This difference in criteria of identification explains some of the differences in reports of the persistence of sperm.

In living individuals, motile sperm are usually seen only up to 6 h, occasionally 12 h and, very rarely, up to 24 h. In the latter case, it is probable that the sperm was obtained from cervical mucus. Thus, it is important when searching for motile sperm in an individual alleged to have been raped only a few hours before to obtain this material from the vaginal pool and not from the cervix.

Nonmotile sperm with tails in the living individual are usually seen up to 26 h, with occasional reports of 2–3 days. In the latter cases, again, these are likely sperm trapped in cervical mucus. The identification of only a single sperm on one or two slides should make the examiner wary that this may represent a case sperm from cervical mucus and may not recent intercourse. In most rape cases with ejaculation and without condom use, numerous sperm will be seen on each smear. The presence of several sperm on a slide, with a history of the last voluntary intercourse 2 or 3 days before, would be inconsistent with the sperm originating at that time, but would be consistent with more recent sexual intercourse.

The best study of the persistence of sperm in the vagina of living individuals is by Willott and Allard.[7] They examined 1332 vaginal swabs taken in alleged rape cases and found 57% positive for sperm. The longest time for identification of sperm with tails was 26 h. Sperm heads were identified up to 120 h. A cervical swab was positive for sperm at 179 h (7 days).

Willott and Allard also examined 225 anal and 212 rectal swabs.[7] Sperm were identified in 37% of the former and in 32% of the latter. They found that it was rare to find sperm with tails, especially after more than 6 h. Sperm heads were identified on an anal swab 45 h after intercourse and on a rectal swab 65 h after intercourse. They also examined 74 oral swabs, of which 12% were positive. Sperm with tails were identified up to 3 h and sperm with heads up to 6 h. One must consider, however, that the times previously quoted for persistence of sperm are for living individuals. Sperm have been identified in the vagina of dead individuals 1–2 weeks after death. In dead individuals, the sperm are destroyed by decomposition, not drainage or the action of the vaginal secretions or cells. Sperm that are deposited on material like cotton, cloth or paper and air-dried can be identified years after the event. However, one must also remember that *failure to demonstrate sperm does not preclude intercourse.*

Analysis for Sperm, Semen and Saliva

If sperm is identified, the collected swabs should also be analyzed for DNA. However, if sperm are not identified, further testing may be performed as sperm are not always identified visually even in cases of undoubted intercourse. This could be caused by use of a condom, failure to ejaculate, drainage of semen or aspermia secondary to disease or a vasectomy. In such cases, the substance most widely analyzed for has been acid phosphatase. Acid phosphatase is found in high concentrations in semen.[8] It is usually present in the vagina for up to 18–24 h after sexual intercourse and occasionally up to 72 h. The highest levels are within the first 12 h, with gradual disappearance by 48–72 h. Because it usually disappears in the first 24 h after intercourse, it is most useful as an indicator of recent intercourse, compared with nonmotile sperm, which can be identified up to 2–3 days after intercourse. In addition to acid phosphatase, tests may be done for semen-specific glycoprotein (P30).[9]

In addition to obtaining rectal, vaginal and oral swabs and slides, any apparent biological stains (i.e., semen, saliva) on the skin of the victim or clothing should be examined. The most commonly used method for recovery of DNA in such instances is the double swab technique.[10] In this technique, the area/stain is first swabbed with a moistened sterile cotton-tipped swab followed by a second dry cotton-tipped swab. Both swabs are then air-dried and submitted to the crime laboratory for analysis. Alternative light sources, such as UV light, can often be utilized to identify such stains.

Bite marks may also be identified on a sexual assault victim (Figure 17.3A, B). If such marks are present, the mark should first be swabbed for recovery of saliva for DNA testing and then documented photographically, with a scale present. When possible, it is best to have all potential bite marks evaluated by a forensic odontologist who may be able to

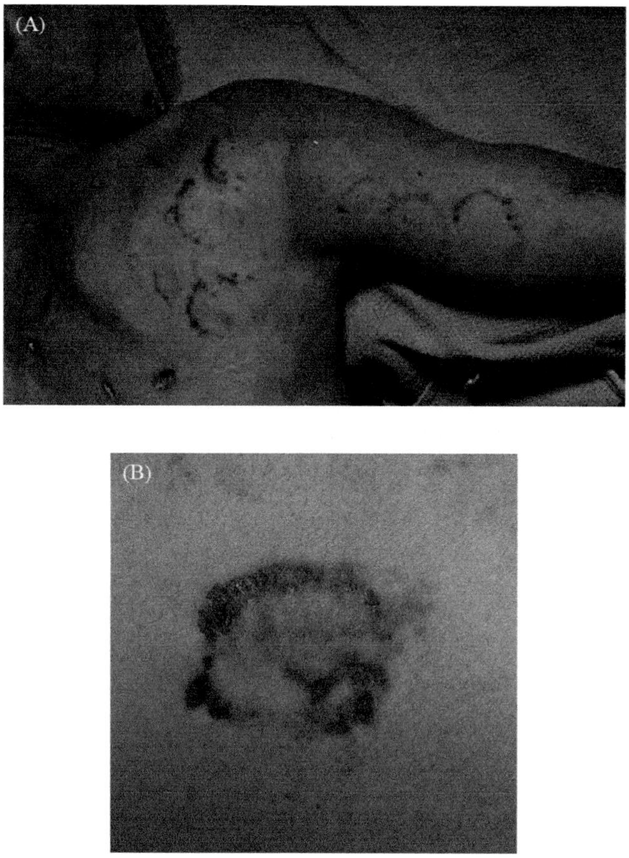

Figure 17.3 (A and B) Bite marks.

create molds of the mark. Like hair, bite marks should never be used to definitively identify a specific assailant, though may still be of assistance in specific cases.

Just as in living victims, male victims of rape-homicide should be examined in much the same fashion though male victims of sexual assault report higher rates of anal penetration and anal injuries than women.[11,12] In a study of 57 male rape victims, 87% reported forced oral and/or anal penetration with 61% having documented anogenital injuries and 35% had extragenital injuries,[11] while another study of 98 male rape victims, 50% reported anal penetration and 24% with compatible genital injuries.[12]

Male victims should be examined in much the same fashion as female victims, the exception of obtaining penile swabs instead of vaginal swabs. If penile swabs are to be obtained, the double swab technique is again preferred. Swabs should be taken around the glans. In an uncircumcised individual, two sets of swabs should be obtained – one set from the outer foreskin and another from the glans.

Homosexual Rape

For completeness, we should mention the victims of homosexual rape. The victims are often children or persons incarcerated in jail or prison. Essentially, the same procedures should be followed for these cases as described previously. Of interest is that these deaths

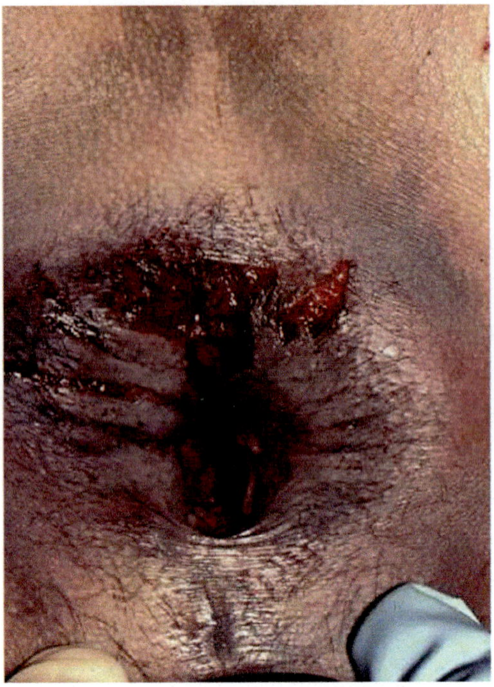

Figure 17.4 Lacerations of the anus. The deceased was beaten and stabbed. A toilet bowl brush was rammed into the rectum and the body set on fire.

tend to be more violent than their heterosexual counterparts as there is often "overkill." The victim is often nude and the number and extent of injuries on the body tend to be greater.[13] The cause of death is usually stabbing, strangulation, blunt force or a combination of all. These cases might be extremely bizarre, with evidence of torture (Figure 17.4).

The Perpetrator

Mention should be made of examination of the suspect in a case of alleged rape. If the individual is apprehended shortly after the incident, their pubic hair should be combed for pubic hair from the victim. Any foreign hair recovered should be submitted for DNA analysis. In addition to collection of foreign pubic hair, swabs of the penis and/or vagina should also be made. In a number of cases, DNA from the victim has been recovered from these swabs. Cina et al. conducted an experimental study on the ability to identify female DNA on postcoital penile swabs.[14] They were able to identify female DNA on swabs taken as long as 24 h after intercourse if the individual did not bathe or shower. Analysis identified the X chromosome.

References

1. U.S. Department of Justice, Office on Violence Against Women, *A National Protocol for Sexual Assault Medical Forensic Examinations Adults/Adolescents* 2nd ed. U.S. Department of Justice, Office on Violence Against Women, Washington DC, NCJ 228119, 2013.
2. Zilkens RR, Smith DA, Kelly MC, et al., Sexual assault and general body injuries: a detailed cross-sectional Australian study of 1163 women. *Forensic Sci Int* 2017; 279:112–120.

3. Zilkens RR, Smith DA, Phillips MA, et al., Genital and anal injuries: a cross-sectional Australian study of 1266 women alleging recent sexual assault. *Forensic Sci Int* 2017; 275:195–202.
4. McLean I, Roberts SA, White C, and Paul S, Female genital injuries resulting from consensual and non-consensual vaginal intercourse. *Forensic Sci Int* 2011; 204(1–3):27–33.
5. Cavness S, Choudhury A, and Sensabaugh G, Hospital wet mount examination for the presence of sperm in sexual assault cases is of questionable value. *J Forensic Sci* 2014; 59(3):729–734.
6. Exline DL, Smith FP, and Drexler SG, Frequency of pubic hair transfer during sexual intercourse. *J Forensic Sci* 1998; 43(3):505–508.
7. Willott GM and Allard JE, Spermatozoa—their persistence after sexual intercourse. *Forensic Sci Int* 1982; 19:135–154.
8. Ricci LR and Hoffman SA, Prostatic acid phosphatase and sperm in the postcoital vagina. *Ann Emerg Med* 1982; 11:530–534.
9. Graves HCB, Sensabaugh GF, and Blake ET, Postcoital detection of a male-specific semen protein. *NEJM* 1985; 312:338–343.
10. Pang BC and Cheung BK, Double swab technique for collecting touched evidence. *Leg Med* 2007; 9(4):181–184.
11. Casali MB, Palazzo E, Blandino A, et al., The adult male rape victim: forensic description of a series of 57 cases. *Am J Forensic Med Pathol* 2017; 38(3):175–179.
12. Duchesne S, Seyller M, and Chariot P, Male sexual assaults in the Paris, France area: an observational study over 8 years. *Forensic Sci Int* 2018; 290:16–28.
13. Bell MD and Vila RI, Homicide and homosexual victims: a study of 67 cases from Broward County, Florida, Medical Examiner's office (1982–1992), with special emphasis on "overkill". *Am J Forensic Med Pathol* 1996; 17(1):65–69.
14. Cina SJ, et al., Isolation and identification of female DNA on postcoital penile swabs. *Am J Forensic Med Pathol*, 2000; 21(2):97–100.

Deaths in the Elderly

18

I'm not afraid of death; I just don't want to be there when it happens.

—Woody Allen

Better health care and improved lifestyles are leading to an increase in the elderly population. In the United States, individuals over the age of 65 years account for approximately 15% of the population and are expected to account for 25% of the population within the next two decades.

Investigating deaths in the elderly can often be difficult since the death is often not unexpected. Disease states such as arteriosclerosis, end-organ damage and cancer become more common as we age. In addition, the elderly are more susceptible to pneumonia and other infectious processes. The elderly are also more susceptible to accidental injuries such as falls and drug overdoses as well as abuse due to their often debilitated state. They can also be the victims of homicide and suicide. Thus, each death should be investigated thoroughly including a review of all available medical records or consultation with the primary physician.

Accidental Deaths

Injuries due to falls are a leading cause of death in persons aged 65 years and above; these include subdural hematomas, hip fractures and rib fractures. Demented patients may also wander away from their home or facility and die due to exposure or dehydration. Elderly patients are also not uncommonly involved in motor vehicle collisions and dwelling fires. Choking and aspiration are also more common in the elderly. Less common accidental deaths may include drinking of cleaning fluids by senile patients or burns caused by immersion in hot bath water.

Drug toxicities are not uncommon in the older populations. As we age, our hepatic and renal functions decrease, as do drug clearance and metabolism. The p450 activity level also decreases, allowing for concentrations of many medications to build up over time. Additionally, senility may lead to an individual accidentally taking too many of their medications unintentionally.

Homicides

The perpetrators of the homicides may be visiting family members, criminals looking for an "easy" target, nursing home (NH) staff or even fellow patients. Homicide may occur even if it was not the intended outcome, meaning an elderly person may be robbed or burglarized and die due to the stress of the event rather than due to any injuries sustained. Thus, the circumstances of death must always be thoroughly reviewed.

Suicides

Suicide in the elderly is not an uncommon occurrence. This may be due to the presence of a debilitating disease or the loss of a loved one such as spouse. In recent years, physician assisted suicide has become more acceptable, with most occurring in individuals over the age of 65 years. Depending upon the applicable state laws, these deaths may or may not be considered as suicides on the death certificate.

Investigation of Abuse or Neglect

Senile Purpura

Often a death in an elderly individual is reported as suspicious due to the individual being "covered in bruises." This is often not to do abuse but to the normal aging process. As we age, our skin becomes thinner, the dermal collagen becomes weaker and the cutaneous vessels weaken allowing for seemingly minor trauma to result in injuries, such as contusions, purpura and epidermal tearing (Figure 18.1).

There is a decrease in the regeneration ability of the keratinocytes which can slow healing. This normal aging process can often be confused with abuse, especially in the setting of anticoagulant use.

Contractures

A contracture is an abnormal, often permanent, condition characterized by flexion and fixation of a limb at a joint (Figure 18.2).

Contractures leave the joint in a nonfunctional position, resistant to bending. They are caused by atrophy and abnormal shortening of muscle fibers. Their primary cause is disuse. Prolonged bed rest, even in "normal" individuals, results in loss of lean muscle mass through lack of use. The muscles become weak, atrophic, change shape and shorten with disuse. The muscle decreases in diameter and in the number of muscle cells. Eventually,

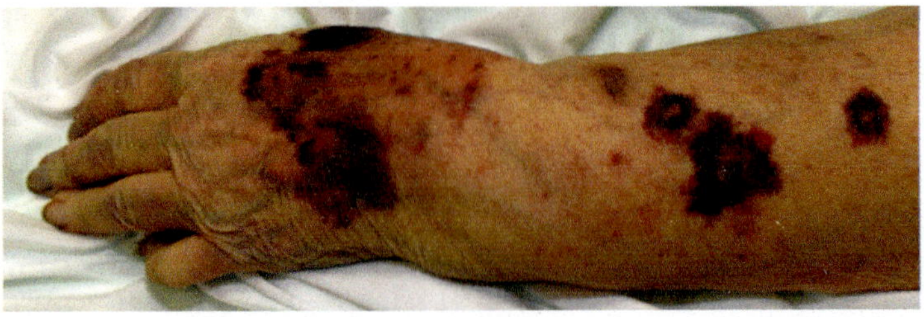

Figure 18.1 Senile purpura on the back of the forearm in an elderly female. This is often confused with abuse, but is merely the result of minor trauma and skin fragility.

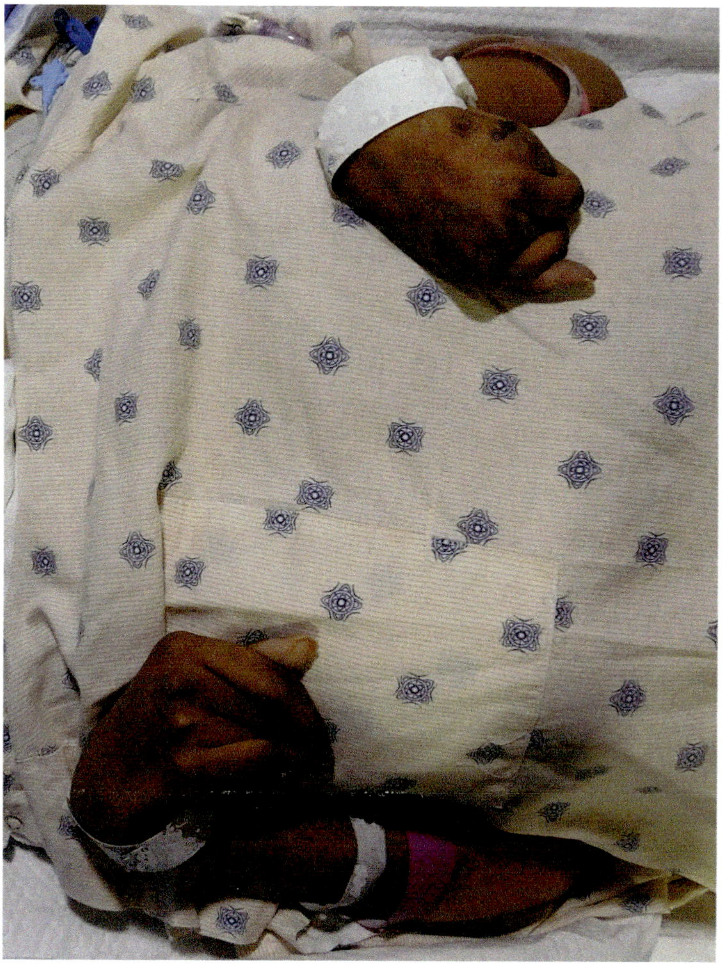

Figure 18.2 Contractures of upper extremities and hands in a decedent with remote head injuries from a motor vehicle collision.

there may be replacement with fibrous connective tissue, progressing to fibrosis and development of contractures.

Contractures are seen in patients with impaired sensorium who are confined to bed. In such patients, a care giver should administer passive range-of-motion exercises on a daily basis to prevent development of contractures. Often, this is not done and contractures develop. Development of contractures may indicate neglect or poor care, especially if admitted to NH or other care facility. Approximately 20% of NH residents nationwide have contractures.[1]

Malnutrition

Malnutrition is manifested by a deficit, excess or imbalance in essential components of a balanced diet. The type of malnutrition seen in elderly patients is usually protein-caloric malnutrition. Thirty-five to 80% of patients in NHs are malnourished, with 30–40% of patients substandard in weight.[1] A weight loss of 5% or greater in 30 days, 7.5% in 3 months and 10% in 6 months, indicates a patient's nutrition should be evaluated.

The amount of nutrition required by a person to live depends on body size, age, health, the environment and degree of activity. The **basal metabolic rate** (BMR) is the amount of energy required of an individual who is awake but at rest, to maintain cellular function at the lowest rate. For a 25-year-old male weighing 154 lb, it is 1744 cal; for a 132-lb, 25-year-old woman, 1281 cal. The number of calories required by a person increases with activity and health problems; however, most elderly patients are not active and health problems are frequent. Stress caused by infections or decubitus ulcers can increase the caloric requirement by a factor of 1.2–1.6. For the 25-year-old male, the calories needed would increase to 2100–2800 cal. The BMR increases 5% for every 1°F rise in body temperature, which necessitates an increase in caloric intake. As to protein intake, in a normal individual, 0.8–1.0 g/kg/day of protein is needed. With infection or decubitus ulcers, this can increase up to 1.2–1.5 g/kg/day.

Malnutrition in the elderly can be caused by the following:

- Chronic disease conditions that make eating difficult, for example, paralysis caused by a stroke
- Lack of appetite due to dementia or other conditions
- Increased caloric or protein requirements due to infection or the healing of wounds
- Medications that impair the desire to eat, for example, psychotropic drugs
- Failure of the caregivers to adequately feed the patients

Unfortunately, differentiating the first four causes from the last can be difficult, which is why a thorough investigation including medical record review may be necessary.

Malnutrition predisposes an individual to the development of decubitus ulcers and infection. These, in turn, lead to increased caloric and protein requirements, thus making the malnutrition worse, which, again, predisposes to decubitus ulcers and infection.

While loss of weight often is an indicator of malnutrition, this is not always the case. The easiest way of determining malnutrition is by measuring serum albumin. The level of albumin in the blood is a reflection of the nutritional status of the patient (Table 21.1). Low levels are associated with protein deprivation (inadequate intake of protein). They are also seen in chronic disease, infection, surgical stress and trauma, all of which result in demand for more protein. Individuals in NHs suffering from these conditions should be given additional food (calories and protein).

Low levels of albumin reflect longstanding malnutrition. The half-life of albumin is 12–20 days, but is shortened in the presence of infection.[5] Thus, low levels of albumin generally reflect what happened to the patient 1–2 months in the past. In contrast, acute starvation reduces the concentrations of proteins that have a short half-life: transferrin (half-life 5 days) and prealbumin (half-life 2 days).[2]

Table 18.1 Blood Albumin*

Normal	3.5–4.5 g/dL
Mild protein depletion	3.0–3.4 g/dL
Moderate depletion	2.5–2.9 g/dL
Severe depletion	<2.5 g/dL

* There is some variation in normal ranges among laboratories.

Dehydration

Dehydration is very common in elderly patients. It can be caused by illness (diarrhea, fever, infection), the effects of medications (e.g., diuretics) and decreased fluid intake. Fluid intake often has to be monitored closely in the elderly debilitated patient to avoid dehydration (see Chapter 4 for more on dehydration).

Decubitus Ulcers

Decubitus ulcers (pressure sores) are the breakdown of tissue due to prolonged mechanical loading and can develop after as little as 4–6 h of sustained loading, though this may be less in a debilitated malnourished individual with additional comorbidities.[3] Factors predisposing to pressure sores are as follows:

- Depressed sensory or motor function
- Altered consciousness
- Pressure over bony prominences
- Malnutrition
- Shearing forces
- Moisture (fecal and urinary incontinence)

The most common cause of decubitus ulcers is **pressure**, usually over bony prominences, in an individual with altered consciousness or impaired motor activity. When the pressure on soft tissue is greater than 32 mm of mercury, it closes both capillary blood and lymphatic flow. This results in deprivation of oxygen to the tissue in this area and accumulation of metabolic end products. If these continue to accumulate for more than 2 h, there is irreversible tissue damage.[3,4] The inability to shift one's body because of depressed sensory or motor function or unconsciousness leads to abnormal pressure and, thus, development of decubitus ulcers. Pressure sores more commonly develop over bony prominences with the most common sites being the sacrum, the coccygeal areas and the greater trochantars from lying in bed, as well as the ischial tuberosities, if the patient is able to sit.

The second major factor in the development of decubitus ulcers is **malnutrition** which results in muscle atrophy and decreased subcutaneous tissue, reducing the padding over the bony prominences, making the pressure more significant and producing ulcers. **Obesity** also contributes to pressure ulcers. A normal amount of fat protects the skin by acting as a cushion. Large quantities of fat, however, lead to ulceration because the adipose tissue is poorly vascularized and the underlying tissue then becomes more susceptible to ischemia.

Another major factor causing ulcers is **shearing forces**.[4] Here, there is sliding of one tissue layer over another with stretching and angulation of blood vessels, which results in injury and thrombosis. This commonly occurs when the head of the bed is raised too high and the individual's body tends to slide downward. Friction and perspiration cause fixation of the skin and the superficial fascia to the sheets, while the deeper fascia slides down. Shearing forces in the elderly are aggravated by the loose skin common in the elderly because of loss of subcutaneous tissue and dehydration.

Moisture, usually caused by urinary and fecal incontinence, is also a major factor predisposing to development of pressure sores. Moisture reduces skin resistance to the other factors and increases the possibility of decubitus ulcers fivefold.

Decubitus ulcers (pressure sores) are divided into four stages based on their clinical appearance and extent.

Stage 1 – The initial lesion seen following compression of skin and tissue is **reactive hyperemia** (reddening of the skin). The redness is caused by sudden increase in blood flow to the area compressed, after relief from the pressure of compression. If there is no injury to the tissue, the redness will disappear in less than 1 h. If the compression is long enough to produce ischemia but not irreversible injury, then you have an abnormal reactive hyperemia, which can last several hours. If the pressure is maintained long enough, one then has a Stage 1 pressure sore manifested by erythema that lasts longer than 24 h, does not blanch on pressure and shows induration of the tissue caused by edema. These sores can occur in a matter of a few hours. In our opinion, while Stage 1 pressure sores are an indication of a potential problem, they do not in themselves indicate neglect. They are readily treatable and should not progress.

Stage 2 – These range in severity from a blister to ulceration of the skin. They may involve the full thickness of the skin but do not penetrate into the subcutaneous fat and are readily treatable.

Stage 3 – These are full-thickness ulcers extending through the skin and subcutaneous fat up to the fascia. There is usually undermining of the skin. The base of the ulcer is usually necrotic, foul-smelling and infected (Figure 18.3).

Stage 4 – Here the ulcer extends down through the fascia into muscle, often to the bone. Osteomyelitis may develop (Figure 18.4A and B).

Stages 3 and 4 ulcers may be indicative of poor or lack of nursing treatment and thus neglect; however, this determination depends upon many factors including the functional state of the individual, the presence of preexisting conditions, the ability of the patient to participate in their medical care (i.e., their refusal to follow medical advice) and the duty of those taking care of the patients (i.e., an NH, an elderly spouse). Preventive measures involve basic nursing techniques. In bed, the patient should be turned or repositioned at least every 2 h; in wheelchairs, every hour. Adequate nutrition and hydration should be given; the skin must be kept dry by preventing patients from lying in their urine and feces; the head of the bed should not be raised to such a degree that the patient will slide down

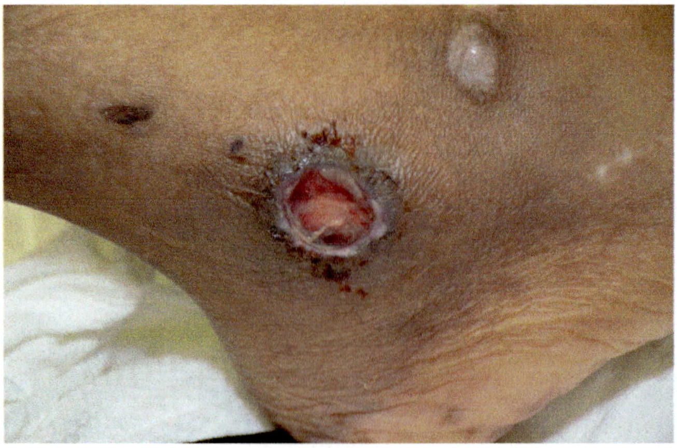

Figure 18.3 Stage 3 decubitus ulcer.

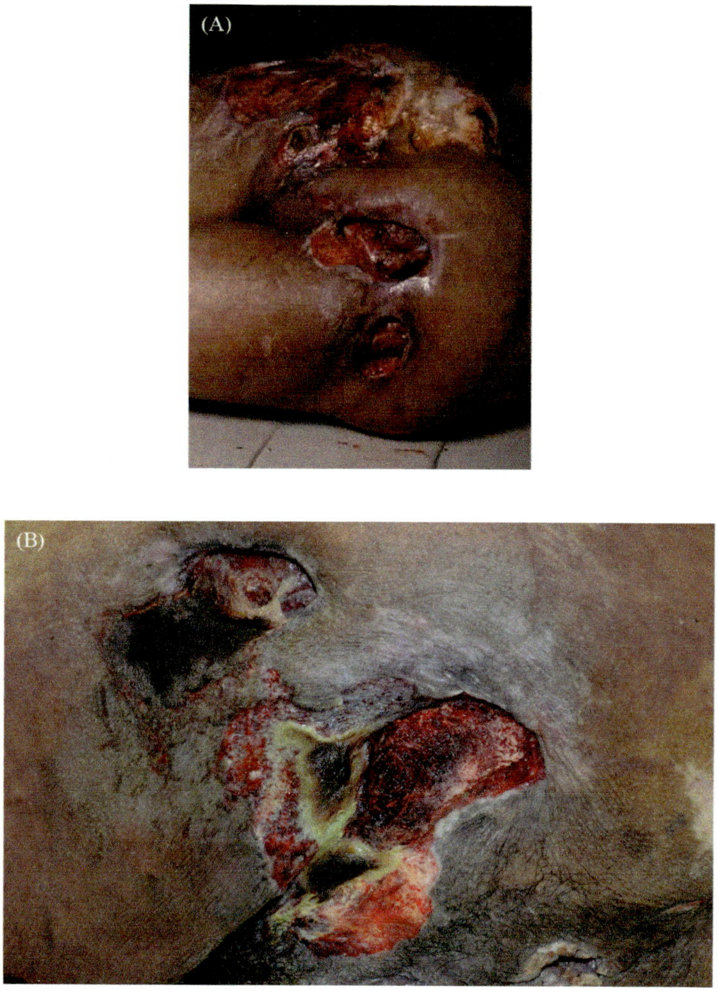

Figure 18.4 (A and B) Stage 4 decubitus ulcers.

and, if necessary, extra padding over bony prominences should be provided. If a sore develops, the physician should be notified immediately.

The incidence of pressure sores in individuals in NHs varies from study to study. A conservative approximation is 7–8%. Tsokos et al. conducted a prospective study of 10,222 bodies coming to cremation in Hamburg, Germany, from various sources including NHs, hospitals and private residences.[5] Pressure sores were observed in 11.2% of the individuals. The distribution of the sores by grades was Stage 1 – 6.1%, Stage 2 – 3%, Stage 3 – 1.1% and Stage 4 – 0.9%. Stages 3 and 4 sores were found principally on the sacrum (69.6%). Seventy-three percent of all Stage 4 sores were in individuals 80 years of age and older. For Stage 4 sores, the place of death was as follows:

- 36.2%: Senior citizen or NH
- 23.4%: Private home
- 17%: Hospital
- 23.4%: Unknown

The site where the individuals developed the sores was not necessarily the same as where they died.

Both the presence of pressure sores and deaths caused by them are underreported. The authors have reviewed hospital admission records of patients with pressure sores where the sores are not mentioned at all in the physical examinations by the physicians or in the diagnoses. Pressure sores are often dismissed as inevitable by many physicians, although pressure sores can often be successfully prevented by determining the patients at risk for development of sores, consistently monitoring them for development of sores and instituting prophylactic procedures to prevent their development. If sores develop, they can be effectively treated by conservative or surgical means.

Decubitus ulcers, Stages 2–4, lose both fluids and proteins; the more severe the lesion, the greater the loss. In addition, the sores can become infected leading to septicemia, the exact incidence of this complication is unknown, as it is often underreported.

Homicide by Decubitus Ulcers

How can one defend a ruling of homicide in a death from decubitus ulcers? In these cases, what one attempts to show is that the patient died of the decubitus ulcers and that the ulcers developed secondary to gross neglect, or failure to provide the most basic nursing services. Quite commonly in such cases, a pattern of falsified records is found, delay in notifying attending physicians of the presence or severity of the ulcer and failure to promptly institute therapy ordered by the physician, though proving this in a noninstitutional setting may be more difficult. In November 2000, the state of Hawaii convicted an individual of manslaughter in the death of a patient at an adult residential care home (a form of NH) for permitting the progression of decubitus ulcers without seeking medical help.[6]

Nursing Home Deaths

There are over 15,000 NHs existing in the United States, housing approximately 1.5 million patients, most of whom are over the age of 65 years. Most deaths in NHs are natural and usually do not fall under the medical examiner's jurisdiction; however, these deaths should still be investigated due to the issues discussed above. Investigation should include a review of all available records and consultation with the supervising physician. A lack of or inconsistent record keeping may indicate a lack of care, and further investigation may be necessary.

Physicians, both clinicians and forensic pathologists, have a tendency to dismiss the deaths of NH patients as inevitable. Some individuals and institutions argue that, because of the patients' condition (i.e., they are bedridden, do not have control of their bowels and cannot feed themselves), it is expected that they will become malnourished and develop contractures and bed sores. Unfortunately, this is not always the case as when some of these same individuals were moved into institutions where they were provided good nursing care, the decubitus ulcers healed, the patients gained weight and their overall health improved. Consider that infants are bedridden, have no control over their bowels and cannot feed themselves. If a caretaker starved a child, leaving it in its urine and feces so that it developed sores and infections, that caretaker would be arrested, charged with child abuse and put in prison, and the death in such a circumstance would be ruled homicide.

Gross Neglect of Patients

NHs or personnel have been charged with homicide for improper and inadequate care of patients.[7,8] In one case involving a death resulting from infected decubitus ulcers (pressure sores), the care-home provider was convicted of manslaughter.[8] In another case, an attending nurse pled guilty to the felony offense of injury to an elderly individual, second degree, because she did not promptly notify a physician or summon emergency medical personnel when a patient was obviously suffering a heart attack.[9] In all probability, if every NH death were properly investigated, the numbers of cases in which individuals and perhaps institutions might be charged with homicide in the death of patients would increase. A careful review of all NH deaths is necessary to identify such cases, though most medical examiner offices do not have the resources do to so.

Drug Overdoses

The authors have investigated a number of cases where a patient was given either too much medication or the wrong medication. This situation is probably fairly common, but, in most instances, does not cause death. When death does occur, the NH is probably often unaware of the mix-up and assumes the death to be natural. In virtually all the cases where death was caused by an inadvertent overdose and the death was investigated, the circumstances of the case came to light only when an employee surreptitiously notified the medical examiner or the family. Insulin seems to be quite commonly involved in these situations.

In rare instances, the drug overdose is intentional. A number cases of health-care workers who believed it their calling to end "suffering" by killing a patient have been reported. Cases such as this often involve potassium chloride or opiate medications such as morphine. In such cases, the medications are often administered orally or via a PEG tube.

Deaths Caused by Hospital Bed Side Rails

Bed side rails are intended to prevent patients from injuring themselves. However, due to the injuries that have been sustained with bed rails, many NHs no longer use them with any patients.

Both indirect and direct injuries have occurred with bed rails. Indirect injuries occur when elderly patients fall while attempting to crawl over the rails. On occasion, bed rails may cause death directly by entrapment.[10,11] The majority of such cases involve NHs, where the patients are elderly and tend to have cognitive and physical disabilities.

Parker and Miles reviewed 74 deaths attributed solely to bed rails. In 52 (70%) of the cases, there was entrapment between the mattress and bed rail, with the face pressed against the mattress.[11] Thirteen (18%) of the deaths were caused by entrapment of the neck within the rails (eight had inserted their heads between the vertical bars; the bed-rail latch failed and the rail dropped on their necks; five patients died because their heads and necks were draped over the top of the rails). Nine (12%) of the 74 patients died when they slid partially off the bed. This resulted in their being suspended by either their heads or pelvises with, in the latter circumstance, the necks hyperflexed or hyperextended by contact with the floor.

In a number of deaths involving bed rails seen by the authors, attempts to conceal the cause of death were made. This involved placing the individual back in bed and notifying the attending physician that the patient had died naturally. Such cases were uncovered only when NH personnel reported the deaths to the medical examiner or a member of the family.

Deaths Caused by Medical Restraints

Restraints are mechanical devices, materials or equipment that restrict individuals' freedom of movement or normal access to their bodies. Like bed rails, many NHs have moved away from using restraints. If individuals attempt to escape from such devices, they run the danger of ligature strangulation or traumatic/positional asphyxia.[12,13] Miles and Irvine reviewed 122 deaths caused by vest and strap restraints, in which 85% occurred in NHs.[13] The victims were elderly, with a median age of 81. They were found suspended from chairs in 58% of the cases and from beds in 42%. Typically, there was a history of sliding down in or escaping restraints. Victims are placed in a vest or strap restraint and left alone. They then slide off the bed or chair, with the restraint catching them across the chest or, less commonly, under the chin. Unfortunately, they do not slide down far enough to reach a weight-bearing surface. If the restraint catches them under the neck, they strangle. If the restraint stops at the chest, their weight on the restraint reduces chest movement, causing traumatic asphyxia.

Medical Records from Nursing Homes

A final note should be made about relying solely on medical records from NHs on which to base an opinion. While the majority of NHs provide excellent care to their patients, the authors have occasionally seen incidents of falsification of the records. Usually these falsifications were done not by the administrative personnel, but by the staffing personnel who cared for the patients. Fortunately, most of the misinformation in itself did not cause death, though it did reveal the unreliability of the records. For example, patients lost a third of their weight after consuming all meals for 2 or 3 months. Or decubitus ulcers did not exist in these patients records, but when discharged to another facility or were autopsied, decubitus ulcers, from Stage 1 ulcers to Stage 4, miraculously appeared. The ulcers also appeared and disappeared depending the nurse caring for the patients.

References

1. Burger SG, Kayser-Jones J, and Bell JP, Malnutrition and dehydration in nursing homes: key issues in prevention and treatment. Research supported by the Commonwealth Fund. June 2000. http://www.cmwf.org/programs/elders/burger_mal_386.asp.
2. Neale G, Diet and disease, in Tomlinson S, Heagerty AM, and Weetman AP (Eds) *Mechanisms of Disease*. Cambridge University Press, Cambridge, UK, 1997.
3. Gejen A, How much time does it take to get a pressure ulcer? *Integrated Evid Hum Anim In Vitro Stud Ostomy Wound Manage* 2008; 54(10):26–35.
4. Bouten CV, Oomens CW, Baaijens FP, and Bader DL, The etiology of pressure ulcers: skin deep or muscle bound? *Arch Phys Med Rehabil* 2003; 84(4):616–619.

5. Tsokos M, Heinemann A, and Puschel K, Pressure sores: epidemiology, medicolegal implications and forensic argumentation concerning causality. *Int J Legal Med* 2000; 113:283–287.
6. DiMaio VJ and DiMaio TG, Homicide by decubitus ulcers. *Am J Forensic Med Pathol* 2002; 23(1):1–4.
7. Long S, *Death Without Dignity*. Texas Monthly Press, Austin, TX, 1987.
8. *State of Hawaii v. Bermissa*, 2000.
9. *State of Texas vs. Jo Ann Maddox*, 1999.
10. Todd JF, Ruhl CE, and Gross TP, Injury and death associated with hospital bed side-rails: reports to the U.S. Food and Drug Administration from 1985 to 1995. *Am J Pub Health* 1997; 87(10):1675–1677.
11. Parker K and Miles SH, Deaths caused by bed rails. *J Am Geriatrics Soc* 1997; 45(7):797–802.
12. Di Maio VJ, Dana SE, and Bux RC, Deaths caused by restraint vests. *JAMA* 1986; 255:905.
13. Miles SH and Irvine P, Deaths cause by physical restraints. *Gerontologist* 1992; 32:762–766.

Sudden Death during or Immediately after a Struggle

19

Some get a kick from cocaine,
I'm sure that if I took even one sniff,
That would bore me terrifically too,
Yet, I get a kick out of you.

—Cole Porter

Deaths during or immediately after a struggle can be a result of many factors: deaths can be due to natural disease exacerbated by the struggle, excited delirium syndrome (EDS), asphyxia or injuries sustained in the struggle itself such as head trauma. However, understanding the dynamics of the struggle, and all the factors involved, is pivotal to an adequate, fair and impartial death investigation.

A struggle, whether with police, other individuals or just oneself, is an intense physical exertion of varying duration. Struggles can be short-lasting only a few minutes, or prolonged. When a medical examiner or coroner encounters a death during or shortly after a struggle, many factors must be considered: the duration and exact nature of the struggle, including issues such as the position of the decedent during the struggle; the use of chemicals such as pepper spray; the deployment of electromuscular disruption devices; the presence or absence of significant internal injuries; and the presence or absence of concomitant natural disease or drugs/medications. All of these factors can affect the outcome, including death, in a struggle and must be considered during the investigation and each will be discussed at length.

The Physiology of a Struggle

During a struggle, or any periods of intense activity, the sympathetic nervous system is activated. The sympathetic nervous system is the controller of the "fight or flight" response. Whenever an individual is exposed to stress, there is a widespread physiological reaction throughout the body. This stress can be physical and or psychological. The reaction of the body to stress is integrated in the brain through the hypothalamus. Signals are transmitted downward from the hypothalamus through the brainstem, into the spinal cord and then to organs, such as the heart, producing massive sympathetic discharge with the release of the neurotransmitters norepinephrine (noradrenalin) and epinephrine (adrenalin).

Neurotransmitters are substances that travel through synapses (a space between the end of the nerve fiber and the cell of the organ) to deliver information to other neurons or cells. They are produced within neurons (nerve cells), stored in vesicles at the end of the axons and released into the synapse upon nerve stimulation. The neurotransmitters we are concerned with are the catecholamines. The principal catecholamines are epinephrine (E), norepinephrine (NE) and dopamine. The main catecholamines in the brain are NE and dopamine; outside the brain NE and E. Outside the brain, sympathetic neurons release NE and the adrenals both NE and E.

Norepinephrine (NE) is released from nerve fibers (axons) into the synapse (a space between the end of the nerve fiber and the cell of the organ) (Figure 19.1).

The NE interacts with receptors on the cell known as adrenoceptors. Adrenoceptors are sites on cell membranes through which norepinephrine and epinephrine (E) act as neurotransmitters in the brain, the cardiovascular system and other organs. The sympathetic nervous system influences the cardiovascular system through changes in the release of NE from sympathetic nerve terminals and NE and E from the adrenals as well as controlling the reuptake mechanisms. Reuptake involves recapturing the neurotransmitters by transport systems, located at the nerve terminals of the releasing neurons and pulling them back into the cells. Neurotransmitters can also be rapidly inactivated and degraded at the synapse itself by the action of specific enzymes. This release and reuptake/destruction balance control the degree of excitation.

The membrane receptors responsible for mediating responses to catecholamines were initially divided into α- and β-adrenoceptors.[1–3] α-Adrenoceptors are differentiated into α_1-adrenoceptors and α_2-adrenoceptors. α_1-Adrenoceptors are usually postsynaptic and in

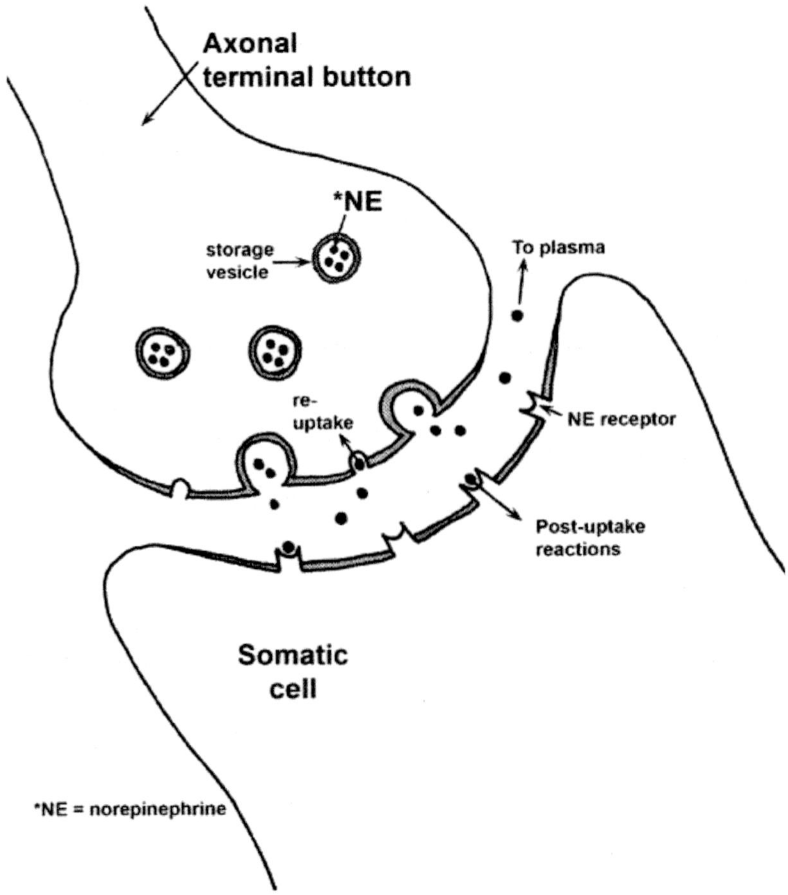

Figure 19.1 Norepinephrine (NE) is released from axons into the synapse and interacts with receptors on the recipient (somatic) cells.

effector organs, while α_2-adrenoceptors are located principally presynaptically and regulate the release of norepinephrine. α_2-Adenoceptors, however, have been identified in both pre- and postsynaptic anatomical locations. α_1-Adrenoceptors were thought to be responsible for excitatory responses; α_2-adrenoceptors for inhibitory responses. While true in general, α_2-adrenoceptors can also mediate excitatory responses. Both α_1- and α_2-adrenoceptors can in turn be divided into three subtypes: α_{1A}, α_{1B}, α_{1D} and α_{2A}, α_{2B} and α_{2C}. In the vascular system, both α_1-adrenoceptors and α_2-adreptors are responsible for vasoconstriction with the α_1-adrenoceptors dominant in arteries and the α_2-adrenoceptors in veins.[4]

There are three β-adrenoceptors: β_1, β_2 and β_3. β_1- and β_2-adrenoceptors mediate the cardiovascular responses to NE released from nerve terminals and to circulating E and NE from the adrenals. The predominate receptor in heart cells is the β_1 subtype. The release of catecholamines causes an increase in the heart rate and force of contraction by way of β_1 receptors in heart cells.

On stimulation of the adrenal glands by the sympathetic nervous system, there is release into the blood of both NE and E, with E predominating (80% E and 20% NE). These are carried by the blood to the organs where they have basically the same effect as does direct sympathetic stimulation. The only difference is that the effects last five to ten times as long because these substances are slowly removed from the blood over a period of 1–3 min.

However, there can be a substantial degree of variation in E and NE responses due to genetic polymorphisms within the general population.[5] Presynaptic α_2 receptors (α_{2A}- and α_{2C}-adrenoceptors) usually inhibit the release of NE from cardiac sympathetic nerves via negative feedback. However, Small et al. demonstrated that some individuals have a polymorphic α_{2C} receptor (α_{2C} Del 322–325) resulting in a substantial loss of the normal negative feedback such that there was an increase in synaptic NE release.[6] In addition, a variant of the β_1 receptors (beta1 Arg 389) has been identified which enhances β_1 receptor activity; activation of the β_1 receptor is results in increased cardiac the rate and strength of muscular contraction. The combination of the two receptor variants in the same individual, resulting in an increase in NE release and enhanced β_1 receptor function at the cardiac myocyte, appeared to act synergistically to increase the risk of heart failure. The presence of polymorphic α_2 and β_1 receptors may also explain why some individuals die following the physical stress, while the bulk of the population does not.

Effects of Catecholamines on the Heart

Upon commencement, high-intensity physical activity (e.g., a struggle) results in secretion of norepinephrine and epinephrine. Norepinephrine's action on the heart is predominantly stimulation of the α_1 and β_1 receptors. Stimulation of β_1 receptors increases heart rate, contractility and velocity of conduction. Norepinephrine interacting with α_1 receptors of the coronary arteries may cause vasoconstriction, thus decreasing the amount of oxygenated blood being supplied to the myocardium at a time when an increased amount is needed due to greater demand being put on the heart resulting from the stimulation of the β_1 receptors. Epinephrine interacts with all four receptors – α_1, α_2, β_1 and β_2 reinforcing the cardiac and coronary actions of NE.

Coronary arteries have in their walls both β_2 and α_1 receptors, with the β_2 more plentiful. Sympathetic activation of normal coronary arteries by either stress or physical activity should result in vasodilatation of both epicardial and microvessels. However, in an abundance of norepinephrine reacting predominantly with the α_1 receptors or in the presence of atherosclerosis or endothelial dysfunction, there may be significant vasoconstriction during exercise,[4] sufficient enough to produce myocardial ischemia.

At the same time that changes in catecholamine concentrations are occurring, there are also changes occurring in the blood potassium concentrations.

Postexercise Peril

Deaths due to a struggle most often occur immediately after the individual is restrained and the struggling has ceased. This time frame corresponds to the time of "post exercise peril" described by Dimsdale et al.[7] It is when an individual is unusually susceptible to developing a fatal cardiac arrhythmia. Dimsdale et al. found that during exercise, an individual's blood NE and E increased, with NE increasing more sharply.[7] Peak concentrations of these catecholamines did not occur during the struggle, however, but in the 3 min immediately following cessation of the exercise. Following cessation of exercise, E and NE continue to rise with NE levels more than tenfold above baseline levels and E threefold.

Compounding the physiological actions of elevated levels of catecholamine are changes in blood potassium levels. Young et al. investigated the relationship between stress and blood catecholamine and potassium levels.[8] Like Dimsdale et al., they found that the highest concentrations of plasma catecholamines occurred during the 3 min post exercise. In their studies, E concentrations peaked 1 min after cessation of exercise, at which point the mean value was more than eightfold mean resting level. Elevated E levels were present for several additional minutes, with a mean value of 1.5 times the resting level at 10 min post exercise. For NE, 1 min following cessation of exercise, the concentration was seven times greater than the resting level. At 10 min, the NE level was twice the resting level.

Blood potassium concentrations have a very narrow range of safety (3.5–5.1 mEq/L). Fatal cardiac arrhythmia is associated with both hyperkalemia and hypokalemia. Hypokalemia occurs when serum potassium is less than 3.5 mmol/L. With mild hypokalemia (serum potassium of 3.0–3.5 mmol/L), there are usually no symptoms.[9] Severe hypokalemia (<2.5 mmol/L) produces symptoms, including muscle necrosis. Both mild and severe hypokalemia increase the incidence of cardiac arrhythmia.[9] Hypokalemia predisposes to prolongation of the QT interval, development of torsade de pointes and sudden cardiac death.[10]

Young et al. found that during exercise, the mean plasma potassium increased slightly more than 1 mEq/L.[8] Following cessation of exercise, the potassium level fell rapidly returning to approximately normal levels in 5 min. The maximum rate of fall occurred within the first- or second-minute post exercise. In some individuals engaged in strenuous exercise, plasma potassium levels of 9 mEq/L may occur if the exercise is carried to exhaustion.[11] Peak levels are proportional to the intensity of the exercise, contracting muscle mass and duration of exercise. There is little evidence, however, that these extremely high levels of potassium due to exercise adversely affect cardiac functioning.[11,12] Such concentrations can only be maintained for 1–2 min before exercise has to be stopped due to exhaustion. Studies suggest that exercise-induced increases in blood catecholamines have a cardioprotective effect on hyperkalemia.[13,14] It is felt, however, that it is the rapid drop to low potassium concentrations following cessation of exercise that produces an arrhythmia. This hypokalemia predisposes to prolongation of the QT interval, development of torsade de pointes and sudden cardiac death.

Sudden Death

Thus, even in the absence of additional factors, to be discussed next, sudden death can occur after a struggle. In individuals who have underlying natural disease processes, such as an enlarged heart or known rhythm disturbances (i.e., Wolff-Parkinson-White syndrome), are even more susceptible. It is much like someone with known ischemic heart disease who runs a marathon, the struggle puts an additional strain on the cardiovascular system that it is unable to compensate for, resulting in fatal ischemia or arrhythmia and death.

Excited Delirium Syndrome

Delirium involves an acute (minutes to hours), transient disturbance in consciousness and cognition. It is manifested by disorientation, disorganized and inconsistent thought processes, an inability to distinguish reality from hallucinations, disturbances in speech, disorientation to time and place and/or misidentification of individuals. When the delirium involves combative and/or violent behavior, it is termed **Excited Delirium. EDS** is the sudden death of an individual, during or immediately following an episode of ED, in which an autopsy fails to reveal evidence of sufficient trauma or natural disease to explain the death. In virtually all such cases, the episode of ED is terminated by a struggle, often with police or medical personnel, and the use of physical restraint. The individual will subsequently go into cardiopulmonary arrest during or within minutes following cessation of the struggle. Attempts at resuscitation are usually unsuccessful. If a cardiac monitor is available at the time of the arrest, the rhythm noted is usually pulseless electrical activity (PEA) or asystole. If resuscitation is "successful," the individual is found to have suffered irreversible hypoxic encephalopathy and death usually occurs in a matter of days.

The entity that we now term "Excited Delirium Syndrome" was first described by Dr. Luther Bell in 1849.[15] Typically, his patients presented with fever, a rapid pulse and a lack of appetite and sleep. They were agitated and anxious, with increasing confusion. Attempts to approach the patients resulted in a violent struggle. The patients continued to deteriorate over a course of weeks before dying. Deaths due to what became known as *Bell's Mania* continued to be reported in the medical literature until the early 1950s when they abruptly disappeared with the introduction of phenothiazines for the treatment of mental illness.[16,17]

While all of Bell's patients had mental disease, and their symptoms progressed over days to weeks prior to death, deaths seen today in association with ED mainly involve abusers of stimulants, for example, cocaine and/ or methamphetamine, with symptoms present for only a few hours. Deaths do still occur in mental patients, though rarely, usually in individuals with schizophrenia and occasionally bipolar disease. In individuals with intrinsic mental disease, death usually occurs following the use of restraint because of an acute psychotic episode, though some have also occurred with the individual present alone in a room; however, the room shows signs of a violent struggle having occurred, including overturned furniture and destroyed items. Deaths occurring in psychiatric patients not on illegal stimulants may be associated with underlying natural disease and/or the presence of psychotropic drugs. Many of these latter drugs are cardiotoxic with some having effects on the cardiovascular system similar to cocaine. Just as with ED due to the use of illegal stimulants, if a patient becomes violent, steps must be taken to protect the safety of both the patient and others. If all nonphysical methods are utilized without avail, then medical personnel have to resort to the use of physical restraints. Deaths due to EDS also occur, though rarely, in association with chronic alcoholism, mental retardation, epilepsy and degenerative diseases of the brain.

The mechanism of death in EDS has been controversial. Since such deaths almost always occur after restraint is either instituted or attempted. The cause of death is often attributed to the application of a choke hold, restraint or positional asphyxia. Because of the circumstances surrounding deaths due to EDS, there are often charges of police or medical misconduct. In some cases, allegations of murder are made. When no physical cause for the death is found at autopsy, this is ascribed to a cover-up. Some groups and individuals find it suspicious that the most deaths due to EDS occur in association with the use of restraint by police; however, this is an association, not necessarily causation. The authors have seen several cases of EDS occurring after a struggle and restraint by bystanders and good Samaritans who are just trying to help. The fact is that if a person goes into ED outside a medical institution, the police are usually called; even if the first responders are Emergency Medical Service personnel, they will call the police. The police are then expected to either arrest the individual or have them transported to a hospital. If the individual becomes violent, the police have to restrain them before transport.

In deaths due to EDS, an autopsy fails to reveal evidence of sufficient trauma or natural disease to explain the death. In regards to trauma, the usual findings are minor abrasions and contusions explainable by the struggle that preceded death. If during the struggle, the individual was either hit in the neck or an arm placed around it, hemorrhage in the neck may be present. In rare instances, fractures of the superior horns of the thyroid cartilage or the hyoid bone may also be found. This leads some individuals to contend that manual strangulation has occurred. What they fail to realize is that both hemorrhage in the neck and the aforementioned fractures do not equate to death due to strangulation. They are only *markers* indicating that pressure or a blow to the neck has occurred. These injuries in themselves are not lethal. Death from manual strangulation involves constant pressure to the neck over a number of minutes – generally more than 2–3 min (see Chapter 8, "Asphyxia").

The two stimulants most commonly associated with death due to EDS are cocaine and methamphetamine, though phencyclidine (PCP), diphenhydramine and acute and chronic ethanol use have also been reported. The authors have also seen a case of EDS due to an overdose of quetiapine in an adolescent male. All of these drugs can result in psychotic behavior with both acute and chronic use and can affect the NE/E, dopamine and/or serotonin systems.

Cocaine is a powerfully addictive drug of abuse whose major routes of administration are sniffing (snorting), injection and smoking (including freebase and crack cocaine). Less commonly, it is taken orally. The effects of cocaine use include paranoia, bizarre, erratic or violent behavior, delusions, and increased temperature, heart rate, myocardial contractility and blood pressure. Cocaine activates the sympathetic nervous system both centrally and peripherally. It blocks the reuptake of norepinephrine at the presynaptic adrenergic terminals, acting as a powerful sympathomimetic agent. Even small doses of cocaine taken intranasally have been associated with vasoconstriction of coronary arteries. In addition to adrenergic stimulation, cocaine has been shown to increase levels of endothelin-1, which is a powerful vasoconstrictor, and to decrease the production of nitric oxide, which is a vasodilator. Thus, cocaine decreases oxygen supply and induces myocardial ischemia through a variety of mechanisms.

Cocaine also strongly binds to the dopamine active transporters (DATs) impairing transport of dopamine back into the nerve terminals after release, with resultant increase in dopamine at the synapse. The resultant elevated levels of dopamine produce "the high" that characterizes cocaine use. In chronic cocaine abusers, in an apparent neuroadaptive measure, there is an increase in the density of DAT binding sites at the nerve terminals, limbic striatum of the brain.[18,19] In chronic cocaine abusers not dying in ED, the number of dopamine transporters (DATs) is found to be normal or increased at the nerve terminals, while in ED has decreased a number of DATs.[19] This possibly explains the occurrence of EDS in these individuals.

Presumably, it is the myocardial ischemia due to the effects of markedly elevated catecholamine levels, in association with hypokalemia that results in a fatal arrhythmia in individuals with EDS due to cocaine. If an electrocardiogram (EKG) is performed immediately after arrest, individuals arresting due to EDS typically show either asystole or PEA. Both these arrhythmias have a grim prognosis with little response to cardiac resuscitation. Though, another prominent effect of cocaine on the heart is a suppression of the delayed rectifier potassium current (IK) that is important for cardiac repolarization. Cocaine inhibits the channels by preferentially binding to a combination of open and inactivated sites. This results in an increase in the QT interval, which is consistent with a general slowing of myocardial repolarization. Prolongation of the QT interval is associated with the development of fatal cardiac arrhythmias.

Like cocaine, methamphetamine is an addictive stimulant drug that may be taken orally intranasally (snorting), intravenously and by smoking. It is related chemically to amphetamine, but the central nervous system effects are greater. The euphoria produced by methamphetamine appears similar to that produced by cocaine but the effects may last much longer. High doses and/or chronic use result in agitation, confusion, hallucinations, paranoia and aggressiveness. Physically, there is increased heart rate and blood pressure due to stimulation of the sympathetic nervous system both centrally and peripherally by increasing levels of dopamine and norepinephrine. Acting on the brain, it causes the accumulation of high levels of the neurotransmitter dopamine by decreasing the number and activity of dopamine transporters.[20,21] In the brain, it also appears to have a direct neurotoxic effect, damaging axons and axon terminals.[20,21] The mechanism of death in EDS due to methamphetamine is the same as with cocaine, myocardial ischemia due to the effects of markedly elevated catecholamine levels, in association with hypokalemia.

The chronic use of stimulants such as cocaine and methamphetamine can also result in cardiomyopathies thought to be due to both direct toxicity on the heart and, indirectly, from drug-induced hypertension, necrosis and ischemia.[22–24] These cardiomyopathies and cardiac enlargement predispose to the development of fatal cardiac arrhythmias.[25,26] Study of individuals who were chronic users of methamphetamine revealed that 27.2% of them demonstrated prolongation of the QT interval. Prolongation of the QT interval is associated with the development of cardiac arrhythmias and sudden death.

Other drugs implicated in potentially causing EDS include marijuana, synthetic marijuana, ethanol, PCP and neuroleptic drugs, all of which have been associated with acute psychoses and stimulation of the sympathetic nervous system. It is believed that all of these drugs cause EDS by the same general mechanisms as cocaine and methamphetamine, creating a psychotic state and a predisposition to cardiac arrhythmias by various mechanisms, including direct cardiac toxicity.

EDS may also occur in the absence of stimulant drugs such as cocaine, methamphetamine or alcohol in individuals with *endogenous* mental disease. Clinically, these are usually referred to as acute psychotic episodes and tend to occur in individuals with schizophrenia, schizoaffective disorders, bipolar disease or delusional disorders. Many such patients have either an inherent dysregulation of the NE/E, dopamine and/or serotonin systems or are taking medications that cause effect in these systems. For example, in schizophrenia, there is a disturbance in the metabolism of norepinephrine (NE) both in the brain and peripherally. Studies in both medicated and non-medicated patients with schizophrenia have found abnormally elevated NE concentrations in samples obtained from plasma, cerebrospinal fluid and postmortem brain. Stress in individuals with schizophrenia results in higher reactive blood levels of NE than in normal individuals. Additionally, many of the medications prescribed for psychotic disorders affect the same systems. For example, the tricyclic antidepressants, like cocaine and methamphetamine, block reuptake of norepinephrine. Haloperidol and other antipsychotics have cardiotoxic properties that may affect the duration of the action potential of ventricular myocytes (heart cells). This duration is based on an equilibrium between inward and outward currents of ions across the cell membrane. These drugs can cause an imbalance in this flow, resulting in a longer action potential and QT prolongation by blocking outward movement of K^+ and thus repolarization, and/or inhibiting inward ionic currents especially Na^+ and Ca^{2+} in heart cells. Prolongation of the QT interval is associated with the ventricular tachyarrhythmia *torsade de pointes* and sudden death.[27,28] Thus, these drugs, in conjunction with a hyperadrenergic state caused by the delirium and struggle and the resultant hypokalemia, may produce a fatal arrhythmia.

Not everyone who uses drugs develops EDS. In death due to EDS, there are no specific autopsy findings that assist in the diagnosis. However, research is currently being conducted to see if some individuals are more susceptible to developing EDS than others. The symptoms of psychosis and mania are both related to dopaminergic hyperactivity in the brain circuits and have long been implicated in neuropsychiatric disorders.[29] The hyperdopaminergia and disordered signaling in dopamine target regions of the brain also serve as a model for schizophrenia and mania, since dopaminergic blocking drugs are effective in alleviating mania and psychosis. This dysregulated dopamine transporter function may also occur in EDS. In EDS victims, there is a loss of dopamine transporter regulation, which causes dopamine overflow in the synapse. The elevated synaptic dopamine leads to a state of hyperdopaminergia, that is associated with the intense motor excitement, paranoia, bizarre and often violent behavior.[29]

Cocaine is the most frequently reported illicit drug in EDS, particularly being chronic cocaine abusers, and often usually engaged in a "binge" pattern of drug use.[19] Often, these individuals have used large amounts of cocaine or methamphetamine for days, which interrupts normal sleep-wake cycles, exacerbating the neuropsychiatric effects. Although EDS is most frequently reported in cocaine abusers, psychostimulants, including methamphetamine, 3,4-methylenedioxymethamphetamine (MDMA), alpha-pyrrolidinovalerophenone (PVP), methylome, and ephedrine, have also been associated with the syndrome.[30] These psychostimulants all directly interact with the dopamine transporter to cause a marked increase in the levels of synaptic dopamine.

Victims of EDS are in an extremely heightened emotional state exhibiting marked paranoia and mounting irrational fear. In addition to the abovementioned discussed physiologic issues, abnormal signaling in the brain-heart axis may be a precipitant of a sudden fatal arrhythmia, since hyperdopaminergic signaling in the limbic system can convert extreme emotional stress into autonomic toxicity. The connection between the hyperdopaminergia and chaotic signaling in higher brain autonomic regulatory centers may explain the abrupt loss of autonomic function that leads to sudden unexpected death in victims of the EDS.

Whether resulting from illicit drugs or inherent mental disease, an individual becomes psychotic and engages in a struggle. The physiologic effects of the struggle are magnified by the drugs/underlying disease process and a fatal arrhythmia more readily ensue. Thus, EDS is a medical emergency. Any individuals presenting with the appearance of EDS should be transported to a medical emergency room even if they have not gone into cardiopulmonary arrest. Unfortunately, immediately following the cessation of the struggle, the individual is generally ignored until suddenly it is realized that they are not breathing. Resuscitation is attempted and is unsuccessful.[31] While most individuals suffer their cardiopulmonary arrest at the end of the struggle or within a few minutes following cessation of their struggling, in others the cardiopulmonary arrest is delayed. The individual may arrest in the vehicle transporting them to jail or a hospital or on arrival at an emergency room. However, even when EDS occurs in a medical environment, resuscitation is almost uniformly unsuccessful.

Positional/Restraint Asphyxia

Often during a struggle, law enforcement officers or emergency medical personnel find it necessary to restrain an individual. First, the responders may attempt to defuse the situation by simply talking to the individual, however, often this fails. If the individual is not being compliant, the officers may attempt to grab the individual and handcuff them with their hands behind their back. This usually elicits a violent struggle. Almost inevitably, as a consequence of the struggle, the individual is brought to the ground. Since the individual has to be handcuffed with his hands behind him, he has to be held prone during the struggle. The struggle will continue on the ground with the individual bucking, twisting, kicking and trying to bite. When they became more violent, ankle shackles are often employed placing the person into the prone maximal restraint position (PMRP), also referred to as hog-tie or hobble position (HTP). Additionally, as one attempts to hold the individual down to handcuff them and place ankle restraints, pressure is often placed on the back by use of knees or someone lying on the individual.

As a result of this positioning and the forces used, restraint asphyxia has also been suggested as a cause or contributory factor in deaths during a struggle. For respiration, one has to have an open airway, lungs capable of gas exchange and the ability to ventilate the lungs. Ventilation involves movement of the chest wall, diaphragm and abdominal wall. It has been proposed by some individuals that placing an individual in a prone position restricts respiration and that, combined with the application of pressure on the back, results in hypoxia and death by interfering with ventilatory efforts. This concern has been the greatest with the PMRP, where an individual is prone with their wrists secured behind the back, ankles bound together and wrists and ankles tied together using handcuffs, cords, chains or hobble devices. As such, the PMRP, is no longer routinely used by law enforcement due to allegations that sudden death could be produced utilizing this position and type of restraint.[31,32,33] Numerous civil suits were filed in regard to prisoners dying while hog-tied. It was alleged that securing an individual in this position while lying prone caused hypoventilatory respiratory failure, that is, positional asphyxia.

While studies have demonstrated a measurable change in pulmonary function tests in prone versus supine patients,[34] their effect has no clinical significance.[35] Studies have also shown that weights up to 102.3 kg (225 lb) applied on the back of individuals restrained prone having no clinically significant impairment in respiration, decrease in oxygenation of the blood or increased carbon dioxide.[36–39] In 1988, Reay et al. conducted a series of experiments to determine the effects on peripheral oxygen saturation and heart rate when an individual is hog-tied and placed prone following exercise.[40] Peripheral oxygen saturation and heart rate were determined using a pulse oximeter. They concluded that hog-tie restraint prolongs recovery from exercise as determined by changes in peripheral oxygen saturation and heart rate. They speculated that restriction of thoracic respiratory movements could be one of the mechanisms for this occurrence and recommended that positional restraint and its effects should be considered in the investigation of individuals restrained in the prone position. In an article published in 1993 by O'Halloran and Lewman, regarding the association of restraint and asphyxiation, hog-tying and death were codified in the concept of "restraint asphyxia" or "positional asphyxia."[41] It was argued that PMRP may prevent adequate chest and abdominal movement, which places the individual at risk of asphyxiation.[31,33,42]

However, studies by Chan et al. refuted these contentions.[35,38] Chan et al. repeated the experiments using a more systematic approach and more sophisticated technology. In experiments involving high-intensity physical activity followed by HTP, Chan et al. demonstrated that, while there was impairment in respiratory activity, both prone and in the HTP but neither resulted in "clinically relevant changes in oxygenation or ventilation."[35] Pulmonary function testing (PFT) (forced vital capacity; forced expiratory volume in 1 s and maximal voluntary ventilation [MVV]) was performed on 15 individuals, ages 18–40 years, in the sitting, supine, prone and restraint position (hog-tying). The subjects were then subjected to two exercise periods and two rest periods. Exercise consisted of 4 min on an exercise bicycle. During the rest periods, determinations of arterial blood gas, pulse rate, oxygen saturation by CO-oximetry and pulse oximetry and PFT, were performed. Determinations at the rest periods were made with the subject alternatively in the sitting position and restrain position. Changes in the heart rate occurred with exercise with a maximum of 164 ± 18.9 beat/m at the beginning of the sitting rest period and 174 ± 15.3 beat/m at the beginning of the restraint rest period. Placing individuals in the restraint position after exercise resulted in restrictive pulmonary functioning as measured by PFT. However, the PFT changes while statistically significant **were not clinically relevant**. Based on arterial PO_2 and CO-oximetry, oxygenation of blood increased with exercise, as one would expect, and in contrast to the findings of Reay et al. Most important was the fact that there was no evidence of hypoxia in the restraint position after exercise with no evidence of hypercapnia either during exercise or in restraint. Chan et al. concluded that there was no evidence that body position while in the "hogtie" or "hobble" restraint position, in and of itself, causes hypoventilation or asphyxiation.[43]

While the use of the hog-tie position as significantly decreased, some individuals now argue that the death may be due to compromise in ventilation occurring when an officer or medical worker applies their body weight to the upper torso of an individual in an attempt to restrain them and/or prevent further struggle. This is usually accomplished by lying across an individual's back, or applying pressure on the back with a knee or hands. This force has been thought to constrict the chest and abdomen more than the PMRP alone[44–46] and lead to asphyxiation.[47] Chan et al. also addressed this issue and examined the effects on pulmonary function from 25 lb (11.4 kg) to 50 lb (22.7 kg) applied to the back of prone subjects.[38] Although the PMRP with or without force applied to the back led to a restrictive pattern on PFT, there was no evidence of hypoxia or hypercapnia.

However, it can be assumed that officers are able, and do, to apply more than 50 lb (22.7 kg) of force to the back of suspects particularly if the individuals are violent. In 2007, Michalewicz et al. addressed this issue in a series of experiments.[48] They investigated ventilatory and metabolic demands in healthy adults when placed in the PMRP and when prone with 90.1–102.3 kg (198–225 lb) of weight on the back. The authors found no clinically important restriction of ventilatory reserve when subjects were placed in the PMRP or when prone with up to 90.2 or 102.3 kg of weight on their back. Likewise, when subjects were maximally struggling for 60 s while in the PMRP, there were no clinically important limitations of metabolic or ventilatory functions. They stated, "Based on these findings, as well as previously published studies, we suggest that factors other than ventilatory failure associated with the restraining process may be responsible for the sudden unexpected deaths of restrained individuals."

Furthermore, Ross and Hazlett[50] also showed that the weight of law enforcement officers on the back of the subject in the prone-restraint position, for about 1–5 min, did not create adverse physiological effects. Kroll et al. assessed the actual forces generated by law enforcement officers during the procedure of handcuffing individuals by exerting weight on the back of prone subjects.[37] The officers used single-knee or double-knee techniques and the weight force was measured for both men and women. The double-knee technique transmitted more weight than single knee averaging 51 lb (23.3 kg) plus 24% of the law enforcement officer's body weight. Single-knee weight force was calculated as 33 lb (15.4 kg) plus 21 lb (9.5 kg) for a male; law enforcement officer body weight is irrelevant to prone-force weight with single-knee techniques.

Thus, several studies have invalidated the positional or restraint asphyxia hypothesis as the prone position does not produce respiratory compromise.[35,51,52] Additionally, it is known that weights of 170–182 kg (375–400 lb) on the chest are survivable because of diaphragmatic breathing.[51] Weight force beyond 260 ± 26 kg (573 ± 57 lb) would cause sufficient rib fractures for fatal flail chest. Applying this to prone restraint suggests that even with significant weight applied with both knees placed on the back of a subject, an individual can breathe well with diaphragmatic or "belly" breathing. However, if both the chest and the abdomen are restricted for more than 4 min, a person may die of asphyxia. That is seen in crowd-crush incidents and is well documented on surveillance videos. These results are supported by prospective field research studies that examined the outcome of prone restraint with violent subjects.[49,53–55]

Restraint Chair

Combative individuals often require physical restraint in the prehospital and law enforcement setting. Specialized restraint chairs have been utilized for this purpose in the latter case, but concern has arisen that restrained individuals are at risk for ventilatory compromise and asphyxiation.

Vilke et al. sought to determine if placement in a restraint chair results in alterations of respiratory or ventilatory function.[56] Ten healthy human volunteers exercised on a cycle ergometer to 85% of the age-predicted maximal heart rate and then were randomized to either a sitting position or restraint chair with arms, legs and chest secured using standard law enforcement protocol. Subjects remained in each position for 30 min, during which PFT of MVV was performed at 11 and 30 min. Arterial oxygen (O_2) saturation and end-tidal PCO_2 levels ($PETCO_2$) were monitored continuously. Subjects repeated the experimental trial in the alternate position after a 45-min rest period. Measures between restraint and sitting positions are then compared and revealed a clinically insignificant decrease in MVV and no evidence of hypoxemia.[56]

Death Due to Choke Holds/Strangulation

During a struggle, the subduing party, often a law enforcement officer, may place an arm around the neck or try to apply a neck hold either to incapacitate the individual or restrain him/her while handcuffs are placed on the individual. In some instances, death by asphyxiation due to such actions has been hypothesized. Asphyxial deaths are discussed in depth in Chapter 6, though a few specific issues that apply directly to deaths during a struggle will be addressed here.

There are two types of neck holds, the choke hold and the carotid sleeper hold. As discussed in Chapter 6, in the **choke (bar arm) hold**, the forearm (or other object such as a flashlight) is placed straight across the front of the neck (Figure 19.2); in the **carotid sleeper hold**, the arm is placed about the neck with the antecubital fossa or crook of the arm centered at the midline of the neck (Figure 19.3).

Figure 19.2 Demonstration of bar arm hold.

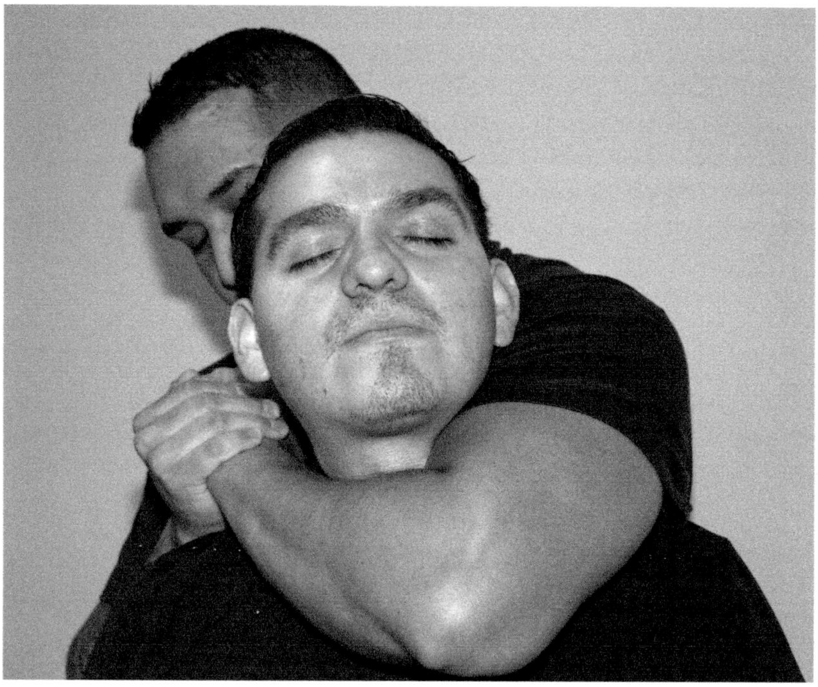

Figure 19.3 Demonstration of a carotid sleeper hold.

With both holds, the arm and forearm are used to compress the neck and, thus, the carotid arteries. If too much force is used, there can be fracture of the larynx or hyoid. These injuries are merely "markers" of force applied to the neck. They indicate that either pressure has been applied or a blow delivered to the neck. The injuries present, either hemorrhage or fractures, are not in themselves the cause of death. It is prolonged compression of the neck that causes death.

Compression of the airway usually does not occur and is not necessary for either one of these holds to be effective. The carotid arteries can be occluded with approximately 11–12 lb of pressure, and the jugular veins at 4.4 lb. Thus, the vessels of the neck would be blocked long before the trachea. Assertions that the trachea was compressed and this was the cause of death because they heard the victim complain that he could not breathe is not possible because you have to breathe to speak as one has to move air over the vocal cords to speak, that is, "breathe."

The majority of the blood supply to the brain is provided by the carotid arteries with the remainder supplied by the vertebral arteries. Compression of the carotid arteries for 10–15 s produces cerebral hypoxia and loss of consciousness. After the choke hold is released, the victim should regain consciousness within 20–30 s. If the carotid arteries are continuously occluded for 2–3 or more minutes, on release of the pressure on the neck, respiration will usually not return spontaneously. The individual, however, should respond to cardiopulmonary resuscitation.

As discussed in Chapter 8, it is sometimes claimed that the death of the healthy individual, following transient pressure applied to the neck, is due to a vasovagal reaction from stimulation of the carotid sinuses, that is, a reflex cardiac death. In normal individuals, pressure on the carotid sinus produces minimal effects with a mild decrease in heart rate (bradycardia) of less than 6 beat a minute and only a slight, insignificant, reduction in blood pressure (less than 10 mm Hg).[57] Some individuals, however, have an extreme reaction to stimulation of the carotid sinuses. In individuals with a hyperactive/ hypersensitive carotid sinus, that is, carotid sinus syndrome, there is an exaggeration of the normal response with syncope and marked hypotension occurring. Occasional, deaths have been referenced.[57] Review of the original literature in regard to the alleged deaths, however, reveals that the individuals dying all had serious underlying cardiovascular disease which in itself could explain death. Additional investigation of this phenomenon has revealed that hyperactive/hypersensitive vasovagal reactions appear to be confined to individuals over the age of 55 years and who also have significant cardiovascular disease.[58-59] In contrast, individuals dying of EDS are usually young males without any natural disease sufficient to explain death.

Pepper Spray

Pepper spray is an extract of hot peppers most often consisting of capsaicin and four derivatives.[60] It is also called oleoresin capsicum or OC spray and is widely available throughout the United States as well as worldwide. Spray canisters usually consist of a carrier for the capsaicin, a propellant, and an aerosol valve nozzle. The carrier is either water or alcohol. The concentration of the capsaicin varies from 1% in canisters sold to the public to 5–10% for police.

When sprayed in an individual's face, it acts within seconds on the membranes of the eyes to cause stinging, tearing and blepharospasm with involuntary closure of the eyes. The substances in pepper spray produce depletion of neurotransmitter substances of the sensory nerves with resultant activation of mast cells and release of histamine resulting in bronchospasm and increased mucus production. Capsaicin also affects the respiratory membranes, causing coughing, bronchoconstriction, mucous secretion and shortness of breath, as well as some brief laryngeal paralysis with resultant inability to speak. The effects usually dissipate after 20–30 min.

The effect of pepper spray has gained wide acceptance in law enforcement as a swift and effective way to subdue violent and dangerous suspects in the field with relatively little force. Despite the success of OC spray, there is growing concern about its safety, particularly when exposure is combined with positional restraint. A number of arrestees exposed to OC, which induces coughing, gagging and shortness of breath, have died in custody – thus prompting the allegation that OC inhalation places individuals at risk for potentially fatal respiratory compromise. However, investigation has failed to reveal conclusive evidence that the pepper spray caused the deaths. Virtually all of the individuals were in the throes of ED at the time of spraying with toxicologic analyses showing the presence of cocaine or methamphetamine. Other individuals gave a history of a psychotic disease. The authors have had a number of cases in which individuals in ED have been sprayed repeatedly with pepper spray with absolutely no effect. This included individuals whose ED was caused by cocaine, as well as other individuals experiencing an acute psychotic episode.

Research findings suggested that inhalation of OC spray does not pose a significant risk to subjects in terms of respiratory and pulmonary function, even when it occurs with positional restraint. Chan et al.[61] showed that inhalation of OC spray does have a significantly detrimental effect on either oxygen or carbon dioxide (CO_2) levels. In fact, the CO_2 levels in some test subjects decreased suggesting OC spray may actually increase ventilation slightly. Studies also failed to detect a difference between the OC and placebo groups in the restraint position; though there was some decline in pulmonary function, it was not enough to be clinically significant. However, OC spray can cause an acute exacerbation underlying pulmonary diseases, such as asthma and chronic obstructive pulmonary; however, this would result in immediate symptoms of respiratory distress and difficulty breathing and autopsy examination in such deaths would demonstrate hyperinflated lungs and mucus plugging.

Electro-Muscular Disruptive Devices (EMDDs)

The most widely known brand of electro-muscular disruptive devices (EMDDs) is TASER®. These devices have a gun-like appearance and house a cartridge containing a pair of electrodes, two darts and propellant (usually compressed nitrogen) for a single shot. The cartridge is replaced after each use. Upon discharge, the compressed nitrogen launches two barbed darts at approximately 50–60 m/s (Figure 19.4).

The cartridges are designated by range, with the maximum at 35 ft (10.6 m) for police and 15 ft (4.5 m) for civilians. The darts (electrodes) are pointed to penetrate clothing and barbed to prevent removal once in place. Each dart usually weighs less than 2 g with a 10-mm tip and approximately 2–3-cm body. The darts are connected by wires to the EMDD, forming an electrical connection to the device.

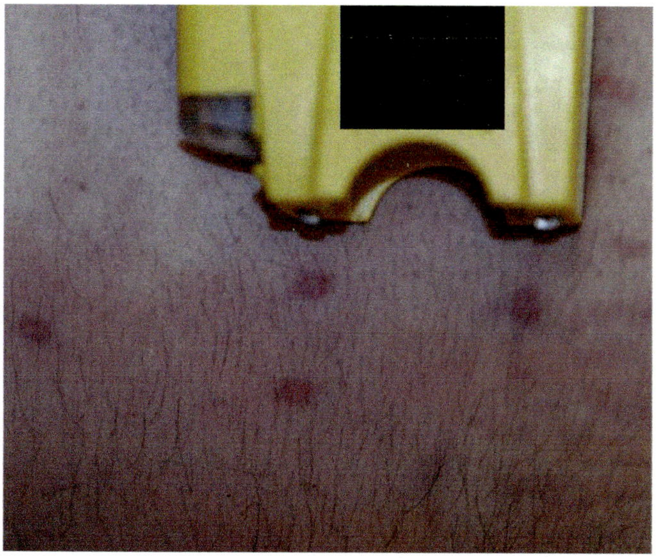

Figure 19.4 Patterned injury on the torso of a decedent from a EMDD used in a contact "stun-gun" mode.

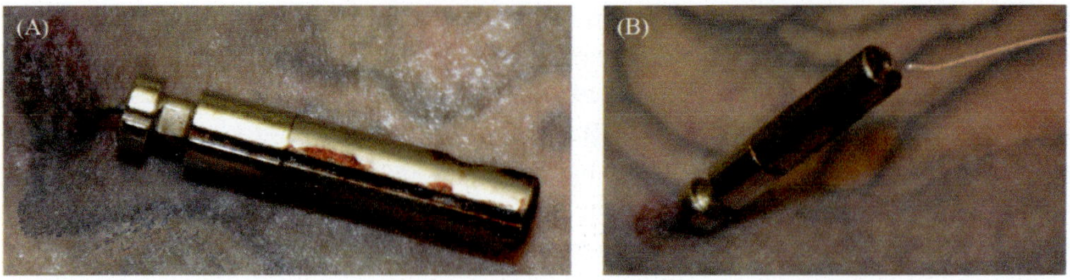

Figure 19.5 (A and B) Barbed darts of an EMDD implanted in the skin of the chest wall of a decedent.

Most EMDD models also have the ability to deliver discharge a current upon contact with the body when used in a "drive-stun" or "stun-gun" mode via electrodes located on the end of the device (Figure 19.5).

The drive-stun mode does not incapacitate an individual but can assist in taking a subject into custody because of induced pain.[62]

When the device is triggered, the electrodes (darts) deliver electrical current to disrupt voluntary control of muscles, causing "neuromuscular incapacitation." The darts are tipped with barbs that grab hold of a target's clothing, and current travels down the wires to the person generating a brief arcing current between the two barbs, causing contraction of the muscle trapped in the circuit. EMDDs are designed to deliver approximately 1200 V in a pulse current, neither direct nor alternating current, causing approximately 0.1-ms shock at 19 shocks per second.[62] The system was also designed to exploit the properties of skeletal muscles so that the current does not penetrate deeper than the skeletal muscle layer.[63] The goal is to deliver a low amperage current to create muscle contraction.[62]

Recall from Chapter 16, that A = V/R and that, in humans, most electrical resistance, comes from the skin, averaging between 100,000 and 1,000,000 ohm depending upon location and thickness. Also recall that in humans, the minimal amount of amperage is perceptible to a human as a tingle at 1 mA. A current of 5 mA will produce tremors of the musculature while 15–17 mA will cause contracture of the muscles, thus the goal for EMDD discharge. However, higher currents can result in contracture of all muscles, respiratory paralysis and death (50 mA), ventricular fibrillation (75–100 mA) or even ventricular arrest (~1 A and higher). Thus, 1200 V generated by an EMDD to 100,000 ohm of resistance results in approximately 12-mA amperage, consistent with the amperage required for musculature contraction, but far below the amperage required to produce death.

It has been hypothesized the EMDD barbs can result in death by producing fatal cardiac arrhythmias. This would not be possible for EMDDs used in stun-gun mode as the current produced only travels approximately 3–4 cm and is of insufficient size to capture the cardiac system. Thus, this claim is mainly for EMDDs firing barbs and has been proffered mainly due to experiments done with swine; however, it has been shown that there are significant differences between the myocardium of swine and that of humans, mainly that swine are three times as sensitive to electrical current as humans. Bharati et al. studied the electrophysiologic and anatomic differences between the pigs and humans and showed that pigs had sinus tachycardia, shortened PR and H-V intervals, and a relatively short sinoatrial conduction time when compared to humans.[64] Because of the above differences from the human, the pig should be used with caution as an experimental model in sudden death where arrhythmias are studied.

Assuming that EMDD barbs could capture the cardiac system, the arrhythmia produced by electrocution would have to be ventricular fibrillation and would have to occur at the time the device was being deployed, as electricity does not accumulate in the body. Ventricular fibrillation would result in loss of consciousness in 5–15 s with cessation of respiration in approximately a minute or two. Others have argued that the electrical current can produce ventricular tachycardia (VT); however, VT is unstable and degenerates into fibrillation within approximately 35 s. While there have been rare reports of VT following electrical injury, none have progressed to cardiac arrest. The majority of deaths after EMDD use are, however, not immediate but occur several minutes after deployment, making cardiac capture very unlikely.

The American Academy of Emergency Medicine (AAEM) recently published updated guidelines on subjects that have received electronic control from law enforcement.[65] These peer-reviewed guidelines are deserving of note as they address several issues apparent in EMDD use and are well researched and cited. The paper concludes, "Clinical evaluation and testing may very well be warranted when evaluating patients after CEW {EMDD} application, not because of the CEW exposure, but as a result of the patient's underlying condition, such as alcohol or drug intoxication, excited delirium syndrome, altered mental status, physical exhaustion, or psychiatric conditions that precipitated the application of the CEW in the first place."[65] The authors have reviewed a number of cases in which EMDD was used in an attempt to subdue a patient with EDS to which the individual showed no effect of the EMDD. The barbs may stick in clothing and fail to reach the skin. The person may simply not react to the current due to the excitation of the NE/E system or the barbs may not function as intended.

Injuries, however, have been documented with EMDD use. Injuries due to falls can occur due to the sudden muscle contraction and loss of ability to protect oneself. Barbs can penetrate the eyes and cranial cavity. Fractures have even been documented to occur due to such forceful muscle contraction.

It should also be kept in mind however that EMDD devices are *less lethal*, not nonlethal, weapons. While there is no evidence that the use of an EMDD has directly caused death by its electrical current, it certainly may contribute to the struggle and activation of the sympathetic nervous system resulting in exacerbation of EDS or underlying natural disease processes. It has been estimated that over 2 million law enforcement individuals have been voluntarily shocked with EMDDs without resulting in death or fatal arrhythmia.

Autopsy, Investigation and Certification of Death

A complete investigation of the circumstances leading up to and surrounding a death occurring during or after a struggle should be conducted, including a timeline of events. It is extremely important to ascertain how long the struggle lasted, what occurred during the struggle (i.e., positioning of the decedent, presence of choke/bar holds, use of pepper spray or EMDDs), what medical treatment was performed and whether any medications were administered before or after the arrest and when exactly the decedent became unresponsive. All medical records of the deceased should be obtained. A complete autopsy, as well as a complete toxicological screen and microscopic survey of all organs, especially the heart should be performed.

In deaths suspected of being due to EDS, the forensic pathologist should never make a determination as to the cause of death until all the facts surrounding the death have been elicited, a complete autopsy has been performed and all toxicological testing is complete. Because of the controversial nature of such deaths, especially when they involve the police, it is recommended that the autopsy be performed by or under the direct supervision of an experienced forensic pathologist if possible. One should take photographs of the body, even if there are no visible injuries.

In deaths that occur during or as a consequence of a struggle, such as those that occur due to EDS, the authors suggest certifying the cause of death in a descriptive manner, such as "Cardiopulmonary arrest during violent struggle in individual under influence of cocaine, alcohol, etc." or "Sudden cardiac arrest during a struggle in the setting of severe atherosclerotic cardiovascular disease." In individuals with psychoses, this can be listed either as a contributory cause or incorporated in the descriptive diagnosis. The manner of death in such cases is usually considered as homicide due to the role of the struggle. In cases where the cause of death is psychosis with the struggle occurring with the decedent alone, the manner of death may be listed as either natural or accident, depending upon local custom.

References

1. Insel PA, Seminars in medicine of the Beth Israel Hospital, Boston: adrenergic receptors – evolving concepts and clinical implications (review article). *New Engl J Med* 1996; 334(9):580–585.
2. Calzada BC and De Artinano AA, Alpha-adrenoceptor subtypes. *Pharm Res* 2001; 44(3):195–208.
3. Guimaraes S and Moura D, Vascular adrenoceptors: an update. *Pharm Rev* 2001; 53:319–356.
4. Heusch G, Baumgart D, Camici P, et al., [Alpha]-adrenergic coronary vasoconstriction and myocardial ischemia in humans. *Circulation* 2000; 101(6):689–694.
5. Hajjar RJ and MacRae CA, Adrenergic-receptor polymorphism and heart failure. *N Engl J Med* 2002; 347(15):1196–1198.
6. Small KM, Wagoner LE, Levin AM, Kardia SLR, and Liggett SB, Synergistic polymorphisms of B_1 and $alpha_{2c}$ adrenergic receptors and the risk of congestive heart failure. *N Engl J Med* 2002; 347(15):1135–1142.
7. Dimsdale JE, et al., Post exercise peril: plasma catecholamine and exercise. *JAMA* 1984; 252:630–632.
8. Young DB, et al., Potassium and catecholamine concentrations in the immediate post exercise period. *Am J Med Sci* 1992; 304(3):150–153.
9. Rastergar A and Soleimani M, Hypokalaemia and hyperkalaemia. *Postgrad Med J* 2001; 77:759–764.
10. Gennar FJ, Current concepts: hypokalemia (review article). *N Engl J Med* 1998; 339(7):451–458.

11. Medbo JI and Sejersted OM, Plasma potassium changes with high intensity exercise. *J Physiol* 1990; 421:105–122.
12. Lindinger MI, Potassium regulation during exercise and recovery in humans: implications for skeletal and cardiac muscle. *J Mol Cell Cardiol* 1995; 27:1011–1022.
13. Paterson DJ, et al., Effect of catecholamines on the ventricular myocyte action potential in raised extracellular potassium. *Acta Physiol Scand* 1993; 148:177–186.
14. Leitch SP and Paterson DJ, Interactive effects of K^+, acidosis, and catecholamines on isolated rabbit heart: implications for exercise. *J Appl Physiol* 1994; 77(3):1164–1171.
15. Bell LV, On a form of disease resembling some advance stages of mania and fever. *Am J Insanity* 1849; 6:97–127.
16. Cancro R, The introduction of neuroleptic: a psychiatric revolution. *Psychiatr Serv* 2000; 51(3):333–5.
17. Lieberman JA, et al., Drugs of the psychopharmacological revolution in clinical. *Psychiatr Serv* 2000; 51(10):1254–8.
18. Staley JK, Hearn WL, Ruttenber AJ, Wetli CV, and Mash DC, High affinity cocaine recognition sites on the dopamine transporter are elevated in fatal cocaine overdose victims. *J Pharmacol Exp Ther* 1994; 271:1678–1685.
19. Mash DC, Pablo J, Ouyang Q, Hearn WL, and Izenwasser S, Dopamine transport function is elevated in cocaine users. *J Neurochem* 2002; 81:292–300.
20. Fleckenstein AE, Gibb JW, and Hanson GR, Differential effects of stimulants on monoaminergic transporters: pharmacological consequences and implications for neurotoxicity. *Eur J Pharmacol* 2000; 406(1):1–13.
21. McCann UD and Ricaurte GA, Amphetamine neurotoxicity: accomplishments and remaining challenges. *Neurosci Biobehav Rev* 2004; 27(8):821–826.
22. Karch SB, Green GS, et al., Myocardial hypertrophy and coronary artery disease in male cocaine users. *J Forensic Sci* 1995; 40(4):591–595.
23. Wiener RS, Lockhart JT, and Schwartz RG, Dilated cardiomyopathy and cocaine abuse: report of two cases. *Am J Med* 1986; 81:699–701.
24. Karch SB (Ed), *Karch's Pathology of Drug Abuse* 3rd ed. CRC Press, Boca Raton, FL, 2002.
25. Silver MD, Gotlieb AI, and Schoen FJ, *Cardiovascular Pathology*. Churchill Livingstone, Philadelphia, PA, 2001.
26. Spitito P, Bellone P, et al., Magnitude of left ventricular hypertrophy and risk of sudden death in hypertrophic cardiomyopathy. *New Eng J Med* 2000; 342(24):1778–1785.
27. Witchel HJ, Hancox JC, and Nutt DJ, Psychotropic drugs, cardiac arrhythmia, and sudden death. *J Clin Psychopharmacol* 2003; 23(1):58–77.
28. Roden DM, Drug-induced prolongation of the QT interval. *N Engl J Med* 2004; 350(10):1013–1022.
29. Mash DC, Excited delirium and sudden death: a syndromal disorder at the extreme end of the neuropsychiatric continuum. *Front Physiol* 2016; 7:435.
30. Mash DC, et al., Brain biomarkers for identifying excited delirium as a cause of sudden death. *Forensic Sci Int* 2009; 190:e13–e19.
31. Stratton SJ, Rogers C, Brickett K, and Gruzinski G, Factors assocaitaed with sudden death of individuals requiring restraint for excited delirium. *Am J Emerg Med* 2001; 19(3):187–191.
32. Pollanen MS, et al., Unexpected deaths related to restraint for excited delirium: a retrospective study of death in police custody and in community. *Can Med Assoc J* 1998; 158:1603–1607.
33. Reay DT, et al., Positional asphyxia during law enforcement transport. *Am J Forensic Med Pathol* 1992; 13:90–97.
34. Palmon SC, Kirsch JR, Depper JA, and Toung TJ, The effect of the prone position on pulmonary mechanics is frame-dependent. *Anesth Analg* 1998; 87(5):1175–1180.

35. Chan TC, et al., Restraint position and positional asphyxia. *Ann Emerg Med* 1997; 30(5):578–586.
36. Eisele JW, et al., Comparison of respiratory function in the prone maximal restraint position with and without additional weight force on the back. Presented at the Annual Meeting of the American Academy of Forensic Science, Reno, NV, Feb. 21–26, 2000.
37. Kroll MW, et al., Applied force during prone restraint is officer weight a factor? *Am J Forensic Med Pathol* 2019; 40:1–7.
38. Chan TC, et.al., Weight force during prone restraint and respiratory function. *Am J Forensic Med Pathol* 2004; 25:185–189.
39. Schmidt P and Snowden T, The effects of positional restraint on the heart rate and oxygen saturation. *J Emerg Med* 1999; 17:777–782.
40. Reay DT, Howard JD, Fligner CL, and Ward RJ, Effects of positional restraint on oxygen saturation and heart rate following exercise. *Am J Forensic Med Pathol* 1988; 9(1):16–18.
41. O'Halloran RL and Lewman LV, Restraint asphyxiation in excited delirium. *Am J Forensic Med Pathol* 1993; 14(4):289–295.
42. Ross DL, Factor associated with excited delirium death in police custody. *Mod Pathol* 1998; 11:1127–1137.
43. Chan TC, Vilke GM, Neuman T, and Clausen L, Restraint positional asphyxia. *Ann Emerg Med* 1997; 30(5):578–586.
44. Lifschultz BD and Donoghue ER, Death in custody, in Welch C (Ed) *Legal Medicine Annual*. Butterworth, Salem, NH, 1991, pp 45–70.
45. Mittleman R and Davis J, Death from custody? *Forensic Pathol* 1991; 22(2):98
46. Reay DT and Howard JD, Restraint position and positional asphyxia. *Am J Forensic Med Pathol* 1999; 20:300–301.
47. Reay DT, Death in custody. *Clin Lab Med* 1998; 18:1–22.
48. Michalewicz BA, Chan TC, Vilke GM, Levy SS, Neuman TS, and Kolkhorst FW, Ventilatory and metabolic demands during aggressive physical restraint in healthy adults. *J Forensic Sci* 2007; 52(1):171–175.
49. Chan TC and Vilke GM, et.al., Reexamination of custody restraint position and positional asphyxia. *Am J Forensic Med Pathol* 1998; 19:201–205.
50. Ross DL and Hazlett MH, Prospective analysis of the outcomes of violent prone restrasint incidents in policing. *Forinsic Res Crim Int J* 2016; 2:1–10.
51. Chan TC, Vilke GM, and Neuman T, Restraint position and positional asphyxia. *Am J Forinsic Med Pathol* 200; 21:93.
52. Siddle BK, Chapter 5, HFRG tactical handcuffing, in Human Factor Research Group Inc. (Ed) *Threat Pattern Recognition Use of Force Student Training Manual*. Millstadt, IL, 2017.
53. Hall CA, Votova K, et al., Restraint in police use of force events: examining sudden in custody death for prone and not-prone positions. *J Forensic Legal Med* 2015; 31:29–35.
54. Lasoff D, Hall C, et al., Outcomes of use of force followed with prone restraint. *J Forensic Med* 2017; 2:119.
55. Bozeman WP, Stopyra JP, et al., Injuries associated with police use of force. *J Trauma Acute Care Surg* 2018; 84:466–472.
56. Vilke GM, et al., Evaluation of the ventilatory effects of a restraint chair on human subjects. *J Emergency Med* 2011; 40(6):714–718.
57. Weiss S and Baker JP, The carotid sinus reflex in health and disease. *Medicine (Baltimore)* 1933; 12:297–354.
58. Thomas JE, Hyperactive carotid sinus reflexes and carotid sinus syncope. *Mayo Clin Proc* 1969; 44:127–139.
59. Walter PF, Crawley IS, and Dorney ER, Carotid sinus hypersensitivity and syncope. *Am J Cardiol* 1978; 42:396–403.
60. Busker RW and van Helden HPM, Toxicologic examination of pepper spray as a possible weapon for the Dutch police. *Am J Forensic Med Pathol* 1998; 19(4):309–316.

61. Chan TC, Vilke GW, Clausen J, et al., *Pepper Spray's Effects on a Suspect'S Ability to Breathe National Institute of Justice Research in Brief.* U.S. Department of Justice Office of Justice Programs, December 2001.
62. Kroll MW, Crafting the perfect shock. *IEEE Spectr* 2008; 44(12):27–31.
63. Panescu D, Nerheim M, Kroll M, et al., New Conducted electrical weapons: electrical safety relative to relevant standards. Conference Proceedings, Annual International Conference of the IEEE Engineering in Medicine and Biology Society, 2017.
64. Bharati S, Levine M, Huang SK, et al., The conduction system of the swine heart. *Chest* 1991; 100(1):207–212.
65. Vilke GM, Bozeman WP, and Chan TC, Emergency department evaluation after conducted energy weapon use: review of the literature for the clinician. *J Emerg Med* 2011; 40(5):598–604.

Medical Misadventures 20

The physician can bury his mistakes, but the architect can only advise his client to plant vines.

—Frank Lloyd Wright

Deaths while undergoing medical treatment are, unfortunately, inevitable. **According to guidance proffered by the National Association of Medical Examiners**, deaths during necessary procedures in high-risk patients or from drug toxicities necessary as part of a therapeutic regimen, would be considered as natural deaths.[1] Examples of such deaths may include deaths occurring during a coronary artery bypass graft procedure or during a colectomy for cancer in an elderly patient with known cardiac disease. Additionally, deaths due to the nontreatment of a disease process due to failure to diagnosis or treat correctly are also considered natural deaths, for example, failure to identify pneumonia in a patient with a cough who eventually dies from sepsis. However, deaths due to improper use of medical equipment, malfunctioning medical equipment or deaths due to grossly negligent medical care may be considered accidental, or even homicidal, depending upon the intent to do harm. For example, instilling air instead of water during an endoscopy procedure resulting in an air embolism may be considered an accident.[1] While deaths caused by the purposeful misuse of such equipment or medications may be determined to be homicide.

The manner of death in such cases and the presence or absence of medical malpractice are separate issues. Families will often sue physicians for medical malpractice due to not following the standard of care, and while this may have occurred, the presence or absence of medical malpractice often has little bearing on the manner of death determination or even the involvement of a medical examiner or coroner. Deaths due to natural disease processes do not necessarily need to fall under the jurisdiction of a medical examiner, even though medical malpractice may have occurred. **All this being said, the classification of the death as to cause and manner is often determined by local custom, health departments and the opinions of the doctors signing the death certificate.**

Drug-Related Deaths

As discussed above, deaths due to drugs may occur in a therapeutic setting. Several drugs are known to have toxic effects, such as chemotherapeutic agents and antiarrhythmic medications, but are used in the course of treatment, often for these very effects. The therapeutic use of such medications, even when toxicities occur, is considered natural deaths. Examples of such reactions include toxic epidermal necrolysis, or Stevens-Johnson syndrome, from an anticonvulsant medication, pulmonary toxicity due to amiodarone prescribed from heart failure or a bleeding diathesis due to warfarin therapy. If these medications are taken or administered in accordance with a prescribed medical use, and not taken in excess, such as an intentional overdose, then the deaths may be considered natural. However, medication errors may also occur. The authors have been involved with several cases where the incorrect medication was unintentionally administered resulting in death, such was the case where propofol was administered instead of propanol in an IV drip and when a pharmacy dispensed methadone instead methylphenidate. This can also occur with dosage errors, such as when 5 cm^3 of morphine was administered instead of 1 cm^3 of a 5 mg/1 cm^3 solution of morphine. In all of these instances, the deaths were considered accidental.

Unfortunately, the authors have also been involved in cases where medications were intentionally administered to either cause death or injury. For instance, a nurse intentionally gave his patient a higher dose of fentanyl than prescribed in order to cause death; this death was determined to be a homicide after a thorough investigation.

Anesthesia Deaths

Anesthesia is usually administered in a monitored clinical setting and in ventilated patients; under such conditions, the risk of death due is minimal. Some anesthetic agents have been associated with toxic effects, such as liver toxicities or prolonged QT interval, which can lead to death, especially in the setting of underlying medical diseases. However, the true anesthesia emergency is malignant hyperthermia that may occur with the use of halogenated anesthetics and succinylcholine.[2] Often the individual has a genetic predisposition, though this condition may not occur every time anesthesia is administered. The onset of signs can be insidious or fulminant, with a rapid rise in body temperature, tachycardia, arrhythmias and skeletal muscle rigidity. The patient might then develop disseminated intravascular coagulopathy, electrolyte abnormalities – especially hyperkalemia – and rhabdomyolysis.

Most anesthetic-related deaths, however, are caused by human error, with the most common problems related to ventilation. An intraoperative death could be caused by as simple a mistake as inserting the intubation tube into the esophagus. There may be unrecognized extubation, disconnection from the ventilator or inadequate ventilation. There may be allergic reaction to the anesthetic agent (rare) or contamination of the gas being administered. In some instances, due to mix-ups in bottled gases, the wrong gas is administered.

Should any of these reactions occur, a thorough investigation should include how the medications were administered, the type of reaction that occurred and the reason for administration. Most anesthesia reactions that occur in a monitored, therapeutic setting, the death may be considered natural. However, when anesthetic agents are administered outside of a monitored therapeutic setting, especially in non-ventilated patients, such reactions may be considered as accidental deaths. Additionally, homicides can also occur, such was the case of a nurse who intentionally injected succinylcholine into the thigh of a 15-month-old girl resulting in death.

When discussing anesthesia related deaths, most physicians think of general anesthesia, though local anesthesia can also result in adverse reactions, including death. In excess, local anesthetics can be cardiotoxic, resulting in arrhythmias and ventricular fibrillation, as well as causing central nervous system (CNS) excitation and seizure activity. Naguib et al. produced an extensive review of adverse effects and drug interactions associated with the use of local anesthetics.[3] They concluded that the adverse effects of local anesthetics were usually caused by excessive dosage, unusually rapid absorption or inadvertent intravascular injection, with the last cause the most common. Severe adverse reactions were caused by either CNS or cardiovascular toxicity. The amount of local anesthetic necessary to produce cardiovascular toxicity is 3.5–6.7 times higher than that needed to produce CNS toxicity. High levels of local anesthetics produce direct depression of the myocardium, with impairment of myocardial contractility, and decreased conduction velocity. There is peripheral vasodilatation with hypotension and bradycardia. This can progress to arrhythmias and cardiac arrest. Bupivacaine and etidocaine are apparently more cardiotoxic than other commonly used local anesthetics, with bupivacaine arrhythmias being more refractory to treatment. CNS toxicity is first manifested by excitement (stimulation), followed by depression, drowsiness, respiratory failure and coma.

The addition of epinephrine will reduce the systemic absorption of the anesthetic injected in such areas and tends to reduce the probability of an overdose. Unfortunately, epinephrine has the potential of being dangerous in itself. If too much epinephrine is used in conjunction with the anesthetic, the epinephrine might be absorbed and, in conjunction with the local anesthetic, cause cardiac arrhythmias. This danger is more theoretical than actual.[4]

Death in the Dental Chair

Deaths associated with dentistry are extremely uncommon. Some deaths are coincidental, caused by the stress, fear and pain of dental procedures precipitating a fatal heart attack. "Few men are heroes … at the moment of visiting their dentist."[5] In any death during a dental procedure, the forensic pathologist must separate the natural coincidental deaths from those that are nonnatural. Most nonnatural deaths are associated with the use of anesthesia.

One of the best studies of deaths associated with dentistry appears to be that of Coplans and Curson in England.[6] They examined 120 deaths over a 10-year period. One hundred were associated with general anesthesia, ten with local anesthesia and six with neither of these, and, in four cases, there was insufficient or inadequate information for classification. Coplans and Curson used the term "general anesthesia" to include not only conventional general anesthesia, but any sedation with analgesia where there was loss of consciousness at some time during the procedure. Of the 100 deaths associated with general anesthesia, in 54 of the cases, the general anesthesia was directly responsible for the death of a healthy individual; in 29 cases, there was some underlying disease that made a significant contribution to the death, but, nonetheless, the general anesthesia provoked the fatal outcome, and, in 17 cases, the general anesthesia was incidental to the outcome.

Some deaths in the dental chair are attributed to allergic reactions to the drugs given, principally local anesthetics. There is controversy as to the validity of this etiology, however. True allergic reactions to a local anesthetic or a substance used as a preservative or stabilizer in the local anesthetic are probably extremely rare.[3,7] Most so-called allergic reactions are probably overdoses of the local anesthetic caused by an intravascular injection of the drug, due to failure to aspirate after placement of the needle; injection of large doses of a local anesthetic into a highly vascular area or unusually rapid absorption.[3,8] This last cause is aided by the fact that local anesthetics by themselves are vasodilators that enhance absorption in vascular areas.

One of the most common causes of death during general anesthesia in a dental office is an overdose of drugs. This could be caused by an error in dosage, ignorance of proper dosage or carelessness. More common, however, is the tendency to give multiple medications during induction and maintenance of general anesthesia or deep sedation, with resultant synergestic action of these drugs. The dentist often gives a barbiturate, a tranquilizer and an opiate (all CNS depressants) and then perhaps uses nitrous oxide. The three CNS depressant drugs produce a synergistic action, so that the combined effect of three different drugs is greater than any one of their individual actions. Another common mistake is failure to take a good medical history or, if it is taken, to appreciate its significance. For example, one must realize that epileptics under general anesthesia may have seizures. In addition, they may already be and, in fact, should be, on CNS depressant drugs such as barbiturates and phenytoin. General anesthetics can also produce asthma-like attacks that are not as apparent in an unconscious patient. Other problems involving anesthesia in the dental office include failure to monitor the patient's vital functions and failure to have the proper drugs and equipment to resuscitate an individual who is having difficulty.

Several deaths due to anesthesia reactions have been historically reported, though, while not common, these types of deaths continue to occur.[9,10] The authors have seen a case of a 6-year child who was administered morphine for pain control after an outpatient dental procedure for dental capping. The child was still lethargic and barely arousable upon discharge home and later succumbed to morphine toxicity. In another case, a middle-aged obese woman was administered 100 μg of fentanyl IV in an outpatient setting and suddenly went unresponsive. Unfortunately, the patient was hypoxic for over 5 min and ultimately died from complications of anoxic encephalopathy.

Botox

Botulinum toxin has been known for over 200 years as a cause of serious food poisoning. It is produced by *Clostridium botulinum* bacterium and is a neurotoxin that prevents the release of acetylcholine at the neuromuscular synapses, resulting in flaccid paralysis. It was first approved in the United States in 1989 for the treatment of strabismus and blepharospasm. Its popularity grew from there and now it is used for everything from cervical dystonia to wrinkles, not to include its many off-label uses. While the half-life of the drug itself is only 4–5 h, its full effects are often not seen for 3–10 days and may last for up to 4 months. Documented side effects range from mild effects such as rash, flu-like syndromes and gastrointestinal discomfort to more severe effects such as muscle weakness, syncope, arrhythmias and respiratory difficulties. Allergic reactions are also not uncommon.

In a review of 1437 adverse events after Botox use, Coté et al. described 28 deaths mainly due to respiratory arrest, myocardial infarct, cerebrovascular accident, pulmonary embolism and pneumonia.[11] Of note, however, is that 26 of the 28 deaths had underlying medical conditions and an elevated risk for mortality. The deaths occurred less than 1 to 120 days after injection with a median of 3 days. Additionally, Li et al. reported a death due to anaphylaxis after a Botox-lidocaine injection.[12] These deaths require a thorough investigation of the timeline since drug administration with careful documentation of all symptomology leading up to death.

Intraoperative Deaths

Deaths during diagnostic or therapeutic procedures can be divided into a number of categories based on etiology. First are the deaths unrelated to the procedures, but caused by the underlying disease for which the procedure is being performed. An example of this involving a diagnostic procedure would be cardiac catheterization following an individual's arrival at the hospital with chest pain. During cardiac angiography, the patient develops a fatal arrhythmia and dies. Surgically, the cases seen most commonly by the authors are deaths during cardiac bypass surgery. The individual is put on a cardiac bypass pump and the surgery is successfully performed, but the patient's heartbeat does not come back when the pump is removed.

As discussed above, intraoperative deaths may be due to anesthesia related issues. They may also be due to other factors, such as blood product administration. Even with all the precautions taken nowadays, sometimes the wrong blood type is administered, with a resultant transfusion reaction.

Death may be caused by inadvertent mechanical disruption of a vital organ. There might be perforation of the coronary artery during angioplasty or angiography, or unrecognized perforation of the uterus during curettage. In individuals with extensive pericardial adhesions, procedures involving splitting the sternum down the middle have occasionally resulted in perforation of the heart. A significant number of deaths have occurred during catheterization of vessels.[13] Catheters have perforated the vena cava, right atrium and ventricle, and the pulmonary arteries. The authors have seen cases of intravenous alimentation where the tubing was inserted into the pleural cavity. Mechanical disruption of vessels during surgery can result in the introduction of air into the vascular system. This occurs most commonly during laminectomy and CNS procedures.[13,14]

Abortion-Related Deaths

The most common causes of maternal death in the United States are hemorrhage, embolism, hypertensive disease of pregnancy and infection, approximately in that order. Death complicating an abortion is uncommon.[16,17] All deaths following an abortion should be reported to a medicolegal office. Under most circumstances, such cases should be autopsied, as they often occur in young healthy women without significant underlying medical illnesses. Abortion is usually performed by one of two methods: abortifacient drugs or instrumentation.

Abortifacient drugs are taken in an attempt to produce an abortion. The most commonly prescribed drugs used for this purpose are mifepristone and misoprostol. Mifepristone blocks the actions of progesterone, a hormone needed to sustain pregnancy, while misoprostol causes uterine contractions and cervical dilatation. Both must be prescribed and monitored by a physician as deaths have been reported.[18]

Prior to the legalization of abortion, other abortifacient drugs were used. Essential oils (oil of pennyroyal, oil of rue, cantharides and purgatives) were often taken to cause pelvic congestion and colonic irritation, which, allegedly, caused excitation and contraction of the adjacent uterus and expulsion of the fetus. Ecbolics, such as ergot, quinine and oxytocin, were also used to directly stimulate the uterine muscle though they were rarely effective. Nowadays, these methods are rarely employed.

Surgical instrumentation is most commonly employed method of abortion in the United States. For early pregnancies (<14 weeks), this most often involves vacuum aspiration, while for later pregnancies, dilation and evacuation is the preferred method. Both of these methods are surgical procedures that require anesthesia and physician oversight.

Deaths due to legal abortion are rare and most commonly results from anesthesia or hemorrhage. While amniotic fluid embolism is typically a complication of term pregnancy, it can also be a cause of death in abortion-related deaths, though it is exceedingly rare.[19] Legal abortions produce seven times less deaths than childbirth,[20] unlike illegal abortions that still result in thousands of deaths per year worldwide.[21]

Unsafe abortions often occur by douching/syringing or direct instrumentation. In induction by douching, a stream of water, hot or cold, with or without an irritant soap or antiseptic solution is injected forcefully into the vagina at the external cervical os. Abortion by syringing is essentially the same principle except a large-capacity syringe or douche syringe is used, with the nozzle inserted into the cervix. The successful abortion depends on the injected fluid's separating the fetal membrane and placenta from the uterine wall attachments. While the mechanical action could be produced just by the injection of ordinary water, most often a soapy solution composed of tap water and household soap was used. The water was usually delivered by a household enema can or bag with attached rubber tubing and a long, slender, hard nozzle. Because of the small cervical opening, failures using douching fluids were unusually high in the primigravida. The injected fluid would enter the vagina, but not the cervical canal. Abortion by douching was often self-induced and was more common among multiparous women. Again, this was a favorite self-induced method of abortion. Deaths due to abortion by douching or syringing were caused by the following:

- Cardiac arrhythmia
- Sepsis
- Air embolism
- Perforation of the uterus or vagina (rare)

Insertion of the douching or syringe nozzle into the cervix, combined with the rapid forceful injection of fluids or the rapid separation of the placenta from the uterine wall, apparently produces a vagal reaction, with a cardiac arrhythmia and death. A number of these deaths were witnessed by relatives of the deceased. The patient died immediately upon insertion of the syringe or tubing into the cervical os and injecting of the fluid. A corrosive endometritis caused by the fluid could also occur resulting in sepsis. On occasion, the soapy/chemical solution enters the uterine veins, initiating a hemolytic anemia, hemoglobinemia and hemoglobinuric nephrosis, with uremia and death.

Air embolism could occur two ways. First is when air became trapped in the rubber tubing and was forcefully injected into the uterine cavity and into torn veins. Second, in the process of separating the fetal membranes from the uterine wall, veins were torn through which air from the atmosphere could be sucked in. While most deaths caused by air embolism occur within a few minutes of the procedure, in some cases, there have been delays of hours. One hypothesis for this delay is that the injected irritating fluid that caused separation and tearing also caused severe contraction of the uterus. Subsequently, as the uterus relaxed, the air then was able to enter the circulation.

Unsafe abortions can also occur by instrumentation. This was usually not self-induced, though in some instances women, especially multiparous women, attempt to use knitting needles or coat hangers. Essentially, this method is a variation on dilatation and uterine curettage. Catheters, soft or hard, and other instruments were used to dilate the cervical os or at least to pass through the cervical os into the uterine cavity. The experienced nonphysicians would typically insert a soft or hard catheter into the cervix and uterus. A cervical packing or tampon was then placed immediately adjacent to the cervix to hold the catheter in place and absorb any blood that might flow from the cervix or uterus during the woman's journey home. The woman was then instructed to go home and expect painful forceful uterine contractions and vaginal bleeding within 24 h, but not later than 48 h. This would indicate expulsion of the fetus and placenta. If the inserted catheter had perforated or ruptured the fetal membrane, causing loss of amniotic fluid and immediate contraction, the fetus and placenta would be expelled within hours. The woman was often instructed that, if she bled profusely, she was to dispose of the catheter and vaginal packing, go to the nearest doctor or hospital and tell them that she had severe vaginal bleeding. She would then attempt to pass this off as a spontaneous abortion.

Deaths from instrumentation are usually caused by the following:

- Primary cardiac arrest caused by a vagal reaction produced by forceful dilation of the cervix and/or insertion of a catheter or sound into the uterus
- Hemorrhage (Figure 20.1)
- Sepsis caused by perforation of the uterus, cervix or vagina (Figure 20.2).
- Air embolus
- Thrombotic embolus

Deaths Due to Cosmetic Procedures

Millions of cosmetic procedures are performed annually just in the United States alone, with breast augmentation, liposuction and gluteal fat grafting ("butt lift") being some of the most common. For many years, the insertion of packs containing medical-grade

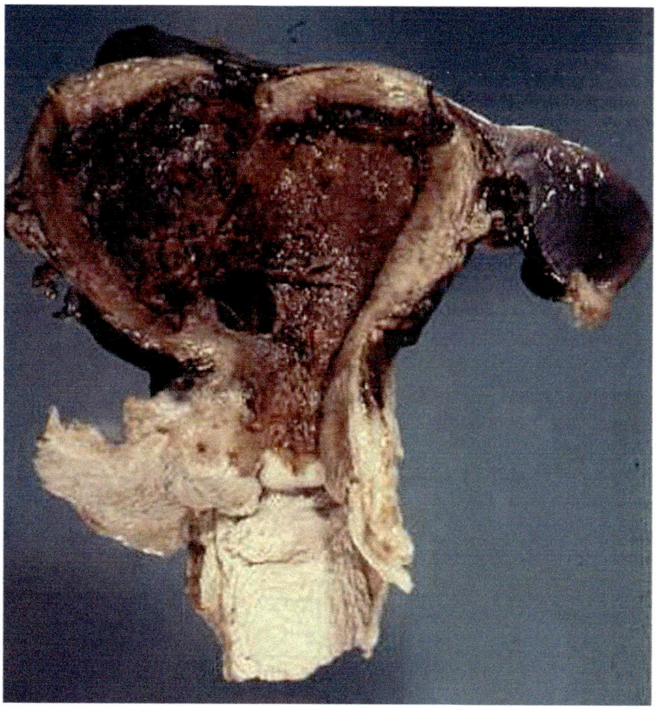

Figure 20.1 A 23-year-old female who died 7 h after a therapeutic abortion. Death was caused by perforation of the uterus. Two liters of blood were found in the retroperitoneal space.

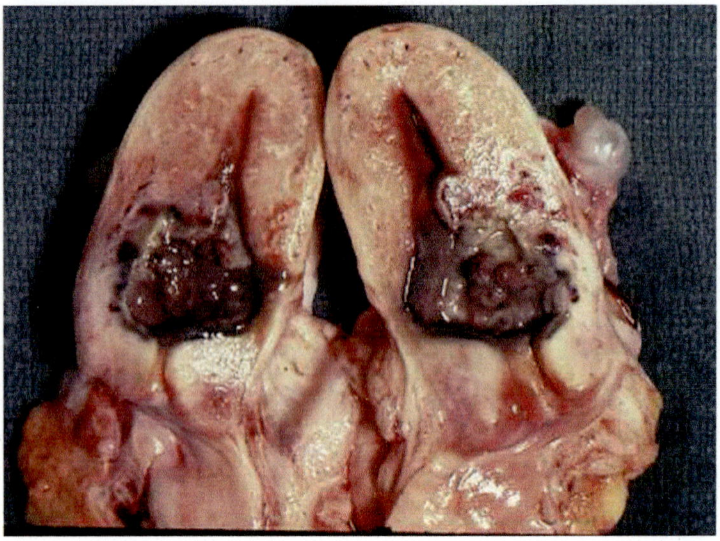

Figure 20.2 Self-induced septic abortion with perforation of the uterus.

silicone to enhance breast and buttocks was routine and believed to be without complication. However, after numerous reports of potential complications,[22] most breast augmentations are now performed utilizing saline containing prostheses. Foreign substances like free-silicon hydrogels, petroleum jelly and oils have also been injected by individuals posing as physicians. Such practices risk complications including pulmonary embolism, kidney failure, infection, scarring and abscess formation, not to mention chest pain, breathing problems and even death. More bizarre and dangerous practices include injecting liquid silicone into the genitalia. This causes a granulomatous foreign body reaction with giant cells, scarring with clear vacuoles without soft tissue with embolization.

Most deaths due to cosmetic surgery, like all other surgical procedures, are related to anesthesia. However, liposuction and fat augmentation have also been associated with fat embolism syndrome resulting in death. This may occur when fat is inadvertently injected directly into a vein or when extravascular fat follows a pressure gradient, entering an injured vein.[23] Visceral perforation can also occur in liposuction, most commonly affecting the abdominal viscera or the small and large intestine which can result in peritonitis and death.[24] One of the authors has seen a death due to aortic perforation during a liposuction procedure which resulting in death due to exsanguination.

Gas Embolism

Death due to gas embolism can result as a complication of medical treatment both surgically and related to anesthesia. Gas emboli may involve either or both the venous and arterial systems and in most instances, the gas involved is air, though, in medical situations, it could be carbon dioxide, nitrous oxide or nitrogen.[25] In the venous system, death from air embolism depends on the size of the bolus and the rate of delivery. In arterial embolism, these factors are not as important, because only a small number of air bubbles occluding a coronary artery or a cerebral vessel can result in death. In venous air embolism, between 75 and 250 cm^3 of air delivered rapidly is necessary to cause death.

Venous air embolism may occur during therapeutic or diagnostic procedures secondary to trauma, during childbirth or abortion. Arterial air embolism occurs secondary to cardiopulmonary bypass, arterial catheterization, surgical procedures involving arteries or injury to the pulmonary veins after chest trauma. One might also incur a paradoxical air embolism, that is, air crossing from the venous to the arterial circulation.

Air entering the venous system is carried to the heart and pulmonary arteries, with resultant mechanical occlusion of the pulmonary arterial vasculature by air bubbles. This is followed by a transient vasoconstriction. Obstruction of the pulmonary blood flow results in churning of the blood and air, producing the frothy appearance of the blood seen at autopsy. This churning can result in the development of complexes of air bubbles, fibrin, platelet aggregates, erythrocytes and fat globules, thus further occluding the vasculature.[26] Death is caused by obstruction of the pulmonary blood flow secondary to obstruction of the pulmonary arterial system by the air bubbles, the pulmonary vasoconstriction and the cellular aggregates. With a very large bolus of air, the obstruction occurs not only in the pulmonary vasculature but also in the right ventricle.

Paradoxical air emboli occur when air or gas that has entered the venous system crosses over to the arterial system. Typically, these have been described in association with septal defects of the heart. These permit air to go from the right side of the heart to the left without passing through the pulmonary vasculature. If a large air embolism is carried to the heart, the sudden rise in the right-sided heart pressure may result in a right-to-left shunt through a probe patent, but physiologically closed, foramen ovale. Increased right-sided heart pressure also causes air to be forced into the epicardial veins on the surface of the heart. Paradoxical emboli can also occur secondary to arteriovenous anastomoses in the lung. In addition, with sufficiently high pressures and delivery of large quantities of air, the ability of the lungs to filter out air can be exceeded, and bubbles of gas may traverse the pulmonary circulation and enter the left atrium. This has been demonstrated by Butler and Hills in experiments on dogs.[27] Air entering the arterial circulation causes death by occluding the cerebral or coronary arteries. Only a very small quantity of air is necessary.

Forensic pathologists will encounter air emboli, as previously discussed, with knife wounds of the neck, but also secondary to surgical procedures. The true incidence of venous air embolism during surgical and diagnostic procedures is unknown, with one exception – craniotomy in the sitting position. Here, air emboli occur in 21–29% of all craniotomies and 40% of all occipital craniotomies.[28,29] Air emboli have also been reported in a host of other therapeutic and diagnostic procedures. Any surgical procedure that causes a negative pressure gradient between the right side of the heart and a vein is a potential risk for venous air embolism. Individuals have been seated or prone, supine, in the lithotomy position and in the lateral knee-chest position at the time they incurred air emboli.[30] In an illustrative case, an obese 40-year-old man who was prone in the semi-knee-chest position for a lumbar laminectomy. Five hours into the procedure, he developed bradycardia and an agonal rhythm. The autopsy revealed air in the right ventricle, with beading of the epicardial veins by air bubbles.

Air emboli were more common when blood and other fluids were delivered in glass bottles rather than the present collapsible plastic bags. Even with plastic bags, there is the possibility, though rare, of an air embolus.[31] Air emboli have also occurred following cesarean section, placenta previa and subclavian venipuncture.[32–34] With a large-bore channel to a vein, a fatal amount of air can pass quickly into a vessel. Theoretically, 100 cm^3 of air per second can enter through a 14-ga needle with a 5-cm water pressure drop across it.[34] Fortunately for people with subclavian lines, this is more theoretical than actual.

Homicides secondary to injection of air into the venous system using a syringe are rare because of the large quantity of air one has to introduce in a bolus (100–250 cm^3), the expertise necessary to administer the injection intravenously and the necessary passivity of the patient. Individuals with established intravenous lines, such as hospital patients, will, of course, be easier to kill in this way. Suicide from an air embolus is rare. The authors have seen it in individuals who have slit their throats, severing their jugular veins, as well as in patients hooked up to dialysis machines who disconnected their tubing and in pregnant females during oral sex, with resultant air embolus.

In a living patient, the diagnosis of venous air embolism to the heart can be made by auscultation of the mill-wheel murmur or by detection of intracardiac air using Doppler ultrasonography or transesophageal echocardiography. In the deceased individual, one must consider the diagnosis prior to the autopsy. The first step may be a chest X-ray to look for air in the heart (Figure 20.3) or postmortem CT or MRI to visualize air emboli within the vascular system.

A Y-shaped incision can then be made into the skin and musculature of the chest and the skin and muscle retracted. Instead of then removing the chest plate in the ordinary way, a "window" should be cut in the sternum and ribs overlying the heart. The bony plate should then be retracted very carefully, so as not to introduce air into the venous system. The pericardial sac can then be cut open and the heart visualized. The epicardial veins should be examined for the presence of air. One or two bubbles in an epicardial vein do not

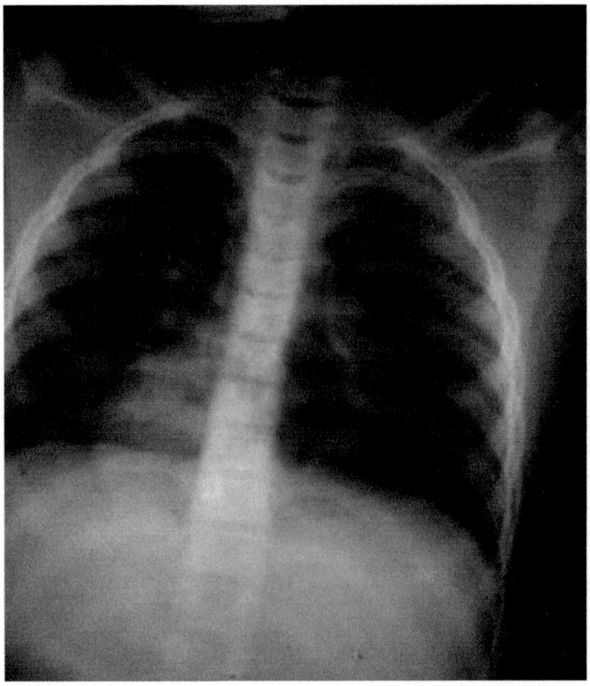

Figure 20.3 Massive air embolus with air in the right atrium and ventricle. Note outline of right ventricular wall.

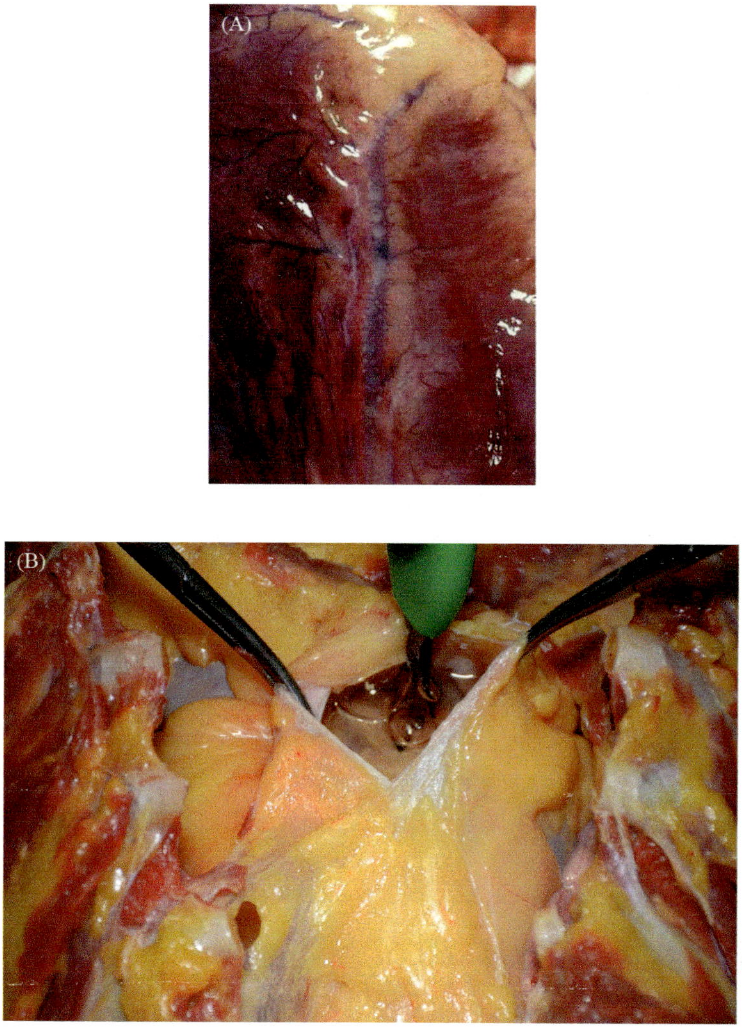

Figure 20.4 (A) Air bubbles in epicardial veins of heart in death caused by air embolism. (B) Air bubbles in flooded heart sac after perforation of right ventricle in air embolus death case. (Photo courtesy of Dr. Rajesh Kannan)

make a diagnosis of air embolism. With air embolism, the epicardial veins usually have a beaded appearance, with numerous air bubbles the length of these vessels (Figure 20.4).

The pericardial sac should then be flooded, the plunger removed from a 50-cm^3 syringe, a large-bore needle attached and the syringe filled with water. The tip of the needle can then be pushed into the right ventricle. If there is air in this chamber, it will be seen to bubble up through the water in the syringe. The water should then be removed and the right side of the heart opened. The blood typically has a frothy appearance.

Following this, the incision can be extended through the anterior abdominal wall to the pubic area. If the air entered in the pelvic region, the inferior vena cava is examined for air bubbles. One should be careful about interpreting one or two bubbles in this vessel as evidence of air embolism. If the deceased has been vigorously resuscitated with a thoracotomy and internal cardiac massage, it is usually impossible to make the diagnosis of air embolus based on the autopsy, because the air observed in vessels could be caused by resuscitation. Air in the coronary arteries cannot be identified at autopsy because air bubbles cannot be seen through the wall of these vessels. In the brain, the process of removing the skull cap, cutting through the dura and putting traction on the brain to see the cerebral circulation might introduce air bubbles into the circulation. Thus, the presence of a few air bubbles in the cerebral circulation does not necessarily indicate an embolus. If individuals survive the initial insult of air in the coronary and cerebral circulation, they might develop myocardial or cerebral infarcts.

The technique described to demonstrate air in the heart using a 50-cm^3 syringe is very basic and very crude. A much better and more sophisticated method is to use an aspirometer. This device not only demonstrates the presence of air but measures the amount and stores it for subsequent analysis by gas chromatography.[35] Embolized air differs from atmospheric air in that CO_2 is less than 15%; N_2 is higher than 70% and O_2 is reduced, usually measuring between 8 and 15%.[32] Detection of CH_4 and H_2 indicates that decomposition has begun. Most individuals feel that decomposition, with its formation of gases of putrefaction, precludes the diagnosis of air emboli, although Bajanowski et al. disagree.[36] They analyzed gas recovered from the ventricles of 15 individuals, exhumed after 10–45 weeks burial, who were believed to have been killed by injection of air. They found that analysis in 8 of the 15 cases gave results typical of air embolism, with only small amounts of the gases of putrefaction present.

References

1. Hanzlick R, Hunsaker JC, and Davis GJ, *A Guide For Manner of Death Classification*. National Association of Medical Examiners, 2002.
2. Hopkins PM, Malignant hyperthermia: advance in clinical management and daignosis. *Br J Anaesth* 2000; 85(1):118–128.
3. Naguib M, et al., Adverse effects and drug interactions associated with local and regional anaesthesia. *Drug Saf* 1998; 18(4):221–250.
4. Pallasch TJ, Vasoconstrictors and the heart. *CDA J* 1998; 26(9):668–676.
5. Christie A, *An Overdose of Death*, Dell Publishing Inc, New York.1940.
6. Coplans MP and Curson I, Deaths associated with dentistry. *Br Dent J* 1982; 153:357–362.
7. Chen AH, Toxicity and allergy to local anesthesia. *CDA J* 1998; 26(9):683–692.
8. Lalli AF and Amaranath L, A critique on mortality associated with local anesthetics. *Anesth Rev* 1982; 9(6):29–36.
9. Hilley MD, Milam SB, Giescke AH, and Giovannitti JA, Fatality associated with the combined use of halothane and gingival retraction cord. *Anesthesiology* 1984; 60:587–588.
10. Garriott JC and DiMaio VJM, Death in the dental chair: three drug fatalities in dental patients. *J Toxicol Clin Toxicol* 1982; 19:987–995.
11. Coté TR, Mohan AK, Polder JA, Walton MK, and Braun MM, Botulinum toxin type a injections: adverse events reported to the US food and drug administration in therapeutic and cosmetic cases. *J Am Acad Dermatol* 2005; 53(3):407–415.
12. Li M, Goldberger B, and Hopkins C, Fatal case of BOTOX®-related anaphylaxis? *J Forensic Sci* 2005; 50(1):169–172
13. Robinson JF, et al., Perforation of the great vessels during central venous line placement. *Arch Intern Med* 1995; 155(11):1225–1228.
14. Palmon SC, et al., Venous air embolism: a review. *J Clin Anesth*, 1997; 9(3):251–257.
15. Albin M, et al., Venous air embolism during lumbar laminectomy in the prone position: report of three cases. *Anesth Analg* 1991; 73:346–349.

16. Lawson HW, Frye A, Atrash HK, et al., Abortion mortality, United States, 1972 through 1987. *Am J Obstet Gynecol* 1995; 171(5):1365–1372.
17. Zane S, Creanga AA, Berg CJ, et al., Abortion-related mortality in the United States 1998–2010. *Obstet Gynecol* 2015; 126(2):258–265.
18. Henriques A, Lourenço AV, Ribeirinho A, et al., Maternal death related to misoprostol overdose. *Obstet Gynecol* 2007; 109(2 Pt2):489–490.
19. Guidotti RJ, Grimes DA, and Cates W, Fatal amniotic fluid embolism during legally induced abortion, United States, 1972 to 1978. *Am J Obstet Gynecol* 1981; 141:257–261.
20. LeBolt SA, Grimes DA, and Cates W, Mortality from abortion and childbirth are the populations comparable? *JAMA* 1982; 248(2):188–191.
21. Haddad L, Unsafe abortion: unnecessary maternal mortality. *Rev Obstet Gynecol* 2009; 2(2):122–126.
22. Ashar B, Assessing the risks of breast implants and FDA's vision for the national breast implant registry *Annals of Surgery*. 2019; 269(1):37–38.
23. Mofid MM, Teitelbaum S, Suissa D, et al., Report on mortality from gluteal fat grafting: recommendations from the ASERF task force. *Aesthet Surg J* 2017; 37(7):796–806.
24. Cárdenas-Camarena L, Andrés Gerardo LP, Durán H, and Bayter-Marin JE, Strategies for reducing fatal complications in liposuction. *Plast Reconstr Surg Glob Open* 2017; 5(10):e1539.
25. Muth CM and Shank ES, Gas embolism. *NEJM* 2000; 342(7):476–482.
26. O'Quin RJ and Lakshminarayn S, Venous air embolism. *Arch Intern Med* 1982; 142:2173–2176.
27. Butler BD and Hills B, Transpulmonary passage of venous air emboli. *J Appl Physiol* 1985; 59:543–547.
28. Hybels C, Venous air embolism in head and neck surgery. *Laryngoscope* 1980; 90:946–954.
29. Tateishi T, Prospective study of air embolism. *Br J Anaesth* 1972; 44:13061310.
30. Albin MS, Venous air embolism and lumbar disk surgery. *JAMA* 1978; 240:1713. (Letter).
31. Yeakel A, Lethal air embolism from plastic blood-storage container. *JAMA* 1968; 204:267–268.
32. Davies DE, Digwood KI, and Hilton IN, Air embolism during cesarean section. *Med J Aust* 1980; 1:644–646.
33. Nelson PK, Pulmonary gas embolism in pregnancy and the puerperium. *Obstet Gynecol Surv* 1960; 15:449–4819.
34. Flannagan JP, et al., Air embolism: a lethal complication of subclavian venipuncture, *NEJM* 1969; 281:488489.
35. Bajanowski T, West A, and Brinkmann B, Proof of fatal air embolism. *Int J Legal Med* 1998; 111:208–211.
36. Bajanowski T, et al., Proof of air embolism after exhumation. *Int J Legal Med* 1998; 112:2–7.

Interpretive Toxicology and Deaths Due to Drugs

21

The three curses of mankind: alcohol, morphine and cocaine.

—19th century, Anonymous

Forensic toxicology is the study and practice of the application of toxicology for the purposes of the law. It involves not just the identification and quantifying of a drug, poison or substance in human tissue, but also the ability to interpret the results of those findings. Every year in the United States, tens of thousands of people die directly or indirectly because of drugs. Because of this, the toxicology laboratory is as important to the medical examiner as the investigative section. It is absolutely necessary for a medicolegal system to have access to a well-equipped, adequately staffed toxicology laboratory. Without this, determinations as to cause and manner of death may be erroneous. The medical examiner must diagnose the cause and manner of death utilizing the circumstances of death, investigative information including medical records, the autopsy findings and the results of the toxicological analyses. Thus, it is imperative that the medical examiner understands the principles of postmortem toxicology and be able to personally interpret the results of the toxicological analyses.

In medical examiner's offices, the results of toxicological testing are correlated with the medical history of the deceased, the autopsy findings and the circumstances leading up to or surrounding the death, so as to determine whether a drug was a cause of death, a contributing factor or played no role. In many instances, drug levels alone cannot be interpreted. All physicians have had cases where an individual was found to have a "fatal" concentration of drug in the blood but was functioning at the time of death, essentially excluding the drug from being a factor in the death. This same situation is seen by clinical physicians – the patient admitted to the emergency room conscious and coherent, with drug concentrations that would be associated with unconsciousness or death in most individuals. This is typically seen in chronic users of drugs where it is possible to develop a physiologic tolerance to the substance, such as occurs with chronic ethanol or opioid use.

No matter how good one's toxicology laboratory, it cannot function if there is failure to collect the proper specimens, in adequate quantity and in the proper containers.

Collection of Tissue for Analysis

In all autopsy cases, at a minimum, blood, urine, bile and vitreous should be collected if available.

Collection of Specimens

- All specimens should be collected with a clean needle and a new syringe.
- The specimens of blood, urine, bile and vitreous should be placed in glass containers, not plastic, as many drugs can bind to the polymers in plastic tubes.

In addition, plastic polymers can also create peaks on chromatography that could mask compounds and interfere with analysis. In some cases, substances such as volatiles can be lost, due to absorption by the plastic.

- Collect the blood from the femoral vessels. If this is not possible, the other sites for collection, in descending order of preference, are as follows:
  - The subclavian vessels
  - The root of the aorta
  - The pulmonary artery
  - The superior vena cava
  - The heart
- Collect a minimum of 40 mL of blood.
  - 20 mL in two 10-mL gray-top glass test tubes (sodium fluoride preservative and potassium oxalate anticoagulant)
  - 10 mL in a purple-top glass test tube (preservative EDTA) for DNA analysis and carbon monoxide testing; can be used for tox testing in the absence of gray-top tubes
  - 10 mL in a red-top tube (no preservative) for serology testing, if needed
  - If volatile testing is desired, fully fill a 10-mL screw-top tube; additionally, it is recommended that brain also be collected in a separate screw-top tube
  - Collect all the vitreous
  - Collect up to 10 mL of urine
  - Collect up to 10 mL of bile
  - Label the specimens with name of deceased; case number; date of collection; name of the person drawing the sample; name of the pathologist; and, in the case of the blood, the source of the blood, for example, femoral.[1]

The practice of opening the pericardial sac, positioning a tube or jar under the heart, then cutting the heart and letting blood drain into the receptacle should be condemned, because it is very easy to contaminate the contents of the jar with pericardial fluid and other material that might be present in the chest cavities. This may dilute the blood (with resultant fallacious low levels) or, if there has been diffusion of a drug from the stomach into pericardial or chest fluid, may actually contaminate it with the drug such that inaccurately high levels are detected in the "heart blood."

Blood is preferentially collected from the femoral vessels to prevent the possibility or contention of postmortem release (redistribution) artifacts. In the case of certain drugs, postmortem concentrations in heart blood can be erroneously elevated due to postmortem drug redistribution. The best examples are the tricyclic antidepressants. In cases involving these drugs, quantitation of the liver has been suggested as being superior to blood levels in determining whether one is dealing with an acute overdose or levels caused by chronic medication.[2] Pounder et al., however, have called this into question by demonstrating postmortem diffusion of drugs from the stomach into the liver, principally the left lobe.[3] Also demonstrated was diffusion into the left lung base, the spleen and the pericardial fluid. To a lesser degree, there was diffusion into the cardiac blood, aortic blood and inferior vena cava.

Diffusion of alcohol into the cardiac chambers, the superior vena cava and the aorta is more controversial. The general feeling is that, while this can occur, it is uncommon. Diffusion appears to be associated with very high concentrations of alcohol in the stomach, failure to refrigerate the body for more than 24 h and an increasing time from death to collection of the blood.[4] Because of the phenomenon of postmortem diffusion, Pounder et al. recommended that, for toxicological purposes, peripheral blood (e.g., that from the femoral vessels) should be used for toxicologic analyses. If tissue is desired, then deep tissue from the right lobe of the liver, the apex of the lung or muscle from an extremity should be used.

In individuals who have died after several hours or days of hospitalization, one would expect that any drugs in the blood at the time of admission would be metabolized. Additionally, fluid resuscitation or the administration of blood products can dilute any drugs which may still be present. In these instances, not only should blood be obtained at autopsy, but the hospital in which the individual was a patient should be contacted to see if any blood obtained at or shortly after hospitalization is still in existence. This should then be obtained for toxicologic analysis. In trauma cases, blood is usually drawn immediately on admission to the emergency room and sent to the blood bank for typing and cross-match; it should then be retained in the blood bank for at least 2 weeks.

In deaths caused by a drug overdose or suspected drug overdose, the pathologist may wish to retain portions of liver, kidney and muscle for subsequent toxicological analysis. Collect at least 50 g of each of the aforementioned tissues. Although with the present-day state of the art in toxicology, testing of tissues is unusually not necessary as, unless there has been unusually prolonged survival, the drug that causes death will be present in the blood. However, even after some time of survival, the drug may be detectable in the vitreous or urine. Drugs tend to be found in higher concentrations in the liver than the blood, as drug metabolism occurs there, so utilizing liver or bile concentrations for interpretation can be difficult. In cases of a suspected oral overdose of drugs, the entire stomach contents should be examined and at least 50 cm^3 retained.

On occasion, in instances of massive trauma to a body, no blood can be collected from the vasculature, though there is free blood in the body cavities. If this blood is collected, tested for alcohol and drugs and found to be negative then one is relatively safe in assuming the individual was not under the effects of alcohol or drugs at the time of death. A positive test, on the other hand, must take into account the possibility of contamination. In such a case, another material such as vitreous or muscle must be analyzed to evaluate the accuracy of the test results on the blood.

If it is elected not to do an autopsy, but rather just an external examination of the body, then blood, urine and vitreous should be collected. Urine can be collected by inserting the needle from a clean syringe through the lower abdominal wall, just above the pubic symphysis. Blood is collected from either the femoral or subclavian vessels. Blood should never be collected by way of a blind stab through the anterior chest wall into the heart. This is to preclude inadvertent contamination of the blood with fluid contents from the esophagus, pericardial sac, stomach or pleural cavity.

Types of Specimens and Their Uses

The specimen of most importance for analysis is blood. This is logical, when one realizes that it is the blood concentration of the drug that has the effect on the individual. A drug detected in the urine or bile had an effect on the individual, but one cannot say that it is having an effect at the time the patient died. Thus, toxicologic analysis should be oriented to analysis of blood. With rare exception, most potentially lethal drugs and their major metabolites can now be detected in blood in any modern toxicology lab. One main exception to this is heroin; however, even in this case, one can use the presence of a metabolite to indicate its presence. Heroin (di-acetylmorphine) is almost immediately metabolized to mono-acetylmorphine and then to morphine. The detection of mono-acetylmorphine in the blood is indicative of recent heroin exposure. Mono-acetylmorphine can often be detected in the vitreous after it has disappeared from the blood. In cases of head trauma, where there is a subdural collection of blood and the individual survives a number of days, subdural blood can often be analyzed for the presence or absence of drugs, though drug concentrations must be interpreted with caution.

After blood, vitreous humor is next in value. Allowing for appropriate distribution ratios, vitreous reflects the drugs and their levels in the blood 1–2 h prior to death. Virtually any drug detectable in the blood is detectable in the vitreous if one uses analytical techniques and equipment of sufficient sensitivity. The significance of the concentration is another matter. Vitreous is analyzed for alcohol when a positive blood alcohol is obtained, as this can often be used to determine if the decedent is in the absorptive or elimination phase of metabolism. Routine electrolyte (sodium, potassium, chloride, urea nitrogen and creatinine) and glucose screens can also be run on the vitreous.

Most drugs are excreted in the urine. Analysis of urine for drugs is easy because there is often minimal protein binding to hinder extraction, and many drugs are concentrated in the urine. It should be realized, however, that the concentration of a drug in the urine is of no significance in the interpretation of the cause of death as it is the concentration in the blood that determines whether an individual lives or dies. Additionally, the presence of a drug in the urine may reflect exposure several days prior to death and not current use or toxicity.

Bile was useful when toxicological procedures were relatively crude because it concentrated drugs as they were excreted, thus making analysis for these drugs relatively easy. Nowadays, it is very rarely of any use other than to detect prior drug use and abuse. An example would be the case of an individual who died of hypoxic encephalopathy believed caused by a heroin overdose. In such a case, an analysis for morphine in the bile is conducted to see if an opiate had been used in the past several days. The authors do not recommend routine use of liver or kidney as there is no direct correlation between concentrations in these organs and those in blood, though kidney can be useful in heavy metal testing as many metals accumulate in the kidneys. Hair and fingernails can be retained for analysis if one suspects arsenic poisoning.

One tissue whose potential for toxicological analysis is not appreciated is muscle. Muscle is of great value in decomposed bodies. Here, one cannot usually collect blood, urine or vitreous. Instead, one tends to rely on the solid organs, such as the liver and kidney. These, however, decompose fairly rapidly and often reflect drug accumulation effect, as previously discussed. The muscle, especially that of the thigh, is often well preserved, in spite of advanced decomposition. Muscle is also believed to reflect the presence or absence of drugs at the time of death and not days prior to death. Muscle concentrations of drugs, however, should be interpreted with caution as they may not accurately reflect blood concentrations.

The National Association of Medical Examiners requires toxicology samples to be retained for a minimum of 2 months after testing, or 1 year for homicides.[5] However, the authors believe the residual specimens should be kept for a minimum of 2 years regardless of case type.

Analysis of insects, for example, maggots, feeding on a severely decomposed body have demonstrated the presence of drugs. In some cases, this has been used to make a diagnosis as to the cause of death. While this may be helpful in specific cases, such as a case reported by Levine et al., where secobarbital was found in maggots recovered from a decomposed and skeletonized body in which a bottle of secobarbital was found nearby.[6] However, in cases that are outside or where there are multiple bodies or sources of feeding, the origination of any drugs detected could be difficult to ascertain and could be suspect in a court of law.

Analysis

Before biological tissues can be analyzed for toxicological purposes, the drugs must be separated from the organic matrix in which they are suspended. Some procedures do not require this separation, such as analysis for drugs of abuse in urine using immunoassay techniques; however, most methodologies utilized for forensic toxicologic testing require separation of the drugs from the biological matrix. Extraction of a drug from the biological sample, for example, blood, can be accomplished using various solvents, buffers and other procedures including protein precipitation, liquid-liquid or solid phase extraction.

Screening Tests

In forensic toxicology, a screening test is first performed to determine the presence or absence of drugs, followed by a confirmatory test, usually performed by different methodologies and on different specimens (i.e., two different blood tubes or aliquots). Screening tests are usually conducted by immunoassay, spectrophotometry or gas or liquid chromatography paired with a detector or mass spectrometer. It must be realized that each of these methods has its limitations.

Immunoassays work by utilizing an antibody-antigen reaction created against a particular drug or drug class. These include radioimmunoassay (RIA), enzyme-linked immunosorbent assay (ELISA), fluorescent polarization immunoassay (FPIA), enzyme-multiplied immunoassay (EMIT) and kinetic interaction of microparticles in solution (KIMS). The major advantages of these systems are that large numbers of tests can be performed relatively easily and quickly using an extremely small volume of specimen, with semiautomated and automated systems to speed the rate of analysis. These assays are usually applied to urine; however, several have been developed for use on blood as well. They also have limited specificity, can show cross reactivity, and are susceptible to interfering substances in the sample leading to false-positive and/or false-negative results. Thus, a negative immunoassay result does not necessarily mean the substance is not present and a positive result always requires confirmation by another method of analysis – *an immunoassay result should never be confirmed by another immunoassay.*

Spectrophotometry is another screening method that utilizes the changes in the wavelength of light as it passes through the sample to identify a substance. While spectrophotometry is easy to use it lacks the required specificity and sensitivity for common use.

In chromatography, drugs are dissolved into a mobile phase (gas or liquid) which is then passed through a stationary phase (i.e., a column) allowing for separation of the constituents of the sample. The time taken to traverse the stationary phase is recorded by a paired detector and compared to an internal standard, allowing for detection of each component within the sample. While chromatography can be very sensitive and specific, it can also be very time consuming, requiring significant sample preparation and expensive equipment.

Confirmatory Tests

Confirmatory tests are performed when a drug has been identified by one of the screening tests. Confirmatory tests should be performed by a different methodology than the screening test and on a different sample, if possible, or, at least, a different extract of the same sample. The confirmatory test should also be more specific than the screening test.

The gold standard for confirmatory testing in forensic toxicology is GC or LC paired with mass spectrometry. This paired method allows for mass spectral analysis of analytes after they have been separated by chromatography. Mass spectrometry is accomplished by fragmenting a molecule by different ionization techniques and analyzing the fragmentation pattern or ion ratios. If mass spectrometry is not available, the American Board of Forensic Toxicology (ABFT) allows for confirmation by the same system as identification as long as a different chemical derivatization and column and, thus, retention time is used. However, this is not recommended by the ABFT and may face scrutiny in a court of law. Confirmation of an immunoassay with another immunoassay is never acceptable.

Testing Panels

Comprehensive toxicological screens should be performed on all deaths where the presence or absence of intoxicating substances may have played a role in the death. In addition, the authors recommend that full toxicology screens be performed on most, if not all, cases requiring autopsy in a medical examiner's office as often substances are found even when not suspected. In particular, all homicides, suicides, accidents, SUID and at work deaths require full toxicology testing, when possible.

Since different laboratories utilize different techniques and testing panels, it is recommended that medical examiners familiarize themselves with the testing panels offered by their laboratories and with which drugs are found on which panels, so that screening can be adequately performed. Ordering of toxicology testing should be done in concert with the toxicologist in charge of the laboratory to make certain the correct tests are performed to screen for the desired drugs. If simply looking for drugs of abuse, an ME may choose to order a comprehensive screen for the common drugs of abuse, but often a more nuanced approach is required. Some drugs, such as digoxin, ethylene glycol, inhalants and the newer "designer drugs" may require special testing others require special samples (i.e., lithium or screw-top tubes). It is recommended that the toxicology laboratory be contacted and consulted regarding the desired testing and any special requirements/samples necessary for performing such testing.

Deaths

Deaths caused by ingestion, injection, snorting or inhalation of drugs fall into four categories by manner: homicide, suicide, accident and undetermined. The last category is used when a decision as to manner of death cannot be made. For the most part, the accidental category is made up of deaths caused by drug abuse. In the 19th century, the "three curses of mankind" were said to be alcohol, morphine and cocaine. Little has changed since then, except that more potent opioids have now replaced heroin and morphine.

The most commonly abused drug in the United States is ethanol, or drinking alcohol. It is responsible for tens of thousands of deaths each year both directly and indirectly. While deaths caused by an acute overdose of ethanol are uncommon, deaths caused by its chronic effects are seen every day. Thus, between 25,000 and 30,000 people a year die of chronic liver disease caused by excessive alcohol intake. Ethanol is the major cause of motor vehicle accidents. Approximately half of all motor vehicle accidents are related to use of alcohol. Alcohol has also been linked to congenital anomalies and the development of malignant tumors.

After alcohol and marijuana, the most commonly abused illicit drugs are cocaine, heroin and methamphetamine. In the early 2000s, the United States also saw a surge in opioid related deaths. However, numerous other drugs can cause death including illicit, prescription and over-the-counter medications.

Autopsy Findings

Unfortunately, there are no pathognomonic findings for a drug overdose death. At autopsy, bodies should be examined closely to identify possible clues to drug use. The nasal septum can become fenestrated with chronic cocaine insufflation. The arms may display "tracks" (raised, hyperpigmented, linear scars overlying veins) indicative of chronic drug injection (Figure 21.1).

With repeated injection into veins, intravenous drug users may develop such scars due to repeated intravenous injection of the solutions, usually with a dull contaminated needle. Needle tracks are often more prominent in geographical areas where the acquisition of clear syringes and needles is difficult, though with the prominence of needle exchange programs and the availability of insulin syringes, needle tracks are not as prominent as they were previously. Scattered irregular often oval scars found on the extremities may be consistent with skin popping (the subcutaneous administration of drugs) (Figure 21.2). Other more uncommon sings of toxicity include darkly pigmented lines across the gums (termed

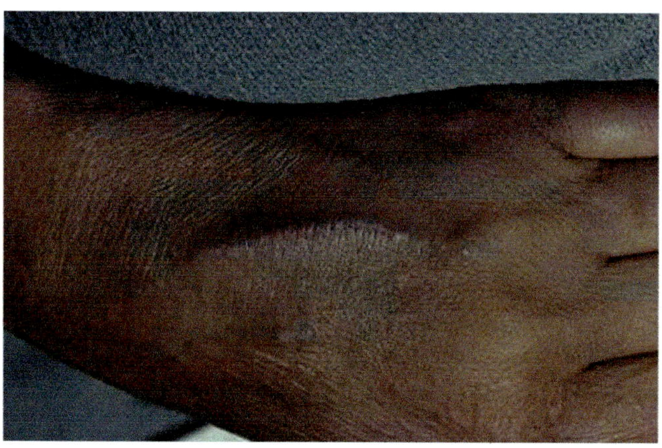

Figure 21.1 Needle track marks on the hand.

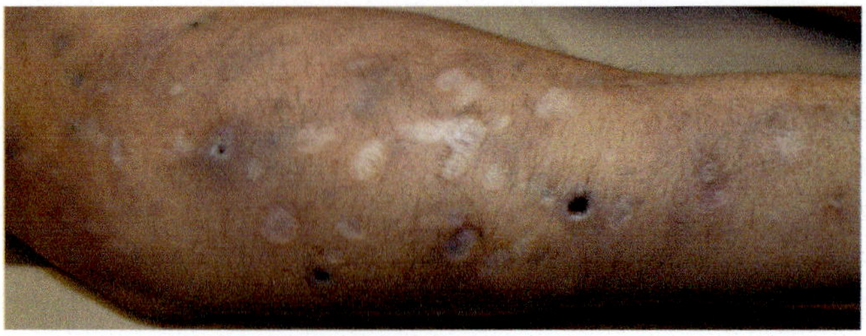

Figure 21.2 Forearm scars due to "skin popping".

"lead lines") in lead poisoning; cherry red lividity seen in carbon monoxide and cyanide poisoning; or even a bitter almond smell which may be present in cyanide poisoning.

Internal clues can also assist in the determination of a drug overdose, but like external findings, are not in and of themselves fully diagnostic. Deaths due to depressant drugs, such as opiates, often kill after a prolonged period of a comatose state, resulting in the classic triad of cerebral edema, pulmonary edema and a full bladder. While this triad is not specific for opiate deaths, the presence of full bladder can assist in interpreting the toxicology results, even in the presence of additional natural disease processes.[7] A large heart in an otherwise healthy, young person may also lead one to suspect chronic sympathomimetic drug use. Intestinal contents should always be examined in suspected drug deaths, as drug "mules" often swallow baggies or condoms filled with illicit substances to transport them and rupture of such an item can lead to sudden death. Additionally, individuals will often swallow such items to conceal them from law enforcement upon arrest (Figure 21.3).

While most medicolegal autopsies do not include a full histologic examination, microscopy can also be helpful when detecting a drug related death. Perivascular foreign body granulomas, often containing polarizable material, seen within the lungs may indicate injection of crushed oral medications. Polarizable crystals can be seen within the vasculature in ethylene glycol toxicity, most notably involving the kidneys, and intranuclear inclusions in hepatocytes and renal epithelium can be seen in cases of lead poisoning.

Figure 21.3 Small baggies containing apparent methamphetamine recovered from a decedent's stomach contents.

By convention, deaths due to natural disease processes, which may be the result of chronic drug use, are still certified as natural. For example, hepatic cirrhosis can be seen with chronic ethanol use, intravenous drug use can lead to endocarditis and vaping can cause vaping-associated lung disease. Known side effects/ reactions, such as pulmonary toxicity with amiodarone or toxic epidermal necrolysis, are also considered natural unless the death is directly due to an acute intoxication. For example, if a heroin addict dies of a combination of endocarditis and acute heroin intoxication, this would be considered an accident.

Interpretation of Results

For postmortem toxicology, the two most important concepts for any death investigator are ***drug concentrations should never be interpreted in a vacuum*** and ***there is no such thing as a "lethal drug concentration."*** The toxicology results alone cannot tell you whether or not the death was due to drug toxicity. The authors have seen numerous traumatic deaths with "lethal" concentrations of various drugs.

Postmortem drug concentrations depend on many variables including postmortem and testing variables, individual variables and drug variables. Postmortem variables include the sample source, methodology used and postmortem interval. As previously discussed, the source of the sample can affect concentration, with peripheral (femoral) sources being preferable over more central sources (i.e., subclavian, iliac or heart). If antemortem specimens are tested, they may be serum samples, rather than whole blood, which can also affect interpretation. Concentrations in liver, urine, bile and stomach contents do not necessarily indicate acute toxicity, only exposure. Methodology can also affect the results and interpretation. Immunoassays may have cross reactivity giving false-positive or false-negative results. The testing panel ordered may not include all drugs of interest or specialized testing may be required. The postmortem interval could also be a factor as some drugs may be metabolized after death or during the agonal period. For example, cocaine is routinely metabolized after death in both the body as well as in the samples if appropriate preservatives are not used. Thus, cocaine may not be detected in an antemortem sample or a decomposed body even though it was present at the time the sample was drawn or at the time of death. The occurrence and amount of postmortem redistribution also increases with an increasing postmortem interval.

Postmortem redistribution can dramatically affect toxicology results and must be understood by pathologists. After death, respiratory and cardiac activity stop and blood flow ceases. The blood begins to separate resulting in changes in the hematocrit and the distribution of drugs within the blood itself; protein bound drugs can be released and proteins can be degraded; cell walls lyze, releasing their contents into the blood; and the presence of microbes can further degrade or alter any drugs present. The environment of the blood and surrounding tissues also changes, pH decreases and solubility and binding properties are altered. These changes can result in the diffusion of drugs both into and out of the blood, or to or from the surrounding tissues – a phenomenon known as postmortem redistribution. In his research, Pounder found that the volume of distribution (V_d) of a specific drug strongly affects this redistribution process, with drugs with higher V_d having a greater tendency toward redistribution.[8] For example, in a case of one of the authors, the following hydrocodone concentrations were obtained: 0.05 mg/L in the femoral blood (therapeutic), 0.12 mg/L in the subclavian blood (possibly therapeutic in chronic user) and

0.52 mg/L in the heart blood, or another case involving citalopram: 0.52-mg/L femoral blood (therapeutic) and 3.01 mg/L in the heart blood. In general, the use of peripheral blood samples for quantification minimizes, but does not eliminate, the inaccuracies due to postmortem redistribution; thus, all postmortem drug concentrations must be interpreted with this principle in mind.

Individual factors focus mainly on drug metabolism and tolerance. Approximately 30% of all drugs are affected by a drug metabolizing enzyme, the majority are part of the CYP450 system, which can lead to concentration variances of a factor of 600 between two individuals given the same dosage. A mutation in a drug metabolizing enzyme, or the presence of an additional inhibiting drug, can lead to accumulation of a drug and toxicity. Genetic factors can also play a role in how an individual absorbs, distributes and metabolizes a drug. Drug metabolism is also dependent on organ function and volume of distribution, both of which can be affected by the presence of additional disease states. For instance, those with cirrhosis or chronic kidney disease may metabolize drugs differently; ill patients may develop fluid accumulations (i.e., ascites, anasarca), which can dramatically affect drug distribution; and hospitalized patients may have decreased organ functionality, which can affect drug metabolism and excretion. For some drugs, this understanding of drug metabolism can assist in interpretation. For example, the concentration of the parent drug can be compared to that of its metabolite to determine acute versus chronic administration, even if both are found at elevated concentrations. Such is the case of amitriptyline (AM) and its metabolite nortriptyline (NO). In a patient taking therapeutic doses of AM, the ratio of AM:NO should be less than one; if AM is taken as an overdose, the ratio is often greater than 2. This can be particularly useful in this situation, as tricyclic antidepressants are particularly susceptible to postmortem redistribution.

Individuals can also develop a tolerance to the physiologic effects of certain drugs. Specifically opiates/opioids, benzodiazepines, barbiturates and ethanol all show a propensity to develop tolerance. To assess tolerance, medical examiners must consider how long have the individual has been taking the drug, at what dose and on what regimen. Additionally, for drugs where tolerance can be an issue, so can withdrawal. Withdrawal from ethanol and benzodiazepines have been shown to result in severe illness and even death.

The intrinsic properties of the drugs themselves can also affect their toxicity. Some prescription and illicit drugs can prolong the QT interval which can result in sudden death especially in the presence of underlying rhythm disturbances. The presence of multiple drugs with similar effects can result in death due to mixed drug toxicity, such as multiple depressant medications like ethanol and benzodiazepines or multiple drugs which affect the serotonin system can result in serotonin syndrome. Many medications have central nervous system effects and their combination can lead to toxicity. For example, toxicity is increased when cocaine and heroin are combined or with the combined use of stimulants and antipsychotic medications.[9] Knowledge of the intrinsic properties of specific drugs is also helpful. For example, GHB can be created in vivo, and their presence alone may not constitute intoxication, while strychnine is significant at any concentration.

When determining a death to be the result of drug toxicity, all available information must be considered not only including the autopsy and toxicology results, but also the investigative information. When was the decedent last seen? What were they doing? How were they acting? Are the terminal events consistent with a drug toxicity? For example, if someone dies suddenly while in mid-conversation, this is likely not the result of a heroin overdose, though it could be indicative of a cocaine toxicity. Are there other disease processes present which may have been a factor?

Specific Drugs/Drug Classes

Alcohols

Ethanol

Ethyl alcohol is the most abused drug in American society and probably the world. Any drink containing from 0.5 to 95% alcohol is considered an alcoholic beverage.[10] The term "proof" is used to describe the strength of an alcoholic beverage. Proof is defined as twice the percentage of the alcohol content of the drink. Thus, an 80-proof beverage is 40% alcohol. The alcohol content of beer ranges between 3.2 and 4%, table wines 7.1 to 14%, whiskey 40–75%, vodka 40–50%, gin 40–85% and rum 40–95%.[10] A standard drink usually consists of a 12-oz beer, a 5-oz glass of wine or a 1.5-oz shot of liquor. In an averaged sized adult, one alcoholic drink will usually result in a peak blood ethanol concentration of 0.02–0.03 g/dL in men and 0.03–0.04 g/dL in women.

Alcohol is rapidly absorbed from all the mucosal surfaces of the gastrointestinal tract. In fasting individuals, 20–25% of a dose of alcohol is absorbed from the stomach and 75–80% from the small intestine.[11] Food delays the absorption of alcohol. Following ingestion of alcohol on an empty stomach, peak blood alcohol concentration occurs within one half to 2 h (average 0.75–1.35 h), whereas with food in the stomach, peak levels are reached within 1–6 h (average 1.06–2.12 h). The delay in reaching peak blood alcohol is directly proportional to the size of the meal and inversely proportional to the amount of time between food and alcohol consumption.

Almost immediately on entering the body, alcohol begins to undergo metabolism. It is metabolized to acetaldehyde, acetaldehyde to acetic acid and acetic acid to carbon dioxide and water. The vast majority of the metabolism (95%) occurs in the liver. Blood alcohol is metabolized at an average rate of 0.015 g/dL/h in males and 0.018 g/dL/h in females.[12] Alcoholics are able to metabolize alcohol at a faster rate than nonalcoholics, apparently because of an increase in liver enzymes. Thus, Clothier et al. reported an average rate of blood alcohol decline of 0.027 g/dL/h (a range of 0.016–0.043 g/dL/h).[13]

Because alcohol is soluble in water, it is present in the body tissue in direct relation to the amount of water content of the tissue or fluid. Specimens with high water content, such as blood or vitreous, will have high concentrations of alcohol compared with tissues such as the liver or brain. Forensic pathologists tend to deal in whole blood when performing alcohol determinations, while clinicians often use serum or plasma. The plasma or serum to whole blood alcohol concentration ratio averages 1.18 (a range of 1.10–1.35). It is often not realized that there may be a significant difference in the alcohol concentration of arterial blood and venous blood in the absorptive phase, with arterial blood up to 40% higher in alcohol concentration than venous blood.[14] There is little difference, however, in the concentration of alcohol in the venous and arterial blood in the postabsorptive phase.

Alcohol is excreted to a small degree unchanged in the urine. The urine in the bladder generally lags behind blood concentration until the blood concentration reaches its peak. The urine concentration then remains higher than the blood values during the declining blood alcohol concentrations. Urine and blood alcohol ratios have been reported as ranging anywhere from 0.32 to 2.44, in spite of the fact that the usually accepted average urine to blood concentration ratio is 1.3.[11] All that the urine concentration reflects is an average over the period of time the urine was produced, and the average is related to a number of factors, including alcohol concentration in the blood. By virtue of this, urine alcohol concentrations are not useful for predicting blood alcohol.[15]

Aside from blood, the best material to analyze for alcohol is vitreous. Alcohol disperses throughout the body in proportion to the water content of the tissue. Vitreous, with a high water content, has proportionally more alcohol than blood when at equilibrium. Thus, at equilibrium, for every unit of alcohol in blood, there are 1.2 units of alcohol in vitreous. A vitreous level of 0.120 g/dL is equivalent to a level of 0.100 g/dL of ethyl alcohol in blood. Because of its isolated location, the equilibration of vitreous alcohol with blood alcohol lags by 1–2 h. Thus, the vitreous alcohol levels provide a method for looking back in time. They will tell what the blood alcohol level was 1–2 h prior to death after one compensates for the greater amount of water in the vitreous. In the absorptive phase of alcohol, vitreous alcohol levels are lower than in the blood. If the individuals stop drinking, their blood alcohol will continue to rise for a short time as absorption continues, plateaus and then begins to go down. Vitreous alcohol, which lags behind blood alcohol, will continue to rise as the blood alcohol plateaus. The vitreous alcohol then plateaus and begins to decline. At the point of equilibration of blood and vitreous, the vitreous alcohol will be higher numerically because of the greater amount of water in the vitreous. This constant ratio of 1.2–1 will continue as the vitreous alcohol declines following the decline in the blood alcohol. Thus, only in the absorptive phase will vitreous alcohol be lower than blood alcohol.

After vitreous, the next-best tissue to analyze for alcohol is muscle. We prefer muscle from the thigh since it is isolated from other organs, unlike psoas muscle, and appears to be fairly resistant to decomposition. Garriott found a blood to muscle ratio of 0.94 ± 0.086 when blood alcohol concentration was greater than 0.10 g/dL; 1.48 ± 0.13 with blood alcohols less than 0.10 g/dL.[16]

If the body is not discovered immediately and decomposition sets in, there may be production of ethyl alcohol by the microbes. The amount of alcohol produced endogenously is to a degree related to the length of decomposition. It should be noted that not in all decomposed bodies will there be endogenous production of alcohol. When it does occur, the alcohol rarely reaches high concentrations; however, concentrations as high as 0.5 g/dL have been reported in diabetics.[17] In the study by Zumwalt et al., 80% of mildly decomposing bodies and 55% of mild to moderately decomposed bodies contained no alcohol.[18] In their study of 130 cases of decomposing bodies, only 23 cases had presumed production of alcohol postmortem in the blood. Of these, 19 had concentrations of 0.07 g/dL or less, with only four having concentrations of between 0.110 and 0.220 g/dL.

In embalming a body, the blood is, for the most part, removed and replaced by embalming fluid. Alcohol determination, however, can still be performed on either the vitreous or muscle. If vitreous is present, it is the preferred specimen. A small amount of embalming fluid will enter the vitreous fluid and produce minor dilution. Embalming fluid contains methanol but not ethyl alcohol. Thus, any ethanol present in the vitreous fluid should be presumed to have been ingested.

Alcohol, being a drug, has measurable effect on many of the physiological activities of the body. Alcohol impairs visual acuity, adaption to both light and darkness, discrimination of colors, persistence or speed of response to visual stimulation, focusing, etc.[19] Decrease in driving skills is measurable with blood alcohol concentrations as low as

0.03 g/dL, though risk of involvement in an accident is not increased. Risk of an accident begins to increase markedly around 0.08 g/dL. By 0.10 g/dL, risk of involvement in a fatal accident increases 12-fold compared with nondrinkers. Alcohol impairs reaction time at blood concentrations in excess of 0.05 g/dL. It has been known since 1919 that the effects of acute alcohol intoxication are more pronounced when the blood level is rising than falling (the Mellanby effect).[19] The individual psychological reaction to acute alcohol intoxication is variable. In all individuals, however, there is some impairment of judgment by 0.10 g/dL. In regard to alcohol's effect on the personality, some people become sleepy, placid and friendly, whereas others become antagonistic, hostile and violent. There is no way to say how individuals will react by blood alcohol level alone.

Of all the organ systems in the body, the most affected by alcohol is the central nervous system. Table 23.1 gives the stages of acute alcohol intoxication, that is, symptomatology versus the actual blood alcohol concentration. Chronic alcoholics are often able to mask many of the signs of acute alcohol intoxication, though there is still physiological impairment. Thus, a chronic alcoholic with a blood level of 0.15 g/dL may superficially appear sober, though there is still impairment in the reflexes, visual acuity, memory, concentration and judgment. Young individuals, inexperienced with alcohol, are more susceptible to the physiological actions of acute alcohol intoxication and to lethal CNS depression.

Most deaths caused by acute alcohol intoxication occur with blood alcohol concentrations of 0.400 g/dL or greater. Inexperienced drinkers are more susceptible than chronic alcoholics. Chronic alcoholics have been apprehended operating motor vehicles with blood alcohol concentrations of 0.45–0.5 g/dL and have actually survived alcohol concentrations as high as 0.6–0.7 g/dL. One must also keep in mind that actual blood alcohol concentration at time of autopsy may be lower than it was prior to death if the individual suffered irreversible hypoxic brain injury caused by the CNS depressant action of the alcohol, yet managed to survive for a period of time, metabolizing the alcohol. In such a case, one may see blood alcohol concentrations between 0.25 and 0.35 g/dL. The vitreous, however, will show significantly higher alcohol concentrations, indicating that the individual is in the metabolizing phase.

Table 21.1 Acute Alcohol Intoxication

Blood Alcohol (g/dL)	Signs/Symptoms
0.01–0.05	Slight physiological impairment detectable on careful testing by 0.05 g/dL.
0.05–0.07	Euphoria; increased self-confidence. Consistent impairment of reaction responses and attention by 0.07 g/dL.
0.07–0.10	Increasing impairment of reaction responses, attention, visual acuity, sensory-motor coordination and judgment. Individual may still appear sober.
0.10–0.20	Increasing impairment of sensory-motor activities, reaction times, attention, visual acuity and judgment. Progressive increase in drowsiness, disorientation and emotional lability. By 0.20 g/dL, loss of coordination, staggering gait, slurred speech.
0.20–0.30	Staggering, grossly impaired, drunk; may be lethargic and sleepy or hostile and aggressive. By 0.30 g/dL, many individuals fall asleep or pass out.
0.30–0.40	Impaired consciousness, stupor, unconsciousness.
0.40+	Unconsciousness, coma. Possible death.

Methanol

Poisoning caused by methyl alcohol is relatively uncommon. Methanol is oxidized by the liver to formaldehyde, which in turn is oxidized to formic acid. Formic acid is six times more toxic than methanol. Symptoms of acute methanol poisoning are weakness, nausea, vomiting, headache, epigastric pain, dyspnea and cyanosis. Inebriation is not a prominent symptom. The symptoms may occur within half an hour after ingestion or may not appear for 24 h. If a fatal amount of methyl alcohol has been ingested, the aforementioned symptoms will be followed by stupor, coma, convulsions, hypothermia and death. Death is nearly always preceded by blindness. If the individual does survive, they may be permanently blind, due to an apparent specific toxicity for the retinal cells. Death in methyl alcohol poisoning is caused by the acidosis from production of organic acids and the CNS depressant action of the alcohol.[20,21]

Formic acid is the primary agent responsible for the severe metabolic acidosis and ocular toxicity of methanol. Ingestion of 70–100 mL of methyl alcohol is usually fatal, though death may occur with ingestion of as little as 30–60 mL. As little as 10 mL of methanol can cause permanent blindness. Of *725* cases of methanol poisoning caused by ingestion reported by Keeney and Mellinkoff, 54% of the individuals died, 12% were blinded and 12% had visual impairment.[21] Methyl alcohol can usually be detected up to 48 h after ingestion because of the slow rate of oxidation. The minimum lethal blood level in methyl alcohol poisoning is approximately 0.08 g/dL. The autopsy findings are nonspecific.

Isopropanol

Isopropanol is available to the public as rubbing alcohol in a 70% aqueous solution. It has twice the CNS depressant potential of ethanol. Unlike methanol, it is not in itself toxic. It is metabolized in the liver to acetone. A lethal dose of isopropanol is estimated at 250 mL for an adult. It should be noted that the appearance of small amounts of isopropanol in the blood is not necessarily indicative of ingestion of this alcohol. In diabetics with ketoacidosis, in alcoholics and in cases of starvation with high levels of acetone, acetone may be converted to isopropyl alcohol. In such cases, there will be a high level of acetone and a low level of isopropyl alcohol.[22] Concentrations less than 0.1 g/dL usually do not indicate exposure or toxicity while concentrations greater than 0.1 g/dL with an Isopropanol: Acetone ratios >1 usually are indicative of ingestion and toxicity.[23] Isopropanol can also be found as a component of embalming fluid and is often used to clean bodies, especially in cases where postmortem tissue procurement occurs. When found due to such contamination (i.e., embalming or cleaning), acetone is usually absent.

Ethylene Glycol

Ethylene glycol is the principal component of most automotive antifreeze solutions. In humans, it is metabolized to a number of compounds, the most important of which is oxalic acid. Upon ingestion, individuals develop central nervous system depression with severe metabolic acidosis. If they survive these, they develop acute renal failure. Microscopic sections of the kidneys viewed under polarized light show deposition of oxalate crystals in the renal tubules and brain.[20,24]

Ethylene glycol itself is not toxic; it is the metabolites (principally oxalic acid) that are. Minimum lethal dose is estimated at 100 mL for an adult, though individuals have survived significantly higher amounts. The clinical manifestations of acute ethylene glycol intoxication can be divided into neurological, cardiorespiratory and renal. Neurological symptoms usually develop within a half hour to 12 h after ingestion. The individual develops nausea, vomiting, convulsions and coma. Cardiorespiratory manifestations usually appear 12–24 h after ingestion. Tachycardia, tachypnea and congestive heart failure are present. If individuals still survive, they then develop acute tubular necrosis. This usually is seen 24–72 h after ingestion.

Opiates/Opioids

Opiates are drugs derived from the opium poppy plant and include morphine, codeine and papaverine. Opioids are drugs, natural or synthetic, that bind to the brain's opioid receptors, having the same actions as opiates. To avoid confusion, the term opioid will be used henceforth to describe the actions of both opiates and opioids.

Opioid drugs normally result in death by causing cardiopulmonary depression often with an antecedent period of coma prior to death. While there are no pathognomonic findings for opioid related deaths, they are traditionally associated with pulmonary edema which often manifests as a "foam cone" of edematous fluid exudating from the nose and mouth (Figure 21.4); additionally, cerebral edema and bladder distention are also seen. It has been hypothesized that pulmonary and cerebral edema as well as the bladder fullness may develop after the prolonged comatose state with impaired respiratory function, or due to a direct toxic effect of opiate drugs on the capillaries, increased vascular permeability

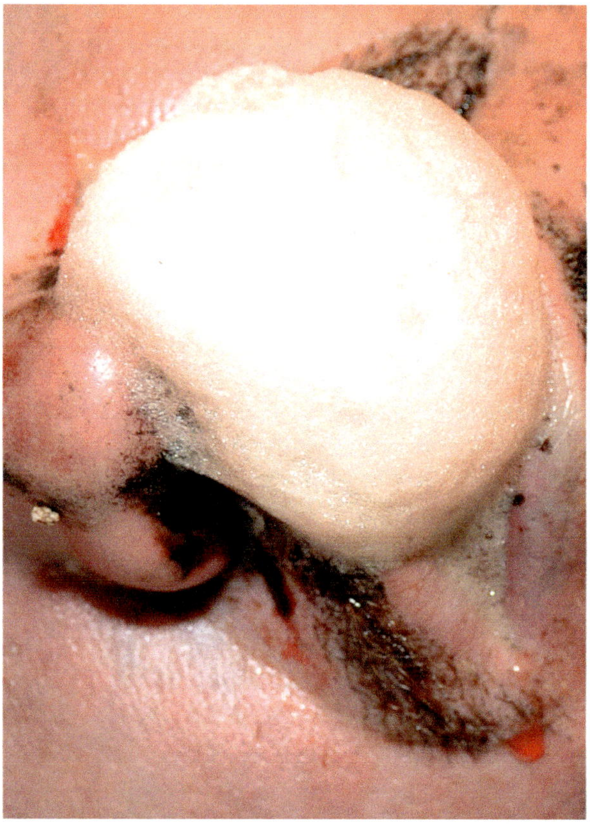

Figure 21.4 Foam cone.

or a central vasomotor effect.[25,26] While it has been shown that pulmonary and cerebral edema also occur with other types of deaths, such as asphyxia and cardiac disease, the triad of pulmonary and cerebral edema with bladder fullness is still a helpful trio when investigating opioid deaths.[7] Opioid toxicity is also known to results in seizures. While the exact mechanism of this association is unclear, research has shown that opioids enhance seizure activity via receptors within the hippocampus, resulting in disinhibition of hippocampal neurons and enhancement of excitatory neurotransmission.[27–29] Additionally, the cardiopulmonary depression caused by opioids may result in cerebral hypoxia leading to seizures.[30]

While opioids are individually toxic, their toxicity can be increased when mixed with other opioids or drugs with similar effects, such as ethanol or benzodiazepines. The toxicity of opioids is also enhanced when mixed with stimulants, likely due the central effects of both.[31,32]

The most important aspect about deaths due to opioids is tolerance. Tolerance can develop with chronic use, and thus, the concentrations of the drugs present at the time of death may not be as helpful in determining lethality. Concentrations may be lower postmortem than there were terminally if the decedent had an antecedent period of a comatose state resulting in drug metabolism or the decedent may exhibit high tolerance to a drug so concentrations may be extremely elevated even though the death is not drug related. Thus, in cases of opioid deaths, it is extremely important in to utilize all investigative and circumstantial findings before certifying a death as a result of an opioid toxicity.

Heroin

Heroin was introduced to medicine and the public in the early part of the 20th century as a replacement for morphine and codeine. When introduced, one of the claims made for it was that it was nonaddictive. While it does have certain therapeutic advantages over morphine and codeine, heroin is much more addictive. Because of this, it is not used therapeutically. Until the widespread introduction of cocaine to the American population, heroin was probably the most popular of the "hard" drugs. Depending on geographical area, it is sold in small plastic envelopes, capsules or balloons. It has typically been cut with a sugar such as lactose or even quinine. The typical "bag" of heroin traditionally contained a 1–2% concentration of the drug. With the introduction of the cheaper black tar form of heroin from Mexico, the quality of heroin being sold increased dramatically. Bags of heroin showing 20–30% purity, with some up to 50%, are now routine in some parts of the country.

Heroin is usually either smoked or injected intravenously. The user usually places the powder in either a bottle cap or spoon, adds water and then heats the mixture over a flame (Figure 21.5).

A piece of cotton may be added to the mixture to "strain out" the impurities. The solution is then taken up into a syringe and injected intravenously. Microscopic examination of the lungs commonly reveals foreign-body granulomas with talc crystals and cotton fibers. The cotton originates from the "strainer." The talc probably has been used as a cutting agent. Recently, heroin is known as H or smack or speedball when combined with cocaine.

Following injection, heroin (diacetylmorphine) is almost immediately metabolized to monoacetylmorphine (half-life 9 min). Monoacetylmorphine is then hydrolyzed to morphine (half-life 38 min). Because of this, if one performs a toxicologic analysis on an individual who died from an overdose of heroin, one does not detect heroin in the blood, but

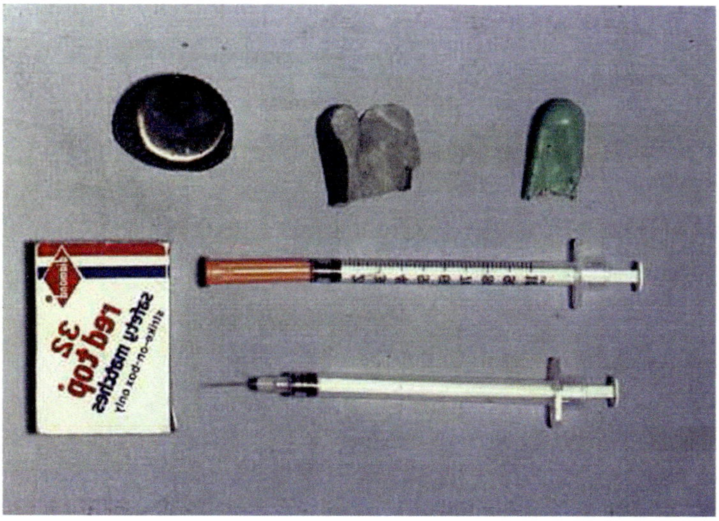

Figure 21.5 Intravenous heroin paraphernalia: syringes, two balloon tips (one opened) that contained heroin and a bottle cap that functioned as a cooker.

rather morphine and monoacetylmorphine. If both monoacetylmorphine and morphine are detected in the blood, this is considered indicative of recent heroin use, though the monoacetylmorphine may only be detected in the vitreous or urine due to its short half-life. Additionally, small amounts of codeine may be detected in the blood or urine in cases of heroin use. Morphine is not metabolized to codeine, rather the codeine detected represents codeine present in the poppy itself. However, it is important to note that codeine is metabolized to morphine via CYP2D6. Thus, in heroin overdoses, on toxicological analysis one may detect morphine, monoacetylmorphine and extremely low concentrations of codeine. If the codeine concentration is higher than that of morphine, this likely indicates codeine ingestion as well. In some very acute deaths from heroin overdose, the urine is negative but the blood positive. Death is not directly related to blood concentration, due to the high tolerance individuals can build up. Thus, a level that makes one individual "high" will kill another.

Methadone

Methadone is a medication previously commonly used for opioid withdrawal patients; however, it has become more commonly used in pain clinics as well due to its long half-life (λ: 8–59 h). Chronic use of methadone often results in extremely high therapeutic concentrations, so extreme care must be utilized when interpreting drug concentrations in a chronic user. Additionally, methadone can result in prolongation of the QT interval and has been associated with development of cardiac rhythm disturbances particularly during the first 3 months of therapy.

Fentanyl and Synthetics Opioids

Fentanyl is a semisynthetic opioid which is 50–100 times more potent than morphine. It is usually prescribed as a transdermal patch or used intravenously for pain control in a hospital setting. Fentanyl is known to undergo significant postmortem redistribution, so extreme caution must be used when interpreting postmortem concentrations.[33] Fentanyl has become an abused drug as well, going by the names China Girl and King Ivory on the street.

In recent years, as part of the opioid epidemic, many synthetic fentanyls have appeared in drug deaths, usually in association with heroin or other illicit drugs. Drugs such as methylfentanyl, alfentanil, acetylfentanyl, carfentanil, sufentanil and U-47700 have been reported to cause death. Drugs such as these have no current therapeutic use and should be considered significant at any concentration.

Sympathomimetics

Sympathomimetic drugs, also known as stimulants, are drugs which stimulate the sympathetic nervous system. These drugs can stimulate the release of catecholamines, including norepinephrine and epinephrine, or inhibit their reuptake or metabolism resulting in activation of both the central nervous and cardiovascular systems. These drugs can result in death by either CNS or cardiovascular toxicity. In the CNS, sympathomimetic drugs stimulate the nervous system, resulting in systemic excitation and a decrease in the seizure threshold. CNS stimulation can also result in hallucinations, aggression, delusions and violent behavior. Cardiovascular effects of such drugs include increasing heart rate, blood pressure and cardiac contractility, resulting in arrythmias. Stimulation of the alpha receptors in the coronary arteries cause contraction, reducing myocardial perfusion, resulting in cardiac ischemia. Since sympathomimetics stimulate the cardiovascular system, they can result in ischemic and hemorrhagic strokes, ruptured aortic and cerebral artery aneurysms, myocardial infarcts (heart attacks) and should be considered as contributing factors if present when any of these presumably natural events occur.

Sequalae of cardiovascular stimulation can often be found in chronic users, such as large, hypertrophic hearts, due to the increases in blood pressure and cardiac contractility, and myocardial fibrosis.[34,35] Accelerated atherosclerosis and/or vasculitis are also commonly seen in younger, chronic users due to the arterial stimulation and injury associated with chronic stimulant use. Habitual, prolonged, heavy use of stimulants can also result in psychosis; individuals may become aggressive, violent and paranoid.[36] Stimulant use is also associated with sudden death during a struggle (see Chapter 19, "Sudden Death during or Immediately after a Struggle".

While individuals can become tolerant to the euphoric effects of stimulants, tolerance is not developed to the CNS or cardiovascular stimulant effects. Thus, deaths due to sympathomimetic drugs are not dose dependent and such drugs can be significant regardless of concentration. There is usually substantial overlap in blood concentrations in individuals dying of a stimulant overdoses and those in whom it is an incidental finding.[35,37]

Cocaine

Cocaine has replaced heroin in some areas as the most commonly abused of the hard drugs. It is one of the most potent of the CNS stimulants. Introduced to medicine and the public in the late 19th century, it soon became the "third scourge of mankind." Cocaine can be sniffed, shot intravenously or smoked as "crack." It is known as coke, snow or speedball, the latter of which when combined with heroin. While originally said to be nonaddictive (just like heroin), it is now realized that it is a very potent addictive compound, especially the crack (free base) form. When smoked as crack, it is immediately absorbed by the lungs and reaches the brain within seconds. It takes slightly longer for its action to affect the brain when injected intravenously. Cocaine is a relatively short-acting drug such that to maintain a high, one has to take it every 15 min to an hour. Since it is a potent vasoconstrictor, snorting the drug can occasionally cause ulceration and perforation of the nasal septum with long-term use.

Cocaine is rapidly hydrolyzed to benzoylecgonine and other derivatives by blood cholinesterases. Breakdown of cocaine will continue in the test tube unless it is inhibited by the addition of sodium fluoride.

Methamphetamine

Methamphetamine is a potent CNS stimulant that is readily produced illicitly. In the brain, it acts by both increasing release of dopamine and blocking its reabsorption, causing hyperstimulation of receptor neurons. Methamphetamine is also a cardiovascular stimulant. It blocks reuptake of norepinephrine and causes an increase in monoamine release. The euphoric effect is similar to cocaine but may last as long as ten times that of cocaine. Methamphetamine is metabolized to amphetamine, its major active metabolite. It is usually taken orally or intravenously though it may be snorted or smoked. Methamphetamine may be transformed into methamphetamine hydrochloride ("ice") which is smoked like crack cocaine. It is also known as chalk, crystal and speed. It has a half-life of 11–12 h, with 45% excreted in urine unchanged over a number of days.

Newer Synthetic Stimulants

In recent years, numerous drugs have emerged that mimic other more commonly known stimulants such as methamphetamine and cocaine, sometimes referred to as "bath salts." Some of these drugs are newly developed compounds, while others are older drugs that have just recently reemerged. Similarly, they act on monoamines by inhibiting their transport and/or inducing their release. Synthetic stimulants are generally amphetamines, cathinones, tryptamines, phenethylamines, piperazines, piperidines or related substances. Some adverse effects can include tachycardia, restlessness, anxiety, agitation, hypertension, nausea, vomiting and diarrhea among others. The in vitro stability of these drugs has been shown to be short, therefore, it is best to keep samples frozen and test as soon as possible. Common drugs in this group include NBOME, mephedrone, pentylone, ethylone and methylenedioxypyrovalerone. Street names include Flakka, Ivory wave, Vanilla Sky and plant food. None of these drugs have known therapeutic uses and their presence should be considered significant regardless of concentration.

Cannabinoids

Marijuana

After alcohol, marijuana is considered the most commonly used drug in the United States. It is derived from the *Cannabis* genus of plants in the *Cannabaceae* family and is known by many names including pot, weed, grass and Mary Jane. In 1996, California became the first state to legalize medicinal marijuana and has subsequently been followed by most other states in the union, which have either legalized medicinal marijuana or recreational marijuana. Cannabinoids, both natural and synthetics, have also been found in numerous over-the-counter vaping products.

Marijuana comes in various preparations and is most often smoked or ingested. The main psychoactive component of marijuana is delta-9-tetrahydrocannabinol (THC) which is rapidly metabolized to the active hydroxymetabolite, 11-OH-THC, and the inactive carboxy metabolite THC-COOH. THC exhibits its effects by interacting with the cannabinoid receptors (CB1 and CB2) and is mainly used for its effect on the emotional and reward systems within the brain, though it also causes altered senses, difficulty with mentation, impaired memory and hallucinations. Chronic use has also been associated with learning difficulties, especially seen in adolescents. While deaths believed to be due to THC have been reported, the authors argue that none have been definitively linked to an overdose of THC. Except those that have choked to death by attempting to swallow a bag of marijuana in an attempt to conceal the evidence in a police arrest. THC can cause tachycardia and is a pulmonary irritant if smoked, possibly exacerbating underlying medical conditions such as coronary artery disease, asthma or emphysema. It has also been associated with intense nausea and vomiting with chronic use, termed hyperemesis syndrome, which only resolves with cessation of use.

The concentrations of THC after smoking are extremely variable. The peak THC concentration is normally reached approximately 10 min after smoking, then rapidly decreases within 1–2 h, with measurable concentrations present for up to 12 h or longer.[38] Although THC rapidly clears the blood stream, it is very lipophilic and accumulates in adipose and brain tissue. THC can be found in measurable concentrations up to 30 days after last use in chronic users.[39] Additionally, THC is known to undergo significant postmortem redistribution and postmortem concentrations should be interpreted with caution.[40] The presence of THC in the blood postmortem does not necessarily indicate recent use or intoxication at the time of death.

It has often been argued that the presence of THC in the blood may be due to passive inhalation, although studies have shown that this is likely not the case. Measurable, though extremely low, concentrations of THC have been reported in nonsmokers; however, the testing involved extreme settings in high-intensity environments.[41,42] Where this effect may be a consideration is if THC is detected in children or SUID deaths, though the presence of THC in such cases may also represent ingestion.

While it has been shown that marijuana can cause driver impairment, the concentration at which this occurs has not been established. While several states and countries have "legal limits" for marijuana, unlike with ethanol, these limits are somewhat arbitrary as a concentration of THC which causes impairment has not been established. For example, legal limits range from 1 ng/mL in Pennsylvania to 5 ng/mL in Colorado, Montana and Washington. Additionally, as discussed above, postmortem concentrations can be significantly affected by postmortem distribution and chronicity of use; thus, the concentrations present in a deceased driver likely do not represent those present at the time the motor vehicle was actually being operated and should not be used to determine impairment.

Synthetic cannabinoids

Synthetic cannabinoids, often termed "K2" or "spice," are a class of drugs manufactured to mimic the effects of delta-9-THC, the active ingredient in marijuana. The term "Synthetic cannabinoids" usually applies to illicitly produced drugs that bind to cannabinoid receptors, same as THC; however, dronabinol (marinol) is also a synthetic cannabinoid that is used as an appetite stimulant in cancer or AIDS patients to induce appetite. However, it is important to note that THC is a weak partial agonist at these receptors while illicit synthetic cannabinoids are full agonists with a greater affinity for the receptors. Thus, these synthetic cannabinoids are highly toxic compounds with effects including seizures, agitation, anxiety, confusion, paranoia, tachycardia, hypertension, hypokalemia, hallucinations, tremors, delusions, vomiting and death. Additionally, some of these compounds have been found to be contaminated with anticoagulants such as warfarin, brodifacoum, difenacoum and bromadiolone.[43] The synthetic cannabinoids are rapidly changing, but some commonly encountered include 5F-AMD, ADBICA, FUBINACA and CHMINACA. Due to the serious toxicities associated with these drugs, they should be considered significant if present, regardless of concentration.

Hallucinogens

Hallucinogenic compounds are a diverse group of drugs that alter the user's perceptions of reality, including their thoughts and feelings, usually by acting on the serotonin receptors in the brain. The most common hallucinogens include D-lysergic acid diethylamide (LSD), psilocybin (mushrooms), mescaline (peyote) and phencyclidine (PCP). Many of these compounds are not found on routine toxicologic analysis and may need to be requested specifically.

Toxicities can result in tachycardia, nausea/vomiting, hypertension, tachypnea, hyperthermia, diaphoresis, psychosis, arrhythmias, seizures and even death. However, while these compounds can result in toxicity, most of them result in death due to injuries sustained while under the influence. For example, a person under the influence of LSD who jumps out of window out of a perception they can fly, when they cannot.

Inhalants

Inhalants are a class of drugs considered forensically when they are intentionally inhaled with the intent of obtaining psychoactive effects; they are also referred to as "volatiles" given their chemical properties. These chemicals are common constituents of fuel gases, propellants, solvents, anesthetics, automotive fuels, refrigerants, paint thinner, glues and dry cleaning agents. Most commonly these compounds include aromatic and halogenated hydrocarbons and fluorocarbons. They are known to be cardiotoxic and are associated with lethal arrhythmias; they can also cause death by oxygen exclusion. Volatile substances are highly lipophilic, so in addition to blood, brain is often a good secondary source. In fact, the authors had a case where they were able to detect 1,1-difluoroethane in the cerebral material of a decedent who died approximately 50 h after exposure and a prolonged hospitalization.[44]

Common volatile compounds include benzene, butane, carbon tetrachloride, chloroform, diethyl ether, enflurane, ether, ethyl ether, fluothane, freon, gasoline, helium, isoflurane, methyl ether, nitrous oxide, oxybismethane, perchloroethylene, propane, tetrachloroethene, tetrafluoroethane, toluene, trichloroethylene, trichloroethane, trichloromethane, trifluoroethane and xylene. Diagnosis of volatile or inhalant toxicity usually depends upon the circumstances of death and the presence of such a substance in the blood or tissue samples, regardless of concentration of the substance. Care must be taken when a death due to an inhalant is suspected and blood must be drawn into a fully filled screw-top tube to prevent aerosolization of the substances into the tube and diffusion through the rubber stopper.

Vaping/e-Cigarettes

Although not truly a toxicologic issue, the use of e-cigarettes (or vaping) has recently been associated with severe lung disease and death. Vaping is essentially inhaled aerosol generated from a device. These devices usually consist of a liquid containing reservoir attached to a heating element and battery.[45] The vaping liquid usually consists of nicotine, CBD or THC, though other substances can also be added including synthetic THC. Additionally, the liquid also contains other chemicals including propylene glycol, glycerin and/or flavoring elements. The liquids come in different flavors, including fruit and candy flavors, and accidental drinking of these liquids by children has resulted in a number of nicotine toxicities.[46]

The main issue with vaping is, again, not a toxicologic issue but a toxicity issue nonetheless. In 2019, an outbreak of severe lung disease known as e-cigarette or vaping-associated lung injury (EVALI) was identified. EVALI is essentially a pneumonitis of unknown origin resulting in a wide range of lung pathology including organizing pneumonia and diffuse alveolar damage.[45] It has been proposed the damage may be due to the inhalation of vitamin E containing THC products, but this link has not been definitively proven.[45]

Toxicology may assist with these deaths, even though the death is due to pulmonary disease, as nicotine or THC identified on toxicology screening may assist the pathologist in understanding the possible etiology of the lung disease.

Metals

Humans are exposed to metals and elements through the environment, food and water, smoking and certain occupations or hobbies. Some metals have also been used not only medicinally but also as poisons, including being components of insecticides or pesticides. Most metals are eliminated by and accumulate in the kidneys, so renal tissue is often the preferred tissue when testing for an acute overdose. Chronic exposure can often be delineated by testing of the hair and/or fingernails. However, the concentrations of metals seen in blood and tissues is often extremely variable due to diet, environment and occupation, making interpretation of postmortem metal concentrations extremely difficult; it is recommended that such interpretation be done with great skepticism and reflection.

Lead

Lead is the major cause of heavy-metal toxicity in present-day society. Lead is found in storage batteries and was used as a constituent of paint and gasoline for many years. The most common causes of lead poisoning in the United States are ingestion of lead-based paint and industrial or environmental exposure. The symptoms of chronic lead poisoning are abdominal cramps, vomiting, constipation, lethargy, anemia, weight loss, muscle paralysis, nephropathy and convulsions. Death is uncommon. When it does occur, it most often involves children in tenement areas who have a history of pica. These children, ages 18 months to 3 years, eat the lead-containing paint peelings that fall off the walls of their homes. The CDC now uses the upper limit 0.05 mg/L for lead exposure in children. Children with concentrations between 0.05 and 0.44 mg/L require close follow up and investigation regarding exposure and chelation therapy is instigating at concentrations greater than 0.45 mg/L.[47]

Lead lines can often be seen on X-ray in cases of lead poisoning; these are dense bands at the ends of the long bones along the growth plates. Burtons' lines (lead lines), a dark line

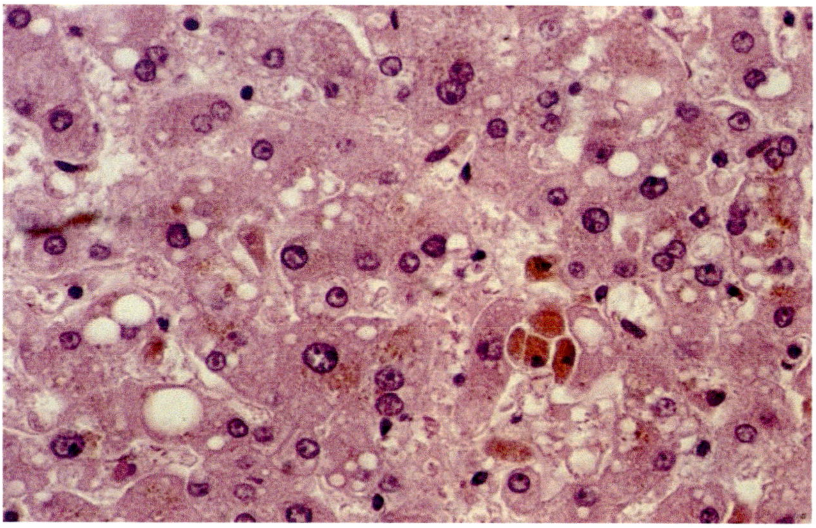

Figure 21.6 Eosinophilic inclusions in nuclei of liver cells in individual with chronic lead poisoning.

along the gum at the dental margin, can also be seen. At autopsy, the most striking finding is the brain, which is massively swollen, with flattening of the gyri, and is extremely pale, almost white. Blood smears show basophilic stippling of erythrocytes. Characteristic eosinophilic intranuclear inclusions may be seen in hepatocytes and cells of the proximal tubules of the kidneys (Figure 21.6).

PAS-positive, pink-staining homogeneous material may be seen in the perivascular spaces in the brain.

Arsenic

The poison with the longest history is arsenic, which has been used since the time of the Roman Empire.[48] It is a metalloid, found throughout the environment, being naturally present in soil in amounts as high as 20 parts per million. It was used medicinally for years and is present in all living organisms, including humans. The average daily human intake of arsenic is between 0.5 and 1 mg contained in food and water. Traditionally, arsenic has been used in herbicides, pesticides and wood preservatives. It is also used as a glass clarifier in the electronics industry. For the most part, arsenic has been replaced by other compounds. The only exceptions are its use as a wood preservative and in the electronics industry, in both of which it is still extensively used.

Arsenic is a popular poison because it is tasteless, odorless and fairly easy to obtain. However, it is not too effective, because death is usually slow and painful rather than instantaneous. Elemental arsenic (As^{o}) is not toxic and can be found in shellfish and seafood. The most common form of arsenic used for poisoning is arsenic trioxide (arsenite [As^{3}+]). Arsenic in this and other forms (arsenate [As^{5}+] and arsine gas [AsH_3]) are cytotoxic, apparently due to the inhibition of sulfhydryl-containing enzymes. Arsenic is almost completely absorbed from the gastrointestinal tract, with excretion primarily through the urine in the form of methylated arsenic. On absorption, it is bound to the protein portion of hemoglobin. Within 24 h of ingestion, large concentrations of it are present in the liver, kidney, spleen, lungs and gastrointestinal tract. It is also deposited in hair, nails and skin.

A fatal dose of arsenic trioxide is somewhere between 200 and 300 mg. Following ingestion, symptoms may begin within 30 min. They tend to be centered about the gastrointestinal tract with nausea, vomiting, colicky abdominal pain and diarrhea with rice-water stools. The patient may have a dry mouth with a metallic taste, a slight garlicky odor to the breath and difficulty swallowing. Damage to the capillary endothelium by the arsenic leads to transudation of plasma. In the bowel, this causes accumulation of fluid in the bowel lumen. Arsenic in the gastrointestinal tract causes sloughing of the mucosa and vesicle formation, not caused by any corrosive action of arsenic, but rather the consequence of its vascular actions. With large doses of arsenic, death can occur in a few hours, caused by shock as a result of the vascular actions. If individuals survive this initial insult, they may develop hepatic and renal failure. Electrocardiographic changes may occur with prolonged QT intervals and nonspecific ST segment changes. At autopsy, in acute deaths, the gastric mucosa is congested and shows some oozing of blood. If the individual lives a day or two, the whole small intestine may have this appearance, with formation of a pseudomembrane in some instances. Within a matter of a few days, there are fatty deposits in the heart, liver and kidneys as well as acute tubular necrosis.

Some poisonings are not accomplished with one large dose, but with multiple smaller doses. Here, the action of the arsenic on the skin causes an initial erythematous flush with subsequent development of melanosis, hyperkeratosis and desquamation. Months after an acute ingestion of arsenic, transverse white bands (Mees's lines) can be seen on the nails. Arsenic can also cause anemia, leukopenia, thrombocytopenia and basophilic stippling.

Individuals may develop a peripheral neuropathy of both the sensory and motor nerves. There is paralysis of the muscles of the hands and feet, with sensory loss. This neuropathy can be seen following both acute and chronic arsenic poisoning. In chronic poisoning, other symptoms may be minor and the person may present just with the neuropathy. In some individuals who take very large doses of arsenic, death may be so rapid that there is no chance to develop gastrointestinal symptoms. Rather, the individual becomes comatose, develops convulsions and dies within several hours. This presentation, however, is unusual. Normal levels of arsenic in the blood range between 0.002 and 0.3 mg/L. Fatal blood levels are from 0.2 to 10 mg/L.

Insulin

Most deaths from insulin are accidental. Suicides are infrequent and homicides rare. Insulin, of course, is used for the treatment of diabetes. Insulin is produced in the beta cells of the islets of Langerhans and, in diabetes, the body either does not produce enough insulin or becomes resistant to the effects of insulin. Classically, diabetes has been treated by the administration of insulin obtained either from cattle or swine. Synthetic human insulin has virtually replaced them.

An overdose of insulin will cause hypoglycemia with irreversible injury to the brain. It was the introduction of RIA that made the measurement of insulin in the body practical. Most large hospital laboratories continue to analyze insulin by this method, though LC/MS/MS methods have also been developed for such testing. Blood glucose levels postmortem are of no help in the diagnosis of hypoglycemia due to both perimortem glucose utilization and release. Thus, one might get decreased, normal or elevated levels of glucose in postmortem blood in an overdose from insulin. The vitreous is of no help either, because abnormally low values of glucose in the vitreous have no significance; only elevated levels of glucose are of any significance.

Insulin is produced in the beta cells of the islets of Langerhans by the enzymatic cleavage of the precursor polypeptide proinsulin. For every molecule of insulin formed, a corresponding molecule of C-peptide is formed. Thus, if an increase in concentration of insulin in the blood is caused by endogenous production either by the pancreas or a tumor, then the concentration of C-peptide should theoretically be elevated as well. Thus, if one finds high insulin and high C-peptide, one assumes that the insulin is endogenous. If, however, one sees high concentrations of insulin and normal or depressed concentrations of C-peptide, then one would conclude that the insulin is of exogenous origin, that is, it was administered. Normally, one would expect the insulin:C-peptide ratio to be less than 1, usually between 0.1 and 0.5; if exogeneous insulin were injected, the ratio should be >1. Unfortunately, this expected ratio of C-peptide is not absolute and both C-peptide and insulin are unstable postmortem.[49] Insulin concentrations may decrease postmortem due to degradation particularly in hemolyzed samples. Insulin is also not found in significant concentrations in tissue (liver, brain, kidney). Thus, a careful investigation is always necessary in these cases. Deaths where the decedent was not prescribed insulin for the treatment of diabetes, yet exogenous insulin is identified, are often easier to identify than cases of insulin overdose where the decedent is a known diabetic treated with exogeneous insulin.

Miscellaneous Drugs

Of course there are many other poisons not discussed in this chapter. Many of which are also not seen on routine toxicology screens. These include plant-based poisons such as ricin, hemlock, oleander and strychnine; acetylcholinesterase inhibitors; manufactured poisons such as VX gas and radiologic agents. The authors would recommend consulting a forensic toxicologist should any of these more uncommon poisons be suspected.

Additionally, before ending this section, it should be noted that just about any drug can be lethal at elevated concentrations. Most antihistamines, antidepressant and antipsychotic medications are cardiotoxic in excess. Anti-inflammatory drugs such as ibuprofen and naprosyn can cause renal failure while acetaminophen is hepatotoxic. Each potential overdose death should receive a thorough death investigation including review of any circumstantial and medical information, a full autopsy examination and a complete toxicology screen looking for drugs of abuse as well as over the counter and prescription medications. The toxicology results should be interpreted in the setting of the investigation and autopsy results.

It is a final suggestion of the authors that in all deaths involving drugs, the medical examiner who performed the autopsy be the one to testify during any procedures regarding the cause and manner of death. While it is likely that the medical examiner did not personally perform the analysis of the drugs implicated in causing the death, the medical examiner is the one who ultimately determined the cause of death and should discuss their rationale regarding the role the drugs may, or may not, have played in such.

References

1. NAME accreditation standards, Section C Morgue Operations, 7e, Specimen Labels. National Association of Medical Examiners. Nov 2018.
2. Apple FS and Bandt CM, Liver and blood postmortem tricyclic antidepressant concentrations. *Am J Clin Pathol* 1988; 89:794–795.

3. Pounder DJ, et al., Postmortem diffusion of drugs from gastric residue: an experimental study. *Am J Forensic Med Pathol* 1996 17(1):1–7.
4. Pounder DJ and Smith DRW, Postmortem diffusion of alcohol from the stomach. *Am J Forensic Med Pathol* 1995; 16(2):89–96.
5. NAME accreditation standards, Section E Toxicology, 4f, Retainment of Specimens. National Association of Medical Examiners. Nov 2018.
6. Levine B, Golle M, and Smialek JE, An unusual drug death involving maggots. *Am J Forensic Med Pathol* 2000; 21(1):59–61.
7. Molina DK, Vance K, Coleman ML, and Hargrove VM, Testing an old adage: can autopsy findings be of assistance in differentiating opioid versus cardiac deaths? *J Forensic Sci* 2019; epub ahead of print.
8. Pounder DJ, The nightmare of postmortem drug changes, in Wecht CH (Ed) *Legal Medicine*. Lexis Law, Albany, NY, 1994, pp 163–93.
9. Molina DK and Hargrove VH, Fatal cocaine interactions: a review of cocaine related deaths in Bexar County Texas. *Am J Forensic Med Pathol* 2011; 32(1):71–77.
10. McAnalley BH, Chemistry of alcoholic beverages. in Garriott JC (Ed) *Medicolegal Aspects of Alcohol* 3rd ed. Lawyers and Judges Pub. Co., Tucson, AZ, 1996.
11. Baselt RC and Danhof IE, Disposition of alcohol in man. in Garriott JC (Ed) *Medicolegal Aspects of Alcohol* 3rd ed. Lawyers and Judges Pub. Co., Tucson, AZ, 1996.
12. Dubowski KM, Human pharmacokinetics of alcohol. *Alcohol Technol Rep* 1976; 5:55–63.
13. Clothier J, et al., Varying rates of alcohol metabolism in relation to detoxication medication. *Alcohol* 1985; 2:443–445.
14. Garriott J, Analysis for alcohol in postmortem specimens. in Garriott JC (Ed) *Medicolegal Aspects of Alcohol* 3rd ed. Lawyers and Judges Pub. Co., Tucson, AZ, 1996.
15. Kuroda N, Williams K, and Pounder DJ, Estimating blood alcohol from urinary alcohol at autopsies. *Am J Forensic Med Pathol* 1995; 16(3):219–222.
16. Garriott JC, Skeletal muscle as an alternative specimen for alcohol and drug analysis. *J Forensic Sci* 1991; 36:60–69.
17. Collison IB, Elevated postmortem ethanol concentrations in an insulin-dependent diabetic. *J Anal Toxicol* 2005; 29:762–764.
18. Zumwalt RE, Bost RO, and Sunshine I, Evaluation of ethanol concentrations in decomposed bodies. *J Forensic Sci* 1982; 27:549–554.
19. Manno JE and Manno BR, Experimental basis of alcohol-induced psychomotor performance impairment (PMPI), in Garriott JC (Ed) *Medicolegal Aspects of Alcohol* 3rd ed. Lawyers and Judges Pub. Co., Tucson, AZ, 1996.
20. Baselt RC, *Disposition of Toxic Drugs and Chemicals in Man* 5th ed. Chemical Toxicology Institute, Foster City, CA, 2000.
21. Keeney AH and Mellinkoff SM, Methyl alcohol poisoning. *Ann Int Med* 1951; 34:331–338.
22. Alexander CB, McBay AJ, and Hudson RP, Isopropanol and isopropanol deaths—ten years' experience. *J Forensic Sci* 1982; 27:541–548.
23. Molina DK, A characterization of sources of isopropanol detected on postmortem toxicologic analysis. *J Forensic Sci* 2010; 55(4):998–1002.
24. Linnanvuo-Laitinen M and Huttunen K, Ethylene glycol intoxication. *Clin Toxicol* 1986; 24:167–174.
25. Wetli CV, Davis JH and Blackbourne BD, Narcotic addiction in Dade County, Florida. *Arch Pathol* 1972; 93:330–342.
26. Gross EM, Autopsy findings in drug addicts. *Pathol Annu* 1978; 13(Pt2):35–67.
27. Saboory E, Derchansky M, Ismaili M, et al., Mechanisms of morphine enhancement of spontaneous seizure activity. *Anesth Analg*, 2007;105:1729–1735.
28. Zieglgansberger W, French ED, Siggins GR, et al., Opioid peptides may excite hippocampal pyramindal neurons by inhibiting adjacent inhibitory interneurons, *Science* 1979;205:415–417.

29. Crain SM, Shen KF, and Chalazonitis A, Opioids excite rather than inhibit sensory neurons after chronic opioid exposure of spinal cord-ganglion cultures. *Brain Res* 1988; 455:99–109.
30. Carlsson C, Smith DS, Keykhah M, et al., The effects of high-dose fentanyl on cerebral circulation and metabolism in rats. *Anesthesiology* 1982;7:375–380.
31. Polettini A, Poloni V, Groppi A, et al., The role of cocaine in heroin-related deaths hypothesis on the interaction between heroin and cocaine, *Forensic Sci Int* 2005;153:23–28.
32. Blumberg H and Ikeda C, Naltrexone, morphine and cocaine interactions in mice and rats. *J Pharmacol Exp Ther* 1978; 206:303–310.
33. Andresen H, Gullans A, Veselinovic M, et al., Fentanyl: toxic or therapeutic? Postmortem and antemortem blood concentrations after transdermal fentanyl application, *J Anal Toxicol* 2012; 36(3):182–194.
34. Hong R, Matsuyama E, and Nur K, Cardiomyopthy associated with the smoking of crystal methamphetamine. *JAMA* 1991; 265:1152–1154.
35. Karch SB, Stephens BG, and Ho C-H, Methamphetamine-related deaths in San Francisco: dermographic, pathologic and toxicologic profiles. *J Forensic Sci* 1999; 44(2):359–368.
36. Iwanami A, et al., Patients with methamphetamine psychosis admitted to a psychiatric hospital in Japan. *Acta Psychiatry Scand* 1994; 89:428–432.
37. Logan BK, Fligner CL, and Haddix T, Cause and manner of death in fatalities involving methamphetamine. *J Forensic Sci* 1998; 43(1):28–34.
38. Huestis MA, Henningfield JE, and Cone EJ, Blood cannabinoids. I. Absorption of THC and formation of 11-OH-THC and THCCOOH during and after smoking marijuana. *J Anal Toxicol* 1992; 16:276–282.
39. Hunt CA and Jones RT, Tolerance and disposition of tetrahydrocannabinol in man. *J Pharm Exp Ther* 1980; 215(1):35–44.
40. Saenz SR, Lewis RJ, Angies MK, and Wagner JR, Postmortem fluid and tissues concentrations of THC, 11-OH-THC and THC-COOH. *J Anal Toxicol* 2017; 41:508–516.
41. Cone EJ, et al., Nonsmoker exposure to secondhand cannabis smoke. III. Oral fluid and blood drug concentrations and corresponding subjective effects, *J Anal Toxicol*, 2015; 39: 497–509.
42. Rohrich J, et al., Concentrations of delta-9-tetrahydrocannabinol and 11-nor-9-carboxytetrahydrocannabinol in blood and urine after passive exposure to cannabis smoke in a coffee shop. *J Anal Toxicol* 2010; 34:196–203.
43. Synthetic THC, Kelkar AH, Smith NA, Martial A, et al., An outbreak of synthetic Cannabinoid-Associated coagulopathy in Illinois *N Engl J Med* 2018;379:1216–1223
44. Molina DK, Limfueco S, and Hargrove VM, Brain: the best specimen for volatile testing? (Letter). *Am J Forensic Med Pathol* 2015; 36(2):122–123.
45. Cecchini MJ, Mukhopadhyay S, Arrossi AV, et al., E-cigarette or vaping product use-associated lung injury: a review for pathologists. *Arch Pathol Lab Med* 2020.
46. Normandin PA and Benotti SA, Pediatric emergency update: lethality of liquid nicotine in E-cigarettes Y. *J Emerg Nurs* 2015; 41(4):357–359.
47. CDC Lead Recommended Actions Based on Blood Lead Level: Summary of Recommendations for Follow-up and Case Management of Children Based on Confirmed Blood Lead Levels, Centers of Disease Control and Prevention. Available at: https://www.cdc.gov/nceh/lead/advisory/acclpp/actions-blls.htm. Accessed 15 Nov 2019
48. Gorby MS. Arsenic poisoning. *West J Med* 1988; 149:308–315.
49. Iwase H, Kobayashi M, Nakajima M, and Takatori T, The ratio of insulin to C-peptide can be used to make a forensic diagnosis of exogenous insulin overdosage. *Forensic Sci Int* 2001; 115(1–2):123–127.

Forensic Science and the Forensic Pathologist

22

To a great mind, nothing is little

—**Sherlock Holmes, Sir Arthur Conan Doyle**

Forensic science is an invaluable partner in death investigations. While a full scope of all the forensic science disciplines and methods are beyond the scope of this book, forensic pathologists should have at least a general understanding of the main areas in which forensic science can assist in medicolegal death investigations. The forensic pathologist, while not a practitioner of the physical and chemical forensic sciences, needs to have a basic understanding of the principles of such and of when a consultation with a forensic scientist is warranted.

Chain of Custody

The type of sample obtained and the method of storage will vary depending upon the testing required; however, regardless of sample type, strict chain of custody is necessary for all forensic testing. Chain of custody simply refers to the documentation (paper or electronic) describing who has care and control of the evidence at all times. In a typical medicolegal death investigation, evidence may go from the forensic pathologist to law enforcement to a secure storage facility to the forensic science laboratory. It is imperative, since the forensic pathologist usually starts the chain, that each step is documented thoroughly and appropriately, from obtaining the evidence from the body to releasing it to either law enforcement or the forensic science laboratory. Additionally, the chain of custody of the body itself should be documented, from the scene or hospital, to the morgue and then release for final disposition.

All collected evidence should be dried and sealed in paper containers, unless otherwise required. The containers should then be sealed with evidence tape and the person sealing the evidence should then initial or sign across the tape to prevent undocumented tampering (Figure 22.1).

At a minimum, the chain of custody should provide a brief description of the evidence, the name and affiliation of the person who has control of the evidence; the name and affiliation of the person who is taking control of the evidence; and the time and date of the exchange of the evidence. Each person involved should also sign the chain of custody form. A copy of the form should be retained by the forensic pathologist in their case file and the original should stay with the evidence.

DNA Analysis

DNA, or deoxyribonucleic acid, testing has become a mainstay of forensic science. Forensic pathology mainly uses this technology as it applies to identification issues, though it is also often used in crime scene and sexual assault kit analysis. These later two analyses do not

Figure 22.1 (A and B) Properly sealed evidence.

usually affect the medicolegal death investigation, though the samples obtained at autopsy are often the basis for such testing.

Since DNA analysis plays such a pivotal role in both the identification of decedents as well as in criminal investigations, it is imperative that forensic pathologists have a basic understanding of its principles and use. Biological fluid analysis has been used in forensics for over 100 years, but up until the late 1980s, it mainly consisted of analysis of blood groups, that is, the ABO blood type system and polymorphic enzyme discrimination.[1] However, DNA typing has virtually eliminated such testing. DNA "fingerprinting," that is, DNA typing for forensic purposes, was developed by Dr. Alec Jeffreys in 1985.[2–4] He determined that, in each strand of DNA, there are thousands of identical DNA sequences that vary in length, constitution and number of the repetitive sequences. The identification and demonstration of the sequences of nucleotides and variable number of tandem repeats (VNTR) possessed by an individual cell is the basis for DNA identification. The technique later became known as restriction fragment length polymorphism (RFLP) and was the catalyst that spurred the growth and progress of forensic DNA analysis.

The importance of forensic DNA analysis is that any tissue containing nucleated cells can potentially be typed to help determine who may or may not have been the donor of biological evidence. Common biological fluids and tissues for forensic DNA analysis include seminal fluid with or without spermatozoa, nucleated blood cells, cells from soft tissue, teeth, bone, fingernails, saliva and hair – essentially any tissue in which there are nucleated cells. DNA can be extracted from these specimens, characterized based on nucleotide composition (sequence polymorphism) or tandem repetitive sequences (length polymorphism) and visualized to determine the donor's genetic profile at the targeted regions of interest. The genetic profile can then be compared with a known reference standard from a person, such as a blood or buccal specimen, or if unavailable, a *deduced* reference known such as the deceased's toothbrush. If these match, and the analysis contains a sufficient number of genetic markers (loci), there is a high degree of probability that the two samples share a common origin. However, instead of source attribution – the identification of a profile to the exclusion of all other possible donors – the rarity of the match estimate is calculated so a weight may be given to the genetic match. The match estimate provides a number of how many times the observed genetic profile is expected to occur in a given population. Due to the discrimination potential of modern day forensic DNA analysis, the ability to exclude an individual who is not the biological donor of the sample has become near absolute. It is only with identical twins that the genetic profile is expected to be the same.

DNA identification can be made using the principles of parentage testing. A child inherits half its DNA from each parent; therefore, DNA obtained from a parent or child of the decedent can be compared to the decedent's DNA to confirm parentage. It is important to note, however, that this use of DNA only confirms that the decedent is a child or parent of the exemplar – the identification is actually made by the comparison source of the DNA when they testify that their father or mother or child is missing. DNA identification can also be made based on other familial relations, such as full-siblings. It is expected that the decedent and a full-sibling will share more genetic material than the decedent and a random, unrelated individual, allowing the forensic DNA analyst to calculate a likelihood of full-sibling kinship. The increase in the number of genetic markers used in the modern forensic DNA laboratory has made this possible.

In addition to the discriminating nature of DNA identification, there are other advantages when compared to the conventional serological techniques. For example, DNA is much more stable than the blood group proteins and enzymes formerly used in biological sample identification. The degradation of sample will not lead to an "altered" genetic profile but likely to a less discriminating, yet usable partial genetic profile. Modern forensic DNA analysis has allowed profiling to be conducted on human remains thousands of years old.

Two basic concepts must be understood in dealing with DNA analyses:

1. If the DNA profile of a known individual (reference standard) does not match the DNA profile of a forensic unknown sample (evidence), the known individual is not the biological donor of the evidence. This is normally conveyed by stating the known individual is *excluded* as a source of the human DNA from the forensic unknown sample.
2. If the DNA profile of a known individual matches the DNA profile of the forensic unknown sample, the known individual may be the biological donor of the evidence. A typical match statement is the known individual *cannot be excluded* as a donor of the evidence. This are three possibilities to explain the match:
   a. The known individual is the source of the evidence DNA.

b. The known individual is not the source of the evidence DNA but coincidentally matches the evidence DNA. The probability of a random match will be provided to the trier of fact so that the appropriate weight may be given to the match.
c. An error was made in either the collection, analysis or reporting of the specimen DNA.

Many individuals misunderstand what is meant by a forensic DNA match. It is accurate to state that every person, except identical twins, has a unique genetic makeup when the totality of his DNA is considered. However, forensic DNA analysis does not analyze a person's entire genetic makeup. It just is not possible to do so in a timely or economical manner. Therefore, regions of DNA that have shown to be highly discriminating, either by nucleotide sequence or nucleotide length, were chosen by the forensic DNA community. The probability of a random match is calculated to demonstrate the rarity or commonality of the genetic profile as observed in the forensic unknown sample. An individual genetic marker may not be very discriminating by itself, but when combined with other genetic markers, the probability of a random match occurrence becomes smaller and smaller. For example, the first genetic marker was typed and the person of interest was not excluded (i.e., the profiles matched). If the person's two alleles (genotype) at that genetic marker (locus) are expected to occur in approximately 10% of the population, it is accurate to state that one in ten individuals would have that genotype. It is also accurate to state that nine out of ten individuals would have a genotype that would not match the evidence, thus excluding them as a possible donor. If a second genetic marker with the same discrimination potential was typed on the evidence DNA, and the person of interest shared that genotype, then the frequency of occurrence from the second locus (one in ten) can be multiplied by the first locus (one in ten). The resulting probability of a random match has now decreased to 1 in 100, or the ability to exclude has risen to 99 out of 100 individuals. This continues for all loci typed, and since each locus genotype is independent from each other's locus genotype, the combined genotype frequency becomes quite discriminating. Given the fact that modern forensic DNA analysis types over 20 genetic markers, the probability of a random match occurring is one in the billions, trillions and beyond.

All nucleated cells in the body contain 23 pairs of chromosomes, except for sperm and ova, which contain 23 chromosomes rather than 23 pairs. Each chromosome consists of a double spiral of DNA in the shape of a twisted ladder, the double helix. The sides of the ladder consist of alternating sugar (deoxyribose) and phosphate molecules; the rungs of the ladder consist of nitrogen bases. The weakest part of the helix or ladder is the rungs, where the nitrogen bases are weakly linked by hydrogen bonds. DNA is composed of units called nucleotides, which consist of a sugar, a phosphate group and a base. Millions of these nucleotides form a single strand. Despite the millions of nucleotides, only four different bases are used. Two of these are purines (adenine and guanine) and two are pyrimidines (thymine and cytosine). In forming the rungs of the ladder, guanine always binds to cytosine and adenine always binds to thymine. These are the only two possible combinations and these are called complementary base pairs. Because of the millions of nucleotides forming a single strand and the fact that there are 23 pairs of chromosomes in each cell, there is an almost infinite variety in the arrangement of the nucleotides. The order or sequence of the bases in a DNA molecule forms a code of the genetic information of the cells.

A gene is a series of these bases that occupies a specific location (locus) on a chromosome, typically producing a specific protein product. There is usually more than one form of a gene for each locus, and these alternate forms are termed alleles. Most of the chromosome, however, serves no known function and does not code for a specific gene product. Many of these noncoding areas consist of multiple copies of identical base sequences, 50–60 base pairs in length, arranged one behind the other, that is, in tandem. The repeated sequences are known as tandem repeats, with the areas made up of tandem repeats known as VNTR. Just like a gene, a VNTR locus can have multiple alleles. An individual will have two alleles, with each allele on a chromosome being inherited. The VNTR loci were the first areas used in DNA typing because of the multiple alleles.

The original method of DNA analysis was RFLP. This was a prolonged, complicated method that took a minimum of 6–8 weeks to conduct. DNA was chemically extracted from the submitted biological specimen and purified. It was then cut into fragments by a restriction enzyme. These substances cut the DNA molecule at specific base sequences. The number of DNA fragments and their length as produced by a particular restriction enzyme depend on how often the enzyme's base sequence occurs in the DNA specimen. Because every individual's DNA sequence is different, the fragments in the DNA specimen from one individual to another may differ in number and length from those in a DNA specimen from another individual.

The DNA fragments were then separated into bands by gel electrophoresis. DNA carries a negative charge and thus travels toward the positive pole in electrophoresis. The distance that each fragment travels depends on its length. The longer the DNA fragment is (in nucleotide bases), the slower its rate of migration through the gel. This creates a number of DNA bands in the gel. These are transferred to a nylon membrane by a technique known as Southern blotting. The membrane is then exposed to a DNA probe having a radioactive tag. The probe looks for a complementary sequence of bases. Thus, adenine looks for thymine, and guanine looks for cytosine. The probe then binds to its complementary sequence. X-ray film is placed next to the membrane to detect the radioactive patterns that appear as a series of bands similar to the bar code on items in grocery stores. Each dark stripe or band represents a point where the DNA probe is bound to its complementary base sequences. While different individuals may share identical patterns at a probe, it is statistically unlikely for random, unrelated individuals to share identical patterns at multiple loci.[4]

RFLP has been replaced by a new technique that utilizes the polymerase chain reaction (PCR). Unlike RFLP where a large quantity of non-degraded DNA was required, PCR is ideal for forensic-type specimens that may be of limited quantity and/or quality. PCR is an enzymatic process in which a specific region of DNA is replicated over and over to yield billions of copies of the original sequence. This replication can be likened to a photocopy machine where the heating and cooling cycles duplicate the original DNA each cycle. This process is used to target and amplify regions of interest termed short tandem repeats (STRs). The STRs are similar to the VNTRs but are typically only 2–6 base pairs in length. They are ideal for forensic DNA analysis due to the number of STR loci available, the number of alleles (8–20) per locus and the short fragment length of the amplified products. Samples that are highly degraded may not yield a full genetic profile, but typically will still provide a partial profile offering some level of discrimination. STR analysis has also become the mainstay of familial testing due the high number of available loci to clearly discriminate related individuals.

In STR analysis, the DNA is extracted from the submitted specimen, quantitated and then replicated by the PCR. Separation of the amplified DNA fragments is by capillary-based electrophoresis (CE) and the identification of the migrating fragments by laser-induced fluorescence detection. This method allows for the amplification (multiplex) of over 20 loci in one sample tube and the semiautomated detection of the amplified DNA fragments in real time. The entire process can be completed in 1–2 work days.

Apart from the discrimination potential and rapid timeframe of STR analysis, its greatest feature is the sensitivity of the technique. It requires very little starting material to obtain a detectible genetic profile so all measures need to be taken to prevent unintentional contamination of a sample. Even using the saw to obtain bone for DNA, if not properly cleaned between patients, can result in DNA contamination. Thus, it is recommended that sterile swabs be used and then dried, without allowing them to come into contact with other collected specimens or DNA material, that is, the collector or assistants. If bones or other equipment are used to obtain the samples, they should be thoroughly cleaned prior to use to limit carry over DNA contamination from other decedents. It may also be a good idea to keep a list of all persons present near the collected material and all cases done in proximity to that collected specimen, should contamination occur.

Combined DNA Index System

The Combined DNA Index System (CODIS) is a nationwide electronic database of DNA profiles. It consists of three levels of databases: the Local DNA Index Systems (LDIS), the State DNA Index Systems (SDIS) and the National DNA Index System (NDIS). Within each database, DNA information can be entered and searched across a variety of indices: the Convicted Offender Index which contains DNA information of those who have been convicted of certain crimes, usually felony offenses; the Forensic Index, which contains profiles from forensic evidence of crimes such as sexual assault kits; and the missing persons index, which contains DNA information from relatives of missing persons. CODIS administrators can input DNA data to be searched against the various databases depending upon their role within the system.

Originally, CODIS had a core set of 13 loci, with at least 8 being required for submission into the system; however, in 2017, that number was increased to 20 required loci (CSF1PO, FGA, THO1, TPOX, VWA, D3S1358, D5S818, D7S820, D8S1179, D13S317, D16S539, D18S51, D21S11, D1S1656, D2S441, D2S1338, D10S1248, D12S391, D19S433, D22S1045).[5] The DNA data contained within these databases is completely confidential; the profiles consist only of the DNA data, the agency identifier, the specimen identifier and the DNA laboratory personnel associated with the analysis. If a match is made, the system notifies the law enforcement or forensic entities involved.

Mitochondrial DNA Analysis

Mitochondrial DNA (mtDNA) analysis is used when the biological evidence recovered is either small in quantity or highly degraded.[6,7] MtDNA typing can be performed on a single hair shaft, old bone and decomposed tissue when nuclear DNA typing is not possible or attempts were unsuccessful. MtDNA differs from nuclear DNA in its location in the cell, its quantity and its mode of inheritance. While the cell nucleus contents may only contain two copies of a gene, one on each of the 23-chromosome pairs, the typical cell contains hundreds, and sometimes thousands, of mitochondria molecules. Thus, there is more mtDNA available for analysis than nuclear DNA.

While nuclear DNA is inherited from both parents, mtDNA is inherited solely from the mother. Because of this, the mtDNA sequences of a mother and her children will exactly match, barring a mutation. This means that mtDNA analysis is limited in that it cannot differentiate between individuals of the same maternal line. However, this lineage attribute makes it valuable in identifying unknown bodies if a maternal relative is available. MtDNA has a higher mutation rate than nuclear DNA, but in spite of this, the transmission of mtDNA is consistent over many generations. It is this reason that it is deemed a lineage marker.

As a rule, mtDNA does not undergo recombination. Individuals, however, can have more than one type of mtDNA (heteroplasmy). This can occur in either a single tissue or different tissues. Variation between the types is usually only one base, though greater variation may occur. Heteroplasmy does not invalidate the use of mtDNA for forensic analysis but must be taken into consideration during interpretation of results.

MtDNA analysis is tedious and labor intensive. The DNA is extracted, amplified by the PCR, purified and quantitated and finally sequenced. The mtDNA sequences are then compared with a standard mtDNA reference, the Anderson sequence. The resultant report is made up of the number of the positions different from the Anderson sequence and the different bases at these positions. Because of its exquisite sensitivity, there is always danger of contamination at the scene, in collection and in analysis. However, mtDNA also seems to be heartier than nuclear DNA, so it may be able to be obtained even when nuclear DNA cannot, such as with older skeletonized or even charred remains.

Touch DNA

In recent years, much has been published on the use of touch DNA in criminal investigations. Touch DNA refers to small amounts of DNA in skin cells that can be transferred, usually to an inanimate object, though handling. For example, the small traces of DNA left behind in a fingerprint when someone touches an object. Previous to PCR techniques, such small quantities of DNA could not be analyzed; however, newer techniques have made such analysis possible. While research has shown that touch DNA may be of assistance in crime scenes[8], there is no evidence that such DNA can be extracted from bodies. For instance, sampling of the neck of a victim of strangulation has not been shown to yield DNA from the perpetrator and has been shown to have considerable contamination.[9]

Firearm Analysis

One of the main areas in which forensic science assists with medicolegal death investigations is in firearm analysis. This includes not only the ballistic comparison of bullets themselves, but range of fire analysis and weapons testing.

Ballistic experts are likely best known for comparing spent bullets to the firearm that discharged them. This is done by comparing the rifling imparted on the bullets as well as unique marks created by the firearm. While this is often extremely helpful in a court of law, this information is not as helpful to the forensic pathologist at the time of the autopsy.

However, ballistic experts are extremely helpful in assisting with issues that may arise during the examination such as the type or caliber of the ammunition used, especially in the setting of unique ammunition or multiple ammunition types. They can also assist in evaluating projectiles for possible ricochet or intermediary target marks or in complex gunshot cases. For example, one of the authors had a case in which the decedent was shot by multiple actors with varying ammunition types, through an intermediary target with multiple shrapnel and ricochet injuries as well as having several older, retained projectiles from previous gunshot injuries (Figure 22.2).

Consultation with the ballistic expert in such cases can assist in determining approximate firearm types and which shrapnel wounds may be related.

Ballistic experts are also essential for evaluating the firearm itself. Many gunshot deaths are suggested to be the result of an accidental misfire of a weapon or are blamed on a child. Ballistic experts can examine the firearm itself to determine if it is in working condition or has a tendency to misfire. They can also determine the trigger pull of a particular weapon to assess whether or not a decedent or another person might possess the ability to fire such a weapon.

Gunshot residue (GSR) testing on the hands of a decedent was discussed in depth in Chapter 7 ("Ballistic Wounds"), and while the utility of GSR testing of the hands of decedents is not helpful, GSR testing on clothing for range of fire analysis can be critical to a

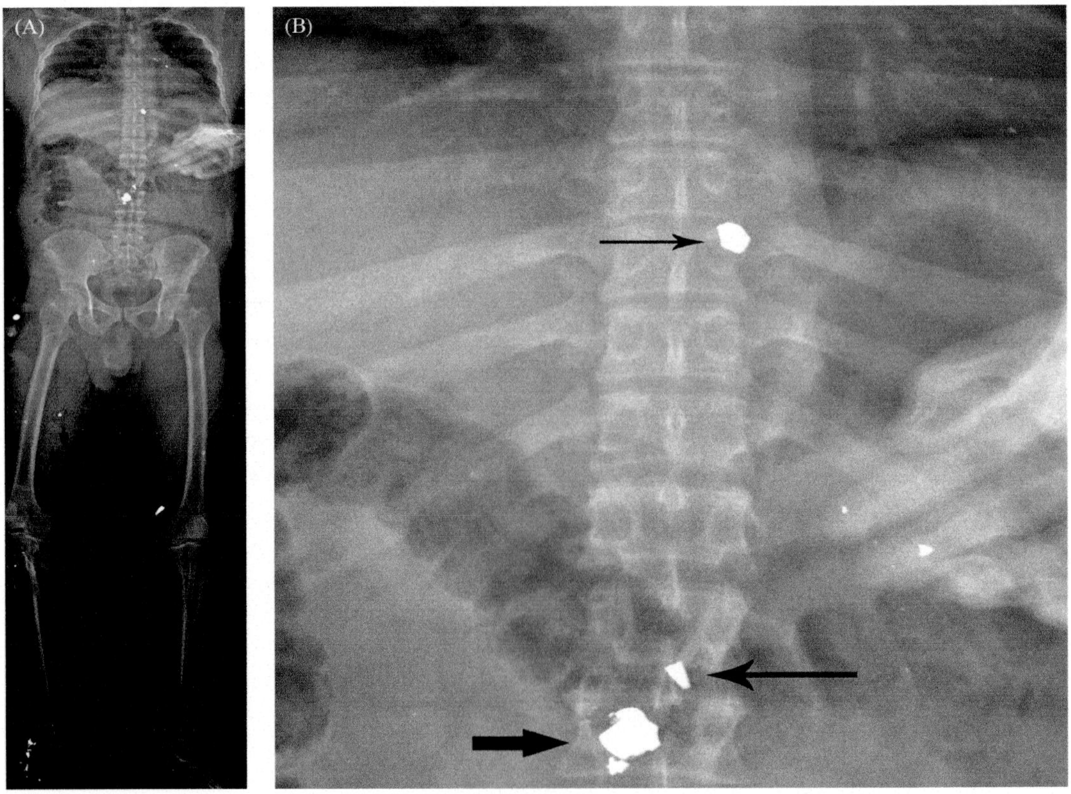

Figure 22.2 (A) Radiograph of decedent shot multiple times with both a rifle and a handgun with shrapnel injuries (ankle) and old, retained projectiles. (B) Close-up of chest of same individual showing older retained projectile (thin arrow), rifle tip (intermediate arrow) and handgun bullet (thick arrow).

case. Gunshot residues may be deposited on clothing in the same manner as they deposit on the hands or mark the skin of a decedent (see Chapter 7); however, they may be difficult to distinguish with the naked eye. Thus, various chemical tests known to react with the main components of GSR, namely, nitrites and lead, can be utilized to obtain a pattern of GSR deposition that can then be analyzed, in much the same way as powder tattooing, to estimate how far the firearm was from the clothing at the time of discharge. Two such common testing methods are the Greiss test that reacts with nitrites to form a pink-orange color and the sodium rhodizonate test that reacts with lead to create a purple coloration. Both of these tests should be conducted by a firearms expert under appropriate laboratory conditions.

In order to allow for the correct analysis of either the clothing or projectiles, care should be taken when collecting the specimens. The clothing should be dried completely then wrapped in paper bags and labeled with the case number and contents of the bag. Projectiles should be cleaned as well as possible of organic material, preferably using water. Bleach and other corrosive chemicals should be avoided as they may etch or otherwise damage the bullet. Similarly, metallic tools, such as forceps, should be avoided when handling such evidence to avoid creating marks on the projectiles which may interfere with analysis.

Tool Mark Analysis

As discussed in Chapter 6, sharp implements may impart characteristics of the implement, called Kerf marks, onto bone or cartilage. These marks may indicate the type of weapon used and, in some cases, identify the actual weapon. The cutting edge of the knife may leave striations on cartilage and bone that can be used for identifying purposes; thus, these surfaces should be collected at autopsy for later comparison.

The sharp teeth of a scavenger or cutting edge of an implement applied to bone with sufficient force will leave a distinctive imprint. This pattern of striations, when examined macroscopically or microscopically, can provide crucial evidence since each tool leaves a characteristic mark that can assist in its identification. Knives are narrow bladed and leave a corresponding narrow "V"-shaped trough in the bone. They are single or double-bladed and leave an opposite "V"-shaped trough in surrounding bone and tend to leave behind only microscopic striations. Axes leave a smooth "V"-shaped trough in the bone, but the defect is very wide and is often significantly deeper due to the lever action of swinging an axe; there is also often accompanying microscopic or macroscopic impact fractures and/or flaking surrounding the contact site.

Chopping weapons cutting through bone can impart characteristic striations on the bone unique to each type of weapon. Humphrey and Hutchinson evaluated hacking trauma on bones produced by cleavers, machetes and axes.[10] Hacking blows produce wounds in bone characterized by at least one smooth, flat side with, in the case of angled impacts, fracturing of the other side. Cleavers produce clean, narrow wounds without fractures at the entry site; machetes wider, less-clean wounds with small fragments of bone at the entry site and fractures in the bed of the cut. Axes make crushing, fragmenting wounds with fractures. Microscopic examination of these wounds by Tucker et al. found that cleavers produce thin, fine striations that are sharp and distinct.[11] Striations produced by machetes were more pronounced but coarse and less distinct. Axe wounds showed no striations on the bone. The authors thought that microscopic analysis of hacking wounds of bone could distinguish different classes of weapons. They also saw a potential to identify specific weapons.

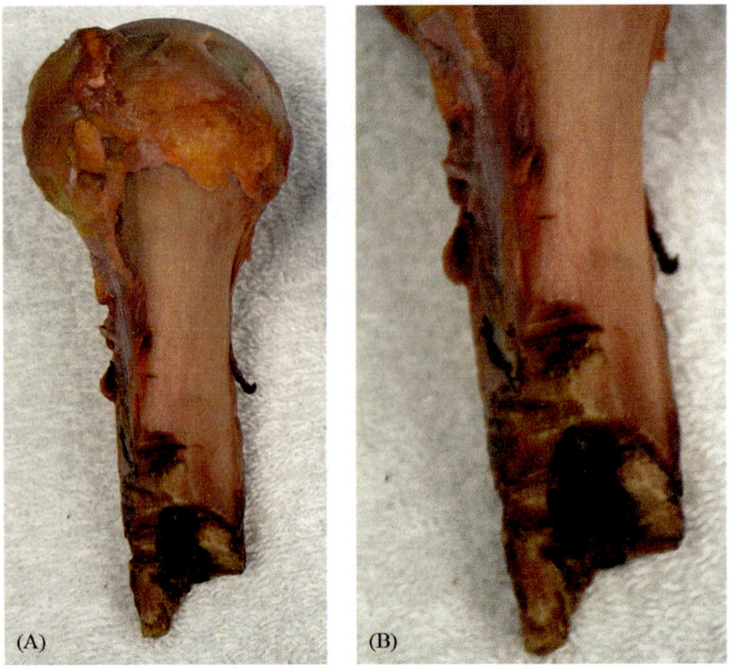

Figure 22.3 (A) Left humerus of dismembered body removed for tool mark analysis; (B) close-up of cut margin showing tool marks.

While serrated blades may leave a pattern of short parallel abrasions along the margin of a wound, distinguishing between a serrated and non-serrated blade may not always be possible. However, it has been shown that serrated blades may leave distinguishing marks along a cartilaginous surface.[12] Pounder et al. studied 136 stab wounds made to porcine and bovine costal cartilage, documented by photography and dental casting, and found that serrated blades created "irregularly regular" patterned striations along the cut surface of the cartilage.[12]

In order to identify such markings, the sample must be collected at autopsy. It is recommended that the bone of cartilage by removed from the body and trimmed of any excess tissue. If possible, it is best to remove the bone by cutting around the adjacent joint, so that the cut aspect is easily identifiable to the examiner (Figure 22.3); if this is not possible, the edge of the bone or cartilage that is cut upon removal should be marked with ink, so the examiner knows this edge does not represent the tool mark for analysis. The samples should be dried or submitted in formalin. It is best to contact the examiner prior to submission to see their preference regarding preservation. The sample should be clearly labeled as to the bone (i.e., humerus) and the desire for tool mark analysis.

Analysis of Trace Evidence

Trace evidence, such as hairs, fibers and other foreign debris, gathered off a body can often assist in the death investigation. Hairs and other fibers can be transferred from an assailant during an assault just as paint chips or fragments of glass can be transferred from a motor vehicle to a body during a collision. It is recommended that bodies be carefully examined for such evidence particularly in cases of homicide, hit and run automobile collisions and possibly dumped bodies. Pulled head hair exemplars should also be obtained in hit and run collisions, as they may be compared to any hair samples recovered from the vehicle itself, though DNA analysis has made this sort of comparison obsolete. Hair exemplars should also be obtained anytime hair is recovered from a body to rule out the decedent as the source. Tissue samples of injuries can also be analyzed via scanning electron microscopy (SEM) to assess for embedded fibers or metallic components that can then be used to match to apparent implement types such as ligatures or knives.[13]

Accelerants and Explosive Testing

In fire and explosion deaths, clothing should be collected for accelerant testing. Due to the volatile nature of these chemicals, these items should not be placed into paper bags as routine, as this may result in loss of the chemicals present. This evidence must be stored in a sealed, nonporous container, such as a paint can, prior to analysis. Accelerant analysis is often pivotal when investigating a fire death as its presence or absence may assist in the determination of manner of death.

References

1. Saferstein R (Ed), *Forensic Science Handbook*, Volume I. Regents/Prentice Hall, New Jersey. 1982.
2. Jeffreys AJ, Wilson V, and Thein SL, Individual-specific fingerprints of human DNA. *Nature* 1985; 316:76–79.
3. Gill P, Jeffreys AJ, and Werret DJ, Forensic application of DNA fingerprints. *Nature* 1985; 318:577–579.
4. Merz B, DNA fingerprints come to court. *JAMA* 1988; 259:2193–2194.
5. CODIS Fact Sheet, Federal Bureau of Investigations. Available at: https://www.fbi.gov/services/laboratory/biometric-analysis/codis/codis-and-ndis-fact-sheet; accessed 19 June 2020.
6. Isenberg AR and Moore JM, Mitochondrial DNA analysis at the FBI laboratory. *Forensic Sci Commun* 1999; 1(2):1–10.
7. Bar W, et al., DNA commission of the international society for forensic genetics: guidelines for mitochondrial DNA typing. *Int J Legal Med* 2000; 113:193–196.
8. Pang BC and Cheung BK, Double swab technique for collecting touched evidence. *Legal Med* 2007; 9(4):181–184.
9. Rutty GN, An investigation into the transference and survivability of human DNA following simulated manual strangulation with consideration of the problem of third party contamination. *Int J Legal Med* 2002; 116(3):170–173.
10. Humphrey JH and Hutchinson DL, Characteristics of hacking trauma. *J Forensic Sci* 2001; 46(2):228–233.
11. Tucker BK, et al., Characteristics of microscopic hacking trauma on bone. *J Forensic Sci* 2001; 46(2):234–240.
12. Pounder DJ, Cormack L, Broadbent E, and Millar J, Class characteristics of serrated knife stabs to cartilage. *Am J Forensic Med Pathol* 2011; 32(2):157–160.
13. Gentile G, Andreola S, Bailo P, et al., A brief review of scanning electron microscopy with energy-dispersive X-ray use in forensic medicine. *Am J Forensic Med Pathol* 2020; 41(4): 280–6.

Appendix A: Forensic Autopsy, Radiography and Photography

The forensic autopsy differs from the hospital autopsy in its objectives and relevance. Besides determining the cause of death, the forensic pathologist must often also establish the manner of death, the identity of the deceased if unknown and the timing of death and/or injury. The forensic autopsy may also involve collection of evidence from the body, which can subsequently be used to either prove or disprove an individual's guilt and confirm or deny his account of how the death occurred.

Because of the possible medicolegal implications of forensic cases, not only must the aforementioned determinations be made, but the findings or lack of them must be documented. In many cases, the cause and manner of death may be obvious. It is the documentation of the injuries or lack of them, as well as the interpretation of how they occurred and the determination or exclusion of other contributory or causative factors that are important.

The forensic autopsy involves not only the actual examination of the body at the autopsy table, but the consideration of other aspects that the general pathologist does not believe to be part of the autopsy — the scene, clothing and toxicology. The forensic autopsy begins at the scene. Pathologists should not perform a forensic autopsy unless they know the circumstances leading up to and surrounding the death. This is a very basic principle that is often violated. What would one think of a physician who examined a patient without asking what the patient's symptoms or complaints were? As in all examinations of patients, one must have a medical history. In the case of the forensic pathologist, the "patient" is unable to render this history. Therefore, the history must be obtained by either the medical examiner or police investigators. This history should be known before the autopsy begins.

The Scene

The scene should be documented either with diagrams or photographs, preferably both. People should be interviewed and a written report should be given to the pathologist prior to the autopsy. It makes good television dramatics to poke and prod a body at the scene, but it does not make sense scientifically. At the scene, there are often multiple people present, including family members and law enforcement, limiting adequate examination. In addition, there is often inadequate lighting and no equipment or proper instrumentation, including running water, to perform an examination. What can be done, however, is to destroy evidence or introduce fallacious findings. Powder can be dislodged from the clothing, primer residue can be wiped away from the hands, the body can be contaminated with the examiner's hair or with the hair of the police officer who helps turn, poke and prod the body, and so on.

The body should be touched and moved as little as possible at the scene. In cases of violent death, paper bags should be secured about the victim's hands so that no trace evidence will be lost. If plastic bags are used and the body is then placed in a cooler, there will be condensation of water vapor on the hands (with possible loss of trace evidence) when it is moved back into a warm environment. Prior to transportation, the body should be either wrapped in a clean white sheet or placed in a clean body bag. It should never be placed directly onto a cart in the back of an ambulance. Who knows what or who was lying on the cart prior to the body transport and trace evidence from a prior body could be deposited on this body, or trace evidence from this body can be lost and subsequently transferred to another body.

At the morgue, the body should never be undressed prior to the medical examiner's seeing it. This includes removing shoes and socks to place toe tags. Examination of the clothing is as much a part of the autopsy as examination of the wounds. The clothing must be examined for blood stains and trace evidence as well as to see if the wounds in the body correlate with the defects in the clothing. How does one know that the individual was not shot and then dressed?

The body should never be embalmed prior to the autopsy. Embalming ruins toxicologic analysis, changes the appearance of the wounds and can induce artifacts. The body should also not be fingerprinted prior to examination of the hands. In fingerprinting, the hands are pried open to ink the fingers. In the process, trace evidence can be lost or false evidence deposited. Tests for firearms residue can be rendered invalid by prying apart fingers and fingerprinting a body.

Forensic Imaging

X-rays should be available in every medical examiner's office, though some offices utilize Computed Tomography (CT) or Magnetic Resonance Imaging (MRI) technology. Regardless of the imaging modality used, all gunshot and sharp force injury deaths, infant deaths, and severely burnt and/or decomposed bodies should be imaged prior to commencing the examination. Postmortem imaging is necessary and especially important in gunshot wound cases in which the bullet appears to have exited. This is because the entire bullet may not have exited but rather only a piece of the bullet or a piece of bone. With the semi-jacketed ammunition now in widespread use, it is common for the lead core to exit the body and the jacket to remain. The core is of no interest ballistically. It is the jacket that is important. The jacket might be retained beneath the skin adjacent to the exit site. It is very easy to miss the jacket material at autopsy, unless one knows, by X-ray, that it is there. Additionally, radiographs can reveal knife tips or other retained implements that not only have forensic value but may pose a safety risk to the examiner.

The Autopsy Examination

After examination of the clothing and personal effects, and after imaging has been performed, the forensic pathologist should then examine the external surfaces of the body, documenting distinguishing characteristics such as eye and hair color and tattoos, and evidence of trauma or natural disease. The presence of medical intervention should also be noted. If necessary, the body should be cleaned in order to fully expose any injuries or other findings, though cleaning of the body should only occur after an initial external examination is performed, and all trace evidence has been collected.

Not all deaths require a full internal examination of the body, such as deaths in elderly patients who have died after sustaining a hip fracture in a fall. In these cases, the examination is complete after review of the medical records and external examination of the body. However, certain deaths should receive a full autopsy including suspected homicides, unknown deaths, unexplained deaths in children, nonnatural deaths, apparent overdose deaths, unidentified persons, skeletonized remains and drowning deaths. If prolonged antecedent medical care has occurred prior to the death, and injuries present have been well documented, an internal examination may not be necessary; however, the authors recommend that every homicide be autopsied regardless of time frame between injury and death.

If an internal examination is deemed necessary, the body is then opened, following standard autopsy protocols, and the internal surfaces of the body are examined in situ and each organ is removed, weighed and examined. Pieces of the organs are retained for possible future microscopic examination, if necessary. After the internal examination is complete and all samples have been obtained, the body can then be closed and released or final disposition. Additional testing, such as microscopy and toxicology, do not require the presence of the body.

Photography

Every body examined at a medical examiner's or coroner's office should, at a minimum, have an identification photograph taken. This is usually a head shot photograph taken with either a placard or other marked indicating the case number of the death being investigated. It is also good practice to take overall photographs of the body as it is received at the office.

Additionally, all significant injuries should be documented photographically. Photographs should be as clear as possible, without obstructing blood or foreign material. Close up photographs of injuries should include a scale and patterned injuries, including bite marks, should be photographed perpendicular to the wound surrounded by a small L-shaped photography scale. Significant defects in clothing should also be photographed as well as any evidence retrieved from the body, such as bullets. Photographs of distinguishing characteristics, such as tattoos, can often be of assistance in cases of unidentified bodies.

With the advent of digital photography, it is now possible to obtain high-quality photographs without much cost or inconvenience. High-quality Single lens reflex (SLR) cameras are reasonably priced and are easy to use. While forensic photographers are greatly helpful in the autopsy suite, often morgue personnel can also be trained to assist with obtaining photographs, and the images can be reviewed in real time. Digital photographs can also be easily stored on computers, though they should also be backed up on a separate device or server.

Appendix B: The Autopsy Report

The first part of the forensic autopsy report should document the body as it was first examined, including any clothing or personal effects. Some physicians choose to include this information in the External Examination section of the report, while others chose to separate it into its own section. Regardless of how it is organized, the physician should describe the age, sex, height, weight and nourishment status of the deceased. Following this, a description of the clothing should be given. This description, initially, does not need to be very detailed. Essentially, a simple listing of the articles found or accompanying the body should be given, for example, a short-sleeved white shirt, or a long-sleeved white shirt unbuttoned down the front, or a bloodstained white T-shirt. If the case is a traumatic death with significant alterations of the garments due to trauma, the clothing will be described in further detail in another section of the autopsy. Personal effects, such as jewelry and/or the contents of the pockets or purses, should also be described and inventoried.

After this description of the general body characteristics, clothing and personal effects, the report should detail the "**External Examination**" of the body. This section should exclude any evidence of trauma, if present, as that will be described in its own section. At a minimum, the external examination section should include:

- The degree and distribution of rigor and livor mortis
- The presence or absence of embalming
- Any changes of decomposition
- Hair and eye color
- The appearance of the eyes, for example, the presence or absence of petechiae or icterus
- Any unusual appearance to the ears, nose, or face, for example, congenital malformations, scarring or severe acne
- The presence and condition of the teeth, including evidence of dentures or significant restorations
- A description of the chest, abdomen, extremities, including the hands, and the back
- A description of the external genitalia
- Significant scars, tattoos or skin lesions
- External evidence of disease
- Old injuries
- Congenital malformations, if present

Evidence of acute medical intervention, such as intravascular cannulae, breathing tubes and thoracotomy incisions, should also be described. It is generally recommended that these interventions be placed into their own section of the report to avoid confusion with injuries; however, if only minor intervention is present, such as an IV line or an endotracheal tube, they can be included in the External Examination section.

If there is injury to the body, it should now be described in the next section, entitled "**Evidence of Injury**." All recent injuries, whether minor or major, external or internal, should be described in this section. There is no need to repeat the description of these injuries in the subsequent Internal Examination section or to describe them in the preceding external description section. Injury descriptions should include their location, type (i.e., abrasion or contusion), size, shape and pattern.

There are many ways to handle the "Evidence of Injury" section. Excluding gunshot wounds and sharp force injuries, it is easiest to divide it into two broad areas: external evidence and internal evidence. Some examiners intermingle these two. They describe the external evidence of injury to the head followed by the internal head injuries. They will then describe the external injuries of the trunk, followed by the internal injuries of the trunk.

Gunshot wounds and sharp force injuries are a different situation. For both, the wounds should include a detailed description of the wound, including the measured wound size and both an anatomic and a measured location of the wound. Each wound should be located on the body (in inches or centimeters) in relation to the top of the head or the sole of the foot and to the right or left of the midline. It should then be described in relation to a local landmark, such as the external auditory canal, nipple or umbilicus.

In gunshot wound cases, if at all possible, each individual wound should be described in its entirety before going on to a second wound and labeled with a unique identifier, such as GSW 1, 2, 3 or A, B, C. The features of the wound that make it an entrance and that determine at what range the bullet was fired should be described—for example, abrasion ring, soot, powder tattooing, muzzle imprint. Pertinent negatives should be noted. The course of the bullet through the body should then be described. All organs perforated or penetrated by the missile should be noted. It is also useful to give an overall description of the missile path through the body in relation to the planes of the body with the body in anatomical position. Thus, one will say, "The bullet traveled from back to front, left to right, and sharply downward." If the bullet exits, the exit wound should be described in relation to the entrance.

If the bullet is found, one should state where it was found, whether it is intact, deformed or fragmented, whether it is lead or jacketed and the approximate caliber (i.e., small, medium or large). A letter or number may be inscribed on the base of the bullet, which should then be sealed into an evidence container, usually an envelope, labeled with the name of the victim, the date of the examination, the case number, the location from which the bullet was recovered, the letter or number assigned it and the name of the prosector.

Like gunshot wounds, when possible, each sharp force injury should be described in its entirety before moving on and each wound should be labeled with a unique identifier, such as SW 1, 2, 3 or IW A, B, C. In some sharp force injuries cases, there are too many injuries to use this approach, or the injuries are clustered together over a small area, hindering identification of separate wound paths; in cases such as this, wounds may be grouped together and described *en masse* rather than separately. For stab wounds, one should indicate whether the wound termini are blunted or pointed, as this may assist in identification of the implement used. It is also useful to give an overall description of the path of the wound through the body in relation to the planes of the body with the body in anatomical position, just like with gunshot wounds.

The last part of the "Evidence of Injury" section should concern the clothing. The location of defects, whether they correspond to the injuries, and the presence of trace evidence, such as powder, soot or car paint, should be described.

Next is the "**Internal Examination**" section. Here, the major organ systems as well as the organ cavities are described. The usual subdivisions of this section are as follows:

- Head and brain
- Body cavities
- Neck
- Respiratory tract
- Cardiovascular system
- Gastrointestinal tract with pancreas
- Liver and biliary tract
- Spleen
- Adrenal glands
- Urinary tract
- Reproductive tract
- Musculoskeletal system

In these sections, one would give organ weights (not necessary for adrenal and pancreas) as well as a brief description of the organs with pertinent negatives. With the pancreas, adrenals and spleen, if there are no positive findings, using the term "unremarkable" as the sole description is acceptable. Do not use the term "normal" as organs are rarely normal – whatever that is.

The next section is the "**Microscopic Examination**." This section should only be included when microscopy was performed and is thus, not present in all reports. It should include a brief description of the organs reviewed and their findings.

The sections after Microscopic Examination may vary by office but may include Radiographs when postmortem radiology is performed or Ancillary Studies section if additional testing such as postmortem cultures are performed. Some pathologists also like to include an Evidence Collected section listing any evidence collected and its disposition.

A toxicology report should also be included as part of the autopsy report, though it may be a separate page from the main report itself.

The final sections of the autopsy report should be "**Findings**" and "**Conclusion**." The Findings should be a summary of the major findings in order of importance. It is not necessary to list every minute, often extraneous finding, as is done in some hospital autopsies. Since this report will most likely be seen by nonphysicians, it is best to list only those significant findings present in a clear and concise format. Examples of findings are listed in the following:

I. Blunt force injuries
   a. Basilar and cranial skull fractures
   b. Intracranial subdural and subarachnoid hemorrhage
   c. Bilateral displaced rib fractures
   d. Hepatic and splenic lacerations
   e. Multiple contusions and abrasions of body

II. Hypertensive and atherosclerotic cardiovascular disease
   a. Cardiomegaly (680 g) with left ventricular hypertrophy
   b. Severe atherosclerosis, coronary arteries
   c. Clinical history of hypertension and previous myocardial infarct

The last section is the **Conclusion** or opinion as to the cause of death. This should briefly describe the cause of death in language as simple as possible. This section is intended for the public, not for physicians. Thus, for example, one can say, "… died of a heart attack due to coronary atherosclerosis ('hardening' of the blood vessels that supply blood and oxygen to the heart muscle)." Or "… died of massive internal bleeding due to a gunshot wound of the aorta (the major blood vessel of the body)." Speculation as to circumstances surrounding the death should be absent or kept to a minimum, though pertinent information in determining the cause and manner of death may be included, as needed.

Appendix C: Normal Organ Weights in Adults and Children

Normal Weights of Organs in Adults

Organ	Male range (g)	Female range (g)
Brain	1179–1621	1033–1404
Heart	233–383	148–296
R lung	155–720	101–589
L lung	112–675	105–515
Liver	968–1860	603–1767
Spleen	28–226	<230
R kidney	81–160	38–174
L kidney	83–176	35–192

Compiled from: Molina DK and DiMaio VJM, Normal organ weights in women: part I – The heart. *Am J Forensic Med Pathol* 2015; 36(3):176–181. Molina DK and DiMaio VJM, Normal organ weights in women: part II – The brain, lungs, liver, spleen and kidneys. *Am J Forensic Med Pathol* 2015; 36(3):182–187. Molina DK and DiMaio VJM, Normal organ weights in men: part I – The heart. *Am J Forensic Med Pathol* 2012; 33(4):362–367. Molina DK and DiMaio VJM, Normal organ weights in men: part II – The brain, lungs, liver, spleen and kidneys. *Am J Forensic Med Pathol* 2012; 33(4):368–372.

Organ Weight Ranges in Infants and Children (Males and Females Combined)

Age	Ave. weight (kg)	Brain range (g)	Heart range (g)	R lung range (g)	L lung range (g)	Liver range (g)	Spleen range (g)	R kidney range (g)	L kidney range (g)
<1 month	3.4	258–576	13–31	17–71	14–60	87–217	4–20	8–22	6–24
1 month	4.3	378–628	17–37	27–85	24–72	106–244	4–24	9–25	8–28
2 months	4.9	411–741	17–41	35–85	27–75	111–271	2–34	10–30	10–30
3 months	6.2	473–833	21–45	39–109	33–95	148–332	8–36	12–36	13–37
4 months	6.6	464–904	24–44	35–97	19–93	137–333	6–38	10–34	13–33
5 months	7.0	542–1004	22–50	38–124	29–107	138–412	7–43	11–35	15–35
6 months	7.6	711–1037	24–52	43–137	35–117	210–386	11–43	18–34	20–36
7 months	8.0	665–1057	23–55	43–145	30–132	182–440	13–49	12–40	15–39
8 months	8.5	712–1120	29–61	42–152	19–149	228–490	17–43	12–47	16–52
9 months	9.4	683–1169	32–60	53–151	27–153	238–496	16–52	15–43	16–64
10 months	10.0	809–1135	37–61	20–212	20–170	233–571	21–53	22–50	18–54
11 months	9.1	761–1177	36–60	52–138	35–129	213–531	10–60	16–48	13–53
12 months	9.9	719–1245	32–64	49–159	39–133	246–544	16–60	18–46	19–47
13 months	10.1	867–1111	34–62	27–175	27–145	293–497	15–63	19–43	22–46
14 months	11.0	765–1303	35–71	27–199	36–158	262–560	19–59	16–52	15–55
15 months	11.4	823–1227	33–73	34–180	23–165	243–549	23–55	16–48	17–53

(Continued)

Organ Weight Ranges in Infants and Children (Males and Females Combined) (*Continued*)

Age	Ave. weight (kg)	Brain range (g)	Heart range (g)	R lung range (g)	L lung range (g)	Liver range (g)	Spleen range (g)	R kidney range (g)	L kidney range (g)
16 months	12.2	908–1252	37–77	47–207	39–177	273–621	21–71	17–57	13–61
17 months	11.4	825–1275	44–68	46–180	38–156	320–548	23–71	23–51	11–65
18 months	12.5	833–1225	38–70	37–163	36–138	320–629	18–72	10–60	17–57
19 months	11.8	858–1316	32–80	36–174	22–168	233–625	17–71	15–55	18–54
20 months	12.7	873–1331	35–85	30–194	40–166	263–651	20–78	18–54	20–56
21 months	13.9	799–1391	42–74	27–203	51–149	318–588	15–73	22–50	21–53
22 months	12.7	868–1416	43–83	39–215	22–190	319–597	18–88	21–57	23–59
23 months	12.9	916–1366	36–90	26–262	16–220	303–667	11–89	16–66	19–67
2 years	14.6	935–1425	42–96	26–262	40–208	289–681	16–86	18–68	20–70
3 years	16.5	971–1509	49–111	41–277	36–244	336–732	20–90	24–71	25–75
4 years	18.9	970–1546	55–121	60–306	54–270	363–833	16–98	22–84	24–82
5 years	20.3	1072–1538	56–142	62–316	53–277	359–881	19–105	30–84	31–85
6 years	26.0	1017–1655	59–185	57–387	44–358	380–1110	20–122	26–100	31–105
7 years	28.9	1020–1620	73–195	54–446	39–419	437–1099	16–162	21–115	23–121
8 years	33.5	1094–1576	71–223	51–497	34–422	462–1206	18–164	29–115	37–111
9 years	37.8	1133–1611	100–230	79–553	71–483	434–1556	27–179	42–120	41–135
10 years	42.2	1093–1637	103–267	49–559	52–498	517–1583	31–161	43–133	39–149
11 years	49.9	1102–1640	113–289	74–600	66–524	469–1813	20–208	45–151	48–158
12 years	58.2	1117–1657	128–336	100–668	64–624	638–1782	32–228	60–150	62–152

Reprinted with permission from Molina DK, Pinneri K, Stash JA, Li L, Vance K, and Cross C, Organ weight reference ranges for ages 0–12 years. *Am J Forensic Med Pathol* Dec 2019.

Index

Note: Locators in *italics* represent figures and **bold** indicate tables in the text.

C

D

E

H

I

N

O

P

W